Dynamic General Equilibrium Modeling

Burkhard Heer · Alfred Maußner

Dynamic General Equilibrium Modeling

Computational Methods and Applications

Second Edition

Professor Burkhard Heer
Free University of Bolzano-Bozen
School of Economics and Management
Via Sernesi 1
39100 Bolzano-Bozen
Italy
Burkhard.Heer@unibz.it

Professor Alfred Maußner
University of Augsburg
Universitätsstraße 16
86159 Augsburg
Germany
Alfred.Maussner@wiwi.uni-augsburg.de

ISBN 978-3-642-03148-9   e-ISBN 978-3-540-85685-6
DOI 10.1007/978-3-540-85685-6
Springer Dordrecht Heidelberg London New York

Library of Congress Control Number: 2009932131

© Springer-Verlag Berlin Heidelberg 2004, 2nd ed. 2009. Corr. 2nd printing
This work is subject to copyright. All rights are reserved, whether the whole or part of the material is concerned, specifically the rights of translation, reprinting, reuse of illustrations, recitation, broadcasting, reproduction on microfilm or in any other way, and storage in data banks. Duplication of this publication or parts thereof is permitted only under the provisions of the German Copyright Law of September 9, 1965, in its current version, and permission for use must always be obtained from Springer. Violations are liable to prosecution under the German Copyright Law.
The use of general descriptive names, registered names, trademarks, etc. in this publication does not imply, even in the absence of a specific statement, that such names are exempt from the relevant protective laws and regulations and therefore free for general use.

Cover design: WMX Design GmbH, Heidelberg

Printed on acid-free paper

Springer is part of Springer Science+Business Media (www.springer.com)

For our families:
Barbara, Sarah, and Carla
Christa, Florian, and Johannes

Preface

Given the huge number of responses and comments to the first edition of our book, we felt obliged to come up with the second edition within such a short period of time. Stochastic Dynamic General Equilibrium modeling is certainly among the most rapidly changing fields in economics and we try to cover the most recent developments.

In this edition, we reorganize and extend the presentation of solution methods in the former Chapters 1 through 4 and add major new material. Different from the first edition Chapter 1 serves as introduction, but does not present any solution techniques. It covers deterministic and stochastic representative agent models, elaborates on their calibration and evaluation, and ends with a characterization of the solution methods presented in Chapters 2 through 6. Chapter 2 now includes a section on the second-order approximation of policy functions, the extended deterministic path algorithm in Chapter 3 is applied to an open economy model with a unit root, and we consider various techniques to speed up value function iteration in Chapter 4. In the second part of the book on heterogenous agent economies we split the former Chapter 7 on overlapping generations (OLG) models. The solution of OLG models with perfect foresight is now covered in Chapter 9, where we also consider different ways to compute the transitional dynamics of these models. A new application deals with a model of the demographic transition. OLG models with aggregate and individual uncertainty are solved in Chapter 10.

Computer Code. As one of our main ambition, we keep the essential feature of this book to make all our programs that we used for the computations available on our website www.wiwi.uni-augsburg.de/vwl/maussner/. Therefore, the reader does not need to download any program code from other websites in order to replicate any of our findings, for example, on the statistics and characteristics of business cycle models or the dynamics of the distribution function in heterogeneous-agent economies. In the email correspondence with our readers this very feature of our book has often been pointed out as a crucial one by the graduate students in order to get started with his or her own research. If you are endowed with the programs for all the basic models of the business cycle, growth, and the distribution that we cover in this book, it is easy to start modifying them and work on your own projects.

Numerical methods are introduced one after the other and every new method is illustrated with the help of an example. This book and its accompanying web page is particularly designed for those students with little or no prior computing experience. We start from the scratch and deliberately concentrate on models that are formulated in discrete time so that we are able to bypass the technical complexities that arise when stochastic elements are introduced into continuous time optimizing models. The computer code is available either in Gauss or Fortran or both. The former computer language is almost identical to Matlab and can be translated without any effort. This way, the reader of this book can easily learn advanced programming techniques and, starting from very simple problems, she or he learns to apply them to more complex models, for example, a stochastic growth model with heterogeneous households.

Dynamic General Equilibrium Models. Dynamic General Equilibrium (DGE) models have become the workhorses of modern macroeconomics. Whatever textbook on advanced macroeconomics you consider you will find three kinds of models: the Solow model, the Ramsey model, and the overlapping generations model. The elementary versions of all three models can be studied with paper and pencil methods. But as soon as the researcher starts asking important questions of economic policy, these methods break down.

There are three questions researcher are most interested in. The first concerns transitional dynamics. For example, in growth theory, we are interested in the question of how countries converge to their long-run equilibrium, or, in public finance, we want to understand the behavior of the economy after an enduring tax cut. The second kind of problem concerns economic fluctuations that are caused by supply and demand shocks. Notably stochastic versions of the Ramsey model have been applied successfully to the study of business cycle dynamics. In these models demand and supply shocks trigger intra- and intertemporal substitution between leisure, consumption, and asset holdings and generate patterns in time series that mimic those found in macroeconomic data. The third issue, which has only received limited attention in the recent textbook literature, concerns models with heterogenous agents. Important applications of heterogeneous-agent economies can be found in the theory of income distribution, in the theory of asset pricing or in the field of public finance, to name but a few. To address any of these economic problems that are formulated as a DGE model, the researcher needs to apply computational methods.

Scope. The book is aimed at graduate students or advanced undergraduates. It may be used for both class-room and self study. It contains a great deal of new research both in the field of computational economics and in the field of macroeconomic theory. In essence, this book makes the following contributions:

1. The book tells the student in a simple way starting from a very basic level how to compute dynamic general equilibrium models. The emphasis is not on formal proofs, but rather on applications with codes and algorithms. Students should be able to start to program their own applications right away. Only some prior knowledge of statistics, linear algebra, and analysis is necessary. The relevant material from numerical analysis is gathered in a separate chapter for those readers who are unfamiliar with these techniques.
2. We also emphasize some problems of the practitioner that have only received limited if any attention at all in the recent text-

book literature. For example, we make an extensive effort to discuss the problem of finding a good initial value for the policy function in complex models so that the algorithm converges to the true solution. Likewise, we discuss the problem of modeling the dynamics of the distribution of the individual state variable in heterogeneous-agent economies in detail. Like econometrics, for example, numerical analysis is also as much an art as a science, and a young researcher in this field may often wonder why his or her particular computer program does not converge to an equilibrium value or fails to produce a sound solution. In other word, experience is important for the solution of numerical problems and our aim is to share as many as possible of our practical knowledge.

3. Our applications also reflect many recent research from the field of business cycle theory. For example, we compute the standard RBC model, monetary business cycle models, or the business cycle dynamics of the asset market. For this reason, the book is also valuable to both the student and the researcher of business cycles.

4. For this reason, the book is also interesting for researchers both in the field of (income and wealth) distribution theory and in the field of public finance.

The presentation in our book is self-contained and the reading of it is possible without the consultation of other material. The field of computational economics, however, is vast and we do not pretend to survey it. Fortunately, there are several other recent good textbooks that are complementary to ours. KENNETH JUDD (1998) is giving a comprehensive survey of computational economics and remains the standard reference, while MIRANDA and FACKLER (2002) have written a book that, like ours, is more directed towards the illustration of examples and algorithms, while their focus, however, is more on continuous time models. MARIMON and SCOTT (1999) have edited a textbook that also illustrates methods in order to compute the stochastic growth model that we have not covered in this book, for example the finite-element method. In our book, we also do not cover the process of calibration and estimation methods of stochastic DGE models with the help of econometric techniques such as maximum likelihood and method of moments. The textbooks of CANOVA (2007) and DEJONG with DAVE (2007) are excellent references for the study of these empirical methods. The textbook by LJUNGQVIST and SARGENT (2004) on recursive macroeconomic theory and the monograph by STOKEY and LUCAS with PRESCOTT (1989) on recursive methods may serve as a helpful reference for the economic theory and mathematical background applied in this book. McCandless (2008) provides a detailed presentation of various monetary and open economy models and their log-linearization together with the Matlab code, while Galí (2008) gives a concise introduction to the New Keynesian framework with an emphasis on monetary theory.

Organization. The book consists of three parts. Part I studies methods in order to compute representative-agent economies, Part II looks at heterogeneous-agent economies, while we collected numerical and other mathematical tools in part III. In the first Chapter, we introduce the benchmark model which is the stochastic Ramsey model and give an overview of possible solution methods. We compare different methods in the following five chapters with a focus on accuracy, speed and ease of implementation. After the study of the Part I, the reader should be able to choose among the different methods the one that suits the computation of his particular business cycle model best. The second part of the book is devoted to the application of numerical methods to the computation of heterogeneous-agent economies. In particular, we consider the heterogeneous-agent extension of the stochastic growth model on the one hand and the overlapping generations model on the other hand. A detailed description of numerical tools from the field of non-linear equations, approximation theory, differential and integration theory or numerical optimization is delegated to Chapter 11 that, together with Chapter 12 on other mathematical tools, constitutes Part III of the book.

We appreciate that this book cannot easily be covered in one semester, but one can conveniently choose parts of it as the basis of a one-semester course. For example, a course on computational methods in business cycle theory may choose the Chapters 1 through 5 or 6 where we covered the methods that we judge to be most useful for the computation of representative-agent business cycle and growth models. Chapter 1 introduces the stochastic growth model and gives an overview of the basic techniques for its computation. Chapter 2 reviews local approximation methods which have been predominantly applied in the analysis of business cycle models. Different from the first edition, we now also look at second-order perturbation methods. Chapters 3 and 4 cover the extended deterministic path approach and discrete state space methods. Chapters 5 and 6 present the parameterized expectations approach and projection methods, respectively. While a standard course on business cycles should minimally cover Chapter 1 with the benchmark model and a description of the basic statistics and calibration exercise as well as the first part of Chapter 2 that covers the computation of the linearized model, the instructor of a more specialized course should cover Chapters 1 and 2 and may pick any one of the remaining chapters. A reading list for a course on monetary economics may also include Chapters 1 and 2 of our book as it enables the student to compute the monetary business cycle model presented in Chapter 2 and, in addition, introduces him to the New Keynesian Phillips curve.

Graduate students with prior knowledge of numerical analysis may use Chapters 7 through 10 for an introduction to the computation of heterogeneous-agent economies and the theory of income distribution. Chapter 7 extends the stochastic growth model to a heterogeneous-agent economy and introduces different ways to compute the stationary distribution of wealth. Chapter 8 considers the dynamics of the income and wealth distribution. In Chapters 9 and 10, we look at overlapping generations models. Chapter 9 considers deterministic models. We compute the stationary equilibrium and transition dynamics in the perfect-foresight Auerbach-Kotlikoff model. Chapter 10 introduces individual and aggregate uncertainty in this model. We compute the stationary distribution of wealth in a model with idiosyncratic shocks to individual productivity and the business cycle dynamics in a model with shocks to total factor productivity. Therefore, a one-semester course in computational public finance that is aimed at the computation of Auerbach-Kotlikoff models can be based on Chapters 1-3, 9 and 10.

Acknowledgements. Finally we would like to thank a large number of individuals. The first edition of the book was written during 2000-2004, while we revised the book during 2006-2008. We would like to thank students in graduate classes in monetary economics and computational economics that were taught at the universities of Augsburg, Bamberg, Innsbruck and Munich and the Deutsche Bundesbank (German Central Bank). We received useful comments from Selahattin İmrohoroğlu, Andreas Irmen, Ken Judd, Paul McNelis, Michael Reiter, José-Victor Ríos-Rull, and Mark Trede. For particular assistance in the preparation of the text, including critical comments on several drafts and helpful suggestions, we like to thank Jürgen Antony, André de Beisac, Hans-Helmut Bünning, Sabine Gunst, Michael Holsteuer, Nikolai Hristov, Torben Klarl, Jana Kremer, Dominik Menno, and Sotir Trambev. Burkhard Heer kindly acknowledges support from the German Science Foundation (Deutsche Forschungsgemeinschaft DFG) during his stay at Georgetown University and Stanford University.

Bolzano *Burkhard Heer*
Augsburg *Alfred Maußner*
October 2008

Table of Contents

Preface VII
List of Figures XXIII
List of Symbols XXVII
List of Programs XXIX

Part I. Representative Agent Models

1 Basic Models 3
  1.1 The Deterministic Finite-Horizon Ramsey Model
     and Non-Linear Programming 4
     1.1.1 The Ramsey Problem 4
     1.1.2 The Kuhn-Tucker Theorem 6
  1.2 The Deterministic Infinite-Horizon Ramsey Model
     and Dynamic Programming 9
     1.2.1 Recursive Utility 9
     1.2.2 Euler Equations 11
     1.2.3 Dynamic Programming 13
     1.2.4 The Saddle Path 16
     1.2.5 Models with Analytic Solution 21
  1.3 The Stochastic Ramsey Model 25
     1.3.1 Stochastic Output 25
     1.3.2 Stochastic Euler Equations 28
     1.3.3 Stochastic Dynamic Programming 30
  1.4 Labor Supply, Growth, and the Decentralized
     Economy 33
     1.4.1 Substitution of Leisure 33
     1.4.2 Growth and Restrictions on Technology and
           Preferences 34

		1.4.3	The Decentralized Economy	40
	1.5	Model Calibration and Evaluation		44
		1.5.1	The Benchmark Model	44
		1.5.2	Calibration	46
		1.5.3	Model Evaluation	51
	1.6	Numerical Solution Methods		59
		1.6.1	Characterization	59
		1.6.2	Accuracy of Solutions	61

Appendices ... 65
A.1 Solution to Example 1.2.1 ... 65
A.2 Restrictions on Technology and Preferences ... 67
Problems ... 72

2 Perturbation Methods ... 75
  2.1 Linear Solutions for Deterministic Models ... 77
  2.2 The Stochastic Linear Quadratic Model ... 84
  2.3 LQ Approximation ... 89
    2.3.1 A Warning ... 89
    2.3.2 An Illustrative Example ... 91
    2.3.3 The General Method ... 95
  2.4 Linear Approximation ... 98
    2.4.1 An Illustrative Example ... 99
    2.4.2 The General Method ... 106
  2.5 Quadratic Approximation ... 114
    2.5.1 Introduction ... 114
    2.5.2 The Deterministic Growth Model ... 116
    2.5.3 The Stochastic Growth Model ... 118
    2.5.4 Generalization ... 124
  2.6 Applications ... 131
    2.6.1 The Benchmark Model ... 131
    2.6.2 Time to Build ... 138
    2.6.3 New Keynesian Phillips Curve ... 143

Appendices ... 158
A.3 Solution of the Stochastic LQ Problem ... 158
A.4 Derivation of the Log-Linear Model of the New Keynesian Phillips Curve ... 160
Problems ... 169

3 Deterministic Extended Path 175
3.1 Solution of Deterministic Models 176
3.1.1 Finite-Horizon Models 176
3.1.2 Infinite-Horizon Models 179
3.2 Solution of Stochastic Models 181
3.2.1 An Illustrative Example 182
3.2.2 The Algorithm in General 184
3.3 Further Applications 186
3.3.1 The Benchmark Model 186
3.3.2 A Small Open Economy 189
Problems 200

4 Discrete State Space Methods 207
4.1 Solution of Deterministic Models 208
4.2 Solution of Stochastic Models 221
4.3 Further Applications 232
4.3.1 Non-Negative Investment 232
4.3.2 The Benchmark Model 235
Problems 238

5 Parameterized Expectations 243
5.1 Characterization of Approximate Solutions 244
5.1.1 An Illustrative Example 244
5.1.2 A General Framework 247
5.1.3 Adaptive Learning 249
5.2 Computation of the Approximate Solution 252
5.2.1 Choice of T and ψ 252
5.2.2 Iterative Computation of the Fixed Point 254
5.2.3 Direct Computation of the Fixed Point 255
5.2.4 Starting Points 257
5.3 Applications 259
5.3.1 Stochastic Growth with Non-Negative Investment 259
5.3.2 The Benchmark Model 265
5.3.3 Limited Participation Model of Money 268
Problems 281

6 Projection Methods 285
6.1 Characterization of Projection Methods 286
6.1.1 An Example 286
6.1.2 The General Framework 289
6.1.3 Relation to Parameterized Expectations 291
6.2 The Building Blocks of Projection Methods 293
6.2.1 Approximating Function 293
6.2.2 Residual Function 294
6.2.3 Projection and Solution 295
6.2.4 Accuracy of Solution 297
6.3 Applications 297
6.3.1 The Deterministic Growth Model 298
6.3.2 The Stochastic Growth Model with Non-Negative Investment 302
6.3.3 The Benchmark Model 309
6.3.4 The Equity Premium Puzzle 311
Problems 324

Part II. Heterogeneous Agent Models

7 Computation of Stationary Distributions 329
7.1 A Simple Heterogeneous-Agent Model with Aggregate Certainty 331
7.2 The Stationary Equilibrium of a Heterogeneous-Agent Economy 338
7.3 Applications 359
7.3.1 The Risk-Free Rate in Economies with Heterogeneous Agents and Incomplete Insurance 359
7.3.2 Heterogeneous Productivity and Income Distribution 367
Problems 384

8 Dynamics of the Distribution Function 389
8.1 Introduction 390
8.2 Transition Dynamics 393

	8.2.1	Partial Information 395
	8.2.2	Guessing a Finite Time Path for the Factor Prices 406
8.3	Aggregate Uncertainty 411	
8.4	Applications 421	
	8.4.1	Costs of Business Cycles with Liquidity Constraints and Indivisibilities 422
	8.4.2	Business Cycle Dynamics of the Income Distribution 431
8.5	Epilogue 446	
Problems 449		

9 Deterministic Overlapping Generations Models ... 451
9.1	The Steady State 453	
	9.1.1	An Illustrative Example 454
	9.1.2	Computation of the Steady State 458
9.2	The Transition Path 469	
	9.2.1	A Stylized 6-Period Model 471
	9.2.2	Computation of the Transition Path 473
9.3	Application: The Demographic Transition 482	
	9.3.1	The Model 483
	9.3.2	Computation 489
	9.3.3	Results 499
Problems 502		

10 Stochastic Overlapping Generations Models 507
10.1 Individual Uncertainty 507
10.2 Aggregate Uncertainty 520
10.2.1 Log-Linearization 522
10.2.2 The Algorithm of Krusell and Smith in Overlapping Generations Models 533
Appendix 549
A.5 Parameters of the AR(1)-Process with Annual Periods 549
Problems 551

Part III. Tools

11 Numerical Methods ... 555
11.1 A Quick Refresher in Linear Algebra ... 555
11.1.1 Complex Numbers ... 555
11.1.2 Vectors ... 557
11.1.3 Norms ... 558
11.1.4 Linear Independence ... 558
11.1.5 Matrices ... 558
11.1.6 Linear and Quadratic Forms ... 563
11.1.7 Eigenvalues and Eigenvectors ... 564
11.1.8 Matrix Factorization ... 565
11.1.9 Givens Rotation ... 570
11.2 Function Approximation ... 570
11.2.1 Taylor's Theorem ... 571
11.2.2 Implicit Function Theorem ... 574
11.2.3 Linear Interpolation ... 575
11.2.4 Cubic Splines ... 577
11.2.5 Families of Polynomials ... 578
11.2.6 Chebyshev Polynomials ... 581
11.2.7 Multidimensional Approximation ... 588
11.2.8 Neural Networks ... 591
11.3 Numerical Differentiation and Integration ... 593
11.3.1 Differentiation ... 593
11.3.2 Numerical Integration ... 598
11.4 Stopping Criteria for Iterative Algorithms ... 603
11.5 Non-Linear Equations ... 606
11.5.1 Single Equations ... 607
11.5.2 Multiple Equations ... 610
11.6 Numerical Optimization ... 622
11.6.1 Golden Section Search ... 623
11.6.2 Gauss-Newton Method ... 626
11.6.3 Quasi-Newton ... 630
11.6.4 Genetic Algorithms ... 633

12 Various Other Tools 645
  12.1 Difference Equations 645
    12.1.1 Linear Difference Equations................. 645
    12.1.2 Non-Linear Difference Equations 648
  12.2 Markov Processes 651
  12.3 DM-Statistic 658
  12.4 The HP-Filter 663

References 667

Name Index 687

Subject Index 693

List of Figures

Figure 1.1:	Boundedness of the Capital Stock	11
Figure 1.2:	Phase Diagram of the Infinite-Horizon Ramsey Model	18
Figure 1.3:	No Path Leaves the Region A_2	19
Figure 1.4:	Convergence of the Stock of Capital in the Infinite-Horizon Ramsey Model	22
Figure 1.5:	Stationary Distribution of the Capital Stock in the Stochastic Infinite-Horizon Ramsey Model	32
Figure 1.6:	Impulse Responses in the Benchmark Model	53
Figure 1.7:	Impulse Responses from an Estimated VAR	54
Figure 1.8:	Productivity Shock in the Benchmark Business Cycle Model	58
Figure 2.1:	Eigenvalues of W	79
Figure 2.2:	Approximate Time Path of the Capital Stock in the Deterministic Growth Model	81
Figure 2.3:	Stationary Distribution of the Capital Stock from the Analytic and the Linear Approximate Solution of the Stochastic Infinite-Horizon Ramsey Model	105
Figure 2.4:	Policy Functions of Consumption of the Deterministic Growth Model	118
Figure 2.5:	Real Effects of a Monetary Shock in the Model Without Nominal Rigidities	153
Figure 2.6:	Impulse Responses to a Monetary Shock in the New Keynesian Phillips Curve Model	154

Figure 3.1:	Example Solutions of the Finite-Horizon Ramsey Model	179
Figure 3.2:	Approximate Time Path of the Capital Stock in the Deterministic Growth Model	181
Figure 3.3:	Simulated Time Path of the Stochastic Ramsey Model	183
Figure 3.4:	Response of State and Costate Variables to a Productivity Shock in the Small Open Economy	196
Figure 3.5:	Response of Control Variables to a Productivity Shock in the Small Open Economy	197
Figure 3.6:	Response to an Interest Rate Shock in the Small Open Economy	198
Figure 4.1:	Policy Functions of the Next-Period Capital Stock of the Infinite-Horizon Ramsey Model	220
Figure 4.2:	Policy Function for Consumption of the Stochastic Growth Model with Non-Negative Investment	234
Figure 5.1:	Impulse Responses to a Monetary Shock in the Limited Participation Model	278
Figure 6.1:	Polynomial Approximation of e^{-t}	288
Figure 6.2:	Euler Equation Residuals from the Deterministic Growth Model	303
Figure 7.1:	Convergence of the Distribution Mean	349
Figure 7.2:	Convergence of K	350
Figure 7.3:	Invariant Density Function of Wealth	351
Figure 7.4:	Invariant Density Function of Wealth for the Employed Worker	353
Figure 7.5:	Next-Period Assets $a'(e_h, a)$ of the Employed Agent	363
Figure 7.6:	Next-Period Assets $a'(e_l, a)$ of the Unemployed Agent	364
Figure 7.7:	Change in Assets $a' - a$	365

Figure 7.8:	Stationary Distribution Function	365
Figure 7.9:	Lorenz Curve of US Wealth, Income, and Earnings in 1992	368
Figure 8.1:	Value Function of the Employed Worker	400
Figure 8.2:	Savings of the Workers	401
Figure 8.3:	Dynamics of the Distribution Function over Time	402
Figure 8.4:	Convergence of the Aggregate Capital Stock	403
Figure 8.5:	The Dynamics of the Distribution Function	410
Figure 8.6:	Goodness of Fit for the Stationary Distribution	411
Figure 8.7:	Distribution Function in Period $T = 3,000$	420
Figure 8.8:	Time Path of the Aggregate Capital Stock K_t	421
Figure 8.9:	Consumption $c(a, s)$ in the Storage Economy	426
Figure 8.10:	Net Savings $a' - a$ in the Storage Economy	427
Figure 8.11:	Invariant Density Function $g(a, s)$ in the Storage Economy	428
Figure 8.12:	Consumption $c(a, s)$ in an Economy with Intermediation	429
Figure 8.13:	Net Savings $a' - a$ in an Economy with Intermediation	430
Figure 8.14:	Invariant Density Function $g(a, s)$ with Intermediation Technology	431
Figure 8.15:	Lorenz Curve of Income	444
Figure 8.16:	Lorenz Curve of Wealth	446
Figure 9.1:	Age-Wealth Profile	462
Figure 9.2:	Age-Labor Supply Profile	463
Figure 9.3:	Age-Capital Profile in the New and in the Old Steady State	474
Figure 9.4:	Age-Labor Supply Profile in the New and in the Old Steady State	475
Figure 9.5:	Capital-Age and Labor-Age Profile in the Old Steady State and for the Household Born in Period $t = -2$	477
Figure 9.6:	Transition from the Old to the New Steady State	479

Figure 9.7: Survival Probabilities in the US in the Year 2000 489
Figure 9.8: Age-Productivity Profile 490
Figure 9.9: Stationary Age Distribution in the Initial Steady State.............................. 494
Figure 9.10: Population Size During the Transition 495
Figure 9.11: Decline of the Labor Force Share During the Transition 496
Figure 9.12: Transition Dynamics of Aggregate Variables and Factor Prices 499
Figure 9.13: Steady State Behavior in the Economy with Constant (solid line) and Growing (broken line) Population............................ 500

Figure 10.1: Lorenz Curve of US and Model Earnings 514
Figure 10.2: Age-Wealth Profile 517
Figure 10.3: Lorenz Curve of US and Model Wealth....... 518
Figure 10.4: Impulse Responses in the OLG Model........ 533
Figure 10.5: Non-Stochastic Steady State Age-Profiles..... 546
Figure 10.6: Time Series Simulation 547

Figure 11.1: Gaussian Plane 556
Figure 11.2: Linear Interpolation 576
Figure 11.3: Chebyshev Polynomials T_1, T_2 and T_3 584
Figure 11.4: Chebyshev Approximation of e^x 587
Figure 11.5: Chebyshev Approximation of $\max\{0, x-1\}$ .. 589
Figure 11.6: Neural Networks 592
Figure 11.7: Bisection Method 607
Figure 11.8: Modified Newton-Raphson Method 609
Figure 11.9: Secant Method............................ 610
Figure 11.10: Gauss-Seidel Iterations..................... 612
Figure 11.11: Dogleg Step 621
Figure 11.12: Golden Section Search 623
Figure 11.13: Stochastic Universal Sampling 638

Figure 12.1: Topological Conjugacy Between $\mathbf{f}$ and $\mathbf{J}(\bar{\mathbf{x}})$ ... 650
Figure 12.2: Local Stable and Unstable Manifold 652

List of Symbols

$\mathbb{Z}$	set of all integers
$\mathbb{R}$	real line
$\mathbb{R}^n$	Euclidean n-space
$\mathbb{C}^n$	complex n-space
C^n	class of functions having n continuous derivatives
f' or $f^{(1)}$	first derivative of a single valued function of a single argument
f'' or $f^{(2)}$	second derivative of a single valued function of a single argument
$f^{(n)}$	nth order derivative of a singe valued function of a single argument
f_i or $D_i f$ or f_{x_i}	first partial derivative of a single valued function with respect to its ith argument
f_{ij} or $D_i D_j f$ or $f_{x_i x_j}$	second partial derivative of a single valued function with respect to argument i and j (in this order)
$A = (a_{ij})$	n by m matrix A with typical element a_{ij}
$A^{-1} = (a^{ij})$	the inverse of matrix A with typical element a^{ij}
A', A^T	the transpose of the matrix $A = (a_{ij})$ with elements $A' = (a_{ji})$
$J(\bar{\mathbf{x}})$	the Jacobian matrix of the vector valued function $\mathbf{f}(\bar{\mathbf{x}})$ at the point $\bar{\mathbf{x}}$

$H(\bar{\mathbf{x}})$	the Hesse matrix of the single valued function $f(\bar{\mathbf{x}})$ at the point $\bar{\mathbf{x}}$
$\nabla f(\mathbf{x})$	the gradient of f at $\mathbf{x}$, that is, the row vector of partial derivatives $\partial f(\mathbf{x})/\partial x_i$
$\|\mathbf{x}\|_2$	the Euclidian norm (length) of the vector $\mathbf{x} \in \mathbb{R}^n$, which is given by $\sqrt{x_1^2 + x_2^2 + \cdots + x_n^2}$
$\operatorname{tr} A$	the trace of the square matrix A, i.e., the sum of its diagonal elements
$\det A$	the determinant of the square matrix A
$\epsilon \sim N(\mu, \sigma^2)$	the random variable ϵ is normally distributed with mean μ and variance σ^2
$\forall$	for all

List of Programs

Name	Programming Language	See Page
Benchmark	Fortran	132, 135, 187, 236, 265, 310
Benchmark_LL	Gauss	52
BLIP	Fortran, Gauss	577
CDHesse	Fortran, Gauss	96, 122, 132, 598
CDJac	Fortran, Gauss	96, 96, 122, 596, 614
ChebCoef	Fortran, Gauss	585
ChebEval1	Gauss	583
cspline	Fortran, Gauss	578
Equity	Fortran	320
Equivec1	Gauss	342, 656
Fixp1	Gauss	613
Fixp2	Gauss	608
FixvMN1	Fortran, Gauss	614
FixvMN2	Fortran, Gauss	187, 614
GaussNewton	Fortran	281
GSS	Gauss	626
HPFilter	Fortran, Gauss	664
LIP	Gauss	575
LP	Fortran	275
NKPK	Gauss	152, 155
MarkovAR	Fortran, Gauss	658
MNRStep	Fortran, Gauss	620
QuasiNewton	Fortran, Gauss	633
QNStep	Fortran, Gauss	620

Name	Programming Language	See Page
Ramsey1	Gauss	178
Ramsey2a	Gauss	80
Ramsey2b	Gauss	117
Ramsey2c	Gauss	181
Ramsey2d	Gauss	217
Ramsey2e	Gauss	300, 301
Ramsey3a	Gauss	104, 114, 306
Ramsey3b	Gauss	122
Ramsey3c	Gauss	183, 200
Ramsey3d	Gauss	229
RCh7_denf	Gauss	352
RCh7_disf1	Gauss	343
RCh7_func	Gauss	357
RCh7_hug	Gauss	362
RCh7_mont	Gauss	354
RCh7_tax	Gauss	379
RCh8_gues	Gauss	409
RCh8_part	Gauss	398
RCh8_unc	Gauss	418
RCh83_cas1	Gauss	437, 439
RCh83_imo	Gauss	425
RCh91d	Gauss	461
RCh91p	Gauss	468
RCh91v	Gauss	466
RCh92AK6	Gauss	473, 481
RCh93	Gauss	491, 497, 498
RCh101	Gauss	515
RCh1021	Gauss	532
RCh1022	Gauss	541
Search1	Fortran	641
Search2	Fortran	642
SGNNI_a	Gauss	234
SGNNI_b	Fortran	262

Name	Programming Language	See Page
SGNNI_c	Fortran	305, 306, 310
SOE	Gauss	196
SolveLA	Fortran, Gauss	76, 83, 99, 106, 113, 113, 113, 132, 133, 134
SolveLA2	Gauss	113
SolveLQA	Fortran, Gauss	76, 89, 96, 96, 134
SolveQA	Fortran, Gauss	130, 133, 133, 134
SolveVI	Fortran, Gauss	228
splint	Fortran, Gauss	578
ToB	Gauss	141

Part I
Representative Agent Models

Chapter 1

Basic Models

Overview. This chapter introduces you to the framework of dynamic general equilibrium models. Our presentation serves two aims: first, we prepare the ground for the algorithms presented in subsequent chapters that use one out of two possible characterizations of a model's solution. Second, we develop standard tools in model building and model evaluation used throughout the book.

The most basic DGE model is the so called Ramsey model, where a single consumer-producer chooses an utility maximizing consumption profile. We begin with the deterministic, finite-horizon version of this model. The set of first-order conditions for this problem is a system of non-linear equations that can be solved with adequate software. Then, we consider the infinite-horizon version of this model. We characterize its solution along two lines: the Euler equations provide a set of difference equations that determine the optimal time path of consumption; dynamic programming delivers a policy function that relates the agent's choice of current consumption to his stock of capital. Both characterizations readily extend to the stochastic version of the infinite-horizon Ramsey model that we introduce in Section 1.3. In Section 1.4 we add productivity growth and labor supply to this model. We use this benchmark model in Section 1.5 to illustrate the problems of parameter choice and model evaluation. Section 1.6 concludes this chapter with a synopsis of the numerical solution techniques presented in Chapters 2 through 6 and introduces measures to evaluate the goodness of the approximate solutions.

Readers who already have experience with the stochastic growth model with endogenous labor supply (our benchmark model) may consider to skip the first four sections and to start with Section 1.5 to become familiar with our notation and to get an idea of the methods presented in subsequent chapters.

1.1 The Deterministic Finite-Horizon Ramsey Model and Non-Linear Programming

1.1.1 The Ramsey Problem

In 1928 Frank Ramsey, a young mathematician, posed the problem "How much of its income should a nation save?"[1] and developed a dynamic model to answer this question. Though greatly praised by Keynes,[2] it took almost forty years and further papers by DAVID CASS (1965), TJALLING KOOPMANS (1965), and WILLIAM BROCK and LEONARD MIRMAN (1972) before Ramsey's formulation stimulated macroeconomic theory. Today, variants of his dynamic optimization problem are the cornerstones of most models of economic fluctuations and growth.

At the heart of the Ramsey problem there is an economic agent producing output from labor and capital who must decide how to split production between consumption and capital accumulation. In Ramsey's original formulation, this agent was a fictitious planning authority. Yet, we may also think of a yeoman growing corn or of a household, who receives wage income and dividends and buys stocks.

In the following we use the farmer example to develop a few basic concepts. Time t is divided into intervals of unit length and extends from the current period $t = 0$ to the farmers planning

---

[1] RAMSEY (1928), p. 543.
[2] KEYNES (1930) wrote:

> ... one of the most remarkable contributions to mathematical economics ever made, both in respect of the intrinsic importance and difficulty of its subject, the power and elegance of the technical methods employed, and the clear purity of illumination with which the writer's mind is felt by the reader to play about its subject.

1.1 Finite-Horizon Ramsey Model and Non-Linear Programming

horizon $t = T$. K_t and N_t denote the amounts of seed and labor available in period t, respectively. They produce the amount Y_t of corn according to

$$Y_t = F(N_t, K_t). \tag{1.1}$$

The production function F has the usual properties:

1. there is no free lunch: $0 = F(0,0)$,
2. F is strictly increasing in both of its arguments,
3. concave (i.e. we rule out increasing returns to scale),
4. and twice continuously differentiable.

At each period the farmer must decide how much corn to produce, to consume and to put aside for future production. The amount of next period's seed is the farmer's future stock of capital K_{t+1}. His choice of consumption C_t and investment K_{t+1} is bounded by current production:

$$C_t + K_{t+1} \leq Y_t.$$

The farmer does not value leisure but works a given number of hours N each period and seeks to maximize the utility function

$$U(C_0, C_1, \ldots, C_T).$$

In the farmer example capital depreciates fully, since seed used for growing corn is not available for future production. When we think of capital in terms of machines, factories, or, even more generally, human knowledge, this is an overly restrictive assumption. More generally, the resource constraint is given by

$$Y_t + (1 - \delta)K_t \geq C_t + K_{t+1},$$

where $\delta \in [0, 1]$ is the rate of capital depreciation. In the following, notation will become a bit simpler if we define the production function to include any capital left after depreciation and drop the constant N:

$$f(K_t) := F(N, K_t) + (1 - \delta)K_t. \tag{1.2}$$

Since production without seed is impossible, we assume $f(0) = 0$, while the other properties of F carry over to f.

We are now in the position to state the finite-horizon deterministic Ramsey problem formally as follows:

$$\max_{(C_0,\ldots,C_T)} U(C_0, \ldots, C_T)$$

s.t.

$$\left.\begin{array}{rcl} K_{t+1} + C_t & \leq & f(K_t), \\ 0 & \leq & C_t, \\ 0 & \leq & K_{t+1}, \end{array}\right\} t = 0, \ldots, T, \qquad (1.3)$$

K_0 given.

There is no uncertainty in this problem: the farmer knows in advance how much corn he will get when he plans to work N hours and has K_t pounds of seed. Furthermore, he is also sure as to how he will value a given sequence of consumption $\{C_t\}_{t=0}^T$. Therefore, we label this problem deterministic. Since we assume $T < \infty$, this is a finite-horizon problem.

1.1.2 The Kuhn-Tucker Theorem

Problem (1.3) is a standard non-linear programming problem: choose an n-dimensional vector $\mathbf{x} \in \mathbb{R}^n$ that maximizes the real-valued function $f(\mathbf{x})$ in a convex set $\mathscr{D}$ determined by l constraints of the form $h^i(\mathbf{x}) \geq 0$, $i = 1, \ldots, l$. The famous Kuhn-Tucker theorem provides a set of necessary and sufficient conditions for a solution to exist:[3]

Theorem 1.1.1 (Kuhn-Tucker) *Let f be a concave C^1 function mapping U into $\mathbb{R}$, where $U \subset \mathbb{R}^n$ is open and convex. For $i = 1, \ldots, l$, let $h^i : U \to \mathbb{R}$ be concave C^1 functions. Suppose there is some $\bar{\mathbf{x}} \in U$ such that*

$$h^i(\bar{\mathbf{x}}) > 0, \quad i = 1, \ldots, l.$$

---

[3] See, for instance, SUNDARAM, 1996, Theorem 7.16, p. 187f.

1.1 Finite-Horizon Ramsey Model and Non-Linear Programming 7

Then $\mathbf{x}^*$ maximizes f over $\mathscr{D} = \{\mathbf{x} \in U | h^i(\mathbf{x}) \geq 0, i = 1, \ldots, l\}$ if and only if there is $\boldsymbol{\lambda}^* \in \mathbb{R}^l$ such that the Kuhn-Tucker first-order conditions hold:

$$\frac{\partial f(\mathbf{x}^*)}{\partial x_j} + \sum_{i=1}^{l} \lambda_i^* \frac{\partial h_i(\mathbf{x}^*)}{\partial x_j} = 0, \quad j = 1, \ldots, n,$$

$$\lambda_i^* \geq 0, \qquad i = 1, \ldots, l,$$

$$\lambda_i^* h^i(\mathbf{x}^*) = 0, \qquad i = 1, \ldots, l.$$

It is easy to see that problem (1.3) fits this theorem if the utility function U and the production function f are strictly concave, strictly increasing, and twice continuously differentiable. Applying Theorem 1.1.1 to problem (1.3) provides the following first-order conditions:[4]

$$0 = \frac{\partial U(C_0, \ldots, C_T)}{\partial C_t} - \lambda_t + \mu_t, \quad t = 0, \ldots, T, \tag{1.4a}$$

$$0 = -\lambda_t + \lambda_{t+1} f'(K_{t+1}) + \omega_{t+1}, \quad t = 0, \ldots, T-1, \tag{1.4b}$$

$$0 = -\lambda_T + \omega_{T+1}, \tag{1.4c}$$

$$0 = \lambda_t \left(f(K_t) - C_t - K_{t+1} \right), \quad t = 0, \ldots, T, \tag{1.4d}$$

$$0 = \mu_t C_t, \quad t = 0, \ldots, T, \tag{1.4e}$$

$$0 = \omega_{t+1} K_{t+1}, \quad t = 0, \ldots, T, \tag{1.4f}$$

where λ_t is the Lagrangean multiplier attached to the resource constraint of period t,

$$f(K_t) - C_t - K_{t+1} \geq 0,$$

and where μ_t and ω_{t+1} are the multipliers related to the non-negativity constraints on C_t and K_{t+1}, respectively. The multipliers value the severeness of the respective constraint. A constraint

---

[4] As usual, a prime denotes the first (two primes the second) derivative of a function $f(x)$ of one variable x. Condition (1.4c) derives from the budget constraint of period T, $f(K_T) - C_T - K_{T+1} \geq 0$, which has the multiplier λ_T, and the non-negativity constraint on K_{T+1}, which has the multiplier ω_{T+1}.

that does not bind has a multiplier of zero. For example, if $C_t > 0$ then (1.4e) implies $\mu_t = 0$. If we want to rule out corner solutions, i.e., solutions where one or more of the non-negativity constraints bind, we need to impose an additional assumption. In the present context this assumption has a very intuitive meaning: the farmer hates to starve to death in any period. Formally, this translates into the statement

$$\frac{\partial U(C_0, \ldots, C_T)}{\partial C_t} \to \infty \text{ if } C_t \to 0 \text{ for all } t = 0, \ldots, T.$$

This is sufficient to imply $C_t > 0$ for all $t = 1, \ldots, T$, $\mu_t = 0$ (from (1.4e)), and the Lagrangean multipliers λ_t equal the marginal utility of consumption in period t and, thus, are also strictly positive:

$$\frac{\partial U(C_0, \ldots, C_t)}{\partial C_t} = \lambda_t.$$

Condition (1.4d), thus, implies that the resource constraints always bind. Furthermore, since we have assumed $f(0) = 0$, positive consumption also requires positive amounts of seed $K_t > 0$ from period $t = 0$ through period T. However, the farmer will consume his entire crop in the last period of his life, since any seed left reduces his lifetime utility. More formally, this result is implied by equations (1.4f) and (1.4c), which yield $\lambda_T K_{T+1} = 0$. Taking all pieces together, we arrive at the following characterization of an optimal solution:

$$K_{t+1} = f(K_t) - C_t, \tag{1.5a}$$

$$\frac{\partial U(C_0, \ldots C_T)/\partial C_t}{\partial U(C_0, \ldots C_T)/\partial C_{t+1}} = f'(K_{t+1}). \tag{1.5b}$$

The lhs of equation (1.5b) is the marginal rate of substitution between consumption in two adjacent periods. It gives the rate at which the farmer is willing to forego consumption in t for consumption one period ahead. The rhs provides the compensation for an additional unit of savings: the increase in future output.

1.2 The Deterministic Infinite-Horizon Ramsey Model and Dynamic Programming

In equation (1.5b) the marginal rate of substitution between two adjacent periods depends on the entire time profile of consumption. For this reason, we must solve the system of $2T - 1$ nonlinear, simultaneous equations (1.5) at once to obtain the time profile of consumption. Though probably difficult in practice this is, in principle, a viable strategy as long as T is finite. However, if we consider an economy with indefinite final period, that is, if T approaches infinity, this is no longer feasible. We cannot solve for infinitely many variables at once. To circumvent this problem, we restrict the class of intertemporal optimization problems to problems that have a recursive structure. Recursive problems pose themselves every period in the same, unchanged way. Their solution is not a time profile of optimal decisions determined at an arbitrary initial period $t = 0$ but consists in decision rules that determine the agent's behavior at each future point in time. The time additive separable (TAS) utility function, which we introduce in the next subsection, allows for a recursive formulation of the Ramsey problem. For this problem we derive first-order conditions via the Kuhn-Tucker method in Subsection 1.2.2. There is, however, an alternative approach available: dynamic programming, which we consider in Subsection 1.2.3. Subsection 1.2.4 provides a characterization of the dynamics of the infinite-horizon Ramsey model. We close this section with a brief digression that considers the few models that admit an analytic solution of the Ramsey problem.

1.2.1 Recursive Utility

The TAS utility function is defined recursively from

$$U_t = u(C_t) + \beta U_{t+1}, \quad \beta \in (0,1). \tag{1.6}$$

In this definition β is a discount factor and $\beta^{-1} - 1$ is known as the pure rate of time preference. The function $u : [0, \infty) \to \mathbb{R}$

is called the one-period, current-period, or felicity function. We assume that u is strictly increasing, strictly concave and twice continuously differentiable.

The solution to the finite-horizon Ramsey model depends upon the chosen terminal date T. Yet, in as far as we want to portray the behavior of the economy with Ramsey type models there is no natural final date T. As a consequence, most models extend the planning horizon into the indefinite future by letting $T \to \infty$. Iterating on (1.6) we arrive at the following definition of the utility function

$$U_t = \sum_{s=0}^{\infty} \beta^s u(C_{t+s}). \tag{1.7}$$

If we want to rank consumption streams according to this criterion function, we must ensure that the sum on the rhs is bounded from above, i.e., $U_t < \infty$ for every admissible sequence of points $C_t, C_{t+1}, C_{t+2}, \ldots$. This will hold, if the growth factor of one-period utility u, $g_u := u(C_{t+s+1})/u(C_{t+s})$, is smaller than $1/\beta$ for all $s = 0, 1, 2, \ldots$. Consider the Ramsey problem (1.3) with infinite time horizon:

$$\max_{C_0, C_1, \ldots} U_0 = \sum_{t=0}^{\infty} \beta^t u(C_t)$$

s.t.

$$\left. \begin{array}{rcl} K_{t+1} + C_t & \leq & f(K_t), \\ 0 & \leq & C_t, \\ 0 & \leq & K_{t+1}, \end{array} \right\} t = 0, 1, \ldots, \tag{1.8}$$

K_0 given.

In this model we do not need to assume that the one-period utility function u is bounded. Since u is continuous, it is sufficient to assume that the economy's resources are finite. In a dynamic context this requires that there is an upper bound on capital accumulation, i.e., there is $\bar{K}$ such that for each $K > \bar{K}$ output is smaller than needed to maintain K:

$$\exists \bar{K} \text{ so that } \forall K_t > \bar{K} \Rightarrow K_{t+1} < K_t. \tag{1.9}$$

For instance, let $f(K) = K^\alpha$, $\alpha \in (0,1)$. Then:

$$K \leq K^\alpha \Rightarrow \bar{K} = 1^{1/(\alpha-1)} = 1.$$

Given condition (1.9), any admissible sequence of capital stocks is bounded by $K^{\max} := \max\{\bar{K}, K_0\}$ and consumption in any period cannot exceed $f(K^{\max})$. Figure 1.1 makes that obvious: consider any point to the left of $\bar{K}$ such as K_1 and assume that consumption equals zero in all periods. Then, the sequence of capital stocks originating in K_1 approaches $\bar{K}$. Similarly, the sequence starting in K_2 approaches $\bar{K}$ from the right.

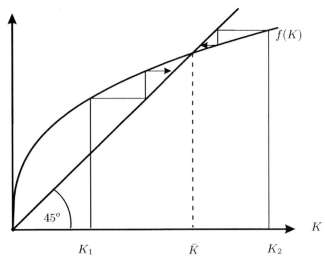

Figure 1.1: Boundedness of the Capital Stock

1.2.2 Euler Equations

There are two approaches to characterize the solution to the Ramsey problem (1.8). The first is an extension of the Kuhn-Tucker method[5] and the second is dynamic programming.[6] According

---
[5] See, e.g., CHOW (1997), Chapter 2 and ROMER (1991).
[6] Here, the standard reference is Chapter 4 of STOKEY and LUCAS with PRESCOTT (1989).

to the first approach necessary conditions may be derived from maximizing the following Lagrangean function with respect to $C_0, C_1, \ldots, K_1, K_2, \ldots$:

$$\mathscr{L} = \sum_{t=0}^{\infty} \beta^t \Big[u(C_t) + \lambda_t \left(f(K_t) - C_t - K_{t+1} \right) + \mu_t C_t + \omega_{t+1} K_{t+1} \Big].$$

Note that in this expression the Lagrangean multipliers λ_t, μ_t, and ω_{t+1} refer to period t values. Period $t = 0$ values are given by $\beta^t \lambda_t$, $\beta^t \mu_t$, and $\beta^t \omega_{t+1}$. The first-order conditions for maximizing $\mathscr{L}$ are given by:

$$u'(C_t) = \lambda_t - \mu_t, \tag{1.10a}$$
$$\lambda_t = \beta \lambda_{t+1} f'(K_{t+1}) + \omega_{t+1}, \tag{1.10b}$$
$$0 = \lambda_t (f(K_t) - C_t - K_{t+1}), \tag{1.10c}$$
$$0 = \mu_t C_t, \tag{1.10d}$$
$$0 = \omega_{t+1} K_{t+1}. \tag{1.10e}$$

We continue to assume that the farmer hates starving to death,

$$\lim_{C \to 0} u'(C) = \infty, \tag{1.11}$$

so that the non-negativity constraints never bind. Since u is strictly increasing in its argument, the resource constraint always binds. Therefore, we can reduce the first-order conditions to a second order difference equation in the capital stock:

$$\frac{u'(f(K_t) - K_{t+1})}{u'(f(K_{t+1}) - K_{t+2})} - \beta f'(K_{t+1}) = 0. \tag{1.12}$$

This equation is often referred to as the Euler equation, since the mathematician Leonhard Euler (1707-1783) first derived it from a continuous time dynamic optimization problem. To find the unique optimal time path of capital from the solution to this functional equation we need two additional conditions. The period $t = 0$ stock of capital K_0 provides the first condition. The second

1.2 Infinite-Horizon Ramsey Model and Dynamic Programming

condition is the so called transversality condition, which is the limit of the terminal condition $\lambda_T K_{T+1} = 0$ from the finite-horizon Ramsey problem (1.3). It requires

$$\lim_{t \to \infty} \beta^t \lambda_t K_{t+1} = 0, \tag{1.13}$$

that is, the present value of the terminal capital stock must approach zero. In the Ramsey model (1.8), condition (1.13), is a necessary condition,[7] as well as conditions (1.10).

1.2.3 Dynamic Programming

We now turn to a recursive formulation of the Ramsey problem. For this purpose we assume that we already know the solution (denoted by a star) $\{K_1^*, K_2^*, \ldots\} \equiv \{K_t^*\}_{t=1}^{\infty}$ so that we are able to compute the life-time utility from

$$v(K_0) := u(f(K_0) - K_1^*) + \sum_{t=1}^{\infty} \beta^t u(f(K_t^*) - K_{t+1}^*).$$

Obviously, the maximum value of life-time utility $v(K_0)$ depends upon K_0 directly – via the first term on the rhs of the previous equation – and indirectly via the effect of K_0 on the optimal sequence $\{K_t^*\}_{t=1}^{\infty}$. Before we further develop this approach, we will adopt the notation that is common in dynamic programming. Since K_0 is an arbitrary initial stock of capital, we drop the time subscript and use K to designate this variable. Furthermore, we use a prime for all next-period variables. We are then able to define the function v recursively via:

$$v(K) := \max_{0 \leq K' \leq f(K)} u(f(K) - K') + \beta v(K'). \tag{1.14}$$

The first term to the right of the max operator is the utility of consumption $C = f(K) - K'$ as a function of the next-period capital stock K'. The second term is the discounted optimal value

---
[7] See KAMIHIGASHI (2002).

of life-time utility, if the sequence of optimal capital stocks starts in the next period with K'. Suppose we know the function v so that we can solve the optimization problem on the rhs of equation (1.14). Obviously, its solution K' depends upon the given value of K so that we may write $K' = h(K)$. The function h is the agent's decision rule or policy function. Note that the problem does not change with the passage of time: when the next period has arrived, the agent's initial stock of capital is $K = K'$ and he has to make the same decision with respect to the capital stock of period $t = 2$, which we denote by K''. In this way he can determine the entire sequence $\{K_t^*\}_{t=1}^{\infty}$.

Yet, we may also view equation (1.14) as an implicit definition of the real-valued function v and the associated function h. From this perspective, it is a functional equation,[8] named Bellman equation after its discoverer the US mathematician Richard Bellman (1920-1984). His principle of optimality states that the solution of problem (1.8) is equivalent to the solution of the Bellman equation (1.14). STOKEY and LUCAS with PRESCOTT(1989), pp. 67-77, establish the conditions for this equivalence to hold. In this context of dynamic programming v is referred to as the value function and h as the policy function, decision rule, or feed-back rule. Both functions are time invariant. The mathematical theory of dynamic programming deals with the existence, the properties, and the construction of v and h. Given that both $u(C)$ and $f(K)$ are strictly increasing, strictly concave and twice continuously differentiable functions of their respective arguments C and K, and that there exists a maximum sustainable capital stock $\bar{K}$ as defined in (1.9), one can prove the following results:[9]

1. The function v exists, is differentiable, strictly increasing, and strictly concave.
2. The policy function g is increasing and differentiable.
3. The function v is the limit of the following sequence of steps $s = 0, 1, \ldots$:

---

[8] As explained in Section 12.1, a functional equation is an equation whose unknown is a function and not a point in $\mathbb{R}^n$.

[9] See, e.g., HARRIS (1987), pp. 34-45 or STOKEY and LUCAS with PRESCOTT (1989), pp. 103-105.

$$v^{s+1}(K) = \max_{0 \leq K' \leq f(K)} u(f(K) - K') + \beta v^s(K'),$$

with $v^0 = 0$.

We illustrate these findings in Example 1.2.1

Example 1.2.1

Let the one-period utility function u and the production function f be given by

$$u(C) := \ln C,$$
$$f(K) := K^\alpha, \quad \alpha \in (0,1),$$

respectively. In Appendix 1 we use iterations over the value function to demonstrate that the policy function $K_{t+1} = h(K_t)$ that solves the Ramsey problem (1.8) is given by

$$K_{t+1} = \alpha \beta K_t^\alpha.$$

Furthermore, the value function is linear in $\ln K$ and given by

$$v(K) = a + b \ln K,$$

$$a := \frac{1}{1-\beta} \left[\ln(1 - \alpha\beta) + \frac{\alpha\beta}{1-\alpha\beta} \ln \alpha\beta \right], \quad b := \frac{\alpha}{1-\alpha\beta}.$$

The dynamic programming approach also provides the first-order conditions (1.12). It requires two steps to arrive at this result. First, consider the first-order condition for the maximization problem on the rhs of equation (1.14):

$$u'(f(K) - K') = \beta v'(K'). \tag{1.15}$$

Comparing this with condition (1.10a) (assuming $\mu_t = 0$) reveals that the Lagrange multiplier $\lambda_t \equiv \beta v'(K_{t+1})$ is a shadow price for newly produced capital (or investment expenditures): it equals the current value of the increase in life-time utility obtained from an additional unit of capital. Second, let $K' = h(K)$ denote the solution of this implicit equation in K'. This allows us to write the Bellman equation (1.14) as an identity,

$$v(K) = u(f(K) - h(K)) + \beta v(h(K)),$$

so that we can differentiate with respect to K on both sides. This yields

$$v'(K) = u'(C)\left(f'(K) - h'(K)\right) + \beta v'(K')h'(K),$$

where $C = f(K) - h(K)$. Using the first-order condition (1.15) provides

$$v'(K) = u'(C)f'(K). \tag{1.16}$$

Since K is an arbitrarily given stock of capital, this equation relates the derivative of the value function $v'(\cdot)$ to the derivative of the one-period utility function $u'(\cdot)$ and the derivative of the (net) production function $f'(\cdot)$ for any value of K. Thus, letting $C' = f(K') - K''$ denote next period's consumption, we may write

$$v'(K') = u'(C')f'(K').$$

Replacing $v'(K')$ in (1.15) by the rhs of this equation yields

$$1 = \beta \frac{u'(f(K') - K'')}{u'(f(K) - K')} f'(K').$$

This equation must hold for any three consecutive stocks of capital (K, K', K'') that establish the optimal sequence $\{K_t^*\}_{t=1}^\infty$ that solves the Ramsey problem (1.8). Thus, it is identical to the Euler equation (1.12), except that we used primes instead of the time indices.

1.2.4 The Saddle Path

To gain insights into the dynamics of the Ramsey model (1.8) we use the phase diagram technique to characterize the solution of the Euler equation (1.12). Substituting the resource constraint $C_t = f(K_t) - K_{t+1}$ into (1.12) yields a first-order, non-linear system of difference equations that governs the optimal time path of capital accumulation:

$$K_{t+1} = f(K_t) - C_t, \tag{1.17a}$$

$$1 = \beta \frac{u'(C_{t+1})}{u'(C_t)} f'(K_{t+1}). \tag{1.17b}$$

Together with the initial capital stock K_0 and the transversality condition (1.13) these equations determine a unique solution. We use Figure 1.2 to construct it.[10]

The thick line in this figure represents the graph of the function $C_t = f(K_t)$ that divides the plane into two regions. All points (K_t, C_t) on and below this graph meet the non-negativity constraint on the future capital stock, $K_{t+1} \geq 0$. No time path that starts in this region can leave it via the abscissa, since for all pairs $(K_t, C_t) > 0$ the solution to equations (1.17) in C_{t+1} is positive due to assumption (1.11). We divide the area below the graph of $C_t = f(K_t)$ into four parts, labeled A_1 through A_4.

Consider first the locus of all pairs (K_t, C_t) along which consumption does not change, i.e., $C_t = C_{t+1}$. According to equation (1.17b) this happens when the capital stock reaches K^*, given by

$$\frac{1}{\beta} = f'(K^*).$$

Since to the right (left) of K^* the marginal product of capital is smaller (larger) than $1/\beta$, consumption decreases (increases) within that region. The vertical arrows in Figure 1.2 designate that behavior.

Consider second the locus of all pairs (K_t, C_t) along which the capital stock does not change. Assuming $K_t = K_{t+1}$ in equation (1.17a) implies:

$$C_t = f(K_t) - K_t.$$

The graph of this function equals the vertical distance between the function $f(K_t)$ and the 45–degree line in Figure 1.1. Thus, it starts

---

[10] The time paths shown in this figure are obtained from a numerical simulation. Since they represent the solution of a system of difference equations and not of a system of differential equations they are connected line segments rather than smooth curves.

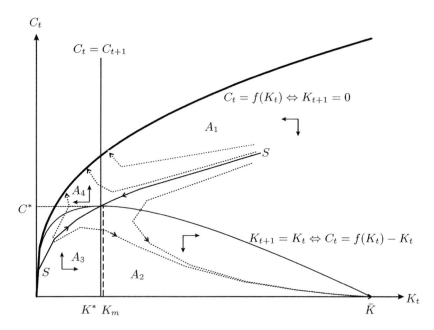

Figure 1.2: Phase Diagram of the Infinite-Horizon Ramsey Model

at the origin, attains a maximum at K_m, defined by $1 = f'(K_m)$, and cuts the K-axis at $\bar{K}$. Points above (below) that locus have a higher (smaller) consumption and, thus, the capital stock declines (increases) in that region, as shown by the horizontal arrows.

The optimal path of capital accumulation is given by the line segment labeled SS, the so called saddle path. Points on that locus converge towards the stationary equilibrium at (K^*, C^*). All other time paths either violate the non-negativity constraint on K_{t+1} in finite time or the transversality condition (1.13). To derive this assertion, we study the behavior of the dynamic system (1.17) in the four different regions. Consider a time path starting in region A_1. According to the arrows, it either

1. moves towards the graph of $C_t = f(K_t)$,
2. enters the region A_4,
3. converges towards the stationary solution (K^*, C^*),
4. converges towards $\bar{K}$,
5. or enters the region A_2.

1.2 Infinite-Horizon Ramsey Model and Dynamic Programming

It can be shown (by a straightforward but somewhat tedious argument) that paths that move towards the graph of $C_t = f(K_t)$ hit that line in finite time, and thus, constitute no feasible paths. Likewise, all paths that originate in the region A_4 violate the non-negativity constraint on K_{t+1} in finite time since they can only move towards the border of the feasible region as designated by the arrows. Time paths that originate in A_3 either

1. enter the region A_4,
2. converge towards the stationary solution,
3. or enter the region A_2.

Consider a path starting in A_2. We already know that it cannot cross the abscissa. In addition, it cannot move into A_1. To see this, consider a point $P_0 := (K_0, C_0)$ on the border – so that $C_0 = f(K_0) - K_0$ – and a point $P_1 := (K_1, C_0), K_1 < K_0$ to the left of P_0 (see Figure 1.3). The length of the horizontal arrow that points from P_1 to the right is given by

$$\Delta_1 := (f(K_1) - C_0) - K_1 = f(K_1) - f(K_0) + K_0 - K_1,$$

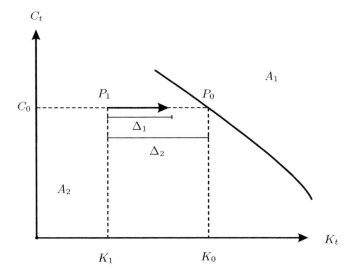

Figure 1.3: No Path Leaves the Region A_2

which is less than the horizontal distance between P_0 and P_1, $\Delta_2 = K_0 - K_1$, since $f(K_1) - f(K_0) < 0$. Therefore, each path in A_3 must converge to $\bar{K}$. Consider what happens along this path. Since A_2 lies to the right of K^* the marginal product of capital along that path decreases from $1/\beta$ at K^* to $f'(\bar{K}) < 1/\beta$. Therefore, there exists a point (K_0, C_0) on that path so that the growth factor of the marginal utility of consumption implied by (1.17b) exceeds $c > 1/\beta$:

$$g_{u'} := \frac{u'(C_1)}{u'(C_0)} = \frac{1}{\beta f'(K_1)} > c,$$

and there is a lower bound on $u'(C_t)$ given by

$$u'(C_t) \geq c^t u'(C_0).$$

This implies

$$\lim_{t \to \infty} \beta^t u'(C_t) K_{t+1} \geq (\beta c)^t u'(C_0) K_{t+1} = \infty,$$

since $\lim_{t \to \infty} K_{t+1} = \bar{K}$ and $\lim_{t \to \infty} (\beta c)^t = \infty$. Thus, we have shown that a path converging to $\bar{K}$ violates the transversality condition. A similar argument applies to all paths that approach $\bar{K}$ from the right.

Summarizing, the only paths left are those that start on the line SS and that converge to the stationary solution at the point (K^*, C^*). From the point of view of dynamic programming, this line is the graph of the policy function for consumption implied by the decision rule for the next-period capital stock via the resource constraint: $C_t = g(K_t) := f(K_t) - h(K_t)$. It relates the capital stock at each date t to the optimal choice of consumption at this date. Given the initial capital stock K_0 the optimal strategy is to choose $C_0 = g(K_0)$ and then to iterate either over the Euler equations (1.17) or, equivalently, over the policy functions h and g.

The problem that we have to deal with is how to derive the function h. Unfortunately, the Ramsey model (1.8) admits an analytical solution of the policy function only in a few special cases, which we consider in the next subsection.[11]

1.2.5 Models with Analytic Solution

Logarithmic Utility and Log-Linear Technology. In Example 1.2.1 we assume a logarithmic utility function $u(C_t) = \ln C_t$ and a net production function of the Cobb-Douglas type $f(K_t) = K_t^\alpha$. If capital depreciates fully, that is, if $\delta = 1$, this function also describes the gross output of the economy. In Appendix 1 we show that the policy function of the next-period capital stock is given by

$$K_{t+1} = h(K_t) := \alpha\beta K_t^\alpha. \tag{1.18}$$

A multi-sector version of this model was used in one of the seminal articles on real business cycles by LONG and PLOSSER (1983) to demonstrate that a very standard economic model without money and other trading frictions is capable to explain many features of the business cycle. RADNER (1966) is able to dispense with the assumption of 100% depreciation. He, instead, assumes that each vintage of capital investment is a separate factor of production in a log-linear technology. The disadvantage of his model is that output is zero if gross investment in any prior period is zero.

Figure 1.4 displays the time path of the stock of capital implied by the solution of Example 1.2.1. We used $\alpha = 0.27$ and $\beta = 0.994$ and set the initial capital stock K_0 equal to one tenth of the stationary capital stock $K^* = (\alpha\beta)^{1/(1-\alpha)}$. It takes only a few periods for K_0 to be close to K^*.

Logarithmic Utility and Log-Linear Adjustment Costs. A second class of models with logarithmic utility and log-linear production function for gross output is provided in an article by HERCOWITZ and SAMPSON (1991). Instead of full depreciation

---

[11] We do not pretend that the following list completely exhausts the class of models with exact solution for the policy function.

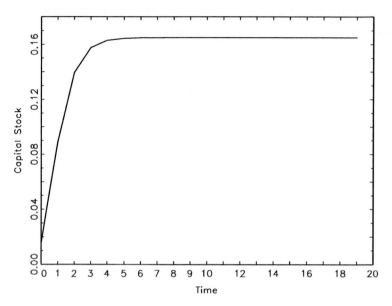

Figure 1.4: Convergence of the Stock of Capital in the Infinite-Horizon Ramsey Model

the authors assume adjustment costs of capital that give rise to the following transition function for the stock of next-period capital:

$$K_{t+1} = K_t^{1-\delta} I_t^{\delta}, \tag{1.19}$$

where gross investment I_t equals output $Y_t = K_t^{\alpha}$ minus consumption:

$$I_t = Y_t - C_t.$$

We ask you in Problem 1.2 to show that the policy functions for the next-period capital stock and for consumption are given by

$$K_{t+1} = k_0 K_t^{\alpha},$$
$$C_t = \left(1 - k_0^{1/\delta}\right) K_t^{\alpha},$$

where the constant k_0 is a unique function of the model's parameters α, β, and δ.

Iso-Elastic Utility and CES-Technology. BENHABIB and RUSTICHINI (1994) provide a class of models where the utility function is not restricted to the logarithmic case but is given by the iso-elastic function

$$u(C_t) = \frac{C_t^{1-\eta} - 1}{1 - \eta}, \quad \eta > 0,$$

which approaches $\ln C_t$ for $\eta \to 1$. There are two vintages of capital, K_{1t} and K_{2t}, respectively, that produce output according to the constant elasticity of substitution function

$$Y_t = \left[aK_{1t}^{1-\epsilon} + (1-a)K_{2t}^{1-\epsilon}\right]^{\frac{1}{1-\epsilon}}.$$

The two vintages are related to each other via the equation

$$K_{2t+1} = \delta K_{1t},$$

that is, capital lasts for two periods and new vintages depreciate at the rate $\delta \in (0,1)$. The economy's resource constraint is given by

$$Y_t = C_t + K_{1t+1}.$$

Assuming $\eta = \epsilon$, the solution of this model is a constant savings rate s determined from

$$1 - s = \left[\beta a + \beta^2 (1-a)\delta^{1-\epsilon}\right]^{\frac{1}{\epsilon}},$$

so that the policy function for K_{1t+1} is given by

$$K_{1t+1} = sY_t.$$

ANTONY and MAUSSNER (2007) argue that this model can be extended and interpreted as a model with adjustment costs of capital that give raise to the transition equation

$$K_{t+1} = \left[aK_t^{1-\epsilon} + (1-a)I_t^{1-\epsilon}\right]^{\frac{1}{1-\epsilon}},$$

with generalizes equation (1.19) to the case $\epsilon \neq 1$. The production function in their model is

$$Y_t = \left[bN^{1-\epsilon} + (1-b)K_t^{1-\epsilon}\right]^{\frac{1}{1-\epsilon}}.$$

N is the given amount of labor used in the production. The savings rate that solves this model is determined from

$$1 - s = \left[\sum_{j=1}^{\infty}(1-b)a(1-a)^{j-1}\beta^j\right]^{\frac{1}{\epsilon}}.$$

The Linear Quadratic Model. In Section 2.2 we consider a special class of models known as linear quadratic models or optimal linear regulator problems. The Ramsey model that we sketch here is an example of this class. We assume a quadratic current period utility function

$$u(C_t) := u_1 C_t - \frac{u_2}{2}C_t^2, \quad u_1, u_2 > 0$$

and a linear (net) production function

$$f(K_t) := AK_t, \quad A > 0.$$

With these functions the system of difference equations (1.17) may be written as:

$$K_{t+1} = AK_t - C_t, \tag{1.20a}$$

$$C_{t+1} = \frac{u_1}{u_2}\left(1 - \frac{1}{\beta A}\right) + \frac{1}{\beta A}C_t. \tag{1.20b}$$

We use the method of undetermined coefficients explained in Appendix 1 to find the policy function. We guess this function for consumption g is linear:

$$C_t = c_1 + c_2 K_t.$$

Substituting this function into (1.20b) provides:

$$c_1 + c_2 K_{t+1} = \frac{u_1}{u_2}\left(1 - \frac{1}{\beta A}\right) + \frac{1}{\beta A}(c_1 + c_2 K_t),$$

$$c_1 + c_2(AK_t - c_1 - c_2 K_t) = \frac{u_1}{u_2}\left(1 - \frac{1}{\beta A}\right) + \frac{1}{\beta A}(c_1 + c_2 K_t).$$

The last equation holds for arbitrary values of K_t if the constant terms on both sides sum to zero:

$$0 = c_1 \left(1 - c_2 - \frac{1}{\beta A}\right) - \frac{u_1}{u_2}\left(1 - \frac{1}{\beta A}\right), \tag{1.21a}$$

and if the coefficients of the variable K_t sum to zero, too. This condition provides the solution for c_2:

$$c_2 = A - \frac{1}{\beta A}, \tag{1.21b}$$

which can be used to infer c_1 from equation (1.21a). Inserting the solution for c_2 in equation (1.20a) delivers the policy function for capital:

$$K_{t+1} = h(K_t) := \frac{1}{\beta A} K_t - c_1.$$

If $1/\beta > A$, the stock of capital approaches the stationary solution

$$K^* = -\frac{c_1}{1 - \frac{1}{\beta A}},$$

from any given initial value K_0, and consumption converges to

$$C^* = u_1/u_2,$$

so that the transversality condition (1.13) holds.

1.3 The Stochastic Ramsey Model

1.3.1 Stochastic Output

In the Ramsey problem (1.8) everything is under the farmer's control. Yet, this is an overly optimistic picture of farming. Less rain during the summer causes harvest failure, whereas the right balance between rainfall and sunshine boosts crop growth. The amount of rainfall is outside the control of the farmer and, usually, he is unable to predict it accurately. The ensuing uncertainty turns the crop and, hence, consumption into stochastic variables. As a consequence, we must restate the farmer's decision problem in the framework of expected utility maximization. We illustrate the points that are involved in this task in Example 1.3.1. Since an in-depth treatment of the analytical framework that underlies stochastic control is beyond the scope of this book we refer the interested reader to STOKEY and LUCAS with PRESCOTT (1989).

Example 1.3.1

Assume the farmer's planing horizon is $T = 1$. His one-period utility function $u(C_t)$ is strictly increasing in consumption C_t. Output in period $t = 0$ is given by $f(K_0)$ and in period $t = 1$ by $Z_1 f(K_1)$, where $Z_1 = \underline{Z}$ with probability π and $Z_1 = \bar{Z} > \underline{Z}$ with probability $1 - \pi$. $f(K_t)$ is strictly increasing in the capital stock K_t. K_0 is given. Since the farmer does not plan beyond $t = 1$, we already know that he will choose $C_1 = Z_1 f(K_1)$. Given his investment decision in the current period K_1 his future consumption is a random variable with realizations $C_1(\underline{Z}) = \underline{Z} f(K_1)$ and $C_1(\bar{Z}) = \bar{Z} f(K_1)$. Hence, the farmer's expected life-time utility is

$$E_0\left[u(C_0) + \beta u(C_1)\right] := u(f(K_0) - K_1) \\ + \beta\left[\pi u(\underline{Z} f(K_1)) + (1-\pi) u(\bar{Z} f(K_1))\right],$$

where E_0 denotes expectations as of period $= 0$. The farmer chooses K_1 to maximize this expression. Differentiating with respect to K_1 and setting to zero the resulting expression yields the following first-order condition:

$$u'(C_0) = \beta \underbrace{\left[u'(\underline{Z} f(K_1)) \underline{Z} f'(K_1) \pi + u'(\bar{Z} f(K_1)) \bar{Z} f'(K_1)(1-\pi)\right]}_{=: E_0[u'(C_1) Z_1 f'(K_1)]}.$$

This equation is the stochastic analog to the respective Euler equation in the deterministic case. It states that the utility loss from increased savings in the current period, $u'(C_0)$, must be compensated by the discounted expected future utility increase.

We will consider the following stochastic infinite-horizon Ramsey model, which is also known as the stochastic growth model:

$$\max_{C_0} \quad E_0 \left[\sum_{t=0}^{\infty} \beta^t u(C_t) \right]$$

s.t. $\qquad\qquad\qquad\qquad\qquad\qquad\qquad\qquad\qquad\qquad$ (1.22)

$$\left. \begin{array}{rcl} K_{t+1} + C_t & \leq & Z_t f(K_t) + (1-\delta)K_t, \\ 0 & \leq & C_t, \\ 0 & \leq & K_{t+1}, \end{array} \right\} \quad t = 0, 1, \ldots,$$

$K_0, Z_0 \quad$ given.

Note that from here on $f(K) \equiv F(N, K)$ for fixed N denotes gross value added and we consider depreciation explicitly. We need to do so, since using our specification of the production function from (1.2), $Z_t f(K_t)$ would imply stochastic depreciation otherwise. Problem (1.22) differs from the deterministic model in two respects: first, output at each period t depends not only on the amount of capital K_t but also on the realization of a stochastic variable Z_t capturing weather conditions. We assume that the farmer knows the amount of rainfall Z_t at harvest time, when he must decide about consumption. Second, and as a consequence of this assumption, in the current period $t = 0$ the farmer chooses only current consumption C_0. In the deterministic case, he gets no new information when the future unfolds. Therefore, he can safely determine consumption from the present to the very distant future. In technical terms, his decision problem is open-loop control, as opposed to close-loop control in the stochastic case. Here, as in Example 1.3.1, future consumption is a stochastic variable from the perspective of the current period. Thus, the farmer does better if he postpones the decision on period t consumption until this period t. As a consequence of the uncertainty with respect to consumption, the farmer aims at maximizing the expected value of his life-time utility. More specifically, the notation $E_0[\cdot]$ denotes expectations with respect to the probability distribution of the sequence of random variables $\{C_t\}_{t=1}^{\infty}$ conditional on information available at $t = 0$. The fact that we use the mathematical expectations operator means that agents use the true – or objective as opposed to subjective – probability distribution of the variables they have to forecast. Since the seminal article of MUTH (1961) economists use the term 'rational expectations' to designate this hypothesis on expectations formation.

The solution of the deterministic, infinite-horizon Ramsey model in terms of a time-invariant policy function rests on the recursive structure of the problem that in turn is implied by the time-additive utility function. To preserve this structure in the context of a stochastic model requires us to restrict the class of probability distributions to stochastic processes that have the Markov property. If you are unfamiliar with Markov processes we recommend to consult Section 12.2, where we sketch the necessary definitions and tools. We proceed to derive the first-order conditions that governs the model's evolution over time. As in the previous section we obtain these conditions via two tracks: the Kuhn-Tucker approach and stochastic dynamic programming.

1.3.2 Stochastic Euler Equations

First order conditions for the stochastic Ramsey model (1.22) can be derived in a manner analogous to the deterministic case. Consider the following Lagrangean function:

$$\mathscr{L} = E_0 \left\{ \sum_{t=0}^{\infty} \beta^t \left[u(C_t) + \mu_t C_t + \omega_{t+1} K_{t+1} \right. \right.$$
$$\left. \left. + \lambda_t \left(Z_t f(K_t) + (1-\delta) K_t - C_t - K_{t+1} \right) \right] \right\}.$$

Since the expectations operator is a linear operator we can differentiate the expression in curly brackets with respect to C_0 and K_1 (see Example 1.3.1). This delivers

$$\frac{\partial \mathscr{L}}{\partial C_0} = E_0 \{ u'(C_0) - \lambda_0 + \mu_0 \} = 0,$$
$$\frac{\partial \mathscr{L}}{\partial K_1} = E_0 \{ -\lambda_0 + \omega_1 + \beta \lambda_1 (1 - \delta + Z_1 f'(K_1)) \} = 0,$$
$$0 = \lambda_0 (Z_0 f(K_0) + (1-\delta) K_0 - C_0 - K_1),$$
$$0 = \mu_0 C_0,$$
$$0 = \omega_1 K_1.$$

Since, as in Example 1.3.1, C_0, K_1, and hence the multipliers λ_0, μ_0, and ω_1 are non-stochastic, we can replace the first condition with

$$u'(C_0) = \lambda_0 - \mu_0$$

and the second with

$$\lambda_0 = \beta E_0 \lambda_1 \{1 - \delta + Z_1 f'(K_1)\} + \omega_1.$$

Now, consider the problem from $t = 1$ onwards, when Z_1 is known and K_1 given. The Lagrangean for this problem is

$$\mathscr{L} = E_1 \left\{ \sum_{t=1}^{\infty} \beta^{t-1} \left[u(C_t) + \mu_t C_t + \omega_{t+1} K_{t+1} \right.\right.$$
$$\left.\left. + \lambda_t \left(Z_t f(K_t) + (1-\delta)K_t - C_t - K_{t+1}\right) \right] \right\}.$$

Proceeding as before, we find

$$u'(C_1) = \lambda_1 - \mu_1,$$
$$\lambda_1 = \beta E_1 \lambda_2 \{1 - \delta + Z_2 f'(K_2)\} + \omega_2.$$

Continuing in this way, we find, since K_t must be optimal at t, that the plan for choosing $C_0, C_1, \ldots$ and $K_1, K_2, \ldots$ must solve the system:

$$u'(C_t) = \lambda_t - \mu_t, \tag{1.23a}$$
$$\lambda_t = \beta E_t \lambda_{t+1} \left[1 - \delta + Z_{t+1} f'(K_{t+1})\right] + \omega_{t+1}, \tag{1.23b}$$
$$0 = \lambda_t(Z_t f(K_t) + (1-\delta)K_t - C_t - K_{t+1}), \tag{1.23c}$$
$$0 = \mu_t C_t, \tag{1.23d}$$
$$0 = \omega_{t+1} K_{t+1}. \tag{1.23e}$$

Thus, an interior solution with strictly positive consumption and capital at all dates t (i.e., $\forall t : \mu_t = \omega_{t+1} = 0$) must satisfy the stochastic analog to the Euler equation (1.12)

$$1 = \beta E_t \frac{u'(Z_{t+1} f(K_{t+1}) + (1-\delta)K_{t+1} - K_{t+2})}{u'(Z_t f(K_t) + (1-\delta)K_t - K_{t+1})} \tag{1.24}$$
$$\times (1 - \delta + Z_{t+1} f'(K_{t+1})).$$

In addition to the stochastic Euler equation (1.24) there is also the stochastic analog of the transversality condition (1.13), namely

$$\lim_{t\to\infty} \beta^t E_t \lambda_t K_{t+1} = 0 \tag{1.25}$$

that provides a boundary condition for the solution to (1.24). KAMIHIGASHI (2005) shows that condition (1.25) is a necessary optimality condition in the following cases:

1. the utility function $u(C_t)$ is bounded,
2. the utility function is logarithmic $u(C_t) = \ln C_t$,
3. the utility function is of the form $u(C_t) = C_t^{1-\eta}/(1-\eta)$, $\eta \in [0, \infty)\backslash\{1\}$ and life-time utility at the optimum is finite.

1.3.3 Stochastic Dynamic Programming

As in the deterministic Ramsey model there is a dynamic programming approach to characterize solutions of the stochastic Ramsey model (1.22). The value function $v(K, Z)$ is now defined as the solution to the following stochastic functional equation:

$$v(K, Z) = \max_{0 \leq K' \leq Zf(K)+(1-\delta)K} u(Zf(K) + (1-\delta)K - K') + \beta E\left[v(K', Z')|Z\right],$$

where expectations are conditional on the given realization of Z and where a prime denotes next period values. In the case of a Markov chain with realizations $[z_1, z_2, \ldots, z_n]$ and transition matrix $P = (p_{ij})$ the expression $E\left[v(K', Z')|Z\right]$ is given by

$$E\left[v(K', Z')|z_i\right] = \sum_{j=1}^n p_{ij} v(K', z_j)$$

and in the case of the continuous valued Markov process with conditional probability density function $\pi(z, Z')$ over the interval $[a, b]$ it is

$$E\left[v(K', Z')|z\right] = \int_a^b v(K', Z')\pi(z, Z')dZ'.$$

It requires some sophisticated mathematics to prove the existence and to find the properties of the value function and the associated policy function $K' = h(K, Z)$. We refer the interested reader to STOKEY and LUCAS with PRESCOTT (1989), Chapter 9 and proceed under the assumption that both the value and the policy function exist and are sufficiently differentiable with respect to K. Under this assumption it is easy to use the steps taken on page 15 to show that the dynamic programming approach also delivers the stochastic Euler equation (1.24). We leave this as an exercise to the reader (see Problem 1.4).

Example 1.3.2 extends Example 1.2.1 to the stochastic case. As in this example, there is an analytic solution for the policy function h.

Example 1.3.2
Let the one-period utility function u and the production function f be given by

$$u(C) := \ln C,$$
$$f(K) := K^\alpha, \quad \alpha \in (0, 1),$$

respectively.

In Example 1.2.1 we find that K' is directly proportional to K^α. So let us try

$$K_{t+1} = h(K_t, Z_t) := A Z_t K_t^\alpha$$

as policy function with the unknown parameter A. If this function solves the problem, it must satisfy the stochastic Euler equation (1.24). To prove this assertion, we replace K_{t+1} in equation (1.24) by the rhs of the previous equation. This gives

$$1 = \beta E_t \left[\frac{(1-A) Z_t K_t^\alpha}{(1-A) Z_{t+1} [A Z_t K_t^\alpha]^\alpha} \alpha Z_{t+1} [A Z_t K_t^\alpha]^{\alpha-1} \right] = \frac{\alpha \beta}{A}.$$

If we put $A = \alpha\beta$ the function $h(Z_t, K_t) = \alpha\beta Z_t K_t^\alpha$ indeed satisfies the Euler equation, and thus is the policy function we look for. ____

The solution of the deterministic Ramsey model is a time path for the capital stock. In the stochastic case $K' = h(K, Z)$ is a random variable, since Z is random. The policy function induces a time-invariant probability distribution over the space of admissible capital stocks. This distribution is the counterpart to the stationary capital stock K^* in the deterministic Ramsey model (1.8). We illustrate this point with the aid of Example 1.3.2 for $\alpha = 0.27$ and $\beta = 0.994$. We assume that Z_t has a uniform distribution over the interval [0.95, 1.05] and employ a random number generator to obtain independent draws from this distribution. Starting with $K^* = (\alpha\beta)^{1/(1-\alpha)}$ we then iterate over $K_{t+1} = \alpha\beta Z_t K_t^\alpha$ to obtain a path with one million observations on K_t. We divide the interval between the smallest and the highest value of K attained along this path into 100 non-overlapping intervals and count the number of capital stocks that lie in each interval. Figure 1.5 displays the result of this exercise. Since it rests on a sample from the distribution of K it provides an approximate picture of the density function of the capital stock implied by the model of Example 1.3.2. Note that despite the fact that each small subinterval $S \subset [0.95, 1.05]$ of length l has the same probability of $l/0.1$, the

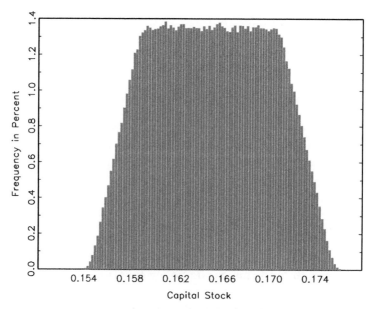

Figure 1.5: Stationary Distribution of the Capital Stock in the Stochastic Infinite-Horizon Ramsey Model

distribution of the capital stock is not uniform. To understand this note that for each fixed $Z \in [0.95, 1.05]$ the capital stock approaches $K(Z) = (\alpha \beta Z)^{1/(1-\alpha)}$. Since the mean of the uniform distribution over $[0.95, 1.05]$ is $Z = 1$, neither very small nor very high values of K have a high chance to be realized.

1.4 Labor Supply, Growth, and the Decentralized Economy

1.4.1 Substitution of Leisure

So far we have taken labor supply as exogenous. Yet, it is well known that there are considerable employment fluctuations over the business cycles. In the context of our farming example, variations in labor input may arise from shocks to labor productivity, if the farmer values both consumption and leisure. To allow for that case we include leisure in the one-period utility function. Leisure L is the farmer's time endowment, which we normalize to 1, minus his working hours N. Thus we may state the one-period utility function now as

$$u(C, 1 - N). \tag{1.27}$$

In the following subsection we will ask what kinds of restrictions we must place on u besides the usual assumptions with respect to concavity and monotonicity when we deal with a growing economy. Before we proceed, we consider briefly what we can expect in general from including leisure into the one-period utility function.

Assume that the farmer observes an increase in today's marginal product of labor that he considers short-lived. How will he react? In the current period the shock increases the farmer's opportunity set, since at any given level of labor input his harvest will be higher than before the shock. At the same time the shock changes the relative price of leisure: the farmer loses more output for each additional unit of leisure he desires. The overall effect of the shock on the intra-temporal substitution between labor and consumption depends upon the relative size of the associated income and substitution effect. If leisure and consumption are normal goods, the farmer wants both more consumption and more leisure (income effect). Yet, since leisure is more costly than before the shock, he also wants to substitute consumption against leisure (substitution effect).

In the intertemporal setting we are considering here, there is an additional, inter-temporal substitution effect. The shock raises the current reward for an additional hour of work vis-à-vis the future return. Consequently, the farmer will want to work more now and less in the future. He can achieve this goal by increasing today's savings and spending the proceeds in subsequent periods. Thus, investment serves as vehicle to the intertemporal substitution of consumption and leisure.

1.4.2 Growth and Restrictions on Technology and Preferences

Labor Augmenting Technical Progress. When we refer to economic growth we think of increases in output at given levels of input brought about by increases in technological knowledge. This kind of technological progress is called disembodied as opposed to embodied progress that operates via improvements in the quality of the factors of production. Disembodied technological progress simply shifts the production function outward. Equivalently, we may think of it as if it redoubled the available physical units of labor and capital. For instance, if N is the amount of physical or raw labor and A its efficiency level, effective labor is AN. Using this concept, output is given by

$$Y_t = Z_t F(A_t N_t, B_t K_t),$$

where the efficiency factors A_t and B_t as well as the productivity shock Z_t are exogenously given time series or stochastic processes. We continue to assume that the production function F has positive but diminishing marginal products, that both factors of production are essential, and that F exhibits constant returns to scale. Formally:[12]

1. $F_i > 0$ and $F_{ii} < 0$ for $i = 1, 2$,
2. $F(AN, 0) = 0$ and $F(0, BN) = 0$,
3. $\lambda Y = F(\lambda AN, \lambda BK)$

In Section 1.2.4 we have seen that the solution to the deterministic, infinite-horizon Ramsey model approaches a stationary equilibrium. There is an appropriate concept of stationarity in models of growth, the so-called balanced growth path. Referring to SOLOW (1988), p. 4, we define a balanced growth path by two requirements:

1. output per working hour grows at a constant rate,
2. and the share of net savings in output is constant.

The motivation for this definition has two different sources. Firstly, from the empirical perspective, the balanced growth path replicates the broad facts about growth of advanced industrial economies.[13] Secondly, from the theoretical perspective, the balanced growth path allows to define variables relative to their trend path that are stationary like the unscaled variables in no-growth models. Therefore, the techniques used to study stationary economies remain valid.

In Appendix 2 we show that for a balanced growth path to exist technical progress must be of the labor augmenting type, i.e., $B_t \equiv 1 \ \forall t$. As a consequence, we specify the production function as

$$Y_t = Z_t F(A_t N_t, K_t). \tag{1.28}$$

Trend versus Difference Stationary Growth. The specification (1.28) leaves two possible modeling choices for the process governing the evolution of the efficiency factor of raw labor. If we

---

[12] Here, and in the following, for any function $F(x_1, \ldots, x_n)$ the expression F_i denotes the first partial derivative of F with respect to x_i, and F_{ij} denotes the derivative of $F_i(x_1, \ldots, x_n)$ with respect to x_j.
[13] See, SOLOW (1988), p. 3ff.

consider growth a deterministic process, the efficiency factor A_t grows at a given and constant growth factor $a > 1$:

$$A_{t+1} = aA_t. \tag{1.29}$$

Variations around the long-run path are induced by the stochastic process $\{Z_t\}_{t=0}^{\infty}$. For this variations to be temporary and not permanent, the process that governs Z_t must be covariance stationary. This requires

1. that the unconditional mean $E(Z_t) = Z$ is independent of time,
2. and that the covariance between Z_t and Z_{t+s}, $\mathrm{cov}(Z_t, Z_{t+s}) = E[(Z_t - Z)(Z_{t+s} - Z)]$, depends upon the time lag s but not on time t itself.

To find the long-run behavior of output assume that Z_t is equal to its unconditional mean $Z \equiv 1$. Since F has constant returns to scale we may write

$$Y_t = A_t F(N_t, K_t/A_t).$$

Note that according to our utility function (1.27) labor supply N_t is bounded above by 1. Since A_t grows at the constant rate $a - 1$, output will grow at the same constant rate, if both labor input and the quantity K_t/A_t are constant. Therefore, capital must grow at the same rate as output.

The assumption of deterministic growth has obvious empirical implications: output is a trend stationary stochastic process, i.e., when we subtract a linear trend from log-output, the resulting time series is a covariance stationary stochastic process.

In an influential paper NELSON and PLOSSER (1982) question this implication. They provide evidence that major macroeconomic aggregates are better modeled as difference stationary stochastic processes. A stochastic process $\{x_t\}_{t \in \mathbb{Z}}$ is difference stationary if the process $\{(x_{t+1} - x_t)\}_{t \in \mathbb{Z}}$ is a covariance stationary stochastic process. In the context of our neoclassical production function we get this result, if we set $Z_t \equiv 1$ and let a difference stationary Markov process govern the evolution of the efficiency level of labor. For instance, we may assume A_t to follow the process

1.4 Labor Supply, Growth, and the Decentralized Economy

$$A_{t+1} = A_t e^{a+\epsilon_t}, \quad \epsilon_t \sim N(0, \sigma^2), a > 0. \tag{1.30}$$

Under this process the growth factor of the efficiency level of labor, A_{t+1}/A_t fluctuates around its long-run mean of e^a and the first difference of log-output, $\ln Y_{t+1} - \ln Y_t$, is covariance stationary. To see this, use

$$Y_t = A_t F(N_t, K_t/A_t)$$

and set $F(\cdot)$ equal to its long-run value $\bar{F} := F(N, K/A)$. Using (1.30), we get

$$\ln Y_{t+1} - \ln Y_t = \ln A_{t+1} - \ln A_t = a + \epsilon_t,$$

which is a white noise process.

Restrictions on Preferences. The restriction to labor augmenting technical progress is not sufficient to guarantee the existence of a balanced growth path when labor supply is endogenous. To see this, we restrict attention to the deterministic case and put $Z \equiv 1$ in (1.28). Using the one-period utility function (1.27), the farmer's maximization problem is

$$\max_{\{C_t, N_t\}_{t=0}^{\infty}} \sum_{t=0}^{\infty} \beta^t u(C_t, 1 - N_t)$$

s.t. $\qquad\qquad\qquad\qquad\qquad\qquad\qquad\qquad\qquad\qquad$ (1.31)

$$\left. \begin{array}{rcl} K_{t+1} + C_t & \leq & F(A_t N_t, K_t) + (1-\delta) K_t, \\ 0 & \leq & C_t, \\ 1 & \geq & N_t \geq 0, \\ 0 & \leq & K_{t+1}, \end{array} \right\} t = 0, 1, \ldots,$$

K_0 given.

Since we are interested in a long-run solution with positive consumption and leisure, we will ignore the non-negativity restrictions and the upper bound on labor in setting up the respective Lagrangean:

$$\mathscr{L} = \sum_{t=0}^{\infty} \beta^t \Big[u(C_t, 1 - N_t) + \Lambda_t \Big(F(A_t N_t, K_t) + (1-\delta) K_t - C_t - K_{t+1} \Big) \Big].$$

Differentiating this expression with respect to C_t, N_t, and K_{t+1} provides the following set of first-order conditions:

$$0 = u_1(C_t, 1 - N_t) - \Lambda_t, \tag{1.32a}$$
$$0 = -u_2(C_t, 1 - N_t) + \Lambda_t F_1(A_t N_t, K_t) A_t, \tag{1.32b}$$
$$0 = -\Lambda_t + \beta \Lambda_{t+1}(1 - \delta + F_2(A_{t+1} N_{t+1}, K_{t+1})). \tag{1.32c}$$

Conditions (1.32a) and (1.32b) imply that the marginal rate of substitution between consumption and leisure, u_2/u_1, equals the marginal product of labor:

$$\frac{u_2(C_t, 1 - N_t)}{u_1(C_t, 1 - N_t)} = A_t F_1(A_t N_t, K_t). \tag{1.33}$$

Conditions (1.32a) and (1.32c) yield

$$\frac{u_1(C_t, 1 - N_t)}{u_1(C_{t+1}, 1 - N_{t+1})} = \beta(1 - \delta + F_2(A_{t+1} N_{t+1}, K_{t+1})). \tag{1.34}$$

Consider the rhs of this equation. Since F is homogenous of degree one, F_2 is homogenous of degree zero, i.e.,

$$F_2(A_{t+1} N_{t+1}, K_{t+1}) = F_2(N_{t+1}, K_{t+1}/A_{t+1}).$$

We have already seen that on a balanced growth path both N_{t+1} and K_{t+1}/A_{t+1} are constants. Thus, in the long run, the rhs of equation (1.34) is constant and the lhs must be, too. Now consider the resource constraint

$$K_{t+1} = Y_t - C_t + (1 - \delta) K_t.$$

If capital and output grow at the common rate $a - 1$, consumption must grow at the same rate, since otherwise the growth factor of capital g_K,

$$g_K := \frac{K_{t+1}}{K_t} = \frac{Y_t}{K_t} - \frac{C_t}{K_t} + (1 - \delta),$$

is not constant. If consumption grows at the rate $a - 1$ the marginal utility of consumption must fall at a constant rate. As we show in Appendix 2 this restricts the one-period utility function u to the class of constant-elasticity functions with respect to consumption. Further restrictions derive from condition (1.33). Since the marginal product of labor increases in the long run at the rate $a-1$ there must be exactly off-setting income and substitution effects with respect to the static labor supply decision. As we demonstrate in Appendix 2 we must restrict the one-period utility function (1.27) to

$$u(C, 1-N) = \begin{cases} C^{1-\eta}v(1-N) \text{ if } \eta \neq 1, \\ \ln C + v(1-N) \text{ if } \eta = 1. \end{cases} \quad (1.35)$$

The function v must be chosen so that $u(C, 1-N)$ is concave. Remember, that a function is concave, if and only if $u_{ii} \leq 0$ and $(u_{11}u_{22} - u_{12}^2) \geq 0$, and that it is strictly concave, if $u_{11} < 0$ and $(u_{11}u_{22} - u_{12}^2) > 0$.[14] For example, in the parameterization of u that we use in Example 1.5.1 below, the restriction of η to $\eta > \theta/(1+\theta)$ implies that u is strictly concave.

Transformation to Stationary Variables. Given the restrictions on technology and preferences it is always possible to choose new variables that are constant in the long run. As an example, consider the deterministic Ramsey model (1.31). Assume $\eta \neq 1$ in (1.35) and deterministic growth of the efficiency level of labor according to (1.29). The static labor supply condition (1.33) can then be written as

$$\frac{v'(1-N_t)}{(1-\eta)v(1-N_t)} \frac{C_t}{A_t} = F_1(N_t, K_t/A_t) \quad (1.36)$$

and the intertemporal condition (1.34) is:

$$\begin{aligned} \frac{C_t^{-\eta}v(1-N_t)}{C_{t+1}^{-\eta}v(1-N_{t+1})} &= \frac{(aA_t)^{\eta}C_t^{-\eta}v(1-N_t)}{A_{t+1}^{\eta}C_{t+1}^{-\eta}v(1-N_{t+1})} \\ &= \frac{a^{\eta}(C_t/A_t)^{-\eta}v(1-N_t)}{(C_{t+1}/A_{t+1})^{-\eta}v(1-N_{t+1})} \\ &= \beta(1-\delta + F_2(N_{t+1}, K_{t+1}/A_{t+1})). \end{aligned} \quad (1.37)$$

---
[14] See, e.g., TAKAYAMA (1985), Theorem 1.E.13.

Since F is homogenous of degree one, we can transform the resource constraint to

$$\frac{K_{t+1}}{A_{t+1}/a} = F(N_t, K_t/A_t) + (1-\delta)(K_t/A_t) - (C_t/A_t). \qquad (1.38)$$

Equations (1.36) through (1.38) constitute a dynamic system in the new variables N_t, $c_t := C_t/A_t$, and $k_t = K_t/A_t$. Their stationary values N, c and k are found as solution to the system of three equations

$$c = \frac{(1-\eta)v(1-N)}{v'(1-N)} F_1(N,k),$$
$$1 = \beta a^{-\eta}(1 - \delta + F_2(N,k)),$$
$$0 = F(N,k) - (1 - \delta - a)k - c.$$

Note, that we can derive the efficiency conditions (1.36) through (1.38) from solving the problem

$$\max_{\{c_t, N_t\}_{t=0}^{\infty}} \sum_{t=0}^{\infty} \tilde{\beta}^t c_t^{1-\eta} v(1 - N_t)$$

s.t.
$$c_t \leq F(N_t, k_t) + (1-\delta)k_t - ak_{t+1},$$
$$k_0 \quad \text{given},$$

with discount factor $\tilde{\beta} := \beta a^{1-\eta}$ in the stationary decision variables $c_t := C_t/A_t$ and $k_{t+1} := K_{t+1}/A_{t+1}$.

1.4.3 The Decentralized Economy

So far we have considered a single agent for ease of exposition. For each of the Ramsey models considered above, it is, however, straightforward to develop a model of a decentralized economy whose equilibrium allocation coincides with the equilibrium allocation of the respective Ramsey model. Since the latter is a utility maximizing allocation, the decentralized equilibrium is optimal in the sense of Pareto efficiency. In the static theory of general equilibrium with a finite-dimensional commodity space the correspondence between a competitive equilibrium and a Pareto efficient allocation of resources is stated in the Two Fundamental Theorems of Welfare Economics.[15] The infinite-horizon Ramsey model has infinitely many commodities. Nevertheless, as shown by DEBREU (1954), it is possible to extend the correspondence between competitive equilibrium and Pareto efficiency to infinite-dimensional commodity spaces.

We illustrate the relation between efficiency and intertemporal equilibrium by means of a simple example.

Firms. The production side of the economy consists of a large number of identical firms $i = 1, 2, \ldots, n$. Each firm uses labor N_i and capital K_i to produce a single output Y_i. The production function $ZF(AN_i, K_i)$ has the usual properties, in particular, it is homogenous of degree one (see page 35). Each firm hires labor and capital services on the respective markets. Let w and r denote the rental rates of labor and capital, respectively, in units of the final good. Since there is no link between successive periods, maximization of the firm's present value is equivalent to maximizing one-period profits

$$\Pi_i := ZF(AN_i, K_i) - wN_i - rK_i.$$

The first-order conditions imply

$$w = ZAF_1(AN_i, K_i) = ZAF_1(A, K_i/N_i),$$
$$r = ZF_2(AN_i, K_i) = ZF_2(A, K_i/N_i),$$

due to the homogeneity of degree zero of F_i. Since all firms face the same factor prices, they choose the same capital-labor ratio $k := K_i/N_i$ from the solution to the above equations. Therefore, output per unit of labor $y_i = Y_i/N_i = ZF(A, K_i/N_i)$ is the same for all firms: $y_i = y = ZF(A, k)$. These results imply the existence of an aggregate production function

---

[15] For a statement, see, e.g., MAS-COLELL, WHINSTON and GREEN (1995) pp. 545ff or STARR (1997), pp. 144ff.

$$Y = \sum_i Y_i = \sum_i N_i y = Ny = NZF(A,k) = ZF(AN, K),$$

where $N = \sum_i N_i$ and $K = \sum_i K_i$. In terms of this function, equilibrium on the markets for labor and capital services is given by

$$\begin{aligned} w &= ZAF_1(AN, K), \\ r &= ZF_2(AN, K), \end{aligned} \qquad (1.39)$$

and the profits of all firms are zero:[16]

$$\begin{aligned} \Pi_i &= Y_i - wN_i - rK_i \\ &= ZF(AN_i, K_i) \underbrace{-ZAF_1 N_i - ZF_2 K_i}_{-ZF(AN_i, K_i)} = 0. \end{aligned}$$

Households. Our example economy is populated by a continuum of households of mass 1, i.e., each individual household is assigned a unique real number h from the interval $[0,1]$. All households have the same one-period utility function and the same time $t = 0$ capital stock. When they face a given path of output and factor prices they choose identical sequences of consumption and labor supply. Let $x(h)$ denote an arbitrary decision variable of household $h \in [0,1]$ and put

$$x(h) = \bar{x} \,\forall h \in [0,1].$$

Since

$$\bar{x} = \int_0^1 x(h) dh = \int_0^1 \bar{x} dh$$

aggregate and individual variables are identical. As a consequence, we can consider a representative member from $[0,1]$ without explicit reference to his index h.

This representative household supplies labor services N_t with efficiency factor A_t and capital services K_t at the given real wage

---

[16] This is just Euler's theorem. For a general statement of this theorem, see, e.g., SYDSÆTER, STRØM and BERCK (1999), p.28.

1.4 Labor Supply, Growth, and the Decentralized Economy

w_t and rental rate of capital r_t, respectively. He saves in terms of capital which depreciates at the rate $\delta \in (0,1]$. Thus, his budget constraint reads:[17]

$$K_{t+1} - K_t \leq w_t N_t + (r_t - \delta)K_t - C_t. \quad (1.40)$$

The household seeks time paths of consumption and labor supply that maximize its life-time utility

$$\sum_{t=0}^{\infty} \beta^t u(C_t, 1 - N_t), \quad \beta \in (0,1), \quad (1.41)$$

subject to (1.40) and the given initial stock of capital K_0. From the Lagrangean of this problem,

$$\mathscr{L} = \sum_{t=0}^{\infty} \beta^t \Big[u(C_t, 1 - N_t) + \Lambda_t(w_t N_t + (1 - \delta + r_t)K_t - C_t - K_{t+1}) \Big]$$

we derive the following first-order conditions:

$$u_1(C_t, 1 - N_t) = \Lambda_t, \quad (1.42a)$$
$$u_2(C_t, 1 - N_t) = \Lambda_t w_t, \quad (1.42b)$$
$$\Lambda_t = \beta \Lambda_{t+1}(1 - \delta + r_{t+1}). \quad (1.42c)$$

Using the factor market equilibrium conditions (1.39) to substitute for w_t and r_{t+1} and applying the Euler theorem to F,

$$Y_t = ZF(A_t N_t, K_t) = ZA_t F_1(A_t N_t, K_t)N_t + ZF_2(A_t N_t, K_t)K_t$$

equations (1.42) reduce to

$$\frac{u_2(C_t, 1 - N_t)}{u_1(C_t, 1 - N_t)} = ZA_t F_1(A_t N_t, K_t), \quad (1.43a)$$

$$\frac{u_1(C_t, 1 - N_t)}{u_1(C_{t+1}, 1 - N_{t+1})} = \beta(1 - \delta + ZF_2(A_{t+1}N_{t+1}, K_{t+1})), \quad (1.43b)$$

$$K_{t+1} = ZF(A_t N_t, K_t) + (1 - \delta)K_t - C_t. \quad (1.43c)$$

---
[17] Here we use the fact that firms' profits are zero. In general, we must include the profits that firms distribute to their shareholders.

This system is identical to the first-order conditions that we derived for the Ramsey model (1.31) in equations (1.33) and (1.34) with the resource constraint being equal to (1.43c). Thus, the equilibrium time path of the decentralized economy is optimal in the sense that it maximizes the utility of all households given the resource constraint of the economy. On the other hand, a benevolent planer who solved the Ramsey problem (1.31) could implement this solution in terms of a competitive equilibrium. He simply has to choose time paths of wages and rental rates equal to the equilibrium sequences of the respective marginal products.

1.5 Model Calibration and Evaluation

The task of numerical DGE analysis is to obtain an approximate solution of the model at hand and to use this solution to study the model's properties. Before this can be done, specific values must be assigned to the model's parameters. In this section we illustrate both the calibration and the evaluation step with the aid of an example that we introduce in the next subsection.

1.5.1 The Benchmark Model

Example 1.5.1 presents our benchmark model. More or less similar models appear amongst others in the papers by HANSEN (1985), by KING, PLOSSER, and REBELO (1988a), and by PLOSSER (1989). It is a stripped down version of the celebrated model of KYDLAND and PRESCOTT (1982), who were awarded the Nobel Price in economics 2004 for their contribution to the theory of business cycles and economic policy. The model provides an integrated framework for studying economic fluctuations in a growing economy. Since it depicts an economy without money it belongs to the class of real business cycle models. The economy is inhabited by a representative consumer-producer who derives utility from consumption C_t and leisure $1 - N_t$ and uses labor N_t and capital services K_t to produce output Y_t. Labor augmenting technical progress at the deterministic rate $a > 1$ accounts for output growth. Stationary shocks to total factor productivity Z_t induce deviations from the balanced growth path of output. Similar models have been used to demonstrate that elementary economic principles may account for a substantial part of observed economic fluctuations. In the following chapters we will apply various methods to solve this model. It thus serves as a point of reference to compare the performance of different algorithms.

Example 1.5.1

Consider the following stochastic Ramsey model. The representative agent solves:

$$\max_{C_0, N_0} E_0 \left[\sum_{t=0}^{\infty} \beta^t \frac{C_t^{1-\eta}(1-N_t)^{\theta(1-\eta)}}{1-\eta} \right],$$

$$\beta \in (0,1), \theta \geq 0, \eta > \theta/(1+\theta),$$

s.t.

$$\left. \begin{array}{rcl} K_{t+1} + C_t & \leq & Z_t(A_t N_t)^{1-\alpha} K_t^{\alpha} + (1-\delta)K_t, \ \alpha \in (0,1), \\ A_{t+1} & = & aA_t, \ a \geq 1, \\ \ln Z_{t+1} & = & \varrho \ln Z_t + \epsilon_{t+1}, \ \varrho \in (0,1), \ \epsilon_t \sim N(0, \sigma^2), \\ 0 & \leq & C_t, \\ 0 & \leq & K_{t+1}, \end{array} \right\} \forall t,$$

K_0, Z_0 given.

First-Order Conditions. From the Lagrangean

$$\mathcal{L} := E_0 \Big\{ \sum_{t=0}^{\infty} \beta^t \Big[\frac{C_t^{1-\eta}(1-N_t)^{\theta(1-\eta)}}{1-\eta} \\ + \Lambda_t \left(Z_t(A_t N_t)^{1-\alpha} K_t^{\alpha} + (1-\delta)K_t - C_t - K_{t+1} \right) \Big] \Big\}$$

we derive the following first-order conditions:

$$0 = C_t^{-\eta}(1-N_t)^{\theta(1-\eta)} - \Lambda_t,$$
$$0 = \theta C_t^{1-\eta}(1-N_t)^{\theta(1-\eta)-1} - \Lambda_t(1-\alpha)Z_tA_t(A_tN_t)^{-\alpha}K_t^{\alpha},$$
$$0 = K_{t+1} - (1+\delta)K_t + C_t - Z_t(A_tN_t)^{1-\alpha}K_t^{\alpha},$$
$$0 = \Lambda_t - \beta E_t\Lambda_{t+1}\left(1-\delta+\alpha Z_{t+1}(A_{t+1}N_{t+1})^{1-\alpha}K_{t+1}^{\alpha-1}\right).$$

In terms of stationary variables $\lambda_t := A_t^{\eta}\Lambda_t$, $c_t := C_t/A_t$, and $k_t := K_t/A_t$ this system is:

$$0 = c_t^{-\eta}(1-N_t)^{\theta(1-\eta)} - \lambda_t, \tag{1.45a}$$
$$0 = \theta c_t^{1-\eta}(1-N_t)^{\theta(1-\eta)-1} - (1-\alpha)\lambda_t Z_t N_t^{-\alpha}k_t^{\alpha}, \tag{1.45b}$$
$$0 = ak_{t+1} - (1-\delta)k_t + c_t - Z_t N_t^{1-\alpha}k_t^{\alpha}, \tag{1.45c}$$
$$0 = \lambda_t - \beta a^{-\eta}E_t\lambda_{t+1}\left(1-\delta+\alpha Z_{t+1}N_{t+1}^{1-\alpha}k_{t+1}^{\alpha-1}\right). \tag{1.45d}$$

Stationary Solution. From these equations we can obtain the balanced growth path of the deterministic counterpart of the model. For that purpose we assume that the productivity shock is equal to its unconditional mean $Z \equiv 1$ for all periods. This allows us to drop the expectation operator E_t from equation (1.45d). Since N_t and all scaled variables are constant in the long-run, we find the stationary solution if we neglect the time indices of all variables. This delivers:[18]

$$\frac{N}{1-N} = \frac{1-\alpha}{\theta}\frac{N^{1-\alpha}k^{\alpha}}{c} = \frac{1-\alpha}{\theta}\frac{y}{c}, \tag{1.46a}$$
$$1 = \beta a^{-\eta}(1-\delta+\alpha N^{1-\alpha}k^{\alpha-1}) \tag{1.46b}$$
$$ = \beta a^{-\eta}(1-\delta+\alpha(y/k)),$$
$$\frac{y}{k} = \frac{N^{1-\alpha}k^{\alpha}}{k} = \frac{c}{k} + (a+\delta-1). \tag{1.46c}$$

1.5.2 Calibration

Definitions. In this book we use the term calibration for the process by which researchers choose the parameters of their DGE models from various sources. The most common ways are:

---

[18] Equation (1.46a) derives from equation (1.45b) after substitution for λ from equation (1.45a).

1. the use of time series averages of the levels or ratios of economic variables,
2. the estimation of single equations,
3. reference to econometric studies based on either macroeconomic or microeconomic data,
4. gauging the parameters so that the model replicates certain empirical facts as second moments of the data or impulse responses from structural vector autoregressions.

Very good descriptions of this process are given by COOLEY and PRESCOTT (1995) and by GOMME and RUPERT (2007). Other authors, for instance CANOVA (2007), p. 249 and DEJONG with DAVE (2007), p. 248ff., use the term calibration in the sense of an empirical methodology that involves the following steps:

1. select an economic question,
2. decide about a DGE model to address this question,
3. choose the functional forms and the parameters of this model,
4. solve the model and evaluate its quality,
5. propose an answer.

In this sense, calibration is an empirical research program distinct from classical econometrics. An econometric model is a fully specified probabilistic description of the process that may have generated the data to be analyzed. The econometric toolkit is employed to estimated this model, to draw inferences about its validity, to provide forecasts and to evaluate certain economic policy measures.

The distinction between calibration and classical econometrics is most easily demonstrated with the aid of Example 1.3.2. The policy function for the next-period capital stock is

$$K_{t+1} = \alpha \beta Z_t K_t^\alpha. \tag{1.47}$$

From this equation we can derive an econometric, single-equation model once we specify the stochastic properties of the productivity shock Z_t. Since, empirically, the stock of capital is a time series with clear upward trend, we could assume that $\ln Z_t$ is a difference stationary stochastic process with positiv drift a, that is

$$\ln Z_{t+1} - \ln Z_t = a + \epsilon_t,$$

where ϵ_t is a serially uncorrelated process with mean $E(\epsilon_t) = 0$ and variance $E(\epsilon_t^2) = \sigma^2$. Then, equation (1.47) implies

$$\ln K_{t+1} - \ln K_t = a + \alpha(\ln K_t - \ln K_{t-1}) + \epsilon_t.$$

This is a first-order autoregressive process in the variable $x_t := \ln K_t - \ln K_{t-1}$. The method of ordinary least squares provides consistent estimates of the parameters a, α, and σ^2. It should come as no surprise that the data will usually reject this model. For instance, using quarterly data for the German capital stock we get an estimate of α of about 0.89 and of $a = 0.00058$. Yet, if capital is rewarded its marginal product, α should be equal to the capital share of income which is about 0.27 (see below). Furthermore, a should be equal to the quarterly growth rate of output, which – between 1974 and 1989 – was about ten times larger than our estimate from this equation. In addition, standard test for homoscedastic and autocorrelation free error terms reject both assumptions, which is an additional sign of a misspecified model. The view that DGE models are too simple to provide a framework for econometric research does not mean that they are useless. In the words of EDWARD PRESCOTT (1986), p. 10:

> *The models constructed within this theoretical framework are necessarily highly abstract. Consequently, they are necessarily false, and statistical hypothesis testing will reject them. This does not imply, however, that nothing can be learned from such quantitative theoretical exercises.*

We have already demonstrated how we can use the model of Example 1.3.2 for 'quantitative theoretical exercises' in Section 1.2.5 where we constructed the distribution of the capital stock implied by the model. For this exercise we set $\alpha = 0.27$ and $\beta = 0.994$. We will explain in a moment on which considerations this choice rests. At this point it should suffice to recognize that these values are not derived from the estimated policy function for capital but rely on time series averages.

Calibration – in the sense of empirically grounded theoretical exercises – is the main use of DGE models. However, there is also a substantial body of more recent work, that employs econometric techniques – such as moment and Likelihood based methods – to estimate DGE models. Since our focus is on numerical solutions, we refer the interested reader to the books by DE JONG with DAVE (2007) and CANOVA (2007) that cover the application of econometric techniques to the estimation of DGE models.

Parameter Choice for the Benchmark Model. We start with the assumption that the real economic data were produced by the model of Example 1.3.2. To account for the representative agent nature of the model it is common to scale the data by the size of the population if appropriate. Since the model from Example 1.5.1 displays fluctuations around a stationary state, a valid procedure to select the model's key parameters is to use long-run time series averages.

We use seasonally adjusted quarterly economic data for the West German economy over the period 1975.i through 1989.iv.[19] We limit our attention to this time period for two reasons. Firstly, between 1960.i and 1975.i the West German average propensity to consume, c/y, has a clear upward trend. Had the German economy been on a balanced growth path this relation had been constant. Yet, the calibration step requires the steady state assumption to be approximately true. Secondly, the German unification in the fall of 1990 is certainly a structural break that violates the steady state assumption for the period after 1989.

In the stationary equilibrium of our model, output per household grows at the rate of labor augmenting technical progress $a-1$. Thus, we can infer a from fitting a linear time trend to gross domestic product at factor prices per capita. This gives $a = 1.005$, implying a quarterly growth rate of 0.5 percent. The second parameter of the production technology, α, equals the average wage share in gross domestic product at factor prices. The national accounts present no data on the wage income of self-employed persons. Yet, from the viewpoint of economic theory, this group of households also receives wage income as well as capital income.

---

[19] Usually, the U.S. economy is taken for this purpose. But since this economy has been the focus of numerous real business cycle models we think it is interesting to use an economy that differs in a number of aspects.

To account for that fact we assume that the self-employed earn wages equal to the average wage of employees. Therefore, we get a higher wage share of $1-\alpha = 0.73$ than the commonly used number of 0.64. The third parameter that describes the economy's production technology is the rate of depreciation δ. We compute this rate as the average ratio of quarterly real depreciation to the quarterly capital stock.[20] As compared to the number of 0.025 commonly used for the U.S. economy[21] our figure of $\delta = 0.011$ is much smaller. With these parameters at hand we can infer the productivity shock Z_t from the production function using the time series on the gross domestic product at factor prices Y_t, on hours H_t and on the stock of capital K_t:

$$Z_t = \frac{Y_t}{((1.005)^t H_t)^{0.73} K_t^{0.27}}.$$

Since our specification of the Markov process for Z_t implies

$$\ln Z_t = \varrho \ln Z_{t-1} + \epsilon_t,$$

where $\ln Z_t \approx (Z_t - Z)/Z$, we fit an AR(1)-process to the percentage deviation of Z_t from its mean. This delivers our estimates of $\varrho = 0.90$ and of $\sigma = 0.0072$.

It is not possible to determine all of the parameters that describe the preferences of the representative household from aggregate time series alone. The critical parameter in this respect is the elasticity of the marginal utility of consumption $-\eta$. Microeconomic studies provide evidence that this elasticity varies both with observable demographic characteristics and with the level of wealth. BROWNING, HANSEN, and HECKMAN (1999) argue that if constancy of this parameter across the population is imposed there is no strong evidence against η being slightly above one. We use $\eta = 2$ which implies that the household desires a smoother

---

[20] For this purpose we construct a quarterly series of the capital stock from yearly data on the stock of capital and quarterly data on investment and depreciation using the perpetual inventory method. The details of this approach can be found in the Gauss program GetPar1.g.

[21] See, e.g., KING, PLOSSER, and REBELO (1988a), p. 214 and PLOSSER (1989), p. 75.

consumption profile than in the case of $\eta = 1$, i.e., the case of logarithmic preferences, which has been used in many studies. The reason for this choice is that a larger η reduces the variability of output, working hours, and investment, and, thus, provides a better match between the model and the respective German macroeconomic variables.

Once the choice of η is made there are several possibilities to select the value of the discount factor β. The first alternative uses the observed average (quarterly) capital-output ratio k/y to solve for β from equation (1.46b). In our case this violates the restriction $\beta < 1$. KING, PLOSSER, and REBELO (1988a), p. 207, equate the average rate of return on equity to $\alpha(y/k) - \delta$ in (1.46b) and solve for $\beta a^{-\eta}$. Other studies, e.g., LUCKE (1998), p. 102, take the ex post real interest rate on short term bonds as estimators of $\alpha(y/k) - \delta$ in equation (1.46b). The average yearly return on the West German stock index DAX was about 8.5 percent, on the FAZ index 11.5 percent, and the ex post real interest rate on three month money market bonds about 2.7 percent. Given a and η, we use $\beta = 0.994$, which implies a yearly return of slightly above 6.5 percent. The final choice concerns the preference parameter θ. We use condition (1.46a) and choose θ so that $N = 0.13$, which is the average quarterly fraction of 1440 ($= 16 \times 90$) hours spend on work by the typical German employee. Note that many other studies put $N = 1/3$ arguing that individuals devote about 8 hours a day to market activities.[22] However, we consider the typical individual to be an average over the total population, including children and retired persons. Therefore, we find a much smaller fraction of a sixteen hours day engaged in income earning activities. Table 1.1 summarizes our choice of parameters.

1.5.3 Model Evaluation

We have already noted above that while formal econometric tests of DGE models are available, they are not the typical way to

---
[22] See, e.g., HANSEN (1985), p. 319f.

Table 1.1

Preferences	Production	
$\beta=0.994$	$a=1.005$	$\alpha=0.27$
$\eta=2.0$	$\delta=0.011$	$\varrho=0.90$
$N=0.13$	$\sigma=0.0072$	

evaluate these models.[23] Instead, it is common to compute impulse responses and second moments from these models and to compare these with the respective empirical counterparts.

Impulse Responses. Impulse responses are the deviations of the model's variables from their stationary solution that occur after a one-time shock that hits the economy. Figure 1.6 displays the response of several variables, measured in percentage deviations from their stationary values. They are computed from the Gauss program `Benchmark_LL.g`.

The time path of productivity is displayed in the upper left panel. It is given by

$$\ln Z_{t+1} = \varrho \ln Z_t + \epsilon_{t+1}.$$

In period $t=1$ the economy is in its stationary equilibrium. In period $t=2$ total factor productivity increases. We set ϵ_t equal to one standard deviation for $t=1$ and to zero thereafter. Since $\ln Z_t$ is highly autocorrelated ($\varrho = 0.9$), Z_t remains above $Z=1$ for many periods. The above average productivity raises the real wage and the representative household substitutes leisure for consumption so that working hours increase (see the upper right panel of Figure 1.6). Both, the increased productivity and the additional supply of labor boost output. Investment expenditures show by far the strongest reaction. To see this, note that the ordinate of all four panels of Figure 1.6 has the same scale. To understand the reaction of investment note first that the household wants to spread

---

[23] Estimation of DGE models is explained, among others, in the books by CANOVA (2007), DE JONG with DAVE (2007) and LUCKE (1998).

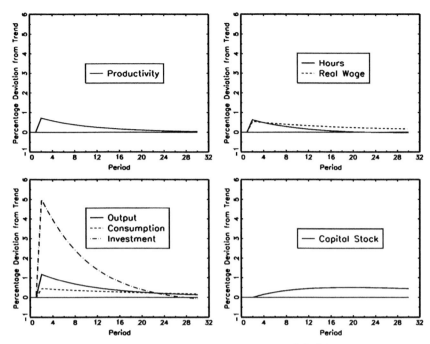

Figure 1.6: Impulse Responses in the Benchmark Model

the extra income earned in period $t = 1$ in order to smooth consumption. Second, the household anticipates higher real interest rates in the future since the productivity increase also raises the future marginal product of capital providing an additional incentive to invest. Since investment expenditures are a small part of the existing capital stock ($I/K = \delta$ in the steady state), we only observe a modest, hump-shaped increase of capital in panel four. However, the above average supply of capital explains why real wages remain high even after the productivity shock has almost faded.

Figure 1.7 displays impulse responses from a vector autoregressive (VAR) model estimated from the same quarterly data that we used to calibrate the parameters of our benchmark model. To maximize the degrees of freedom, we used the sample period from 1960.i through 1989.iv for which consistent data are available. The variables of the model are (in this order) real gross domestic product at factor prices per capita y, real private consumption per

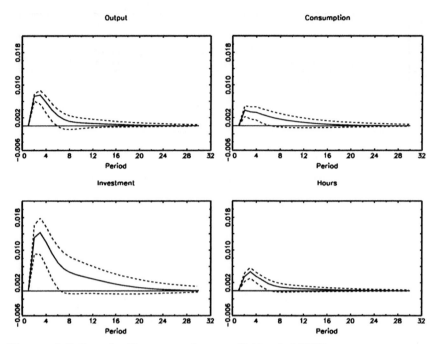

Figure 1.7: Impulse Responses from an Estimated VAR

capita c, real investment expenditures per capita i, and working hours per capita n. The VAR was estimated with two lags as indicated by the Schwarz information criterion. We used HP-filtered variables to remove the apparent trend in the data. Identification of the productivity shock was achieved by placing y at the top and by using the Cholesky factorization of the covariance matrix of the estimated residuals to obtain orthogonal shocks. 95-percent confidence bounds (the broken lines in Figure 1.7) were obtained from a bootstrap procedure.[24]

Similar to our theoretical model investment expenditures display the largest amplitude. According to our model the relation

---

[24] Readers that are unfamiliar with structural vector autoregressive models may want to consult, for instance, AMISANO and GIANNINI (1997), CANOVA (2007), Chapter 4, FAVERO (2001), Chapter 6 or HAMILTON (1994), Chapters 10 and 11. The Gauss program SVar.g and the data set used for this estimation can be downloaded from the web side of this book.

between the maximum increase of investment and the maximum increase of output is about five. In the estimated impulse responses of Figure 1.7, however, this relation is just about two. There is another striking difference between the model and the data. In the model, the maximum increase of all variables occurs in the period of the shock. In the data, the maximum increase of output, investment, and working hours takes place in the period after the shock hit the economy. The failure of the benchmark model to replicate this hump-shaped pattern has been a concern among researchers since it was pointed out first by COGLEY and NASON (1995).

Second Moments. A second typical tool to evaluate small scale DGE models is to compare the second moments of the time series obtained from simulations of the model to those of the respective macroeconomic aggregates. Most of these aggregates have an upward trend that must be removed to render the time series stationary. Most applications subject the logs of these aggregates to the Hodrick-Prescott or – for short – HP-filter that we describe in more detail in Section 12.4. The cyclical component of a time series that the filter returns is then the percentage deviation of the original series from its HP-trend component. The solution of our model consists of time paths of stationary variables $x_t := X_t/A_t$, where X_t denotes the level of the respective variable. Therefore, given our specification of the evolution of labor augmenting technical progress,

$$A_{t+1} = aA_t \quad \Leftrightarrow \quad A_t = A_0 a^t,$$

we can recover the time paths of the logs of the levels from

$$\ln X_t = \ln x_t + \ln A_t = \ln x_t + \ln A_0 + at.$$

To get comparable results, we must apply the HP-filter to $\ln X_t$. Yet, we can bypass the computation of $\ln X_t$, since, as we demonstrate in 12.4, the cyclical component of $\ln x_t$ is equal to the cyclical component of $\ln X_t$.

Table 1.2 displays the results from solving and simulating the model from Example 1.5.1 using the most widely employed log-linear solution method that we describe in Chapter 2. The second moments from the model are averages over 500 simulations. The length of the simulated time series is equal to the number of quarterly observations from 1975.i through 1989.iv. At the beginning of the first quarter our model economy is on its balanced growth path. In this and in the following 59 quarters it is hit by productivity shocks that drive the business cycle.

Consider the match between the data and the model's time series. The numbers in Table 1.2 reveal well known results. The model is able to reproduce the fact that investment is more volatile than output and consumption, but it exaggerates this stylized fact of the business cycle. Consumption is too smooth as compared to its empirical counterpart. The autocorrelations, however, are quite in line with the data. The cross correlations between output and the other variables are almost perfect in the model, quite in contrast to the cross-correlations found in the data.

The quite obvious mismatch between the data and the artificial time series can be traced to two different sources. First, we have not attempted to construct aggregates from the national income and product accounts (NIPA) that are consistent with the

Table 1.2

Variable	s_x	r_{xy}	r_x
Output	1.44	1.00	0.64
	(1.14)	(1.00)	(0.80)
Investment	6.11	1.00	0.64
	(2.59)	(0.75)	(0.79)
Consumption	0.56	0.99	0.66
	(1.18)	(0.79)	(0.84)
Hours	0.77	1.00	0.64
	(0.78)	(0.40)	(0.31)
Real Wage	0.67	0.99	0.65
	(1.17)	(0.41)	(0.91)

Notes: Empirical values from HP-filtered German data in parenthesis. s_x:=standard deviation of HP-filtered simulated series of variable x, r_{xy}:=cross correlation of variable x with output, r_x:=first order autocorrelation of variable x.

definition of output, capital, and labor in our model. Second, the benchmark model may be too simple to give an adequate account of the empirical facts.

COOLEY and PRESCOTT (1995) and GOMME and RUPERT (2007) present nice accounts of consistent measurement. Let us just consider two examples. The first one relates to consumption, the second to the capital stock.

In our model consumption is the flow of non-durables, whereas the German NIPA only report the sum of the quarterly expenditures on consumer durables and non-durables. From the viewpoint of our model, consumer durables are capital goods, and their purchases represent investment expenditures. Since the model predicts the latter to be more volatile than consumption, it should come as no surprise that the consumer aggregate taken from the NIPA is more volatile than the consumption series from our model. As a second example take the capital stock. Since our model gives no explicit account of the government sector our measure of the capital stock includes the public stock of capital. Yet, the NIPA provide no data on depreciation for the public infrastructure. As a consequence, our measure of the rate of capital depreciation is biased downwards. Yet, with lower user costs of capital, the household's incentive for intertemporal substitution increases and investment becomes more volatile. For instance, if we increase δ from 0.011 to 0.025, the ratio between the standard deviations of investment and output declines from about 4.3 to 3.5, which is much closer to the empirical ratio of 2.3.

To understand in what respects our benchmark model may be too simple, consider the household's first-order conditions with respect to consumption and labor supply given in equation (1.45a), which may also be written as:

$$w_t := (1-\alpha) Z_t N_t^{-\alpha} k_t^{\alpha},$$
$$w_t = \theta \lambda_t^{-1/\eta} (1-N_t)^{\frac{\theta(1-\eta)}{\eta} - 1}.$$

The first line posits that the real wage per efficiency unit of labor w_t equals the marginal product of effective labor N_t. For a given capital stock k_t this relation defines a downward sloping labor demand schedule (see Figure 1.8). The second line defines an

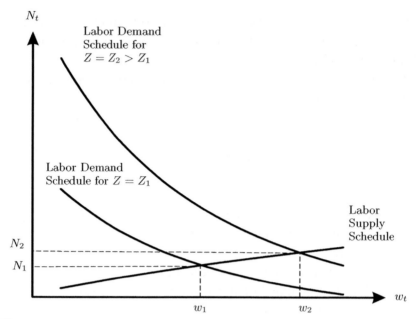

Figure 1.8: Productivity Shock in the Benchmark Business Cycle Model

upward sloping labor supply schedule for a fixed multiplier λ_t.[25] A productivity shock raising Z from Z_1 to Z_2 shifts the labor demand schedule outward. Equilibrium in the labor market requires higher wages, and, as a result, the representative household supplies more hours. Thus, the immediate impact of the shock is to raise the real wage, hours, and output. Since current consumption is a normal good, it increases as a consequence of the higher current income. Investment increases for several reasons: Firstly, future consumption as well as future leisure are normal goods. Thus, the household wants to spend part of his higher current income on future consumption and future leisure. He builds up his stock of capital over the next periods so that future production is potentially higher. Secondly, since the productivity shock is highly autocorrelated, the household expects above normal returns to capital. Thus, all variables in the model move closely

---

[25] Note, that we restricted η to $\eta > \theta/(1+\theta)$ so that the one-period utility function is strictly concave.

together with income which, in turn, is driven by a single shock. In reality, however, there may be additional shocks. For instance, think of a preference shock that shifts the labor supply curve to the left. That shock increases the real wage and reduces employment and output. As a consequence, the tight positive correlation between output, hours, and the real wage loosens.

In subsequent chapters you will see how these and other extensions help to bring artificial and empirical data closer together. Before we close this chapter we present an overview of the solution techniques to be introduced in the following chapters and relate them to the different characterizations of a model's solution presented in the preceding sections.

1.6 Numerical Solution Methods

We have seen in Sections 1.2.4 and 1.3.3 that only very special DGE models admit an exact solution. Thus, usually we must resort to numerical methods that provide approximate solutions. What are the general ideas behind these solutions and how are we able to determine how close they are to the true but unknown solution? The next two subsections deal with these issues.

1.6.1 Characterization

We characterize solutions along two dimensions (see Table 1.3). First, we distinguish between techniques that provide approximate solutions to the model's Euler equations and methods that deliver approximations to the model's policy functions. Second, we discern local from global methods. Local methods use information about the true model at a certain point in the model's state space. One such point, for instance, is the stationary equilibrium. Global methods incorporate information from the model's entire state space.

There is a long tradition in mathematics to characterize the solution of a system of non-linear difference equations locally by the

Table 1.3

	Local methods	Global methods
Euler Equations	Log-linear approximation → Chapter 2	Extended path → Chapter 3
Policy Function	LQ-approximation, Second order approximation → Chapter 2	Value function iteration → Chapter 4, Parameterized expectations → Chapter 5, Projection methods → Chapter 6

dynamics of a linear system, since linear systems admit an exact solution. The methods presented in Chapter 2 rest on this tradition. They linearize (or log-linearize) the model's Euler equations and solve the ensuing linear system using well-known techniques from linear algebra. This delivers linear approximations to the model's policy functions.

Closely related to this approach is the LQ-approximation. The linear-quadratic (LQ) model features a quadratic one-period utility function and a linear transition function that relates the current state of the system to the state of the system in the next period. The LQ-approximation incorporates all non-linear restrictions of the model in the one-period utility function and obtains a quadratic Taylor-series expansion of this function at the model's stationary equilibrium. It then solves for the linear policy functions of this approximate model.

It is well known from calculus that any sufficiently differentiable function can be approximated arbitrarily well by a Taylor series expansion around a given point in its domain. Second-order (or even higher-order) approximations of the model's policy functions rest on this result. They infer the magnitudes of the (partial) derivatives in this expansion from the model's properties at the stationary solution.

The extended path method, which we consider in Chapter 3, replaces the system of difference equations formed by the model's Euler equations by a large but finite-dimensional non-linear system of equations. In the stochastic case a related deterministic system of equations is solved repeatedly to trace out the time path of the model under a given sequence of shocks.

In Chapter 4 we consider methods that approximate the state space of the model by a denumerable grid of points. On this grid it is relatively easy to compute the value and the associated policy function via elementary mathematical operations.

The methods considered in Chapter 5 and Chapter 6 resort to functional analysis. The parameterized expectations approach recognizes that agent's conditional expectations are time invariant functions of the model's state variables and approximates these functions by polynomial functions or neural networks. The parameters of the approximating function are determined using information from the entire state space of the model. Projection methods approximate the policy functions predominantly by families of orthogonal polynomials. They also use global information.

1.6.2 Accuracy of Solutions

How shall we compare the solutions obtained from different methods and decide which one to use? In this subsection we consider three different criteria.

Second Moments. In as much as we are interested in the kind of model evaluation considered in Section 1.5 the second moments of time series obtained from simulating the model provide a first benchmark. For this reason, each of the following chapters provides the results from the solution of the benchmark model of Example 1.5.1. Our simulations use the same sequence of shocks so that differences in the results can be traced to differences in the solution procedure. As in HEER and MAUSSNER (2008), we will find that there are no noteworthy differences in second moments that favor the more advanced global methods over the local ones.[26]

Euler Equation Residuals. There are, however, considerable differences with respect to a measure of accuracy known as Euler equation residuals. To develop this measure we will introduce a more general framework.

Suppose we want to approximate a function $h : X \to Y$ that maps the subset X of $\mathbb{R}^n$ into the subset Y of $\mathbb{R}$. The function h is implicitly defined by the functional equation

$$G(h) = 0.$$

The operator $G : C_1 \to C_2$ maps the elements of the function space C_1 to the function space C_2. Examples of functional equations are the Bellman equation (1.14) of the deterministic growth model and the Euler equation of the stochastic growth model (1.24). The unknown function of the former is the value function $v(K)$, the policy function $h(K, Z)$ is the unknown of the latter. Suppose we have found an approximation $\hat{h}$. Then, for each $\mathbf{x} \in X$ we can compute the residual

$$R(\mathbf{x}) := G(\hat{h}(\mathbf{x})).$$

Since $\hat{h}$ approximates h, $R(\mathbf{x})$ will in general not be equal to zero, and we can use the maximum absolute value of R over all $\mathbf{x} \in X$ as a measure of the goodness of our approximation.

For instance, let $\hat{h}(K)$ denote an approximate solution of the policy function of the next-period capital stock in the deterministic growth model. Then, we can compute the residual of the Euler equation (1.12) from

$$R(K) = 1 - \frac{\beta u'(f(\hat{h}(K)) - \hat{h}(\hat{h}(K)))}{u'(f(K) - \hat{h}(K))} f'(\hat{h}(K)).$$

---

[26] A related but independent study with similar results is ARUOBA, FERNÁNDEZ-VILLAVERDE, and RUBIO-RAMÍREZ (2006).

A more interpretable definition of the Euler equation residual is due to CHRISTIANO and FISHER (2000). In the context of equation (1.12) it is given by

$$\tilde{R}(K) := \frac{\tilde{C}}{C} - 1,$$
$$C = f(K) - \hat{h}(K), \quad (1.48)$$
$$1 = \frac{\beta u'(f(\hat{h}(K)) - \hat{h}(\hat{h}(K)))}{u'(\tilde{C})} f'(\hat{h}(K)).$$

Thus, $\tilde{R}(K)$ is the rate by which consumption $\tilde{C}$ had to be raised above consumption given by the policy function $\hat{h}$ in order to deliver an Euler equation residual equal to zero.

In HEER and MAUSSNER (2008) we find for the benchmark model that both the extended path and the projection method provide very accurate results. The second-order approximation of the policy functions also delivers good results and outperforms the solutions obtained from value function iteration and the parameterized expectations approach. The least accurate solutions are linear approximations of the policy functions.

DM-Statistic. Euler equation residuals can be computed for both deterministic and stochastic DGE models. The measure proposed by DEN HAAN and MARCET (1994) is related to stochastic models only. They propose to compute the residuals e_t from the model's Euler equations along a simulated time path. For instance, if $\hat{h}(K_t, Z_t)$ is the approximate policy function of the next-period capital stock in the stochastic Ramsey model in equation (1.22), e_t is given by

$$e_t = u'(C_t) - \beta u'(C_{t+1})(1 - \delta + Z_{t+1} f'(\hat{h}(K_t, Z_t))),$$
$$C_t = Z_t f(K_t) + (1-\delta)K_t - \hat{h}(K_t, Z_t),$$
$$C_{t+1} = Z_{t+1} f(\hat{h}(K_t, Z_t)) + (1-\delta)\hat{h}(K_t, Z_t)$$
$$\qquad - \hat{h}(Z_{t+1}, \hat{h}(K_t, Z_t)).$$

The variable e_t is an ex-post forecast error of

$$\beta E_t u'(C_{t+1})(1 - \delta + Z_{t+1} f'(K_{t+1})).$$

With rational expectations this forecast error should be uncorrelated with past observation. This assertion can be tested by regressing e_t on lagged variables. The estimated coefficients should be statistically insignificant. We provide the details of this test in Section 12.3. The test statistic, the so called DM-statistic,[27] is asymptotically distributed as a χ^2-variable. If this test rejects the null of independence, this may stem from an inaccurate solution that gives raise to systematic ex-post forecast errors. DEN HAAN and MARCET (1994) propose to run a large number of simulations of the model and to record the simulations where the DM-statistic is either smaller than the 2.5-percent critical value or larger than the 97.5-percent critical value. From a good solution we expect that about 5 percent of the simulations fall into these two regions.

---

[27] There is another statistic labeled DM-statistic that should not be confused with the statistic considered here. The statistic developed by DIEBOLD and MARIANO (1995) is used to evaluate the predictive accuracy of different econometric forecasts.

Appendix 1: Solution to Example 1.2.1

We derive the solution to Example 1.2.1 using iterations over the value function. Thus, letting $v^0 = 0$ we solve

$$v^1 = \max_{K'} \ln(K^\alpha - K')$$

yielding $K' = 0$ and $v^1 = \alpha \ln K$. In the next step we seek K' that solves

$$v^2 = \max_{K'} \ln(K^\alpha - K') + \beta \alpha \ln K'.$$

From the first order condition

$$\frac{1}{K^\alpha - K'} = \frac{\alpha\beta}{K'}$$

we get

$$K' = \frac{\alpha\beta}{1+\alpha\beta} K^\alpha,$$
$$v^2 = \alpha(1+\alpha\beta)\ln K + A_1,$$
$$A_1 := \ln(1/(1+\alpha\beta)) + \alpha\beta \ln(\alpha\beta/(1+\alpha\beta)).$$

The value function in step $s = 3$ is given by

$$v^3 = \max_{K'} \ln(K^\alpha - K') + \beta\alpha(1+\alpha\beta)\ln K' + \beta A_1$$

yielding

$$K' = \frac{\alpha\beta + (\alpha\beta)^2}{1 + \alpha\beta + (\alpha\beta)^2} K^\alpha,$$
$$v^3 = \alpha(1 + \alpha\beta + (\alpha\beta)^2)\ln K + A_2,$$
$$A_2 = \ln\left[\frac{1}{1+\alpha\beta+(\alpha\beta)^2}\right] + (\alpha\beta + (\alpha\beta)^2)\ln\left[\frac{\alpha\beta+(\alpha\beta)^2}{1+\alpha\beta+(\alpha\beta)^2}\right] + \beta A_1.$$

Continuing in this fashion we find the policy function in step s given by

$$K' = \frac{\sum_{i=1}^{s-1}(\alpha\beta)^s}{\sum_{i=0}^{s-1}(\alpha\beta)^s} K^\alpha$$

with limit $s \to \infty$ equal to

$$K' = \alpha\beta K^\alpha.$$

Obviously, from the first two steps, the value function is a linear function of $\ln K$. To infer the parameters of $v := \lim_{s \to \infty} v^s$, we use the method of undetermined coefficients.

This method postulates a functional form for the solution with unknown parameters, which are also called the undetermined coefficients. The parameterized function is inserted into the equations that are describing our model and solved for the unknown coefficients. Thus, assume $v = a + b \ln K$ with a and b as yet undetermined coefficients. Solving

$$\max_{K'} \ln(K^\alpha - K') + \beta(a + b \ln K')$$

yields

$$K' = \frac{\beta b}{1 + \beta b} K^\alpha.$$

Therefore

$$v = \underbrace{\alpha(1 + \beta b)}_{b} \ln K + \underbrace{\beta a + \ln\left[\frac{1}{1 + \beta b}\right] + \beta b \ln\left[\frac{\beta b}{1 + \beta b}\right]}_{a}.$$

Equating the constant on the rhs of this equation to a and the slope parameter to b, we get:

$$b = \alpha(1 + \beta b) \Rightarrow b = \frac{\alpha}{1 - \alpha\beta},$$

$$a = \beta a + \ln\left[\frac{1}{1 + \beta b}\right] + \beta b \ln\left[\frac{\beta b}{1 + \beta b}\right],$$

$$\Rightarrow a = \frac{1}{1 - \beta}\left[\ln(1 - \alpha\beta) + \frac{\alpha\beta}{1 - \alpha\beta} \ln \alpha\beta\right].$$

Appendix 2: Restrictions on Technology and Preferences

Here we derive formally the restrictions that we must place on technology and preferences to ensure the existence of a balanced growth path. We draw heavily on the Appendix to KING, PLOSSER, and REBELO (1988) and, like SOLOW (1988), p. 35f., define a balanced growth path as an equilibrium that features (see page 35)

1. a constant rate of output growth,
2. and a constant share of savings in output.

Technology. The constant share of savings S_t in output implies that output and capital must grow at the same rate: using the economy's resource constraint, we find:[28]

$$g_K = \frac{K_{t+1}}{K_t} = \frac{\overbrace{Y_t - C_t}^{S_t} + (1-\delta)K_t}{K_t} = \frac{S_t}{Y_t}\frac{Y_t}{K_t} + (1-\delta).$$

So, if S_t/Y_t is constant, so must be Y_t/K_t, and, hence, output and capital must grow at the same rate.

Now, consider the general case of labor and capital augmenting technical progress:

$$Y_t = F(A_t N_t, B_t K_t), \quad A_t = A_0 a^t, \quad B_t = B_0 b^t.$$

Since F is linear homogenous, the growth factor of output, g_Y, can be factored as follows

$$g_Y = \frac{Y_{t+1}}{Y_t} = \frac{B_{t+1} K_{t+1}}{B_t K_t} \frac{F(X_{t+1}, 1)}{F(X_t, 1)} = b g_K g_F, \quad \text{(A.2.1a)}$$

$$X_t := (A_0/B_0)(a/b)^t (N_t/K_t) \Rightarrow g_X = \frac{a g_N}{b g_K}. \quad \text{(A.2.1b)}$$

Since $g_Y = g_K$ we get from (A.2.1a)

$$1 = b g_F.$$

There are two cases to consider:

1) $b = g_F \equiv 1$

---

[28] In the following the symbol g_X denotes the growth factor of the variable X.

2) and $g_F = 1/b, b > 1$.

In the first case technical progress is purely labor augmenting and for $g_F \equiv 1$ we must have $g_X = 1$, implying $g_K = ag_N$. Now, in our representative agent framework with a constant population size, N is bounded between zero and one. Thus, a constant rate of capital and output growth requires $g_N = 1$ (otherwise $N \to 1$ or $N \to 0$). Therefore, output and capital grow at the rate of labor augmenting technical progress $a - 1$. For the share of savings to remain constant, consumption must also grow at this rate.

Now consider the second case. For

$$g_F := \frac{F(X_{t+1}, 1)}{F(X_t, 1)} = \text{constant} < 1$$

X_t must grow at the constant rate

$$g_X = \frac{ag_N}{bg_K} \overset{g_N=1}{\Longrightarrow} g_X = \frac{a}{bg_K}.$$

Let

$$X_t = X_0 c^t, \quad c = \frac{a}{bg_K},$$

and define $f(X_t) := F(X_t, 1)$ so that the condition reads

$$\frac{f(X_0 c^{t+1})}{f(X_0 c^t)} = \text{constant}.$$

Since this must hold for arbitrary given initial conditions X_0, differentiation with respect to X_0 implies

$$0 = \frac{1}{f(X_t)^2} \left\{ f(X_t) f'(X_{t+1}) \frac{X_{t+1}}{X_0} - f(X_{t+1}) f'(X_t) \frac{X_t}{X_0} \right\} dX_0,$$

$$0 = \left\{ \frac{f'(X_{t+1}) X_{t+1}}{f(X_{t+1})} - \frac{f'(X_t) X_t}{f(X_t)} \right\} \frac{f(X_{t+1})}{f(X_t)} \frac{dX_0}{X_0}.$$

For the term in curly brackets to be zero, the elasticity of f with respect to X_t must be a constant, say α:

$$\frac{f'(X_t) X_t}{f(X_t)} = \alpha.$$

Yet, the only functional form with constant elasticity is

$$f(X) = ZX^\alpha$$

with Z an arbitrary constant of integration. Thus, output must be given by a Cobb-Douglas function

$$Y = F(AN, BK) = BK(f(AN/BK)) = BKZ(AN/BK)^\alpha$$
$$= Z(AN)^\alpha (BK)^{1-\alpha}.$$

Yet, if F is Cobb-Douglas, technical progress can always be written as purely labor-augmenting, since

$$Y_t = Z(A_t N_t)^\alpha (B_t K_t)^{1-\alpha} = Z(\tilde{A}_t N_t)^\alpha K_t^{1-\alpha}, \quad \tilde{A}_t := A_t B_t^{(1-\alpha)/\alpha}.$$

Preferences. Consider equation (1.34) which determines the farmer's savings decision. We reproduce it here for convenience:

$$\frac{u_1(C_t, 1-N_t)}{u_1(C_{t+1}, 1-N_{t+1})} = \beta(1-\delta + F_2(A_{t+1}N_{t+1}, K_{t+1})). \qquad (\text{A.2.2})$$

On a balanced growth path with constant supply of labor the right hand side of this equation is a constant, since A_t and K_t grow at the same rate and $F_2(AN, K) = F_2(N, K/A)$. On that path the resource constraint is given by

$$C_t = F(A_t N_t, K_t) + (1-\delta)K_t - K_{t+1}$$
$$= A_t \big[F(N, K/A) + (1-\delta)(K/A) - a(K/A) \big].$$

Since the term in brackets is constant, consumption grows at the rate $a - 1$, and we may write:

$$C_t = C_0 a^t.$$

On the balanced growth path equation (A.2.2), thus, may be written as:

$$\frac{u_1(C_0 a^t, 1-N)}{u_1(C_0 a^{t+1}, 1-N)} = \Delta = \text{constant}.$$

This must hold irrespective of the arbitrary constant C_0. Differentiating with respect to C_0 yields:

$$\Delta \frac{dC_0}{C_0} \left\{ \frac{u_{11}(C_t, 1-N)}{u_1(C_t, 1-N)} C_t - \frac{u_{11}(C_{t+1}, 1-N)}{u_1(C_{t+1}, 1-N)} C_{t+1} \right\} = 0.$$

The term in curly brackets is zero, if the elasticity of the marginal utility of consumption $(u_{11}/u_1)C$, is a constant, say $-\eta$. Integrating

$$\frac{du_1(C, 1-N)}{u_1(C, 1-N)} = -\eta \frac{dC}{C}$$

on both sides gives

$$\ln u_1(\cdot) = -\eta \ln C + \ln v_1(1-N), \Rightarrow u_1(\cdot) = C^{-\eta} v_1(1-N)$$

where v_1 is an arbitrary function of leisure $1 - N$. Integrating once more with respect to C yields

$$u(C, 1-N) = \begin{cases} \frac{C^{1-\eta} v_1(1-N)}{1-\eta} + v_2(1-N) & \text{if } \eta \neq 1, \\ v_1(1-N) \ln C + v_2(1-N) & \text{if } \eta = 1. \end{cases} \quad (A.2.3)$$

Restrictions on the functions v_1 and v_2 derive from the static condition on labor supply in equation (1.33). Remember, this condition is

$$\frac{u_2(C_t, 1-N_t)}{u_1(C_t, 1-N_t)} = A_t F_1(A_t N_t, K_t),$$

in general, and

$$\frac{u_2(C, 1-N)}{u_1(C, 1-N)} = A F_1(N, K/A)$$

along the balanced growth path. Write this as

$$\ln[u_2(C, 1-N)] = \ln[u_1(C, 1-N)] + \ln A + \ln[F_1(N, K/A)],$$

and differentiate with respect to C and A. The result is

$$\underbrace{\frac{u_{21}(\cdot)}{u_2(\cdot)}}_{\xi} C \frac{dC}{C} = \underbrace{\frac{u_{11}(\cdot)}{u_1(\cdot)}}_{-\eta} C \frac{dC}{C} + \frac{dA}{A},$$

where ξ denotes the elasticity of the marginal utility of leisure with respect to consumption. Since $dC/C = dA/A$ in the long-run, this condition restricts ξ to

$$\xi = 1 - \eta.$$

Using (A.2.3) this implies that

- $v_2(1-N)$ is a constant in the case of $\eta \neq 1$,
- $v_1(1-N)$ is a constant in the case of $\eta = 1$.

Setting the respective constants equal to zero and 1, respectively, yields the functional forms of the one-period utility function given in (1.35).

Problems

1.1 Finite-Horizon Ramsey Model. Prove that the finite horizon Ramsey model stated in (1.3) meets the assumptions of the Kuhn-Tucker theorem 1.1.1.

1.2 Infinite-Horizon Ramsey Model with Adjustment Costs. Consider the following Ramsey model: A fictitious planer maximizes

$$\sum_{t=0}^{\infty} \beta^t \ln C_t, \quad \beta \in (0,1),$$

subject to

$$K_{t+1} = K_t^{1-\delta} I_t^{\delta}, \quad \delta \in (0,1),$$
$$I_t = K_t^{\alpha} - C_t, \quad \alpha \in (0,1),$$
$$K_0 \text{ given.}$$

The symbols have the usual meaning: C_t is consumption, K_t is the stock of capital, and I_t is investment.

a) State the Lagrangian of this problem and derive the first-order conditions of this problem. (Hint: Substitute for I_t in the transition equation for capital from the definition of I_t.)

b) Suppose the policy function for capital is given by

$$K_{t+1} = k_0 K_t^{k_1}.$$

Use this equation to derive the policy functions for investment and consumption.

c) Assume that the policy function for consumption can be written as

$$C_t = c_0 K_t^{c_1}.$$

If this guess is true, how are c_0, c_1, k_0 and k_1 related to the model's parameters α, β, and δ?

d) Substitute the policy functions into the Euler equation for capital. Show that the assumptions made thus far hold, if k_0 meets the condition

$$k_0^{1/\delta}\left(k_0^{-\alpha} - \beta(1-\delta)\right) = \alpha\beta\delta.$$

e) Prove that there is a unique k_0 that solves this equation.

1.3 A Vintage Model of Capital Accumulation. In Section 1.2.5 we consider the problem

$$\max \sum_{t=0}^{\infty} \beta^t \frac{C_t^{1-\eta}-1}{1-\eta}, \quad \beta \in (0,1),\ \eta > 0,$$

subject to

$$K_{2t+1} = \delta K_{1t}, \quad \delta \in (0,1),$$

$$Y_t = \left[aK_{1t}^{1-\eta} + (1-a)K_{2t}^{1-\eta}\right]^{\frac{1}{1-\eta}}, \quad a \in (0,1),$$

$$Y_t = C_t + K_{1t+1},$$

K_{10} and K_{20} given.

a) Use dynamic programming to derive the first-order conditions for this problem. (Hint: Use $v(K_1, K_2)$ as value function, note that $K_2' = \delta K_1$, and substitute for K_1' the economy's resource constraint.)

b) Prove that $K_{1t+1} = sY_t$, where s is determined from

$$1 - s = \left[\beta a + \beta^2(1-a)\delta^{1-\eta}\right]^{\frac{1}{\eta}},$$

solves this problem.

1.4 Dynamic Programming and the Stochastic Ramsey Model. The stochastic Euler equations of the Ramsey model (1.22) are given in (1.24). Use stochastic dynamic programming as considered in Section 1.3.3 to derive these conditions.

1.5 Analytic Solution of the Benchmark Model. Consider the benchmark model of Example 1.5.1. Assume $\eta = 1$ so that the current period utility function is given by

$$u(C_t, N_t) := \ln C_t + \theta \ln(1 - N_t).$$

Furthermore, suppose $\delta = 1$, that is, full depreciation. Use the method of undetermined coefficients (see Appendix 1) to verify that

$$k_{t+1} = AZ_t N_t^{1-\alpha} k_t^{\alpha},$$

with A to be determined, is the policy function for the next-period capital stock. Show that working hours N_t are constant in this model.

1.6 A Model With Flexible Working Hours and Analytic Solution
In Section 1.2.5 we considered a model with adjustment costs. We extend this model to a stochastic model with endogenous labor supply. Assume the current period utility function

$$u(C_t, N_t) = \ln\left(C_t - \frac{\theta}{1+\omega} N_t^{1+\omega}\right), \quad \theta, \omega > 0.$$

The transition equation for the capital stock is

$$K_{t+1} = K_t^{1-\delta} I_t^\delta, \quad \delta \in (0,1).$$

The production function is

$$Y_t = Z_t N_t^{1-\alpha} K_t^\alpha.$$

Determine the coefficients of the following guesses for the policy functions for consumption C_t working hours N_t, and the next-period capital stock K_{t+1}:

$$C_t = c_1 Z_t^{c_2} K_t^{c_3},$$
$$N_t = n_1 Z_t^{n_2} K_t^{n_3},$$
$$K_{t+1} = k_1 Z_t^{k_2} K_t^{k_3}.$$

Chapter 2

Perturbation Methods

Overview. In the previous chapter we have seen that the solution of a DGE model with a representative agent is given by a set of policy functions that relate the agent's choice variables to the state variables that characterize the agent's economic environment. In this chapter we explore methods that use local information to obtain either a linear or a quadratic approximation of the agent's policy function. To see what this means, remember from elementary calculus that a straight line that is tangent to a function $y = f(x)$ at x^* locally approximates f: according to Taylor's theorem (see Section 11.2.1) we may write

$$f(x^* + h) = \underbrace{f(x^*) + f'(x^*)h}_{\text{linear function in } h} + \phi(h),$$

where the error $\phi(h)$ has the property

$$\lim_{\substack{h \to 0 \\ h \neq 0}} \frac{\phi(h)}{h} = 0.$$

Thus, close to x^*, f equals a slightly perturbed linear function. To set up the linear function, we only need to know (i) the value of f at x^* and (ii) the value of its first derivative f' at the same point.

Probably less well known is the following result. If $x_t = f(x_{t-1})$ is a non-linear difference equation and $\bar{x}_t = f'(x^*)\bar{x}_{t-1}$, $\bar{x}_t = x_t - x^*$ its linear approximation at x^* defined by $x^* = f(x^*)$, then the solution of the linear model provides a local approximation of the solution of the non-linear equation.[1] Perturbation methods

---

[1] See Section 12.1 on difference equations, if you are unfamiliar with this subject.

rest on these observations. As we will see, they are not limited to linear approximations. If f is n-times continuously differentiable, we may use a polynomial in h of degree up to $n-1$ to build a local model of f.

In this chapter we mainly consider linear approximations. They are the most frequently used solutions in applied research and are easy to apply. As you will see in later chapters they also provide a first guess for more advanced, non-local methods.

The next section considers deterministic models. In this context it is relatively easy to demonstrate by means of an example (the Ramsey model of Section 1.2) that we can get linear approximations to the policy functions by either solving the linearized system of Euler equations or by applying the implicit function theorem to the steady state conditions of the model. We use this result to provide a procedure that computes the solution of an arbitrary deterministic model with n variables from the linearized system of Euler equations.

Before we turn to the solution of stochastic DGE models in Sections 2.3 and 2.4, we consider a model where the linear policy functions provide an exact solution. This is the linear-quadratic (LQ) model outlined in Section 2.2. Two different approximation methods derive from the LQ problem. The first approach, considered in Section 2.3, approximates a given model so that its return function is quadratic and the law of motion is linear and solves the approximate model by value function iterations. The second approach, taken up in Section 2.4, relies on a linear approximation of the model's Euler equations and solves the ensuing system of linear stochastic difference equations.

We close the methodological part of this chapter in Section 2.5 with the quadratic approximation of the policy functions of an arbitrary stochastic DGE model. The bottom line of Sections 2.3 through 2.5 are three programs: SolveLA and SolveLQA compute linear approximations to deterministic as well as stochastic DGE models. The difference between the two programs is the way you must set up your model. SolveLA is a general purpose routine, while SolveLQA is limited to models whose solution can be obtained by solving a central planing problem. Yet, in some kinds of problems it is much easier to cast your model into the framework of SolveLQA. The third program, SolveQA, computes quadratic approximations of the policy functions of an arbitrary DGE model. Various applications illustrate the use of these programs in Section 2.6.

2.1 Linear Solutions for Deterministic Models

This Section applies two tools. The implicit function theorem, sketched in Section 11.2.2, allows us to compute the derivatives of a system of policy functions that is implicitly determined by a system of non-linear Euler equations. The close relation between the local solution of a system of non-linear, first-order difference equations and the solution of the related linearized system, outlined in Section 12.1, provides a second route to compute linear approximations of a model's policy functions. If you are unfamiliar with any of these tools, you might consider reading the respective sections before proceeding.

We use the deterministic growth model from Section 1.2 to illustrate both techniques before we turn to the general approach. We begin with the solution of the system of non-linear difference equations that governs the model's dynamics.

Approximate Computation of the Saddle Path. Consider equations (1.17) that characterize the solution of the Ramsey problem (1.8) from Section 1.2:

$$K_{t+1} - f(K_t) + C_t =: g^1(K_t, C_t, K_{t+1}, C_{t+1}) = 0, \tag{2.1a}$$

$$u'(C_t) - \beta u'(C_{t+1}) f'(K_{t+1}) =: g^2(K_t, C_t, K_{t+1}, C_{t+1}) = 0. \tag{2.1b}$$

Equation (2.1a) is the farmer's resource constraint.[2] It states that seed available for the next period K_{t+1} equals production $f(K_t)$

---

[2] Remember, that in the notation of Section 1.2 $f(K) := (1-\delta)K + F(N, K)$, where N are the farmer's exogenously given working hours.

minus consumption C_t. The first-order condition with respect to the next-period stock of capital K_{t+1} is equation (2.1b). These two equations implicitly specify a non-linear system of difference equations $\mathbf{x}_{t+1} = \boldsymbol{\Psi}(\mathbf{x}_t)$ in the vector $\mathbf{x}_t := [K_t, C_t]'$:

$$\mathbf{g}(\mathbf{x}_t, \boldsymbol{\Psi}(\mathbf{x}_t)) = \mathbf{0}_{2\times 1}, \ \mathbf{g} = [g^1, g^2]'.$$

The stationary solution defined by

$$1 = \beta f'(K^*), \tag{2.2a}$$
$$K^* = f(K^*) - C^* \tag{2.2b}$$

is a fixed point of $\boldsymbol{\Psi}$. We obtain the linear approximation of $\boldsymbol{\Psi}$ at $\mathbf{x}^* = [K^*, C^*]'$ via equation (11.38):

$$\bar{\mathbf{x}}_{t+1} = J(\mathbf{x}^*)\bar{\mathbf{x}}_t, \quad \bar{\mathbf{x}}_t := \mathbf{x}_t - \mathbf{x}^*. \tag{2.3}$$

with the Jacobian matrix J determined by

$$J(\mathbf{x}^*) = \begin{bmatrix} \frac{\partial g^1(\mathbf{x}^*,\mathbf{x}^*)}{\partial K_{t+1}} & \frac{\partial g^1(\mathbf{x}^*,\mathbf{x}^*)}{\partial C_{t+1}} \\ \frac{\partial g^2(\mathbf{x}^*,\mathbf{x}^*)}{\partial K_{t+1}} & \frac{\partial g^2(\mathbf{x}^*,\mathbf{x}^*)}{\partial C_{t+1}} \end{bmatrix}^{-1} \begin{bmatrix} \frac{\partial g^1(\mathbf{x}^*,\mathbf{x}^*)}{\partial K_t} & \frac{\partial g^1(\mathbf{x}^*,\mathbf{x}^*)}{\partial C_t} \\ \frac{\partial g^2(\mathbf{x}^*,\mathbf{x}^*)}{\partial K_t} & \frac{\partial g^2(\mathbf{x}^*,\mathbf{x}^*)}{\partial C_t} \end{bmatrix}. \tag{2.4}$$

The derivatives of $\mathbf{g}$ at the fixed point are easily obtained from (2.1a) and (2.1b) (we suppress the arguments of the functions and write f' instead of $f'(K^*)$ and so forth):

$$J(\mathbf{x}^*) = -\begin{bmatrix} 1 & 0 \\ -\beta u' f'' & -u'' \end{bmatrix}^{-1} \begin{bmatrix} -\frac{1}{\beta} & 1 \\ 0 & u'' \end{bmatrix} = \begin{bmatrix} \frac{1}{\beta} & -1 \\ -\frac{u' f''}{u''} & 1 + \frac{\beta u' f''}{u''} \end{bmatrix}.$$

In computing the matrix on the rhs of this equation we used the definition of the inverse matrix given in (11.14). The eigenvalues λ_1 and λ_2 of J satisfy (see (11.24)):

$$\det J = \frac{1}{\beta} = \lambda_1 \lambda_2,$$

$$\operatorname{tr} J = \underbrace{1 + \frac{1}{\beta} + \frac{\beta u' f''}{u''}}_{=:\Delta} = \lambda_1 + \lambda_2.$$

2.1 Linear Solutions for Deterministic Models

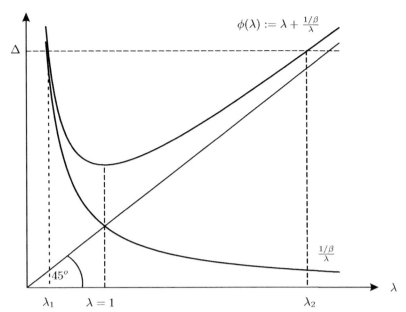

Figure 2.1: Eigenvalues of W

Therefore, they solve equation

$$\phi(\lambda) := \lambda + \frac{1/\beta}{\lambda} = \Delta.$$

The solutions are the points of intersection between the horizontal line through Δ and the hyperbola $\phi(\lambda)$ (see Figure 2.1). The graph of ϕ obtains a minimum at $\lambda_{min} = 1/\sqrt{\beta} > 1$, where $\phi'(\lambda_{min}) = 1 - (1/\beta)\lambda^{-2} = 0$.[3] Since $\phi(1) = 1 + (1/\beta) < \Delta$, there must be one intersection to the right of $\lambda = 1$ and one to the left, proving that J has one real eigenvalue $\lambda_1 < 1$ and another real eigenvalue $\lambda_2 > 1$.

Let $J = TST^{-1}$ with

$$S = \begin{bmatrix} \lambda_1 & s_{12} \\ 0 & \lambda_2 \end{bmatrix}$$

denote the Schur factorization of J (see (11.27) in Section 11.1.8). In the new variables (where $T^{-1} = (t^{ij})$)

---

[3] In Figure 2.1 λ_{min} is so close to $\lambda = 1$ that we do not show it.

$$\mathbf{y}_t = T^{-1}\bar{\mathbf{x}}_t \Leftrightarrow \begin{bmatrix} y_{1t} \\ y_{2t} \end{bmatrix} = \begin{bmatrix} t^{11} & t^{12} \\ t^{21} & t^{22} \end{bmatrix} \begin{bmatrix} K_t - K^* \\ C_t - C^* \end{bmatrix} \quad (2.5)$$

the system of equations (2.3) is given by

$$\mathbf{y}_{t+1} = S\mathbf{y}_t.$$

The second line of this matrix equation is

$$y_{2t+1} = \lambda_2 y_{2t}.$$

Since $\lambda_2 > 1$, the variable y_{2t} will diverge unless we set $y_{20} = 0$. This restricts the system to the stable eigenspace. Using $y_{2t} = 0$ in (2.5) implies

$$0 = t^{21}\bar{x}_{1t} + t^{22}\bar{x}_{2t}, \quad (2.6a)$$
$$y^{1t} = (t^{11} - t^{12}(t^{21}/t^{22}))x_{1t}. \quad (2.6b)$$

The first line is the linearized policy function for consumption:

$$C_t - C^* = -\frac{t^{21}}{t^{22}}[K_t - K^*]. \quad (2.7a)$$

The second line of (2.6) implies via $y_{1t+1} = \lambda_1 y_{1t}$ the linearized policy function for savings:

$$K_{t+1} - K^* = \lambda_1 [K_t - K^*]. \quad (2.7b)$$

We illustrate these computations in the program Ramsey2a.g, where we use $u(C) = [C^{1-\eta} - 1]/(1 - \eta)$ and $F(N, K) = K^\alpha$. In this program we show that it is not necessary to compute the Jacobian matrix analytically as we have done here. You may also write a procedure that receives the vector $[K_t, C_t, K_{t+1}, C_{t+1}]'$ as input and that returns the rhs of equations (2.1). This procedure can be passed to a routine that numerically evaluates the partial derivatives at the point (K^*, C^*, K^*, C^*). From the output of this procedure you can extract the matrices that appear on the rhs of equation (2.4).

Figure 2.2 compares the time path of the capital stock under the analytic solution $K_{t+1} = \alpha\beta K_t^\alpha$ (which requires $\eta = \delta = 1$)

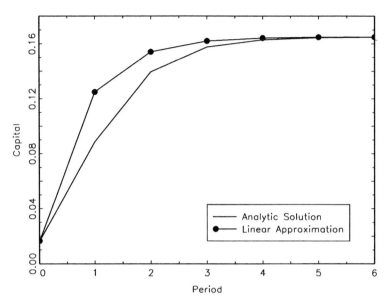

Figure 2.2: Approximate Time Path of the Capital Stock in the Deterministic Growth Model

with the path obtained from the approximate linear solution. The parameters are set equal to $\alpha = 0.27$ and $\beta = 0.994$, respectively. The initial capital stock equals one-tenth of the stationary capital stock. As we would have expected, far from the fixed point, the linear approximation is not that good. Yet, after about five iterations it is visually indistinguishable from the analytic solution.

Approximate Policy Functions. We now apply the implicit function theorem directly to find the linear approximation of the policy function for optimal savings. Let $K_{t+1} = h(K_t)$ denote this function. Since $K^* = h(K^*)$, its linear approximation at K^* is given by

$$K_{t+1} = h(K_t) \simeq K^* + h'(K^*)(K_t - K^*). \tag{2.8}$$

Substituting equation (2.1a) for $C_t = f(K_t) - h(K_t)$ into equation (2.1b) delivers:

$$g(K_t) := u'\left[(f(K_t) - h(K_t)\right] \\ - \beta u'\left[(f(h(K_t)) - h(h(K_t))\right] f'(h(K_t)).$$

We know that $g(K^*) = 0$. Theorem 11.2.3 allows us to compute $h'(K^*)$ from $g'(K^*) = 0$. Differentiating with respect to K_t and evaluating the resulting expression at K^* provides the following quadratic equation in $h'(K^*)$ (we suppress the arguments of all functions):

$$(h')^2 - \underbrace{\left(1 + (1/\beta) + (\beta u' f'')/u''\right)}_{=:\Delta} h' + (1/\beta) = 0 \tag{2.9}$$

Let h'_1 and h'_2 denote the solutions. Since (by Viète's rule) $h'_1 + h'_2 = \Delta$ and $h'_1 h'_2 = 1/\beta$, the solutions of equation (2.9) equal the eigenvalues of the Jacobian matrix λ_1 and λ_2 obtained in the previous paragraph. The solution is, thus, given by $h'(K^*) = \lambda_1$ and the approximate policy function coincides with equation (2.7a). Note that we actually do not need to compute the approximate policy function for consumption: given the approximate savings function (2.7a) we obtain the solution for consumption directly from the resource constraint (2.1a).

Observe further that this way to compute $h'(K^*)$ is less readily implemented on a computer. In order to set up (2.9) we need software that is able to do symbolic differentiation. Our general procedure for non-linear, deterministic DGE models therefore relies on the approach considered in the previous paragraph.

The General Method. It is straightforward to generalize the method outlined above to compute the linear approximate solution of a non-linear system of difference equations implied by a deterministic DGE model. Suppose the map

$$\mathbf{g}(\mathbf{x}_t, \mathbf{x}_{t+1}) = \mathbf{0}_{n \times 1}, \quad \mathbf{x}_t \in \mathbb{R}^n$$

implicitly describes the model's dynamics. Assume, further, that n_1 of the elements in $\mathbf{x}_t$ have given initial conditions (as the capital stock in the deterministic growth model) and that $n_2 = n - n_1$ are jump variables (as consumption), whose initial conditions must be chosen in order to satisfy the model's transversality conditions. Let $\mathbf{x}^*$ denote the fixed point. Since the analytic computation of the Jacobian matrix is usually very cumbersome and failure prone, it is advisable to write a procedure that returns the rhs of $\mathbf{g}(\mathbf{x}_t, \mathbf{x}_{t+1})$. This procedure serves as input to a program that performs numeric differentiation. Given the matrices $A := \mathbf{g}_{\mathbf{x}_{t+1}}(\mathbf{x}^*, \mathbf{x}^*)$ and $B := \mathbf{g}_{\mathbf{x}_t}(\mathbf{x}^*, \mathbf{x}^*)$, the Jacobian matrix of the linearized system (2.3) is given by $J = A^{-1}B$. This matrix must have n_1 eigenvalues inside and n_2 eigenvalues outside the unit circle.

Let $\mathbf{y}_t := T^{-1}\bar{\mathbf{x}}_t$ with $J = TST^{-1}$ denote the new variables in which the system is decoupled

$$\begin{bmatrix} \mathbf{y}_{1t+1} \\ \mathbf{y}_{2t+1} \end{bmatrix} = \begin{bmatrix} S_{11} & S_{12} \\ 0_{n_2 \times n_1} & S_{22} \end{bmatrix} \begin{bmatrix} \mathbf{y}_{1t} \\ \mathbf{y}_{2t} \end{bmatrix}.$$

Since all the eigenvalues on the main diagonal of S_{22} are outside the unitUnit circle circle, we must set $\mathbf{y}_{2t} = \mathbf{0}_{n_2 \times 1}$ to secure convergence. Thus, the second block of the matrix equation

$$\begin{bmatrix} \mathbf{y}_{1t} \\ \mathbf{0}_{n_2 \times 1} \end{bmatrix} = \begin{bmatrix} T^{11} & T^{12} \\ T^{21} & T^{22} \end{bmatrix} \begin{bmatrix} \bar{\mathbf{x}}_{1t} \\ \bar{\mathbf{x}}_{2t} \end{bmatrix}$$

implies the policy function for the jump variables:

$$\bar{\mathbf{x}}_{2t} = -(T^{22})^{-1}T^{21}\bar{\mathbf{x}}_{1t}. \tag{2.10a}$$

Using this result to substitute for $\bar{\mathbf{x}}_{2t}$ in the first block of equations yields:

$$\mathbf{y}_{1t} = \left(T^{11} - T^{12}(T^{22})^{-1}T^{21}\right)\bar{\mathbf{x}}_{1t}.$$

Observe that the inverse of the matrix in parenthesis is T_{11} (apply the formula for the inverse of a partitioned matrix (11.15a) to the matrix T^{-1}). Thus,

$$\mathbf{y}_{1t+1} = (T_{11})^{-1}\bar{\mathbf{x}}_{1t+1} = S_{11}\mathbf{y}_{1t} = S_{11}T_{11}^{-1}\bar{\mathbf{x}}_{1t}$$

so that the policy function for $\bar{\mathbf{x}}_{1t+1}$ is given by

$$\bar{\mathbf{x}}_{1t+1} = T_{11}S_{11}T_{11}^{-1}\bar{\mathbf{x}}_{1t}. \tag{2.10b}$$

You will see in Section 2.4 that our procedure SolveLA that computes the linear approximate solution of stochastic DGE models provides the policy functions (2.10) as a special case.

2.2 The Stochastic Linear Quadratic Model

This section presents the stochastic linear quadratic model and derives some of its important properties. Since its main purpose is to provide a framework for both linear quadratic and linear approximation methods, we postpone detailed algorithms for the computation of the policy function until Section 2.3 and Section 2.4, respectively.

Description. Consider an economy governed by the following stochastic linear law of motion:

$$\mathbf{x}_{t+1} = A\mathbf{x}_t + B\mathbf{u}_t + \boldsymbol{\epsilon}_t. \tag{2.11}$$

The n-dimensional column vector $\mathbf{x}_t$ holds those variables that are predetermined at period t. A fictitious social planner sets the values of the variables stacked in in the m-dimensional column vector $\mathbf{u}_t$. We refer to $\mathbf{x}$ as the state vector and to $\mathbf{u}$ as the control vector. $A \in \mathbb{R}^{n \times n}$ and $B \in \mathbb{R}^{n \times m}$ are matrices. Due to the presence of shocks, the planner cannot control this economy perfectly. The n vector of shocks $\boldsymbol{\epsilon}$ has a multivariate normal distribution with $E(\boldsymbol{\epsilon}) = \mathbf{0}$ and covariance matrix[4] $E(\boldsymbol{\epsilon}\boldsymbol{\epsilon}') = \Sigma$. The planner must choose $\mathbf{u}_t$ before he can realize the size of the shocks.

Given $\mathbf{x}_0$ the planner's objective is to maximize

$$E_0 \sum_{t=0}^{\infty} \beta^t \left[\mathbf{x}_t' Q \mathbf{x}_t + \mathbf{u}_t' R \mathbf{u}_t + 2\mathbf{u}_t' S \mathbf{x}_t \right], \quad \beta \in (0,1), \tag{2.12}$$

subject to (2.11). The current period objective function

$$g(\mathbf{x}_t, \mathbf{u}_t) := \begin{bmatrix} \mathbf{x}_t', & \mathbf{u}_t' \end{bmatrix} \begin{bmatrix} Q & S' \\ S & R \end{bmatrix} \begin{bmatrix} \mathbf{x}_t \\ \mathbf{u}_t \end{bmatrix} \tag{2.13}$$

is quadratic and concave in $(\mathbf{x}_t', \mathbf{u}_t')$. This requires that both the symmetric $n \times n$ matrix Q and the symmetric $m \times m$ matrix R are negative semidefinite.

Note that this specification encompasses non-stochastic state variables and first-order (vector) autoregressive processes.

---

[4] Remember that a prime denotes transposition, i.e., $\boldsymbol{\epsilon}'$ is a row vector and $\boldsymbol{\epsilon}$ a column vector.

Derivation of the Policy Function. The Bellman equation for the stochastic LQ problem is given by

$$v(\mathbf{x}) := \max_{\mathbf{u}} \quad \mathbf{x}'Q\mathbf{x} + 2\mathbf{u}'S\mathbf{x} + \mathbf{u}'R\mathbf{u} \\ + \beta E\left[v(A\mathbf{x} + B\mathbf{u} + \epsilon)\right], \tag{2.14}$$

where we used (2.11) to replace next-period state variables in $Ev(\cdot)$ and where we dropped the time indices for convenience, because all variables refer to the same date t. Expectations are taken conditional on the information contained in the current state $\mathbf{x}$. We guess that the value function is given by $v(\mathbf{x}) := \mathbf{x}'P\mathbf{x} + d$, P being a n dimensional symmetric, negative semidefinite square matrix and $d \in \mathbb{R}$ an unknown constant.[5] Thus, we may write (2.14) as follows:[6]

$$\mathbf{x}'P\mathbf{x} + d = \\ \max_{\mathbf{u}} \quad \mathbf{x}'Q\mathbf{x} + 2\mathbf{u}'S\mathbf{x} + \mathbf{u}'R\mathbf{u} \\ + \beta E\left[((A\mathbf{x} + B\mathbf{u} + \epsilon)'P(A\mathbf{x} + B\mathbf{u} + \epsilon) + d)\right]. \tag{2.15}$$

Evaluating the conditional expectations on the rhs of (2.15) yields:

$$\mathbf{x}'P\mathbf{x} + d = \\ \max_{\mathbf{u}} \quad \mathbf{x}'Q\mathbf{x} + 2\mathbf{u}S\mathbf{x} + \mathbf{u}'R\mathbf{u} \\ + \beta \mathbf{x}'A'PA\mathbf{x} + 2\beta \mathbf{x}'A'PB\mathbf{u} + \beta \mathbf{u}'B'PB\mathbf{u} \\ + \beta \operatorname{tr}(P\Sigma) + \beta d. \tag{2.16}$$

In the next step we differentiate the rhs of (2.16) with respect to the control vector $\mathbf{u}$, set the result equal to the zero vector, and solve for $\mathbf{u}$. This provides the solution for the policy function:

---

[5] Note, since $\mathbf{x}'_t P\mathbf{x}_t$ is a quadratic form, it is not restrictive to assume that P is symmetric. Furthermore, since the value function of a well defined dynamic programming problem is strictly concave, P must be negative semidefinite.

[6] If you are unfamiliar with matrix algebra, you may find it helpful to consult Section 11.1. We present the details of the derivation of the policy function in Appendix 3.

$$\mathbf{u} = -\underbrace{(R+\beta B'PB)^{-1}(S+\beta B'PA)}_{F}\mathbf{x}. \tag{2.17}$$

To find the solution for the matrix P and the constant d, we eliminate $\mathbf{u}$ from the Bellman equation (2.16) and compare the quadratic forms and the constant terms on both sides. It turns out that P must satisfy the following implicit equation, known as algebraic matrix Riccati equation:

$$\begin{aligned}P = Q + \beta A'PA \\ - (S+\beta B'PA)'[R+\beta B'PB]^{-1}(S+\beta B'PA),\end{aligned} \tag{2.18}$$

and that d is given by:

$$d = \frac{\beta}{1-\beta}\operatorname{tr}(P\Sigma).$$

The solution of (2.18) can be obtained by iterating on the matrix Riccati difference equation

$$\begin{aligned}P_{s+1} = Q + \beta A'P_s A \\ - (S+\beta B'P_s A)'[R+\beta B'P_s B]^{-1}(S+\beta B'P_s A)\end{aligned}$$

starting with some initial negative definite matrix P_0.[7] Other methods to solve (2.18) rely on matrix factorizations. Since we will use iterations over the value function later on, we will not explore these methods any further. Once the solution for P has been computed, the dynamics of the model is governed by

$$\mathbf{x}_{t+1} = A\mathbf{x}_t + B\mathbf{u}_t + \epsilon_{t+1} = (A-FB)\mathbf{x}_t + \epsilon_t.$$

Certainty Equivalence. The solution of the stochastic LQ problem has a remarkable feature. Since the covariance matrix of the shocks Σ appears neither in equation (2.17) nor in equation (2.18), the optimal control is independent of the stochastic properties of the model summarized by Σ. Had we considered a deterministic

---
[7] For example $P_0 = -0.01 I_n$.

linear quadratic problem by assuming $\epsilon_t = \mathbf{0} \forall t$, we would have found the same feedback rule (2.17). You may want to verify this claim by solving Problem 2.1. This property of the stochastic LQ problem is called certainty equivalence principle. It is important to note that if we use the LQ approximation to solve an arbitrary economic model we enforce the certainty equivalence principle on this solution. This may hide important properties of the model. For instance, consider two economies A and B which are identical in all respects except for the size of their productivity shocks. If economy's A shock has a much larger standard deviation than economy B's shock, it is hard to believe that the agents in both economies use the same feed-back rules.

Derivation of the Euler Equations. As we have seen in Chapter 1 an alternative way to derive the dynamic path of an optimizing model is to consider the model's Euler equations. It will be helpful for the approach taken in Section 2.4 to separate the state variables into two categories. Variables that have a given initial condition but are otherwise determined endogenously are stacked in the n dimensional vector $\mathbf{x}$. Purely exogenous shocks are summarized in the l dimensional vector $\mathbf{z}$. As in the previous subsection $\mathbf{u}$ is the m dimensional vector of controls. The planner's current period return function is the following quadratic form:

$$g(\mathbf{x}_t, \mathbf{u}_t, \mathbf{z}_t) := \mathbf{x}_t' A_{xx} \mathbf{x}_t + \mathbf{u}_t' A_{uu} \mathbf{u}_t + \mathbf{z}_t' A_{zz} \mathbf{z}_t \\ + 2\mathbf{u}_t' A_{ux} \mathbf{x}_t + 2\mathbf{u}_t' A_{uz} \mathbf{z}_t + 2\mathbf{x}_t' A_{xz} \mathbf{z}_t. \quad (2.19)$$

$A_{ij}, i, j \in \{x, u, z\}$ are given matrices. The transition law of the endogenous state variables is

$$\mathbf{x}_{t+1} = B_x \mathbf{x}_t + B_u \mathbf{u}_t + B_z \mathbf{z}_t, \quad (2.20)$$

where $B_x \in \mathbb{R}^{n \times n}$, $B_u \in \mathbb{R}^{n \times m}$, and $B_z \in \mathbb{R}^{n \times l}$ are given matrices. The shocks follow a first-order vector autoregressive process

$$\mathbf{z}_{t+1} = \Pi \mathbf{z}_t + \boldsymbol{\epsilon}_{t+1}, \quad \boldsymbol{\epsilon} \sim N(\mathbf{0}, \Sigma). \quad (2.21)$$

The eigenvalues of $\Pi \in \mathbb{R}^{l \times l}$ lie inside the unit circle. The planner maximizes

$$E_0 \sum_{t=0}^{\infty} \beta^t g(\mathbf{x}_t, \mathbf{u}_t, \mathbf{z}_t) \tag{2.22}$$

subject to (2.20) and (2.21).

Let $\boldsymbol{\lambda}_t$ denote the n vector of Lagrange multipliers. The Lagrangian of this LQ problem is

$$\mathscr{L} = E_0 \sum_{t=0}^{\infty} \beta^t \Big[g(\mathbf{x}_t, \mathbf{u}_t, \mathbf{z}_t) + 2\boldsymbol{\lambda}'_t (B_x \mathbf{x}_t + B_u \mathbf{u}_t + B_z \mathbf{z}_t - \mathbf{x}_{t+1}) \Big].$$

Differentiating this expression with respect to $\mathbf{u}_t$ and $\mathbf{x}_{t+1}$ provides the following set of first-order conditions:

$$0 = A_{uu} \mathbf{u}_t + A_{ux} \mathbf{x}_t + A_{uz} \mathbf{z}_t + B'_u \boldsymbol{\lambda}_t,$$
$$\boldsymbol{\lambda}_t = \beta E_t \left[A_{xx} \mathbf{x}_{t+1} + A_{xz} \mathbf{z}_{t+1} + A'_{ux} \mathbf{u}_{t+1} + B'_x \boldsymbol{\lambda}_{t+1} \right].$$

The first of these equations may be rewritten as:

$$C_u \mathbf{u}_t = C_{x\lambda} \begin{bmatrix} \mathbf{x}_t \\ \boldsymbol{\lambda}_t \end{bmatrix} + C_z \mathbf{z}_t, \tag{2.23a}$$

whereas the second equation and the transition law (2.20) can be summarized in the following matrix difference equation:

$$D_{x\lambda} E_t \begin{bmatrix} \mathbf{x}_{t+1} \\ \boldsymbol{\lambda}_{t+1} \end{bmatrix} + F_{x\lambda} \begin{bmatrix} \mathbf{x}_t \\ \boldsymbol{\lambda}_t \end{bmatrix} = D_u E_t \mathbf{u}_{t+1} + F_u \mathbf{u}_t \tag{2.23b}$$
$$+ D_z E_t \mathbf{z}_{t+1} + F_z \mathbf{z}_t.$$

The matrices in these equations relate to those of the original problem as follows:

$$C_u := A_{uu}, \qquad\qquad C_{x\lambda} := -[A_{ux}, B'_u],$$
$$C_z := -A_{uz},$$

$$D_{x\lambda} := \begin{bmatrix} \beta A_{xx} & \beta B'_x \\ I_n & 0_{n \times n} \end{bmatrix}, \quad F_{x\lambda} := \begin{bmatrix} 0_{n \times n} & -I_n \\ -B_x & 0_{n \times n} \end{bmatrix},$$

$$D_u := \begin{bmatrix} -\beta A'_{ux} \\ 0_{n \times m} \end{bmatrix}, \quad F_u := \begin{bmatrix} 0_{n \times m} \\ B_u \end{bmatrix},$$

$$D_z := \begin{bmatrix} -\beta A_{xz} \\ 0_{n \times l} \end{bmatrix}, \quad F_z := \begin{bmatrix} 0_{n \times l} \\ B_z \end{bmatrix},$$

where I_n and $0_{n\times m}$ denote the n dimensional identity matrix and the $n \times m$ zero matrix, respectively.

Equations (2.23) describe a system of stochastic linear difference equations in two parts. The first part (2.23a) determines the control variables as linear functions of the model's state variables, $\mathbf{x}_t$, exogenous shocks $\mathbf{z}_t$, and the vector of Lagrange multipliers $\boldsymbol{\lambda}_t$, often referred to as the vector of costate variables. The second part (2.23b) determines the dynamics of the vector of state and costate variables. In Section 2.4 equations (2.23) will serve as framework to study the approximate dynamics of non-linear models. Before we explore this subject and discuss the solution of (2.23), we consider the computation of the policy function via value function iterations in the next section.

2.3 LQ Approximation

This section provides the details of an algorithm proposed by HANSEN and PRESCOTT (1995). Their approach rests on a linear quadratic approximation of a given model and they device a simple to program iterative procedure to compute the policy function of the approximate model. In Section 2.3.2, we use the deterministic Ramsey model from Example 1.2.1 to illustrate the various steps. Section 2.3.3 outlines the general approach and its implementation in the Gauss program `SolveLQA`.

2.3.1 A Warning

Before we begin, we must warn you. As has been pointed out by JUDD (1998), pp. 506-508 and, more recently, by BENIGNO and WOODFORD (2007), the method provides a correct linear approximation to the policy function only when the constraints are linear. A different policy function arises from maximizing a quadratic approximation of the objective function subject to linearized constraints. To see this, consider a simple static problem.

Maximize $U(x_1, x_2)$ subject to $x_2 = f(x_1, \epsilon)$, where ϵ is a parameter of the problem. Let $x_1 = h(\epsilon)$ denote the policy function that solves this problem and assume that a solution at $\epsilon = 0$ exists. This solution solves

$$g(\epsilon = 0) := U_1\left[h(\epsilon), f(h(\epsilon), \epsilon)\right]$$
$$+ U_2\left[h(\epsilon), f(h(\epsilon), \epsilon)\right] f_1(h(\epsilon), \epsilon) = 0.$$

The implicit function theorem 11.2.3 allows us to compute $h'(0)$ from $g'(0) = 0$. This provides[8]

$$h'(0) = -\frac{U_{12}f_2 + U_{22}f_1f_2 + U_2f_{12}}{U_{11} + 2U_{12}f_1 + U_{22}f_1^2 + U_2f_{11}}. \tag{2.24}$$

The quadratic approximation of U at $x_1^* = h(0)$ and $x_2^* = f(x_1^*, 0)$ is obtained from applying equation (11.32) to U at (x_1^*, x_2^*):

$$U^Q = U(x_1^*, x_2^*) + U_1\bar{x}_1 + U_2\bar{x}_2 + \frac{1}{2}\begin{bmatrix}\bar{x}_1, & \bar{x}_2\end{bmatrix}\begin{bmatrix}U_{11} & U_{12} \\ U_{21} & U_{22}\end{bmatrix}\begin{bmatrix}\bar{x}_1 \\ \bar{x}_2\end{bmatrix}.$$

Maximizing this expression with respect to $\bar{x}_1 := x_1 - x_1^*$ subject to the linearized constraint

$$\bar{x}_2 = x_2 - x_2^* = f_1\bar{x}_1 + f_2\epsilon$$

provides (since $U_1 + U_2f_1 = 0$)

$$\bar{x}_1 = -\frac{U_{12}f_2 + U_{22}f_1f_2}{U_{11} + 2U_{12}f_1 + U_{22}f_1^2}\epsilon. \tag{2.25}$$

This solution differs from (2.24) with respect to the rightmost terms in the numerator and the denominator in the solution for $h'(0)$, U_2f_{12} and U_2f_{11}, respectively. Both terms vanish, if the constraint is linear.

BENIGNO and WOODFORD (2007) propose to use the quadratic approximation of the constraint to replace the linear terms in U^Q. Indeed, if we replace $\bar{x}_2$ by

$$\bar{x}_2 = f_1\bar{x}_1 + f_2\epsilon + \frac{1}{2}[\bar{x}_1, \epsilon]\begin{bmatrix}f_{11} & f_{12} \\ f_{21} & f_{22}\end{bmatrix}\begin{bmatrix}\mathbf{x}_1 \\ \epsilon\end{bmatrix}$$

in the expression for U^Q and optimize this new function, we obtain the same linear policy function as given in equation (2.24).

---
[8] We used $U_{12} = U_{21}$, which holds, if U is twice continuously differentiable. See, e.g., Theorem 1.1 on p. 372 in LANG (1997).

2.3.2 An Illustrative Example

The Model. We know from Section 2.2 that the policy function of the LQ problem is independent of the second moments (and, a fortiori, of any higher moments) of the shocks. Therefore, nothing is lost but much is gained in notational simplicity, if we use the deterministic Ramsey model from example 1.2.1 to illustrate the approach of HANSEN and PRESCOTT (1995). In this example the farmer solves

$$\max_{\{C_t\}_{t=0}^\infty} \sum_{t=0}^\infty \beta^t \ln C_t, \quad \beta \in (0,1),$$
$$\text{s.t. } K_{t+1} + C_t \leq K_t^\alpha, \ \alpha \in (0,1), \ t = 0, 1, \ldots,$$
$$K_0 \text{ given.}$$

C_t denotes consumption at time t, and K_t is the stock of capital. The dynamics of this model is determined by two equations:

$$1 = \beta \frac{C_t}{C_{t+1}} \alpha K_{t+1}^{\alpha-1}, \tag{2.26a}$$

$$K_{t+1} = K_t^\alpha - C_t. \tag{2.26b}$$

The first equation is a special case of the Euler equation (1.12) in the case of logarithmic preferences and a Cobb-Douglas production function. The second equation is the economy's resource constraint.

Approximation Step. We want to approximate this model by a linear quadratic problem. Towards this end we must look for a linear law of motion and put all remaining nonlinear relations into the current period return function $\ln C_t$. We achieve this by using investment expenditures $I_t = K_t^\alpha - C_t$ instead of consumption as a control variable. Remember, this model assumes 100 percent depreciation (i.e., $\delta = 1$), so that the linear transition law is:

$$K_{t+1} = I_t. \tag{2.27}$$

Let $g(K_t, I_t) := \ln(K_t^\alpha - I_t)$ denote the current period utility function. We approximate this function by a quadratic function in (K, I) at the point of the stationary solution of the model. This solution derives from equations (2.26) and (2.27) for $K_{t+1} = K_t = \bar{K}$ and $C_{t+1} = C_t = \bar{C}$. Thus,

$$\bar{K} = (\alpha\beta)^{(1/(1-\alpha))}, \tag{2.28a}$$
$$\bar{I} = \bar{K}. \tag{2.28b}$$

A second order Taylor series approximation of g yields:

$$\begin{aligned} g(K, I) &\simeq g(\bar{K}, \bar{I}) + g_K(K - \bar{K}) + g_I(I - \bar{I}) \\ &+ (1/2)g_{KK}(K - \bar{K})^2 + (1/2)g_{II}(I - \bar{I})^2 \\ &+ (1/2)(g_{KI} + g_{IK})(K - \bar{K})(I - \bar{I}). \end{aligned} \tag{2.29}$$

For latter purposes, we want to write the rhs of this equation by using matrix notation.[9] To take care of the constant and the linear terms we define the vector $(1, K, I)^T$ and the 3×3 matrix $Q = (q_{ij})$ and equate the rhs of (2.29) to the product

$$[1, K, I] Q \begin{bmatrix} 1 \\ K \\ I \end{bmatrix}.$$

Comparing terms on both sides of the resulting expression and using the symmetry of the second order mixed partial derivatives ($g_{KI} = g_{IK}$) yields the elements of Q:

$$\begin{aligned} q_{11} &= g - g_K \bar{K} - g_I \bar{I} + (1/2)g_{KK}\bar{K}^2 + g_{KI}\bar{K}\bar{I} + (1/2)g_{II}\bar{I}^2, \\ q_{12} &= q_{21} = (1/2)(g_K - g_{KK}\bar{K} - g_{KI}\bar{I}), \\ q_{13} &= q_{31} = (1/2)(g_I - g_{II}\bar{I} - g_{KI}\bar{K}), \\ q_{23} &= q_{32} = (1/2)g_{KI}, \\ q_{22} &= (1/2)g_{KK}, \\ q_{33} &= (1/2)g_{II}. \end{aligned}$$

In the next step we use Q and the even larger vector $\mathbf{w} = [1, K, I, 1, K']$ (where K' denotes the next-period stock of capital) to write the rhs of the Bellman equation, $g(K, I) + \beta v(K')$, in matrix notation. This gives:

---

[9] To prevent confusion, we depart from our usual notation temporarily and let the superscript T denote the transpose operator. As usual in dynamic programming, the prime ' denotes next-period variables.

$$[1, K, I, 1, K'] \underbrace{\begin{bmatrix} Q & 0_{3\times 2} \\ 0_{2\times 3} & \beta V^0_{2\times 2} \end{bmatrix}}_{R_{5\times 5}} \begin{bmatrix} 1 \\ K \\ I \\ 1 \\ K' \end{bmatrix}, \quad V^0 := \begin{bmatrix} v^0_{11} & v^0_{12} \\ v^0_{21} & v^0_{22} \end{bmatrix}. \quad (2.30)$$

We initialize V^0 with a negative definite matrix, e.g., $V^0 = -0.001 I_2$, where I_2 denotes the two-dimensional identity matrix. Our aim is to eliminate all future variables (here it is just K') using the linear law of motion. Then, we perform the maximization step that allows us to eliminate the controls (here it is just I). After that step we have a new guess for the value function, say V^1. We use this guess as input in a new round of iterations until V^0 and V^1 are sufficiently close together.

Reduction Step. We begin to eliminate K' and the constant from (2.30) so that the resulting quadratic form is reduced to a function of the current state K and the current control I. Note that $K' = I$ can be written as dot product:

$$K' = [0, 0, 1, 0] \begin{bmatrix} 1 \\ K \\ I \\ 1 \end{bmatrix},$$

and observe that

$$\begin{bmatrix} 1 \\ K \\ I \\ 1 \\ K' \end{bmatrix} = \begin{bmatrix} I_4 \\ 0\ 0\ 1\ 0 \end{bmatrix} \begin{bmatrix} 1 \\ K \\ I \\ 1 \end{bmatrix}.$$

Thus, we may express (2.30) equivalently as:

$$[1, K, I, 1, K'] R_{5\times 5} \begin{bmatrix} 1 \\ K \\ I \\ 1 \\ K' \end{bmatrix} = [1, K, I, 1] R_{4\times 4} \begin{bmatrix} 1 \\ K \\ I \\ 1 \end{bmatrix},$$

where

$$R_{4\times 4} = \begin{bmatrix} I_4 \\ 0\,0\,1\,0 \end{bmatrix}^T R_{5\times 5} \underbrace{\begin{bmatrix} I_4 \\ 0\,0\,1\,0 \end{bmatrix}}_{S_{5\times 4}}.$$

So what was the trick? In words: use the rightmost variable in $\mathbf{w}^T = [1, K, I, 1, K']$ and write it as linear function of the remaining variables. This gives a row vector with 4 elements. Append this vector to the identity matrix of dimension 4 to get the transformation matrix $S_{5\times 4}$. The matrix of the Bellman equation with K' eliminated is $R_{4\times 4} = S_{5\times 4}^T R_{5\times 5} S_{5\times 4}$.

In the same way we can eliminate the second constant. The constant in terms of the remaining variables $[1, K, I]$ is determined by the dot product:

$$1 = [1, 0, 0] \begin{bmatrix} 1 \\ K \\ I \end{bmatrix}.$$

Thus, the matrix $S_{4\times 3}$ is now

$$S_{4\times 3} = \begin{bmatrix} I_3 \\ 1\,0\,0 \end{bmatrix},$$

and the rhs of the Bellman equation in terms of $[1, K, I]$ is

$$g(K, I) + \beta v(I) = [1, K, I] R_{3\times 3} \begin{bmatrix} 1 \\ K \\ I \end{bmatrix}, \quad R_{3\times 3} = S_{4\times 3}^T R_{4\times 4} S_{4\times 3}.$$

Maximization Step. In this last step we eliminate I from the rhs of the Bellman equation to find

$$[1, K] R_{2\times 2} \begin{bmatrix} 1 \\ K \end{bmatrix}.$$

The matrix $R_{2\times 2}$ will be our new guess of the value function. After the last reduction step, the quadratic form is:

$$[1, K, I] \begin{bmatrix} r_{11} & r_{12} & r_{13} \\ r_{21} & r_{22} & r_{23} \\ r_{31} & r_{32} & r_{33} \end{bmatrix} \begin{bmatrix} 1 \\ K \\ I \end{bmatrix}$$

$$= r_{11} + (r_{12} + r_{21})K + (r_{13} + r_{31})I + (r_{23} + r_{32})KI + r_{22}K^2 + r_{33}I^2.$$

Setting the derivative of this expression with respect to I equal to zero and solving for I gives:

$$I = \underbrace{-\frac{r_{13} + r_{31}}{2r_{33}}}_{i_1} - \underbrace{\frac{r_{23} + r_{32}}{2r_{33}}}_{i_2} K = -\frac{r_{13}}{r_{33}} - \frac{r_{23}}{r_{33}} K,$$

where the last equality follows from the symmetry of R. Thus, we can use

$$S = \begin{bmatrix} & & I_2 & \\ -i_1 & & -i_2 & \end{bmatrix}$$

to reduce $R_{3\times 3}$ to the new guess of the value function:

$$V^1 = S^T R_{3\times 3} S.$$

We stop iterations, if the maximal element in $|V^1 - V^0|$ is smaller than $\epsilon(1-\beta)$ for some small positive ϵ (see (11.84) in Section 11.4 on this choice).

2.3.3 The General Method

Notation. Consider the following framework: There is a n vector of state variables $\mathbf{x}$, a m vector of control variables $\mathbf{u}$, a current period return function $g(\mathbf{x}, \mathbf{u})$, and a discount factor $\beta \in (0,1)$. As you will see in a moment, it will be helpful to put $x_1 = 1$. All non-linear relations of the model are part of the specification of g, and the remaining linear relations define the following law of motion:

$$\mathbf{x}' = A\mathbf{x} + B\mathbf{u}. \tag{2.31}$$

Furthermore, there is a point $[\mathbf{x}^{*T}, \mathbf{u}^{*T}]^T$. Usually, this will be the stationary solution of the deterministic counterpart of the model under consideration.

Approximation Step. Let $Q \in \mathbb{R}^{l \times l}$, $l = n + m$, denote the matrix of the linear quadratic approximation of the current period return function $g(\cdot)$, and define the $n + m$ column vector $\mathbf{y} = [\mathbf{x}^T, \mathbf{u}^T]^T$. From a Taylor series expansion of g at $\mathbf{y}^*$, we get:

$$\mathbf{y}^T Q \mathbf{y} = g(\mathbf{y}^*) + \sum_{i=1}^{n+m} g_i(y_i - y_i^*) + \frac{1}{2} \sum_{i=1}^{n+m} \sum_{j=1}^{n+m} g_{ij}(y_i - y_i^*)(y_j - y_j^*),$$

where g_i and g_{ij} are first and second partial derivatives of g at $\mathbf{y}^*$, respectively.[10] Comparing terms on both sides of this expression delivers the elements of $Q = (q_{ij})$:

$$q_{11} = g(\mathbf{y}^*) + \sum_{i=1}^{n+m} g_i y_i^* + \frac{1}{2} \sum_{i=1}^{n+m} \sum_{j=1}^{n+m} g_{ij} y_i^* y_j^*,$$
$$q_{1i} = q_{i1} = \frac{1}{2} g_i - \frac{1}{2} \sum_{j=1}^{n+m} g_{ij} y_j^*, \quad i = 2, 3, \ldots, n+m,$$
$$q_{ij} = q_{ji} = \frac{1}{2} g_{ij}, \quad i, j = 2, 3, \ldots, n+m.$$

Except in very rare cases, where g_i and g_{ij} are given by simple analytic expressions, one will use numeric differentiation (see Section 11.3.1). For instance, to use our program SolveLQA, the user must supply a procedure gproc that returns the value of g at an arbitrary point $[\mathbf{x}^T, \mathbf{u}^T]^T$. Note that you must pass $(1, x_2, \ldots, x_n, u_1, \ldots, u_n)^T$ to that procedure, even if the 1 is not used in gproc. This ensures that any procedure that computes the gradient of g returns a vector with l elements and that any procedure that returns the Hesse matrix returns a $l \times l$ matrix. Given this procedure, our Gauss programs CDJac and CDHesse compute the gradient vector $\nabla g = [0, g_2, g_3, \ldots, g_{n+m}]$ and the Hesse matrix $H := (h_{ij}) \equiv (g_{ij})$, $i, j = 1, 2, \ldots, n+m$ from which SolveLQA builds Q using the above formulas. All of this is done without any further intervention of the user. If higher accuracy in the computation of the Hesse matrix is desired, the user can supply a routine MyGrad that returns the gradient vector of g. He must then set the flag _MyGrad=1 to let the program know that an analytic gradient is available. SolveLQA will then use MyGrad to compute the Hesse matrix by using the forward difference Jacobian programmed in CDJac.

---

[10] Note, since $x_1 = 1$, we have $g_1 = 0$ and $g_{1i} = g_{i1} = 0$ for $i = 1, 2, \ldots, l$.

Reduction Steps. Let R^s denote the matrix that represents the quadratic form on the rhs of the Bellman equation at reduction step s, where

$$R^1 := \begin{bmatrix} Q_{n+m \times (n+m)} & 0_{(n+m) \times n} \\ 0_{n \times (n+m)} & \beta V^0_{n \times n} \end{bmatrix}.$$

In addition, let $\mathbf{c}_s^T$ denote the $n+1-s$-th row of the matrix

$$C_s = \begin{bmatrix} A & B & 0_{n \times (n-s)} \end{bmatrix}.$$

Then, for $s = 1, 2, \ldots, n$ iterate on

$$R^{s+1} = \begin{bmatrix} I_{2n+m-s} \\ \mathbf{c}_s^T \end{bmatrix}^T R^s \begin{bmatrix} I_{2n+m-s} \\ \mathbf{c}_s^T \end{bmatrix}.$$

Maximization Steps. After the last reduction step the matrix R is reduced to a square matrix of size $n+m$. There are m maximization steps to be taken until R is reduced further to a square matrix of size n, which is our new guess of the value function. At step $s = 1, 2, \ldots, m$ the optimal choice of the control variable u_{m+1-s} as a linear function of the variables $[x_1, \ldots, x_n, u_1, \ldots, u_{m-s}]$ is given by the row vector

$$\mathbf{d}_s^T = \begin{bmatrix} -\dfrac{r_{1k}}{r_{kk}}, & -\dfrac{r_{2k}}{r_{kk}}, & \ldots, & -\dfrac{r_{k-1,k}}{r_{kk}} \end{bmatrix}, \quad k = n+m-s.$$

Therefore, we iterate on

$$R^{s+1} = \begin{bmatrix} I_{n+m-s} \\ \mathbf{d}_s^T \end{bmatrix}^T R^s \begin{bmatrix} I_{n+m-s} \\ \mathbf{d}_s^T \end{bmatrix}, \quad s = 1, 2, \ldots, m.$$

If R is reduced to size n, we have found a new guess of the value function $V^1 = R^{m+1}$, and we compare its elements to those of V^0. If they are close together,

$$\max_{ij} |v_{ij}^0 - v_{ij}^1| < \epsilon(1-\beta),$$

we stop iterations. Otherwise we replace V^0 with V^1 and restart.

Computation of the Policy Function. It is a good idea to store the vectors $\mathbf{d}_s$ in a $m \times (n + m - 1)$ matrix D. After convergence, we can use $D = (d_{ij})$ to derive the policy matrix $F \in \mathbb{R}^{m \times n} = (f_{ij})$ that defines the controls as functions of the states. This works as follows: The policy vector $\mathbf{d}_m$ (i.e., the last row of D) holds the coefficients that determine the first control variable u_1 as function of the n state variables:

$$u_1 = \sum_{i=1}^{n} d_{mi} x_i \quad \Rightarrow \quad f_{1i} = d_{mi}.$$

The second control is given by

$$u_2 = \sum_{i=1}^{n} d_{m-1,i} x_i + d_{m-1,n+1} u_1$$
$$\Rightarrow f_{2i} = d_{m-1,i} + d_{m-1,n+1} f_{1i}.$$

Therefore, we may compute the coefficients of F recursively from:

$$f_{ji} = d_{m+1-j,i} + \sum_{k=1}^{j-1} d_{m+1-j,n+k} f_{ki},$$
$$j = 1, \ldots, m, \ i = 1, \ldots, n.$$

As a final check of the solution, we can use

$$|\mathbf{u}^* - F\mathbf{x}^*|.$$

i.e. the discrepancy between the stationary solution of the controls from the original model and those computed using the linear policy function.

2.4 Linear Approximation

In this section we return to the system of stochastic difference equations (2.23). Remember, this system is one way to characterize the solution of the linear quadratic problem. However, we are by no means restricted to this interpretation. More generally, we may consider this system as an approximation of an arbitrary non-linear model. In the next subsection we explain this approximation by means of the stochastic growth model. Our discussion closely parallels the presentation in Section 2.1. First, we demonstrate that both, the solution to a linearized system of stochastic difference equations and the application of the implicit function theorem provide the same set of equations for the coefficients of the policy function. Second, we obtain these coefficients from the solution of a linear system of stochastic difference equations. Section 2.4.2 presents the solution method for the general case of equations (2.23) and explains the use of our program SolveLA that implements this method.

2.4.1 An Illustrative Example

There are two equations that determine the time path of the stochastic Ramsey model from Section 1.3 with strictly positive consumption. They are obtained from equations (1.23):

$$0 = K_{t+1} - (1-\delta)K_t - Z_t f(K_t) + C_t, \tag{2.32a}$$
$$0 = u'(C_t) - \beta E_t u'(C_{t+1})(1 - \delta + Z_{t+1} f'(K_{t+1})). \tag{2.32b}$$

We assume that the productivity shock Z_t follows the process

$$\ln Z_t = \varrho \ln Z_{t-1} + \sigma \epsilon_t, \quad \epsilon_t \sim N(0,1). \tag{2.32c}$$

Since $\ln Z_t \simeq \bar{Z}_t, \bar{Z}_t = Z_t - Z^*, Z^* \equiv 1$ this equation may be approximated by

$$\bar{Z}_t = \varrho \bar{Z}_{t-1} + \sigma \epsilon_t. \tag{2.32d}$$

Note, that for $\sigma = 0$ and $Z^* = 1$ this model reduces to the deterministic growth model with the stationary equilibrium determined from

$$C^* = f(K^*) - \delta K^*, \tag{2.33a}$$
$$1 = \beta(1 - \delta + f'(K^*)). \tag{2.33b}$$

More generally, equations (2.32) may be written as $E_t \mathbf{g}(\mathbf{x}_t, \mathbf{x}_{t+1}) = \mathbf{0}_{2 \times 1}$, $\mathbf{x}_t := [K_t, C_t, Z_t]'$.

Linear Stochastic Difference Equations. At (K^*, C^*, Z^*) the linearized version of this system of equations is given by:

$$\begin{bmatrix} 0 \\ 0 \end{bmatrix} = \begin{bmatrix} g_1^1 & g_2^1 \\ g_1^2 & g_2^2 \end{bmatrix} \begin{bmatrix} \bar{K}_t \\ \bar{C}_t \end{bmatrix} + \begin{bmatrix} g_4^1 & g_5^1 \\ g_4^2 & g_5^2 \end{bmatrix} E_t \begin{bmatrix} \bar{K}_{t+1} \\ \bar{C}_{t+1} \end{bmatrix} + \begin{bmatrix} g_3^1 \\ g_3^2 \end{bmatrix} \bar{Z}_t + \begin{bmatrix} g_6^1 \\ g_6^2 \end{bmatrix} E_t \bar{Z}_{t+1},$$
(2.34)

where $\bar{x}_t$ denotes $x_t - x^*$. Since equation (2.32d) implies $E_t \bar{Z}_{t+1} = \varrho \bar{Z}_t$ the last term in equation (2.34) may also be written as $\varrho[g_6^1, g_6^2]' \bar{Z}_t$. We assume that the linear policy functions for $\bar{K}_{t+1}$ and $\bar{C}_t$ are of the form

$$\bar{K}_{t+1} = h_K^K \bar{K}_t + h_Z^K \bar{Z}_t,$$
(2.35a)
$$\bar{C}_t = h_K^C \bar{K}_t + h_Z^C \bar{Z}_t,$$
(2.35b)

where h_j^i, $i, j \in \{K, C\}$ denotes the derivative of the policy function of variable i with respect to its jth argument. Substituting this guess in equation (2.34) yields

$$\begin{bmatrix} a_1 \\ a_2 \end{bmatrix} \bar{K}_t + \begin{bmatrix} b_1 \\ b_2 \end{bmatrix} \bar{Z}_t = \begin{bmatrix} 0 \\ 0 \end{bmatrix},$$

where a_i and b_i, $i = 1, 2$ are collections of coefficients to be given in a moment. Obviously, if (2.35) is a solution to (2.34), this requires $a_i = b_i = 0$, $i = 1, 2$ and, thus, provides four (non-linear) equations in the unknown coefficients $h_K^K, h_Z^K, h_K^C, h_Z^C$. A modest amount of algebra reveals these relations:

$$a_1 = g_1^1 + g_2^1 h_K^C + (g_4^1 + g_5^1 h_K^C) h_K^K = 0,$$
(2.36a)
$$a_2 = g_1^2 + g_2^2 h_K^C + (g_4^2 + g_5^2 h_K^C) h_K^K = 0,$$
(2.36b)
$$b_1 = (g_3^1 + g_6^1 \varrho) + (g_2^1 + g_5^1 \varrho) h_Z^C + (g_4^1 + g_5^1 h_K^C) h_Z^K = 0,$$
(2.36c)
$$b_2 = (g_3^2 + g_6^2 \varrho) + (g_2^2 + g_5^2 \varrho) h_Z^C + (g_4^2 + g_5^2 h_K^C) h_Z^K = 0.$$
(2.36d)

Application of the Implicit Function Theorem. We will now demonstrate that the same set of conditions emerges, if we apply the implicit function theorem to the system $E_t \mathbf{g}(\mathbf{x}_t, \mathbf{x}_{t+1}) = \mathbf{0}_{2 \times 1}$.

This allows us also to show that the linear policy functions are indeed independent of the parameter σ. We assume non-linear policy functions $K_{t+1} = h^K(K_t, Z_t, \sigma)$ and $C_t = h^C(K_t, Z_t, \sigma)$ with the property $K^* = h^K(K^*, Z^*, 0)$, $C^* = h^C(K^*, Z^*, 0)$ so that a solution of $\mathbf{g}(\cdot) = \mathbf{0}_{2\times 1}$ at $(K^*, Z^*, 0)$ exists. It is not difficult to see that differentiating $\mathbf{g}$ with respect to K_t and Z_t provides the same conditions on the derivatives of h^C and h^K at the stationary solution as presented in equations (2.36). Just note, that g^i, $i = 1, 2$ can be written as

$$g^i\Big(K_t, h^C(K_t, Z_t, \sigma), Z_t, h^K(K_t, Z_t, \sigma),$$
$$h^C\big(h^K(K_t, Z_t, \sigma), e^{\varrho \ln Z_t + \sigma \epsilon_{t+1}}, \sigma\big), e^{\varrho \ln Z_t + \sigma \epsilon_{t+1}}\Big),$$

so that, for instance,

$$\frac{\partial g^1(\cdot)}{\partial K_t} = g_1^1 + g_2^1 h_K^C + g_4^1 h_K^K + g_5^1 h_K^C h_K^K \equiv a_1.$$

Consider the derivatives with respect to σ. They imply:[11]

$$\begin{bmatrix} (g_4^1 + g_5^1 h_K^C) & (g_2^1 + g_5^1) \\ (g_4^2 + g_5^2 h_K^C) & (g_2^2 + g_5^2) \end{bmatrix} \begin{bmatrix} h_\sigma^K \\ h_\sigma^C \end{bmatrix} = \begin{bmatrix} 0 \\ 0 \end{bmatrix}.$$

This is a system of homogenous equations in h_σ^K and h_σ^C. Since its matrix of coefficients is regular, the only possible solution is $h_\sigma^K = h_\sigma^C = 0$.

We have, thus, seen by means of an example that the application of perturbation methods to a stochastic DGE model allows us to derive linear approximations of the policy functions via the solution of the linearized system of stochastic difference equations.[12]

---

[11] The derivative of the term $Z_{t+1} = e^{\varrho \ln Z_t + \sigma \epsilon_{t+1}}$ with respect to σ evaluated at $Z^* = 1$ and $\sigma = 0$ is ϵ_{t+1}. The expectation of this term as of time t, $E_t \epsilon_{t+1}$, equals zero, the mean of $N(0, 1)$.

[12] The generalization of this result is obvious but involves either intricate formulas or the use of tensor notation so that we have decided not to pursue it here. See SCHMITT-GROHÉ and URIBE (2004) for a proof.

Derivation of the Solution. Rather than solving (2.36), we determine the coefficients of the policy functions via the same procedure that we used in Section 2.1. From (2.32) and (2.34) we obtain the following system of linear, stochastic difference equations:

$$E_t \begin{bmatrix} \bar{K}_{t+1} \\ \bar{C}_{t+1} \end{bmatrix} = \underbrace{\begin{bmatrix} \frac{1}{\beta} & -1 \\ -\frac{u'f''}{u''} & 1 + \frac{\beta u' f''}{u''} \end{bmatrix}}_{=:W} \begin{bmatrix} \bar{K}_t \\ \bar{C}_t \end{bmatrix} + \underbrace{\begin{bmatrix} f \\ -\frac{\beta u' f f'' + \varrho u'}{u''} \end{bmatrix}}_{=:R} \bar{Z}_t. \tag{2.37}$$

The matrix W equals the Jacobian matrix of the deterministic system (2.3), and, thus, has eigenvalues $\lambda_1 < 1$ and $\lambda_2 > 1$. In the new variables[13]

$$\begin{bmatrix} \tilde{K}_t \\ \tilde{C}_t \end{bmatrix} := T^{-1} \begin{bmatrix} \bar{K}_t \\ \bar{C}_t \end{bmatrix} \Leftrightarrow T \begin{bmatrix} \tilde{K}_t \\ \tilde{C}_t \end{bmatrix} := \begin{bmatrix} \bar{K}_t \\ \bar{C}_t \end{bmatrix} \tag{2.38}$$

the system of difference equations may be written as:[14]

$$E_t \begin{bmatrix} \tilde{K}_{t+1} \\ \tilde{C}_{t+1} \end{bmatrix} = \underbrace{\begin{bmatrix} \lambda_1 & s_{12} \\ 0 & \lambda_2 \end{bmatrix}}_{S} \begin{bmatrix} \tilde{K}_t \\ \tilde{C}_t \end{bmatrix} + \underbrace{\begin{bmatrix} q_1 \\ q_2 \end{bmatrix}}_{Q=T^{-1}R} \hat{Z}_t. \tag{2.39}$$

Consider the second equation of this system, which is a relation in the new variable $\tilde{C}_t$ and the exogenous shock:

$$E_t \tilde{C}_{t+1} = \lambda_2 \tilde{C}_t + q_2 \bar{Z}_t. \tag{2.40}$$

We can solve this equation for $\tilde{C}_t$ via repeated substitution: from (2.40) we get

$$\tilde{C}_t = \frac{1}{\lambda_2} E_t \tilde{C}_{t+1} - \frac{q_2}{\lambda_2} \bar{Z}_t. \tag{2.41}$$

Shifting the time index one period into the future yields:

---

[13] Remember, T is the matrix that puts W into Schur form $W = TST^{-1}$.
[14] Pre-multiply (2.37) by T^{-1} and use the definitions in (2.38) to arrive at this representation.

$$\tilde{C}_{t+1} = \frac{1}{\lambda_2} E_{t+1}\tilde{C}_{t+2} - \frac{q_2}{\lambda_2}\bar{Z}_{t+1}.$$

Taking expectations as of period t on both sides and noting that (via the law of iterated expectations) $E_t(E_{t+1}\tilde{C}_{t+2}) = E_t\tilde{C}_{t+2}$ yields:

$$E_t\tilde{C}_{t+1} = \frac{1}{\lambda_2} E_t\tilde{C}_{t+2} - \frac{q_2}{\lambda_2} E_t\bar{Z}_{t+1} = \frac{1}{\lambda_2} E_t\tilde{C}_{t+2} - \frac{q_2}{\lambda_2}\varrho\bar{Z}_t, \quad (2.42)$$

due to (2.32d). Substitution of this solution for $E_t\tilde{C}_{t+1}$ into (2.41) results in:

$$\tilde{C}_t = \frac{1}{\lambda_2^2} E_t\tilde{C}_{t+2} - \left[\frac{q_2}{\lambda_2} + \frac{q_2}{\lambda_2}\frac{\varrho}{\lambda_2}\right]\bar{Z}_t.$$

We can use (2.42) to get an expression for $\tilde{C}_{t+3}$ and so on up to period $t + \tau$:

$$\tilde{C}_t = \left[\frac{1}{\lambda_2}\right]^\tau E_t\tilde{C}_{t+\tau} - \frac{q_2}{\lambda_2}\sum_{i=0}^{\tau-1}\left[\frac{\varrho}{\lambda_2}\right]^i \bar{Z}_t. \quad (2.43)$$

Suppose that the sequence

$$\left\{\frac{1}{\lambda_2^\tau} E_t\tilde{C}_{t+\tau}\right\}_{\tau=0}^\infty$$

converges towards zero for $\tau \to \infty$. This is not very restrictive: since $1/\lambda_2 < 1$, it is sufficient to assume that $E_t\tilde{C}_{t+\tau}$ is bounded. Intuitively, this assumption rules out speculative bubbles along explosive paths and renders the solution unique. In addition, it guarantees that the transversality condition (1.25) is met. In this case we can compute the limit of (2.43) for $\tau \to \infty$:

$$\tilde{C}_t = -\frac{q_2/\lambda_2}{1 - (\varrho/\lambda_2)}\bar{Z}_t. \quad (2.44)$$

We substitute this solution into the second equation of (2.38),[15]

---
[15] We denote the elements of T^{-1} by (t^{ij}).

$$\tilde{C}_t = t^{21}\bar{K}_t + t^{22}\bar{C}_t,$$

to get the solution for $\bar{C}_t$ in terms of $\bar{K}_t$ and $\bar{Z}_t$:

$$\bar{C}_t = \underbrace{-\frac{t^{21}}{t^{22}}}_{=:h_K^C} \bar{K}_t - \underbrace{\frac{q_2/\lambda_2}{t^{22}(1-(\varrho/\lambda_2))}}_{=:h_Z^C} \bar{Z}_t. \tag{2.45}$$

From the first equation of (2.37),

$$\bar{K}_{t+1} = \frac{1}{\beta}\bar{K}_t - \bar{C}_t + f\bar{Z}_t,$$

we can derive the solution for $\bar{K}_{t+1}$:

$$\bar{K}_{t+1} = \frac{1}{\beta}\bar{K}_t - \underbrace{(h_K^C \bar{K}_t + h_Z^C \bar{Z}_t)}_{=\bar{C}_t} + f\bar{Z}_t$$

$$\bar{K}_{t+1} = \underbrace{\left(\frac{1}{\beta} - h_K^C\right)}_{=:h_K^K}\bar{K}_t + \underbrace{(f - h_Z^C)}_{=:h_Z^K}\bar{Z}_t.$$

Thus, given a sequence of shocks $\{\epsilon_t\}_{t=0}^T$ and an initial $\bar{K}_0$ we may compute the entire time path of consumption and the stock of capital by iteration over

$$\bar{C}_t = h_K^C \bar{K}_t + h_Z^C \bar{Z}_t, \tag{2.46a}$$
$$\bar{K}_{t+1} = h_K^K \bar{K}_t + h_Z^K \bar{Z}_t, \tag{2.46b}$$
$$\bar{Z}_{t+1} = \varrho \bar{Z}_t + \epsilon_{t+1}. \tag{2.46c}$$

The Gauss program Ramsey3a.g computes the linear approximations of the policy function of the stochastic growth model from Section 1.3 along the lines described above. The utility function is parameterized as $u(C) = [C^{1-\eta} - 1]/(1-\eta)$ and the production function as $f(K) = K^\alpha$. The program shows how to derive the coefficients of the matrices in equation (2.34) by using numeric differentiation. In the case with logarithmic preferences, complete depreciation $\delta=1$, $\alpha = 0.27$, $\beta = 0.994$ $\varrho = 0.90$, and $\sigma = 0.0072$ the program delivers the following policy functions:

$$\bar{C}_t = 0.736\bar{K}_t + 0.450\bar{Z}_t,$$
$$\bar{K}_{t+1} = 0.270\bar{K}_t + 0.165\bar{Z}_t.$$

In this case, the exact analytic solution is

$$C_t = 0.268 Z_t K_t^{0.27},$$
$$K_{t+1} = 0.732 Z_t K_t^{0.27}$$

Figure 2.3 shows the histograms of the distribution for the capital stock that result from the simulation of both solutions. The simulations use the same sequence of shocks to prevent random differences in the results. By and large, the linear model implies the same stationary distribution of the capital stock as does the true, non-linear model.

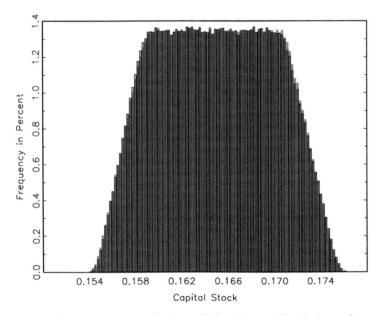

Figure 2.3: Stationary Distribution of the Capital Stock from the Analytic and the Linear Approximate Solution of the Stochastic Infinite-Horizon Ramsey Model

In most applications we want a unit free measure of deviations around the deterministic steady state. Given the linear approximations from above, this is easy to obtain: Just divide both sides of the policy function by the stationary value of the respective lhs variable and rearrange. For instance, using (2.46a), we may write:

$$\hat{C}_t := \frac{C_t - C^*}{C^*} = h_K^C \frac{K^*}{C^*} \underbrace{\frac{K_t - K^*}{K^*}}_{=:\hat{K}_t} + h_Z^C \frac{Z^*}{C^*} \underbrace{\frac{Z_t - Z^*}{Z^*}}_{=:\hat{Z}_t}.$$

Since $\ln(X_t/X^*) \simeq (X_t - X^*)/X^*$, this is a log-linear approximation of the policy function for consumption that relates the percentage deviation of consumption to the percentage deviations of the stock of capital and the productivity shock, respectively.

In the next subsection we basically use the same steps to derive the policy functions for the general system (2.23). If you dislike linear algebra, you may skip this section and note that the program SolveLA performs the above explained computations for the general case. The program requires the matrices from (2.23) as input and returns matrices L_j^i that relate the vectors $\mathbf{u}_t$, $\boldsymbol{\lambda}_t$ and $\mathbf{x}_{t+1}$ to the model's state variables in the vectors $\mathbf{x}_t$ and $\mathbf{z}_t$.

2.4.2 The General Method

In this subsection we consider the solution of a system of linear stochastic difference equations given in the form of (2.23), which derives from the LQ problem. There are related ways to state and solve such systems. The list of references includes the classical paper by BLANCHARD and KAHN (1980), Chapter 3 of the book by FARMER (1993), the papers of KING and WATSON (1998), (2002), KLEIN (2000) and the approach proposed by UHLIG (1999). Our statement of the problem is the one proposed by BURNSIDE (1999), but we solve it along the lines of KING and WATSON (2002).

The Problem. Consider the system of stochastic difference equations (2.47):

2.4 Linear Approximation

$$C_u \mathbf{u}_t = C_{x\lambda} \begin{bmatrix} \mathbf{x}_t \\ \boldsymbol{\lambda}_t \end{bmatrix} + C_z \mathbf{z}_t, \qquad (2.47a)$$

$$D_{x\lambda} E_t \begin{bmatrix} \mathbf{x}_{t+1} \\ \boldsymbol{\lambda}_{t+1} \end{bmatrix} + F_{x\lambda} \begin{bmatrix} \mathbf{x}_t \\ \boldsymbol{\lambda}_t \end{bmatrix} = D_u E_t \mathbf{u}_{t+1} + F_u \mathbf{u}_t \qquad (2.47b)$$
$$+ D_z E_t \mathbf{z}_{t+1} + F_z \mathbf{z}_t.$$

To ease notation we use $n(x)$ to denote the dimension (i.e., the number of elements) of the vector $\mathbf{x}$. We think of the $n(u)$ vector $\mathbf{u}_t$ as the collection of variables that are determined within period t as linear functions of the model's state variables. We distinguish between three kinds of state variables: those with given initial conditions build the $n(x)$ vector $\mathbf{x}_t$; the $n(\lambda)$ vector $\boldsymbol{\lambda}_t$ collects those variables, whose initial values may be chosen freely. In the LQ problem these are the costate variables. In the stochastic growth model it is just the Lagrange multiplier of the budget constraint. Purely exogenous stochastic shocks are stacked in the $n(z)$ vector $\mathbf{z}_t$. We assume that $\mathbf{z}_t$ is governed by a stable vector autoregressive process of first-order with normally distributed innovations ϵ_t:

$$\mathbf{z}_t = \Pi \mathbf{z}_{t-1} + \epsilon_t, \quad \epsilon_t \sim N(\mathbf{0}, \Sigma). \qquad (2.48)$$

Stability requires that the eigenvalues of the matrix Π lie within the unit circle.

System Reduction. We assume that the first equation can be solved for the vector $\mathbf{u}_t$:

$$\mathbf{u}_t = C_u^{-1} C_{x\lambda} \begin{bmatrix} \mathbf{x}_t \\ \boldsymbol{\lambda}_t \end{bmatrix} + C_u^{-1} C_z \mathbf{z}_t. \qquad (2.49)$$

Shifting the time index one period into the future and taking expectations conditional on information as of period t yields:

$$E_t \mathbf{u}_{t+1} = C_u^{-1} C_{x\lambda} E_t \begin{bmatrix} \mathbf{x}_{t+1} \\ \boldsymbol{\lambda}_{t+1} \end{bmatrix} + C_u^{-1} C_z E_t \mathbf{z}_{t+1}. \qquad (2.50)$$

The solutions (2.49) and (2.50) allow us to eliminate $\mathbf{u}_t$ and $E_t \mathbf{u}_{t+1}$ from (2.47b):

$$\left(D_{x\lambda} - D_u C_u^{-1} C_{x\lambda}\right) E_t \begin{bmatrix} \mathbf{x}_{t+1} \\ \boldsymbol{\lambda}_{t+1} \end{bmatrix} = -\left(F_{x\lambda} - F_u C_u^{-1} C_{x\lambda}\right) \begin{bmatrix} \mathbf{x}_t \\ \boldsymbol{\lambda}_t \end{bmatrix}$$
$$+ \left(D_z + D_u C_u^{-1} C_z\right) E_t \mathbf{z}_{t+1}$$
$$+ \left(F_z + F_u C_u^{-1} C_z\right) \mathbf{z}_t.$$

Assume that this system can be solved for $E_t(\mathbf{x}_{t+1}, \boldsymbol{\lambda}_{t+1})'$. In other words, the matrix $D_{x\lambda} - D_u C_u^{-1} C_{x\lambda}$ must be invertible. Using $E_t \mathbf{z}_{t+1} = \Pi \mathbf{z}_t$, which is implied by (2.48), we get the following reduced dynamic system:

$$E_t \begin{bmatrix} \mathbf{x}_{t+1} \\ \boldsymbol{\lambda}_{t+1} \end{bmatrix} = W \begin{bmatrix} \mathbf{x}_t \\ \boldsymbol{\lambda}_t \end{bmatrix} + R \mathbf{z}_t,$$
$$W = -\left(D_{x\lambda} - D_u C_u^{-1} C_{x\lambda}\right)^{-1} \left(F_{x\lambda} - F_u C_u^{-1} C_{x\lambda}\right),$$
$$R = \left(D_{x\lambda} - D_u C_u^{-1} C_{x\lambda}\right)^{-1}$$
$$\times \left[\left(D_z + D_u C_u^{-1} C_z\right) \Pi + \left(F_z + F_u C_u^{-1} C_z\right)\right]. \tag{2.51}$$

Change of Variables. Consider the Schur factorization of the matrix W:

$$S = T^{-1} W T,$$

which gives raise to the following partitioned matrices:

$$S = \begin{bmatrix} S_{xx} & S_{x\lambda} \\ 0 & S_{\lambda\lambda} \end{bmatrix}$$
$$= \underbrace{\begin{bmatrix} T^{xx} & T^{x\lambda} \\ T^{\lambda x} & T^{\lambda\lambda} \end{bmatrix}}_{T^{-1}} \underbrace{\begin{bmatrix} W_{xx} & W_{x\lambda} \\ W_{\lambda x} & W_{\lambda\lambda} \end{bmatrix}}_{W} \underbrace{\begin{bmatrix} T_{xx} & T_{x\lambda} \\ T_{\lambda x} & T_{\lambda\lambda} \end{bmatrix}}_{T}. \tag{2.52}$$

We assume that the eigenvalues of W appear in ascending order on the main diagonal of S (see 11.1). To find a unique solution, $n(x)$ eigenvalues must lie inside the unit circle and $n(\lambda)$ eigenvalues must have modulus greater than one. In the new variables

$$\begin{bmatrix} \tilde{\mathbf{x}}_t \\ \tilde{\boldsymbol{\lambda}}_t \end{bmatrix} := \begin{bmatrix} T^{xx} & T^{x\lambda} \\ T^{\lambda x} & T^{\lambda\lambda} \end{bmatrix} \begin{bmatrix} \mathbf{x}_t \\ \boldsymbol{\lambda}_t \end{bmatrix} \tag{2.53}$$

the dynamic system (2.51) can be rewritten as

$$E_t \begin{bmatrix} \tilde{\mathbf{x}}_{t+1} \\ \tilde{\boldsymbol{\lambda}}_{t+1} \end{bmatrix} = \begin{bmatrix} S_{xx} & S_{x\lambda} \\ 0 & S_{\lambda\lambda} \end{bmatrix} \begin{bmatrix} \tilde{\mathbf{x}}_t \\ \tilde{\boldsymbol{\lambda}}_t \end{bmatrix} + \begin{bmatrix} Q_x \\ Q_\lambda \end{bmatrix} \mathbf{z}_t, \qquad (2.54)$$
$$Q = [Q_x, Q_\lambda]' = T^{-1} R.$$

Policy Function for λ_t. Consider the second line of (2.54), which is a linear system in $\tilde{\boldsymbol{\lambda}}$ alone:

$$E_t \tilde{\boldsymbol{\lambda}}_{t+1} = S_{\lambda\lambda} \tilde{\boldsymbol{\lambda}}_t + Q_\lambda \mathbf{z}_t. \qquad (2.55)$$

Its solution is given by:

$$\tilde{\boldsymbol{\lambda}}_t = \Phi \mathbf{z}_t. \qquad (2.56)$$

There is a quick and a more illuminating way to compute the matrix Φ. Here is the quick one: Substitute (2.56) into equation (2.55) to obtain

$$E_t \Phi \mathbf{z}_{t+1} = \Phi \Pi \mathbf{z}_t = S_{\lambda\lambda} \Phi \mathbf{z}_t + Q_\lambda \mathbf{z}_t.$$

Thus, Φ must solve the matrix equation

$$\Phi \Pi = S_{\lambda\lambda} \Phi + Q_\lambda.$$

Applying the vec operator to this equations yields (see the rule (11.10b))

$$\text{vec}\,\Phi = \left[\Pi' \otimes I_{n(\lambda)} - I_{n(z)} \otimes S_{\lambda\lambda} \right]^{-1} \text{vec}\, Q_\lambda.$$

One may also compute the rows of the matrix Φ in the following steps: The matrix $S_{\lambda\lambda}$ is upper triangular with all of its eigenvalues μ_i on the main diagonal being larger than one in absolute value:

$$S_{\lambda\lambda} = \begin{bmatrix} \mu_1 & s_{12} & \cdots & s_{1n(\lambda)} \\ 0 & \mu_2 & \cdots & s_{2n(\lambda)} \\ \vdots & \vdots & \ddots & \vdots \\ 0 & 0 & \cdots & \mu_{n(\lambda)} \end{bmatrix}.$$

Therefore, the last line of (2.55) is a stochastic difference equation in the single variable $\tilde{\lambda}_{n(\lambda)}$, just like equation (2.40):

$$E_t \tilde{\lambda}_{n(\lambda)\,t+1} = \mu_{n(\lambda)} \tilde{\lambda}_{n(\lambda)\,t} + \mathbf{q}'_{n(\lambda)} \mathbf{z}_t, \tag{2.57}$$

where $\mathbf{q}'_{n(\lambda)}$ denotes the last row of the matrix Q_λ. Note, that $\tilde{\lambda}_{n(\lambda)\,t}$ – as every other component of $\tilde{\boldsymbol{\lambda}}_t$ – may be a complex variable. Yet, since the modulus (i.e., the absolute value) of the complex number $\mu_{n(\lambda)}$ is larger than one, the sequence

$$\left\{ \frac{1}{\mu_{n(\lambda)}^\tau} E_t \tilde{\lambda}_{n(\lambda)\,t+\tau} \right\}_{\tau=0}^{\infty}$$

will converge to zero if the sequence

$$\left\{ E_t \tilde{\lambda}_{n(\lambda)\,t+\tau} \right\}_{\tau=0}^{\infty}$$

is bounded (see Section 12.1). Given this assumption, we know from equation (2.44) that the solution to (2.57) is a linear function of $\mathbf{z}_t$:

$$\tilde{\lambda}_{n(\lambda)\,t} = \underbrace{(\phi_{n(\lambda)\,1}, \phi_{n(\lambda)\,2}, \ldots, \phi_{n(\lambda),n(z)})'}_{\boldsymbol{\phi}'_{n(\lambda)}} \mathbf{z}_t.$$

To determine the yet unknown coefficients of this function, i.e., the elements of the row vector $\boldsymbol{\phi}'_{n(\lambda)}$, we proceed as follows: we substitute this solution into equation (2.57). This yields:

$$\boldsymbol{\phi}'_{n(\lambda)} E_t \mathbf{z}_{t+1} = \mu_{n(\lambda)} \boldsymbol{\phi}'_{n(\lambda)} \mathbf{z}_t + \mathbf{q}'_{n(\lambda)} \mathbf{z}_t,$$
$$\left(\boldsymbol{\phi}'_{n(\lambda)} \Pi - \boldsymbol{\phi}'_{n(\lambda)} \mu_{n(\lambda)} \right) \mathbf{z}_t = \mathbf{q}'_{n(\lambda)} \mathbf{z}_t,$$
$$\boldsymbol{\phi}'_{n(\lambda)} \left(\Pi - \mu_{n(\lambda)} I_{n(z)} \right) \mathbf{z}_t = \mathbf{q}'_{n(\lambda)} \mathbf{z}_t,$$

where the second line follows from (2.48). Equating the coefficients on both sides of the last line of the preceding expression gives the solution for the unknown vector $\boldsymbol{\phi}_{n(\lambda)}$:

$$\boldsymbol{\phi}'_{n(\lambda)} = \mathbf{q}'_{n(\lambda)} \left(\Pi - \mu_{n(\lambda)} I_{n(z)} \right)^{-1}. \tag{2.58}$$

2.4 Linear Approximation

Since the eigenvalues of Π are inside the unit circle, this solution exists.

Now, consider the next to last line of (2.55):

$$E_t \tilde{\lambda}_{n(\lambda)-1\,t+1} = \mu_{n(\lambda)-1} \tilde{\lambda}_{n(\lambda)-1\,t} + s_{n(\lambda)-1,n(\lambda)} \tilde{\lambda}_{n(\lambda)\,t} + \mathbf{q}'_{n(\lambda)-1} \mathbf{z}_t,$$

$$E_t \tilde{\lambda}_{n(\lambda)-1\,t+1} = \mu_{n(\lambda)-1} \tilde{\lambda}_{n(\lambda)-1\,t} + s_{n(\lambda)-1,n(\lambda)} \boldsymbol{\phi}'_{n(\lambda)} \mathbf{z}_t + \mathbf{q}'_{n(\lambda)-1} \mathbf{z}_t.$$

The solution to this equation is given by the row vector $\boldsymbol{\phi}'_{n(\lambda)-1}$. Repeating the steps from above, we find:

$$\boldsymbol{\phi}'_{n(\lambda)-1} = \left(\mathbf{q}'_{n(\lambda)-1} + s_{n(\lambda)-1\,n(\lambda)} \boldsymbol{\phi}'_{n(\lambda)} \right) \left(\Pi - \mu_{n(\lambda)-1} I_{n(z)} \right)^{-1}. \tag{2.59}$$

Proceeding from line $n(\lambda)-1$ to line $n(\lambda)-2$ and so forth until the first line of (2.55) we are able to compute all of the rows $\boldsymbol{\phi}'_i$ of the matrix Φ. The respective formula is:

$$\boldsymbol{\phi}'_i = \left[\mathbf{q}'_i + \sum_{j=i+1}^{n(\lambda)} s_{i,j} \boldsymbol{\phi}'_j \right] \left(\Pi - \mu_i I_{n(z)} \right)^{-1}, \tag{2.60}$$

$$i = n(\lambda), n(\lambda)-1, \ldots, 1.$$

Given the solution for $\tilde{\boldsymbol{\lambda}}_t$ we can use (2.53) to find the solution for $\boldsymbol{\lambda}_t$ in terms of $\mathbf{x}_t$ and $\mathbf{z}_t$. The second part of (2.53) is:

$$\tilde{\boldsymbol{\lambda}}_t = T^{\lambda x} \mathbf{x}_t + T^{\lambda \lambda} \boldsymbol{\lambda}_t.$$

Together with (2.56) this gives:

$$\boldsymbol{\lambda}_t = \underbrace{-\left(T^{\lambda\lambda}\right)^{-1} T^{\lambda x}}_{L_x^\lambda} \mathbf{x}_t + \underbrace{\left(T^{\lambda\lambda}\right)^{-1} \Phi}_{L_z^\lambda} \mathbf{z}_t. \tag{2.61}$$

Policy Function for $\mathbf{x}_{t+1}$. In obvious notation the first part of (2.51) may be written as:

$$\mathbf{x}_{t+1} = W_{xx} \mathbf{x}_t + W_{x\lambda} \boldsymbol{\lambda}_t + R_x \mathbf{z}_t.$$

Substitution for $\boldsymbol{\lambda}_t$ from (2.61) gives:

$$\mathbf{x}_{t+1} = \underbrace{\left(W_{xx} - W_{x\lambda}\left(T^{\lambda\lambda}\right)^{-1}T^{\lambda x}\right)}_{L_x^x}\mathbf{x}_t$$
$$+ \underbrace{\left(W_{x\lambda}\left(T^{\lambda\lambda}\right)^{-1}\Phi + R_x\right)}_{L_z^x}\mathbf{z}_t. \tag{2.62}$$

The expression for L_x^x may be considerably simplified. In terms of partitioned matrices the expression $W = TST^{-1}$ may be written as:

$$\begin{bmatrix} W_{xx} & W_{x\lambda} \\ W_{\lambda x} & W_{\lambda\lambda} \end{bmatrix} = \begin{bmatrix} T_{xx} & T_{x\lambda} \\ T_{\lambda x} & T_{\lambda\lambda} \end{bmatrix} \begin{bmatrix} S_{xx} & S_{x\lambda} \\ 0 & S_{\lambda\lambda} \end{bmatrix} \begin{bmatrix} T^{xx} & T^{x\lambda} \\ T^{\lambda x} & T^{\lambda\lambda} \end{bmatrix},$$

which implies:

$$W_{xx} = T_{xx}S_{xx}T^{xx} + T_{xx}S_{x\lambda}T^{\lambda x} + T_{x\lambda}S_{\lambda\lambda}T^{\lambda x},$$
$$W_{x\lambda} = T_{xx}S_{xx}T^{x\lambda} + T_{xx}S_{x\lambda}T^{\lambda\lambda} + T_{x\lambda}S_{\lambda\lambda}T^{\lambda\lambda}.$$

Substituting the rhs of these equations into the expression for L_{xx} from (2.62) gives:

$$L_x^x = T_{xx}S_{xx}\left(T^{xx} - T^{x\lambda}\left(T^{\lambda\lambda}\right)^{-1}T^{\lambda x}\right).$$

Since

$$\begin{bmatrix} T_{xx} & T_{x\lambda} \\ T_{\lambda x} & T_{\lambda\lambda} \end{bmatrix} = \begin{bmatrix} T^{xx} & T^{x\lambda} \\ T^{\lambda x} & T^{\lambda\lambda} \end{bmatrix}^{-1}$$

the formula for the inverse of a partitioned matrix (11.15a) implies:

$$\left(T_{xx}\right)^{-1} = T^{xx} - T^{x\lambda}\left(T^{\lambda\lambda}\right)^{-1}T^{\lambda x}.$$

Putting all pieces together, we find:

$$L_x^x = T_{xx}S_{xx}T_{xx}^{-1}.$$

Policy Function for $\mathbf{u}_t$. Using equation (2.49) the solutions for $\mathbf{x}_t$ and $\boldsymbol{\lambda}_t$ imply the following policy function for the vector $\mathbf{u}_t$:

$$\mathbf{u}_t = \underbrace{C_u^{-1} C_{x\lambda} \begin{bmatrix} I_{n(x)} \\ L_x^\lambda \end{bmatrix}}_{L_x^u} \mathbf{x}_t \\
+ \underbrace{\left(C_u^{-1} C_{x\lambda} \begin{bmatrix} 0_{n(x) \times n(z)} \\ L_z^\lambda \end{bmatrix} + C_u^{-1} C_z \right)}_{L_z^u} \mathbf{z}_t. \qquad (2.63)$$

Implementation. Our Gauss program SolveLA performs the computation of the policy matrices according to the formulas given by equations (2.61), (2.62), and (2.63). It uses the Gauss intrinsic command Schtoc to get the matrices S and T. However, the eigenvalues on the main diagonal of S are not ordered. We use the Givens rotation described in Section 11.1 to sort the eigenvalues in ascending order. The program's input are the matrices from (2.47), the matrix Π from (2.48), and the number of elements $n(x)$ of the vector $\mathbf{x}_t$. The program checks whether $n(x)$ of the eigenvalues of W are inside the unit circle. If not, it stops with an error message. Otherwise it returns the matrices L_x^x, L_z^x, L_x^λ, L_z^λ, L_x^u, and L_z^u. A second version of this program, SolveLA2, uses the Gauss foreign language interface and calls a routine (written in Fortran) that returns S and T so that the eigenvalues of the complex matrix S with modulus less than one appear in the upper left block of S. This routine in turn calls the program ZGEES from the Fortran LAPACK library. Our Fortran version of SolveLA also uses ZGGES to get the Schur decomposition with sorted eigenvalues. The Gauss version of SolveLA (and SolveLA2) also solves purely deterministic models. Just set the matrices C_z, F_z, D_z and Π equal to the Gauss missing value code.

The matrices that are an input to both programs can be obtained in two ways. The first and probably more cumbersome approach is to use paper and pencil to derive the coefficients of the matrices analytically. If the differentiation is done with respect to the (natural) logs of the variables, SolveLA returns the coefficients of the log-linear policy functions. Otherwise the coefficients refer to the linear approximation. One may, however, also use numeric differentiation to obtain the matrices from (2.47). We provide an example in the Gauss program `Ramsey3a.g` where we show how to solve the stochastic growth model by using `SolveLA`.

2.5 Quadratic Approximation

In this section we consider quadratic approximations of the policy functions of DGE models. We introduce you to this topic in the next subsection. Then, we consider two examples before we provide the general algorithm in Subsection 2.5.4.

2.5.1 Introduction

We begin with the quadratic approximation of the solution of a system of static equilibrium conditions. Consider the equilibrium condition $g(x,y)=0$ and suppose that a solution exists at (x^*, y^*). Let $y=h(x)$ be the solution in an ϵ neighborhood of x^*. A second-order Taylor series approximation of h at x^* is given by

$$h(x^* + \epsilon) \simeq y^* + h'(x^*)\epsilon + \frac{1}{2}(h'')^2(x^*)\epsilon^2.$$

Differentiating $g(x, h(x))$ once provides

$$g_1(x, h(x)) + g_2(x, h(x))h'(x). \qquad (2.64)$$

At (x^*, y^*) this expression must equal zero, from which we obtain the solution

$$h'(x^*) = -\frac{g_1(x^*, y^*)}{g_2(x^*, y^*)}.$$

Differentiating (2.64) again and setting the result equal to zero yields:

$$h''(x^*) = -\frac{g_{11} + (g_{12} + g_{21})h' + g_{22}(h')^2}{g_2}.$$

This formula still looks pretty simple. Though straight forward, the generalization to the case of n exogenous and m endogenous variables $\mathbf{g}(\mathbf{x}, \mathbf{y}) = \mathbf{0}_{m \times 1}$ produces formulas with lots of indices. First note that in this context the quadratic approximation of the solution $h^j(\mathbf{x})$, $j = 1, 2, \ldots, m$ is given by

$$\hat{h}^j(\mathbf{x}) = h^j(\mathbf{x}^*) + \mathbf{h}_{\mathbf{x}}^j \bar{\mathbf{x}} + \frac{1}{2}\bar{\mathbf{x}}' H^j \bar{\mathbf{x}}, \qquad (2.65)$$

where $\mathbf{h}_{\mathbf{x}}^j = [h_{x_1}^j, h_{x_2}^j, \ldots, h_{x_n}^j]'$ is the vector of linear coefficients and $H^j = (h_{il}^j)$ is the n-by-n matrix of quadratic coefficients. The vectors $\mathbf{h}_{\mathbf{x}}^j$ are determined from the matrix equation

$$\mathbf{h}_x = -D_{\mathbf{y}}^{-1} D_{\mathbf{x}}$$

where $D_{\mathbf{y}}$ ($D_{\mathbf{x}}$) is the matrix of partial derivatives of $\mathbf{g}(\mathbf{x}, \mathbf{y})$ with respect to the variables in the vector $\mathbf{y}$ ($\mathbf{x}$) (see equation (11.38)). Note, that a single element in this matrix equation is given by

$$0 = g_{x_k}^j(\mathbf{x}, \mathbf{h}(\mathbf{x})) + \sum_{l=1}^m g_{y_l}^j(\mathbf{x}, \mathbf{h}(\mathbf{x})) h_{x_k}^l,$$

$$j = 1, 2, \ldots, m, \quad k = 1, 2, \ldots, n.$$

Differentiating this expression with respect to variable x_i provides

$$0 = g_{x_k x_i}^j + \sum_{l=1}^m g_{x_k y_l}^j h_{x_i}^l + \sum_{l=1}^m g_{y_l}^j h_{x_k x_i}^l + \sum_{l=1}^m g_{y_l x_i}^j h_{x_k}^l$$

$$+ \sum_{s=1}^m \sum_{l=1}^m g_{y_l y_s}^j h_{x_i}^s h_{x_k}^l, \quad j = 1, \ldots, m; \; i, k = 1, \ldots, n.$$

These mn^2 equations can be arranged to n^2 matrix equations in the coefficients $h_{x_k x_j}^j$, $j = 1, 2, \ldots, m$. Due to the symmetry of the Hesse matrices $n(n+1)/2$ of these equations are redundant. As you will see in the next examples, since the structure of the equilibrium conditions of DGE models is not as simple as $\mathbf{g}(\mathbf{x}, \mathbf{h}(\mathbf{x})) = \mathbf{0}_{m \times 1}$, the respective formulas to compute the Hesse matrices H^j are more involved.

2.5.2 The Deterministic Growth Model

We return to the deterministic growth model considered in Sections 1.2 and 2.1. We let $K_{t+1} = h^K(K_t)$ and $C_t = h^C(K_t)$ denote the policy functions for the next-period capital stock and consumption, respectively. For both functions we seek a second order approximation at the stationary solution K^* of the form

$$\bar{K}_{t+1} = h_K^K \bar{K}_t + \frac{1}{2} h_{KK}^K \bar{K}_t^2,$$

$$\bar{C}_t = h_K^C \bar{K}_t + \frac{1}{2} h_{KK}^C \bar{K}_t^2,$$

where h_K^i and h_{KK}^i, $i \in \{K, C\}$ denote the first and second derivative of the policy function of variable i with respect to the stock of capital K. Of course, all derivatives are evaluated at the stationary solution K^*. To obtain the coefficients h_K^i and h_{KK}^i, we use a more general exposition. Observe that the resource constraint $g^1(\cdot)$ and the Euler equation for the optimal next-period capital stock $g^2(\cdot)$, equations (2.1a) and (2.1b), have the following structure:

$$g^i(K, C, K', C')$$
$$\equiv g^i(K, h^C(K), h^K(K), h^C(h^K(K))) = 0, \quad i = 1, 2,$$

where we have omitted the time indices. To distinguish between current period variables and next-period variables we used a prime to denote the latter. Differentiating with respect to K yields (we suppress the arguments of g^i but not of h^i)

$$g_K^i + g_C^i h_K^C(K) + g_{K'}^i h_K^K(K) + g_{C'}^i h_K^C(K') h_K^K(K) = 0, \qquad (2.66)$$
$$i = 1, 2.$$

We have already solved these two equations in Section 2.1, so let us assume here that we know h_K^K and h_K^C. To obtain equations in h_{KK}^K and h_{KK}^C, we must differentiate (2.66) with respect to K. This yields:

$$\begin{bmatrix} g_{K'}^1 + g_{C'}^1 h_K^C & g_C^1 + g_{C'}^1 \left(h_K^K\right)^2 \\ g_{K'}^2 + g_{C'}^2 h_K^C & g_C^2 + g_{C'}^2 \left(h_K^K\right)^2 \end{bmatrix} \begin{bmatrix} h_{KK}^K \\ h_{KK}^C \end{bmatrix} = \begin{bmatrix} \mathbf{h}_K^T H(g^1) \mathbf{h}_K \\ \mathbf{h}_K^T H(g^2) \mathbf{h}_K \end{bmatrix}, \quad (2.67)$$

2.5 Quadratic Approximation

where

$$\mathbf{h}_K^T = \left[1, h_K^C, h_K^K, h_K^C h_K^K\right], \quad H(g^i) := \begin{bmatrix} g^i_{KK} & \cdots & g^i_{KC'} \\ \vdots & \ddots & \vdots \\ g^i_{C'K} & \cdots & g^i_{C'C'} \end{bmatrix}.$$

Since (2.67) is a system of two linear equations it is easily solved for h_{KK}^K and h_{KK}^C. Usually, we will use numeric differentiation to obtain the coefficients of equation (2.67). If $u(C) := (C^{1-\eta} - 1)/(1-\eta)$ and $f(K) = (1-\delta)K + K^\alpha$, the matrix on the lhs of (2.67) is given by

$$\left[\frac{1}{[\eta h_K^C + \alpha\beta(1-\alpha)C^*(K^*)^{\alpha-2}]} \quad \frac{1}{\eta\left[\left(h_K^K\right)^2 - 1\right]} \right]$$

and the vector on the rhs, say **b**, has elements

$$b_1 := \alpha(\alpha - 1)(K^*)^{\alpha-2}$$

and

$$b_2 := \eta(1+\eta)\frac{1}{C^*}\left[\left(h_{KK}^K\right)^2 - 1\right]\left(h_K^C\right)^2$$
$$+ \alpha\beta(1-\alpha)(K^*)^{\alpha-2}\left(h_K^K\right)^2\left(2\eta h_K^C + (2-\alpha)\frac{C^*}{K^*}\right).$$

In the Gauss program Ramsey2b.g we compute the coefficients of the quadratic policy functions using both analytic and numeric derivatives. Figure 2.4 displays the policy function for consumption from the linear, the quadratic solution and the analytic solution ($\alpha = 0.27$ and $\beta = 0.994$).

To compare the accuracy of the linear with the accuracy of the quadratic approximation this program also computes the residuals of the Euler equation (2.1b) over a grid of 200 points in the interval $[0.9K^*, 1.1K^*]$. For the parameter values $\alpha = 0.27$, $\beta = 0.994$, $\eta = 2$, and $\delta = 0.011$ we find that the maximum absolute Euler equation residual from the linear solution is about 13 times larger than that obtained from the quadratic policy function which is 2.4×10^{-6}, and, thus, very small. We also find that there is no noteworthy difference in accuracy, if we use analytic instead of numeric derivatives.

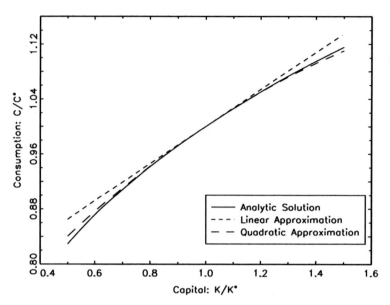

Figure 2.4: Policy Functions of Consumption of the Deterministic Growth Model

2.5.3 The Stochastic Growth Model

The Framework. We return to the stochastic growth model considered in Sections 1.3 and 2.4.1 assuming $u(C) = [C^{1-\eta} - 1]/(1-\eta)$ and $f(K) = K^\alpha$. As in the previous subsection, we drop the time indices from all variables and use a prime to designate variables that pertain to the next period. This allows us to the write the equilibrium conditions as[16]

$$0 = Eg^i(K, C, z, K', C', z'), \quad i = 1, 2, \qquad (2.68a)$$
$$C = h^C(K, z, \sigma),$$
$$C' = h^C(h^K(K, z, \sigma), z', \sigma),$$

---

[16] You may probably wonder why we use $z = \ln Z$ as a state variable and not Z itself. In the present context, in which we know what the equilibrium conditions look like, we could indeed have used Z. Yet, when writing a general purpose routine, we have no information about the structure of the equilibrium conditions. In this case, we are bound to assume that the shocks evolve according to a linear first-order autoregressive process.

$$K' = h^K(K, z, \sigma),$$
$$z' = \varrho z + \sigma \epsilon', \quad \epsilon' \sim N(0,1),$$

where

$$g^1(\cdot) = K' - (1-\delta)K - e^z K^\alpha + C, \tag{2.68b}$$
$$g^2(\cdot) = C^{-\eta} - \beta(C')^{-\eta}\left(1 - \delta + \alpha e^{z'}(K')^{\alpha-1}\right). \tag{2.68c}$$

The operator E denotes expectations with respect to information available at the current period.

As in Section 2.4.1 we consider the model in a neighborhood of $\sigma = 0$, where it reduces to the deterministic growth model with stationary solution $(K^*, C^*, z^* = 0)$ determined by equations (2.33). For $i \in \{C, K\}$ we look for quadratic approximations of the policy function h^i given by

$$\begin{aligned}h^i(K, z, \sigma) = &\, h^i(K^*, z^*, \sigma = 0) \\ &+ h^i_K \bar{K} + h^i_z \bar{z} + h^i_\sigma \sigma \\ &+ \frac{1}{2}\begin{bmatrix}\bar{K}, \bar{z}, \sigma\end{bmatrix}\begin{bmatrix}h^i_{KK} & h^i_{Kz} & h^i_{K\sigma} \\ h^i_{zK} & h^i_{zz} & h^i_{z\sigma} \\ h^i_{\sigma K} & h^i_{\sigma z} & h^i_{\sigma\sigma}\end{bmatrix}\begin{bmatrix}\bar{K} \\ \bar{z} \\ \sigma\end{bmatrix},\end{aligned} \tag{2.69}$$

where the bar denotes deviations from the stationary solution. Note that the Hesse matrix in (2.69) is a symmetric matrix, i.e., $h^i_{jk} = h^i_{kj}$, $j, k \in \{K, z, \sigma\}$. To determine the coefficients of these functions we closely follow SCHMITT-GROHÉ and URIBE (2004).[17]

As in Section 2.4.1 we differentiate (2.68a) with respect to K, z, and σ. To represent the respective formulas we define the vector function

$$\mathbf{h} := \begin{bmatrix} h^C(K, z, \sigma) \\ h^K(K, z, \sigma) \\ h^C(h^K(K, z, \sigma), \varrho z + \sigma\epsilon', \sigma) \end{bmatrix}$$

with the vector of derivatives denoted by $\mathbf{h}_K$, $\mathbf{h}_z$, and $\mathbf{h}_\sigma$, respectivley. In addition, we use $g^i_{[i]}$ for the (column) vector of first

---

[17] In a recent paper LOMBARDO and SUTHERLAND (2007) outline an algorithm that also provides second-order accurate solutions. Their procedure relies on methods developed for the solution of linear models.

120   Chapter 2: Perturbation Methods

derivatives of g^i with respect to the indices in the vector $\mathbf{i}$ and $g^i_{[\mathbf{i}_1][\mathbf{i}_2]}$ for the matrix of second partial derivatives with respect to the indices in $\mathbf{i}_1$ (for the rows of the matrix) and $\mathbf{i}_2$ (for the columns). To avoid confusion, we denote the transpose of a vector by the superscript T.

Consider the derivatives of conditions (2.68a) with respect to K, z, and σ:

$$0 = E\left\{\left[1, \mathbf{h}_K^T\right] g^i_{[K,C,K',C']}\right\}, \tag{2.70a}$$

$$0 = E\left\{\left[\mathbf{h}_z^T, 1, \varrho\right] g^i_{[C,K',C',z,z']}\right\}, \tag{2.70b}$$

$$0 = E\left\{\left[\mathbf{h}_\sigma^T, \epsilon'\right] g^i_{[C,K',C',z']}\right\}. \tag{2.70c}$$

Since we have already seen how we can compute the coefficients of the linear part of (2.69) in Section 2.4.1, we proceed to the coefficients of the quadratic part. For the following derivations we will keep in mind that we found $h^i_\sigma = 0$.

Coefficients of the Hesse Matrices. Differentiating equation (2.70a) with respect to K provides two linear equations in the coefficients h^i_{KK}:

$$0 = \mathbf{h}_{KK}^T g^i_{[C,K',C']} + \left[1, \mathbf{h}_K^T\right] g^i_{[K,C,K',C'][K,C,K',C']} \begin{bmatrix} 1 \\ \mathbf{h}_K \end{bmatrix}, \tag{2.71a}$$

where $\mathbf{h}_{KK}$ is the vector of second derivatives of $\mathbf{h}$ with respect to K. This equation corresponds to equation (2.67) in the deterministic case.

To determine h^i_{Kz}, we differentiate (2.70a) with respect to z, yielding

$$0 = \mathbf{h}_{Kz}^T g^i_{[C,K',C']} + \left[1, \mathbf{h}_K^T\right] g^i_{[K,C,K',C'][C,K',C',z]} \begin{bmatrix} \mathbf{h}_z \\ 1 \end{bmatrix} \tag{2.71b}$$

$$+ \varrho \left[1, \mathbf{h}_K^T\right] g^i_{[K,C,K',C'][z']}.$$

The first term in this equation equals

$$\left(g^i_{K'} + g^i_{C'} h_K^C\right) h_{KZ}^K + \left(g^i_C + \varrho g^i_{C'} h_K^K\right) h_{KZ}^C + g^i_{C'} h_K^K h_{KK}^C h_Z^K.$$

Thus, (2.71b) provide two linear equations in h_{KZ}^K and h_{KZ}^C.

Differentiating conditions (2.70a) with respect to σ provides conditions on $h^i_{K\sigma}$:

$$0 = E\left\{\mathbf{h}^T_{K\sigma} g^i_{[C,K'C']} + \left[1, \mathbf{h}^T_K\right] g^i_{[K,C,K',C'][C,K',C']} \mathbf{h}_\sigma \right. \quad (2.71c)$$

$$\left. + \left[1, \mathbf{h}^T_K\right] g^i_{[K,C,K',C'][z']} \epsilon' \right\}.$$

The expectation of the first term in curly brackets is

$$E\left\{\mathbf{h}^T_{K\sigma} g^i_{[C,K',C']}\right\} = \left(g^i_{K'} + g^i_{C'} h^C_K\right) h^K_{K\sigma} + \left(g^i_C + g^i_{C'} h^K_K\right) h^C_{K\sigma},$$

since $h^K_\sigma = 0$ and $E(h^K_K h^C_{KZ} \epsilon') = 0$. At the stationary solution the second term in (2.71c) is obviously zero, since $\mathbf{h}_\sigma$ is a vector with zeros. The expectation of the third term is also zero since $E(\epsilon') = 0$. Thus, system (2.71c) is a linear homogeneous system with solution $h^i_{K\sigma} = 0$.

To determine the coefficients h^i_{zz}, we differentiate (2.70b) with respect to z. The result is:

$$0 = \mathbf{h}^T_{zz} g^i_{[C,K',C']}$$

$$+ \left[\mathbf{h}^T_z, 1, \varrho\right] g^i_{[C,K',C',z,z'][C,K',C',z,z']} \begin{bmatrix} \mathbf{h}_z \\ 1 \\ \varrho \end{bmatrix}. \quad (2.71d)$$

The first term on the rhs of this equation equals

$$\mathbf{h}^T_{zz} g^i_{[C,K',C']} = \left(g^i_{K'} + g^i_{C'} h^C_K\right) h^K_{ZZ} + \left(g^i_C + g^i_{C'} \varrho^2\right) h^C_{ZZ}$$
$$+ g^i_{C'} h^K_Z \left(h^C_{KK} h^K_Z + 2\varrho h^C_{KZ}\right).$$

Differentiating (2.70b) with respect to σ provides

$$0 = E\left\{\mathbf{h}^T_{z\sigma} g^i_{[C,K',C']} \right.$$

$$\left. + \left[\mathbf{h}^T_z, 1, \varrho\right] g^i_{[C,K',C',z,z'][C,K',C',z']} \begin{bmatrix} \mathbf{h}_\sigma \\ \epsilon' \end{bmatrix} \right\}. \quad (2.71e)$$

As in equation (2.71c) all terms except the coefficients of $h^K_{Z\sigma}$ and $h^C_{Z\sigma}$ are equal to zero. Therefore, $h^K_{Z\sigma} = h^C_{Z\sigma} = 0$.

Finally, we turn to the coefficients $h^i_{\sigma\sigma}$. They are obtained from differentiating equations (2.70c) with respect to σ. This delivers:

$$0 = E\left\{\mathbf{h}^T_{\sigma\sigma} g^i_{[C,K',C']}\right.$$
$$\left. + \left[\mathbf{h}^T_\sigma, \epsilon'\right] g^i_{[C,K',C',z'][C,K',C',z']} \begin{bmatrix} \mathbf{h}_\sigma \\ \epsilon' \end{bmatrix}\right\}, \quad (2.71f)$$
$$\mathbf{h}^T_{\sigma\sigma} = \left[h^C_{\sigma\sigma}, h^K_{\sigma\sigma}, h^C_{\sigma\sigma} + h^C_K h^K_{\sigma\sigma} + \Delta\right],$$
$$\Delta := h^K_\sigma \left(h^C_{KK} h^K_\sigma + h^C_{KZ}\epsilon' + h^C_{K\sigma}\right)$$
$$+ \epsilon' \left(h^C_{ZK} h^K_\sigma + h^C_{ZZ}\epsilon' + h^C_{z\sigma}\right) + h^C_{\sigma K} h^K_\sigma + h^C_{\sigma z}\epsilon'.$$

To evaluate this expression, observe that

1. at $\sigma = 0$ the vector of derivatives $\mathbf{h}^T_\sigma$ equals $[0, 0, h^C_Z \epsilon]$, since $h^i_\sigma = 0$,
2. $h^i_{\sigma j} = h^i_{j\sigma} = 0$ for $i \in \{K, C\}$ and $j \in \{K, z\}$,
3. $E(\epsilon')^2 = 1$ and $E(\epsilon') = 0$.

Thus, equations (2.71f) reduce to

$$0 = \left(g^i_{K'} + g^i_{C'} h^C_K\right) h^K_{\sigma\sigma} + \left(g^i_C + g^i_{C'}\right) h^C_{\sigma\sigma}$$
$$+ g^i_{C'C'} (h^C_Z)^2 + 2 g^i_{C'z'} h^C_Z + g^i_{z'z'} + g^i_{C'} h^C_{ZZ}.$$

Our Gauss program `Ramsey3b.g` computes the quadratic approximation of the policy function from these formulas. It employs numeric differentiation to compute $g^i_{[\cdot]}$ as well as the Hesse matrices that appear in (2.71).

Table 2.1 presents the coefficients from this exercise for the parameter values $\alpha = 0.27$, $\beta = 0.994$, $\eta = 1$, and $\delta = 1$. The second column shows solutions obtained from using the Gauss commands `gradp` and `hessp` that provide forward difference approximations of the first and second partial derivatives, respectively.[18] Our own procedures `CDJac` and `CDHesse` imple-

---

[18] See Section 11.3.1 on numeric differentiation, where we explain forward difference as well as central difference formulas for the numeric computation of derivatives.

Table 2.1

Coefficient	Forward Differences	Central Differences	Analytic solution
h_K^K	0.270000	0.270000	0.270000
h_Z^K	0.164993	0.164993	0.164993
h_{KK}^K	−1.194628	−1.194595	−1.194595
h_{KZ}^K	0.269781	0.270000	0.270000
h_{ZZ}^K	0.156787	0.164995	0.164993
$h_{\sigma\sigma}^K$	−0.023160	0.000001	0.000000
h_K^C	0.736036	0.736036	0.736036
h_Z^C	0.449782	0.449781	0.449781
h_{KK}^C	−3.256642	−3.256537	−3.256538
h_{KZ}^C	0.735831	0.736036	0.736036
h_{ZZ}^C	0.479034	0.449782	0.449781
$h_{\sigma\sigma}^C$	0.023160	−0.000001	0.000000

ment central difference formulas that involve a smaller approximation error. The fourth column presents the coefficients computed from the quadratic approximation of the analytic solutions $h^K = \alpha\beta e^z K^\alpha$ and $h^C = (1 - \alpha\beta)e^z K^\alpha$, respectively. There is no noteworthy difference in the linear coefficients as well as in h_{KK}^i. There is a small difference between the solutions for h_{KZ}^K, but the numeric value of $h_{\sigma\sigma}^i$ is far from its true value of zero when we use forward difference formulas. This imprecision can also be seen from the residuals of the Euler equation

$$C_t^{-\eta} = E_t \beta C_{t+1}^{-\eta} \left(1 - \delta + \alpha(e^{\varrho z_t + \sigma \epsilon_{t+1}}) K_{t+1}^{\alpha-1}\right). \quad (2.72)$$

We compute the residuals on a grid of 400 equally spaced points on the square $[0.9K^*, 1.2K^*] \times [\ln(0.95), \ln(1.05)]$. With respect to the maximum absolute value of these residuals the solution displayed in the second column of Table 2.1 is about 2.5 times worse than the solution based on the numbers in column four. The Euler equation residual from the linear solution is almost 37 times larger than the Euler equation residual from the quadratic solution displayed in column four. When we use the parameter values from Table 1.1 for α, β, η, δ, ϱ, and σ, the linear solution is about 13 times less accurate than the quadratic solution, whose maximum absolute Euler equation residual is 4.6×10^{-6}.

Computation of the Euler Equation Residual. Here we briefly explain our computation of the residual in the stochastic growth model. Given the approximate policy functions $\hat{h}^K$ and $\hat{h}^C$ the term to the right of the expectations operator E_t in equation (2.72) can be written as

$$\phi(K, Z, \sigma, \epsilon) := \beta \left(\hat{h}^C(\hat{h}^K(K, Z, \sigma), e^{\varrho z_t + \sigma \epsilon}, \sigma) \right)^{-\eta}$$
$$\times \left(1 - \delta + \alpha e^{\varrho z_t + \sigma \epsilon} \left(\hat{h}^K(K, Z, \sigma) \right)^{\alpha - 1} \right).$$

For given values of K, z, and σ this is a function of the stochastic variable ϵ that has a standard normal distribution. Therefore, the rhs of equation (2.72) is given by

$$\Delta := \int_{-\infty}^{\infty} \phi(K, Z, \sigma, \epsilon) \frac{e^{-\frac{\epsilon^2}{2}}}{\sqrt{2\pi}} d\epsilon.$$

We use the Gauss-Hermite four point integration formula given in equation (11.77) to compute this expectation. Given Δ, the Euler equation residual at (K, Z) is defined as

$$\tilde{R} = \frac{\Delta^{-1/\eta}}{\hat{h}^C(K, Z, \sigma)} - 1.$$

2.5.4 Generalization

Framework. Equations (2.68a) are readily generalized. Just replace K by an $n(x)$ vector **x** of state variables, C by a $n(y)$ vector **y** of control and costate variables, Z by an $n(z)$ vector of shocks **z**, and ϵ by a $n(z)$ vector ϵ of $N(\mathbf{0}_{n(z)}, I_{n(z)})$ distributed innovations so that $\mathbf{z}_t = \Pi \mathbf{z}_{t-1} + \sigma \Omega \epsilon$. The $n(z)$ by $n(z)$ matrix Ω allows for possible correlations between the elements of **z**. To see this, note that the conditional variance of $\mathbf{z}_t$ given $\mathbf{z}_{t-1}$ is given by $E(\sigma\Omega\epsilon)(\sigma\Omega\epsilon)^T = \sigma^2\Omega\Omega^T$, where the superscript T denotes the transposition of a matrix or a vector.

The $n(x) + n(y)$ equilibrium conditions are

$$0 = Eg^i(\mathbf{x},\mathbf{y},\mathbf{z},\mathbf{x}',\mathbf{y}',\mathbf{z}'), \quad i = 1, 2, \ldots, n(x) + n(y), \quad (2.73a)$$

where

$$\mathbf{y} = \mathbf{h}^y(\mathbf{x},\mathbf{z},\sigma), \qquad (2.73b)$$
$$\mathbf{x}' = \mathbf{h}^x(\mathbf{x},\mathbf{z},\sigma), \qquad (2.73c)$$
$$\mathbf{y}' = \mathbf{h}^y(\mathbf{x}',\mathbf{z}',\sigma), \qquad (2.73d)$$
$$\mathbf{z}' = \Pi\mathbf{z} + \sigma\Omega\epsilon' \qquad (2.73e)$$

The quadratic approximation of the policy function h^i, $i \in \{x_1, \ldots, x_{n(x)}, y_1, \ldots, y_{n(y)}\}$ is an expression of the form

$$h^i = h^i(\mathbf{x}^*, \mathbf{z}^*, \sigma = 0) + (\mathbf{l}^i)^T \begin{bmatrix} \bar{\mathbf{x}} \\ \bar{\mathbf{z}} \end{bmatrix}$$
$$+ \frac{1}{2}[\bar{\mathbf{x}}^T, \bar{\mathbf{z}}^T, \sigma] \underbrace{\begin{bmatrix} H^i_{xx} & H^i_{xz} & 0 \\ H^i_{zx} & H^i_{zz} & 0 \\ 0 & 0 & H^i_{\sigma\sigma} \end{bmatrix}}_{H^i} \begin{bmatrix} \bar{\mathbf{x}} \\ \bar{\mathbf{z}} \\ \sigma \end{bmatrix}. \quad (2.74)$$

The row vector $\mathbf{l}^i$ holds the coefficients of the linear part and the matrices H^i_{xx}, H^i_{xz}, and H^i_{zz} contain the coefficients of the quadratic part with respect to the state variables $\mathbf{x}$ and $\mathbf{z}$. As before, the bar denotes deviations from the equilibrium $\mathbf{x}^*$ and $\mathbf{z}^*$, respectively. The scalar $H^i_{\sigma\sigma}$ is the coefficient of σ^2. Note that in the general model both the linear coefficients of σ are zero and the matrices $H^i_{x\sigma}$ and $H^i_{z\sigma}$ are zero matrices as in the example of the previous subsection.[19]

Computation of the Quadratic Part. To obtain these matrices we proceed as in our example. Given the vector

---
[19] See SCHMITT-GROHÉ and URIBE (2004) for a proof.

$$\mathbf{h} := \begin{bmatrix} h^{y_1}(\mathbf{x}, \mathbf{z}, \sigma) \\ \vdots \\ h^{y_{n(y)}}(\mathbf{x}, \mathbf{z}, \sigma) \\ h^{x_1}(\mathbf{x}, \mathbf{z}, \sigma) \\ \vdots \\ h^{x_{n(x)}}(\mathbf{x}, \mathbf{z}, \sigma) \\ h^{y_1}(\mathbf{x}', \mathbf{z}', \sigma) \\ \vdots \\ h^{y_{n(y)}}(\mathbf{x}', \mathbf{z}', \sigma) \end{bmatrix}, \qquad (2.75)$$

we use $\mathbf{h}_i$ to denote the vector whose elements are the derivatives of the elements of $\mathbf{h}$ with respect to variable i.

We begin with the coefficients of the matrices $H_{\mathbf{xx}}$. We differentiate equations (2.73a) with respect to x_j and evaluate the result at the point $(\mathbf{x}^*, \mathbf{z}^*, \sigma = 0)$:

$$0 = [1, \ \mathbf{h}_{x_j}^T] \, g^i_{[x_j, \mathbf{y}, \mathbf{x}', \mathbf{y}']}, \quad i = 1, 2, \ldots, n(x) + n(y). \qquad (2.76)$$

Differentiating this expression with respect to x_k provides a set of $(n(x) + n(y))n(x)^2$ conditions in the unknown coefficients of the matrices $H^i_{\mathbf{xx}}$:

$$\mathbf{h}_{x_j x_k}^T g^i_{[x_j, \mathbf{y}, \mathbf{x}', \mathbf{y}']} = -[1, \mathbf{h}_{x_j}^T] \, g^i_{[x_j, \mathbf{y}, \mathbf{x}', \mathbf{y}'][x_k, \mathbf{y}, \mathbf{x}', \mathbf{y}']} \begin{bmatrix} 1 \\ \mathbf{h}_{x_k} \end{bmatrix}, \qquad (2.77a)$$

$i = 1, \ldots, n(x) + n(y), \ j = 1, \ldots, n(x), \ k = 1, \ldots, n(x),$

where

$$\mathbf{h}_{x_j}^T = \left[h_{x_j}^{y_1}, \ldots, h_{x_j}^{y_{n(y)}}, h_{x_j}^{x_1}, \ldots, h_{x_j}^{x_{n(x)}}, \Delta_1^1, \ldots, \Delta_{n(y)}^1 \right], \qquad (2.77b)$$

$$\Delta_i^1 = \sum_{l=1}^{n(x)} h_{x_l}^{y_i} h_{x_j}^{x_l}.$$

and

$$\mathbf{h}_{x_j x_k}^T = \left[h_{x_j x_k}^{y_1}, \ldots, h_{x_j x_k}^{y_{n(y)}}, h_{x_j x_k}^{x_1}, \ldots, h_{x_j x_k}^{x_{n(x)}}, \Delta_1^2, \ldots, \Delta_{n(y)}^2 \right], \qquad (2.77c)$$

$$\Delta_i^2 = \sum_{l=1}^{n(x)} h_{x_l}^{y_i} h_{x_j x_k}^{x_l} + \sum_{l=1}^{n(x)} h_{x_j}^{x_l} \sum_{r=1}^{n(x)} h_{x_l x_r}^{y_i} h_{x_k}^{x_r}.$$

2.5 Quadratic Approximation

Different from our example in the previous subsection the system of equations (2.77a) cannot be factored into smaller systems in the pairs of coefficients (x_j, x_k), since all the unknown coefficients $h^{y_i}_{x_l x_r}$ appear in each equation. The huge linear system (2.77a) may be written as $A\mathbf{w} = \mathbf{q}$, where

$$\mathbf{w} := \text{vec}\left[H^{x_1}_{\mathbf{xx}}, \ldots, H^{x_{n(x)}}_{\mathbf{xx}}, H^{y_1}_{\mathbf{xx}}, \ldots, H^{y_{n(y)}}_{\mathbf{xx}} \right].$$

The element $h^{x_i}_{x_j x_k}$ in this vector has the index $ix(i, j, k) = (i-1)n(x)^2 + (j-1)n(x) + k$. The index of $h^{y_i}_{x_j x_k}$ is $iy(i, j, k) = n(x)^3 + ix(i, j, k)$. Using the functions ix and iy it is easy to loop over $j = 1, \ldots, n(x)$, $k = 1, \ldots, n(x)$, and $i = 1, \ldots, n(x) + n(y)$ to set up the matrix A and the vector $\mathbf{q}$ from (2.77a).

The elements of the matrices $H^i_{\mathbf{xz}}$ solve

$$\mathbf{h}^T_{x_j z_k} g^i_{[\mathbf{y}, \mathbf{x}', \mathbf{y}']} = -\left[1, \mathbf{h}^T_{x_j}\right] g^i_{[x_j, \mathbf{y}, \mathbf{x}', \mathbf{y}'][\mathbf{y}, \mathbf{x}', \mathbf{y}', z_k, \mathbf{z}']} \begin{bmatrix} \mathbf{h}_{z_k} \\ 1 \\ \pi_{1k} \\ \vdots \\ \pi_{n(z)k} \end{bmatrix}, \quad (2.78)$$

$i = 1, \ldots, n(x) + n(y)$, $j = 1, \ldots, n(x)$, $k = 1, \ldots, n(z)$,

where π_{lk} is the element in the lth row and kth column of the matrix Π from equation (2.73e). This system is derived from differentiating (2.76) with respect to z_k. The elements of the vector $\mathbf{h}_{z_k}$ are the derivatives of (2.75) with respect to z_k:

$$\mathbf{h}^T_{z_k} := \left[h^{y_1}_{z_k}, \ldots, h^{y_{n(y)}}_{z_k}, h^{x_1}_{z_k}, \ldots, h^{x_{n(x)}}_{z_k}, \Delta^3_1, \ldots, \Delta^3_{n(y)} \right],$$

$$\Delta^3_i = \sum_{l=1}^{n(x)} h^{y_i}_{x_l} h^{x_l}_{z_k} + \sum_{l=1}^{n(z)} h^{y_i}_{z_l} \pi_{lk}. \quad (2.79)$$

Differentiating the elements of (2.77b) with respect to z_k provides the vector $\mathbf{h}_{x_j z_k}$:

$$\mathbf{h}^T_{x_j z_k} := \left[h^{y_1}_{x_j z_k}, \ldots, h^{y_{n(y)}}_{x_j z_k}, h^{x_1}_{x_j z_k}, \ldots, h^{x_{n(y)}}_{x_j z_k}, \Delta^4_1, \ldots, \Delta^4_{n(y)} \right],$$

$$\Delta^4_i := \sum_{l=1}^{n(x)} h^{y_i}_{x_l} h^{x_l}_{x_j z_k} + \sum_{l=1}^{n(x)} h^{x_l}_{x_j} \left[\sum_{r=1}^{n(x)} h^{y_i}_{x_l x_r} h^{x_r}_{z_k} + \sum_{r=1}^{n(z)} h^{y_i}_{x_l z_r} \pi_{rk} \right].$$

The system of equations (2.78) may also be written as $A\mathbf{w} = \mathbf{q}$. But note that different from (2.77a) the lhs of (2.78) not only contains the elements of $H^i_{\mathbf{xz}}$ but also terms that belong to the vector $\mathbf{q}$.

To obtain the matrices $H^i_{\mathbf{zz}}$ we first differentiate (2.73a) with respect to z_j and then with respect to z_k. The result is:

$$\mathbf{h}^T_{z_j z_k} g^i_{[\mathbf{y},\mathbf{x}',\mathbf{y}']} = -\left[\mathbf{h}^T_{z_j}, 1, \pi_{1j}, \ldots, \pi_{n(z),j}\right]$$

$$\times g^i_{[\mathbf{y},\mathbf{x}',\mathbf{y}',z_j,\mathbf{z}'][\mathbf{y},\mathbf{x}',\mathbf{y}',z_k,\mathbf{z}']} \begin{bmatrix} \mathbf{h}_{z_k} \\ 1 \\ \pi_{1k} \\ \vdots \\ \pi_{n(z),k} \end{bmatrix}, \qquad (2.80)$$

$$\mathbf{h}^T_{z_j z_k} = \left[h^{y_1}_{z_j z_k}, \ldots, h^{y_{n(y)}}_{z_j z_k}, h^{x_1}_{z_j z_k}, \ldots, h^{x_{n(x)}}_{z_j z_j}, \Delta^5_1, \ldots, \Delta^5_{n(y)}\right],$$

$$\Delta^5_i = \sum_{l=1}^{n(x)} h^{y_i}_{x_l} h^{x_l}_{z_j z_k}$$

$$+ \sum_{l=1}^{n(x)} h^{x_l}_{z_j} \left[\sum_{r=1}^{n(x)} h^{y_i}_{x_l x_r} h^{x_r}_{z_k} + \sum_{r=1}^{n(z)} h^{y_i}_{x_l z_r} \pi_{rk}\right]$$

$$+ \sum_{l=1}^{n(z)} \pi_{lj} \left[\sum_{r=1}^{n(x)} h^{y_i}_{z_l x_r} h^{x_r}_{z_k} + \sum_{r=1}^{n(z)} h^{y_i}_{z_l z_r} \pi_{rk}\right].$$

In the last step, we determine $H^i_{\sigma\sigma}$. Differentiating (2.73a) twice with respect to σ yields

$$0 = E\left\{\mathbf{h}^T_{\sigma\sigma} g^i_{[\mathbf{y},\mathbf{x}',\mathbf{y}']}\right\}$$

$$+ E\left\{\left[\mathbf{h}^T_\sigma, \Delta^6_1, \ldots, \Delta^6_{n(z)}\right] g^i_{[\mathbf{y},\mathbf{x}',\mathbf{y}',\mathbf{z}'][\mathbf{y},\mathbf{x}',\mathbf{y}',\mathbf{z}']} \begin{bmatrix} \mathbf{h}_\sigma \\ \Delta^6_1 \\ \vdots \\ \Delta^6_{n(z)} \end{bmatrix}\right\},$$

$$\Delta^6_i := \sum_{s=1}^{n(z)} \omega_{is} \epsilon'_s, \qquad (2.81)$$

2.5 Quadratic Approximation

where ω_{is} is the element in the ith row and sth column of the matrix Ω from equation (2.73e). At the stationary equilibrium, the vector $\mathbf{h}_\sigma$ is given by

$$\mathbf{h}_\sigma^T = \left[\underbrace{0,\ldots,0,}_{n(y) \text{ elements}} \underbrace{0,\ldots,0,}_{n(x) \text{ elements}} \Delta_1^7,\ldots,\Delta_{n(y)}^7 \right],$$

$$\Delta_i^7 = \sum_{s=1}^{n(z)} h_{z_s}^{y_i} \sum_{r=1}^{n(z)} \omega_{sr} \epsilon_r',$$

since in the general model as well as in our example $h_\sigma^{y_i} = h_\sigma^{x_j} = 0$. The vector $\mathbf{h}_{\sigma\sigma}$ is given by

$$\mathbf{h}_{\sigma\sigma}^T = \left[h_{\sigma\sigma}^{y_1},\ldots,h_{\sigma\sigma}^{y_{n(y)}}, h_{\sigma\sigma}^{x_1},\ldots,h_{\sigma\sigma}^{x_{n(x)}}, \Delta_1^8,\ldots,\Delta_{n(y)}^8 \right],$$

$$\Delta_i^8 = \sum_{s=1}^{n(x)} h_{x_s}^{y_i} h_{\sigma\sigma}^{x_s}$$

$$+ \sum_{s=1}^{n(x)} h_\sigma^{x_s} \left(\sum_{r=1}^{n(x)} h_{x_s x_r}^{y_i} h_\sigma^{x_r} + \sum_{r=1}^{n(z)} h_{x_s z_r}^{y_i} \sum_{t=1}^{n(z)} \omega_{rt} \epsilon_t' + h_{x_s \sigma}^{y_i} \right)$$

$$+ \sum_{s=1}^{n(z)} \left(\sum_{r=1}^{n(z)} \omega_{sr} \epsilon_r' \right) \left[\sum_{t=1}^{n(x)} h_{z_s x_t}^{y_i} h_\sigma^{x_t} + \sum_{t=1}^{n(z)} h_{z_s z_t}^{y_i} \sum_{u=1}^{n(z)} \omega_{tu} \epsilon_u' \right]$$

$$+ \sum_{s=1}^{n(x)} h_{\sigma x_s}^{y_i} h_\sigma^{x_s} + \sum_{s=1}^{n(z)} h_{\sigma z_s}^{y_i} \sum_{r=1}^{n(z)} \omega_{sr} \epsilon_r' + h_{\sigma\sigma}^{y_i}.$$

Consider the expectation of the first term on the rhs of (2.81) and note that

1. the vector $g_{[\mathbf{y},\mathbf{x}',\mathbf{y}']}^i$ does not contain any stochastic variables,
2. in addition to $h_\sigma^{y_i} = 0$ and $h_\sigma^{x_i} = 0$ also $h_{\sigma z_s}^{y_i} = h_{\sigma x_s}^{y_i} = 0$,
3. $E(\epsilon_i' \epsilon_j') = 0$ for all $i \neq j$ and $E(\epsilon_i' \epsilon_i') = 1$.

Therefore, we get

$$E\left\{\mathbf{h}_{\sigma\sigma}^{T} g_{[\mathbf{y},\mathbf{x'},\mathbf{y'}]}^{i}\right\}$$
$$=\left[h_{\sigma\sigma}^{y_{1}},\ldots,h_{\sigma\sigma}^{y_{n(y)}},h_{\sigma\sigma}^{x_{1}},\ldots,h_{\sigma\sigma}^{x_{n(x)}},\Delta_{1}^{9},\ldots,\Delta_{n(y)}^{9}\right]g_{[\mathbf{y},\mathbf{x'},\mathbf{y'}]}^{i},$$

$$\Delta_{i}^{9}=\sum_{s=1}^{n(x)} h_{x_{s}}^{y_{i}} h_{\sigma\sigma}^{x_{s}} + h_{\sigma\sigma}^{y_{i}} + \sum_{s=1}^{n(z)}\sum_{r=1}^{n(z)} h_{z_{s}z_{r}}^{y_{i}} \sum_{t=1}^{n(z)} \omega_{st}\omega_{rt}.$$

By using a well known property of the trace operator, the expectation of the second term on the rhs of (2.81) equals[20]

$$\operatorname{tr}\left\{g_{[\mathbf{y'},\mathbf{z'}][\mathbf{y'},\mathbf{z'}]}^{i} E\left[\Delta_{1}^{7},\ldots,\Delta_{n(y)}^{7},\Delta_{1}^{6},\ldots,\Delta_{n(z)}^{6}\right]\begin{bmatrix}\Delta_{1}^{7}\\ \vdots \\ \Delta_{n(y)}^{7} \\ \Delta_{1}^{6} \\ \vdots \\ \Delta_{n(z)}^{6}\end{bmatrix}\right\}.$$

The expectation of the cross-products involved in this expression are readily evaluated to be

$$E\left[\Delta_{i}^{7}\Delta_{j}^{7}\right]=\sum_{q=1}^{n(z)}\sum_{s=1}^{n(z)} h_{z_{q}}^{y_{i}} h_{z_{s}}^{y_{j}} \sum_{r=1}^{n(z)} \omega_{qr}\omega_{sr},$$

$$E\left[\Delta_{i}^{7}\Delta_{j}^{6}\right]=\sum_{s=1}^{n(z)} h_{z_{s}}^{y_{i}} \sum_{r=1}^{n(z)} \omega_{sr}\omega_{jr},$$

$$E\left[\Delta_{i}^{6}\Delta_{j}^{6}\right]=\sum_{r=1}^{n(z)} \omega_{ir}\omega_{jr}.$$

Implementation. Our Gauss program `SolveQA` implements the computation of the Hesse matrices H^i in (2.74). It requires the coefficients of the linear part, the matrices Π, Ω, the Jacobian matrix of **g** stored in a matrix `gmat`, say, and the $n(x)+n(y)$ Hesse matrices of g^i as input. The latter must be gathered in a three-dimensional array `hcube`, say. The program returns two

---

[20] The second term on the rhs of (2.81), say a, is a scalar so that $a = \operatorname{tr}(a)$. Yet, for any two conformable matrices A and B, it holds that $\operatorname{tr}(AB) = \operatorname{tr}(BA)$.

three-dimensional arrays: xcube contains the $n(x)$ Hesse matrices H^{x_i} and ycube stores the $n(y)$ Hesse matrices H^{y_i}.

Of course, there is other software available on the world wide web. SCHMITT-GROHÉ and URIBE (2004) provide Matlab programs that compute the matrices of the quadratic part in our equation (2.74). An advantage of their program is its ability to handle symbolic differentiation if you own the respective Matlab toolbox. Other programs that can handle quadratic approximations are Dynare[21] mainly developed by JUILLARD and Gensys written by SIMS.[22]

2.6 Applications

In this section we consider three applications of the methods presented in the previous sections. First, we solve the benchmark model introduced in Chapter 1, second, we consider a simplified version of the time-to-build model of KYDLAND and PRESCOTT (1982), and third, we develop a monetary model with nominal rigidities that give raise to what has been called the New Keynesian Phillips curve.

2.6.1 The Benchmark Model

In Example 1.5.1, we present the benchmark model, in which a representative agent chooses feed-back rules for consumption and labor supply that maximize his expected live time utility over an infinite time horizon. This section shows how we can obtain linear and quadratic approximations of these feed-back rules by using the methods introduced in Sections 2.2 through 2.5.

Linear and Quadratic Policy Functions. Our starting point is the system of stochastic difference equations which we obtained

---
[21] See the user's guide written by GRIFFOLI (2007).
[22] See KIM, KIM, SCHAUMBURG, and SIMS (2005) on this program.

in Section 1.5. We repeat these equations for your convenience:[23]

$$0 = c_t^{-\eta}(1-N_t)^{\theta(1-\eta)} - \lambda_t, \tag{2.82a}$$
$$0 = \theta c_t^{1-\eta}(1-N_t)^{\theta(1-\eta)-1} - (1-\alpha)\lambda_t Z_t N_t^{-\alpha} k_t^\alpha, \tag{2.82b}$$
$$0 = ak_{t+1} - (1-\delta)k_t + c_t - Z_t N_t^{1-\alpha} k_t^\alpha, \tag{2.82c}$$
$$0 = \lambda_t - \beta a^{-\eta} E_t \lambda_{t+1}\left(1 - \delta + \alpha Z_{t+1} N_{t+1}^{1-\alpha} k_{t+1}^{\alpha-1}\right). \tag{2.82d}$$

Equation (2.82a) states that the shadow price of an additional unit of capital, λ_t, must equal the agent's marginal utility of consumption. Condition (2.82b) equates the marginal rate of substitution between consumption and leisure with the marginal product of labor. Equation (2.82c) is the economy's resource constraint. According to equation (2.82d) the marginal utility of consumption must equal the discounted expected utility value of the return on investment in the future stock of capital. We complete the model by specifying the law of motion for the natural log of the productivity shock $z_t := \ln Z_t$:

$$z_t = \varrho z_{t-1} + \epsilon_t, \quad \epsilon_t \sim N(0, \sigma^2). \tag{2.82e}$$

In Section 1.5 we explain the choice of the model's parameters α, β, δ, η, and θ. With these values at hand, we can compute the stationary solution (k, λ, c, N) from equations (1.46). The vectors $\mathbf{x}_t$, $\mathbf{u}_t$, and $\boldsymbol{\lambda}_t$ from equations (2.47) are then given by $\mathbf{x}_t \equiv k_t - k$, $\boldsymbol{\lambda}_t \equiv \lambda_t - \lambda$, $\mathbf{u}_t := [c_t - c, N_t - N]'$, and $\mathbf{z}_t \equiv \ln Z_t$. In our Fortran program Benchmark.for we use numeric differentiation of (2.82) at (k, λ, c, N) to obtain the Jacobian matrix gmat. From this matrix we derive the coefficients of the matrices C_u, $C_{x\lambda}$, C_z, $D_{x\lambda}$, $F_{x\lambda}$, D_u, F_u, D_z, and F_z, that appear in (2.47). A call to SolveLA returns the coefficients of the linear approximate policy functions. To obtain the coefficients of the quadratic part, we differentiate each equation of (2.82) twice using CDHesse. This

---

[23] The symbols have the following meaning: C_t is consumption, N_t are working hours, K_t is the stock of capital, Λ_t is the shadow price of an additional unit of capital and Z_t is the level of total factor productivity. Except for $\lambda_t := A_t^\eta \Lambda_t$, the other lower case variables are scaled by the level of labor-augmenting technical progress A_t, that is, $c_t := C_t/A_t$ and $k_t := K_t/A_t$.

provides the three dimensional array hcube that is an input to SolveQA. Thus, it requires four steps to compute the solutions:

Step 1: solve for (k, λ, c, n),
Step 2: write a procedure that receives the vector of 10 elements $(k, \lambda, c, n, z, k', \lambda', c', n', z')$ and that returns the lhs of (2.82),
Step 3: compute gmat and hcube by using CDJac and CDHesse, respectively,
Step 4: set up the matrices required by SolveLA and SolveQA.

Linear Quadratic Algorithm. At first sight, it seems that the law of motion of the productivity shock z_t in equation (2.82e) is the only linear equation of the benchmark model. Yet, if we use investment expenditures

$$i_t = Z_t N_t^{1-\alpha} k_t^\alpha - c_t \qquad (2.83)$$

instead of consumption c_t, equation (2.82c) can be written as:

$$k_{t+1} = \frac{1}{a} i_t + \frac{1-\delta}{a} k_t, \qquad (2.84)$$

which is linear in k_{t+1}, k_t, and i_t. Let $\mathbf{x}_t := [1, k_t, z_t]'$ denote the vector of states and $\mathbf{u}_t := [i_t, N_t]'$ the vector of controls. Then, for our model, the transition equation (2.31) is given by:

$$\mathbf{x}_{t+1} = \underbrace{\begin{bmatrix} 1 & 0 & 0 \\ 0 & (1-\delta)/a & 0 \\ 0 & 0 & \varrho \end{bmatrix}}_{A} \mathbf{x}_t + \underbrace{\begin{bmatrix} 0 & 0 \\ 1/a & 0 \\ 0 & 0 \end{bmatrix}}_{B} \mathbf{u}_t + \begin{bmatrix} 0 \\ 0 \\ \epsilon_t \end{bmatrix}. \qquad (2.85)$$

The remaining non-linearities are handled by the algorithm. The current period return function in the scaled variables is given by:

$$g(\mathbf{x}, \mathbf{u}) := \frac{1}{1-\eta} \left(e^{z_t} N_t^{1-\alpha} k_t^\alpha - i_t \right)^{1-\eta} (1 - N_t)^{\theta(1-\eta)}.$$

You must write a subroutine, say GProc, that takes the vector ybar=$[1, k, z, i, N]'$ as input and returns the value of g at this point.

There is a final issue that concerns the appropriate discount factor. The value function v that solves the Bellman equation

$$v(k,z) = \max_{k',N} \; u\left(e^z N^{1-\alpha} k^\alpha + (1-\delta)k - ak', 1 - N\right)$$
$$+ \tilde{\beta} E\left[v(k',z')|z\right]$$

is a function in the scaled variables. It is, thus, inappropriate to use β which pertains to the original variables. $\tilde{\beta}$ is found by observing that equations (2.82) solve the following scaled problem:

$$\max_{c_0, N_0} \sum_{t=0}^{\infty} \tilde{\beta}^t \left\{ \left[\frac{c_t^{1-\eta}(1-N_t)^{\theta(1-\eta)}}{1-\eta} \right. \right.$$
$$\left. \left. + \lambda_t \left(Z_t N_t^{1-\alpha} k_t^\alpha + (1-\delta)k_t - c_t - ak_{t+1}\right) \right] \right\}, \quad (2.86)$$

$$\tilde{\beta} := \beta a^{1-\eta}.$$

Other Variables of Interest. Both the program SolveLA and SolveQA provide approximations of the policy functions for k_{t+1}, c_t, and N_t. From these we obtain the solution for output y_t, investment i_t, and the real wage w_t, respectively, via

$$y_t = Z_t N_t^{1-\alpha} k_t^\alpha, \quad (2.87a)$$
$$i_t = y_t - c_t, \quad (2.87b)$$
$$w_t = (1-\alpha) Z_t N_t^{-\alpha} k_t^\alpha. \quad (2.87c)$$

The program SolveLQA provides linear approximate solutions for i_t and N_t from which we derive c_t via equation (2.87b). Given c_t the resource constraint (2.82c) yields the solution for k_{t+1}.

Time series for output y_t, consumption c_t, investment i_t, hours N_t, and the real wage w_t are derived by iterations that start at the stationary solution $k_1 = k$. We use a random number generator to obtain a sequence of innovations $\{\epsilon_t\}_{t=1}^T$. The sequence of capital stocks and the sequence of productivity shocks follow from

$$\left. \begin{array}{l} k_{t+1} = \hat{h}^k(k_t, z_t), \\ z_{t+1} = \varrho z_t + \epsilon_{t+1}, \end{array} \right\} t = 1, 2, \ldots, T-1,$$

where $\hat{h}^k(\cdot)$ denotes the approximate policy function for the next-period stock of capital. Once we have computed the sequences $\{k_t\}_{t=1}^T$ and $\{z_t\}_{t=1}^T$, the sequences for the other variables of the model are obtained from the respective approximate policy functions and from (2.87).

Results. Table 2.2 summarizes the results of our simulations carried out with the Fortran program Benchmark.for. We used the parameter values from Table 1.1. The length T of our artificial time series for output, investment, consumption, working hours, and the real wage is 60 quarters.[24] The second moments displayed in Table 2.2 refer to HP-filtered percentage deviations from a variable's stationary solution.[25] They are averages over 500 simulations. We use the same sequence of shocks for all three solution methods to prevent random differences in the results.

The first message from Table 2.2 is that except for the small difference in the standard deviation of investment of 0.01 between the linear and the linear quadratic solution there are virtually no differences in the second moments across our three different methods. There are, however, differences in accuracy. As explained in Section 1.6.2, we use two measures of accuracy: the residuals of the Euler equation (2.82d) and the DM-statistic.

The Euler equation residuals are computed over a grid of 400 equally spaced points over the square $[\underline{k}; \overline{k}] \times [\underline{z}; \overline{z}]$. We choose $\underline{z} = \ln 0.95$ and $\overline{z} = \ln 1.05$ because in more than ninety percent of our simulations z_t remains in this interval. The largest interval for the stock of capital that we consider is $\mathscr{K} = [0.8; 1.2]k$, where k is the stationary solution. Yet, even the much smaller interval $[0.9; 1.1]k$ covers all simulated sequences of the capital stock. We compute the Euler equation residual as the rate by which consumption had to be raised over $\hat{h}^c(k, z)$ so that the lhs of equation (2.82d) matches its rhs. The numbers displayed in Table 2.2 are the maximum absolute values over the square indicated in the left-most column of the table.

---

[24] See Section 1.5 on the issues of parameter choice and model evaluation.
[25] See Section 12.4 on the HP-Filter.

Table 2.2

	Linear			Linear Quadratic			Quadratic		
	\multicolumn{9}{c}{Second Moments}								
Variable	s_x	r_{xy}	r_x	s_x	r_{xy}	r_x	s_x	r_{xy}	r_x
Output	1.44	1.00	0.64	1.44	1.00	0.64	1.44	1.00	0.64
Investment	6.11	1.00	0.64	6.12	1.00	0.64	6.11	1.00	0.64
Consumption	0.56	0.99	0.66	0.56	0.99	0.66	0.56	0.99	0.66
Hours	0.77	1.00	0.64	0.77	1.00	0.64	0.77	1.00	0.64
Real Wage	0.67	0.99	0.65	0.67	0.99	0.65	0.67	0.99	0.65
				Euler Equation Residuals					
$[0.90; 1.10]k$	1.835E-4			7.656E-4			1.456E-5		
$[0.85; 1.15]k$	3.478E-4			9.322E-4			4.085E-5		
$[0.80; 1.20]k$	5.670E-4			1.100E-3			8.845E-5		
				DM-Statistic					
<3.816	2.0			1.3			2.7		
>21.920	3.4			8.9			3.0		

Notes: s_x:=standard deviation of variable x, r_{xy}:=cross correlation of variable x with output, r_x:=first order autocorrelation of variable x. All second moments refer to HP-filtered percentage deviations from a variable's stationary solution. Euler equation residuals are computed as maximum absolute value over a grid of 400 equally spaced points on the square $\mathscr{K} \times [\ln 0.95; \ln 1.05]$, where $\mathscr{K}$ is defined in the respective row of the left-most column. The 2.5 and the 97.5 percent critical values of the $\chi^2(11)$-distribution are displayed in the last two lines of the first column. The table entries refer to the percentage fraction out of 1,000 simulations where the DM-statistic is below (above) its respective critical value.

First, note that all residuals are quite small. Even in the worst case, the required change of consumption is merely 0.11 percent. Second, and as expected from a local method, accuracy diminishes with the distance from the stationary solution. For instance, consider the linear policy function. The Euler equation residual over $[0.85; 1.15]k$ ($[0.8; 1.2]k$) is almost two times (three times) larger than the maximum residual over $[0.9; 1.1]k$. Third, the Euler equation residuals of the linear quadratic approach are worse than those of the linear approach. For the former, the maximum absolute Euler equation residual over $[0.9; 1.1]k$ is more than four times larger than the Euler equation residual of the linear solution method. Fourth, although the quadratic policy function delivers a more accurate solution than the linear policy function, the difference between the respective Euler equation residuals becomes smaller as one moves further away from the stationary solution: Over $[0.9; 1.1]k$ the Euler equation residual of the linear solution is more than twelve times larger than the Euler equation residual of the quadratic solution. Yet over $[0.8; 1.2]k$ it is only six times larger. Fifth, there are several possible ways to compute the Euler equation residuals. For instance, since both the linear and the quadratic perturbation method deliver a policy function for λ, we could use this function in the computation. We, however, used the policy functions for consumption and hours and inferred λ from equation (2.82a), since the linear quadratic approach delivers only policy functions for investment and hours. The difference is considerable: When we use the linear approximate policy function for λ we find a maximum Euler equation residual over $[0.9; 1.1]k$ that is 26 times larger than that displayed in Table 2.2.

As explained in Section 1.6.2 (and more formally in Section 12.3), the DM-statistic aims to detect systematic forecast errors with respect to the rhs of the Euler equation (2.82d). For this purpose, we simulate the model and compute the ex-post forecast error

$$e_t := \beta a^{-\eta} \lambda_{t+1} \left(1 - \delta + \alpha Z_{t+1} N_{t+1}^{1-\alpha} k_{t+1}^{\alpha-1}\right) - \lambda_t,$$

where λ_t is given by equation (2.82a). We use simulated time series with many periods so that the asymptotic properties of the test statistic will apply. The simulations always start at the stationary solution. To prevent the influence of the model's transitional dynamics on our results, we discard a small fraction of the initial observations. In effect, we use 3,000 points. We regress e_t on a constant, five lags of consumption, and five lags of the productivity shock and compute the Wald-statistic (which is the DM-statistic in this context) of the null that all coefficients from this regression are equal to zero. We use White's (1980) heteroscedasticity robust covariance estimator. Under the null the Wald-statistic has a χ^2-distribution with 11 degrees of freedom. We run 1,000 tests and computed the fraction of the DM-statistic below (above) the 2.5 (97.5) percent critical value (displayed in the first column of Table 2.2). If systematic errors are not present, about 2.5 percent of our simulations should yield test statistics below (above) the respective critical values. Both, the linear and the quadratic policy functions provide satisfactory results. Yet, the linear policy functions obtained from the linear-quadratic approach are less good. The null is far more often rejected than can be expected, namely in almost 9 percent of our simulations.

Finally, note that the second moments as well as the DM-statistic depend on the random numbers used for the productivity shock z_t. Thus, when you repeat our calculations, you will find at least small differences to our results.

2.6.2 Time to Build

Gestation Period. In the benchmark model investment projects require one quarter to complete. In their classic article KYDLAND and PRESCOTT (1982) use a more realistic gestation period. Based on published studies of investment projects they assume that it takes four quarters for an investment project to be finished. The investment costs are spread out evenly over this period. Yet, the business cycle in this extended model is similar to the business cycle in their benchmark model with a one quarter lag. We introduce the time-to-build assumption into the benchmark model of the previous section. Our results confirm their findings. Nevertheless, we think this venture is worth the while, since it nicely demonstrates the ease of applying the linear quadratic solution algorithm to a rather tricky dynamic model.

The model that we consider uses the same specification of the household's preferences and production technology as the model in the previous section. The timing of investment expenditures differs from this model in the following way. In each quarter t the representative household launches a new investment project. After four quarters this project is finished and adds to the capital stock. The investment costs are spread out over the entire gestation period. More formally, let S_{it}, $i = 1, 2, 3, 4$ denote an investment project that is finished after i periods and that requires the household to pay the fraction ω_i of its total costs. At any period, there are four unfinished projects so that total investment expenditures I_t amount to

$$I_t = \sum_{i=1}^{4} \omega_i S_{it}, \quad \sum_{i=1}^{4} \omega_i = 1. \tag{2.88}$$

Obviously, the S_{it} are related to each other in the following way:

$$\begin{aligned} S_{1t+1} &= S_{2t}, \\ S_{2t+1} &= S_{3t}, \\ S_{3t+1} &= S_{4t}, \end{aligned} \tag{2.89}$$

and the capital stock evolves according to

$$K_{t+1} = (1-\delta)K_t + S_{1t}. \tag{2.90}$$

First-Order Conditions. Since the model exhibits growth, we transform it to a stationary problem. As in Section 2.6.1 we put $c_t := C_t/A_t$, $i_t := I_t/A_t$, $k_t := K_t/A_t$, $\lambda_t := \Lambda_t A_t^\eta$, $s_{it} = S_{it}/A_t$, and $\tilde{\beta} := \beta a^{1-\eta}$. In this model, the vector of states is $\mathbf{x}_t = [1, k_t, s_{1t}, s_{2t}, s_{3t}, \ln Z_t]'$ and the vector of controls is $\mathbf{u} = [s_{4t}, N_t]'$. From (2.89) and (2.90) we derive the following law of motion of the stationary variables:

$$\mathbf{x}_{t+1} = \underbrace{\begin{bmatrix} 1 & 0 & 0 & 0 & 0 & 0 \\ 0 & \frac{1-\delta}{a} & \frac{1}{a} & 0 & 0 & 0 \\ 0 & 0 & 0 & \frac{1}{a} & 0 & 0 \\ 0 & 0 & 0 & 0 & \frac{1}{a} & 0 \\ 0 & 0 & 0 & 0 & 0 & 0 \\ 0 & 0 & 0 & 0 & 0 & \rho \end{bmatrix}}_{:=A} \mathbf{x}_t + \underbrace{\begin{bmatrix} 0 & 0 \\ 0 & 0 \\ 0 & 0 \\ 0 & 0 \\ \frac{1}{a} & 0 \\ 0 & 0 \end{bmatrix}}_{=:B} \mathbf{u}_t + \begin{bmatrix} 0 \\ 0 \\ 0 \\ 0 \\ 0 \\ \epsilon_t \end{bmatrix}. \tag{2.91}$$

The remaining task is to compute the stationary equilibrium. Consider the Lagrangean of the stationary problem:

$$\mathcal{L} = E_0 \sum_{t=0}^{\infty} \tilde{\beta}^t \left\{ \frac{c_t^{1-\eta}(1-N_t)^{\theta(1-\eta)}}{1-\eta} \right.$$
$$+ \lambda_t \left(Z_t N_t^{1-\alpha} k_t^{\alpha} - \sum_{i=1}^{4} \omega_i s_{it} - c_t \right)$$
$$\left. + \gamma_t ((1-\delta)k_t + s_{1t} - a k_{t+1}) \right\},$$

where γ_t is the Lagrange multiplier of the transformed constraint (2.90). Differentiating this expression with respect to c_t, N_t, s_{4t} and k_{t+4} provides the following conditions:[26]

$$\lambda_t = c_t^{-\eta}(1-N_t)^{\theta(1-\eta)}, \qquad (2.92a)$$

$$\frac{\theta c_t}{1-N_t} = (1-\alpha) Z_t N_t^{-\alpha} k_t^{\alpha}, \qquad (2.92b)$$

$$0 = E_t \big[-\omega_4 \lambda_t - (\tilde{\beta}/a)\omega_3 \lambda_{t+1} - (\tilde{\beta}/a)^2 \omega_2 \lambda_{t+2} \qquad (2.92c)$$
$$- (\tilde{\beta}/a)^3 \omega_1 \lambda_{t+3} + (\tilde{\beta}/a)^3 \gamma_{t+3} \big],$$
$$0 = E_t \big[-(\tilde{\beta}/a)^3 \gamma_{t+3} + (\tilde{\beta}/a)^4 (1-\delta)\gamma_{t+4} \qquad (2.92d)$$
$$+ (\tilde{\beta}/a)^4 \lambda_{t+4} \alpha Z_{t+4} N_{t+4}^{1-\alpha} k_{t+4}^{\alpha-1} \big].$$

The first and the second condition are standard and need no comment. The third and the fourth condition imply the following Euler equation in the shadow price of capital:

$$0 = E_t \big\{ \omega_4 [(\tilde{\beta}/a)(1-\delta)\lambda_{t+1} - \lambda_t]$$
$$+ \omega_3 (\tilde{\beta}/a)[(\tilde{\beta}/a)(1-\delta)\lambda_{t+2} - \lambda_{t+1}]$$
$$+ \omega_2 (\tilde{\beta}/a)^2 [(\tilde{\beta}/a)(1-\delta)\lambda_{t+3} - \lambda_{t+2}]$$
$$+ \omega_1 (\tilde{\beta}/a)^3 [(\tilde{\beta}/a)(1-\delta)\lambda_{t+4} - \lambda_{t+3}]$$
$$+ (\tilde{\beta}/a)^4 \alpha \lambda_{t+4} Z_{t+4} N_{t+4}^{1-\alpha} k_{t+4}^{\alpha-1} \big\}.$$

---

[26] To keep track of the various terms that involve s_{4t} and k_{t+4}, it is helpful to write out the sum for $t = 0, 1, 2, 3, 4$.

2.6 Applications

Stationary Equilibrium. On a balanced growth path, where $Z_t = 1$ and $\lambda_t = \lambda_{t+1}$ for all t, this expression reduces to

$$\frac{y}{k} = \frac{a - \tilde{\beta}(1-\delta)}{\alpha\tilde{\beta}}\left[\omega_1 + (a/\tilde{\beta})\omega_2 + (a/\tilde{\beta})^2\omega_3 + (a/\tilde{\beta})^3\omega_4\right]. \tag{2.93}$$

Given a, β, δ, and η, we can solve this equation for the output-capital ratio y/k. From $(1-\delta)k + s_1 = ak$ we find $s_1 = (a+\delta-1)k$, the stationary level of new investment projects started in each period. Total investment per unit of capital is then given by

$$\frac{i}{k} = \frac{1}{k}\sum_{i=1}^{4}\omega_i s_i = (a+\delta-1)\sum_{i=1}^{4}a^{i-1}\omega_i.$$

Using this, we can solve for

$$\frac{c}{k} = \frac{y}{k} - \frac{i}{k}.$$

Since $y/c = (y/k)/(c/k)$, we can finally solve the stationary version of (2.92b) for N. This solution in turn provides $k = N(y/k)^{1/(\alpha-1)}$, which allows us to solve for i and c. The final step is to write a procedure that returns the current period utility as a function of **x** and **u**. The latter is given by:

$$g(\mathbf{x}, \mathbf{u}) := \frac{1}{1-\eta}\left(e^{\ln Z_t}N_t^{1-\alpha}k_t^{\alpha} - \sum_{i=1}^{4}s_{it}\right)^{1-\eta}(1-N_t)^{\theta(1-\eta)}.$$

Results. The Gauss program ToB.g implements the solution. We use the parameter values from Table 1.1 and assume $\omega_i = 0.25$, $i = 1,\ldots,4$. Table 2.3 displays the averages of 500 time series moments computed from the simulated model. We used the same random numbers in both the simulations of the benchmark model and the simulations of the time-to-build model. Thus, the differences revealed in Table 2.3 are systematic and not random.

In the time-to-build economy output, investment, and hours are a little less volatile than in the benchmark economy. The intuition behind this result is straightforward. When a positive technological shock hits the benchmark economy the household takes

Table 2.3

	Benchmark			Time to Build		
Variable	s_x	r_{xy}	r_x	s_x	r_{xy}	r_x
Output	1.45	1.00	0.63	1.37	1.00	0.63
Investment	6.31	0.99	0.63	5.85	0.99	0.65
Consumption	0.57	0.99	0.65	0.58	0.97	0.56
Hours	0.78	1.00	0.63	0.71	0.98	0.65
Real Wage	0.68	0.99	0.64	0.68	0.98	0.58

Notes: s_x:=standard deviation of HP-filtered simulated series of variable x, r_{xy}:=cross correlation of variable x with output, r_x:=first order autocorrelation of variable x.

the chance, works more at the higher real wage and transfers part of the increased income via capital accumulation into future periods. Since the shock is highly autocorrelated, the household can profit from the still above average marginal product of capital in the next quarter. Yet in the time-to-build economy intertemporal substitution is not that easy. Income spent on additional investment projects will not pay out in terms of more capital income until the fourth quarter after the shock. However, at this time a substantial part of the shock has faded. This reduces the incentive to invest and, therefore, the incentive to work more.

LAWRENCE CHRISTIANO and RICHARD TODD (1996) embed the time-to-build structure in a model where labor augmenting technical progress follows a random walk. They use a different parameterization of the weights ω_i. Their argument is that investment projects typically begin with a lengthy planning phase. The overwhelming part of the project's costs are spent in the construction phase. As a consequence, they set $\omega_1 = 0.01$ and $\omega_2 = \omega_3 = \omega_4 = 0.33$. This model is able to account for the positive autocorrelation in output growth, whereas the KYDLAND and PRESCOTT (1982) parameterization of the same model – $\omega_i = 0.25$, $i = 1, \ldots, 4$ – is not able to replicate this empirical finding. However, the random walk assumption does not lent itself to the linear quadratic approach, and, therefore we will not pursue this matter any further.

2.6.3 New Keynesian Phillips Curve

Money in General Equilibrium. So far we have restricted our attention to non-monetary economies. In this subsection we focus on the interaction of real and monetary shocks to explain the business cycle.

Introducing money into a dynamic general equilibrium model is not an easy task. As a store of value money is dominated by other interest bearing assets like corporate and government bonds or stocks, and in the basically one-good Ramsey model there is no true need for a means of exchange. So how do we guarantee a positive value of pure fiat outside money in equilibrium?

Monetary theory has pursed three approaches (see, e.g., WALSH (2003)). The first device is to assume that money yields direct utility, the second strand of the literature imposes transaction costs, and the third way is to guarantee an exclusive role for money as a store of value. We will pursue the second approach in what follows and assume transaction costs to be proportional to the volume of trade. Moreover, a larger stock of real money balances relative to the volume of trade reduces transaction costs (see LEEPER and SIMS (1994)). Different from other approaches, as, e.g., the cash-in-advance assumption, our particular specification implies the neutrality of monetary shocks in the log-linear model solution. This allows us to focus on other deviations from the standard model that are required to explain why money has short-run real effects.

The most prominent explanation for the real effects of money that has been pursued in the recent literature are nominal rigidities that arise from sticky wages and/or prices.[27] Among the var-

---

[27] A non-exhaustive list of models of nominal rigidities includes BERGIN and FEENSTRA (2000), CHARI, KEHOE, and MCGRATTAN (2000), CHO and COOLEY (1995), COOLEY and HANSEN (1995, 1998), CHRISTIANO, EICHENBAUM, and EVANS (1997), HAIRAULT and PORTIER (1995).

ious models probably the CALVO (1983) model has gained the most widespread attention. For this reason we use the discrete time version of his assumption on price setting to introduce nominal frictions into the monetary economy that we consider in the following paragraphs.

The CALVO (1983) hypothesis provides a first-order condition for the optimal relative price of a monopolistically competitive firm that is able to adjust its price optimally whereas a fraction of other firms is not permitted to do so. The log-linear version of this condition (see equation (A.4.11e) in Appendix 4) relates the current inflation rate to the expected inflation rate and a measure of labor market tension. It thus provides solid microfoundations for the well-known Phillips curve that appears in many textbooks. This curve plays the role of a short-run aggregate supply function and relates inflation to expected inflation and cyclical unemployment.[28] In the CALVO (1983) model the deviation of marginal costs from their average level measures labor market tension. Since this equation resembles the traditional Phillips curve it is sometimes referred to as the New Keynesian Phillips curve.

The Household Sector. The representative household has the usual instantaneous utility function u defined over consumption C_t and leisure $1 - N_t$, where N_t are working hours:

$$u(C_t, 1 - N_t) := \frac{C_t^{1-\eta}(1 - N_t)^{\theta(1-\eta)}}{1 - \eta}. \tag{2.94}$$

The parameters of this function are non-negative and satisfy $\eta > \theta/(1 + \theta)$. The household receives wages, rental income from capital services, dividends D_t and a lump-sum transfer from the government T_t. We use P_t to denote the aggregate price level. The wage rate in terms of money is W_t and the rental rate in terms of consumption goods is r_t. The household allocates its income net of transaction costs TC_t to consumption, additional holdings of physical capital K_t and real money balances M_t/P_t, where M_t is the beginning-of-period stock of money. This produces the following budget constraint:

---

[28] See, e.g., MANKIW (2000), pp. 364.

$$\frac{M_{t+1} - M_t}{P_t} + K_{t+1} - (1-\delta)K_t \leq \frac{W_t}{P_t}N_t + r_t K_t + D_t \qquad (2.95)$$
$$+ T_t - TC_t - C_t.$$

Transactions costs are given by the following function

$$TC_t = \gamma \left(\frac{C_t}{M_{t+1}/P_t} \right)^\kappa C_t, \quad \gamma, \kappa > 0. \qquad (2.96)$$

Importantly, the assumption that the costs TC_t depend upon the ratio of consumption to real end-of-period money holdings M_{t+1}/P_t is responsible for the neutrality of money in our model. The household maximizes the expected discounted stream of future utility

$$E_0 \sum_{t=0}^{\infty} \beta^t u(C_t, 1 - N_t)$$

subject to (2.95) and (2.96).

Money Supply. The government sector finances the transfers to the household sector from money creation. Thus,

$$T_t = \frac{M_{t+1} - M_t}{P_t}. \qquad (2.97)$$

We assume that the monetary authority is not able to monitor the growth rate of money supply perfectly. In particular, we posit the following stochastic process for the growth factor of money supply $\mu_t := M_{t+1}/M_t$:

$$\hat{\mu}_{t+1} = \rho^\mu \hat{\mu}_t + \epsilon_t^\mu, \quad \hat{\mu}_t := \ln \mu_t - \ln \mu, \quad \epsilon_t^\mu \sim N(0, \sigma^\mu). \qquad (2.98)$$

In the stationary equilibrium money grows at the rate $\mu - 1$.

Price Setting. To motivate price setting by individual firms we assume that there is a final goods sector that assembles the output of a large number J_t of intermediary producers to the single good Y_t according to

$$Y_t = \left[J_t^{-1/\epsilon} \sum_{j=1}^{J_t} Y_{jt}^{(\epsilon-1)/\epsilon} \right]^{\epsilon/(\epsilon-1)}, \quad \epsilon > 1. \qquad (2.99)$$

The money price of intermediary product j is P_{jt} and final output sells at the price P_t. The representative firm in the final sector takes all prices as given. Maximizing its profits $P_t Y_t - \sum_{j=1}^{J_t} P_{jt} Y_j$ subject to (2.99) produces the following demand for good j:

$$Y_{jt} = \left(\frac{P_{jt}}{P_t}\right)^{-\epsilon} \frac{Y_t}{J_t}. \tag{2.100}$$

Accordingly, ϵ is the price elasticity of demand for good j. It is easy to demonstrate that the final goods producers earn no profits if the aggregate price index P_t is given by the following function:

$$P_t = \left[\frac{1}{J_t} \sum_{j=1}^{J_t} P_{jt}^{1-\epsilon}\right]^{1/(1-\epsilon)}. \tag{2.101}$$

An intermediary producer j combines labor N_{jt} and capital services K_{jt} according to the following production function:

$$Y_{jt} = Z_t (A_t N_{jt})^{1-\alpha} K_{jt}^{\alpha} - F, \quad \alpha \in (0,1), F > 0. \tag{2.102}$$

F is a fixed cost in terms of forgone output. We will use F to determine the number of firms on a balanced growth path from the zero profit condition. As in all our other models A_t is an exogenous, deterministic process for labor augmenting technical progress,

$$A_{t+1} = a A_t, \quad a \geq 1,$$

and Z_t is a stationary, stochastic process for total factor productivity that follows

$$\hat{Z}_{t+1} = \rho^Z \hat{Z}_t + \epsilon_t^Z, \quad \hat{Z}_t = \ln Z_t, \quad \epsilon_t^Z \sim N(0, \sigma^Z).$$

Note that α, F, A_t, and Z_t are common to all intermediary producers, who also face the same price elasticity ϵ.

From now on we must distinguish between two types of firms, which we label A and N, respectively. Type A firms are allowed to set their price P_{At} optimally, whereas type N firms are not. To prevent their relative price P_{Nt}/P_t from falling short of the aggregate price level, type N firms are permitted to increase their price according to the average inflation factor π. This is the inflation factor on a balanced growth path without any uncertainty. Thus

$$P_{Nt} = \pi P_{Nt-1}. \qquad (2.103)$$

To which type an individual firm j belongs is random. At each period $(1-\varphi)J_t$ of firms receive the signal to choose their optimal relative price P_{At}/P_t. The fraction $\varphi \in [0,1]$ must apply the rule (2.103). Those firms that are free to adjust their price solve the following problem:

$$\max_{P_{At}} E_t \sum_{\tau=t}^{\infty} \varphi^{\tau-t} \varrho_\tau \left[\left(\frac{\pi^{\tau-t} P_{At}}{P_\tau} \right) Y_{A\tau} - g_\tau (Y_{A\tau} + F) \right]$$

$$\text{s.t.} \quad Y_{A\tau} = \left(\frac{\pi^{\tau-t} P_{At}}{P_\tau} \right)^{-\epsilon} \frac{Y_\tau}{J_\tau}. \qquad (2.104)$$

The sum to the right of the expectations operator E_t is the discounted flow of real profits earned until the firm will be able to reset its price optimally again. Real profits are given by the value of sales in units of the final good $[(\pi^{\tau-t}P_{At})/P_\tau]Y_\tau$ minus production cost $g_\tau(Y_{A\tau}+F)$, where g_τ are the firm's variable unit costs.[29] The term $\varphi^{\tau-t}$ captures the probability that in period τ the firm is still a type N producer. ϱ_τ is the discount factor for time τ profits. We show in Section 6.3.4 that this factor is related to the household's discount factor β and marginal utility of wealth Λ_τ by the following formula:

$$\varrho_\tau = \beta^{\tau-t} \frac{\Lambda_\tau}{\Lambda_t}. \qquad (2.105)$$

Intermediary producers distribute their profits to the household sector. Thus,

---

[29] We show in Appendix 4 that g_τ also equals the firm's marginal costs. Note further that equation (2.102) implies that the firm must produce the amount $Y_{jt} + F$ in order to sell Y_{jt}.

$$D_t := \sum_{j=1}^{J_t} \frac{P_{jt}}{P_t} Y_{jt} - \frac{W_t}{P_t} N_{jt} - r_t K_{jt}. \tag{2.106}$$

This equation closes the model. To streamline the presentation we restrict ourselves to the properties of the stationary equilibrium and the simulation results. Appendix 4 provides the mathematical details of the analysis and the loglinear model used for the simulation.

Stationary Equilibrium. The model of this section depicts a growing economy. For this reason we must scale the variables so that they are stationary on a balanced growth path. As previously, we use the following definitions: $c_t := C_t/A_t$, $y_t := Y_t/A_t$, $k_t := K_t/A_t$, $\lambda_t := \Lambda_t A_t^\eta$. In addition, we define the inflation factor $\pi_t := P_t/P_{t-1}$ and real end-of-period money balances $m_t := M_{t+1}/(A_t P_t)$. The stationary equilibrium of the deterministic model has the following properties:

1. The productivity shock and the money supply shock equal their respective means $Z_t = Z \equiv 1$ and $\mu_t = \mu$ for all t.
2. Inflation is constant: $\pi = \frac{P_t}{P_{t-1}}$ for all t.
3. All (scaled) variables are constant.
4. All firms in the intermediary sector earn zero profits.

There are two immediate consequences of these assumptions. First, inflation is directly proportional to the growth rate of money supply $\mu - 1$:[30]

$$\pi = \frac{\mu}{a}.$$

Second, the optimal relative price of type A firms satisfies

$$\frac{P_A}{P} = \frac{\epsilon}{\epsilon - 1} g,$$

i.e., it is determined as a markup on the firm's marginal costs g. Furthermore, the formula for the price index given in equation (A.4.5) implies $P_A = P$ so that $g = (\epsilon - 1)/\epsilon$ and $P_N = P$. Since

---
[30] See equation (A.4.2c) for $m_t = m_{t+1}$.

2.6 Applications 149

all firms charge the same price, the market share of each producer is Y/J. Therefore, working hours and capital services are equal across firms, $N_j = N/J$, and $K_j = K/J$, and profits amount to

$$D_j = \frac{Y}{J} - g\left(\frac{Y}{J} + F\right).$$

Imposing $D_j = 0$ for all j and using $Y/J = (AN/J)^{1-\alpha}(K/J)^\alpha - (F/J)$ yields

$$j := \frac{J_t}{A_t} = \frac{N^{1-\alpha}k^\alpha}{\epsilon F}.$$

Thus, to keep profits at zero, the number of firms must increase at the rate $a - 1$ on the balanced growth path.[31] The production function (2.102) thus implies

$$y = \frac{\epsilon - 1}{\epsilon} N^{1-\alpha} k^\alpha.$$

Using this in the first-order condition for cost minimization with respect to capital services (see equation (A.4.3b)) implies

$$r = \alpha(y/k).$$

Eliminating r from the Euler equation for capital delivers the well known relation between the output-capital ratio and the household's discount factor β:

$$\frac{y}{k} = \frac{a^\eta - \beta(1-\delta)}{\alpha\beta}. \qquad (2.107a)$$

This result allows us to solve for the consumption-output ratio via the economy's resource constraint (see (A.4.9)):

$$\frac{c}{y} = \left(1 + \frac{1-a-\delta}{y/k}\right)\left[1 + \gamma\left(\frac{C}{\mu(M/P)}\right)^\kappa\right]^{-1}.$$

---
[31] Alternatively, we could have assumed that fixed costs are given by $A_t F$ so that the number of firms does not grow without bounds.

The stationary version of the Euler condition for money balances (see equation (A.4.2e)) delivers:

$$\frac{\beta a^{1-\eta}}{\mu} = 1 - \kappa\gamma \left(\frac{C}{\mu(M/P)}\right)^{1+\kappa}. \qquad (2.107b)$$

We need a final equation to determine the stationary level of working hours. Using the results obtained so far we derive this relation from the household's first-order condition with respect to labor supply (see equation (A.4.2b)):

$$\frac{N}{1-N} = \frac{1-\alpha}{\theta}\left(1+\frac{1-a-\delta}{y/k}\right)^{-1} h(c/x), \qquad (2.107c)$$

$$h(c/x) := \frac{1+\gamma(c/x)^\kappa}{1+\gamma(1+\kappa)(c/x)^\kappa}, \quad \frac{c}{x} := \frac{PC}{\mu M}.$$

It is obvious from equation (2.107a) that the output-capital ratio and therefore also the capital-labor ratio k/N and labor productivity y/N are independent of the money growth rate. As can be seen from (2.107b), the velocity of end-of-period money balances $c/x \equiv C/(\mu(M/P))$ is an increasing function of the money growth rate. In the benchmark model of Section 2.6.1 working hours are determined by the first two terms on the rhs of (2.107c). The presence of money adds the factor $h(c/x)$. It is easy to show that $h(c/x)$ is an decreasing function of the velocity of money (c/x). Since $N/(1-N)$ increases with N, steady-state working hours are a decreasing function of the money growth rate.

Calibration. We do not need to assign new values to the standard parameters of the model. The steady state relations presented in the previous paragraph show that the usual procedure to calibrate β, α, a, and δ is still valid. We will also use the empirical value of N to infer θ from (2.107c). This implies a slightly smaller value of θ as compared to the value of this parameter in the benchmark model. Nothing is really affected from this choice.

Unfortunately, there is no easy way to determine the parameters of the productivity shock, since there is no simple aggregate production function that we could use to identify Z_t. The problem becomes apparent from the following equation, which we derive in Appendix 4:

$$\hat{y}_t = \vartheta(1-\alpha)\hat{N}_t + \vartheta\alpha\hat{k}_t + \vartheta\hat{Z}_t(1-\vartheta)\hat{j}_t, \quad \vartheta = \frac{\epsilon}{\epsilon-1}. \quad (2.108)$$

This equation is the model's analog to the log-linear aggregate production function in the benchmark model given by

$$\hat{y}_t = (1-\alpha)\hat{N}_t + \alpha\hat{k}_t + \hat{Z}_t.$$

Since $\vartheta > 1$ we overstate the size of $\hat{Z}_t$, when we use this latter equation to estimate the size of the technology shock from data on output, hours, and the capital stock. Furthermore, in as much as the entry of new firms measured by $\hat{j}_t$ depends upon the state of the business cycle, the usual measure of $\hat{Z}_t$ is further spoiled. We do not consider this book to be the right place to develop this matter further. Possible remedies have been suggested for instance by ROTEMBERG and WOODFORD (1995) and HAIRAULT and PORTIER (1995). Instead, we continue to use the parameters from the benchmark model so that we are able to compare our results to those obtained in the Section 2.6.1 and Section 2.6.2.

What we further need are the parameters of the money supply process, of the transaction costs function, and of the structure of the monopolistic intermediary goods sector.

Our measure of money supply is the West-German monetary aggregate M1 per capita. As in Section 1.5 we focus on the period 1975.i through 1989.iv. The average quarterly growth rate of this aggregate was 1.67 percent. We fitted an AR(1) process to the deviations of μ_t from this value. The autocorrelation parameter from this estimation is not significantly different from zero and the estimated standard deviation of the innovations is $\sigma^\mu = 0.0173$. We use the average velocity of M1 with respect to consumption of 0.84 to determine γ from (2.107b). Finally, we can use the following observation to find an appropriate value of κ: The lhs of equation (2.107b) is equal to

$$\frac{1}{\pi(1-\delta+r)}.$$

The term in the denominator is the nominal interest rate factor, i.e., one plus the nominal interest rate q, say. This implies the following long run interest rate elasticity of the demand for real money balances:

$$\frac{d(M/P)/(M/P)}{dq/q} = \frac{-1}{(1+\kappa)\pi(1-\delta+r)}.$$

The estimate of this elasticity provided by HOFFMAN, RASCHE, and TIESLAU (1995) is about -0.2. Since $1/R \approx 1$ we use $\kappa = 4$.

Table 2.4

Preferences	Production	
β=0.994	a=1.005	α=0.27
η=2.0	δ=0.011	ρ^Z=0.90
N=0.13	σ^Z=0.0072	

Money Supply	Transactions Costs	Market Structure
μ=1.0167	$C/(M/P)$=0.84	φ=0.25
ρ^μ=0.0	κ=4.0	ϵ=6.0
σ^μ=0.0173		

The degree of nominal rigidity in our model is determined by the parameter φ. According to the estimates found in ROTEMBERG (1987) it takes about four quarters to achieve full price adjustment. Therefore, we use $\varphi = 0.25$. LINNEMANN (1999) presents estimates of markups for Germany, which imply a price elasticity of $\epsilon = 6$. Table 2.4 summarizes this choice of parameters.

Results. The Gauss program NKPK.g implements the solution. To understand the mechanics of the model, we consider the case without nominal frictions first. Figure 2.5 displays the time paths of several variables after a one-time shock to the money supply process (2.98) in period $t = 3$ of size σ^μ. Before this shock the economy was on its balanced growth path, after this shock the growth factor of money follows (2.98) with $\epsilon_t^\mu = 0$.

The case $\rho^\mu = 0$ highlights the unanticipated effect of the shock, since after period 3 the money growth rate is back on its

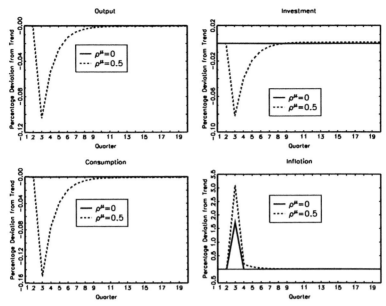

Figure 2.5: Real Effects of a Monetary Shock in the Model Without Nominal Rigidities

stationary path. The money transfer in period 3 raises the household's income unexpectedly. Since both consumption and leisure are normal goods the household's demand for consumption increases and its labor supply decreases. The latter raises the real wage so that marginal costs increase. Higher costs and excess demand raise inflation. This increase just offsets the extra amount of money so that the real stock of money does not change. Therefore, none of the real variables really changes. Money is neutral. This can be seen in Figure 2.5 since the impulse responses of output, consumption, and investment coincide with the zero line.

Things are different when the shock is autocorrelated. In this case there is also an anticipated effect. Households know that money growth will remain above average for several periods and expect above average inflation. This in turn increases the expected costs of money holdings and households reduce their cash holdings. As a consequence, the velocity of money with respect to consumption increases. To offset this negative effect on transaction costs the households reduce consumption. Their desire to smooth consumption finally entails less investment. Note however that these effects are very small. For instance, consumption in period 3 is 0.16 percent below its stationary value, and investment is 0.08 percent below its steady state level.

We find very different impulse responses, if nominal rigidities are present. This can be seen in Figure 2.6. Since inflation cannot adjust fully, households expect above average inflation even in the case of $\rho^\mu = 0$. This creates a desire to shift consumption to the current period so that there is excess demand. Monopolistically competitive firms are willing to satisfy this demand since their price exceeds their marginal costs. Thus output increases. The household's desire to spread the extra income over several periods spurs investment into physical capital.

There is another noteworthy property of the model: The spike-like shape of the impulse responses. Consumption, hours, output, and investment are almost back on their respective growth paths

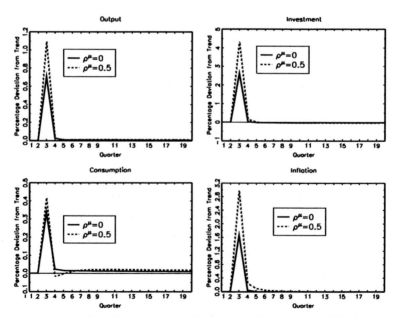

Figure 2.6: Impulse Responses to a Monetary Shock in the New Keynesian Phillips Curve Model

after period 3, irrespective of whether or not the monetary shock is autocorrelated. This is in stark contrast to the findings of empirical studies. For instance, according to the impulse responses estimated by COCHRANE (1998) and, more recently, by CHRISTIANO, EICHENBAUM, and EVANS (2005) the response of output is hump shaped and peaks after eight quarters. The apparent failure of the model to explain the persistence of a monetary shock has let many researches to question the usefulness of the New Keynesian Phillips curve. In a recent paper EICHENBAUM and FISHER (2004) argue that the CALVO (1983) model is able to explain persistent effects of monetary shocks if one abandons the convenient but arbitrary assumption of a constant price elasticity. WALSH (2005) argues that labor market search, habit persistence in consumption, and monetary policy inertia together can explain the long-lasting effects of monetary shocks. However, as HEER and MAUSSNER (2007) point out, this result may be due to the assumption of prohibitively high costs of capital adjustment. In CHRISTIANO, EICHENBAUM, and EVANS (2005) wage staggering and variable capacity utilization account for the close fit between the estimated and the model-implied impulse responses of output and inflation.

Table 2.5 reveals the contribution of monetary shocks to the business cycle. To fully understand the model we must disentangle several mechanisms that work simultaneously. For this reason, columns 2 to 4 present simulations, where neither monetary shocks, nor nominal rigidities, nor monopolistic elements are present. This requires to set $\vartheta = 1$, $\varphi = 0$, and $\sigma^\mu = 0$ in the program NKPK.g. Obviously, this model behaves almost like the benchmark model (see Table 2.2).

Next consider columns 5 to 7. In this model, there are no monetary shocks, but there are monopolistic price setters facing nominal rigidities. The most immediate differences are: output is more volatile and hours are less volatile than in the benchmark model. How can this happen? Note that under monopolistic price setting the marginal product of labor is larger than it is under perfect competition. The same is true for the marginal product of capital. Thus, a technology shock that shifts the production function

Table 2.5

Variable	$\vartheta=1, \varphi=0, \sigma^\mu=0$			$\sigma^\mu=0$			$\sigma^\mu=0.0173$		
	s_x	r_{xy}	r_x	s_x	r_{xy}	r_x	s_x	r_{xy}	r_x
Output	1.43	1.00	0.63	1.55	1.00	0.68	1.69	1.00	0.56
	(1.14)	(1.00)	(0.80)	(1.14)	(1.00)	(0.80)	(1.14)	(1.00)	(0.80)
Consump-tion	0.53	0.99	0.65	0.55	0.98	0.72	0.64	0.98	0.52
	(1.18)	(0.79)	(0.84)	(1.18)	(0.79)	(0.84)	(1.18)	(0.79)	(0.84)
Invest-ment	6.16	1.00	0.63	6.87	1.00	0.67	7.31	1.00	0.58
	(2.59)	(0.75)	(0.79)	(2.59)	(0.75)	(0.79)	(2.59)	(0.75)	(0.79)
Hours	0.76	1.00	0.63	0.59	0.99	0.75	0.97	0.86	0.23
	(0.78)	(0.40)	(0.31)	(0.78)	(0.40)	(0.31)	(0.78)	(0.40)	(0.31)
Real Wage	0.67	0.99	0.65	0.66	0.99	0.72	0.81	0.97	0.45
	(1.17)	(0.41)	(0.91)	(1.17)	(0.41)	(0.91)	(1.17)	(0.41)	(0.91)
Inflation	0.27	−0.53	−0.07	0.31	−0.48	−0.05	1.62	0.30	−0.06
	(0.28)	(0.04)	(−0.03)	(0.28)	(0.04)	(−0.03)	(0.28)	(0.04)	(−0.03)

Notes: s_x:=standard deviation of HP-filtered simulated series of variable x, r_{xy}:=cross correlation of variable x with output, r_x:=first order autocorrelation of variable x. Empirical magnitudes in parenthesis.

outward boosts output more than it would do in a competitive environment. Due to the fixed costs of production, the shock also raises profits and thus dividend payments to the household. This in turn increases the household's demand for leisure. Since prices do not fully adjust, these effects are a bit smaller than they are in a purely real model without nominal frictions.[32]

Columns 8 to 10 present the results from simulations where both technology shocks and monetary shocks are present. The most noteworthy effect concerns working hours. The standard deviation of this variable increases by 64 percent. The wealth effect that we identified above now works in the opposite direction: A monetary shock squeezes the profits of firms, since marginal costs rise and prices cannot fully adjust. As a consequence, the house-

---

[32] A detailed comparison between a real and a monetary model of monopolistic price setting appears in MAUSSNER (1999).

hold's demand for leisure falls. But note, most of the shock is absorbed by inflation, which increases substantially.

Appendix 3: Solution of the Stochastic LQ Problem

In this Appendix we provide the details of the solution of the stochastic linear quadratic (LQ) problem. If you are unfamiliar with matrix algebra, you should consult 11.1 before proceeding.

Using matrix algebra we may write the Bellman equation (2.15) as follows:

$$\begin{aligned}\mathbf{x}'P\mathbf{x} + d = \max_{\mathbf{u}} \Big[&\mathbf{x}'Q\mathbf{x} + \mathbf{u}'R\mathbf{u} + 2\mathbf{u}'S\mathbf{x} \\ &+ \beta E\Big(\mathbf{x}'A'PA\mathbf{x} + \mathbf{u}'B'PA\mathbf{x} + \epsilon'PA\mathbf{x} \\ &+ \mathbf{x}'A'PB\mathbf{u} + \mathbf{u}'B'PB\mathbf{u} + \epsilon'PB\mathbf{u} \\ &+ \mathbf{x}'A'P\epsilon + \mathbf{u}'B'P\epsilon + \epsilon'P\epsilon + d\Big)\Big].\end{aligned} \quad (A.3.1)$$

Since $E(\epsilon) = \mathbf{0}$ the expectation of all linear forms involving the vector of shocks ϵ evaluate to zero. The expectation of the quadratic form $\epsilon'P\epsilon$ is:

$$E\left(\sum_{i=1}^{n}\sum_{i=1}^{n} p_{ij}\epsilon_i\epsilon_j\right) = \sum_{i=1}^{n}\sum_{j=1}^{n} p_{ij}\sigma_{ij},$$

where σ_{ij} (σ_{ii}) denotes the covariance (variance) between ϵ_i and ϵ_j (of ϵ_i). It is not difficult to see that this expression equals $\text{tr}(P\Sigma)$. Furthermore, since $P = P'$ and

$$z := \mathbf{u}'B'PA\mathbf{x} = z' = (\mathbf{x}'A'PB'\mathbf{u})'$$

we may write the Bellman equation as

$$\begin{aligned}\mathbf{x}'P\mathbf{x} + d = \max_{\mathbf{u}} \Big[&\mathbf{x}'Q\mathbf{x} + 2\mathbf{u}S\mathbf{x} + \mathbf{u}'R\mathbf{u} + \beta\mathbf{x}'A'PA\mathbf{x} \\ &+ 2\beta\mathbf{x}'A'PB\mathbf{u} + \beta\mathbf{u}'B'PB\mathbf{u} + \beta\,\text{tr}(P\Sigma) + \beta d\Big].\end{aligned} \quad (A.3.2)$$

This is equation (2.16) in the main text. Differentiation of the rhs of this expression with respect to $\mathbf{u}$ yields

$$2S\mathbf{x} + 2R\mathbf{u} + 2\beta(\mathbf{x}'A'PB)' + 2\beta(B'PB)\mathbf{u}.$$

Setting this equal to the zero vector and solving for $\mathbf{u}$ gives

$$\underbrace{(R+\beta B'PB)}_{C^{-1}}\mathbf{u} = -\underbrace{(S+\beta B'PA)}_{D}\mathbf{x} \qquad \text{(A.3.3)}$$

$$\Rightarrow \quad \mathbf{u} = -CD\mathbf{x}.$$

If we substitute this solution back into (A.3.2), we get:

$$\begin{aligned}\mathbf{x}'P\mathbf{x}+d &= \mathbf{x}'Q\mathbf{x} - 2(CD\mathbf{x})'S\mathbf{x} + (CD\mathbf{x})'RCD\mathbf{x} + \beta \mathbf{x}'A'PA\mathbf{x}\\ &\quad - 2\beta\mathbf{x}'A'PBCD\mathbf{x} + \beta(CD\mathbf{x})'B'PBCD\mathbf{x} + \beta\operatorname{tr}(P\Sigma) + \beta d\\ &= \mathbf{x}'Q\mathbf{x} + \beta\mathbf{x}'A'PA\mathbf{x}\\ &\quad - 2\mathbf{x}'D'C'S\mathbf{x} - 2\beta\mathbf{x}'A'PBCD\mathbf{x}\\ &\quad + \mathbf{x}'D'C'RCD\mathbf{x} + \beta\mathbf{x}'D'C'B'PBCD\mathbf{x}\\ &\quad + \beta\operatorname{tr}(P\Sigma) + \beta d.\end{aligned}$$

The expression on the fourth line can be simplified to

$$-2\mathbf{x}'D'C'S\mathbf{x} - \underbrace{2\beta\mathbf{x}'A'PBCD\mathbf{x}}_{=2\beta\mathbf{x}'D'C'B'PA\mathbf{x}}$$

$$= -2\mathbf{x}'D'C'\underbrace{(S+\beta B'PA)}_{D}\mathbf{x} = -2\mathbf{x}'D'C'D\mathbf{x}.$$

The terms on the fifth line add to

$$\mathbf{x}'D'C'\underbrace{(R+\beta B'PB)C}_{I}D\mathbf{x} = \mathbf{x}'D'C'D.$$

Therefore,

$$\mathbf{x}'P\mathbf{x}+d = \mathbf{x}'Q\mathbf{x}+\beta\mathbf{x}'A'PA\mathbf{x}-\mathbf{x}'D'C'D\mathbf{x}+\beta\operatorname{tr}(P\Sigma)+\beta d. \quad \text{(A.3.4)}$$

For this expression to hold, the coefficient matrices of the various quadratic forms on both sides of equation (A.3.4) must satisfy the matrix equation

$$P = Q + \beta A'PA + D'C'D,$$

and the constant d must be given by

$$d = \frac{\beta}{1-\beta}\operatorname{tr}(P\Sigma).$$

This finishes the derivation of the solution of LQ the problem.

Appendix 4: Derivation of the Log-Linear Model of the New Keynesian Phillips Curve

In this appendix we provide the details of the solution of the model from Section 2.6.3.

The Household's Problem. The Lagrangean of the household's problem is:

$$\mathscr{L} = E_0 \sum_{t=0}^{\infty} \beta^t \left\{ \frac{C_t^{1-\eta}(1-N_t)^{\theta(1-\eta)}}{1-\eta} \right.$$

$$+ \Lambda_t \left[\frac{W_t}{P_t} N_t + (r_t - \delta) K_t + D_t + T_t \right.$$

$$\left. \left. - \gamma \left(\frac{C_t}{M_{t+1}/P_t} \right)^\kappa C_t - C_t - (K_{t+1} - K_t) - \frac{M_{t+1} - M_t}{P_t} \right] \right\}.$$

Differentiating this expression with respect to C_t, N_t, K_{t+1} and M_{t+1} provides the following first-order conditions:

$$0 = C_t^{-\eta}(1-N_t)^{\theta(1-\eta)} - E_t \Lambda_t \left[1 + \gamma(1+\kappa) \left(\frac{C_t}{M_{t+1}/P_t} \right)^\kappa \right],$$

$$0 = \theta C_t^{1-\eta}(1-N_t)^{\theta(1-\eta)-1} - \Lambda_t \frac{W_t}{P_t}, \quad \text{(A.4.1)}$$

$$0 = \Lambda_t - \beta E_t \Lambda_{t+1}(1 - \delta + r_{t+1}),$$

$$0 = E_t \left\{ -\frac{\Lambda_t}{P_t} + \kappa\gamma \left(\frac{C_t}{M_{t+1}/P_t} \right)^{\kappa+1} \frac{\Lambda_t}{P_t} + \beta \frac{\Lambda_{t+1}}{P_{t+1}} \right\}.$$

As usual, we must define variables that are stationary. We choose $c_t := C_t/A_t$, $k_t := K_t/A_t$, $\lambda_t := \Lambda_t A_t^\eta$, $w_t := W_t/(P_t A_t)$, $m_{t+1} := M_{t+1}/(A_t P_t)$, and $j_t := J_t/A_t$. The inflation factor is $\pi_t := P_t/P_{t-1}$. Since the price level is determined in period t, this variable is also a period t variable. The growth factor of money supply, also determined in period t, is given by $\mu_t := M_{t+1}/M_t$, where M_t is the beginning-of-period money stock and M_{t+1} the end-of-period money stock. In these variables, we can rewrite the system (A.4.1) as follows:

$$c_t^{-\eta}(1-N_t)^{\theta(1-\eta)} = \lambda_t \left(1 + \gamma(1+\kappa) \left(\frac{c_t}{m_{t+1}} \right)^\kappa \right), \quad \text{(A.4.2a)}$$

$$\lambda_t w_t = \theta c_t^{1-\eta}(1-N_t)^{\theta(1-\eta)-1}, \quad \text{(A.4.2b)}$$

$$m_{t+1} = \frac{\mu_t}{a\pi_t} m_t, \quad (A.4.2c)$$

$$\lambda_t = \beta a^{-\eta} E_t \lambda_{t+1} (1 - \delta + r_{t+1}), \quad (A.4.2d)$$

$$\beta a^{-\eta} E_t \frac{\lambda_{t+1}}{\pi_{t+1}} = \lambda_t \left(1 - \kappa\gamma \left(\frac{c_t}{m_{t+1}}\right)^{\kappa+1}\right). \quad (A.4.2e)$$

Price Setting. To study the price setting behavior, it is convenient to first solve the firm's cost minimization problem

$$\min_{N_{jt}, K_{jt}} \frac{W_t}{P_t} N_{jt} + r_t K_{jt} \quad \text{s.t. (2.102)}.$$

The first-order conditions for this problem are easy to derive. They are:

$$w_t = g_t(1-\alpha) Z_t N_{jt}^{-\alpha} (K_{jt}/A_t)^{\alpha} = g_t(1-\alpha) Z_t (k_t/N_t)^{\alpha}, \quad (A.4.3a)$$

$$r_t = g_t \alpha Z_t N_{jt}^{1-\alpha} (K_{jt}/A_t)^{\alpha-1} = g_t \alpha Z_t (k_t/N_t)^{\alpha-1}, \quad (A.4.3b)$$

where g_t is the Lagrange multiplier of the constraint (2.102), and $w_t := W_t/(P_t A_t)$ is the real wage rate per unit of effective labor.[33] It is well known from elementary production theory that g_t equals the marginal costs of production. Furthermore, the constant scale assumption with respect to $Y_{jt} + F$ also implies that g_t are the variable unit costs of production:

$$g_t = \frac{(W_t/P_t) N_{jt} + r_t K_{jt}}{Y_{jt} + F}.$$

Marginal costs as well as the capital-output ratio are the same in all intermediary firms due to the symmetry that is inherent in the specification of the demand and production function. For later use we note the factor demand functions that are associated with this solution:

---

[33] Note that g_t is equal for all firms. This can be seen by using

$$\frac{w_t}{r_t} = \frac{1-\alpha}{\alpha} \frac{K_{jt}}{N_{jt}},$$

which implies that all firms choose the same capital-labor ratio $k_t/N_t \equiv K_{jt}/N_{jt}$, since all firms face the same real wages and rental rates. Via equation (A.4.3b) this also implies $g_t = g_{jt}$ for all j.

$$N_{jt} = \frac{Y_{jt} + F}{A_t Z_t} \left(\frac{1-\alpha}{\alpha}\right)^{\alpha} \left(\frac{w_t}{r_t}\right)^{-\alpha}, \qquad \text{(A.4.4a)}$$

$$K_{jt} = \frac{Y_{jt} + F}{Z_t} \left(\frac{1-\alpha}{\alpha}\right)^{\alpha-1} \left(\frac{w_t}{r_t}\right)^{1-\alpha}. \qquad \text{(A.4.4b)}$$

In each period $(1-\varphi)J_t$ firms choose their optimal money price P_{At} and φJ_t firms increase their price according to average inflation,

$$P_{Nt} = \pi P_{Nt-1}.$$

Therefore, the aggregate price level given in equation (2.101) is:

$$P_t = \left[(1-\varphi)P_{At}^{1-\epsilon} + \varphi(\pi P_{Nt-1})^{1-\epsilon}\right]^{\frac{1}{1-\epsilon}}.$$

Now observe that the pool of firms that are not allowed to choose their price optimally consists itself of firms that were able to set their optimal price in the previous period and those unlucky ones that were not allowed to do so. Thus, P_{Nt-1} is in turn the following index:

$$P_{Nt-1} = \left[(1-\varphi)P_{At-1}^{1-\epsilon} + \varphi(\pi P_{Nt-2})^{1-\epsilon}\right]^{\frac{1}{1-\epsilon}}.$$

Using this formula recursively establishes:

$$P_t = \left[(1-\varphi)\left\{P_{At}^{1-\epsilon} + \varphi(\pi P_{At-1})^{1-\epsilon} + \varphi^2(\pi^2 P_{At-2})^{1-\epsilon} + \ldots\right\}\right]^{\frac{1}{1-\epsilon}},$$

which implies

$$\varphi(\pi P_{t-1})^{1-\epsilon} = \left[(1-\varphi)\{\varphi(\pi P_{At-1})^{1-\epsilon} + \varphi^2(\pi^2 P_{At-2})^{1-\epsilon} + \ldots\}\right].$$

Thus, the aggregate price level can equivalently be written as

$$P_t = \left[(1-\varphi)P_{At}^{1-\epsilon} + \varphi(\pi P_{t-1})^{1-\epsilon}\right]^{\frac{1}{1-\epsilon}}. \qquad \text{(A.4.5)}$$

We now turn to the first-order conditions that determine the optimal price of type A firms. Maximizing the expression in (2.104) with respect to P_{At} provides the following condition:

$$\underbrace{\frac{\epsilon-1}{\epsilon}}_{=:1/\vartheta} P_{At} E_t \sum_{\tau=t}^{\infty} \varphi^{\tau-t} \varrho_\tau \left(\frac{\pi^{\tau-t}}{P_\tau}\right)^{(1-\epsilon)} \frac{Y_\tau}{J_\tau}$$

$$= E_t \sum_{\tau=t}^{\infty} \varphi^{\tau-t} \varrho_\tau \left(\frac{\pi^{\tau-t}}{P_\tau}\right)^{-\epsilon} g_\tau \frac{Y_\tau}{J_\tau}.$$

We multiply both sides by $P_t^{-\epsilon}$ and replace ϱ_τ by the rhs of equation (2.105). The result is:

$$\frac{1}{\vartheta}\left(\frac{P_{At}}{P_t}\right) E_t \sum_{\tau=t}^{\infty}(\varphi\beta a^{-\eta})^{\tau-t}\frac{\lambda_\tau}{\lambda_t}\pi^{(1-\epsilon)(\tau-t)}\left(\frac{P_\tau}{P_t}\right)^{\epsilon-1}\frac{Y_\tau}{J_\tau}$$
$$= E_t \sum_{\tau=t}^{\infty}(\varphi\beta a^{-\eta})^{\tau-t}\frac{\lambda_\tau}{\lambda_t}\pi^{-\epsilon(\tau-t)}g_\tau\left(\frac{P_\tau}{P_t}\right)^{\epsilon}\frac{Y_\tau}{J_\tau}. \quad (A.4.6)$$

Our next task is to determine aggregate output and employment. Note from (2.100) that final goods producers use different amounts of type A and N goods since the prices of these inputs differ. Therefore, aggregate output is:

$$Y_t = (1-\varphi)J_t\frac{P_{At}}{P_t}Y_{At} + \varphi J_t\frac{\pi}{\pi_t}Y_{Nt}$$
$$= (1-\varphi)J_t\left[\frac{P_{At}}{P_t}\left(Z_t A_t N_{At}(K_{At}/A_t N_{At})^{1-\alpha} - F\right)\right]$$
$$+ \varphi J_t\left[\frac{\pi}{\pi_t}\left(Z_t A_t N_{Nt}(K_{Nt}/A_t N_{Nt})^{1-\alpha} - F\right)\right].$$

Using the fact that all producers choose the same capital-labor ratio k_t/N_t provides:

$$Y_t = A_t\left[\frac{P_{At}}{P_t}Z_t\underbrace{(1-\varphi)J_t N_{At}}_{n_t N_t}(k_t/N_t)^{1-\alpha} + \frac{\pi}{\pi_t}Z_t\underbrace{\varphi J_t N_{Nt}}_{(1-n_t)N_t}(k_t/N_t)^{1-\alpha}\right]$$
$$- J_t F\left[(1-\varphi)\frac{P_{At}}{P_t} + \varphi\frac{\pi}{\pi_t}\right],$$

where the fraction of workers employed by type A firms n_t is given by:

$$n_t := \frac{(1-\varphi)J_t N_{At}}{N_t}. \quad (A.4.7)$$

From this we derive the following equation in terms of aggregate output per efficiency unit A_t:

$$y_t := \frac{Y_t}{A_t} = Z_t N_t^{1-\alpha}k_t^{\alpha}\left[n_t\frac{P_{At}}{P_t} + (1-n_t)\frac{\pi}{\pi_t}\right]$$
$$- j_t F\left[(1-\varphi)\frac{P_{At}}{P_t} + \varphi\frac{\pi}{\pi_t}\right]. \quad (A.4.8)$$

In the log-linear version of this equation the variable n_t drops out. Thus, there is no need to derive the equation that determines this variable.

Finally, consider the household's budget constraint (2.95). In equilibrium it holds with equality. Using the government's budget constraint (2.97) and the definition of dividends (2.106), we end up with the following resource constraint:

$$ak_{t+1} = y_t + (1-\delta)k_t - \gamma \left(\frac{c_t}{m_{t+1}}\right)^\kappa c_t - c_t. \tag{A.4.9}$$

The Log-Linear Model. The dynamic model consists of equations (A.4.2), (A.4.3), (A.4.5),(A.4.6), (A.4.8), and (A.4.9). The stationary equilibrium of this system is considered in the main text so that we can focus on the derivation of the log-linear equations. First, consider the variables that play the role of the control variables in the system (2.47). These are the deviations of consumption, working hours, output, the inflation factor, the real wage rate, and the rental rate of capital from their respective steady state levels:

$$\mathbf{u}_t := [\hat{c}_t, \hat{N}_t, \hat{y}_t, \hat{\pi}_t, \hat{w}_t, \hat{r}_t]'.$$

The state variables with predetermined initial conditions are the stock of capital and beginning-of-period money real money balances. Thus, in terms of (2.47):

$$\mathbf{x}_t = [\hat{k}_t, \hat{m}_t]'.$$

Purely exogenous are the technological shock $\hat{Z}_t$, the monetary shock $\hat{\mu}_t$, and the entrance rate of firms $\hat{j}_t$ into the intermediary goods sector. For the latter we will assume it is independent of the state of the business cycle so that $\hat{j}_t = 0$ for all t.[34] Thus,

$$\mathbf{z}_t = [\hat{Z}_t, \hat{\mu}_t]'.$$

The remaining variables are the shadow price of capital λ_t, firms' marginal costs g_t, and real end-of-period money balances m_{t+1}. Note, that we cannot determine the latter from equation (A.4.2c), since we

---

[34] For instance, ROTEMBERG and WOODFORD (1995) link $\hat{j}_t$ to the technological shock.

Appendix 4

need this equation to determine π_t. Thus, in addition to λ_t and g_t, this variable is a costate. To keep to the dating convention in (2.47) we define the auxiliary variable $x_t \equiv m_{t+1}$. Hence, our vector of costate variables comprises:

$$\lambda_t = [\hat{\lambda}_t, \hat{g}_t, \hat{x}_t]'.$$

We first present the static equations that relate control variables to state and costate variables. The log-linear versions of equations (A.4.2a) through (A.4.2c) are

$$-(\eta + \xi_1)\hat{c}_t - \xi_2 \hat{N}_t = \hat{\lambda}_t - \xi_1 \hat{x}_t, \quad \text{(A.4.10a)}$$

$$(1-\eta)\hat{c}_t - \xi_3 \hat{N}_t - \hat{w}_t = \hat{\lambda}_t, \quad \text{(A.4.10b)}$$

$$\hat{\pi}_t = \hat{m}_t - \hat{x}_t + \hat{\mu}_t, \quad \text{(A.4.10c)}$$

$$\xi_1 := \frac{\kappa\gamma(1+\kappa)(c/x)^\kappa}{1+\gamma(1+\kappa)(c/x)^\kappa}, \quad \frac{c}{x} = \frac{C}{\mu(M/P)},$$

$$\xi_2 := \theta(1-\eta)\frac{N}{1-N},$$

$$\xi_3 := [\theta(1-\eta) - 1]\frac{N}{1-N}.$$

The log-linear cost-minimizing conditions (A.4.3) deliver two further equations:

$$\alpha \hat{N}_t + \hat{w}_t = \alpha \hat{k}_t + \hat{g}_t + \hat{Z}_t, \quad \text{(A.4.10d)}$$

$$(\alpha - 1)\hat{N}_t + \hat{r}_t = (\alpha - 1)\hat{k}_t + \hat{g}_t + \hat{Z}_t. \quad \text{(A.4.10e)}$$

To derive the sixth equation we use the formula for the price level to write

$$\pi_t = \frac{P_t}{P_{t-1}} = \left[(1-\varphi)\left(\underbrace{\frac{P_{At}}{P_t}\frac{P_t}{P_{t-1}}}_{\pi_t}\right)^{1-\epsilon} + \varphi\pi^{1-\epsilon} \right]^{\frac{1}{1-\epsilon}}.$$

Log-linearizing at $P_A/P = 1$ provides:

$$\hat{\pi}_t = \frac{1-\varphi}{\varphi}\widehat{P_{At}/P_t}.$$

We use this relation to derive

$$\hat{y}_t - \vartheta(1-\alpha)\hat{N}_t = \vartheta\alpha\hat{k}_t + \vartheta\hat{Z}_t + (1-\vartheta)\hat{j}_t. \tag{A.4.10f}$$

from equation (A.4.8). The six equations (A.4.10a) through (A.4.10f) determine the control variables. We now turn to the dynamic equations that determine the time paths of $\hat{k}_t$, $\hat{m}_t$, $\hat{x}_t \equiv \hat{m}_{t+1}$, $\hat{\lambda}_t$, and $\hat{g}_t$. The log-linear versions of the resource constraint (A.4.9), the Euler equations for capital and money balances (A.4.2d) and (A.4.2e), and the definition $x_t := m_{t+1}$ are:

$$aE_t\hat{k}_{t+1} - (1-\delta)\hat{k}_t - \xi_4 \hat{x}_t = \frac{y}{k}\hat{y}_t - \xi_5 \hat{c}_t, \tag{A.4.11a}$$

$$-E_t\hat{\lambda}_{t+1} + \hat{\lambda}_t = \xi_6 E_t \hat{r}_{t+1}, \tag{A.4.11b}$$

$$E_t\hat{\lambda}_{t+1} - \hat{\lambda}_t - \xi_7 \hat{x}_t = -\xi_7 \hat{c}_t + E_t \hat{\pi}_{t+1}, \tag{A.4.11c}$$

$$E_t \hat{m}_{t+1} - \hat{x}_t = 0, \tag{A.4.11d}$$

$$\xi_4 := \kappa\gamma(c/x)^\kappa (c/k),$$

$$\xi_5 := (1 + \gamma(1+\kappa)(c/x)^\kappa)(c/k),$$

$$\xi_6 := 1 - \beta a^{-\eta}(1-\delta),$$

$$\xi_7 := \frac{\kappa\gamma(1+\kappa)(c/x)^{1+\kappa}}{1 - \gamma\kappa(c/x)^{1+\kappa}}.$$

The remaining fifth equation is the log-linear condition for the firms' optimal price:

$$\frac{(1-\varphi)(1-\varphi\beta a^{-\eta})}{\varphi}\hat{g}_t = -\beta a^{-\eta} E_t \hat{\pi}_{t+1} + \hat{\pi}_t. \tag{A.4.11e}$$

This looks nice and resembles a Phillips curve since it relates the current inflation rate to the expected future rate of inflation and a measure of labor market tension, which is here given by the deviation of marginal costs from their steady state level. It requires a substantial amount of algebra to get this relation and it is this task to which we turn next. Considering (A.4.6) we find:

$$\widehat{(P_{At}/P_t)}\frac{1}{\vartheta}\frac{y}{j}\underbrace{\left(1 + \varphi\beta a^{-\eta} + (\varphi\beta a^{-\eta})^2 + \ldots\right)}_{(1-\varphi\beta a^{-\eta})^{-1}}$$

$$+ \frac{1}{\vartheta}\frac{y}{j}\sum_{\tau=t}^{\infty}(\varphi\beta a^{-\eta})^{\tau-t} E_t \left[\widehat{(\lambda_\tau/\lambda_t)} + (\epsilon-1)\widehat{(P_\tau/P_t)} + \widehat{(y_\tau/j_\tau)}\right]$$

$$= g\frac{y}{j}\sum_{\tau=t}^{\infty}(\varphi\beta a^{-\eta})^{\tau-t} E_t \left[\widehat{(\lambda_\tau/\lambda_t)} + \epsilon\widehat{(P_\tau/P_t)} + \widehat{(y_\tau/j_\tau)} + \hat{g}_\tau\right].$$

Since $\vartheta g = 1$ and $\widehat{P_{At}/P_t} = [\varphi/(1-\varphi)]\hat{\pi}_t$ (see above), we can simplify this expression to

$$\frac{\varphi}{(1-\varphi)(1-\varphi\beta a^{-\eta})}\hat{\pi}_t = \sum_{\tau=t}^{\infty}(\varphi\beta a^{-\eta})^{\tau-t} E_t\left[\widehat{(P_\tau/P_t)} + \hat{g}_\tau\right].$$
(A.4.12)

Next, we shift the time index one period into the future, multiply through by $\varphi\beta a^{-\eta}$, and compute the conditional expectation of the ensuing expression:[35]

$$\left(\frac{\varphi}{1-\varphi}\right)\left(\frac{\varphi\beta a^{-\eta}}{1-\varphi\beta a^{-\eta}}\right) E_t\hat{\pi}_{t+1}$$
$$= E_t\left[(\varphi\beta a^{-\eta})^2\left(\widehat{\frac{P_{t+2}}{P_{t+1}}}\right) + (\varphi\beta a^{-\eta})^3\left(\widehat{\frac{P_{t+3}}{P_{t+1}}}\right) + \cdots + \varphi\beta a^{-\eta}\hat{g}_{t+1}\right.$$
$$\left. + (\varphi\beta a^{-\eta})^2 \hat{g}_{t+2} + \cdots \right].$$

We subtract this equation from (A.4.12) to arrive at:

$$\frac{\varphi}{(1-\varphi)(1-\varphi\beta a^{-\eta})}\left(\hat{\pi}_t - \varphi\beta a^{-\eta}E_t\hat{\pi}_{t+1}\right)$$
$$= \hat{g}_t + E_t\left[\varphi\beta a^{-\eta}\left(\widehat{\frac{P_{t+1}}{P_t}}\right) + (\varphi\beta a^{-\eta})^2\left\{\left(\widehat{\frac{P_{t+2}}{P_t}}\right) - \left(\widehat{\frac{P_{t+2}}{P_{t+1}}}\right)\right\}\right.$$
$$\left. + (\varphi\beta a^{-\eta})^3\left\{\left(\widehat{\frac{P_{t+3}}{P_t}}\right) - \left(\widehat{\frac{P_{t+3}}{P_{t+1}}}\right)\right\} + \cdots \right]. \quad \text{(A.4.13)}$$

Since

$$\widehat{\left(\frac{P_\tau}{P_t}\right)} = \sum_{s=t+1}^{\tau}\hat{\pi}_s,$$

the terms in curly brackets reduce to $\hat{\pi}_{t+1}$ so that the sum in brackets equals

---

[35] Here we use the law of iterated expectations according to which $E_t x_{t+1} = E_t(E_{t+1}x_{t+1})$.

$$\hat{\pi}_{t+1} \underbrace{\left[\varphi\beta a^{-\eta} + (\varphi\beta a^{-\eta})^2 + \ldots\right]}_{(\varphi\beta a^{-\eta})/(1-\varphi\beta a^{-\eta})}.$$

Substituting these results back into (A.4.13) delivers equation (A.4.11e).

To determine the time path of investment, we start from

$$i_t = y_t - \left(1 + \gamma \left(\frac{c_t}{x_t}\right)^\kappa\right) c_t, \quad x_t \equiv m_{t+1}.$$

The log-linearized version of this equation is:

$$\hat{i}_t = \iota_1 \hat{y}_t - \iota_2 \hat{c}_t + \iota_3 \hat{x}_t,$$

$$\iota_1 := (y/i) = \frac{y/k}{a+\delta-1}, \quad \iota_2 := \left(1 + (1+\kappa)\gamma \left(\frac{c}{x}\right)^\kappa\right) \frac{c}{i},$$

$$\iota_3 := \kappa\gamma \left(\frac{C}{\mu(M/P)}\right)^\kappa \frac{c}{i}, \quad \frac{c}{i} = \frac{y}{i} - 1.$$

Problems

2.1 Certainty Equivalence
Consider the deterministic linear quadratic optimal control problem of maximizing

$$\sum_{t=0}^{\infty} \beta^t [\mathbf{x}_t' Q \mathbf{x} + \mathbf{u}_t' R \mathbf{u}_t + 2\mathbf{u}_t' S \mathbf{x}_t]$$

subject to the linear law of motion

$$\mathbf{x}_{t+1} = A\mathbf{x}_t + B\mathbf{u}_t.$$

Adapt the steps followed in Section 2.2 and Appendix 3 to this problem and show that the optimal control as well as the matrix P are the solutions to equations (2.17) and (2.18), respectively.

2.2 Relation Between the LQ Problems (2.12) and (2.19)
Show that the linear quadratic problem with the current period return function

$$g(\mathbf{x}_t, \mathbf{u}_t, \mathbf{z}_t) := \mathbf{x}_t' A_{xx} \mathbf{x}_t + \mathbf{u}_t' A_{uu} \mathbf{u}_t + \mathbf{z}_t' A_{zz} \mathbf{z}_t$$
$$+ 2\mathbf{u}_t' A_{ux} \mathbf{x}_t + 2\mathbf{u}_t' A_{uz} \mathbf{z}_t + 2\mathbf{x}_t' A_{xz} \mathbf{z}_t$$

and the law of motion

$$\mathbf{x}_{t+1} = B_x \mathbf{x}_t + B_u \mathbf{u}_t + B_z \mathbf{z}_t$$

is a special case of the problem stated in equations (2.12) and (2.11). Toward that purpose define

$$\tilde{\mathbf{x}}_t = \begin{bmatrix} \mathbf{x}_t \\ \mathbf{z}_t \end{bmatrix}, \quad \tilde{\epsilon}_t = \begin{bmatrix} 0_{n \times 1} \\ \epsilon_t \end{bmatrix}$$

and show how the matrices A, B, Q, R, and S must be chosen so that both problems coincide.

2.3 Convex Costs of Price Adjustment
Instead of the CALVO (1983) model, consider the following model of price setting introduced in HAIRAULT and PORTIER (1995). Intermediate producers face convex costs of adjusting their price given by

$$PC_{jt} := (\psi/2) \left(\frac{P_{jt}}{P_{jt-1}} - \pi \right)^2.$$

Thus they solve the following problem:

$$\max \quad E_0 \sum_{t=0}^{\infty} \varrho_t \left[(P_{jt}/P_t) Y_{jt} - (W_t/P_t) N_{jt} - r_t K_{jt} - PC_{jt} \right],$$

s.t.

$$Y_{jt} = (P_{jt}/P_t)^{-\epsilon} (Y_t/J_t),$$
$$Y_{jt} = Z_t (A_t N_{jt})^\alpha K_{jt}^{1-\alpha} - F.$$

Calibrate the parameter ψ so that a one percent deviation of the firm's inflation factor P_{jt}/P_{jt-1} from average the average inflation factor entails costs of 0.01 percent of the firm's value added. Do you find more persistence of a money supply shock with this alternative specification of nominal rigidities? What happens, if you increase ψ?

2.4 Government Spending in a Real Business Cycle Model

In most OECD countries, wages and labor productivity are acyclic or even negatively correlated with output and working hours, while, in the stochastic Ramsey model, however, these correlations are positive and close to one (please compare table 2.2). One possible remedy for this shortcoming of the stochastic growth model is the introduction of a government spending shock. The following model is adapted from BAXTER and KING (1993) and AMBLER and PAQUET (1996).

Consider the stochastic growth model where the number of agents is normalized to one. Assume that utility is also a function of government consumption, where due to our normalization per capita government spending G_t is also equal to total government spending G_t. In particular, government consumption substitutes for private consumption C_t^p:

$$C_t = C_t^p + \vartheta G_t,$$

with $\vartheta < 1$ as some forms of government spending, for example military spending, do not provide utility for private consumption. The household maximizes her intertemporal utility:

$$\max_{C_0^p, N_0} \quad E_0 \left[\sum_{t=0}^{\infty} \beta^t \frac{C_t^{1-\eta}(1-N_t)^{\theta(1-\eta)}}{1-\eta} \right],$$
$$\beta \in (0,1), \eta \geq 0, \theta \geq 0, \eta > \theta/(1+\theta),$$

subject to the budget constraint

$$C_t^p + I_t^p = (1-\tau)(w_t N_t + r_t K_t^p) + Tr_t.$$

Both wage income $w_t N_t$ and interest income $r_t K_t$ are taxed at the constant rate τ. The household also receives lump-sum transfers Tr_t from the government. The private capital stock evolves according to:

$$K_{t+1}^p = (1-\delta)K_t^P + I_t^p,$$

where δ denotes the depreciation rate. Production is described by a Cobb-Douglas Production Function, $Y_t = Z_t N_t^\alpha K_t^{1-\alpha}$, where the productivity Z_t follows an AR(1) process, $Z_{t+1} = Z_t^\varrho e^{\epsilon_t}$, with $\epsilon_t \sim N(0, \sigma^2)$ and $\varrho = 0.90$ and $\sigma = 0.007$. Factors are rewarded by their marginal products. Government consumption $G_t = g_t \bar{G}$ follows a stochastic process:

$$\ln g_t = \rho_g \ln g_{t-1} + \epsilon_t^g,$$

with $\epsilon_t^g \sim N(0, \sigma_g^2)$ and $\rho_g = 0.95$ and $\sigma_g = 0.01$. In the steady state, government consumption is constant and equal to 20% of output, $\bar{G} = 0.2\bar{Y}$. In equilibrium, the government budget is balanced:

$$\tau(w_t N_t + r_t K_t^p) = G_t + Tr_t.$$

The model is calibrated as follows: $\beta = 0.99$, $\eta = 2.0$, $\psi = 0.5$, $\alpha = 0.6$, $\delta = 0.02$. θ and τ are chosen so that the steady state labor supply $\bar{N}$ and transfers $\overline{Tr}$ are equal to 0.30 and 0, respectively.
a) Compute the steady state.
b) Compute the log-linear solution. Simulate the model and assume that ϵ_t and ϵ_t^g are uncorrelated. What happens to the correlation of labor productivity and wages with output and employment?
c) Assume that transfers are zero, $Tr_t = 0$, and that the income tax τ_t always adjusts in order to balance the budget. How are your results affected?
d) Assume now that the government expenditures are split evenly on government consumption G_t and government investment I_t^G. Government capital K_t^G evolves accordingly

$$K_{t+1}^G = (1-\delta)K_t^G + I_t^G,$$

and production is now given by

$$Y_t = Z_t = Z_t N_t^\alpha K_t^{1-\gamma} \left(K_t^G\right)^{1-\alpha-\gamma}$$

with $\alpha = 0.6$ and $\gamma = 0.3$. Recompute the model.

2.5 Government Spending and Nominal Rigidities

In the previous problem, you have learned about the 'wealth effect' of government demand. An increase in government expenditures results in a reduction of transfers and, hence, wealth of the households is decreased. Consequently, the households increase their labor supply and both employment and output increase. In this problem, you will learn about the traditional Keynesian IS-LM effect. Expansionary fiscal policy increases aggregate demand and demand-constrained firms increases their output as prices are fixed in the short run. The model follows LINNEMANN and SCHABERT (2003).

Households maximize the expected value of a discounted stream of instantaneous utility:

$$\max_{C_0, N_0} E_0 \left[\sum_{t=0}^{\infty} \beta^t \frac{C_t^{1-\eta}(1-N_t)^{\theta(1-\eta)}}{1-\eta} \right],$$

$\beta \in (0,1), \eta \geq 0, \theta \geq 0, \eta > \theta/(1+\theta)$.

A role for money is introduced into the model with the help of a cash-in-advance constraint:

$$P_t C_t \leq M_t + P_t Tr_t,$$

Nominal consumption purchases $P_t C_t$ are constrained by nominal beginning-of period money balances M_t and nominal government transfers $P_t Tr_t$.[36] The household holds two kinds of assets, nominal money M_t and nominal bonds, B_t. Bonds yield a gross nominal return R_t. In addition, agents receive income from labor, $P_t w_t N_t$, government transfers, $P_t Tr_t$, and from firm profits, $\int_0^1 \Omega_{it} \, di$. The budget constraint is given by:

$$M_{t+1} + B_{t+1} + P_t c_t = P_t w_t N_t + R_t B_t + M_t + P_t Tr_t + \int_0^1 \Omega_{it} di.$$

The number of firms i is one, $i \in (0,1)$. Firms are monopolistically competitive and set their prices in a staggered way as in the model of Section 2.6.3. Accordingly, profit maximization of the firms implies the New Keynesian Phillips curve:

$$\hat{\pi}_t = \psi \widehat{mc}_t + \beta E_t \{\hat{\pi}_{t+1}\}, \quad \psi = (1-\varphi)(1-\beta\varphi)\varphi^{-1},$$

where mc_t denotes marginal costs (compare (A.4.11e)).

Firms produce with labor only:

$$y_{it} = N_{it}.$$

Cost minimization implies that the real wage is equal to marginal costs:

---

[36] Government transfers are included in this cash-in-advance specification in order to avoid the following: an expansionary monetary policy consisting in a rise of M_{t+1} already increases prices P_t due to the expected inflation effect. Accordingly, real money balances M_t/P_t fall and so does real consumption C_t if government transfers do not enter the cash-in-advance constraint. This, however, contradicts empirical evidence.

$$w_t = mc_t.$$

The government issues money and nominal riskless one-period bonds and spends its revenues on government spending, G_t, and lump-sum transfers:

$$P_t Tr_t + P_t G_t + M_t + R_t B_t = B_{t+1} + M_{t+1}.$$

Real government expenditures follow an AR(1)-process:

$$\ln G_t = \rho \ln G_{t-1} + (1-\rho) \ln G + \epsilon_t$$

with $\epsilon_t \sim N(0, \sigma^2)$ and $\rho = 0.90$ and $\sigma = 0.007$.
Monetary policy is characterized by a forward-looking interest-rate rule:

$$\hat{R}_{t+1} = \rho_\pi E - t\hat{\pi}_{t+1} + \rho_y E_t \hat{y}_{t+1}, \quad \rho_{pi} > 1.$$

The restriction ρ_π is imposed in order to ensure uniqueness of the equilibrium.

a) Compute the first-order conditions of the household.
b) Compute the stationary equilibrium that is characterized by a zero-supply of bonds, $B_t = 0$,[37] and $R > 1$ (in this case, the cash-in-advance constraint is always binding). Furthermore, in equilibrium, the aggregate resource constraint is given by $y_t = c_t + G_t$ and firms are identical, $y_{it} = y_t = N_t = N_{it}$. Define the equilibrium with the help of the stationary variables $\{\pi_t, w_t, m_t \equiv \frac{M_t}{P_{t-1}}, R_t, y_t, G_t\}$.
c) Compute the steady-state.
d) Calibrate the model as in the previous problem. In addition, set $\rho_\pi = 1.5$, $\rho_y \in \{0, 0.1, 0.5\}$, $\pi = 1$, and $\varphi = 0.75$.
e) Log-linearize the model and compute the dynamics. How does consumption react to an expansionary fiscal policy? Does it increase (as IS-LM implies) or decrease (due to the wealth effect)?
f) Assume now that the interest-rate rule is subject to an exogenous autocorrelated shock with autoregressive parameter $\rho_R \in \{0, 0.5\}$. How does a shock affect the economy?
g) Assume that monetary policy is described by a money-growth rule that is subject to an autoregressive shock. Recompute the model for an autoregressive parameter $\rho_\mu \in \{0, 0.5\}$ and compare the impulse responses to those implied by an interest-rate rule.

---

[37] Why can we set the nominal bonds supply equal to zero?

Chapter 3

Deterministic Extended Path

Overview. We know from Section 1.1 that the first-order conditions of the deterministic finite-horizon Ramsey model constitute a system of non-linear equations. The first section of this chapter employs a non-linear equations solver to obtain the approximate time profile of the optimal capital stock. We then extend this approach to the infinite-horizon deterministic Ramsey model of Section 1.2. At first sight this may seem impossible since this model has an infinite number of unknowns. However, we know from Section 1.2.4 that the optimal time profile of the capital stock converges monotonically to the stationary solution. We use this observation to reduce the system of first-order conditions to a finite number of equations. In Section 3.2 we turn to the stochastic Ramsey model (1.22). We use the property of this model to converge after a one-time productivity shock, to trace out a Rational expectations path for its variables. From this path we obtain the solution for the decision variables of the current period. This observation dates back to FAIR and TAYLOR (1983) and was applied to the stochastic Ramsey model by GAGNON (1990) from whom we borrowed the label 'deterministic extended path'. More broadly speaking, the method is a forward iteration method, since we solve for current-period variables by determining a specific future path of the economy. We sketch the general structure of this approach at the end of Section 3.2 and close the chapter with two further applications in Section 3.3: our benchmark model of Example 1.5.1 and the small open economy model of CORREIA, NEVES and REBELO (1995). This latter model is less suited for the methods of Chapter 2, since it has no uniquely determined stationary solution. This feature, however, poses no problem for the deterministic extended path algorithm.

The mathematical tools that we employ in this chapter are algorithms that obtain approximate numeric solutions to systems of non-linear equations. We explain the mathematical background behind the most common routines in Section 11.5. It is the task of each researcher to prepare the system of non-linear equations to which her or his model gives rise so that a non-linear equations solver is able to obtain the solution. For this reason, this chapter is a collection of example applications that demonstrate the use of the deterministic extended path approach. Since the solution of non-linear equations with numerical methods is a delicate business, we hope nevertheless that it will be useful for the reader to go through the following pages.

3.1 Solution of Deterministic Models

In this section we use the finite-horizon deterministic Ramsey model (1.3) to illustrate the use of non-linear equation solvers. We then explain the computation of the saddle path of the infinite-horizon Ramsey model (1.8).

3.1.1 Finite-Horizon Models

The Model. Consider the first-order conditions of the finite-horizon Ramsey model (1.5), which we here repeat for your convenience:

$$K_{t+1} = f(K_t) - C_t, \qquad (3.1a)$$

$$\frac{\partial U(C_0, \ldots, C_T)/\partial C_t}{\partial U(C_0, \ldots, C_T)/\partial C_{t+1}} = f'(K_{t+1}). \qquad (3.1b)$$

The first equation is the economy's resource constraint, the second condition determines the farmer's savings. As usual, K_t denotes the capital stock of period $t = 0, 1, \ldots, T$ and C_t consumption.

3.1 Solution of Deterministic Models

To determine the time path of capital and consumption from this system, we must specify functional forms for U and f. We assume that U is given by the time-separable utility function

$$U(C_0,\ldots,C_T) := \sum_{t=0}^{T} \beta^t \frac{C_t^{1-\eta} - 1}{1-\eta}, \quad \beta \in (0,1), \eta > 0,$$

and that

$$f(K_t) := (1-\delta)K_t + K_t^\alpha, \quad \alpha \in (0,1), \delta \in [0,1],$$

where β is the discount factor and δ the rate of capital depreciation. Using these two functions, equations (3.1) simplify to

$$0 = [(1-\delta)K_t + K_t^\alpha - K_{t+1}]^{-\eta}$$
$$- \beta \left[(1-\delta)K_{t+1} + K_{t+1}^\alpha - K_{t+2}\right]^{-\eta} \left(1 - \delta + \alpha K_{t+1}^{\alpha-1}\right),$$
$$t = 0, 1, \ldots, T-1,$$
$$0 = K_{T+1}. \tag{3.2}$$

For a given initial capital stock K_0, this is a system of T non-linear equations in the T unknown capital stocks $K_1, K_2, \ldots, K_T$. Thus, it is an example of the general non-linear system of equations $\mathbf{f(x)} = \mathbf{0}$, $\mathbf{x} \in \mathbb{R}^n$ considered in Section 11.5 and can be solved by using the algorithms considered there.

Non-Linear Equations Solvers. For their proper use, you should know how non-linear equations solvers work. The common structure of the algorithms that we employ in this book is the iterative scheme:

$$\mathbf{x}_{s+1} = \mathbf{x}_s + \mu \Delta \mathbf{x}_s, \quad s = 0, 1, \ldots.$$

They start with an initial guess of the solution $\mathbf{x}_0$, determine a direction of change $\Delta \mathbf{x}$ and a step length μ, and proceed to the next guess of the solution $\mathbf{x}_1$. This process is continued until either $f(\mathbf{x}_s) \simeq \mathbf{0}$, in which case the problem is solved, or $\mathbf{x}_{s+1} - \mathbf{x}_s \simeq \mathbf{0}$ so that no further progress can be achieved. The algorithms differ in the way they determine both μ and $\Delta \mathbf{x}$.

The first problem that one, thus, encounters, is the choice of the initial value x_0. In the problems of this chapter, the stationary solution of the model is usually an adequate choice. In subsequent chapters, where we will face more complicated non-linear systems, we will employ genetic search algorithms to tackle the initial value problem. At least, we must find an x_0 so that f is defined at this point. In our model, this amounts to ensure that consumption is positive at x_0, because in the set of real numbers it is an undefined operation to raise a negative number to an arbitrary power. In our Gauss program Ramsey1.g we set the starting value equal to a fraction of $(1 - \delta)K_0 + K_0^\alpha$ for all initial K_t, $t = 1,\ldots,T$ guaranteeing $C_t > 0$, where K_0 is the capital stock inherited from the past – an exogenously given, arbitrary number.

The second problem that may surface is that the algorithm selects a point x_{s+1} at which f cannot be evaluated. Note, that many algorithms do not control for undefined operations, should they occur during the course of iterations. Usually, the program will stop with an error message. To prevent this, our own non-linear equation solvers keep track of an error flag that you can set before an undefined operation will be executed. If possible, the algorithm then reduces μ accordingly to way around this problem. A second work around is to tell the algorithm that there are upper and lower bounds for x. In the problems considered in this chapter this will usually be the case.

Solutions. Figure 3.1 displays four different solutions for the time path of the capital stock. They differ in the values of δ and K_0 but rest on the same choice of $\alpha = 0.27$, $\beta = 0.994$, and $T = 60$. The left panel displays solutions for the case $\delta = 1$. If the initial capital stock K_0 is small, the farmer quickly builds up his capital to a certain level, to which he sticks until shortly before the end of his planning horizon. Then he rapidly depletes this stock to the terminal value of $K_{T+1} = 0$. The farmer displays a similar behavior if his initial capital stock is very high. He dissaves to reach a target level, which he again maintains almost up to the end of his planning horizon.

The right panel displays solutions which rest on a more realistic value of $\delta = 0.011$ so that the farmer's savings are small relative

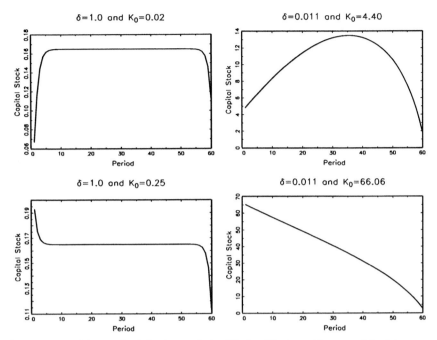

Figure 3.1: Example Solutions of the Finite-Horizon Ramsey Model

to his wealth K_t. Under this assumption the time path of the capital stock is hump-shaped if the given initial capital stock K_0 is small. If the farmer starts with a high capital stock, he continually depletes his resources over his entire planning period.

3.1.2 Infinite-Horizon Models

It is easy to extend the approach of the previous subsection to obtain approximate solutions of the transitional dynamics of infinite-horizon deterministic models. We take advantage of a model's property to approach a stationary solution from arbitrary initial conditions. An example of this property is the saddle path of the Ramsey model (1.8), which we study in Section 1.2.4. To approximate this path, we simply replace the terminal condition $K_{T+1} = 0$ in (3.2) with the stationary capital stock $K_{T+1} = K^*$. In this way, we obtain a finite-dimensional system of non-linear equations from the infinite number of equations that determine the true solution.

The Model. The Euler equations of the Ramsey model (1.8) are given in (1.17). Using the same functional forms as in the previous subsection, these equations also simplify to the system given in (3.2) except that they hold for all $t = 0, 1, \ldots$. This is a system with an infinite number of unknown variables. However, we know that this system determines a convergent path to the stationary capital stock determined by the condition $1 = \beta f'(K^*)$ (see Section 1.2.4 on this point). Using the definition of f given above, we can solve this condition for K^* resulting in

$$K^* = \left[\frac{1 - \beta(1 - \delta))}{\alpha\beta}\right]^{\frac{1}{\alpha-1}}. \tag{3.3}$$

To reduce the infinite number of equations, we assume that the economy will be close to K^* in period $t = T$. This allows us to replace $K_{T+1} = 0$ by $K_{T+1} = K^*$ in (3.2).

Solution. To generate a reliable approximation of the true saddle path, we must set T large enough so that K_{T+1} is indeed close to K^*. An appropriate method to determine T is to start with some small T, increase this to T', solve the larger system and compare the first T elements of this solution to the T elements of the previous solution. Should they differ by a small amount only, the proper T has been found. Otherwise this process is continued until sufficiently close solutions are found.

In the infinite-horizon model, the choice of the starting value is more delicate than in the finite-horizon model. The strategy that was successful in the latter model does not work if the economy's inherited capital stock K_0 (remember, this is a parameter of our model!) is small relative to K^*, because it implies $C_T < 0$. On the other hand, if we set all initial values equal to K^*, and K_0 is small, we get $C_0 < 0$. Instead of using different starting values for each K_t, we employ a homotopy method to approach K_0: We use K^* for all K_t to initialize the non-linear equations solver. This works, if we set K_0 very close to K^*. We then use this solution as starting value for a smaller K_0 and continue in this fashion until

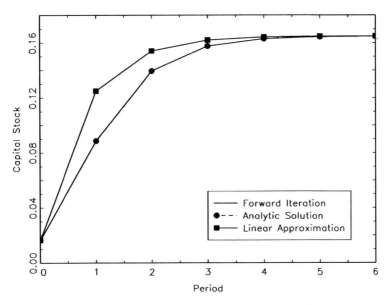

Figure 3.2: Approximate Time Path of the Capital Stock in the Deterministic Growth Model

K_0 has reached the value we desire. In our program Ramsey2c.g we reduce K_0 in this way to ten percent of the stationary capital stock. Figure 3.2 displays the time path of the capital stock for the case where an analytical solution is available, that is for $\eta = 1$ and $\delta = 1$. It is, thus, similar to Figure 2.2. Very obviously, the forward iteration method produces a much better approximation of the saddle path than the linear solution which we computed in Section 2.1. It is visually indistinguishable from the path obtained from the analytic solution $K_{t+1} = \alpha \beta K_t^\alpha$ (see Section 1.2.5).

3.2 Solution of Stochastic Models

In this section we use forward iterations to solve for the time path of stochastic DGE models. We use the infinite-horizon stochastic Ramsey model (1.22) to develop this method before we outline the algorithm in general.

3.2.1 An Illustrative Example

The time path of the stochastic infinite-horizon Ramsey model (1.22) is determined from the Euler equations (1.24). Let $u(C_t) := (C_t^{1-\eta} - 1)/(1-\eta)$ and $f(K_t) = K_t^\alpha$ denote the current-period utility function and the production function, respectively. In this case, these conditions may be written as:

$$\begin{aligned} 0 = & \left[(1-\delta)K_t + Z_t K_t^\alpha - K_{t+1}\right]^{-\eta} \\ & - \beta E_t \Big\{ \left[(1-\delta)K_{t+1} + Z_{t+1} K_{t+1}^\alpha - K_{t+2}\right]^{-\eta} \\ & \quad \times \left(1 - \delta + \alpha Z_{t+1} K_{t+1}^{\alpha-1}\right) \Big\}, \quad t = 0, 1, 2, \ldots. \end{aligned} \quad (3.4)$$

As previously, we assume that the natural log of the productivity level Z_t, $\ln Z_t$, is governed by a first-order autoregressive process:

$$\ln Z_t = \varrho \ln Z_{t-1} + \epsilon_t, \quad \varrho \in [0,1), \ \epsilon_t \sim N(0, \sigma^2). \quad (3.5)$$

Assume that the farmer observes the initial Z_0. His expected value of Z_1, then, is

$$E_0(\ln Z_1) = E_0(\varrho \ln Z_0 + \epsilon_1) = \varrho \ln Z_0$$

since $E_0(\epsilon_1) = 0$. Iterating on equation (3.5), he is, thus, able to determine the expected future path of Z_t:

$$\{Z_0, Z_1, \ldots\} = \{Z_t\}_{t=0}^\infty = \left\{Z_0^{\varrho^t}\right\}_{t=0}^\infty.$$

Given this path, we can determine the time path of the capital stock under the assumption that no further shocks will occur, that is $\epsilon_t = 0, \forall t = 1, 2, \ldots$. Under this assumption Z_t will approach $Z = 1$, and, consequently, K_t will converge to K^*, as given by equation (3.3). We can obtain an approximation of this path from the solution of the system of T non-linear equations

$$\begin{aligned} 0 = & \left[(1-\delta)K_t + Z_0^{\varrho^t} K_t^\alpha - K_{t+1}\right]^{-\eta} \\ & - \beta \left[(1-\delta)K_{t+1} + Z_0^{\varrho^{t+1}} K_{t+1}^\alpha - K_{t+2}\right]^{-\eta} \\ & \quad \times \left(1 - \delta + \alpha Z_0^{\varrho^{t+1}} K_{t+1}^{\alpha-1}\right), \end{aligned} \quad (3.6)$$

$$t = 0, 1, 2, \ldots T-1,$$
$$K_{T+1} = K^*.$$

This solution approximates the Rational expectations equilibrium of the model from the point of view of period $t = 0$. From this solution the farmer chooses K_1 as his next-period capital stock. At $t = 1$ he will observe a new shock ϵ_1 that will alter the expected path of Z_t. From this new path, we can again compute the Rational expectations equilibrium and obtain K_2. Proceeding in this way, we are able to compute the approximate dynamics of the model for an arbitrary number of periods.

Figure 3.3 plots a time path computed from the Gauss model Ramsey3c.g. The parameters are $\alpha = 0.27$, $\beta = 0.994$, $\varrho = 0.9$, $\sigma = 0.0072$, $\eta = 1$, and $\delta = 1$ so that an analytic solution $K_{t+1} = \alpha\beta Z_t K_t^\alpha$ exists. The time path obtained from the deterministic extended path (DEP) method is so close to the true solution that it is virtually impossible to distinguish them from each other with the naked eye. Numerically, the maximum absolute relative distance between the two paths,

$$\max_{t=0,1,\ldots,100} \left| \frac{K_t^{DEP} - K_t^{True}}{K_t^{True}} \right|$$

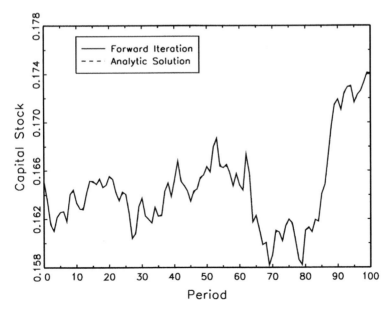

Figure 3.3: Simulated Time Path of the Stochastic Ramsey Model

is about 1.7E-08. In Problem 3.1 we ask you to compute the linear solution and to compare it to those shown in Figure 3.3. You will find that the maximum absolute relative distance of the linear solution to the true one is about 1.4E-3, and, thus, several orders of magnitude worse than the DEP solution.

3.2.2 The Algorithm in General

In this subsection we provide the general structure of the deterministic extended path algorithm. We resort to the notation of Section 2.5.4 to describe an arbitrary stochastic DGE model.

Notation. $\mathbf{x}_t \in \mathbb{R}^{n(x)}$ is the vector of those state variables that have given initial conditions $\mathbf{x}_0$ but are otherwise determined endogenously. $\mathbf{y}_t \in \mathbb{R}^{n(y)}$ is the vector of control and costate variables. Sometimes – as in our example consumption C_t – it may be easy to substitute these variables out of the dynamic system, but in general this will not be the case. The vector of purely exogenous variables, the vector of shocks, is denoted by $\mathbf{z}_t \in \mathbb{R}^{n(z)}$. The system of stochastic difference equations that governs this model is

$$\begin{aligned} 0 &= E_t \left[g^i(\mathbf{x}_t, \mathbf{y}_t, \mathbf{z}_t, \mathbf{x}_{t+1}, \mathbf{y}_{t+1}, \mathbf{z}_{t+1}) \right], \\ \mathbf{z}_t &= \Pi \mathbf{z}_{t-1} + \sigma \Omega \epsilon_t, \quad \epsilon_t \sim N(\mathbf{0}_{n(z)}, I_{n(z)}), \sigma \geq 0, \\ i &= 1, 2, \ldots, n(x) + n(y), \\ t &= 0, 1, \ldots. \end{aligned} \quad (3.7)$$

The eigenvalues of the matrix Π are all within the unitUnit circle circle so that $\mathbf{z}_t$ will approach $\mathbf{0}_{n(z)}$, if $\epsilon_t = \mathbf{0}_{n(z)} \forall t$. We further assume that in this case $\mathbf{x}_t$ and $\mathbf{y}_t$ converge to the stationary values $\mathbf{x}^*$ and $\mathbf{y}^*$, respectively. The local convergence of the model can be verified from the linearized model at $(\mathbf{x}^*, \mathbf{y}^*, \mathbf{0})$. In the notation of the reduced system (2.51) the matrix W must have $n(x)$ eigenvalues within the unitUnit circle circle.

The Algorithm. Given these properties, we can obtain a finite-dimensional system of non-linear equations from (3.7) which allows us to compute the Rational expectations path of the model for each given $\mathbf{z}_t$.

Algorithm 3.2.1 (Deterministic Extended Path)

Purpose: *Simulation of the stochastic DGE model (3.7)*

Steps:

Step 1: *Initialize: Let p denote the number of periods to consider and $(\mathbf{x}_0, \mathbf{z}_0)$ the initial state of the model.*

  Step 1.1: Use a random number generator and draw a sequence of shocks $\{\epsilon_t\}_{t=0}^{p}$.

  Step 1.2: Compute the time path $\{\mathbf{z}_t\}_{t=1}^{p}$ from $\mathbf{z}_t = \Pi \mathbf{z}_{t-1} + \sigma \Omega \epsilon_t$.

  Step 1.3: Choose T large enough so that $(\mathbf{x}^*, \mathbf{y}^*)$ is a good approximation of $(\mathbf{x}_T, \mathbf{y}_T)$ under the maintained assumption that after $t = 0, 1, \ldots, p$ the vector of innovations equals its unconditional mean: $\epsilon_{t+s} = \mathbf{0} \; \forall s = 1, 2, \ldots, T$. (Iterate over T to see whether this condition holds.)

Step 2: *For $t = 0, 1, \ldots, p$ repeat these steps:*

  Step 2.1: Compute the expected time path of $\{\mathbf{z}_{t+s}\}_{s=0}^{t+T}$ from $\mathbf{z}_{t+s} = \Pi^s \mathbf{z}_t$.

  Step 2.2: Solve the system of $T(n(x) + n(y))$ equations

  $$0 = g^i(\mathbf{x}_{t+s}, \mathbf{y}_{t+s}, \Pi^s \mathbf{z}_t, \mathbf{x}_{t+s+1}, \mathbf{y}_{t+s+1}, \Pi^{s+1} \mathbf{z}_t),$$
  $$i = 1, 2, \ldots, n(x) + n(y),$$
  $$s = 0, 1, \ldots, T-1,$$
  $$\mathbf{x}^* = \mathbf{x}_{t+T},$$

  for $\{\mathbf{x}_{t+s}\}_{s=1}^{T}$ and $\{\mathbf{y}_{t+s}\}_{s=0}^{T}$. From the solution, keep $\mathbf{x}_{t+1}$ and $\mathbf{y}_t$.

  Step 2.3: Use $\mathbf{x}_{t+1}$ as starting value for period $t+1$.

Note that it is not possible to set $\mathbf{y}_{t+T}$ equal to $\mathbf{y}^*$ in Step 2.2, since this would yield a system with more equations than unknown variables. As a consequence, it is, thus, not possible to iterate backwards starting from

$$0 = g^i(\mathbf{x}_{t+T-1}, \mathbf{y}_{t+T-1}, \Pi^{T-1}\mathbf{z}, \mathbf{x}^*, \mathbf{y}^*, \Pi^T),$$
$$i = 1, 2, \ldots, n(x) + n(y).$$

We must, indeed, solve the entire system of interdependent equations. Even with a moderate number of variables this systems will comprise several hundreds of equations. Algorithms which compute the Jacobian of the system to determine the direction of progress will consume a considerable amount of computation time. It is, thus, advisable to reduce the system as far as possible. For instance, one may use static equations to substitute out a part or even all of the control variables of the model. The applications of the next section illustrate this approach.

3.3 Further Applications

The first application which we consider is the benchmark model of Example 1.5.1.

3.3.1 The Benchmark Model

Our starting point is the system of stochastic difference equations from Section 1.5. We repeat these equations for your convenience but assume that you are familiar with our notation. If not, please refer either to Chapter 1 or to footnote 23 in Chapter 2 for a quick reference.

$$0 = c_t^{-\eta}(1 - N_t)^{\theta(1-\eta)} - \lambda_t, \tag{3.8a}$$
$$0 = \theta c_t^{1-\eta}(1 - N_t)^{\theta(1-\eta)-1} - (1-\alpha)\lambda_t Z_t N_t^{-\alpha} k_t^{\alpha}, \tag{3.8b}$$
$$0 = ak_{t+1} - (1-\delta)k_t + c_t - Z_t N_t^{1-\alpha} k_t^{\alpha}, \tag{3.8c}$$
$$0 = \lambda_t - \beta a^{-\eta} E_t \lambda_{t+1} \left(1 - \delta + \alpha Z_{t+1} N_{t+1}^{1-\alpha} k_{t+1}^{\alpha-1}\right). \tag{3.8d}$$

This system is an example of the general model defined in equations (3.7), with $\mathbf{x}_t \equiv k_t$, $\mathbf{y}_t \equiv [c_t, N_t, \lambda_t]'$, and $\mathbf{z}_t \equiv \ln Z_t$. For a given T, for example $T = 150$, we have to solve a system of 600 unknown variables. This is a pretty large number. In Problem 3.2 we ask you to write a program that solves this system. We, instead, will use the two static equations (3.8a) and (3.8b) to reduce the above system to a system with $2T$ variables. Substituting for λ_t in equation (3.8b) from equation (3.8a) yields:

$$c_t = \frac{1-\alpha}{\theta}(1-N_t)Z_t N_t^{-\alpha} k_t^{\alpha}.$$

This allows us to eliminate consumption c_t from the resource constraint (3.8c). In addition, we solve (3.8a) for λ_t and use the solution to replace this variable from equation (3.8d). In the ensuing equation we eliminate c_t with the help of the resource constraint (3.8c). The result is a system of $2T$ equations in the unknown variables $\{N_{t+s}\}_{s=0}^{T}$ and $\{k_{t+s}\}_{s=1}^{T-1}$:

$$0 = Z_t^{\varrho^s} N_{t+s}^{1-\alpha} k_{t+s}^{\alpha} + (1-\delta)k_{t+s} - ak_{t+s+1}$$
$$- \frac{1-\alpha}{\theta}(1-N_{t+s})Z_t^{\varrho^s} N_{t+s}^{-\alpha} k_{t+s}^{\alpha},$$

$$0 = \left(\frac{Z_t^{\varrho^{s+1}} N_{t+s+1}^{1-\alpha} k_{t+s+1}^{\alpha} + (1-\delta)k_{t+s+1} - ak_{t+s+2}}{Z_t^{\varrho^s} N_{t+s}^{1-\alpha} k_{t+s}^{\alpha} + (1-\delta)k_{t+s} - ak_{t+s+1}} \right)^{\eta}$$
$$\times \left(\frac{1-N_{t+s}}{1-N_{t+s+1}} \right)^{\theta(1-\eta)} - \beta a^{-\eta} \left(1-\delta + \alpha Z_t^{\varrho^{s+1}} N_{t+s+1}^{1-\alpha} k_{t+s+1}^{\alpha-1} \right),$$

$s = 0, \ldots, T-1, \quad k_T = k_{T+1} = k.$

Our program Benchmark.for solves this system with our non-linear equations solver FixvMN2. This program takes care of the upper and lower bounds for both the capital stock and working hours. In addition, we use a flag that signals the program if consumption becomes negative. If this should occur during the simulations, the program computes a homotopy path: The distance between (k_t, z_t) – the state of the system at period t from which the rational expectations path is to be computed – and the stationary solution $(k, \ln Z = 0)$ is divided into n small steps $(\Delta k, \Delta \ln Z)$. The non-linear equations solver is restarted from $(k + \Delta k, \Delta \ln Z)$ using the stationary solution as initial value. This always works if Δk and ΔZ are small enough. The solution is then taken as starting value for the next pair of states $(k + 2\Delta k, 2\Delta \ln Z)$. In this way, the algorithm proceeds until it arrives at (k_t, z_t).

Table 3.1 compares the results of our simulations to those obtained in Chapter 2 from the linear policy functions (see Table 2.2).

Table 3.1

	Linear			DEP		
Variable	s_x	r_{xy}	r_x	s_x	r_{xy}	r_x
		Second Moments				
Output	1.44	1.00	0.64	1.44	1.00	0.64
Investment	6.11	1.00	0.64	6.11	1.00	0.64
Consumption	0.56	0.99	0.66	0.56	0.99	0.66
Hours	0.77	1.00	0.64	0.77	1.00	0.64
Real Wage	0.67	0.99	0.65	0.67	0.99	0.65
		Euler Equation Residuals				
$[0.90; 1.10]k$		1.835E-4			8.370E-7	
$[0.85; 1.15]k$		3.478E-4			9.130E-7	
$[0.80; 1.20]k$		5.670E-4			1.101E-6	
		DM-Statistic				
<3.816		5.0			2.8	
>21.920		3.0			3.0	

Notes: s_x:=standard deviation of variable x, r_{xy}:=cross correlation of variable x with output, r_x:=first order autocorrelation of variable x. All second moments refer to HP-filtered percentage deviations from a variable's stationary solution. Euler equation residuals are computed as maximum absolute value over a grid of 400 equally spaced points on the square $\mathscr{K} \times [\ln 0.95; \ln 1.05]$, where $\mathscr{K}$ is defined in the respective row of the first column. The 2.5 and the 97.5 percent critical values of the $\chi^2(11)$-distribution are displayed in the last two lines of the first column. The table entries refer to the percentage fraction out of 1,000 simulations where the DM-statistic is below (above) its respective critical value.

The parameters of the model are those presented in Table 1.1. The length of the deterministic extended path (DEP) is $T = 150$. We have chosen this number, because it implies a high degree of accuracy. When we reduced T to 100, the maximum absolute Euler equation residual increased by a factor of 14. Table 3.1 confirms our first finding in Section 2.6.1: There are no numeric differences (up to the second digits) between the second moments. However, the DEP method provides a remarkable increase in the degree of accuracy. The respective Euler equation residuals are about 500 times smaller than those of the linear method. This comes, however, at the cost of computing time. It requires less than a second to compute the second moments by using the linear policy functions. The DEP method consumes more than two and half an hour for the same task. There is a second difference between the two methods. The Euler equation residuals of the DEP method do not change much if we increase the interval around the stationary solution. The DEP is not a local method. It computes a Rational expectations path from the given state of the system to the stationary solution implied by this state. If T is reasonably large, this path will be very close to the true saddle path, even if the initial state is far from the stationary solution. The smaller fraction of simulations that result in a DM-statistic below the 2.5 percent critical value also indicates that the DEP method provides a more accurate solution than the linear method. However, it took almost two weeks to compute the DM-statistic.

3.3.2 A Small Open Economy

As a second example we present the small open economy model of CORREIA, NEVES, and REBELO (1995). We portray this economy from the perspective of a representative household who is both a consumer and a producer. This will streamline the derivation of the necessary equations. Problem 3.3 sketches a decentralized economy with the same dynamic properties.

The Model. Consider a consumer-producer in a small open economy who uses domestic labor N_t and domestic capital K_t to produce output Y_t according to

$$Y_t = Z_t F(A_t N_t, K_t).$$

The natural logarithm of total factor productivity Z_t follows the AR(1) process

$$\ln Z_t = \varrho \ln Z_{t-1} + \epsilon_t, \quad \varrho \in [0, 1), \; \epsilon_t \sim N(0, \sigma^2),$$

while the level of labor augmenting technical progress A_t grows deterministically

$$A_{t+1} = aA_t, \quad a \geq 1.$$

Capital formation is subject to frictions, that is, investment expenditures I_t do not produce additional capital one-to-one. Instead, it becomes more and more difficult to build up capital, if investment expenditures increase. This is captured by

$$K_{t+1} = \phi(I_t/K_t)K_t + (1-\delta)K_t, \quad \delta \in (0,1), \qquad (3.10)$$

where $\phi(\cdot)$ is a concave function. The usual, frictionless process of capital accumulation, $K_{t+1} = I_t + (1-\delta)K_t$, is a special case of (3.10) for $\phi(I_t/K_t) \equiv I_t/K_t$.

The consumer in this economy can freely borrow or lend on the international capital market at the real interest rate r_t. At period t, his net foreign wealth is B_t. Accordingly, his budget constraint is given by

$$B_{t+1} - B_t \leq TB_t + r_t B_t, \qquad (3.11)$$

where

$$TB_t = Y_t - C_t - I_t$$

is the country's trade balance. However, there are legal restrictions on the amount of international borrowing that prevent the consumer from accumulating debt at a rate that exceeds the respective interest rate, that is:

$$\lim_{t \to \infty} \frac{B_{t+1}}{(1+r_0)(1+r_1)(1+r_2)\cdots(1+r_t)} \geq 0.$$

A country that is initially a net debtor ($B_0 < 0$) must therefore allow for future trade surpluses so that the inequality

$$-B_0 \leq \sum_{t=0}^{\infty} \frac{TB_t}{(1+r_0)(1+r_1)\cdots(1+r_t)} \qquad (3.12)$$

will be satisfied. The consumer-producer chooses consumption C_t, investment I_t, working hours N_t, his future domestic capital stock K_{t+1} and net foreign wealth B_{t+1} to maximize

$$U_t = E_t \sum_{s=0}^{\infty} \beta^s u(C_{t+s}, N_{t+s}), \quad \beta \in (0,1)$$

subject to his budget constraint (3.11), the capital accumulation equation (3.10), the solvency condition (3.12), and given initial stocks K_t and B_t, respectively.

First-Order Conditions. The Lagrangian of this problem is

$$\mathscr{L} = E_t \sum_{s=0}^{\infty} \beta^s \Big\{ u(C_{t+s}, N_{t+s}) \\
+ \Lambda_{t+s}\big[Z_{t+s}F(A_{t+s}N_{t+s}, K_{t+s}) + (1+r_{t+s})B_{t+s} \\
\qquad - C_{t+s} - I_{t+s} - B_{t+s+1}\big] \\
+ \Lambda_{t+s}q_{t+s}\big[\phi(I_{t+s}/K_{t+s})K_{t+s} + (1-\delta)K_{t+s} \\
\qquad - K_{t+s+1}\big] \Big\}.$$

The multiplier q_t is the price of capital in terms of the consumption good so that $\Lambda_t q_t$ is the price in utility terms (that is, in the units in which we measure utility u). Differentiating this expression with respect to C_t, N_t, I_t, K_{t+1} and B_{t+1} provides the first-order conditions

$$0 = u_C(C_t, N_t) - \Lambda_t, \tag{3.13a}$$
$$0 = u_N(C_t, N_t) + \Lambda_t Z_t F_{AN}(A_t N_t, K_t) A_t, \tag{3.13b}$$
$$0 = q_t - \frac{1}{\phi'(I_t/K_t)}, \tag{3.13c}$$
$$0 = q_t - \beta E_t \frac{\Lambda_{t+1}}{\Lambda_t}\Big[Z_{t+1}F_K(A_{t+1}N_{t+1}, K_{t+1}) \tag{3.13d}$$
$$\qquad + q_{t+1}\big(1 - \delta + \phi(I_{t+1}/K_{t+1})\big) - (I_{t+1}/K_{t+1})\Big],$$
$$0 = \Lambda_t - \beta E_t \Lambda_{t+1}(1 + r_{t+1}). \tag{3.13e}$$

The first two equations and the last equation are standard and need no further comment. The third equation determines investment expenditures as a function of the current capital stock and the price of capital q_t. According to the fourth equation (3.13d), the current price of capital must equal the expected discounted future reward from an additional unit of capital. This reward has several components: the increased output as given by the marginal product of capital $Z_{t+1}F_K(A_{t+1}N_{t+1}, K_{t+1})$, the residual value of the remaining unit of capital $q_{t+1}(1-\delta)$, and the increased productivity of future investment

$$q_{t+1}\phi(\cdot) - \underbrace{q_{t+1}\phi'(\cdot)}_{=1}(I_{t+1}/K_{t+1}).$$

Functional Forms. CORREIA, NEVES, and REBELO (1995) assume that F is the usual Cobb-Douglas function

$$F(A_tN_t, K_t) = (A_tN_t)^{1-\alpha}K_t^{\alpha}, \quad \alpha \in (0,1). \tag{3.14}$$

For the current period utility function they consider the specification proposed by GREENWOOD, HERCOWITZ and HUFFMAN (1988):

$$u(C_t, N_t) = \frac{\left(C_t - \frac{\theta}{1+\nu}A_tN_t^{1+\nu}\right)^{1-\eta}}{1-\eta}, \quad \theta, \nu > 0. \tag{3.15}$$

They do not need to specify the function ϕ, because they resort to the linear solution method, which only requires the elasticity of ϕ'. We, however, need an explicit function to solve for the deterministic extended path and use

$$\phi(I_t/K_t) = \frac{\phi_1}{1-\zeta}\left(\frac{I_t}{K_t}\right)^{1-\zeta} + \phi_2, \quad \zeta \geq 0. \tag{3.16}$$

This is an increasing, concave function of its argument I_t/K_t. The parameter ζ is the elasticity of ϕ' and determines the degree of concavity. For ζ close to zero, adjustment costs play a minor role.

Temporary Equilibrium. The model depicts a growing economy. Therefore, we must define new variables that are stationary. As in the benchmark model this is accomplished by scaling the original variables (in as far as they are not themselves stationary) by the level of labor augmenting technical progress A_t. We think by now your are familiar with this procedure and able to derive the following system from (3.13) and the functional specifications (3.14), (3.15), and (3.16), respectively.

$$0 = \left(c_t - \frac{\theta}{1+\nu} N_t^{1+\nu}\right)^{-\eta} - \lambda_t, \tag{3.17a}$$

$$0 = \theta N_t^\nu - (1-\alpha) Z_t N_t^{-\alpha} k_t^\alpha, \tag{3.17b}$$

$$0 = i_t - (\phi_1 q_t)^{1/\zeta} k_t, \tag{3.17c}$$

$$0 = q_t - \beta a^{-\eta} E_t \frac{\lambda_{t+1}}{\lambda_t} \Big[\alpha Z_{t+1} N_{t+1}^{1-\alpha} k_{t+1}^{\alpha-1} \tag{3.17d}$$
$$\qquad + q_{t+1} \left(1 - \delta + \phi(i_{t+1}/k_{t+1})\right) - (i_{t+1}/k_{t+1}) \Big],$$

$$0 = \lambda_t - \beta a^{-\eta} E_t \lambda_{t+1}(1 + r_{t+1}), \tag{3.17e}$$

$$0 = a k_{t+1} - \phi(i_t/k_t) k_t - (1-\delta) k_t, \tag{3.17f}$$

$$0 = a b_{t+1} - Z_t N_t^{1-\alpha} k_t^\alpha - (1+r_t) b_t + c_t + i_t. \tag{3.17g}$$

The lower case variables are defined as $x_t := X_t/A_t$, $X_t \in \{C_t, I_t, K_t, B_t\}$ except for $\lambda_t := A_t^\eta \Lambda_t$. Equation (3.17b) follows from (3.13b) if Λ_t is replaced by (3.13a). It determines working hours N_t as a function of the marginal product of labor. In a decentralized economy the latter equals the real wage per efficiency unit of labor w_t. Viewed from this perspective, equation (3.17b) is a static labor supply equation with w_t as its single argument so that there is no operative income effect. This is an implication of the utility function (3.15). Equation (3.17f) is the scaled transition law of capital (3.10), and equation (3.17g) derives from the households budget constraint (3.11).

Calibration. We do not intend to provide a careful, consistent calibration of this model with respect to a specific small open economy (say, the Portuguese one to which CORREIA, NEVES, and REBELO (1995) refer), since we left out a few details of the original model (as government spending and international transfers) and since our focus is on the technical details of the solution but not on the model's descriptive power. For this reason we continue to use the values of the parameters a, α, β, η, δ, ϱ, σ, N from Table 1.1. As we have just noted, (3.17b) defines a labor supply schedule with $1/\nu$ as the elasticity of labor supply with respect to the real wage. As in HEER and MAUSSNER (2008), we use $\nu = 5$ and calibrate θ so that the stationary fraction of working hours equals $N = 0.13$. We borrow the value of $\zeta = 1/30$ from the authors of the original model and choose the remaining parameters of (3.16) so that adjustment costs play no role on the model's balanced growth path. This requires $i = (a + \delta - 1)k$ and $q = 1$, implying

$$\phi_1 = (a + \delta - 1)^\zeta,$$

$$\phi_2 = (a + \delta - 1)\frac{\zeta}{\zeta - 1}.$$

Balanced Growth Path. Given the choices made so far, we can solve equations (3.17) for the economy's balanced growth path by ignoring the expectations operator and by setting $x_t = x_{t+1} = x$ for all variables x. Equation (3.17e) then implies

$$r = \frac{a^\eta}{\beta} - 1. \tag{3.18a}$$

This is a restriction on the parameters of our model, since the real interest rate r is exogenous to the small open economy. The properties of the function ϕ imply the solution for the output-capital ratio from equation (3.17d):

$$\frac{y}{k} = \frac{a^\eta - \beta(1 - \delta)}{\alpha\beta}. \tag{3.18b}$$

Given N we can infer k and y from this solution. This, in turn, allows us to solve (3.17c) for i. It is, however, not possible to obtain definite solutions for both b and c: on the balanced growth path the budget constraint (3.17g) simplifies to

$$(a - (1 + r))b = y - c - i. \tag{3.18c}$$

Formally, the parameter restriction (3.18a) deprives the model of one equation. Economically, the possibility to borrow on the international capital market allows consumption smoothing to a degree that imposes a unit root. To understand this, consider equation (3.17e) and assume a constant real interest rate r and perfect foresight. This implies

$$\frac{\lambda_{t+1}}{\lambda_t} = 1$$

so that there is no tendency for λ_t to return to its initial value λ, say, after a shock. However, N is determined from a, α, β, δ, θ, and ν, and will converge, if the stock of capital will converge to k. As a consequence, any permanent jump of λ_t translates into a permanent jump of consumption and – via the budget constraint – into a permanent change of b_t.

This unit root is an obstacle for any local solution method. After all, these methods determine the parameters of the policy function from the stationary solution. A model without tendency to return to its balanced growth path can be driven far apart from it, even by a sequence of shocks that are themselves generated from a stationary stochastic process. The policy functions that are used to simulate this model, thus, might become more and more unreliable. As we will demonstrate in the next paragraph, the deterministic extended path algorithm is immune to this problem.

Before we turn to the solution of our model, we resolve the problem with c and b. We simply assume that the economy starts with zero net foreign debt, $b = 0$, so that $c = y - i$.

Solution and Results. The system of equations (3.17) fits into the general structure of equations (3.7). The shocks are $z_t = [\ln Z_t, r_t]'$, the state variable with initial conditions are $\mathbf{x}_t = [k_t, b_t]'$, the control and costate variables are $\mathbf{y}_t = [c_t, i_t, N_t, \lambda_t, q_t]'$. As in the previous subsection, we reduce this system by substituting out the control variables (c_t, i_t, N_t). This is easily accomplished since equations (3.17a) through (3.17c) can be solved analytically for these three variables. We can further reduce the number of unknown variables by noting that equation (3.17e) determines the entire path of $\{\lambda_t\}_{t=0}^T$ from the exogenous path $\{r_t\}_{t=0}^T$ of the world interest rate and from λ_0. We assume – without proof – that the capital stock approaches k, but invite you to use the methods from Section 2.4.2 and check numerically that at $(k, 0, \lambda, 1)$ the model has indeed one root equal to unity, one root between zero and one

196 Chapter 3: Deterministic Extended Path

and two roots outside the unitUnit circle circle. As noted above, this implies that N_t, y_t, and i_t also approach their stationary values. For the model to be consistent with the solvency condition (3.12), it must hold that b_t does not grow without bounds but converges to a certain limit in response to a shock. We induce this condition by assuming $b_T = b_{T-1}$ for some large T. In this way we reduce (3.17) to a system of $3T$ equations in $\{k_t\}_{t=1}^{T-1}$, $\{b_t\}_{t=1}^{T-1}$, $\{q_t\}_{t=0}^{T}$, and λ_0. The Gauss program SOE.g computes impulse responsesImpulse response function to productivity and interest rate shocks from this system.

Consider, first, a productivity shock. Figure 3.4 plots the response of the model's state and costate variables, Figure 3.5 shows the time paths of several other variables.

The figures confirm what we have noted in the previous paragraph. The shock boosts the current – and since it is highly autocorrelated – the expected future rewards of labor. In Figure 3.5 this appears as a temporary increase of the real wage. Due to the

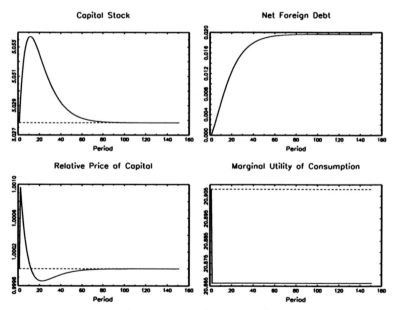

Figure 3.4: Response of State and Costate Variables to a Productivity Shock in the Small Open Economy

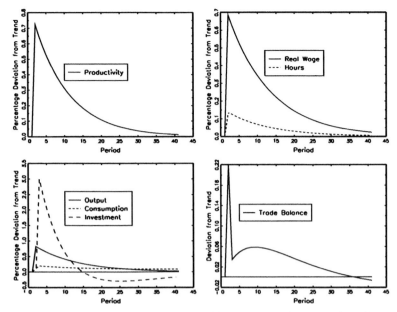

Figure 3.5: Response of Control Variables to a Productivity Shock in the Small Open Economy

small elasticity of labor supply, working hours increase slightly, and raise output beyond the level which is implied by the increased total factor productivity. The household also anticipates a temporary increase of the marginal product of capital. This higher reward raises investment and induces the hump-shaped response of the capital stock seen in Figure 3.4. Note that the shadow price of capital falls below unity on its way back to the stationary value of $q = 1$. Consider, now the reaction of consumption. Different from the closed economy, where the interest rate will approach its former level after a temporary productivity shock, the household can earn the rate r on his savings forever. This allows him to increase consumption permanently – a much stronger way to smooth consumption. To achieve this, the household sells part of the domestic production on the world market in exchange for bonds. After domestic production and investment have returned to their respective pre-shock values, the interest income allows for a permanently higher level of consumption. The mirror image of this exchange is the development of the trade balance: initially, we observe a surplus that finally turns into a permanent deficit. Corresponding to the permanent increase of consumption is the once and for all drop of the marginal utility of consumption displayed in the lower left panel of Figure 3.4, where the broken line indicates the pre-shock value of λ.

Consider, second, a shock to the world interest rate. If this shock is not autocorrelated, and if – as assumed here – the domestic economy is initially neither a net debtor nor a net creditor, this shock has no impact: the current income does not change (since $r_0 b_0 = 0$), so λ does not need to adjust, and in $t = 1$ the world interest rate is back to its initial value so that there are no further, anticipated effects. In Figure 3.6 we display the consequences of an autocorrelated, positive interest rate shock (see the upper left panel) that hits the economy in period $t = 1$. The autocorrelation coefficient of the shock equals 0.90 and the shock increases the world interest rate by one percent in $t = 1$. The prospect of

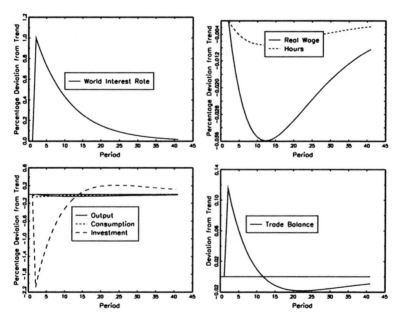

Figure 3.6: Response to an Interest Rate Shock in the Small Open Economy

temporarily higher returns on the international capital market increases savings (see the small, but visible fall of consumption) and triggers a portfolio adjustment. Temporarily, investment in the home country stock of capital declines in favor of foreign bonds. The reduced stock of capital decreases the marginal product of labor so that the real wage and employment shrink. This occurs no sooner than in period $t = 2$, so that output begins to decline in the period after the incidence of the shock. In the end, we observe a permanent increase of consumption financed from the interest income on foreign bonds. Therefore, the initial trade surplus is being replaced by a permanent trade deficit in the long-run.

Problems

3.1 Stochastic Ramsey Model. Figure 3.3 displays a simulated time path of the stochastic Ramsey model 1.22 obtained from the deterministic extended path method. Use our program `Ramsey3c` and the vector of productivity levels `zvec_Figure3_3` to recompute this path. In addition, compute the linear solution as explained in Section 2.4. Compare the linear solution to the analytic solution and to the deterministic extended path solution.

3.2 Benchmark Model. In Section 3.3.1 we use a reduced system of equations to compute the deterministic extended path solution of the Benchmark model from Example 1.5.1. Use the system of equations (3.8) instead of this system and recompute the solution. Compare the run-time of your program to the run-time of our program.

3.3 A Small Open Economy with Consumers and Producers. The economy is populated by a unit mass of identical consumers. The representative consumer supplies labor services N_t and allocates his wealth between the stocks S_t of domestic firms and an internationally traded bond B_t. The rate of return of this bond is determined on the world capital market and denoted by r_t. Domestic firms are distributed on the unit interval and are identical. As a result, the consumer must choose how much of his wealth he wants to put in the stocks of domestic firms, but he has no need to decide about the allocation of funds invested into specific firms. The stock price of the representative firm is v_t. Each stock yields a dividend payment of d_t. The consumer's budget constraint, thus, is:

$$B_{t+1} - B_t + v_t(S_{t+1} - S_t) = w_t A_t N_t + (1+r_t)B_t + d_t S_t - C_t,$$

where C_t denotes consumption, w_t is the real wage per efficiency unit of labor $A_t N_t$. At period $t = 0$ the consumer chooses C_0, N_0, S_1, and B_1 to maximize

$$E_0 \sum_{t=0}^{\infty} \beta^t \frac{\left(C_t - \frac{\theta}{1+\nu} N_t^{1+\nu}\right)^{1-\eta} - 1}{1-\eta}, \quad \beta \in (0,1),\ \theta > 0,\ \nu > 0,$$

subject to his budget constraints and given his initial portfolio (B_0, S_0). The consumer is not allowed to accumulate debt at an ever increasing rate. Thus

$$\lim_{t \to \infty} \frac{B_{t+1}}{(1+r_0)(1+r_1)\cdots(1+r_t)} \geq 0.$$

The representative firm produces output Y_t according to the function

$$Y_t = Z_t(A_t N_t)^{1-\alpha} K_t^{\alpha}, \quad \alpha \in (0,1).$$

Z_t is a stationary random process and the level of labor augmenting technical progress A_t is governed by

$$A_{t+1} = a A_t, \quad a \geq 1.$$

The firm is not able to rent capital services but must accumulate capital according to

$$K_{t+1} = \phi(I_t/K_t)K_t + (1-\delta)K_t.$$

The firm funds its investment expenditures I_t from retained earnings RE_t and the emission of new stocks $v_t(S_{t+1} - S_t)$:

$$I_t = RE_t + v_t(S_{t+1} - S_t).$$

Profits $Y_t - w_t A_t N_t$ which are not retained for investment are distributed to its share holders:

$$d_t S_t = Y_t - w_t A_t N_t - RE_t.$$

Let $R_t = (v_t + d_t)/v_{t-1}$ denote the gross return on shares. At $t = 0$ the firm maximizes

$$V_0 := E_0 \sum_{t=0}^{\infty} \frac{Y_t - w_t A_t N_t - I_t}{R_0 R_1 \cdots R_t}$$

subject to the above given constraints with respect to N_0, I_0, and K_1. Show that the first-order conditions of the consumer's and the firm's problem together with the various constraints specified above imply the system of stochastic difference equations given in (3.17).

3.4 **Consumption Smoothing in the Small Open Economy.** According to our findings in Section 3.3.2, a small open economy should display more consumption smoothing than an otherwise identical closed economy. To confirm this assertion, we ask you to write a program that computes second moments of consumption from simulated time series. To stick as close to our benchmark model of Example 1.5.1 use the traditional utility function

$$u(C_t, N_t) = \frac{C_t^{1-\eta}(1-N_t)^{\theta(1-\eta)} - 1}{1-\eta}$$

instead of equation (3.15). Assume a constant world interest rate given by $r = (a^{\eta}/\beta) - 1$ so that productivity shocks are the single cause of the business cycle. Calibrate ζ from equation (3.16) so that the standard deviation of investment equals the standard deviation of investment in the benchmark model.

Chapter 3: Deterministic Extended Path

3.5 **Productivity and Preference Shocks.** Empirically the correlation between working hours and the real wage is close to zero. The benchmark model, however, predicts a strong positive correlation. In the following model, which is adapted from HOLLAND and SCOTT (1998), we introduce a preference shock in the benchmark model of Example 1.5.1. Specifically, we assume that the parameter θ in the momentary utility function of the representative household is not a constant but a random variable θ_t that is governed by a first-order autoregressive process:

$$\theta_t = \theta^{1-\gamma}\theta_{t-1}^{\gamma}e^{\xi_t}, \quad \gamma \in [0,1], \; \xi_t \sim N(0, \sigma_\xi^2).$$

The innovations ξ_t induce shifts of the labor supply schedule along a given labor demand schedule. By this, they counteract the positive correlation between the real wage and working hours introduced by shocks to total factor productivity Z_t. The planer's problem is as follows:

$$\max_{C_0, N_0} E_0 \left\{ \sum_{t=0}^{\infty} \beta^t \frac{C_t^{1-\eta}(1-N_t)^{\theta_t(1-\eta)}}{1-\eta} \right\}$$

s.t.

$$\left.\begin{array}{rcl} K_{t+1} + C_t & \leq & Z_t(A_t N_t)^{1-\alpha} K_t^{\alpha} + (1-\delta)K_t, \\ A_t & = & aA_{t-1}, \quad a \geq 1, \\ Z_t & = & Z_{t-1}^{\varrho}e^{\epsilon_t}, \quad \epsilon_t \sim N(0, \sigma_\epsilon^2), \\ 0 & \leq & C_t, \\ 1 & \geq & N_t \geq 0, \\ 0 & \leq & K_{t+1}, \end{array}\right\} t = 0, 1, \ldots,$$

K_0, A_0 Z_0 given.

Use the parameter values given in Table 1.1 to calibrate this model. In addition, put $\gamma = 0.9$ and $\sigma_\xi = 0.01$ and calibrate θ so that the stationary fraction of working hours equals $N = 0.13$.

a) Derive the first-order conditions for the planer's problem and write it down in terms of stationary variables. Modify the extended path algorithm 3.2.1 to suit this model.
b) Simulate the model several hundred times. Pass the time series for working hours and the real wage to the HP-filter and compute the average cross-correlation between those two variables.
c) Repeat this exercise for a value of σ_ξ close to zero.

3.6 **Transition Dynamics and Endogenous Growth.** The following endogenous growth model is based on LUCAS (1990). The description of the dynamics is adapted from GRÜNER and HEER (2000).

Consider the following deterministic Ramsey problem that is augmented by a human capital sector. Households live infinitely maximizing intertemporal utility:

$$\sum_{t=0}^{\infty} \beta^t \frac{\left(c_t l_t^\theta\right)^{1-\eta}}{1-\eta}, \quad 0 < \beta < 1, \ 0 < \theta,$$

where c_t and l_t denote consumption and leisure in period t. The individual can allocate his time endowment B to work n, learning v and leisure l:

$$B = n_t + v_t + l_t.$$

The human capital of the representative individual h is determined by the time v he allocates to learning according to:

$$h_{t+1} = h_t\left(1 + Dv_t^\gamma\right).$$

Physical capital k_t accumulates according to:

$$k_{t+1} = (1-\tau_w)n_t h_t w_t + (1+(1-\tau_r)r_t)k_t + b_t - c_t,$$

where wage income and interest income are taxed at the rates τ_w and τ_r, respectively. Pre-tax wage income is given by the product of the wage rate w_t, the working hours n_t, and the human capital h_t. r_t and b_t denote the real interest rate and government transfers, respectively.

Production per capita y is a function of capital k and effective labor nh. Output is produced with a CES technology:

$$y_t = F(k, nh) = a_0 \left(a_1 k^{\sigma_p} + a_2 (nh)^{\sigma_p}\right)^{\frac{1}{\sigma_p}},$$

where σ_p denotes the elasticity of substitution in production. Define the state variable $z \equiv \frac{k}{nh}$. The production per effective labor is defined by $f(z) \equiv F(z, 1)$. In a factor market equilibrium, factors are rewarded with their marginal products:

$$w = f(z) - zf'(z),$$
$$r = f'(z).$$

The government receives revenues from taxing labor income and capital income. The government budget is balanced so that government consumption g and transfers b equal tax revenues in any period:

$$g_t + b_t = \tau_w n_t h_t w_t + \tau_r r_t k_t.$$

Periods t correspond to years. The model is calibrated as follows: $\eta = 2.0$, $\theta = 0.5$, $\eta = 0.97$, $B = 2.13$, $D = 0.035$, $\gamma = 0.8$, $\sigma_p = -2/3$, $a_0 = 0.77$, $a_1 = 0.36$, $a_2 = 0.64$, $\tau_w = 0.36$, $\tau_r = 0.40$. The share of government consumption in output is $g/y = 0.21$.

a) Derive the first-order conditions of the household and the equilibrium conditions of the model.
b) On a balanced growth path, consumption, output, physical capital, and human capital grow at a constant rate μ, while the time allocation is constant. Derive the equations that characterize the balanced growth equilibrium. For this reason, express the equations with the help of stationary variables. For example, divide the government budget constraint by y_t.
c) Use our non-linear equation solver to compute the stationary equilibrium.
d) How does the growth rate react to a reduction of the capital income tax rate τ_r from 40% to 25% that is financed i) by a reduction in transfers b_t and ii) by an increase in the wage income tax rate τ_w? Explain why the growth rate decreases in the latter case.
e) Compute the dynamics for the transition between the old steady state that is characterized by a capital income tax rate $\tau_r = 40\%$ and the new steady state that is characterized by $\tau_r = 25\%$. Assume that during the transition and in the new steady state, g/y and b/y are constant and that the wage income tax rate τ_w adjusts in order to balance the government budget. Use forward iteration to compute the dynamics. (difficult)

3.7 Business Cycle Fluctuations and Home Production.

In the US economy, hours worked fluctuate considerably more than productivity, and the correlation is close to zero. The standard real business cycle model presented in Section 1.4 has considerable difficulties to replicate this fact. For our German calibration, forCalibration example, hours worked and productivity have approximately equal standard deviations (0.77% and 0.72%, respectively). The following extension of the stochastic growth model is based on BENHABIB, ROGERSON, and WRIGHT (1991). In their model, agents work in the production of both a market-produced good M and a home-produced good H.

Households maximize intertemporal utility

$$E_0 \left\{ \sum_{t=0}^{\infty} \beta^t \left[\frac{C_t^{1-\eta}(L_t)^{\theta(1-\eta)}}{1-\eta} \right] \right\}$$

where C_t is the following composite of the consumptions of good M and H:

$$C_t = \left(a C_{Mt}^{\phi} + (1-a) C_{Ht}^{\phi} \right)^{\frac{1}{\phi}}.$$

The time endowment of one unit is allocated to market and home production according to:

$$1 = L_t - N_{Mt} - N_{Ht}.$$

Notice that the two types of work are assumed to be perfect substitutes, while the two consumption goods are combined by an aggregator that implies a constant elasticity of substitution equal to $\phi/(1-\phi)$.
The model has two technologies:

$$Y_{Mt} = F(Z_{Mt}, K_{Mt}, N_{Mt}) = Z_{Mt} K_{Mt}^{\alpha} N_{Mt}^{1-\alpha},$$
$$Y_{Ht} = G(Z_{Ht}, K_{Ht}, N_{Ht}) = Z_{Ht} K_{Ht}^{\gamma} N_{Ht}^{1-\gamma}.$$

The technology shocks follows the processes:

$$\ln Z_{M,t+1} = \rho \ln Z_{Mt} + \epsilon_{Mt},$$
$$\ln Z_{H,t+1} = \rho \ln Z_{Ht} + \epsilon_{Ht},$$

where $\epsilon_{it} \sim N(0, \sigma_i^2)$ are normally i.i.d. for $i = M, H$ and have a contemporaneous correlation $r_{MH} = cor(\epsilon_{Mt}, \epsilon_{Ht})$.
Total capital $K_t = K_{Mt} + K_{Ht}$ accumulates according to

$$K_{t+1} = (1-\delta)K_t + I_t.$$

New capital is produced only in the market sector implying the constraints:

$$C_{Mt} + I_t = Y_{Mt},$$
$$C_{Ht} = Y_{Ht}.$$

Model periods correspond to quarters. The model is calibrated as follows: $\beta = 0.99$, $\alpha = 0.36$, $\delta = 0.025$, $\eta = 1.5$, $\phi = 0.8$, $\gamma = 0.08$, $r_{MH} = 0.66$, $\rho = 0.9$, $\sigma_M = \sigma_H = 0.007$. The steady state leisure $\bar{L} = 0.7$ is used to calibrate θ. a is set so that $C_H/C_M = 1/4$.

a) Derive the first-order conditions of the model.
b) Compute the steady state and calibrate the parameters a and θ.
c) Compute the standard deviation of hours worked in the market activity, N_{Mt}, and productivity, Z_{Mt}, as well as the correlation of N_{Mt} and Z_{Mt}. Apply the HP-filter to the simulated time series. Explain why the variance of hours worked has increased. Vary ϕ and analyze the sensitivity of your result with regard to this parameter. Explain your result.

Chapter 4

Discrete State Space Methods

Overview. In this chapter we explore methods that replace the original model by a model whose state space consists of a finite number of discrete points. In this case, the value function is a finite dimensional object. For instance, if the state space is one-dimensional and has elements $\mathscr{X} = \{x_1, x_2, \ldots, x_n\}$, the value function is just a vector of n elements where each element gives the value attained by the optimal policy if the initial state of the system is $x_j \in \mathscr{X}$. We can start with an arbitrary vector of values representing our initial guess of the value function and then obtain a new vector by solving the maximization problem on the rhs of the Bellman equation. This procedure will converge to the true value function of this discrete valued problem. Though simple in principle, this approach has a serious drawback. It suffers from the curse of dimensionality. On a one-dimensional state space, the maximization step is simple. We just need to search for the maximal element among n. Yet, the value function of an m-dimensional problem with n different points in each dimension is an array of n^m different elements and the computation time needed to search this array may be prohibitively high.

For this reason we will confine ourselves in this chapter to problems where the maximization step can be reduced to search a vector of n elements. While this limits the class of representative agents models to which we can apply this method, this endeavor is nevertheless worth the while. As you will learn in the second part of the book, there are many heterogenous agent models in which discrete state space methods play an integral part of the solution procedure.

In Section 4.1 we use the infinite-horizon Ramsey model (1.8) to discuss the choice of the set $\mathscr{X}$, the choice of the initial value function, the maximization step, and the termination of the sequence of iterations. In addition, we consider methods to speed up convergence and to increase precision. Section 4.2 extends these methods to the stochastic growth model (1.22). Additional applications in Section 4.3 cover the stochastic growth model with irreversible investment and our benchmark model of Example 1.5.1.

4.1 Solution of Deterministic Models

In this section we introduce discrete state space methods. The deterministic infinite-horizon Ramsey model of Section 1.2 serves as our point of departure. We repeat its main properties in the next paragraph. Then we present a simple algorithm that computes the value function of a discrete version of this model. Subsequently we consider several improvements of this algorithm with respect to computation time and precision.

The Model. In the model of Section 1.2 a fictitious planer (or farmer) equipped with initial capital K_0 chooses a sequence of future capital stocks $\{K_t\}_{t=1}^{\infty}$ that maximizes the life-time utility of a representative household

$$U_0 = \sum_{t=0}^{\infty} \beta^t u(C_t), \quad \beta \in (0,1),$$

subject to the economy's resource constraint

$$f(K_t) \geq C_t + K_{t+1},$$

and non-negativity constraints on consumption C_t and the capital stock K_{t+1}. The utility function $u(C_t)$ is strictly concave and twice continuously differentiable. The function $f(K_t) = F(N, K_t) + (1-\delta)K_t$ determines the economy's current resources as the sum of output $F(N, K_t)$ produced from a fixed amount of labor N and capital services K_t and the amount of capital left after depreciation, which occurs at the rate $\delta \in (0,1)$. The function f is also strictly concave and twice continuously differentiable.

The method that we employ rests on a recursive formulation of this maximization problem in terms of the Bellman equation (1.14):

$$v(K) = \max_{0 \leq K' \leq f(K)} u(f(K) - K') + \beta v(K'). \tag{4.1}$$

This is a functional equation in the unknown value function v. Once we know this function, we can solve for K' as a function h of the current capital stock K. The function $K' = h(K)$ is known as the policy function.

Discrete Approximation. We know from the analysis of Section 1.2.4 that the optimal sequence of capital stocks monotonically approaches the stationary solution K^* determined from the condition $\beta f'(K^*) = 1$. Thus, the economy will stay in the interval $[K_0, K^*]$ (or in the interval $[K^*, K_0]$ if $K_0 > K^*$). Instead of considering this uncountable set, we use n discrete points of this set to represent the state space. In this way, we transform our problem from solving the functional equation (4.1) in the space of continuous functions (an infinite dimensional object) to the much nicer problem of determining a vector of n elements. Note, however, that the stationary solution of this new problem will differ from K^*. For this reason we will use $\bar{K} > K^*$ as an upper bound of the state space.

Our next decision concerns the number of points n. A fine grid $\mathscr{K} = \{K_1, K_2, \ldots K_n\}$, $K_i < K_{i+1}$, $i = 1, 2, \ldots, n$, provides a good approximation. On the other hand, the number of function evaluations that are necessary to perform the maximization step on the rhs of the Bellman equation increases with n so that computation time places a limit on n. We will discuss the relation between accuracy and computation time below. For the time being, we consider a given number of grid-points n.

A related question concerns the distance between neighboring points in the grid. In our applications we will work with equally spaced points $\Delta = K_{i+1} - K_i$ for all $i = 1, 2, \ldots, n-1$. Yet, as the policy and the value function of the original problem are more curved for low values of the capital stock, the approximation is less accurate in this range. As one solution to this problem one might choose an unequally-spaced grid with more points in the lower interval of state space; for instance $K_i = K_1 + \Delta(i-1)^2$, $\Delta = (K_n - K_1)/(n-1)^2$, or choose a grid with constant logarithmic distance, $\Delta = \ln K_{i+1} - \ln K_i$. However, one can show that neither grid type dominates uniformly across applications.

In our discrete model the value function is a vector $\mathbf{v}$ of n elements. Its ith element holds the life-time utility U_0 obtained from a sequence of capital stocks that is optimal given the initial capital stock $K_0 = K_i \in \mathcal{K}$. The associated policy function can be represented by a vector $\mathbf{h}$ of indices. As before, let i denote the index of $K_i \in \mathcal{K}$, and let $j \in 1, 2, \ldots, n$ denote the index of $K' = K_j \in \mathcal{K}$, that is, the maximizer of the rhs of the Bellman equation for a given K_i. Then, $h_i = j$.

The vector $\mathbf{v}$ can be determined by iterating over

$$v_i^{s+1} = \max_{K_j \in \mathscr{D}_i} \; u(f(K_i) - K_j) + \beta v_j^s, \quad i = 1, 2, \ldots, n,$$

$$\mathscr{D}_i := \{K \in \mathcal{K} : K \leq f(K_i)\}.$$

Successive iterations will converge to the solution $\mathbf{v}^*$ of the discrete valued infinite-horizon Ramsey model according to the contraction mapping theorem.[1]

A Simple Iterative Procedure. The following steps describe an algorithm that is very simple to program. It computes $\mathbf{v}^*$ iteratively. Since the solution to

$$\max_{K'} \; u(f(K) - K') + \beta \times 0$$

is obviously $K' = 0$, we start the iterations with $v_i^0 = u(f(K_i))$ for all $i = 1, \ldots, n$. In the next step we find a new value and policy function as follows: For each $i = 1, \ldots, n$:

Step 1: compute

$$w_j = u(f(K_i) - K_j) + \beta v_j^0, \; j = 1, \ldots, n.$$

---

[1] See, e.g., Theorem 12.1.1 of JUDD (1998), p. 402.

Step 2: Find the index j^* such that

$$w_{j^*} \geq w_j \,\forall j = 1, \ldots, n.$$

Step 3: Set $h_i^1 = j^*$ and $v_i^1 = w_{j^*}$.

In the final step, we check if the value function is close to its stationary solution. Let $\|\mathbf{v}^0 - \mathbf{v}^1\|_\infty$ denote the largest absolute value of the difference between the respective elements of $\mathbf{v}^0$ and $\mathbf{v}^1$. The contraction mapping theorem implies that $\|\mathbf{v}^0 - \mathbf{v}^1\|_\infty \leq \epsilon(1-\beta)$ for each $\epsilon > 0$. That is, the error from accepting $\mathbf{v}^1$ as solution instead of the true solution $\mathbf{v}^*$ cannot exceed $\epsilon(1-\beta)$.

If one uses a standard programming language (as, e.g., C, Fortran, Gauss, or Matlab) there is no need to care about finding the maximal element of $\mathbf{w} = [w_1, w_2, \ldots, w_n]'$ in Step 2, since there are built-in subroutines (as. e.g., the `maxindc` command in Gauss or the `MaxLoc` function in Fortran 95).

Exploiting Monotonicity and Concavity. The algorithm that we have just described is not very smart. We can do much better, if we exploit the structure of our problem. The first thing we can do is to select the initial value function more carefully. We can save on iterations, if the initial value function is closer to its final solution. Using K^* from the continuous valued problem as our guess of the stationary solution, the stationary value function is defined by

$$v_i^* = u(f(K^*) - K^*) + \beta v_i^*, \quad \forall i = 1, 2, \ldots, n,$$

and we can use $v_i^* = u(f(K^*) - K^*)/(1-\beta)$ as our initial guess.

Second, we can exploit the monotonicity of the policy function (see Section 1.2.3 on this result), that is:

$$K_i \geq K_j \Rightarrow K_i' = h(K_i) \geq K_j' = h(K_j).$$

As a consequence, once we find the optimal index j_1^* for K_1, we need no longer consider capital stocks smaller than $K_{j_1^*}$ in the search for j_2^*. More generally, let j_i^* denote the index of the maximization problem in step 2 for i. Then, for $i+1$ we evaluate $u(F(N, K_i) - K_j) + \beta v_j^0$ only for indices $j \in \{j_i^*, \ldots n\}$.

Third, we can shorten the number of computations in the maximization Step 2, since the function

$$\phi(K') := u(f(K) - K') + \beta v(K') \tag{4.2}$$

is strictly concave.[2] A strictly concave function ϕ defined over a grid of n points either takes its maximum at one of the two boundary points or in the interior of the grid. In the first case the function is decreasing (increasing) over the whole grid, if the maximum is the first (last) point of the grid. In the second case the function is first increasing and then decreasing. As a consequence, we can pick the mid-point of the grid, K_m, and the point next to it, K_{m+1}, and determine whether the maximum is to the left of K_m (if $\phi(K_m) > \phi(K_{m+1})$) or to the right of K_m (if $\phi(K_{m+1}) > \phi(K_m)$). Thus, in the next step we can reduce the search to a grid with about half the size of the original grid. KREMER (2001), pp. 165f, proves that search based on this principle needs at most $\log_2(n)$ steps to reduce the grid to a set of three points that contains the maximum. For instance, instead of 1000 function evaluations, binary search requires no more than 13! We describe this principle in more detail in the following algorithm:

Algorithm 4.1.1 (Binary Search)

Purpose: *Find the maximum of a strictly concave function $f(x)$ defined over a grid of n points $\mathscr{X} = \{x_1, ..., x_n\}$*

Steps:

Step 1: Initialize: Put $i_{min} = 1$ and $i_{max} = n$.
Step 2: Select two points: $i_l = floor((i_{min}+i_{max})/2)$ and $i_u = i_l+1$, where $floor(i)$ denotes the largest integer less than or equal to $i \in \mathbb{R}$.
Step 3: If $f(x_{i_u}) > f(x_{i_l})$ set $i_{min} = i_l$. Otherwise put $i_{max} = i_u$.
Step 4: If $i_{max} - i_{min} = 2$, stop and choose the largest element among $f(x_{i_{min}})$, $f(x_{i_{min}+1}})$, and $f(x_{i_{max}})$. Otherwise return to Step 2.

---

[2] Since the value function, as well as the utility and the production function, is strictly concave. See Section 1.2.3.

Finally, the closer the value function gets to its stationary solution, the less likely it is that the policy function changes with further iterations. So usually one can terminate the algorithm, if the policy function has remained unchanged for a number of consecutive iterations.

Putting all pieces together we propose the following algorithm to solve the infinite horizon deterministic Ramsey problem via value function iteration on a discrete state space:

Algorithm 4.1.2 (Value Function Iteration 1)

Purpose: *Find an approximate solution of the policy function for the Ramsey model (1.8)*

Steps:

Step 1: Choose a grid

$$\mathcal{K} = \{K_1, K_2, \ldots, K_n\}, \ K_i < K_j, \ i < j = 1, 2, \ldots n.$$

Step 2: Initialize the value function: $\forall i = 1, \ldots, n$ *set*

$$v_i^0 = \frac{u(f(K^*) - K^*)}{1 - \beta},$$

where K^* denotes the stationary solution to the continuous-valued Ramsey problem.

Step 3: Compute a new value function and the associated policy function, $\mathbf{v}^1$ and $\mathbf{h}^1$, respectively: Put $j_0^* \equiv 1$. For $i = 1, 2, \ldots, n$, and j_{i-1}^* use Algorithm 4.1.1 to find the index j_i^* that maximizes

$$u(f(K_i) - K_j) + \beta v_j^0$$

in the set of indices $\{j_{i-1}^*, j_{i-1}^* + 1, \ldots, n\}$. Set $h_i^1 = j_i^*$ and $v_i^1 = u(f(K_i) - K_{j_i^*}) + \beta v_{j_i^*}^0.$

Step 4: Check for convergence: If $\|\mathbf{v}^0 - \mathbf{v}^1\|_\infty < \epsilon(1 - \beta), \ \epsilon > 0$ (or if the policy function has remained unchanged for a number of consecutive iterations) stop, else replace $\mathbf{v}^0$ with $\mathbf{v}^1$ and $\mathbf{h}^0$ with $\mathbf{h}^1$ and return to step 3.

Policy Function Iteration. Value function iteration is a slow procedure since it converges linearly at the rate β (see Section 11.4 on rates of convergence), that is, successive iterates obey

$$\|\mathbf{v}^{s+1} - \mathbf{v}^*\| \leq \beta\|\mathbf{v}^s - \mathbf{v}^*\|,$$

for a given norm $\|x\|$. Howard's improvement algorithm or policy function iteration is a method to enhance convergence. Each time a policy function $\mathbf{h}^s$ is computed, we solve for the value function that would occur, if the policy were followed forever. This value function is then used in the next step to obtain a new policy function $\mathbf{h}^{s+1}$. As pointed out by PUTERMAN and BRUMELLE (1979), this method is akin to Newton's method for locating the zero of a function (see Section 11.5) so that quadratic convergence can be achieved under certain conditions.

The value function that results from following a given policy $\mathbf{h}$ forever is defined by

$$v_i = u(f(K_i) - K_j) + \beta v_j, \quad i = 1, 2, \ldots, n.$$

This is a system of n linear equations in the unknown elements v_i. We shall write this system in matrix-vector notation. Towards this purpose we define the vector $\mathbf{u} = [u_1, u_2, \ldots, u_n]$, $u_i = u(f(K_i) - K_j))$, where, as before, j is the index of the optimal next-period capital stock K_j given the current capital stock K_i. Furthermore, we introduce a matrix Q with zeros everywhere except for its row i and column j elements, which equal one. The above equations may then be written as

$$\mathbf{v} = \mathbf{u} + \beta Q \mathbf{v}, \tag{4.3}$$

with solution $\mathbf{v} = [I - \beta Q]^{-1}\mathbf{u}$.

Policy function iterations may either be started with a given value function or a given policy function. In the first case, we compute the initial policy function by performing Step 3 of Algorithm 4.1.2 once. The difference occurs at the end of Step 3, where we set $\mathbf{v}^1 = [I - \beta Q^1]\mathbf{v}^0$. Q^1 is the matrix obtained from the policy function $\mathbf{h}^1$ as explained above.

If n is large, Q is a sizeable object and you may encounter a memory limit on your personal computer. For instance, if your grid contains 10,000 points Q has 10^8 elements. Stored as double precision (that is eight bytes of memory for each element) this matrix requires 0.8 gigabyte of memory. Fortunately, Q is a sparse matrix (that is a matrix with few non-zero elements) and many linear algebra routines are able to handle this data type. For instance, using the Gauss sparse matrix procedures allows to store Q in an $n \times 3$ matrix which occupies just 240 kilobyte of memory.

If it is not possible to implement the solution of the large linear system or if it becomes too time consuming to solve this system, there is an alternative to full policy iteration. Modified policy iteration with k steps computes the value function $\mathbf{v}^1$ at the end of Step 3 of Algorithm 4.1.2 in these steps:

$$\begin{aligned} \mathbf{w}^1 &= \mathbf{v}^0, \\ \mathbf{w}^{l+1} &= \mathbf{u} + \beta Q^1 \mathbf{w}^l, \quad l = 1, \ldots, k, \\ \mathbf{v}^1 &= \mathbf{w}^{k+1}. \end{aligned} \quad (4.4)$$

As proved by PUTERMAN and SHIN (1978) this algorithm achieves linear convergence at rate β^{k+1} (as opposed to β for value function iteration) close to the optimal value of the current-period utility function.

Interpolation Between Grid-Points. In the Ramsey model that we have considered so far, we are able to restrict the state space to a small interval. This facilitates a reasonably accurate solution with a moderate number of grid-points so that convergence is achieved in a few minutes. Yet, in the heterogenous agent models of the second part, we will encounter problems, where the relevant state space is large and where we repeatedly need to compute the value function. In these situations, computation time on a grid with many points may become a binding constraint. We, thus, look for methods that increase precision for a given number of grid-points without a compensating rise in computation time.

How do we accomplish this? Consider Step 3 of Algorithm 4.1.2, where we maximize the rhs of the Bellman equation (4.2) with respect to K'. Assume that K_j is this solution. Since the value function is increasing and concave, the true maximizer must lie in the interval $[K_{j-1}, K_{j+1}]$. If we were able to evaluate the rhs of the Bellman equation at all $K' \in [K_{j-1}, K_{j+1}]$, we could pick the maximizer of $\phi(K')$ in this interval. Two things are necessary to achieve this goal: an approximation of the value function over the interval $[K_{j-1}, K_{j+1}]$ and a method to locate the maximum of a continuous function.

We consider function approximation in Section 11.2. The methods that we will employ here assume that a function $y = f(x)$ is tabulated for discrete pairs (x_i, y_i). Linear interpolation computes $\hat{y} \simeq f(x)$ for $x \in [x_i, x_{i+1}]$ by drawing a straight line between the points (x_i, y_i) and (x_{i+1}, y_{i+1}). The cubic spline determines a function $\hat{f}_i(x) = a_i + b_i x + c_i x^2 + d_i x^3$ that connects neighboring points and puts $\hat{y} = \hat{f}_i(x)$, $x \in [x_i, x_{i+1}]$. The first method provides a smooth function between grid-points that is continuous (but not differentiable) at the nodes (x_i, y_i). The second methods determines a smooth (continuously differentiable) function over the complete set of points (x_i, y_i). Since the current-period utility function is smooth anyway, these methods allow us to approximate the rhs of the Bellman equation (4.2) by a continuous function $\hat{\phi}(K)$:

$$\hat{\phi}(K) := u(f(K_i) - K) + \hat{v}(K), \qquad (4.5)$$

where $\hat{v}$ is determined by interpolation, either linearly or cubically.

In the interval $[K_{j-1}, K_{j+1}]$ the maximum of $\hat{\phi}$ is located either at the end-points or in the interior. For this reason, we need a method that is able to deal with both boundary and interior solutions of a one-dimensional optimization problem. The golden-section search considered in Section 11.6.1 satisfies this requirement.

We are now able to modify Step 3 of Algorithm 4.1.2 in the following way: we determine j_i^* as before and then refine the solution. First, assume that j_i^* is the index neither of the first nor of the last grid-point so that the optimum of (4.2) is bracketed by $I_j = [K_{j_i^*-1}, K_{j_i^*+1}]$. Instead of storing the index j_i^*, we now locate the maximum of (4.5) in I_j with the aid of Algorithm (11.6.1) and store the maximizer $\tilde{K}_{j_i^*} \in I_j$ in the vector $\mathbf{h}$ in position i. $\hat{\phi}(\tilde{K}_{j_i^*})$

is stored in v_i. If $j_i^* = 1$, we evaluate (4.5) at a point close to K_1. If this returns a smaller value than at K_1, we know that the maximizer is equal to K_1. Otherwise, we locate $\tilde{K}_{j_i^*}$ in $[K_1, K_2]$. We proceed analogously, if $j_i^* = n$.

Evaluation. In the preceding paragraphs, we introduced six different algorithms:

1. Simple value function iteration, which maximizes the rhs of the Bellman equation by picking the maximizer from the list of all possible values,
2. value function iteration (Algorithm 4.1.2), which exploits the monotonicity of the policy function and the concavity of the value function,
3. policy function iteration, i.e., Algorithm 4.1.2, where we use $\mathbf{v}^1 = \mathbf{u} + [I - \beta Q^1]^{-1}\mathbf{v}^0$ in Step 3,
4. modified policy function iteration, i.e., Algorithm 4.1.2, where $\mathbf{v}^1$ in Step 3 is computed via (4.4),
5. value function iteration according to Algorithm 4.1.2 with linear interpolation between grid-points,
6. value function iteration according to Algorithm 4.1.2 with cubic interpolation between grid-points.

We use these six algorithms to compute the approximate solution of the infinite-horizon Ramsey model with $u(C) = [C^{1-\eta} - 1]/(1-\eta)$ and $F(N, K) = K^\alpha$ and evaluate their performance with respect to computation time and accuracy as measured by the residuals of the Euler equation (see (1.48) for the definition of this variable)

$$u'(C_t) = \beta u'(C_{t+1}) f'(K_{t+1}).$$

We used a notebook with a dual core 2 gigahertz processor. The source code is available in the Gauss program Ramsey2d.g. The parameters of the model are set equal to $\alpha = 0.27$, $\beta = 0.994$, $\eta = 2.0$, and $\delta = 0.011$. The value and the policy function are computed on a grid of n points over the interval $[0.75K^*, 1.25K^*]$. We stopped iterations if the maximum absolute difference between successive approximations of the value function became smaller than $0.01(1-\beta)$ or if the policy function remained unchanged in 30 consecutive iterations. (This latter criterium is only applicable for methods 1 through 4.) Modified policy iterations use $k=30$. The Euler equation residuals are computed for 200 equally spaced points in the smaller interval $[0.8K^*, 1.2K^*]$. Linear – and in the case of method 6 – cubic interpolation was used to compute the policy function between the elements of the vector **h**. Table 4.1 presents the maximum absolute value of the 200 residuals.

Table 4.1

	Run Time				
Method	n=250	$n=500$	$n=1,000$	$n=5,000$	$n=10,000$
1	0:00:43:06	0:03:04.44	0:12:39:51	7:16:36:28	
2	0:00:05:63	0:00:12:91	0:00:28.94	0:04:00:67	0:09:16:91
3	0:00:02:08	0:00:05:02	0:00:14:22	0:06:18:61	0:22:11:48
4	0:00:02:31	0:00:04:47	0:00:08:31	0:01:18:53	0:04:39:17
5	0:01:05:97	0:02:34:89	0:06:36:89	1:25:07:61	7:43:13:78
6	0:01:15:92	0:02:27:94	0:04:48:80	0:22:41:84	0:44:14:28

	Euler Equation Residuals				
Method	$n=250$	$n=500$	$n=1,000$	$n=5,000$	$n=10,000$
1	4.009E-2	2.061E-2	9.843E-3	1.835E-3	
2	4.009E-2	2.061E-2	9.843E-3	1.835E-3	8.542E-4
3	4.026E-2	2.061E-2	9.363E-3	2.562E-3	8.722E-4
4	4.026E-2	2.061E-2	8.822E-3	3.281E-3	8.542E-4
5	5.814E-4	4.605E-4	2.339E-4	4.093E-5	2.013E-5
6	3.200E-7	3.500E-7	3.200E-7	3.800E-7	3.600E-7

Notes: Method numbers are explained in the main text. Run time is given in hours:minutes:seconds:hundreth of seconds on a dual core 2 gigahertz processor. The empty entry pertains to a simulation which we interrupted after 8 hours of computation time. Euler equation residuals are computed as maximum absolute value of 200 residuals computed on an equally spaced grid of 200 points over the interval $[0.8K^*, 1.2K^*]$.

As can be seen from the first row of this table, computation time becomes prohibitive for simple value function iteration if n is large. Even on a grid of 5,000 points the algorithm requires more than 7 hours to converge. For the same n, Algorithm 4.1.2 needs just 4 minutes and modified policy iteration (method 4) 1 minute and 18 seconds! The rows labeled 3 and 4 in the upper panel of Table 4.1 convey a second finding. Policy iteration requires more time than modified policy iteration if n is reasonably large. In our example, this occurs somewhere between $n = 250$ and $n = 500$. The time needed to solve the large linear system (4.3) considerably slows down the algorithm. For a sizable grid of $n = 10,000$ points, method 4 is about five times faster than method 3. It should come as no surprise that adding interpolation between grid-points to Step 3 of Algorithm 4.1.2 increases computation time. After all, we must determine the line connecting two points of the grid and must locate the maximizer of (4.5) via a search routine. Method 5 requires almost eight hours to converge, if n equals 10,000. It is, however, surprising, that cubic interpolation, which requires additional computations as compared to linear interpolation, is nevertheless quite faster for large grids. In the case of $n = 10,000$ the algorithm converged after about three quarters of an hour. It seems that the smoother cubic function – though more expensive to compute – allows a quicker determination of $\tilde{K}_{j_i^*}$.

In the case of methods 1 through 4 the Euler equation residuals decrease from about 4.E-2 to about 9.E-4, if n increases from 250 to 10,000. It, thus, requires a sizable grid to obtain an accurate solution. Linear interpolation (method 5) achieves residuals of size 6.E-4 already with $n = 250$. In the case of $n = 10,000$ (i.e., with 40 times more points), the Euler residual shrinks by a factor of 20 at the cost of many hours of patience before we could discover this result. Cubic interpolation achieves very high accuracy at $n = 250$ that cannot be increased by making the grid finer. The high degree of accuracy that can be achieved with this method even for a small number of grid-points is further illustrated in Figure 4.1.

The upper panel of this figure plots the analytic policy function of the model, which is given by $K' = \alpha\beta K^\alpha$ in the case of

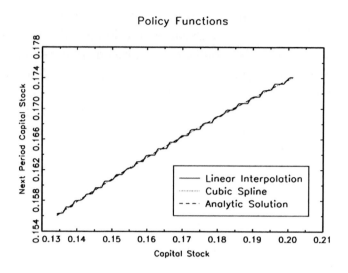

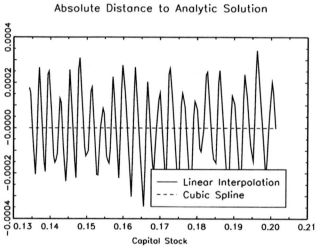

Figure 4.1: Policy Functions of the Next-Period Capital Stock of the Infinite-Horizon Ramsey Model

$\eta = \delta = 1$ (see (1.18)) together with two approximate solutions. Both use a grid of $n = 100$ points over $[0.75K^*, 1.25K^*]$. The solution obtained from linear interpolation between the grid-points wriggles around the true solution, whereas the solution based on cubic interpolation is visually not distinguishable from the latter. Although even the first approximate solution is close to the true one (the maximum absolute value of the distance to the true solution is less than 4.E-4), the second approximation is so close that the distance to the analytic solution is almost zero (see the lower panel of Figure 4.1).

The cubic interpolation between grid-points, thus, outperforms the other five methods. It needs only slightly more than a minute (see Table 4.1) to compute a highly accurate approximate solution of the deterministic growth model (see the column $n = 250$ in Table 4.1).

4.2 Solution of Stochastic Models

In this section we adapt the methods presented in the previous section to the stochastic growth model (1.22). This model belongs to a more general class of recursive problems that we will describe in the next paragraph. We then develop a flexible algorithm that solves a discrete version of this problem via value function iteration.

The Framework. Let K denote the endogenous state variable of the model and Z a purely exogenous shock governed by a stationary stochastic process. The current-period return u depends on the triple (Z, K, K'), where K' denotes the next-period value of K. The choice of K' is restricted to lie in a convex set $\mathscr{D}_{K,Z}$ that may depend on K and Z. In the stochastic growth model of Section 1.3 u is the current-period utility of consumption $C = Zf(K) + (1-\delta)K - K'$ and $\mathscr{D}_{K,Z} := \{K' : 0 \leq K' \leq Zf(K)+(1-\delta)K\}$. The solution of the problem is a value function $v(K, Z)$ that solves the Bellman equation

$$v(K, Z) = \max_{K' \in \mathscr{D}_{K,Z}} u(Z, K, K') + \beta E\left[v(K', Z')|Z\right], \quad (4.6)$$

where $E[\cdot|Z]$ is the mathematical expectations operator conditional on the realization of Z at the time the decision on K' is to be made.

Approximations of $E[\cdot|Z]$**.** As in Section 4.1 we replace the original problem by a discrete valued problem and approximate the value function by an $n \times m$ matrix $V = (v_{ij})$, whose row i and column j argument gives the value of the optimal policy, if the current state of the system is the pair (K_i, Z_j), $K_i \in \mathscr{K} = \{K_1, K_2, \ldots, K_n\}$, $Z_j \in \mathscr{Z} = \{Z_1, Z_2, \ldots, Z_m\}$.

The further procedure depends on the model's assumptions with respect to Z. There are models that assume that Z is governed by a Markov chain with realizations given by the set $\mathscr{Z}$ and transition probabilities given by a matrix $P = (p_{jl})$, whose row j and column l element is the probability of moving from Z_j to state Z_l (see Section 12.2 on Markov chains). For instance, in Section 7.1 you will encounter a model with just two states. A household is either employed ($Z_1 = 1$) or unemployed ($Z_2 = 0$), and he faces given probabilities p_{12} to loose his job (if he is employed) or p_{21} to find a job (if he is unemployed). Since the probability to stay employed p_{11} must equal $1 - p_{12}$ and the probability not to find a job must equal $p_{22} = 1 - p_{21}$, the matrix P is fully determined. Given $\mathscr{Z}$ and the matrix P, the Bellman equation of the discrete valued problem is

$$v_{ij} = \max_{K_k \in \mathscr{D}_{ij}} \ u(Z_j, K_i, K_k) + \beta \sum_{l=1}^{m} p_{jl} v_{kl}, \qquad (4.7)$$

$$i = 1, 2, \ldots, n, \ j = 1, 2, \ldots, m,$$

where we use $\mathscr{D}_{ij}$ as a shorthand for the set $\mathscr{D}_{K_i, Z_j}$. As in the previous section, we can use iterations over this equation to determine the matrix V.

Suppose, as it is the case in the benchmark model of Example 1.5.1, that $\ln Z$ follows an AR(1)-process:

$$\ln Z' = \varrho \ln Z + \sigma \epsilon', \quad \varrho \in [0, 1), \ \epsilon' \sim N(0, 1). \qquad (4.8)$$

The first approach to tackle this case is to use Algorithm 12.2.1 (see Section 12.2) that provides a Markov chain approximation of the continuous-valued AR(1)-process. To use this algorithm, you must provide the size of the interval $I_Z = [Z_1, Z_m]$ and the number of grid-points m. The algorithm determines the grid

$\mathscr{Z} = \{Z_1, Z_2, \ldots, Z_m\}$ and the matrix of transition probabilities $P = (p_{jl})$ so that the discrete-valued Bellman equation (4.7) still applies. The boundaries of $\mathscr{Z}$ must be chosen so that Z remains in the interval I_Z. The usual procedure is to set $Z_m - Z_1$ equal to a multiple of the unconditional standard deviation of the process (4.8), which equals[3]

$$\sigma_Z = \sqrt{\frac{\sigma^2}{1-\varrho^2}}.$$

One can use simulations of this process to find out if it leaves a given interval. Usually, an interval of size equal to $9\sigma_Z$ or $10\sigma_Z$ is large enough. TAUCHEN (1986) provides evidence that even 9 grid-points are sufficient for a reasonably good approximation of (4.8).

The second approach to approximate the conditional expectation on the rhs of the Bellman equation (4.6) rests on the analytic expression for $E(\cdot|Z)$. In the case of the process (4.8) this equals

$$E\left[v(K', Z')|Z\right] = \int_{-\infty}^{\infty} v\left(K', e^{\varrho \ln Z + \sigma \epsilon'}\right) \frac{e^{\frac{-(\epsilon')^2}{2}}}{\sqrt{2\pi}} d\epsilon'.$$

If the value function is tabulated in the matrix $V = (v_{ij})$, we can interpolate between the row-elements of V to obtain an integrable function of Z, which allows us to employ numeric integration techniques to obtain $E[\cdot|Z]$. As explained in Section 11.3.2, Gauss-Hermite quadrature is a suitable method. In HEER and MAUSSNER (2008), we point to a serious drawback of this approach. Gauss-Hermite quadrature requires a much larger interval for Z than it will be necessary for simulations of the model. I_Z must contain the integration nodes $\pm\sqrt{2}\sigma x$, where x denotes the largest node used by the respective Gauss-Hermite formula. For instance, $x \simeq 1.65$ in the four-nodes formula that we usually employ to compute a conditional expectation. Thus, instead of using an interval of size $10\sigma_Z$, say, you must use an interval of size $21\sigma_Z$. In particular, we have to ascertain that $\varrho \ln Z_m + \sqrt{2}\sigma x \leq \ln Z_m$

---

[3] See, e.g., HAMILTON (1994), pp. 53-56 for a derivation of this formula.

and $\varrho \ln Z_1 - \sqrt{2}\sigma x \geq \ln Z_1$. For given ϱ, σ, and x these equations can be solved for the lower and the upper bound $\ln Z_1$ and $\ln Z_m$, respectively. For our parameter values this delivers $|\ln Z_m - \ln Z_1| \simeq 21\sigma_Z$. Yet, as explained below, the boundaries of $\mathscr{K}$ will usually depend on the boundaries of $\mathscr{Z}$. For a given number of grid-points n, a larger interval $I_K = [K_1, K_n]$ implies a less accurate solution that may outweigh the increase of precision provided by the continuous-valued integrand. With respect to the benchmark model of Example 1.5.1 we indeed find that the Markov chain approximation allows a much faster computation of the value function for a given degree of accuracy.[4] For this reason, we will consider this approach only.

The Basic Algorithm. The problem that we, thus, have to solve, is to determine V iteratively from

$$v_{ij}^{s+1} = \max_{K_k \in \mathscr{D}_{ij}} \; u(Z_j, K_i, K_k) + \beta \sum_{l=1}^{m} p_{jl} v_{kl}^s, \tag{4.9}$$
$$i = 1, 2, \ldots, n, \; j = 1, 2, \ldots, m.$$

This process will also deliver the policy function $H = (h_{ij})$. In our basic algorithm, this matrix stores the index k_{ij}^* of the optimal next-period state variable $K_k' \in \mathscr{K}$ in its ith row and jth column element. The pair of indices (i, j) denotes the current state of the system, that is, (K_i, Z_j). We assume that the value function v of our original problem is concave in K and that the policy function h is monotone in K so that we can continue to use all of the methods encountered in Section 4.1. As we have seen in this section, a reasonable fast algorithm should at least exploit the concavity of v and the monotonicity of h. Our basic algorithm, thus, consists of steps 1, 2.1, and 2.2i of Algorithm 4.2.1 (see below). We first discuss the choice of $\mathscr{K}$ and V^0 before we turn to methods that accelerate convergence and increase precision.

Choice of $\mathscr{K}$ and V^0. This choice is a bit more delicate than the respective step of Algorithm 4.1.2. In the deterministic growth model considered in the previous section the optimal sequence of

---
[4] See HEER and MAUSSNER (2008).

capital stocks is either increasing or decreasing, depending on the given initial capital stock K_0. This makes the choice of $\mathscr{K}$ easy. In a stochastic model, the future path of K depends on the expected path of Z, and we do not know in advance whether for any given pair (K_i, Z_j) the optimal policy is to either increase or decrease K. For this reason, our policy to choose $\mathscr{K}$ is "guess and verify". We will start with a small interval. If the policy function hits the boundaries of this interval, that is, if $h_{ij} = 1$ or $h_{ij} = n$ for any pair of indices, we will enlarge $\mathscr{K}$. In the case of the stochastic growth model (1.22) an educated guess is the following: If the current shock is Z_j and we assume that $Z = Z_j$ forever, the sequence of capital stocks will approach K_j^* determined from

$$1 = \beta(1 - \delta + Z_j f'(K_j^*)). \tag{4.10}$$

Approximate lower and upper bounds are, thus, given by K_1^* and K_m^*, respectively. Since, the stationary solution of the discrete-valued problem will not be equal to the solution of the continuous-valued problem, K_1 (K_n) should be chosen as a fraction (a multiple) of K_1^* (K_m^*).

As we already know from Section 4.1 computation time also depends on the initial V^0. Using the zero matrix is usually not the best choice, but it may be difficult to find a better starting value. For instance, in the stochastic growth model we may try $v_{ij}^0 = u(Z_j f(K_i) - \delta K_i)$, that is, the utility obtained from a policy that maintains the current capital stock for one period. Or, we may compute V^0 from the m different stationary solutions that result if Z equals Z_j forever:

$$v_{ij}^0 = u(Z_j f(K_j^*) - \delta K_j^*) + \beta \sum_{l=1}^{m} p_{jl} v_{il}^0,$$

where K_j^* solves (4.10). This is a system of linear equations in the nm unknowns v_{ij}^0 with solution

$$V^0 = (I - \beta P')^{-1} U,$$
$$U = (u_{ij}), \ u_{ij} = u(Z_j f(K_j^*) - \delta K_j^*) \ \forall i, j.$$

A third choice is $v_{ij}^0 = u(f(K^*) - \delta K^*)/(1-\beta)$, that is, the value obtained from the stationary solution of the deterministic growth model.

There is, however, an even better strategy: i) start with a coarse grid on the interval $[K_1, K_n]$; ii) use the basic algorithm to compute the value function V^* on this grid; iii) make the grid finer by using more points n. iv) interpolate column-wise between neighboring points of the old grid and the respective points of V^* to obtain an estimate of the initial value function on the finer grid. Since on a coarse grid the algorithm will quickly converge, the choice of V^0 in step i) is not really important and $V^0 = 0$ may be used.

Acceleration. In Section 4.1 we discovered that policy function iteration is a method to accelerate convergence. This method assumes that a given policy H^1 is maintained forever. In the context of the Bellman equation 4.7 this provides a linear system of equation in the nm unknowns v_{ij} (for the moment, we suppress the superscript of V):

$$v_{ij} = u_{ij} + \beta \sum_{l=1}^{m} p_{jl} v_{h_{ij} l}, \qquad (4.11)$$

$$u_{ij} := u(Z_j, K_i, K_{h_{ij}}), \ i = 1, 2, \ldots, n, \ j = 1, 2, \ldots, m.$$

In matrix notation, this may be written as

$$\text{vec } V = \text{vec } U + \beta Q \text{ vec } V, \quad U = (u_{ij}). \qquad (4.12)$$

vec V (vec U) is the nm column vector obtained from vertically stacking the rows of V (U). The $nm \times nm$ matrix Q is obtained from H and P: Its row $r = (i-1)m + j$ elements in columns $c_1 = (h_{ij} - 1)m + 1$ through $c_m = (h_{ij} - 1)m + m$ equal the row j elements of P. All other elements of Q are zero. Even for a grid $\mathscr{L}$ with only a few elements m, Q is much larger than its respective counterpart in equation (4.3). In the previous section we have seen that for $n > 500$ (and, in the notation of this section $m = 1$), modified policy iteration is faster than full policy iteration. For this reason, we only will implement modified policy iteration into our algorithm. This is done in Step 2.3 of Algorithm 4.2.1

Interpolation. We know from the results obtained in Section 4.1 that interpolation between the points of $\mathcal{K}$ is one way to increase the precision of the solution. Within the current framework the objective is to obtain a continuous function $\hat{\phi}(K)$ that approximates the rhs of the Bellman equation (4.6) given the tabulated value function in the matrix V and the grid $\mathcal{K}$. We achieve this by defining

$$\hat{\phi}(K) = u(Z_j, K_i, K) + \beta \sum_{l=1}^{m} p_{jl}\hat{v}_l(K). \tag{4.13}$$

The function $\hat{v}_l(K)$ is obtained from interpolation between two neighboring points K_i and K_{i+1} from $\mathcal{K}$ and the respective points v_{il} and $v_{i+1\,l}$ from the matrix V. Thus, each time the function $\hat{\phi}(K)$ is called by the maximization routine, m interpolation steps must be performed. For this reason, interpolation in the context of a stochastic model is much more time consuming than in the case of a deterministic model. Our algorithm allows for either linear or cubic interpolation in the optional Step 2.2.ii.

Algorithm 4.2.1 (Value Function Iteration 2)

Purpose: *Find an approximate policy function of the recursive problem (4.6) given a Markov chain with elements $\mathscr{Z} = \{Z_1, Z_2, \ldots, Z_m\}$ and transition matrix P.*

Steps:

Step 1: Choose a grid

$$\mathcal{K} = \{K_1, K_2, \ldots, K_n\},\ K_i < K_j,\ i < j = 1, 2, \ldots n,$$

and initialize V^0.

Step 2: Compute a new value function V^1 and an associated policy function H^1: For each $j = 1, 2, \ldots, m$ repeat these steps:

Step 2.1: Initialize: $k_{0j}^* = 1$.

Step 2.2: i) For each $i = 1, 2, \ldots, n$ and $k_{i-1\,j}^*$ use Algorithm 4.1.1 to find the index k^* that maximizes

$$w_k = u(Z_j, K_i, K_k) + \beta \sum_{l=1}^{m} p_{jl} v_{kl}^0$$

in the set of indices $k \in \{k^*_{i-1j}, k^*_{i-1j}+1, \ldots, n\}$. Set $k^*_{ij} = k^*$. If interpolation is not desired, set $h^1_{ij} = k^*$ and $v^1_{ij} = w_{k^*}$, else proceed as follows:

ii) (optional) If $k^* = 1$ evaluate the function $\hat{\phi}$ defined by equation (4.13) at a point close to K_1. If this returns a smaller value than at K_1, set $\tilde{K} = K_1$, else use Algorithm 11.6.1 to find the maximizer $\tilde{K}$ of $\hat{\phi}$ in the interval $[K_1, K_2]$. Store $\tilde{K}$ in h^1_{ij} and $\hat{\phi}(\tilde{K})$ in v^1_{ij}. Proceed analogously if $k^* = n$. If k^* equals neither 1 nor n, find the maximizer $\tilde{K}$ of $\hat{\phi}$ in the interval $[K_{k^*-1}, K_{k^*+1}]$ and put $h^1_{ij} = \tilde{K}$ and $v^1_{ij} = \hat{\phi}(\tilde{K})$.

Step 2.3: (optional, if Step 2.2.i was taken) Set $\mathbf{w}^1 = \text{vec } V^1$, and for $l = 1, 2, \ldots, k$ iterate over

$$\mathbf{w}^{l+1} = \text{vec } U + \beta Q^1 \mathbf{w}^l,$$

and replace $\mathbf{V}^1$ by the respective elements of $\mathbf{w}^{k+1}$.

Step 3: Check for convergence: if

$$\max_{\substack{i=1,\ldots n \\ j=1,\ldots m}} |v^1_{ij} - v^0_{ij}| \leq \epsilon(1-\beta), \quad \epsilon \in \mathbb{R}_{++}$$

(or if the policy function has remained unchanged for a number of consecutive iterations) stop, else replace V^0 with V^1 and H^0 with H^1 and return to Step 2.

We provide both a Gauss and a Fortran version of this algorithm in the program `SolveVI`. The program facilitates four different methods:

1. Value function iteration (Step 1, Step 2.1, Step 2.2.i, and Step 3),
2. modified policy function iteration (method 1 amended by Step 2.3)
3. value function iteration with linear interpolation (Step 2.2.ii in addition to Step 2.2.i),
4. value function iteration with cubic interpolation.

Evaluation. We apply these four methods to the stochastic growth model presented in (1.22). As in the previous chapters, we use

$$u(C) = \frac{C^{1-\eta} - 1}{1 - \eta},$$
$$f(K) = K^\alpha,$$

and measure the accuracy of the solution by the residuals of the Euler equation[5]

$$C^{-\eta} = \beta E\left\{ \left[(C')^{-\eta} \left(1 - \delta + \alpha(e^{\varrho \ln Z + \sigma \epsilon'})(K')^{\alpha-1}\right)\right] \Big| Z \right\}.$$

The residual is computed by replacing C and C' in this equation by the approximate policy function for consumption,

$$\hat{h}^C(K, Z) = ZK^\alpha + (1-\delta)K - \hat{h}^K(K, Z),$$

where the policy function for the next-period capital stock $\hat{h}^K$ is obtained from bilinear interpolation between the elements of the matrix H. The residuals are computed over a grid of 200^2 points over the interval $[0.8K^*, 1.2K^*] \times [0.95, 1.05]$. Table 4.2 displays the maximum absolute value of the 200^2 residuals. We used a notebook with a dual core 2 gigahertz processor. The source code is available in the Gauss program `Ramsey3d.g`. The parameters of the model are set equal to $\alpha = 0.27$, $\beta = 0.994$, $\eta = 2.0$, $\delta = 0.011$, $\varrho = 0.90$, and $\sigma = 0.0072$. The value and the policy function are computed on a grid of $n \times m$ points. The size of the interval $I_Z = [Z_1, Z_m]$ equals 11 times the unconditional standard deviation of the AR(1)-process in equation (4.8). We stopped iterations, if the maximum absolute difference between successive approximations of the value function became smaller than $0.01(1-\beta)$ or if the policy function remained unchanged in 50 consecutive iterations. (This latter criterium is only applicable for methods 1 and 2.) Modified policy iterations use $k = 30$.

---

[5] See Section 1.3.2, where we derive this equation and Section 2.5.3 where we explain the computation of the residuals in more detail.

Table 4.2

Method	n	m	Run Time i	Run Time ii	Euler Equation Residual
2	250	9	0:00:22:06		7.407E-2
4	250	9	0:00:22:94		7.407E-2
5	250	9	2:13:37:84	0:13:31:16	1.272E-3
6	250	9	2:04:01:67	0:21:01:69	1.877E-4
6	500	9	5:12:58:44	0:23:17:52	1.876E-4
6	250	15		1:04:39:22	4.930E-6
2	10,000	9	2:33:26:16	0:20:10:94	1.933E-3
4	10,000	9	1:06:48:58	0:03:52:42	1.933E-3
4	10,000	31	1:06:49:52	0:13:40:80	1.931E-3
4	100,000	15		0:17:59:56	2.089E-4
4	500,000	15		3:43:03:81	4.387E-5

Notes: The method numbers are explained in the main text. Run time is given in hours:minutes:seconds:hundreth of seconds on a dual core 2 gigahertz processor. The column labeled i gives the run time where the initial value function was set equal to $u(f(K^*) - \delta K^*)/(1-\beta)$, column ii presents computation time from a sequential approach: we start with a coarse grid of $n = 250$ and increase the number of grid points in a few steps to the desired value of n given in the second column. Except in the first step – where we use the same initial V^0 as in the third column – each step uses the value function obtained in the previous step to initialize V^0. Euler equation residuals are computed as maximum absolute value of 200^2 residuals computed on an equally spaced grid over the interval $[0.8K^*, 1.2K^*] \times [0.95, 1.05]$. Empty entries indicate simulations, which we have not performed for obvious reasons.

On a coarse grid for the capital stock, $n = 250$, the first four rows in Table 4.2 confirm our intuition. Interpolation increases computation time drastically, from about 25 seconds (for methods 1 and 2) to over 2 hours but provides reasonably accurate solutions. In the case of method 3 (method 4) the Euler equation residual is about 50 times (400 times) smaller than that obtained from methods 1 and 2. The run times given in column ii highlight the importance of a good initial guess for the value function. The results presented there were obtained in the following way.

We used method 2 to compute the value function on a grid of $n = 250$ points (given the choice of m as indicated in the table). For this initial step we use $v_{ij} = u(f(K^*) - \delta K^*)/(1 - \beta)$ as our guess of V. In successive steps we made the grid finer until the number of points given in column 2 was reached. Each step used the previous value function, employed linear interpolation to compute the additional points in the columns of V, and took the result as initial guess of the value function. The computation time in column ii is the cumulative sum over all steps. In the case of method 3 this procedure reduced computation time by about 2 hours! The entries for method 1 and 2 and $n = 10,000$ in column i confirm our findings from the deterministic Ramsey model that modified policy iteration is an adequate way to reduce computation time (by almost one and half an hour). Since it is faster close to the true solution, it clearly outperforms method 1 in successive iterations (compare the entries for $n = 10,000$ and $n = 9$ in column i and ii): it is about 5 times faster as compared to 2.3 times in the simulations without a good initial value function.

The entries for method 4 document that increased precision does not result from additional points in the grid for the capital stock but in the grid for the productivity shock. In the case $n = 250$ and $m = 15$ the Euler equation residual of about 5.E-6 indicates a very accurate solution. However, even with good starting values, it takes about an hour to compute this solution.

There are two adequate ways to compute a less precise but still sufficiently accurate solution with Euler equation residuals of magnitude of about 2.E-4: either with method 4 on a coarse grid, $n = 250$ and $m = 9$ or with method 2 on a much finer grid, $n = 100,000$ and $m = 15$. Both methods require about 20 minutes to compute the policy function. Thus, different from our findings in the previous section, cubic interpolation is not unambiguously the most favorable method.

However, if high precision is needed, cubic interpolation on a coarse grid is quite faster than method 2. As the last row of Table 4.2 shows, even on a fine grid of $n = 500,000$ points the Euler equation residual is still about 10 times larger than that from method 4 for $n = 250$ and $m = 15$. Yet, whereas method 4 requires about an hour to compute the policy function, method 2 needs almost four hours.

4.3 Further Applications

In this section we consider two applications of Algorithm 4.2.1. First, we consider the stochastic growth model under the assumption that the given stock of capital cannot be transferred into consumption goods. This places a non-negativity constraint on investment. Second, we compute a discrete approximation of the policy function of our benchmark model.

4.3.1 Non-Negative Investment

The methods presented in Chapters 2 and 3 are not suitable for models with binding constraints. The local methods of Chapter 1 require that the system of equations that determines the model's dynamics is sufficiently differentiable at a certain point. This will not hold with binding constraints. If the constraints do not bind at this point but nearby, the true policy functions will have kinks that the approximate policy functions do not display. Thus, as soon as the model leaves the close vicinity of the stationary point, the approximate policy functions are no longer applicable. The non-linear methods that we employ to solve for the model's Rational expectations path in Chapter 3 also rely on differentiable functions. Yet, even if one resorts to derivative-free methods, constraints are hard to embed. Each time when a constraint binds it creates a different branch of the economy's future time path. All these different paths must be compared to each other to single out the correct one. Even in models with one state variable this a formidable task, which easily encounters reasonable limits on computation time.

Within the recursive approach taken in this chapter, however, it is not very difficult to take care of constraints. The stochastic growth model with a binding constraint on investment is a good example to make that point.

The Model. Suppose that it is not possible to eat up the current stock of capital so that consumption cannot exceed production. This places the restriction

$$K' \geq (1-\delta)K$$

on the choice of the future capital stock. Equivalently, investment $i = K' - (1-\delta)K$ cannot be negative. The problem, thus, is to find a value function that solves the Bellman equation

$$v(K,Z) = \max_{K' \in \mathscr{D}_{K,Z}} u(Zf(K) + (1-\delta)K - K')$$
$$+ \beta E\left[v(K', Z')|Z\right], \qquad (4.14)$$

$$\mathscr{D}_{K,Z} = \{K' : (1-\delta)K \leq K' \leq Zf(K) + (1-\delta)K\}.$$

In Problem 4.1 we ask you to derive the first-order conditions for this maximization problem from the Kuhn-Tucker Theorem 1.1.1 under the assumption of a given value function v. These conditions are required to compute Euler equation residuals for this model. Yet, in order to find v, it is not necessary to know these conditions at all.

Modifications of the Algorithm. It requires just one line of additional programming code to adapt Step 2.2.i of Algorithm 4.2.1 to take care of the constraint on investment. Consider the set of indices $\{k^*_{i-1j}, k^*_{i-1j}+1, \ldots, n\}$ which we search to find the maximizer $K_k \in \mathscr{K}$ of the rhs of the Bellman equation. Instead of starting the search with $k = k^*_{i-1j}$, we first check if $K_k \geq (1-\delta)K_i$. If K_k violates this condition, we try K_{k+1} and so forth until we arrive at a point K_{k+r}, $r = 1, 2, \ldots, n-k$ that meets this condition. Since $(1-\delta)K_i < K_i$, there is always an r that meets this requirement. Then, we locate k in the set $\{k^*_{i-1j} + r, \ldots, n\}$.

Similar changes must be made to Step 2.2.ii. We think this is a good exercise, and leave these changes to the reader (see Problem 4.1).

Results. You will find the modified Algorithm 4.2.1 in the Gauss program SGNNI_a.g . For the constraint to bind, it requires large productivity shocks. Instead of $\sigma = 0.0072$ (the value that we used in the model of the previous section), we set $\sigma = 0.05$ and left all other parameter values unchanged. We use a Markov chain of $m = 31$ points on a grid of size $9\sigma_Z$ to approximate the AR(1)-process of the natural log of the level of productivity Z. Our grid of the capital stock has $n = 50,000$ elements.

Figure 4.2 displays the policy function of consumption $\hat{h}^C(K, Z)$ in the domain $[0.6K^*, 1.6K^*] \times [0.6, 1.6]$. In simulations of the model with a large number of periods, both K and Z never left this square. The policy function was computed at 100^2 pairs (K, Z) via bilinear interpolation from the policy function of the next-period capital stock. The graph displays a clear kink. For each K there is a threshold value of the level of total factor productivity (TFP). Below this point the household would like to consume some of his capital stock to smooth consumption. Above this point, the con-

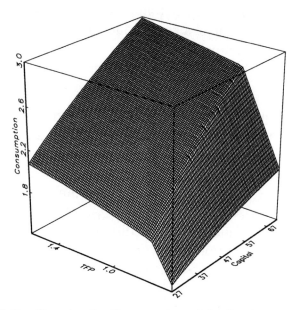

Figure 4.2: Policy Function for Consumption of the Stochastic Growth Model with Non-Negative Investment

straint does not bind and the consumption function is identical to the function of the model without constraint.

4.3.2 The Benchmark Model

We have already encountered the recursive formulation of the benchmark model of Example 1.5.1 in Section 2.6.1. For your convenience, we restate the Bellman equation of this model:

$$v(k,z) = \max_{k',N} \; u\left(e^z N^{1-\alpha} k^\alpha + (1-\delta)k - ak', 1-N\right)$$
$$+ \tilde{\beta} E\left[v(k', z')|z\right],$$

where the utility function u is specified as

$$u(c, 1-N) := \frac{c^{1-\eta}(1-N)^{\theta(1-\eta)} - 1}{1-\eta}.$$

Remember,

$$c = e^z N^{1-\alpha} k^\alpha + (1-\delta)k - ak'$$

and k refer to consumption C and capital K per unit of labor augmenting technical progress A, and $\tilde{\beta} = \beta a^{1-\eta}$. The next-period capital k' stock must lie in the interval

$$0 < k' \leq (e^z N^{1-\alpha} k^\alpha + (1-\delta)k)/a$$

and working hours N are restricted to $(0,1)$.

It is easy to apply Algorithm 4.2.1 to this model. There is just one change compared with the stochastic growth model of Section 4.2: Inside the procedure that returns the household's utility as a function of $(Z = e^z, k, k')$, we must solve for N. We can use the first-order condition with respect to working hours for this purpose. Differentiating the rhs of the Bellman equation with respect to N and setting the result equal to zero yields

$$\theta(e^z N^{1-\alpha} k^\alpha + (1-\delta)k - ak') = (1-\alpha)(1-N)e^z N^{-\alpha} k^\alpha. \quad (4.15)$$

Table 4.3

	Linear Approximation			Value Function Iteration					
				$n=5,000$ $m=9$			$n=250$ $m=19$		
Second Moments									
Variable	s_x	r_{xy}	r_x	s_x	r_{xy}	r_x	s_x	r_{xy}	r_x
Output	1.44	1.00	0.64	1.40	1.00	0.64	1.44	1.00	0.64
Investment	6.11	1.00	0.64	5.79	1.00	0.64	6.11	1.00	0.64
Consumption	0.56	0.99	0.66	0.58	0.99	0.66	0.56	0.99	0.66
Hours	0.77	1.00	0.64	0.72	0.99	0.63	0.77	1.00	0.64
Real Wage	0.67	0.99	0.65	0.68	0.99	0.65	0.67	0.99	0.65
Euler Equation Residuals									
$[0.90; 1.10]k$	1.835E-4			1.373E-3			2.390E-6		
$[0.85; 1.15]k$	3.478E-4			1.277E-3			2.370E-6		
$[0.80; 1.20]k$	5.670E-4			1.691E-3			2.396E-6		
DM-Statistic									
<3.816	2.0			0.0			2.7		
>21.920	3.4			54.8			3.1		

Notes: s_x:=standard deviation of variable x, r_{xy}:=cross correlation of variable x with output, r_x:=first order autocorrelation of variable x. All second moments refer to HP-filtered percentage deviations from a variable's stationary solution. Euler equation residuals are computed as maximum absolute value over a grid of 400 equally spaced points on the square $\mathscr{K} \times [\ln 0.95; \ln 1.05]$, where $\mathscr{K}$ is defined in the respective row of the left-most column. The 2.5 and the 97.5 percent critical values of the $\chi^2(11)$-distribution are displayed in the last two lines of the first column. The table entries refer to the percentage fraction out of 1,000 simulations where the DM-statistic is below (above) its respective critical value.

For each $k' < (e^z k^\alpha + (1-\delta)k)/a$ this equation has a unique solution in $(0,1)$. We use the modified Newton-Raphson method described in Section 11.5.2 to solve this equation. From this solution, we can compute c and, thus, $u(c, 1-N)$.

Table 4.3 depicts the results from two simulations of the model with our program `Benchmark.for`. The first one rests on a policy function for the next-period capital stock k' computed on a grid of $n=5,000$ and $m=9$ points without interpolation between these points. The second was computed on a grid of $n = 250$ and $m = 19$ points with cubic interpolation between the points of the grid of the capital stock. To reduce run-time, we first solved the problem on a grid of $n = 250$ and $m = 9$ points and used the result to initialize the value function for subsequent computations. It took about six and half a minute to find the first solution and two hours to compute the second policy function.

The first solution is obviously inferior to the linear solution, whose results are reproduced from Table 2.2. The Euler equation residuals are about three times larger and the DM-statistic clearly indicates that the errors are correlated with past information. The differences in the second moments, however, are insignificant. For instance, the standard deviation of output (computed as the average from 500 simulations) has itself a standard deviation of 0.24 so that the difference of 0.04 is between two standard error bounds. The same is true for the differences between the other second moments. The reason for these relatively bad results is the coarse grid for the productivity shock. A simulation (the results of which are not presented in the table) with the same n but $m = 19$ performs better. From 1,000 simulations 3.1 (2.5) percent have a DM-statistic below (above) the 2.5-percent (97.5-percent) critical value, and except for the standard deviation of investment (which differs by 0.01) the other standard deviations match those from the linear solution. Cubic interpolation between the points of a coarse grid provides an even more accurate solution. There is no difference to the second moments obtained from the linear solution. Yet, the Euler equation residuals are about 200 times smaller and, thus, indicate a highly accurate solution. Note, finally, that the size of the Euler equation residual is almost independent of the length of the interval on which it is computed. We have already seen this property of non-linear, global methods in the chapter on the deterministic extended path method and it is confirmed here.

Problems

4.1 Stochastic Growth Model with Non-Negative Investment. In Section 4.3.1 we consider the stochastic growth model with non-negative investment.
   a) Use the Kuhn-Tucker-Theorem 1.1.1 and the procedure outlined in Section 1.2.3 to derive the Euler equation of this model from the Bellman equation (4.14).
   b) Devise a procedure to compute the residuals of this equation.
   c) Modify the program SolveVIS so that it can handle the non-negativity constraint on investment in the case of interpolation between gridpoints.

4.2 Stochastic Growth. In the benchmark model of Example 1.5.1 labor-augmenting technical progress grows deterministically. Suppose instead the following production function

$$Y_t = (A_t N_t)^{1-\alpha} K_t^{\alpha},$$

where the log of labor augmenting technical progress A_t is a random walk with drift μ:

$$\ln A_t = \mu + \ln A_{t-1} + \epsilon_t, \quad \epsilon_t \sim N(0, \sigma^2).$$

The household's preferences are the same as those presented in Example 1.5.1. Use $\mu = 0.00465$ and $\sigma = 0.006$ and the parameter values given in Table 1.1 to calibrate the model. Except for the stock of capital define stationary variables as in Section 1.4.2. For the capital stock define $k_t := K_t / A_{t-1}$. This ensures that the stationary capital stock k_t is still a predetermined variable at the beginning of period t.

   a) Derive the first-order conditions for the planers problem:

$$\max_{C_0, N_0} E_0 \left\{ \sum_{t=0}^{\infty} \beta^t \frac{C_t^{1-\eta}(1-N_t)^{\theta(1-\eta)}}{1-\eta} \right\}$$

s.t.

$$\left. \begin{array}{rcl} K_{t+1} + C_t & \leq & (A_t N_t)^{1-\alpha} K_t^{\alpha} + (1-\delta) K_t, \\ A_t & = & A_{t-1} e^{\mu + \epsilon_t}, \\ 0 & \leq & C_t, \\ 1 & \geq & N_t \geq 0, \\ 0 & \leq & K_{t+1}, \end{array} \right\} t = 0, 1, \ldots,$$

K_0, A_0 given.

   b) State this set of equations in terms of stationary variables and compute the balanced growth path.

c) Place a grid over k_t and solve the model via value function iteration. (Hint: Don't forget to use the correct discount factor!).
d) Use a random number generator and simulate the model. Compute second moments from first-differences of the logged variables (why?) and compare their empirical analogs obtained from German data (see the following table).

Variable	s_x	r_{xy}	r_x
Output	0.75	1.00	0.24
Consumption	0.76	0.56	0.04
Investment	1.99	0.68	0.25
Hours	0.97	0.59	−0.26
Real Wage	1.01	−0.14	−0.23

Notes: Second moments from first differences of logged German data, 70.i to 89.iv. s_x:= standard deviation of variable x, s_{xy}:=cross correlation of x with output y, r_x:=first order autocorrelation.

4.3 **Wealth Allocation.** EROSA and VENTURA (2002) analyze the money demand of households in a heterogeneous-agent economy. In order to compute the optimal household decision they cannot rely upon perturbation methods because households differ with regard to their individual asset holdings. Instead, they use value function iteration. In order to facilitate the computation, they apply a nice trick that may become handy whenever you consider household optimization problems where the households hold different kinds of assets. In the present problem, households can choose to allocate their wealth w on real money m and capital k. In the following, we will compute the steady state for a simple representative-agent economy.

The household supplies one unit of labor inelastically. The individual consumes a continuum of commodities indexed by $i \in [0,1]$. The representative household maximizes intertemporal utility

$$\sum_{t=0}^{\infty} \beta^t u(c), \quad u(c) = \frac{c^{1-\eta}}{1-\eta},$$

where c denotes a consumption aggregator $c = \inf_i c(i)$. As a consequence, the household consumes the same amount of all goods i. Following DOTSEY and IRELAND (1996) the households chooses whether to buy the goods with cash or credit. Let $s \geq 0$ denote the fraction of goods that are purchased with credit. The cash goods are purchased with the help of real money balances giving rise to the cash-in-advance constraint:

$$c(1-s) = m.$$

In order to purchase the good i by credit, the household must purchase $w\gamma(i)$ of financial services:

$$\gamma(i) = \gamma_0 \left(\frac{i}{1-i}\right)^\theta,$$

with $\theta > 0$. w denotes the wage rate, and the financial services are provided by competitive financial intermediaries who only use labor L^f as an input. Clearly, some goods will be purchased with cash as the credit costs go to infinity for $i \to 1$. Therefore, real money balances m will not be zero. Likewise, credit costs go to zero for $i \to 0$ and some goods will be purchased with credit as long as nominal interest rates are above zero, which will be the case in our economy. Therefore, we have an interior solution for $0 < s < 1$.

Let π denote the exogenous inflation rate that characterizes monetary policy. The decision problem can be formulated by the following Bellman equation

$$v(k,m) = \max_{c,s,m',k'} \{u(c) + \beta v(k', m')\}$$

subject to the cash-in-advance constraint and the budget constraint

$$c + w \int_0^s \gamma(c,i) \; di + k' + m'(1+\pi) = (1+r)k + w + m,$$

where r denotes the interest rate.
Production uses capital K and labor L^y:

$$Y = K^\alpha (L^y)^{1-\alpha}.$$

Capital depreciates at rate δ. In a factor market equilibrium,

$$w = (1-\alpha)K^\alpha (L^y)^{-\alpha},$$

$$r = \alpha K^{\alpha-1} (L^y)^{1-\alpha} - \delta.$$

In general equilibrium, the government spends the seignorage πM on government consumption G. The equilibrium conditions are given by

$$\begin{aligned} G &= \pi M, \\ M &= m, \; , C = c, \; K = k, \\ 1 &= L^y + L^f, \\ Y &= G + \delta K + C. \end{aligned}$$

Periods correspond to quarters. The model parameters are set as follows: $\beta = 0.99$, $\eta = 2.0$, $\delta = 0.02$, $\alpha = 0.36$, $\pi = 0.01$, $\gamma_0 = 0.0421$, $\theta = 0.3232$. The algorithm consists of the following steps:

Step 1: Choose initial values for K, M, and L^y and compute w and r.
Step 2: Solve the household decision problem.
Step 3: Compute the steady state with $k' = k'(k,m) = k$ and $m' = m'(k,m) = m$.
Step 4: Return to step 1 if $k \neq K$ and $m \neq M$.

Compute the steady state of the model as follows:

a) Use value function iteration over the state space (k,m).[6] Provide a good initial guess for K and M (Hint: 1) assume that $r = 1/\beta$ and $L^y \approx 1$ implying a value for K from the first-order condition of the firm. 2) Assume that $c = Y - \delta K$ and that households finance about 82% of consumption with M1, which is the approximate number for the US.)

b) Use the following two-step procedure in order to solve the household optimization problem (as suggested by EROSA and VENTURA (2002) in their Appendix A):

  i. Assume that the household allocates his wealth $w \equiv k + (1+\pi)m$ on capital and money according to the optimal portfolio functions $m = g_m(w)$ and $k = g_k(w)$. As an initialization of these functions in the first iteration over K and M, use a linear function that represents the weights of K and M in total wealth $K + (1+\pi)M$. Solve the following Bellman equation in the first stage:

  $$v(w) = \max_{c,s,w'} \{u(c) + \beta v(w')\}$$

  subject to the cash-in-advance constraint

  $$c(1-s) = g_m(w)$$

  and the budget constraint:

  $$c + w \int_0^s \gamma(c,i) \, di + w' = (1+r)g_k(w) + w + g_m(w).$$

  This provides the policy function $w' = g_w(w)$.

  ii. In the second stage, solve the optimization problem:

  $$(g_k(w), g_m(w)) = \arg\max_{k,m} \left\{ \max_{c,s} u(c) \right\}$$

---

[6] In order to compute the optimum, you need to know the *Leibniz rule*:

$$\int_{a(x)}^{b(x)} f(t,x) \, dt = f(b(x),x)b'(x) - f(a(x),x)a'(x) + \int_{a(x)}^{b(x)} \frac{\partial}{\partial x} f(t,x) \, dt.$$

subject to

$$(1+\pi)m + k = \omega$$

$$c(1-s) = m,$$

$$c + w\int_0^s \gamma(c,i)\ di + w' = (1+r)k + w + m,$$

where $w' = g_w(\omega)$.

Iterate until convergence and compare the policy functions, Euler equation residuals and the computational time of the two procedures.

c) How does an increase of the quarterly inflation rate from 1% to 2% affect the equilibrium allocation?

Chapter 5

Parameterized Expectations

Overview. We know from Chapter 1 that there are two ways to characterize the solution of a Ramsey problem or, more generally, of a recursive dynamic general equilibrium (DGE) model: (1) in terms of a policy function that relates the model's decision or control variables to the model's state variables or (2) in terms of a system of stochastic difference equations that determines the time paths of the model's endogenous variables. The method presented in this chapter rests on yet a third solution concept. In the Rational expectations equilibrium of a recursive DGE model agents' conditional expectations are time invariant functions of the model's state variables. The parameterized expectations approach (PEA) applies methods from function approximation (see Section 11.2) to these unknown functions. In particular, it uses simple functions instead of the true but unknown expectations and employs Monte Carlo techniques to determine their parameters.

The PEA has several advantages vis-a-vis both the value function iteration approach and the extended path algorithm. In contrast to the former, it does not suffer as easily from the curse of dimensionality and, therefore, can be applied to models with many endogenous state variables. Unlike the latter, it deals easily with binding constraints. Our applications in Section 5.3 illustrate these issues.

We describe the PEA in two steps. (1) In the next section we look at the solution of a Ramsey problem from a different angle. Instead of focusing on agents' policy functions, we consider their conditional expectations of future prices, quantities, and shocks. Except in our discussion of the deterministic extended path algorithm considered in Chapter 3, we have tacitly assumed that these expectations are consistent with the model. It is now the time to make this more obvious. The ensuing concept of a rational expectations equilibrium is yet another way to describe the solution of a DGE model. Its feature is a time invariant (possibly vector-valued) function $\mathscr{E}$ used by agents to predict their future economic environment. An approximate solution is a simple function $\hat{\mathscr{E}}$, for example a finite degree polynomial, that approximates $\mathscr{E}$ sufficiently well. We will see that the definition of conditional expectations provides the clue to compute the parameters of $\hat{\mathscr{E}}$. This naturally implies a general framework for the PEA.

(2) Section 5.2 considers the single steps of this algorithm in more detail. Specifically, we will deal with two approaches to solve the fixed-point problem that defines the PEA solution. The first approach is iterative, the second solves a non-linear equations problem. Both approaches require good starting values and so we will consider this problem subsequently.

Having read this chapter you will have seen applications of almost every tool from the collection of numerical methods presented in Chapter 11.

5.1 Characterization of Approximate Solutions

This section provides a general description of the parameterized expectations approach (PEA). In the first subsection we use the stochastic growth model of Section 1.3 to illustrate the basic idea. The second subsection provides the general framework and the third subsection highlights the relation between the PEA and models of adaptive learning.

5.1.1 An Illustrative Example

The Model. The dynamics of the stochastic Ramsey model from (1.22) is governed by two equations:[1]

---
[1] See Section 1.3.2 for their derivation.

$$K_{t+1} = Z_t f(K_t) + (1-\delta)K_t - C_t, \qquad (5.1a)$$
$$u'(C_t) = \beta E_t \big[u'(C_{t+1})\left(1-\delta+\alpha Z_{t+1} f'(K_{t+1})\right)\big]. \qquad (5.1b)$$

C_t denotes consumption, K_t the stock of capital, and Z_t the total factor productivity that evolves over time according to

$$Z_t = Z_{t-1}^\varrho e^{\epsilon_t}, \quad \epsilon_t \sim N(0,\sigma^2). \qquad (5.1c)$$

Equation (5.1a) is the economy's resource constraint. Implicit in the Euler equation (5.1b) is the statement that the expected marginal rate of substitution between current and future consumption must equal the expected gross return on investment, i.e., one plus the marginal product of capital net of depreciation δ.

Conditional Expectations. We know from Chapter 1 that the solution to this set of equations can be written in terms of a time invariant policy function $K_{t+1} = h^K(K_t, Z_t)$. Accordingly, the conditional expectation on the rhs of equation (5.1b) is also a time invariant function $\mathscr{E}$ of the model's state variables K_t and Z_t. To see this, let

$$h^C(K_t, Z_t) := Z_t f(K_t) + (1-\delta)K_t - h^K(K_t, Z_t)$$

denote the solution for consumption given K_t and Z_t. Therefore, $C_{t+1} = h^C(h^K(K_t, Z_t), Z_{t+1})$. Using (5.1c) to replace Z_{t+1}, we may summarize the expression inside the expectations operator E_t in a function $\phi(K_t, Z_t, \epsilon_{t+1})$:

$$\begin{aligned}\phi(K_t, Z_t, \epsilon_{t+1}) :=& u'\left(h^C(h^K(K_t, Z_t), Z_t^\varrho e^{\epsilon_{t+1}})\right) \\ &\times \left(1-\delta + Z_t^\varrho e^{\epsilon_{t+1}} f'\left(h^K(K_t, Z_t)\right)\right).\end{aligned}$$

Since the innovations to (5.1c) are normal variates, we get $\mathscr{E}$ via integration:

$$\mathscr{E}(K_t, Z_t) := \int_{-\infty}^{\infty} \phi(K_t, Z_t, \epsilon_{t+1}) \frac{e^{-\frac{(\epsilon_{t+1})^2}{2\sigma^2}}}{\sqrt{2\pi\sigma^2}} d\epsilon_{t+1}.$$

Approximation of $\mathscr{E}$. Suppose we knew $\mathscr{E}$. Then, given an arbitrary initial capital stock K_0 and an arbitrary initial level of the total factor productivity Z_0, we can compute the rhs of equation (5.1b) and solve the system of two equations (5.1) for K_1 and C_0. With K_1 at hand, Z_1 derived from Z_0, and a draw from the $N(0, \sigma^2)$-distribution, we can use $\mathscr{E}(K_1, Z_1)$ and (5.1) again to solve for (K_2, C_1). Repeating these steps over and over, we can trace out an entire time path for the variables of our model economy.

As with the policy function h^K, there is generally no analytic solution for $\mathscr{E}$. The idea behind the PEA is to approximate the unknown function $\mathscr{E}$ by a simple function ψ. For instance, DEN HAAN and MARCET (1990) use $\psi(\gamma_1, \gamma_2, \gamma_3, K_t, Z_t) = \gamma_1 K_t^{\gamma_2} Z_t^{\gamma_3}$ to approximate the solution of the stochastic difference equation (5.1).

Given the choice of the approximating function, the remaining task is to fix its parameters. Remember the definition of conditional expectations: let y denote a random variable that we wish to forecast using observations on $(x_1, x_2, \ldots, x_n)$. We seek a function h that minimizes the expected mean quadratic error

$$E[(y - h(x_1, x_2, \ldots, x_n))^2].$$

The solution to this problem is the conditional expectation:[2]

$$E[y|(x_1, x_2, \ldots, x_n)] := \arg\min_{h} E[(y - h(x_1, x_2, \ldots, x_n))^2].$$

The parameter choice mimics this definition. We need some additional notation to describe this procedure. For simplicity, we collect the model's variables in the vector $\mathbf{s}_t := [C_t, K_t, K_{t+1}, Z_t]'$ and stack the model's state variables in the vector $\mathbf{w}_t := [K_t, Z_t]'$. We use $\psi(\boldsymbol{\gamma}, \mathbf{w}_t)$ to denote the function approximating $\mathscr{E}$ for a given p-vector of parameters $\boldsymbol{\gamma} := [\gamma_1, \gamma_2, \ldots, \gamma_p]$ and assume that a time path $\{\mathbf{s}_t\}_{t=0}^{T}$ of length $T+1$ has been computed based on a given (K_0, Z_0) and T draws from the $N(0, \sigma^2)$-distribution. To emphasize the dependence on $\boldsymbol{\gamma}$ we write $\mathbf{s}_t(\boldsymbol{\gamma})$ and $\mathbf{w}_t(\boldsymbol{\gamma})$. Given this, let

---

[2] See, e.g., Sargent (1987), p. 224.

$$\phi(\mathbf{s}_{t+1}(\boldsymbol{\gamma})) := u'(C_{t+1})\left(1 - \delta + Z_{t+1}f'(K_{t+1})\right)$$

denote the (ex post) rhs of equation (5.1b) associated with this time path so that $\phi(\mathbf{s}_{t+1}(\boldsymbol{\gamma})) - \psi(\boldsymbol{\gamma}, \mathbf{w}_t(\boldsymbol{\gamma}))$ is the time $t+1$ prediction error. Next, define the map $\Gamma : \mathbb{R}^p \to \mathbb{R}^p$ by

$$\Gamma(\boldsymbol{\gamma}) := \arg\min_{\boldsymbol{\xi}} \sum_{t=0}^{T-1} \left[\phi(\mathbf{s}_{t+1}(\boldsymbol{\gamma})) - \psi(\boldsymbol{\xi}, \mathbf{w}_t(\boldsymbol{\gamma}))\right]^2.$$

Thus, $\Gamma(\boldsymbol{\gamma})$ is the parameter vector $\boldsymbol{\xi}$ that minimizes the sum of squared prediction errors associated with the time path that results from predictions of the rhs of equation (5.1b) using the function $\psi(\boldsymbol{\gamma}, \cdot)$. The fixed point $\boldsymbol{\gamma}_{p,T}$ of this mapping,

$$\boldsymbol{\gamma}_{p,T} = \Gamma(\boldsymbol{\gamma}_{p,T}),$$

is the approximate model solution. It depends on the length of the time path T and the function $\psi(\cdot)$.

5.1.2 A General Framework

This section describes the parameterized expectations approach in more general terms. Each of the representative agent models that you will encounter in this book fits the following framework.

Let $\mathbf{s}_t$ denote an $n(s)$-dimensional vector that collects all of the model's variables. This vector belongs to some subset U of $\mathbb{R}^{n(s)}$.[3] It is convenient to consider two further subsets of the variables in $\mathbf{s}_t$. The first subset, the $n(z)$-vector $\mathbf{z}_t$, includes all exogenous stochastic processes with the Markov property that drive the model.[4] The second subset collects the model's state variables in the $n(w)$-dimensional vector $\mathbf{w}_t \in X \subset \mathbb{R}^{n(w)}$. Note that $\mathbf{w}_t$ includes $\mathbf{z}_t$ and

---
[3] Many of the variables of an economic model are restricted to belong to a given subinterval of the real line. For instance, output, consumption, investment, and the stock of capital cannot be negative. For this reason, we restrict $\mathbf{s}_t$ to a subset U of $\mathbb{R}^{n(s)}$. This set implicitly imposes the restrictions on the values which the variables can take.

[4] See Section 12.2 on this property.

all those variables from the vector $\mathbf{s}_t$ that have given initial conditions but are otherwise determined endogenously. In the notation of Section 2.5.4, $\mathbf{w}_t = [\mathbf{x}_t', \mathbf{z}_t']'$. The variables in $\mathbf{w}_t$ summarize the information that is relevant to predict the future economic environment. In addition, there are two vector-valued functions that govern the model's dynamics. The function $\boldsymbol{\phi}$ with argument $\mathbf{s}_{t+1}$ maps U to V, a subset of $\mathbb{R}^k$. The function $\mathbf{g}$ with arguments $E_t[\boldsymbol{\phi}(\mathbf{s}_{t+1})]$ and $\mathbf{s}_t$ collects the model's Euler equations, definitions, resource constraints, and so forth. In the example from the previous subsection $\boldsymbol{\phi}$ equals the single-valued expression to the right of the conditional expectations operator E_t while $\mathbf{g}$ is given by equations (5.1), and V is the one-dimensional space of positive real numbers $\mathbb{R}_+$. Accordingly, the system of stochastic difference equations that drive the model can be written as follows:

$$\mathbf{g}\left(E_t\left[\boldsymbol{\phi}(\mathbf{s}_{t+1})\right], \mathbf{s}_t\right) = \mathbf{0} \text{ for all } t = 0, 1, \ldots, \infty. \tag{5.2}$$

Due to the recursive nature of the model (that allows for its solution in terms of a time invariant policy function) there is a time invariant conditional expectations function $\mathscr{E}$ given as the solution to

$$\mathscr{E} := \arg\min_{\mathbf{h}: X \to V} E\left[\left(\boldsymbol{\phi}(\mathbf{s}_{t+1}) - \mathbf{h}(\mathbf{w}_t)\right)'\left(\boldsymbol{\phi}(\mathbf{s}_{t+1}) - \mathbf{h}(\mathbf{w}_t)\right)\right]$$

that solves (5.2), i.e.,

$$\mathbf{g}\left(\mathscr{E}(\mathbf{w}_t), \mathbf{s}_t\right) = \mathbf{0} \text{ for all } t = 0, 1, \ldots, \infty. \tag{5.3}$$

The parameterized expectations approach approximates this solution in the following steps:

Algorithm 5.1.1 (PEA)

Purpose: *Approximate the solution to (5.3)*

Steps:

Step 1: Choose a function $\boldsymbol{\psi}(\boldsymbol{\gamma}, \cdot) : X \to V$ that depends on the vector of parameters $\boldsymbol{\gamma} \in \mathbb{R}^p$.

Step 2: Draw a sequence of shocks $\{\mathbf{z}_t\}_{t=0}^T$.

Step 3: Iterate on

$$\mathbf{g}\left(\boldsymbol{\psi}(\boldsymbol{\gamma}, \mathbf{w}_t(\boldsymbol{\gamma})), \mathbf{s}_t(\boldsymbol{\gamma})\right) = 0$$

to find the sequence $\{\mathbf{w}_t(\boldsymbol{\gamma})\}_{t=0}^T$.
Step 4: Find the fixed point $\boldsymbol{\gamma}_{p,T} = \Gamma(\boldsymbol{\gamma}_{p,T})$ *of the map* Γ *defined by*

$$\Gamma(\boldsymbol{\gamma}) := \arg\min_{\boldsymbol{\xi}} \frac{1}{T} \sum_{t=0}^{T-1} \|\boldsymbol{\phi}(\mathbf{s}_{t+1}(\boldsymbol{\gamma})) - \boldsymbol{\psi}(\boldsymbol{\xi}, \mathbf{w}_t(\boldsymbol{\gamma}))\|^2,$$

where $\|\cdot\|$ *denotes the Euclidean norm.*
Step 5: Decide whether $\boldsymbol{\psi}(\boldsymbol{\gamma}_{p,T}, \cdot)$ *is close to the true but unknown solution* $\mathscr{E}$. *If not, change either* T *or* $\boldsymbol{\psi}(\cdot)$ *and return to Step 1.*

MARCET and MARSHALL (1992, 1994) provide conditions on the functions $\mathbf{g}$, $\boldsymbol{\phi}$, $\boldsymbol{\psi}$ as well as on the process $\{\mathbf{z}_t\}_{t=0}^\infty$ that make the PEA a meaningful concept. Using a weaker definition of an approximate solution than that given in Step 4 they are able to show that the approximation can be made arbitrarily close to the true solution (5.3) by letting $T \to \infty$ and $p \to \infty$. Since we will be dealing with the computation of $\boldsymbol{\gamma}_{p,T}$ for a fixed T and p we can sidestep the involved technical details and can proceed with the definition given in Step 4.

5.1.3 Adaptive Learning

Models of Learning. There is an interesting relation between the approximate solution discussed in the previous section and attempts to formalize how agents learn about their environment.

The rational expectations equilibrium defined in (5.3) presupposes two requirements: individual rationality and mutual consistency of perceptions of the environment. The agents in the model use the true conditional expectations function for their forecasts. They have somehow solved estimation and inference problems that an econometrician must deal with. Models of learning depict economic agents as econometricians that use current and past observations to estimate the parameters of the economy's law of motion. Since the actual law of motion depends upon the law perceived by agents, this is like chasing a moving target. Agents that act like econometricians are not as smart as those that populate the rational expectations equilibrium. For that reason, SARGENT (1993) refers to the former as agents with 'bounded rationality', a term coined by HERBERT SIMON (1957). Others use the term 'adaptive learning' to characterize this approach. EVANS and HONKAPOHJA (2001) provide an introduction into the related methods and present many applications. In the following paragraphs we will sketch an adaptive learning process whose stationary point is the approximate solution discussed in the previous subsection.

Recursive Least Squares. Assume that you want to estimate the linear equation

$$y_i = \gamma' \mathbf{x}_i + \epsilon_i, \quad i = 1, 2, ..., t,$$

where γ is a p-dimensional column vector of parameters related to the observations of p independent variables collected in the column vector $\mathbf{x}_i = [x_{i1}, x_{i2}, \ldots, x_{ip}]'$. Put $\mathbf{y} = [y_1, y_2, \ldots, y_t]'$ and $X = [\mathbf{x}_1, \mathbf{x}_2, \ldots, \mathbf{x}_t]'$. The well-known formula for the least squares estimator gives:[5]

$$\gamma_t = (X'X)^{-1} X' \mathbf{y} = \left(\sum_{i=1}^{t} \mathbf{x}_i \mathbf{x}_i' \right)^{-1} \left(\sum_{i=1}^{t} \mathbf{x}_i y_i \right). \quad (5.4)$$

Suppose you have estimated γ from $t-1$ observations and now you are given one additional observation $(y_t, x_{t1}, x_{t2}, ..., x_{tp})$. There is a convenient formula that updates your estimate as follows:[6]

---

[5] This formula is derived in most introductory and advanced textbooks on econometrics. See, e.g., GREENE (2003), pp. 19ff. or JUDGE, HILL, GRIFFITHS, and LÜTKEPOHL (1988), p. 164ff.

[6] You can verify this formula by substituting the definitions of γ_t from (5.4) and of R_t into (5.5).

$$\gamma_t = \gamma_{t-1} + \frac{1}{t}R_t^{-1}\mathbf{x}_t(y_t - \gamma'_{t-1}\mathbf{x}_t),$$
$$R_t = R_{t-1} + \frac{1}{t}(\mathbf{x}_t\mathbf{x}'_t - R_{t-1}),$$
(5.5)

where

$$R_t := \frac{1}{t}\left(\sum_{i=1}^{t}\mathbf{x}_i\mathbf{x}'_i\right)$$

is a square matrix of dimension p and R_t^{-1} its inverse. The update of γ in the first line of (5.5) uses the most recent forecast error $y_t - \gamma'_{t-1}\mathbf{x}_t$.

Learning Dynamics and the PEA. Suppose the agents in our model economy were not able to compute the true conditional expectations function $\mathscr{E}$. For ease of exposition assume that the range of $\phi : X \to V$ is a subset of the real line (as in the Ramsey model of Section 5.1.1). Let $\psi(\gamma_t, \cdot)$ denote the agents' forecast of $\phi(\cdot)$ using their most recent estimate of the parameter vector γ_t. Since the entire history of the model economy depends upon the sequence of estimates $\{\gamma_\tau\}_{\tau=0}^{t}$ the time sequence of the model's variables is different from the sequence $\{s_\tau\}_{\tau=0}^{t}$ obtained for a given and constant vector γ. To emphasize this difference, we use $\tilde{\mathbf{s}}_t$ and $\tilde{\mathbf{w}}_t$ to denote the vector of variables and the vector of states, respectively, that are associated with a given sequence of estimates $\{\gamma_\tau\}_{\tau=0}^{t}$. Assume that agents use non-linear least squares to estimate γ, i.e., at period t they choose γ_t to minimize

$$\frac{1}{t}\sum_{i=0}^{t-1}[\phi(\tilde{\mathbf{s}}_{i+1}) - \psi(\gamma_t, \tilde{\mathbf{w}}_i)]^2.$$

A solution to this problem that fits into the framework of recursive least squares can be found as follows. Linearize $\psi(\gamma, \cdot)$ at the previous estimate γ_{t-1}:

$$\psi(\gamma_t, \cdot) \simeq \psi(\gamma_{t-1}, \cdot) + \nabla\psi(\gamma_{t-1})(\gamma_t - \gamma_{t-1}),$$

where the symbol $\nabla\psi(\gamma_{t-1})$ denotes the row vector of first derivatives of the function ψ evaluated at the point γ_{t-1}. Put

$$\bar{y}_i := \phi(\tilde{\mathbf{s}}_{i+1}) - \psi(\boldsymbol{\gamma}_{t-1}, \tilde{\mathbf{w}}_i) + \nabla\psi(\boldsymbol{\gamma}_{t-1})\boldsymbol{\gamma}_{t-1},$$
$$\bar{\mathbf{w}}'_i := \nabla\psi(\boldsymbol{\gamma}_{t-1}),$$

and solve

$$\min_{\boldsymbol{\gamma}_t} \quad \frac{1}{t}\sum_{i=0}^{t-1}[\bar{y}_i - \boldsymbol{\gamma}'_t\bar{\mathbf{w}}_i]^2.$$

The solution is given by (5.4) with y_i and $\mathbf{x}_i$ replaced by $\bar{y}_i$ and $\bar{\mathbf{w}}_i$, respectively. Now, we are able to apply the recursive formula (5.5) to formulate the dynamics of our model under non-linear least squares learning:

$$\begin{aligned}\boldsymbol{\gamma}_t &= \boldsymbol{\gamma}_{t-1} + \frac{1}{tR_t}\nabla\psi(\boldsymbol{\gamma}_{t-1})'(\phi(\tilde{\mathbf{s}}_t) - \psi(\boldsymbol{\gamma}_{t-1}, \tilde{\mathbf{w}}_{t-1})), \\ R_t &= R_{t-1} + \frac{1}{t}\left(\nabla\psi(\boldsymbol{\gamma}_{t-1})'\nabla\psi(\boldsymbol{\gamma}_{t-1}) - R_{t-1}\right), \\ 0 &= g(\psi(\boldsymbol{\gamma}_t, \tilde{\mathbf{w}}_t), \tilde{\mathbf{s}}_t).\end{aligned} \quad (5.6)$$

MARCET and MARSHALL (1994) show, that the approximate solution defined in Step 4 of Algorithm 5.1.1 for $t \to \infty$, denoted by $\boldsymbol{\gamma}_p$, is a rest point of this process. Furthermore, if the absolute values of the eigenvalues of $\Gamma(\boldsymbol{\gamma})$ evaluated at $\boldsymbol{\gamma}_p$ are less than one, there is a neighborhood $\mathcal{N}(\boldsymbol{\gamma}_p)$ such that all $\boldsymbol{\gamma} \in \mathcal{N}(\boldsymbol{\gamma}_p)$ converge to this rest point.

5.2 Computation of the Approximate Solution

This section considers the single steps of the PEA Algorithm 5.1.1 in more detail. We start with the choice of the sample size T and the approximating function ψ in the next subsection.

5.2.1 Choice of T and ψ

Sample Size. We note in Section 5.1.2 that the accuracy of the approximation increases with T. The underlying intuition is as follows. Suppose we would compute the time sequence of $\Omega_T := \{\mathbf{s}_t\}_{t=0}^T$ from the true function $\mathscr{E}$. In this case Ω_T is a sample drawn from the ergodic distribution that is the solution of the system of stochastic difference equations defined in (5.3). As usual in sampling, the larger Ω_T is, the better does it represent the properties of the underlying distribution. In particular, those parts of the space U where the solution spends most of its time receive a high frequency count in Ω_T, whereas those parts of U which are visited very rarely appear hardly in Ω_T. As a consequence, the non-linear least squares estimator invoked in Step 4 of the PEA will be eager to keep the expectational errors small on those subsets of U, which we are most interested in. Of course, this property carries over to any sufficiently good approximation ψ of $\mathscr{E}$.

Applications of the PEA to solve the stochastic growth model therefore use large integer values of T. For instance, DUFFY and MCNELIS (2001) use $T = 2,000$, DEN HAAN and MARCET (1990) choose $T = 2,500$, the Fortran programs of MARCET and LORENZONI (1999) allow for a maximum of 10,000 data points, and CHRISTIANO and FISHER (2000) even put $T = 100,000$. To eliminate the influence of the initial value $\mathbf{w}_0$ one can disregard the first 0.5 or 1.0 percent of the data points from the simulated time series and choose the parameter vector $\boldsymbol{\gamma}_{p,T}$ with respect to the remaining sample.

Function Approximation. More challenging is the choice of ψ. Remember that this function is vector-valued, as it maps points from a subset of $\mathbb{R}^{n(w)}$ to points in a subset of $\mathbb{R}^k$. If we think of the j-th coordinate of ψ as a map $\psi_j : X \subset \mathbb{R}^n \to \mathbb{R}$ we can reduce this problem to the simpler one of approximating a real-valued function. In Section 11.2 we present various ways to approximate a given function. In our applications of the PEA we use a complete set of polynomials of degree p in the $n(w)$ variables $(w_{1t}, \ldots, w_{n(w)t})$ to build ψ_j. The members of the set are either products of monomials $(w_1^{k_1} w_2^{k_2} \cdots w_n(w)^{k_n})$ or Chebyshev polynomials (see Section 11.2.6), where $\sum_{i=1}^n (w) k_i = p$. Monomials are easy to deal with in the PEA for the following reason: in many applications we do not know the boundaries of X in advance. However, the domain of orthogonal families of polynomials, as for the Chebyshev polynomials, are certain compact intervals of the real line. When we use bases from members of these families, we must specify a compact region X before we start the computations. This is not necessary in the case of monomials, since their domain is the entire real line. The drawback from using monomials that we will encounter later is the problem of multicollinearity. Very often, higher order terms of a variable w_i appear to be indistinguishable from one another on the computer so that it is impossible to regress the errors $\phi(\mathbf{s}_{t+1}, \boldsymbol{\gamma}) - \psi(\boldsymbol{\gamma}, \mathbf{w}_t)$ on $\mathbf{w}_t$. Hence, even if the theory tells us that we get a more accurate solution if we increase the degree of the polynomial, we will not be able to achieve this on the computer with monomials. Since the orthogonality of Chebyshev polynomials in discrete applications pertains to the zeros of these polynomials (see (11.56)) only, their use does not really provide a work around of this problem. Of course, the PEA is not restricted to a certain class of functions, and you may want to redo our examples using, e.g., neural networks (see Section 11.2).

5.2.2 Iterative Computation of the Fixed Point

Convergence. There is a last step to be taken in order to implement the parameterized expectations approach: the actual computation of the parameters of the expectations function $\psi(\boldsymbol{\gamma}, \cdot)$. Probably the most obvious thing to do is to iterate on the mapping Γ defined in Step 4 of Algorithm 5.1.1,

$$\boldsymbol{\gamma}_{s+1} = \Gamma(\boldsymbol{\gamma}_s), s = 0, 1, \ldots, \tag{5.7}$$

starting with an arbitrary $\boldsymbol{\gamma}_0$. However, since (5.7) is essentially a non-linear difference equation, this procedure need not converge, even if the fixed point exists. DEN HAAN and MARCET (1990) as well as MARCET and MARSHALL (1994) propose to iterate on

$$\boldsymbol{\gamma}_{s+1} = (1-\lambda)\boldsymbol{\gamma}_s + \lambda\Gamma(\boldsymbol{\gamma}_s) \tag{5.8}$$

for some $\lambda \in (0,1]$ to foster convergence. Indeed, if the related adaptive learning model is locally stable, there are starting values $\boldsymbol{\gamma}_0$ such that for a sufficiently small λ (5.8) will converge.

Non-Linear Least Squares. If we use this iterative procedure we have to solve

$$\min_{\boldsymbol{\xi}} \frac{1}{T} \sum_{t=0}^{T-1} \|\boldsymbol{\phi}(\mathbf{s}_{t+1}(\boldsymbol{\gamma})) - \boldsymbol{\psi}(\boldsymbol{\xi}, \mathbf{w}_t(\boldsymbol{\gamma}))\|^2$$

at each step. This breaks down to solving k non-linear least squares problems. To see this let $\phi_j(\cdot)$ and $\psi_j(\cdot)$ denote the j-th component of $\boldsymbol{\phi}$ and $\boldsymbol{\psi}$, respectively, and partition the parameter vector $\boldsymbol{\gamma}$ so that $\boldsymbol{\gamma}_j := [\gamma_{1j}, \ldots, \gamma_{pj}]$, $j = 1, 2, \ldots, k$. With this notation the minimization problem can be rewritten as

$$\min_{\boldsymbol{\xi}} \frac{1}{T} \sum_{t=0}^{T-1} \sum_{j=1}^{k} [\phi_j(\mathbf{s}_{t+1}(\boldsymbol{\gamma})) - \psi_j(\boldsymbol{\xi}_j, \mathbf{w}_t(\boldsymbol{\gamma}))]^2,$$

$$\equiv \min_{\boldsymbol{\xi}} \sum_{j=1}^{k} \frac{1}{T} \sum_{t=0}^{T-1} [\phi_j(\mathbf{s}_{t+1}(\boldsymbol{\gamma})) - \psi_j(\boldsymbol{\xi}_j, \mathbf{w}_t(\boldsymbol{\gamma}))]^2,$$

$$\equiv \sum_{j=1}^{k} \min_{\boldsymbol{\xi}_j} \frac{1}{T} \sum_{t=0}^{T-1} [\phi_j(\mathbf{s}_{t+1}(\boldsymbol{\gamma})) - \psi_j(\boldsymbol{\xi}_j, \mathbf{w}_t(\boldsymbol{\gamma}))]^2.$$

In our applications we use the damped Gauss-Newton method explained in Section 11.6.2 to solve this problem. In the early stages of the iterations over (5.7) it is not necessary to compute the minimum with great accuracy. Thus one can make the algorithm faster by choosing very generous stopping criteria. For instance, the programs by MARCET and LORENZONI (1999) bypass the convergence test (11.86) (see Section 11.4 on this criterion).

5.2.3 Direct Computation of the Fixed Point

In this subsection we consider the PEA as solution to a complicated system of $k \times p$ non-linear equations.

Remember the following notation used so far. $\psi_j(\gamma_j, \mathbf{w}_t(\gamma))$, $j = 1, 2, \ldots, k$ is the time t forecast of the j-th conditional expectation given the vector of states $\mathbf{w}_t$ and the parameter vector $\gamma = [\gamma_1, \gamma_2, \ldots, \gamma_k]$, where $\gamma_j = [\gamma_{1j}, \gamma_{2j}, \ldots, \gamma_{pj}]$. Accordingly, $\phi_j(\mathbf{s}_{t+1}(\gamma))$, is the time $t+1$ value of the expression to the right of the expectations operator that defines the j-th conditional expectation.

In this notation, the $k \times p$ first-order conditions for the minimization problem in Step 4 of Algorithm 5.1.1 may be written as follows:

$$0 = \frac{-2}{T} \sum_{t=0}^{T-1} [\phi_j(\mathbf{s}_{t+1}(\gamma)) - \psi_j(\xi_j, \mathbf{w}_t(\gamma))] \frac{\partial \psi_j}{\partial \xi_{ij}}(\xi_j, \mathbf{w}_t(\gamma)),$$

for all $i = 1, 2, \ldots, p$, and $j = 1, 2, \ldots, k$.

The iterative procedure of the previous subsection solves this problem for $\xi = [\xi_1, \xi_2, \ldots, \xi_k]$ given γ and stops if $\xi \simeq \gamma$. Here we replace ξ in the above system with γ to get:

$$0 = \underbrace{\frac{-2}{T} \sum_{t=0}^{T-1} [\phi_j(\mathbf{s}_{t+1}(\gamma)) - \psi_j(\gamma_j, \mathbf{w}_t(\gamma))] \frac{\partial \psi_j}{\partial \gamma_{ij}}(\gamma_j, \mathbf{w}_t(\gamma))}_{=: \varphi_{ij}(\gamma)},$$

for all $i = 1, 2, \ldots, p$, and $j = 1, 2, \ldots, k$. (5.10)

The zero of this non-linear system of equations in γ is an equivalent characterization of the approximate model solution. Thus, instead of the iterative procedure outlined above, we can apply a non-linear equation solver to (5.10).

This sounds nice and easy! But think of the following issues. Routines that solve non-linear equations, as the modified Newton-Raphson method with line search, require a starting value. With an arbitrary γ_0, however, it may not be possible to perform the simulations in Step 3 of Algorithm 5.1.1 at all. For instance, it may happen that at some t a non-negativity constraint implicit in the definition of $\mathbf{g}(\cdot)$ is violated so that it is impossible to compute $\{\mathbf{s}_t\}_{t=0}^T$. Even if this does not happen at the given γ_0 the algorithm may want to try a vector where it is not possible to simulate the model for all T. For this reason any procedure that performs the simulation step must return an error flag that signals the calling program to stop. Otherwise your program will crash because of overflows, underflows or other run-time errors arising from undefined numerical operations. By the same token, the procedure that computes the rhs of (5.10) must return an error flag to the non-linear equations solver telling it to stop or to look for a different γ if it is not possible to evaluate all the $\varphi_{ij}(\gamma)$. Yet, standard software usually assumes that it is possible to evaluate a given non-linear system everywhere and there is no way to tell the program to do otherwise. So, unless you write your own non-linear equations solver (or trust our routines) you are bound to find very good starting values. It is this issue that we turn to next.

5.2.4 Starting Points

Good starting values are essential to both the iterative and the direct approach to locate the PEA solution. The iterations over (5.8) may not converge if the initial point is outside of the basin of attraction of the respective learning algorithm, and non-linear equations solvers easily get stuck if the simulation step fails. There are several ways to handle this problem.

Homotopy. In mathematics two vector-valued functions $\mathbf{f}: X \to Y$ and $\mathbf{g}: X \to Y$ are said to be homotopic if $\mathbf{f}$ can be continuously deformed into $\mathbf{g}$. A function $\mathbf{h}(\mathbf{x}, s)$ that performs this task, i.e., that equals $\mathbf{f}$ for $s = 0$ and $\mathbf{g}$ for $s = 1$, is called a homotopy function. For instance,

$$\mathbf{h}(\mathbf{x}, s) := (1 - s)\mathbf{f}(\mathbf{x}) + s\mathbf{g}(\mathbf{x}) \tag{5.11}$$

is a homotopy function.

Suppose we want to solve $\mathbf{g}(\mathbf{x}) = \mathbf{0}$ and know the solution $\mathbf{x}_0$ of $\mathbf{f}(\mathbf{x}) = \mathbf{0}$. The idea behind homotopy methods is to construct a path in $X \times \mathbb{R}$ that takes us from the known solution to the solution of the problem of interest. Simple continuation methods use the linear homotopy (5.11), form an increasing sequence $0 < s_1 < s_2 < \cdots < 1$ and solve the related sequence of problems $\mathbf{h}(\mathbf{x}, s_i) = \mathbf{0}$. If the homotopy path in $X \times \mathbb{R}$ has peaks and troughs along the s dimension, simple continuation methods can fail. More advanced methods construct the homotopy path by solving a related system of differential equations.[7]

As regards DGE models the problem is to construct a simple model whose solution is either known or has been found in previous work and to move gradually from this model to the model of interest. This may be simple, as it is in the stochastic growth model, where an analytic solution exists for log-preferences and full depreciation of capital (see Example 1.3.2). As you will see in Section 5.3.1, in this case we can also derive an analytic expression for the conditional expectations function $\mathscr{E}(K_t, Z_t)$. We can then use small steps to move from $\delta = 1$ and $\eta = 1$ to a version of this model where the rate of capital depreciation δ is in the range of empirical estimates and where the elasticity of the marginal utility of consumption η is different from one. However, if we think of a model with capital and real balances of money as a second asset, it is less obvious from where to start. Moreover, if the model of interest departs significantly from the simple stochastic growth model it may be very cumbersome to trace out a sequence of more and more complicated models. For this reason, we consider search methods that are easy to implement for any kind of model and that have been found effective in quite different areas, such as automatic programming, machine learning, game theory, and numerical optimization.

Genetic Algorithms. In Section 11.6.4 we introduce genetic algorithms as a tool to minimize a given function. Here, our problem is to find the zeros of a set of non-linear functions $f^1(\mathbf{x}), f^2(\mathbf{x}), \ldots, f^n(\mathbf{x})$. But the solution to this problem is also a minimum of

$$g(\mathbf{x}) := \sum_{i=1}^{n} (f^i(\mathbf{x}))^2.$$

---

[7] See, e.g., JUDD (1998), pp. 176ff.

Though the converse is not true, a solution to this minimization problem might be a good starting point for a non-linear equations solver.

Using the Linear Policy Functions. In Section 2.4 we consider the linear approximation method. Very often it is possible to obtain the solution from this method with little additional effort. The extra work to be done is to obtain the linearized equations of the model. One can then use the linear policy functions to trace out a path for the vector $\mathbf{s}_t$ and solve the non-linear regression problem

$$\min_{\gamma_0} \frac{1}{T} \sum_{t=0}^{T-1} [\boldsymbol{\phi}(\mathbf{s}_{t+1}) - \boldsymbol{\psi}(\boldsymbol{\gamma}_0, \mathbf{w}_t)]^2 .$$

At this point one can also apply econometric tests to check whether the chosen degree of $\boldsymbol{\psi}$ is appropriate. For instance, if the t-ratio of a regressor is smaller than unity, one might exclude it from the regression.

5.3 Applications

In this section we consider three applications of the PEA. First, we illustrate its ability to implement constraints on some of the model's variables. For this purpose we resolve the stochastic growth model with a non-negativity constraint on investment, which we have already encountered in Section 4.3.1. Second, we obtain the PE solution of the benchmark model of Example 1.5.1, and third, we show how the PEA can be applied to models with more than one conditional expectations function.

5.3.1 Stochastic Growth with Non-Negative Investment

The Model. To apply the PEA to the model of Section 4.3.1, we must first derive the set of difference equations that governs the time path of this model. While we are quite aware that you have already mastered this task (see Problem 4.1), we will repeat the necessary steps for your convenience. In terms of the Lagrangian the problem is to maximize

$$\mathscr{L} = \sum_{s=0}^{\infty} \beta^{s-t} E_t \bigg[\frac{C_{t+s}^{1-\eta} - 1}{1-\eta} + \mu_{t+s} \left(K_{t+s+1} - (1-\delta) K_{t+s} \right) \\ + \Lambda_{t+s} \left(Z_{t+s} K_{t+s}^{\alpha} + (1-\delta) K_{t+s} - C_{t+s} - K_{t+s+1} \right) \bigg].$$

Differentiating this expression with respect to C_t and K_{t+1} and setting the results equal to zero provides the conditions:

$$0 = C_t^{-\eta} - \mu_t - \beta E_t \big[C_{t+1}^{-\eta} (1 - \delta + \alpha Z_{t+1} K_{t+1}^{\alpha-1}) - \mu_{t+1}(1-\delta) \big], \tag{5.12a}$$
$$0 = Z_t K_t^{\alpha} + (1-\delta) K_t - C_t - K_{t+1}, \tag{5.12b}$$
$$0 = \mu_t [K_{t+1} - (1-\delta) K_t], \tag{5.12c}$$
$$0 \leq \mu_t, \tag{5.12d}$$
$$0 \leq K_{t+1} - (1-\delta) K_t. \tag{5.12e}$$

Line (5.12c) to (5.12e) are the Kuhn-Tucker conditions associated with the non-negativity constraint on investment: either the constraint does not bind, in which case $\mu_t = 0$ (from (5.12c)) or gross investment is zero, in which case $\mu_t \geq 0$. Equation (5.12a) is the model's Euler equation and equation (5.12b) the economy's resource restriction.

Implementation. We already know from Example 1.3.2 that this model has an analytic solution for the policy function if $\eta = \delta = 1$, which is given by

$$K_{t+1} = \alpha \beta Z_t K_t^{\alpha}.$$

Since, in this case,

$$C_t = (1 - \alpha \beta) Z_t K_t^{\alpha},$$

the non-negativity constraint never binds, irrespective of the size of the productivity shock. Therefore, we can evaluate the rhs of

(5.12a) to find the analytic solution for the conditional expectations function $\mathscr{E}(K_t, Z_t)$. We ask you to perform this task in Problem 5.1. Here, we just report the result:

$$\mathscr{E}(K_t, Z_t) = \frac{1}{(1-\alpha\beta)\beta} K_t^{-\alpha} Z_t^{-1}.$$

We use this information to approximate $\mathscr{E}$ in the general case $\eta > 0$ and $\delta \in [0,1]$ by an exponential polynomial in (K_t, Z_t). We use a complete set of base functions, which either consist of monomials or of Chebyshev polynomials. For instance, the first degree, complete polynomial with monomial base functions is

$$\psi(\boldsymbol{\gamma}, K_t, Z_t) := \exp\bigl(\gamma_1 + \gamma_2 \ln K_t + \gamma_3 \ln Z_t\bigr),$$

while the second degree polynomial is

$$\psi(\boldsymbol{\gamma}, K_t, Z_t) := \exp\bigl(\gamma_1 + \gamma_2 \ln K_t + \gamma_3 \ln Z_t \\ + \gamma_4 (\ln K_t)^2 + \gamma_5 \ln K_t \ln Z_t + \gamma_6 (\ln Z_t)^2\bigr).$$

In the case of a base of Chebyshev polynomials the terms in $\ln K$ and $\ln Z$ in the equations above are replaced by $T_i(X(\ln K))$ and $T_j(X(\ln Z))$, where $X : [a,b] \to [-1,1]$ defines the function that maps points from the interval $[a,b]$ to the interval $[-1,1]$, which is the domain of the Chebyshev polynomial T_i of degree i (see Section 11.2.6).

The Kuhn-Tucker conditions in the simulation are implemented as follows: given (K_t, Z_t) we first solve for

$$C_t = (\beta\psi(\boldsymbol{\gamma}, K_t, Z_t))^{-1/\eta},$$

and compute

$$K_{t+1} = Z_t K_t^\alpha + (1-\delta)K_t - C_t.$$

We then test the non-negativity constraint. If

$$K_{t+1} - (1-\delta)K_t < 0,$$

we set

$$\bar{C}_t = Z_t K_t^\alpha < C_t,$$

and

$$K_{t+1} = (1-\delta)K_t.$$

The Lagrange multiplier μ_t is found by solving

$$\mu_t = \bar{C}_t^{-\eta} - \beta\psi(\gamma, K_t, Z_t).$$

This solution is always positive, if $C_t > \bar{C}_t$, i.e., if the constraint binds. Indeed, setting up the model with a non-negativity constraint is computationally easier than without this restriction. Otherwise we would have to check for $K_{t+1} < 0$ and terminate the computations with the given vector of parameters γ. This introduces a discontinuity that must be handled explicitly in the non-linear equations solver. Nevertheless, it may happen that this routine tries a vector γ for which it is not possible to evaluate $\psi(\cdot)$, either because of an over- or an underflow. So the program must take this into account (see below).

Our Fortran program SGNNI_b.for determines the parameter vector γ by solving the non-linear equation (5.10). In Problem 5.2 we ask you to find the PE solution via fixed-point iterations. Our program either accepts an initial γ_0 to start computations or uses a genetic algorithm to find reasonable starting values from scratch.

Results. Table 5.1 presents accuracy statistics from several simulations. The parameter values are $\alpha = 0.27$, $\beta = 0.994$, $\delta = 0.011$, $\eta = 2$, and $\varrho = 0.90$. We consider two different values of the standard deviation of the innovations in the process (5.1c). If σ equals 0.072, the non-negativity constraint never binds so that the solution equals the solution of the stochastic growth model without any constraint. In the case $\sigma = 0.05$, the non-negativity constraint binds occasionally. Our simulations further distinguish between a small T of 5,000 points, and a large T of 100,000 (or even 1,000,000) points. As we have pointed out above, we expect the precision of the solution to increase with T. Finally, we consider different degrees p. Note in this respect that for $p = 1$ the monomial and the Chebyshev base functions are identical (except for the different domain). Our measures of accuracy are the residuals of the Euler equation (5.12a) and the fraction of the DM-statistic below (above) the 2.5 (97.5) percent critical value of the $\chi^2(11)$-distribution. We compute this statistic from a regression of the prediction error on a constant, five lags of consumption, and five lags of the total factor productivity. The Euler equations are computed over a square that is chosen so that 90 (80) percent of the realizations of (K_t, Z_t) obtained in 1,000 simulations with as many as 3,000 periods lie in this square.

Consider, first, the choice of T. For both the small and the high value of σ the DM-statistic indicates that the solution based on only $T = 5,000$ points is less good than the one obtained from a time series of length $T = 100,000$. The Euler equation residuals are less sensitive to this parameter. The largest reduction occurs in the case of $\sigma = 0.0072$ for $p = 2$ in the 80% interval. The maximum Euler equation residual for $T = 5,000$ is about 8 times larger than that for $T = 100,000$. In the case of $\sigma = 0.05$ for $p = 1$ the Euler equation residual computed in both intervals is almost unchanged when T is increased from $5,000$ to $100,000$. Note, however, that these results rest on the random draw of Z_t so that you may find somewhat different results if you redo our experiment.

Consider, second, the degree p of the polynomial. If σ is small, there is no noteworthy gain in accuracy from increasing p. In some cases – see line one and two in the first panel and line four and five in the second panel – accuracy even decreases. The reason is that additional, higher-order terms in the polynomial contribute more noise than further information. In the terminology of regression analysis these additional elements are almost linear combinations of the already present lower-order terms. This is known as the problem of multicollinearity. In a linear regression model the solution will be highly imprecise. Yet, as we have seen in Section 5.2.3, the non-linear regression step that is involved in the computation of the fixed point can be reduced to a series of linear regression problems (the Gauss-Newton algorithm). If we determine the PE solution from the non-linear system of equations (5.10), we may

Table 5.1

Base Function	Euler Equation Residual 90%	80%	DM-Statistic < 3.816	> 21.920
\multicolumn{5}{c}{$\sigma = 0.0072, T = 5,000$}				
Monomial: $p = 1$	5.779E-5	4.668E-5	0.7	11.1
Monomial: $p = 2$	1.501E-4	9.630E-5	0.7	26.8
Chebyshev: $p = 2$	1.501E-4	9.630E-5	0.7	26.8
\multicolumn{5}{c}{$\sigma = 0.0072, T = 100,000$}				
Monomial: $p = 1$	2.011E-5	1.224E-5	1.4	4.1
Monomial: $p = 2$	1.981E-5	1.200E-5	1.6	3.5
Chebyshev: $p = 2$	1.981E-5	1.200E-5	1.6	3.5
Chebyshev: $p = 3$	2.705E-5	1.668E-5	1.6	3.5
\multicolumn{5}{c}{$\sigma = 0.05, T = 5,000$}				
Monomial: $p = 1$	1.141E-3	7.133E-4	1.0	9.0
Monomial: $p = 2$	5.850E-4	3.721E-4	1.0	11.7
Chebyshev: $p = 2$	5.850E-4	3.721E-4	1.0	11.7
\multicolumn{5}{c}{$\sigma = 0.05, T = 100,000$}				
Monomial: $p = 1$	9.993E-4	5.673E-4	2.2	5.2
Monomial: $p = 2$	2.289E-4	1.189E-4	2.0	3.7
Chebyshev: $p = 2$	2.289E-4	1.189E-4	2.0	3.7
\multicolumn{5}{c}{$\sigma = 0.05, T = 1000,000$}				
Chebyshev: $p = 2$	2.608E-4	1.040E-4	2.8	3.7
Chebyshev: $p = 3$	1.941E-4	7.137E-5	2.9	3.6

Notes: T is the length of the time series from which the coefficients are computed, p is the degree of the polynomial. Euler equation residuals are computed as maximum absolute value of 200^2 residuals computed on an equally spaced grid $\mathscr{K} \times \mathscr{Z}$. The size of the interval for K was chosen so that 90 (80) percent of the realizations of K out of 1,000 simulations with 3,000 points each are within the respective interval. The interval for Z was likewise determined.

not be able to find a solution in this case. Indeed, we were not able to solve the model with $p = 3$ in a base of monomials in reasonable time. If the size of the shocks is larger, higher-order terms provide additional information. Moving from $p = 1$ to $p = 2$ almost halves the residual (see lines one and two in panel three).

The increase in accuracy is even more pronounced for a large T. However accuracy does not improve noteworthy, if we move from $p = 2$ to $p = 3$ in a base of Chebyshev polynomials.

Also note, third, that for a given degree, where we were able to compute both the solution with respect to a monomial and a Chebyshev base, the solutions coincide: While the parameters differ due to the different domains, both functions predict the same value of the rhs of the Euler equation (5.12a) for a given pair (K_t, Z_t).

Summarizing the results, one can be confidential to compute a reasonably accurate solution of the model in either base with a degree $p = 2$ polynomial and a sample size of $T = 100,000$.

5.3.2 The Benchmark Model

In this subsection we provide the details of the PE solution of the benchmark model of Example 1.5.1. The time path of this model is determined from the system of equations

$$\lambda_t = c_t^{-\eta}(1 - N_t)^{\theta(1-\eta)}, \tag{5.13a}$$
$$0 = \theta c_t^{1-\eta}(1 - N_t)^{\theta(1-\eta)-1} - (1-\alpha)\lambda_t Z_t N_t^{-\alpha} k_t^{\alpha}, \tag{5.13b}$$
$$ak_{t+1} = Z_t N_t^{1-\alpha} k_t^{\alpha} + (1-\delta)k_t - c_t, \tag{5.13c}$$
$$\lambda_t = \beta a^{-\eta} E_t \lambda_{t+1}(1 - \delta + \alpha Z_{t+1} N_{t+1}^{1-\alpha} k_{t+1}^{\alpha-1}). \tag{5.13d}$$

Remember the definitions: $c_t := C_t/A_t$, $k_t := K_t/A_t$, and $\lambda_t = A_t^{\eta}\Lambda_t$, where Λ_t is the Lagrange multiplier of the budget constraint, which equals the marginal utility of consumption (see (5.13a)). The second line in (5.13) is the optimality condition with respect to labor supply, the third line gives the budget constraint, and the fourth line represents the Euler equation for the capital stock. We can eliminate consumption from the first two equations of (5.13). The result is an implicit equation for N_t:

$$((1-\alpha)/\theta)Z_t N_t^{-\alpha} k_t^{\alpha} = \lambda_t^{-1/\eta}(1 - N_t)^{[\theta(1-\eta)/\eta]-1}. \tag{5.14}$$

Its solution determines N_t as a function of (k_t, Z_t, λ_t). In our program Benchmark.for we use the modified Newton-Raphson algorithm 11.5.2 to find this solution.

The program allows you to either choose a complete polynomial in a base of monomials or a product base polynomial with Chebyshev polynomials as base functions (see Section 11.2.7 on the respective definitions) to parameterize the conditional expectation on the rhs of (5.13d). Let $\lambda_t = \beta a^{-\eta} \psi(\gamma, k_t, Z_t)$ denote this parameterization. Given λ_t as well as k_t and Z_t, we can solve equation (5.14) for N_t. In the next step we determine consumption from equation (5.13a). Finally, the budget constraint (5.13c) provides the next-period capital stock k_{t+1}.

To find good starting values γ_0 for the non-linear equations solver that determines the PE solution from equation (5.10) we use the linear policy function computed in Section 2.6.1 to trace out an initial time path for λ_t, k_t, and Z_t. We then use Algorithm 11.6.2 to regress λ_t on $\psi(\gamma_0, K_t, Z_t)$. The program also allows you to employ a genetic search algorithm to find γ_0.

Table 5.2 presents the results of our simulations for the same set of parameters used in Chapter 2 through Chapter 4 (see Table 1.1). We used a second degree complete polynomial with monomial base functions to parameterize the rhs of the Euler equation (5.12d). The table displays results obtained from two different PE solutions and from the linear policy functions.

Consider, first, the accuracy of the solutions. The small sample size of $T = 5000$ yields a solution that is less accurate than the linear solution: its Euler equation residuals are about 10 times larger. There is, however, a remarkable gain in precision, from increasing T from 5,000 to one million observations. The maximum Euler equation residual out of 400 residuals computed over the square $[0.8k^*, 1.2k^*] \times [0.95, 1.05]$ shrinks by a factor of $1/80$. It required about 12 minutes to compute this second solution as compared to about five seconds for the first one. The reason is the time consuming computation of the Jacobian matrix if T is large. Recall from Section 4.3.2 that it takes about six minutes to compute an equally precise solution from value function iteration and about two hours to obtain a solution with Euler equation residuals that are an order of magnitude smaller than those from the PE solution with a sample size of one million. While the PEA is a non-linear, global approach to solve DGE models, it is never-

Table 5.2

	Linear Approximation			Parameterized Expectations $T=5,000$			$T=1,000,000$		
				Second Moments					
Variable	s_x	r_{xy}	r_x	s_x	r_{xy}	r_x	s_x	r_{xy}	r_x
Output	1.44	1.00	0.64	1.45	1.00	0.64	1.44	1.00	0.64
Investment	6.11	1.00	0.64	6.19	1.00	0.64	6.11	1.00	0.64
Consumption	0.56	0.99	0.66	0.55	0.99	0.66	0.56	0.99	0.66
Hours	0.77	1.00	0.64	0.78	1.00	0.64	0.77	1.00	0.64
Real Wage	0.67	0.99	0.65	0.67	0.99	0.65	0.67	0.99	0.65
				Euler Equation Residuals					
$[0.90; 1.10]k$	1.835E-4			1.404E-3			3.687E-5		
$[0.85; 1.15]k$	3.478E-4			2.864E-3			5.110E-5		
$[0.80; 1.20]k$	5.670E-4			5.215E-3			6.531E-5		
				DM-Statistic					
<3.816	2.0			0.4			3.1		
>21.920	3.4			27.5			3.1		

Notes: s_x:=standard deviation of variable x, r_{xy}:=cross correlation of variable x with output, r_x:=first order autocorrelation of variable x. All second moments refer to HP-filtered percentage deviations from a variable's stationary solution. Euler equation residuals are computed as maximum absolute value over a grid of 400 equally spaced points on the square $\mathscr{X} \times [\ln 0.95; \ln 1.05]$, where $\mathscr{X}$ is defined in the respective row of the left-most column. The 2.5 and the 97.5 percent critical values of the $\chi^2(11)$-distribution are displayed in the last two lines of the first column. The table entries refer to the percentage fraction out of 1,000 simulations where the DM-statistic is below (above) its respective critical value.

theless more precise in those areas of the state space which have a higher probability of being visited by the sampled time path. Therefore, the Euler equation residuals increase with the area of the square over which they are computed.

Consider, second, the time series moments. What we already know from Chapter 2 through Chapter 4 is confirmed here. Even a relatively bad solution in terms of the Euler equation residuals and the DM-statistic provides second moments that are very similar to those obtained from a more accurate solution.

5.3.3 Limited Participation Model of Money

In this subsection we develop a monetary model that features three expectational equations. This allows us to demonstrate the usefulness of the PEA in models with many state variables. We begin with a motivation of this model.

Motivation. In the textbook IS-LM model an expansionary monetary shock lowers the nominal interest rate. Since inflationary expectations do not adjust immediately, the real interest rate also declines. This spurs investment expenditures, which in turn raise aggregate spending. Given a sufficiently elastic short-run supply function output and employment increase. This story is in line with the empirical evidence provided by vector autoregressions.[8] Yet, most monetary DGE models do not reproduce this liquidity effect. Consider, for instance, the model presented in Section 2.6.3. In this model there is only an anticipated inflation effect on the nominal interest rate: when agents learn about a temporarily high money growth rate, they expect a rise of future inflation and demand a higher nominal interest rate.

In this section we present a model of a monetary economy that is able to account for both the liquidity and the inflationary expectations effect.[9] The model includes a rudimentary banking sector. Households face a cash-in-advance constraint and can lend part of their financial wealth M_t to the banking sector at the gross nominal interest q_t (one plus the nominal interest rate). The firms in this model pay wages to the household sector before they sell their output. To finance their wage bill they borrow money from the banking sector. The government injects money into the economy via the banking sector. The crucial assumption is that banks receive the monetary transfer after households have decided about the volume of their banking deposits. Given the additional money, banks lower the nominal interest rate to increase their loans to

---

[8] See, e.g, CHRISTIANO, EICHENBAUM, and EVANS (1999).
[9] The model is based on a paper by LAWRENCE CHRISTIANO, MARTIN EICHENBAUM, and CHARLES EVANS (1997). Different from their model, we also include capital services as a factor of production.

firms. At the reduced credit costs firms hire more labor and increase production. The fact that households cannot trade on the market for deposits after the monetary shock has been observed has given the model its name: limited participation model.

The Banking Sector. At the beginning of period t banks receive deposits of size B_t from households. Government transfers amount to $M_{t+1} - M_t$, where M_t are beginning-of-period money balances. Banks, thus, are able to lend $B_t + (M_{t+1} - M_t)$ to firms. At the end of the period they pay interest and principal $q_t B_t$ to their creditors and distribute the remaining profits,

$$D_t^B = \frac{q_t(B_t + M_{t+1} - M_t)}{P_t} - \frac{q_t B_t}{P_t} = q_t \frac{M_{t+1} - M_t}{P_t} \quad (5.15)$$

to the household sector. As in Section 2.6.3 P_t denotes the money price of output.

Producers. The representative producer employs labor N_t and capital services K_t to produce output according to

$$Y_t = Z_t(A_t N_t)^{1-\alpha} K_t^\alpha, \quad \alpha \in (0,1). \quad (5.16)$$

As in the benchmark model A_t is the level of labor-augmenting technical progress that grows deterministically at the rate $a - 1 \geq 0$. Total factor productivity Z_t is governed by the stochastic process

$$Z_t = Z_{t-1}^{\rho^Z} e^{\epsilon_t^Z}, \quad \epsilon_t^Z \sim N(0, \sigma^Z). \quad (5.17)$$

Producers hire workers at the money wage rate W_t and capital services at the real rental rate r_t. Since they have to pay workers in advance, they borrow $W_t N_t$ at the nominal rate of interest $q_t - 1$ from banks. Hence, their profits are given by

$$D_t^P = Y_t - q_t \frac{W_t}{P_t} N_t - r_t K_t. \quad (5.18)$$

Maximizing (5.18) with respect to N_t and K_t provides the following first-order conditions:

$$q_t w_t = (1-\alpha) Z_t N_t^{-\alpha} k_t^\alpha, \quad w_t := \frac{W_t}{A_t P_t}, \quad k_t := \frac{K_t}{A_t}, \quad (5.19a)$$

$$r_t = \alpha Z_t N_t^{1-\alpha} k_t^{\alpha-1}. \quad (5.19b)$$

Consequently, profits in the production sector are zero.

Money Supply. Money supply is governed by the same process that we used in Section 2.6.3. Thus,

$$\mu_t := \frac{M_{t+1}}{M_t}, \quad \mu_t = \mu^{1-\rho^\mu} \mu_{t-1}^{\rho^\mu} e^{\epsilon_t^\mu}, \quad \epsilon_t^\mu \sim N(0, \sigma^\mu). \tag{5.20}$$

Households. The households' total financial wealth at the beginning of period t is given by $M_t = B_t + X_t$, where B_t is the amount deposited at banks and X_t are cash balances kept for the purchase of consumption goods. Since households receive wages before they go shopping, their cash-in-advance constraint is

$$C_t \leq \frac{X_t + W_t N_t}{P_t}. \tag{5.21}$$

The real income of households consists of wages $W_t N_t / P_t$, net rental income $(r_t - \delta) K_t$ from capital services (where capital depreciates at the rate δ), interest on banking deposits $(q_t - 1) B_t / P_t$, and dividends from banks D_t^B. This income is split between consumption C_t and savings S_t. Savings are used to increase financial wealth M_t and the stock of physical capital K_t. Accordingly, the budget constraint is given by:

$$\begin{aligned} K_{t+1} - K_t &+ \frac{(X_{t+1} - X_t) + (B_{t+1} - B_t)}{P_t} \\ &\leq \frac{W_t}{P_t} N_t + (r_t - \delta) K_t + (q_t - 1) \frac{B_t}{P_t} + D_t^B - C_t. \end{aligned} \tag{5.22}$$

We depart from our usual specification of the household's preferences over consumption and leisure and follow CHRISTIANO, EICHENBAUM, EVANS (1997) who use the instantaneous utility function:

$$u(C_t, N_t) := \frac{1}{1-\eta} \left[(C_t - \theta A_t N_t^\nu)^{1-\eta} - 1 \right], \quad \theta > 0, \nu > 1$$

that we have already encountered in the small open economy model of Section 3.3.2. As you will see in a moment, this function implies a labor supply schedule that depends on the real wage only. In particular, labor supply does not depend on wealth. Technically, this makes it easy to solve for N_t given the real wage and to separate the role of the elasticity of labor supply $1/(\nu-1)$ from other factors.

The household maximizes the expected stream of discounted utility

$$E_0 \sum_{t=0}^{\infty} \beta^t u(C_t, N_t)$$

with respect to C_0, N_0, K_1, X_1, and B_1 subject to (5.21) and (5.22). Since the household must decide on the size of its nominal deposits before the monetary shock is observed, X_t and B_t are state variables of the model. The Lagrangean for this problem is:

$$\mathcal{L} = E_0 \sum_{t=0}^{\infty} \beta^t \left\{ \frac{1}{1-\eta} \left[(C_t - \theta A_t N_t^\nu)^{1-\eta} - 1 \right] \right.$$
$$+ \Lambda_t \left[\frac{W_t}{P_t} N_t + (r_t - \delta) K_t + \frac{(q_t - 1) B_t}{P_t} + D_t^B - C_t \right.$$
$$\left. - (K_{t+1} - K_t) - \frac{(X_{t+1} - X_t) + (B_{t+1} - B_t)}{P_t} \right]$$
$$\left. + \Xi_t \left[\frac{X_t + W_t N_t}{P_t} - C_t \right] \right\}.$$

From this expression we can derive the set of first-order conditions that describes the household's decisions. In the following, we present these conditions in terms of the stationary variables $y_t := Y_t/A_t$, $c_t := C_t/A_t$, $k_t := K_t/A_t$, $w_t := W_t/(A_t P_t)$, $\pi_t := P_t/P_{t-1}$, $\lambda_t := \Lambda_t A_t^\eta$, $x_t := X_t/(A_{t-1} P_{t-1})$, $m_t := M_t/(A_{t-1} P_{t-1})$, and $\xi_t := \Xi_t A_t^\eta$. The definitions of x_t and m_t guarantee that these variables are pre-determined at the beginning of period t.

$$\lambda_t + \xi_t = (c_t - \theta N_t^\nu)^{-\eta}, \tag{5.24a}$$

$$N_t = \left(\frac{w_t}{\theta \nu} \right)^{\frac{1}{\nu-1}}, \tag{5.24b}$$

$$\lambda_t = \beta a^{-\eta} E_t \lambda_{t+1} \left(1 - \delta + \alpha Z_{t+1} N_{t+1}^{1-\alpha} k_{t+1}^{\alpha-1} \right), \tag{5.24c}$$

$$\lambda_t = \beta a^{-\eta} E_t \left(\frac{\lambda_{t+1} q_{t+1}}{\pi_{t+1}} \right), \tag{5.24d}$$

$$\lambda_t = \beta a^{-\eta} E_t \left(\frac{\lambda_{t+1} + \xi_{t+1}}{\pi_{t+1}} \right), \tag{5.24e}$$

$$0 = \xi_t (x_t/(a\pi_t) + w_t N_t - c_t). \tag{5.24f}$$

Equation (5.24a) shows that the marginal utility of consumption departs from the shadow price of wealth λ_t as long as the cash-in-advance constraint binds, i.e., if $\xi_t > 0$. The related Kuhn-Tucker condition is equation (5.24f). Equation (5.24b) is the labor supply schedule. The well-known Euler equation for capital is given in (5.24c). Together with equations (5.24d) and (5.24e) it implies equal expected rewards on the holdings of physical capital, of banking deposits, and of cash balances.

In addition to these equations the household's budget constraint is satisfied with the equality sign and the cash-in-advance constraint holds. Since

$$w_t N_t = \frac{B_t + M_{t+1} - M_t}{A_t P_t} = m_{t+1} - x_t/(a\pi_t),$$

we may write the latter in the following way:

$$c_t = m_{t+1}, \quad \text{if } \xi_t > 0, \tag{5.25a}$$

$$c_t \leq m_{t+1}, \quad \text{if } \xi_t = 0, \tag{5.25b}$$

$$m_{t+1} = \frac{\mu_t m_t}{a\pi_t}, \tag{5.25c}$$

where the third equation is implied from the definition of m_t. In equilibrium, the household's budget constraint reduces to the well-known resource restriction:

$$ak_{t+1} = Z_t N_t^{1-\alpha} k_t^{\alpha} + (1-\delta)k_t - c_t. \tag{5.26}$$

Stationary Equilibrium. In a stationary equilibrium all shocks equal their unconditional means, $Z_t \equiv 1$ and $\mu_t \equiv \mu$ for all t, and all (scaled) variables are constant. Equation (5.25c) implies that the inflation factor π (one plus the rate of inflation) is proportional to the money growth factor:

$$\pi = \frac{\mu}{a}. \qquad (5.27a)$$

The Euler equation for capital (5.24c) delivers

$$1 = \beta a^{-\eta} \underbrace{(1-\delta + \alpha(y/k))}_{1-\delta+r} \Rightarrow \frac{y}{k} = \frac{a^{\eta} - \beta(1-\delta)}{\alpha\beta}. \qquad (5.27b)$$

Together with (5.24d) this implies the Fisher equation, here written in terms of gross rates:

$$q = \pi(1 - \delta + r). \qquad (5.27c)$$

Given this, the stationary version of (5.24e) implies:

$$\xi = \lambda(q-1). \qquad (5.27d)$$

Accordingly, the cash-in-advance constraint binds in equilibrium if the nominal interest rate is positive: $q - 1 > 0$. Combining (5.27a) and (5.27c), we find that this condition is satisfied, if the growth rate of money is not too small:

$$\mu > \beta a^{1-\eta}.$$

Finally note that equation (5.24b) and equation (5.19a) imply

$$N^{\nu-1} = \frac{1}{q}\left(\frac{1-\alpha}{\nu\theta}\frac{y}{N}\right). \qquad (5.27e)$$

Since y/N is a function of y/k, it is independent of the money growth rate. Yet, according to (5.27c) and (5.27a) q is an increasing function of μ. Thus, steady-state working hours depend inversely on the rate of money growth. As in the model of Section 2.6.3 money is not superneutral.

The PEA Solution. Our model has two exogenous shocks, Z_t and μ_t, and three variables with given initial conditions, k_t, m_t, and x_t. However, there are not enough equations to determine consumption, working hours, the rate of inflation, the nominal interest rate, and the Lagrange multiplier of the cash-in-advance constraint given the former variables. We must define additional co-state variables. However, there is no easy way to do so, since the three Euler equations (5.24c) through (5.24e) have the same lhs. Technically speaking, the system of stochastic difference equations $\mathbf{g}(\cdot)$ is not easily invertible. There are various possible ways to deal with this situation. The following is the solution that really works.

As in the applications above we parameterize the rhs of the Euler equation for capital:

$$\lambda_t = \beta a^{-\eta} \psi^1(\boldsymbol{\gamma}_1, k_t, m_t, x_t, Z_t, \mu_t). \tag{5.28a}$$

Since $m_t > 0$ in any solution where money has a positive value, we multiply the second Euler equation (5.24d) on both sides by m_{t+1} and parameterize the ensuing rhs of this equation:

$$m_{t+1}\lambda_t = \beta a^{-\eta} \psi^2(\boldsymbol{\gamma}_2, k_t, m_t, x_t, Z_t, \mu_t). \tag{5.28b}$$

Analogously, we multiply the third Euler equation by x_{t+1} and put

$$x_{t+1}\lambda_t = \beta a^{-\eta} \psi^3(\boldsymbol{\gamma}_3, k_t, m_t, x_t, Z_t, \mu_t). \tag{5.28c}$$

We are now able to trace out a time path as follows: Given the five-tuple $(k_t, m_t, x_t, Z_t, \mu_t)$ we use (5.28a) to solve for λ_t. We use this solution to infer m_{t+1} and x_{t+1} from (5.28b) and (5.28c), respectively. Given m_t and m_{t+1} equation (5.25c) delivers π_t. Since

$$w_t N_t = \frac{\mu_t m_t - x_t}{a\pi_t}.$$

we can solve for $w_t N_t$ and use this in (5.24b) to solve for N_t. In the next step we use the first-order condition for labor demand (5.19a) to solve for q_t. Finally we check the Kuhn-Tucker conditions: assume $\xi_t = 0$. This implies

$$\bar{c}_t = \lambda_t^{-1/\eta} + \theta N_t^\nu,$$

from (5.24a). If $\bar{c}_t < m_{t+1}$ we accept this solution. Otherwise we put $\tilde{c}_t = m_{t+1}$ and solve for ξ_t from (5.24a):

$$\xi_t = (\tilde{c}_t - \theta N_t^\nu)^{-\eta} - \lambda_t.$$

Since $\bar{c}_t > \tilde{c}_t$, we also have $\xi_t > 0$. In the last step we compute k_{t+1} from the resource constraint (5.26).

Implementation. The Fortran program LP.for implements the PEA solution. As in the previous applications we use exponentials of simple polynomials for ψ^i, $i = 1, 2, 3$. The program allows the user to find the solution either iteratively or in one step by solving the related system of non-linear equations. In both cases the program obtains starting values from the solution of the log-linearized model. We do this for the following reason. Since we have five state variables and three expectational equations the potential number of coefficients in the expectational equations is large. For instance, a complete second degree polynomial in five variables has 21 coefficients. Accordingly, the potential of multicollinearity among the 21 regressors is high and we do not consider higher degree polynomials. Given the log-linear solution, we compute time paths for the relevant variables. In a first step we look at the correlation matrix between the potential regressors and exclude those that are highly correlated with others.[10] In a second step we regress the error terms from the log-linear solution on the remaining regressors. For this step, we use the Gauss-Newton method presented in Algorithm 11.6.2. Given these initial values we either invoke our non-linear equations solver or compute new time paths and estimates until the estimates converge. In a third step we reduce the set of regressors further: we exclude all regressors whose t-ratios from the solution of step 2 are smaller than one in absolute value. As it turns out, we get good results with a small number of coefficients.

Note also that the number of regressors depends on your assumptions with regard to monetary policy. If the monetary authority is able to control money supply perfectly, i.e., $\sigma^\mu = 0$, the vector $\boldsymbol{\mu} := [\mu_1, \ldots, \mu_T]'$ is a vector of constants. Neither $\boldsymbol{\mu}$ nor any of its integer powers or cross-products with other variables can be used as regressor. To see this, consider the case

$$\psi(k_t, \mu_t) := \exp(\gamma_1 + \gamma_2 \ln(k_t) + \gamma_3 \ln(\mu_t)).$$

The Jacobian matrix of ψ with respect to γ_i is given by:

---

[10] The program allows you to write this matrix to a file without doing any further computations.

$$\begin{bmatrix} \psi(k_1,\mu_1) & \psi(k_1,\mu_1)\ln(k_1) & \psi(k_1,\mu_1)\ln(\mu_1) \\ \psi(k_2,\mu_2) & \psi(k_2,\mu_2)\ln(k_2) & \psi(k_2,\mu_2)\ln(\mu_2) \\ \vdots & \vdots & \vdots \\ \psi(k_T,\mu_T) & \psi(k_T,\mu_T)\ln(k_T) & \psi(k_T,\mu_T)\ln(\mu_T) \end{bmatrix}.$$

Thus, if $\mu_t = \mu$ for all t, the third column of this matrix is a multiple $\ln(\mu)$ of the first and the Jacobian is singular. Accordingly, the Gauss-Newton step cannot be computed.

Concluding this paragraph, we strongly advice you to go through steps one to three from above for every parameter set that you wish to consider.

Table 5.3

Preferences	Production		Money Supply
$\beta=0.994$	$a=1.005$	$\alpha=0.27$	$\mu=1.0167$
$\eta=2.0$	$\delta=0.011$	$\rho^Z=0.90$	$\rho^\mu=0.0$
$N=0.13$	$\sigma^Z=0.0072$		$\sigma^\mu=0.0173$
$\nu=5.0$			

Results. If not mentioned otherwise the following results are computed for the calibrationCalibration displayed in Table 5.3. The parameters for the production side and for money supply are the same as those used in Section 2.6.3 and are, therefore, reproduced from Table 2.3. The preference parameters β and η are the same as in the benchmark model. Furthermore, we choose θ so that stationary working hours are $N=0.13$. The parameter that determines the labor supply elasticity ν is taken from HEER and MAUSSNER (2008).

Table 5.4 displays the arguments and estimated coefficients of the functions that we use to parameterize expectations. They are the results of the steps described in the previous paragraph.

We will first consider the relative strength between the liquidity and the anticipated inflation effect. If the monetary shock is not autocorrelated – as our estimates of this process from German data indicate – there is no anticipated inflation effect. This effect

Table 5.4

Regressors	$\sigma^\mu = 0.0173$			$\sigma^\mu = 0$		
	ψ^1	ψ^2	ψ^3	ψ^1	ψ^2	ψ^3
c	4.1457	2.4675	−8.5449	4.1161	2.3547	−3.7464
	(56.45)	(18.70)	(−23.03)	(54.70)	(87.23)	(−59.33)
k	−1.4201	−0.8764	1.2091	−1.2503	−0.6635	0.0492
	(−36.28)	(−3.68)	(6.17)	(−32.01)	(−13.80)	(1.51)
x	−0.1440		−4.8323	−0.1033	0.0016	−2.1977
	(−3.43)		(−22.76)	(−2.39)	(1.64)	(−60.54)
Z	−0.4868	−0.1099	−3.6561	−0.4859	−0.1046	−3.7700
	(−183.87)	(−14.31)	(−275.13)	(−183.33)	(−31.95)	(−1692.54)
μ	−0.0040	0.0140	−0.1237			
	(−2.21)	(2.06)	(−13.68)			
k^2	0.2333	0.1841	−0.5130	0.1570	0.0880	0.0225
	(13.20)	(1.71)	(−5.80)	(8.90)	(4.05)	(1.53)
x^2	−0.0227		−0.7571	−0.0164		−0.3410
	(−3.50)		(−22.96)	(−2.45)		(−60.36)
Z^2	−0.1063		−5.0438	−0.1023		−5.7785
	(−1.74)		(−16.58)	(−1.66)		(−112.73)
μ^2	0.0734		3.9122			
	(1.61)		(17.30)			

Notes: c refers to the intercept, t-ratios of estimated coefficients at final solution in parenthesis.

gains importance, if the autocorrelation parameter ρ^μ increases. The impulse responsesImpulse response function displayed in Figure 3.1 show this very clearly. The monetary shock hits the economy in period $t = 3$. The solid lines correspond to the case $\rho^\mu = 0$. The liquidity effect is obvious from the lower right panel of Figure 5.1. The additional supply of money lowers the nominal interest rate. The costs of hiring labor decrease, working hours and production increase. Part of the extra income is consumed and part is transferred to future periods via additional capital accumulation. The positive effect on consumption is very small, and, thus, not visible in Figure 5.1.

The dotted lines correspond to an autocorrelated money supply process. In addition to the liquidity effect, there is also an inflationary expectations effect. As can be seen from Figure 5.1 the latter dominates the former for our choice of parameters. Since

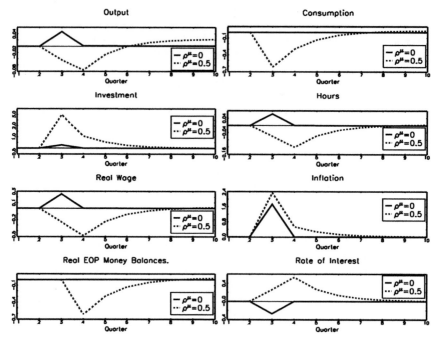

Figure 5.1: Impulse Responses to a Monetary Shock in the Limited Participation Model

households expect higher inflation, their costs of holding money balances increase. They substitute physical capital for financial wealth so that there is a stronger increase in investment. Since the cash-in-advance constraint binds, the reduced money holdings entail lower consumption. On the production side the increased nominal interest rate reduces working hours and output. This negative income effect puts additional pressure on consumption.

Table 5.5 presents second moments from two different simulations of the model. The first run considers the case of steady money growth, i.e., $\sigma^\mu = 0$, the second simulation assumes monetary shocks of the size observed in the data.

First, consider columns 2 to 4. They show one obvious difference between the benchmark model and the present model (compare Table 5.2). The standard deviation of working hours in the benchmark model is more than four times larger, and, as a consequence, output fluctuations are more pronounced. This dif-

Table 5.5

Variable	PEA Solution						Loglinear Solution		
	$\sigma^\mu = 0$			$\sigma^\mu = 0.0173$			$\sigma^\mu = 0.0173$		
	s_x	r_{xy}	r_x	s_x	r_{xy}	r_x	s_x	r_{xy}	r_x
Output	0.98	1.00	0.68	0.98	1.00	0.68	0.98	1.00	0.68
Investment	4.47	1.00	0.69	4.47	1.00	0.69	4.45	1.00	0.69
Consumption	0.34	0.98	0.67	0.34	0.98	0.67	0.34	0.98	0.67
Hours	0.17	0.87	0.78	0.18	0.83	0.67	0.18	0.83	0.67
Real Wage	0.69	0.87	0.78	0.74	0.83	0.67	0.73	0.83	0.67
Inflation	0.27	−0.43	−0.09	1.69	−0.02	−0.07	1.70	−0.02	−0.09

Notes: s_x:=standard deviation of HP-filtered simulated series of variable x, r_{xy}:=cross correlation of variable x with output, r_x:=first order autocorrelation of variable x.

ference is easily traced to the small elasticity of labor supply of $1/(\nu - 1) = 0.25$. In the benchmark model the Frisch elasticity of labor supply is determined implicitly, and is about 1.7.[11]

Given our calibration, the real effects of monetary shocks in the limited participation model are quite small and negligible. The standard deviations in column 5 differ from those in column 2 only in two instances: due to the liquidity effect, the standard deviation of the real wage is about 7 percent higher, which translates into a greater variability of hours. Of course, inflation is substantially more volatile if monetary shocks are present. The standard deviation of this variable is almost equal to σ^μ.

Finally, consider columns 7 to 9. They present the second moments obtained from the simulation of the loglinear solution of the

---

[11] The Frisch elasticity measures the relative change of working hours to a one-percent increase of the real wage, given the marginal utility of wealth λ. In the steady state of the benchmark model it is given by

$$\frac{dN/N}{dw/w} = \frac{1-N}{N}\left(\frac{1-\eta}{\eta}\theta - 1\right)^{-1}.$$

model. Both the loglinear and the PEA simulations use the same random numbers, so that differences between the two solutions are non-random.[12] Compared to columns 4 to 6, no noteworthy difference is discernible.

---

[12] They are random only in so far as the PEA solution depends itself on a long sequence of random numbers.

Problems

5.1 Analytic Solution to the Expectations Function
Consider the stochastic Ramsey Model from Example 1.3.2. The problem is to solve

$$\max \sum_{t=0}^{\infty} \beta^t \ln C_t$$

subject to $K_{t+1} = Z_t K_t^\alpha - C_t,$

K_0, Z_0 given.

We already know that the policy function g is given by

$$g(K_t, Z_t) = \alpha \beta Z_t K_t^\alpha.$$

Use this information to find the analytic solution for the expectations function $\mathscr{E}$.

5.2 Fixed-Point Iterations
Consider the stochastic growth model with irreversible investment from Section 5.3.1. Write a program that determines the PE solution of this model from fixed-point iterations. For this purpose you can use the relevant parts of our program `SGNNI_b.for`. Your program should implement these steps:
  i) Given an initial γ_0, and a sequence of productivity shocks $\{Z_t\}_{t=0}^T$, compute the time path of consumption, the capital stock and the Lagrange multiplier μ_t.
  ii) Use the damped Gauss-Newton algorithm in `GaussNewton.for` to estimate a new parameter vector γ_1 from a non-linear regression of the error terms $C_{t+1}^{-\eta}(1-\delta) + \alpha Z_{t+1} K_{t+1}^\alpha - (1-\delta)\mu_{t+1}$ on $\psi(\gamma_1, K_t, Z_t)$.
  iii) Iterate on equation (5.8) until convergence. Choose different values of λ to how this choice affects convergence.

5.3 A Cash-in-Advance Model
A less complicated DGE model of a monetary economy than the limited participation model of Section 5.3.3 is the model of COOLEY and HANSEN (1989). This paper introduces money into the model of HANSEN (1985) via a cash-in-advance constraint. The authors demonstrate that a policy of constant money growth does not alter the business cycle characteristics of the original model and that an erratic money supply resembling the US historical experience alters the behavior of real variables slightly.
COOLEY and HANSEN (1989) solve their model with a variant of the linear-quadratic method of Section 2.3. We ask you to employ the PEA to solve their model and to reproduce their results.

Chapter 5: Parameterized Expectations

We use the same symbols for consumption, capital, working hours, money balances, and so forth as in the model of Section 5.3.3. The representative household solves the following problem:

$$\max_{C_0, N_0, K_1, M_1} E_0 \sum_{t=0}^{\infty} \beta^t (\ln C_t - \theta N_t)$$

subject to

$$K_{t+1} - K_t + \frac{M_{t+1} - M_t}{P_t} \leq \frac{W_t}{P_t} N_t + (r_t - \delta) K_t + T_t - C_t,$$

$$C_t \leq \frac{M_t}{P_t} + T_t.$$

Money supply is determined by

$$T_t = \frac{M_{t+1} - M_t}{P_t}, \quad M_{t+1} = \mu_t M_t.$$

The policy of a constant money supply implies $\mu_t = \mu$ for all t, whereas

$$\hat{\mu}_t = (1 - \rho^\mu)\mu + \rho^\mu \hat{\mu}_{t-1} + \epsilon_t^\mu, \quad \epsilon_t^\mu \sim N(0, \sigma^\mu), \quad \hat{\mu}_t := \ln(\mu_t/\mu)$$

describes an erratic money supply.
The representative firm solves

$$\max_{N_t, K_t} Z_t N_t^\alpha K_t^{1-\alpha} - \frac{W_t}{P_t} N_t - r_t K_t,$$

where Z_t is governed by

$$\ln Z_t = \rho^Z \ln Z_{t-1} + \epsilon_t^Z, \quad \epsilon_t^Z \sim N(0, \sigma^Z).$$

a) Set up the Lagrangean of the household's problem and derive the first-order conditions for this problem.
b) Use the first-order conditions of the firm's problem to substitute for the wage rate and the rental rate in the household's optimality conditions and derive the system of stochastic difference equations that govern the model's dynamics.
c) Solve for the model's balanced growth path and show that working hours are a decreasing function of the steady state growth rate of money.
d) Consult the Appendix of DEN HAAN and MARCET (1994) to find out how they solve this model using the PEA.
e) COOLEY and HANSEN (1989) calibrate their model as follows: $\beta = 0.99$, $\theta = 2.86$, $\alpha = 0.64$, $\rho^Z = 0.95$, $\sigma^Z = 0.00721$, $\rho^\mu = 0.48$, and $\sigma^\mu = 0.009$. Use a polynomial in K_t, Z_t, and μ_t to parameterize the conditional expectation appearing in the Euler equation of capital and solve the model.

f) Use the solution and simulate the model. As in the original paper use time series with 115 observations and compute seconds moments as averages over 50 simulations from the HP-filtered time series.
g) Consider the COOLEY and HANSEN (1989) model with current period utility given by

$$u(C_t, N_t) := \frac{1}{1-\eta} C_t^{1-\eta}(1-N_t)^{\theta(1-\eta)}, \quad \eta \neq 1,\ \theta > 0, \eta > \frac{\theta}{1+\theta}.$$

Put $\eta = 2$ and choose θ so that working hours in the steady state equal $N = 0.33$.

With these preferences it is no longer possible to solve the model along the lines of DEN HAAN and MARCET (1994). To solve the model you must parameterize the conditional expectations not only in the Euler equation for capital but also in the Euler equation for money balances. Solve the model and compare your results to those of the original model.

(Hint: Use $\Lambda_t m_{t+1} = \psi^2(K_t, Z_t, m_t, \mu_t)$ as the second parameterized equation.)

Chapter 6

Projection Methods

Overview. The parameterized expectations approach (PEA) considered in the previous chapter solves DGE models by approximating the agents' conditional expectations and determines the best approximation via Monte-Carlo simulations. In this chapter, we also employ methods from function approximation. Yet, these methods are not limited to functions that determine the agents' conditional expectations, nor do they necessarily resort to simulation techniques to find a good approximation. These methods, known as projection or weighted residual methods, may, thus, be viewed as generalizations of the PEA along certain dimensions. 1) The functions that we approximate do not need to be the conditional expectations that characterize the first-order conditions of the agents in our model. Instead, we may approximate the agent's policy function, or the value function of the problem at hand. 2) We use different criteria to determine the goodness of the fit between the true but unknown function and its polynomial representation. These criteria prevent the problem that we encountered in the previous chapter, namely, that it may be difficult to increase precision by using a higher degree polynomial. 3) Some of these criteria require numerical integration. The Monte-Carlo simulation is just one way to do this. Other techniques exist and often are preferable.

This chapter is structured as follows. First, the general idea of projection methods is presented. Second, we consider the various steps that constitute this class of methods in more detail. It will become obvious that we need several numerical tools to implement a particular method. Among them are numerical integration and optimization as well as finding the zeros of a set of non-linear equations. Third, we apply projection methods to the deterministic and the simple stochastic growth model and compare our results to those of Chapter 2 and Chapter 4. As an additional application, we study the equity premium puzzle, i.e. the (arguably) missing explanation for the observation that the average return on equities has been so much higher than the one on bonds over the last century. For this reason, we consider asset pricing within the stochastic growth model.

6.1 Characterization of Projection Methods

6.1.1 An Example

Projection methods derive approximate solutions to functional equations.[1] The unknown of a functional equation is not a point in $\mathbb{R}^n$ but a function f that maps $\mathbb{R}^n$ to $\mathbb{R}^m$. Since an appropriately defined set of functions is itself a vector space, the problem is to pick an element from a function space. Different from $\mathbb{R}^n$, however, function spaces have infinite dimensions, and in many circumstances it is impossible to derive analytic solutions. Projection methods use a family of polynomials $\mathcal{P} := \{\varphi_i\}_{i=0}^{\infty}$ and approximate f by a finite sum of members of this family.

To be concrete, consider the ordinary differential equation[2]

$$\dot{x}(t) + x(t) = 0, \quad x(0) = 1, \tag{6.1}$$

with solution

---

[1] Early expositions of projection methods are provided by JUDD (1992,1998) and REDDY (1993). McGRATTAN (1996) also considers so-called finite-element methods that approximate the solution over non-overlapping subdomains of the state-space. In these methods, low-polynomials are fitted on subdomains rather than high polynomials on the entire state-space. Our piecewise linear or cubic approximation of the value function in Algorithm 4.2.1 can be interpreted as a finite-element method. In the following, we will not consider these methods and refer the interested reader to REDDY (1993) and McGRATTAN (1996).
[2] In the following, we draw on McGRATTAN (1999).

$$x(t) = e^{-t}. \tag{6.2}$$

Suppose we use the monomials $(1, t, t^2)$ to approximate the solution in the interval $[0, 2]$:[3]

$$\hat{x}(t) = 1 + \gamma_1 t + \gamma_2 t^2. \tag{6.3}$$

How shall we choose the unknown parameters γ_i, $i = 1, 2$? In econometrics, we approximate a given set of points $(x_i, y_i) \in \mathbb{R}^2$ by drawing a line so that the sum of squared distances of (x_i, y_i) from this line attains a minimum. Something similar to this also works here. Let us define the residual function

$$R(\boldsymbol{\gamma}, t) := \underbrace{\gamma_1 + 2\gamma_2 t}_{d\hat{x}/dt} + \underbrace{1 + \gamma_1 t + \gamma_2 t^2}_{\hat{x}(t)}. \tag{6.4}$$

This function describes the error that results, if we use our guess of the solution (6.3) instead of the true solution (6.2) in the functional equation (6.1). By analogy, we could choose the parameters so that in the interval $[0, 2]$ $\hat{x}(t)$ is as close as possible to $x(t)$ in the sense of

$$\min_{\gamma_1, \gamma_2} \int_0^2 R(\boldsymbol{\gamma}, t)^2 dt. \tag{6.5}$$

The first-order conditions for this problem are given by the following two equations:

$$0 = \int_0^2 R(\boldsymbol{\gamma}, t) \frac{\partial R(\boldsymbol{\gamma}, t)}{\partial \gamma_1} dt,$$

$$0 = \int_0^2 R(\boldsymbol{\gamma}, t) \frac{\partial R(\boldsymbol{\gamma}, t)}{\partial \gamma_2} dt.$$

By using (6.4) and the derivatives of this function with respect to γ_1 and γ_2, it is easy to compute the integrals. This delivers the following linear system of equations in the two unknowns γ_1 and γ_2:

---

[3] Note that we set $\gamma_0 = 1$ to satisfy the boundary condition $x(0) = 1$.

288   Chapter 6: Projection Methods

$$-4 = 8\frac{2}{3}\gamma_1 + 16\gamma_2,$$
$$-6\frac{2}{3} = 16\gamma_1 + 33\frac{1}{15}\gamma_2.$$

Figure 6.1 shows that the approximate solution is not too far from the true function e^{-t}. Of course, we can get a better approximation if we use a higher degree polynomial.

Using a well known property of the least squares estimator delivers another solution concept, the Galerkin method. Remember, the least squares residuals are orthogonal to the space spanned by the vectors that represent the observations of the independent variables. Here, the functions t and t^2 play the role of these vectors. Thus, we demand

$$0 = \int_0^2 R(\boldsymbol{\gamma}, t) t \, dt,$$
$$0 = \int_0^2 R(\boldsymbol{\gamma}, t) t^2 \, dt.$$
(6.6)

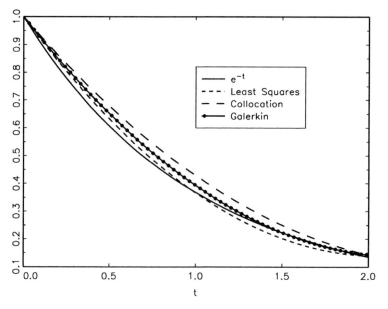

Figure 6.1: Polynomial Approximation of e^{-t}

Computing the integrals on the rhs of (6.6) gives a second set of linear equations in the unknown parameters γ_1 and γ_2:

$$-2 = 4\frac{2}{3}\gamma_1 + 9\frac{1}{3}\gamma_2,$$
$$-2\frac{2}{3} = 6\frac{2}{3}\gamma_1 + 14\frac{2}{5}\gamma_2.$$

The dotted line in Figure 6.1 represents the Galerkin approximate solution of the differential equation (6.1).

Finally, we may want that the residual function is equal to zero at a given set of points. Suppose we choose $t_1 = 1$ and $t_2 = 2$. This gives the linear system

$$-1 = 2\gamma_1 + 3\gamma_2,$$
$$-1 = 3\gamma_1 + 8\gamma_2.$$

The solution based on this principle is known as collocation method. Figure 6.1 reveals that this approximation is about as close to the true curve as the other solutions.

6.1.2 The General Framework

The three different solutions that we have just considered may be obtained from the following setting. We want to approximate an unknown function $f : X \to Y$, where X and Y are subsets of $\mathbb{R}^n$ and $\mathbb{R}^m$, respectively. This function is implicitly defined by the functional equation $F(f) = 0$, where $F : C_1 \to C_2$. C_1 and C_2 are given spaces of functions, e.g., the set of all continuously differentiable functions on $[a, b]$. Examples of functional equations are the Bellman equation (1.14) of the deterministic growth model considered in Chapter 1 and the Euler equation of the stochastic growth model (1.45c) also presented in Chapter 1. Given a family of polynomials $\mathcal{P} := \{\varphi_i\}_{i=0}^{\infty}$, we approximate f by a finite linear combination of the first $p+1$ members of this family:

$$\hat{f}(\mathbf{x}) = \sum_{i=0}^{p} \gamma_i \varphi_i(\mathbf{x}), \quad \mathbf{x} \in X \subset \mathbb{R}^n. \tag{6.7}$$

The residual function is obtained by substituting $\hat{f}$ into the functional equation:

$$R(\boldsymbol{\gamma}, \mathbf{x}) := F(\hat{f}(\boldsymbol{\gamma}, \mathbf{x})), \quad \boldsymbol{\gamma} := (\gamma_0, \ldots, \gamma_p). \tag{6.8}$$

Suppose there is a set of test functions $\{g_i(\mathbf{x})\}_{i=0}^p$ and a weighting function $w(\mathbf{x})$. Together with R they define an inner product given by

$$\int_X w(\mathbf{x}) R(\boldsymbol{\gamma}, \mathbf{x}) g_i(\mathbf{x}) d\mathbf{x}.$$

On a function space, this inner product induces a norm (i.e., a measure of distance) on this space and we choose the vector of parameters $\boldsymbol{\gamma}$ so that

$$\int_X w(\mathbf{x}) R(\boldsymbol{\gamma}, \mathbf{x}) g_i(\mathbf{x}) d\mathbf{x} = 0, \quad \forall i = 0, 1, \ldots, n. \tag{6.9}$$

It is easy to see that the three different solutions considered above are derived from (6.9) for special choices of g_i and w.

1. The least squares solution puts $g_i \equiv \partial R / \partial \gamma_i$ and $w \equiv 1$.
2. The Galerkin solution chooses $g_i \equiv \varphi_i$ and $w \equiv 1$.
3. The collocation method uses the Dirac delta function as weighting function,

$$w(\mathbf{x}) = \begin{cases} 0 \text{ if } \mathbf{x} \neq \mathbf{x}_i, \\ 1 \text{ if } \mathbf{x} = \mathbf{x}_i, \end{cases}$$

and puts $g_i \equiv 1$.

In the following, we restrict ourselves to these three definitions of a solution being close to the true function. Before we consider the different steps to implement a specific solution in more detail, we summarize the general procedure that underlies projection methods in an algorithm.

Algorithm 6.1.1 (Projection Method)

Purpose: *Approximate the solution $f : X \to Y$ of a functional equation $F(f) = 0$.*

Steps:

Step 1: Choose a bounded state-space $X \subset \mathbb{R}^n$ and a family of functions $\varphi_i(\mathbf{x}) : X \to Y$, $i = 0, 1, \ldots$.

Step 2: Choose a degree of approximation p and let

$$\hat{f}(\boldsymbol{\gamma}, \mathbf{x}) = \sum_{i=0}^{p} \gamma_i \varphi_i(\mathbf{x}).$$

Step 3: Define the residual function:

$$R(\boldsymbol{\gamma}, \mathbf{x}) := F(\hat{f}(\boldsymbol{\gamma}, \mathbf{x})).$$

Step 4: Choose a projection function g_i, a weighting function w and compute the inner product:

$$G_i := \int_X w(\mathbf{x}) R(\boldsymbol{\gamma}, \mathbf{x}) g_i(\mathbf{x}) d\mathbf{x}, \quad i = 0, \ldots, n.$$

Find the value of $\boldsymbol{\gamma}$ that solves $G_i = 0$, or, in the case of least squares projection ($g_i = \partial R / \partial \gamma_i$ and $w \equiv 1$), that minimizes

$$\int_X R(\boldsymbol{\gamma}, \mathbf{x})^2 d\mathbf{x}.$$

Step 5: Verify the quality of the candidate solution $\boldsymbol{\gamma}$. If necessary, return to step 2 and increase the degree of approximation p or even return to step 1 and choose a different family of basis functions.

6.1.3 Relation to Parameterized Expectations

LAWRENCE CHRISTIANO and JONAS FISHER (2000) point out that the conventional parameterized expectations approach (PEA) presented in Chapter 5 is a particular projection method. Consider again the non-linear regression step 4 of algorithm 5.1.1. In this step, we solve the non-linear equation system (5.10), which we restate for your convenience:

$$0 = \frac{-2}{T}\sum_{t=0}^{T-1}[\phi_j(\mathbf{s}_{t+1}(\boldsymbol{\gamma})) - \psi_j(\boldsymbol{\gamma}_j, \mathbf{w}_t(\boldsymbol{\gamma}))]\frac{\partial \psi_j}{\partial \gamma_{ij}}(\boldsymbol{\gamma}_j, \mathbf{w}_t(\boldsymbol{\gamma})),$$

for all $i = 1, 2, \ldots, p$, and $j = 1, 2, \ldots, k$.

In this equation, the $n(w)$-vector of states $\mathbf{w}_t \in X \subset \mathbb{R}^{n(w)}$ contains all relevant information to predict the conditional expectation $\boldsymbol{\phi}(\mathbf{s}_{t+1})$. The function that approximates $\phi_j(\cdot)$ is given by $\psi_j(\cdot)$ and parameterized by $\boldsymbol{\gamma}_j$.

In order to generate the time series for $\mathbf{w}_t$ and for $\mathbf{s}_{t+1}$ in the stochastic growth model, for example, a random sample of the technology shock Z_t is drawn. If the time horizon T is getting large, the probability distribution of the state variables $\mathbf{w}_t \in X \subset \mathbb{R}^{n(w)}$ approaches the ergodic distribution, say $\pi(\mathbf{w})$, induced by the choice of $\boldsymbol{\phi}(\cdot)$ and the distribution of Z_t. The PEA can now readily be identified with a specific projection method. The residual is given by

$$R_j(\boldsymbol{\gamma}, \mathbf{x}) = \phi_j(\mathbf{s}_{t+1}(\boldsymbol{\gamma})) - \psi_j(\boldsymbol{\gamma}_j, \mathbf{w}_t(\boldsymbol{\gamma}))$$

and the weight for the i-th component of $\boldsymbol{\gamma}$ is simply

$$w^i(\mathbf{w}_t, \boldsymbol{\gamma}) = \pi(\mathbf{w}_t)\frac{\partial \psi_j}{\partial \gamma_{ij}}(\boldsymbol{\gamma}_j, \mathbf{w}_t(\boldsymbol{\gamma})).$$

In particular, the residual at point $\mathbf{w}_t \in X$ is also weighted by its probability $\pi(\mathbf{w}_t) = 1/T$. The Monte-Carlo simulation used in the conventional PEA more likely generates data points near the steady state for two reasons. First, since the innovations in the AR(1)-process are drawn from a normal distribution, realizations far from the mean of 0 are less likely. Second, the economy tends to return to the steady state after a shock.

This property of the Monte-Carlo simulation, however, also constitutes a major weakness of the conventional PEA. If we numerically approximate a function, we use nodes that are not concentrated in a certain area of the interval over which we want to approximate this function.[4] For example, with Chebyshev regres-

---
[4] See Section 11.2.

sion a relatively large proportion of the nodes is distributed close to the limits of the interval $[-1, 1]$. Therefore, we could get a much better quality of fit with much less fitting points if we modify the PEA accordingly. We will show this in Section 6.3.2, where we solve the stochastic growth model.

6.2 The Building Blocks of Projection Methods

In this subsection we consider the separate steps of Algorithm 6.1.1 in more detail. We begin with the choice of the family of functions.

6.2.1 Approximating Function

In the applications of Chapter 5 we use the family of monomials $\{1, x, x^2, ...\}$ to approximate the conditional expectations function. There, we already encountered the problem that the fitting step may fail due to the fact that higher degree monomials may be nearly indistinguishable from each other numerically. We can circumvent this problem by using a family of orthogonal polynomials, as, e.g., the Chebyshev polynomials described in Section 11.2.6. There are further considerations that make Chebyshev polynomials a prime candidate for projection methods. Some of them are mentioned in Section 11.2.6 and others will become obvious in the next paragraphs.

One further issue must be resolved at this step. Polynomials are single valued functions. So, how are we going to interpret the term $\varphi_i(\mathbf{x})$ in equation (6.7)? As we explain in Section 11.2.7, $\varphi_i(\mathbf{x})$ is the i–th member of a so called product base, which consists of products of members of a family of polynomials. If $\mathbf{x} \in X \subset \mathbb{R}^n$, let $(k_1, k_2, \ldots k_n)$ denote the n-tuple of integers from the set $\mathcal{I} := \{0, 1, 2, \ldots, p\}$. Then:

$$\varphi_i(\mathbf{x}) := \prod_{j=1}^{n} \varphi_{k_j}(x_j).$$

Note that there are $(1+p)^n$ different n-tuples that can be built from the set $\mathcal{I}$. The respective product space is called the n-fold tensor product base. A smaller set, the complete set of polynomials, derives from the condition $\sum_{j=1}^{n} k_j = p$. For instance, if $n = 2$, this set consists of $(p+1)(p+2)/2$ members, whereas the tensor product base has $(1+p)^2$ members.

6.2.2 Residual Function

In many economic applications there are several ways to solve the model. For instance, in Chapter 5 we approximate the agent's conditional expectations function. Yet, we can solve the models considered there also by computing the agent's policy function. In some cases it is not always obvious, which way is best, and some experimentation with different solution concepts may be warranted. In other cases a particular solution may suggest itself on a priori reasons. In the stochastic growth model with a binding constraint on investment the agent's policy function will have a kink at the point where the constraint becomes binding. As we demonstrate in Section 11.2.6, it is difficult to approximate a kinked function with a linear combination of differentiable functions as the Chebyshev polynomials. Thus, in this case it is better to solve the model by computing the agent's conditional expectations function.

Even if we have decided on the function that we wish to approximate it is not always obvious how to define the residual function in step 3 of Algorithm 6.1.1. Consider the Euler equation of the deterministic growth model from (1.12):

$$0 = \frac{u'(C_t)}{u'(C_{t+1})} - \beta f'(K_{t+1}),$$
$$K_{t+1} = f(K_t) - C_t,$$

where C_t is consumption in period t, K_t the agent's stock of capital, $u'(\cdot)$ the marginal utility of consumption, and $f'(\cdot)$ the marginal product of capital. Assume we want to solve this model in terms of the policy function $C(K_t)$. Letting $\hat{C}(\gamma, K)$ denote the approximate solution, the residual function may be computed from

$$R(\gamma, K) := \frac{u'[\hat{C}(\gamma, K)]}{u'[\hat{C}(\gamma, f(K) - \hat{C}(\gamma, K))]} \qquad (6.10)$$
$$- \beta f'[f(K) - \hat{C}(\gamma, K)].$$

Notice that by this formulation we do not put more weight on low asset values K (and, hence, low consumption C) with a corresponding high value of marginal utility because we form the fraction of current and next-period marginal utilities. However, if we chose the alternative residual function

$$R(\gamma, K) := u'(\hat{C}(\gamma, K))$$
$$- \beta u'[\hat{C}(\gamma, f(K) - \hat{C}(\gamma, K))] f'[f(K) - \hat{C}(\gamma, K)]$$

small errors in the approximation of the true consumption function $C(K)$ would result in large residuals at low values of the capital stock K, while relatively larger deviations of the approximated function from the true solution for high values of K would result in a much smaller residual. As we aim to find a good uniform approximation of the policy function over the complete state-space, we should be careful with respect to the choice of the residual function and rather use (6.10).

6.2.3 Projection and Solution

Depending on the choice of the projection function and the weighting function this step may become more or less involved. Note that for $\mathbf{x} \in X \subset \mathbb{R}^n$ the shorthand $\int_X$ denotes the n-fold integral:

$$\int_X w(\mathbf{x}) R(\gamma, \mathbf{x}) g_i(\mathbf{x}) d\mathbf{x}$$
$$:= \int_{\underline{x}_1}^{\bar{x}_1} \int_{\underline{x}_2}^{\bar{x}_2} \cdots \int_{\underline{x}_n}^{\bar{x}_n} w(\mathbf{x}) R(\gamma, \mathbf{x}) g_i(\mathbf{x}) dx_1 dx_2 \ldots dx_n. \qquad (6.11)$$

If the dimension of the state-space is small, we can use one of several methods to compute numeric approximations to these integrals. For instance, in Section 11.3.2 we consider the Gauss-Chebyshev quadrature that replaces the integral by a weighted sum of m function values, computed at the zeros of the m-th degree Chebyshev polynomial. Suppose $\mathbf{x} = (x_1, x_2)$ so that the double integral is approximated by a double sum over the pairs (x_i, x_j), $i, j = 1, 2, \ldots, m$. If we use $m = 100$ nodes to compute the integral, this amounts to adding up 10,000 elements. In general, using Gauss-Chebyshev quadrature to evaluate (6.11), requires $m^n - 1$ summations. In higher dimensional problems, the integration step can become a binding constraint. For instance, HEER and MAUSSNER (2004) use the Galerkin method to solve a multi-country, representative agent model. For eight countries with idiosyncratic productivity shocks the state-space of this model has dimension $n = 16$. Even with only 3 nodes Gauss-Chebyshev quadrature requires 43,046,721 evaluations of the integrand. In this paper we employ an integration formula that uses $2^n + 2n + 1$ points. On a personal computer with Pentium III, 846 MHz processor it takes 14 days, 16 hours and 32 minutes to find the solution.

If we project the residual against the Dirac delta function, we circumvent the computation of integrals. Of course, this will save a lot of computer time if the state-space is large. Instead, the task is to solve the non-linear equation system

$$R(\boldsymbol{\gamma}, \mathbf{x}_j) = 0, \quad j = 0, 1, \ldots, p.$$

But at which set of points $\mathbf{x}_j$ should the residual function equal zero? It is well known from the so called Chebyshev interpolation theorem[5] that the Chebyshev zeros minimize the maximal interpolation error. For this reason, one should use the Chebyshev nodes of the Chebyshev polynomial of order $p+1$. This particular projection method is called Chebyshev collocation.

We have seen that the least squares projection derives from minimizing $\int_X R(\boldsymbol{\gamma}, \mathbf{x})^2 d\mathbf{x}$. Thus, instead of solving the set of $p+1$

---

[5] See, e.g., JUDD (1998), Theorem 6.7.2, p. 221.

non-linear equations

$$\int_X R(\boldsymbol{\gamma}, \mathbf{x}) \frac{\partial R(\boldsymbol{\gamma}, \mathbf{x})}{\partial \gamma_j} d\mathbf{x} = 0, \quad \forall j = 0, 1, \ldots, p,$$

we can also employ numerical optimization techniques to find the minimizer of $\int_X R(\boldsymbol{\gamma}, \mathbf{x})^2 d\mathbf{x}$. Otherwise we must compute the partial derivatives of the residual function either analytically or numerically. Depending on the structure of the problem, the latter approach — though not as accurate as the former — may be preferable since it requires less programming. What is required is just passing the function $R(\cdot)$ to a subroutine that returns the gradient of a user supplied function.

6.2.4 Accuracy of Solution

A first and simple to perform check of the accuracy of the solution is to compute the residuals $R(\boldsymbol{\gamma}, \mathbf{x})$ over a grid of points in X. To get an idea of how good your solution is, you must compare it to a second solution. This second solution could use different projection functions $\tilde{g}_i$ or a more accurate, but perhaps more time-consuming integration routine.

A second accuracy check is to simulate the model. From this simulation the second moments of important economic variables and the DM-statistic (see Section 12.3) can be computed. Hints at a bad solution are implausible second moments or signs of correlation of expectational errors with past information.

In the case of Chebyshev polynomials, there is a third, easy to use criterium. From Theorem 11.2.4 we know that the coefficients γ_j drop off rapidly and that γ_p is small. If your solution does not display this pattern, you should return to step 2 or even step 1 of Algorithm 6.1.1.

6.3 Applications

In this section, we present several applications. First, we compute the policy function of the deterministic growth model that we also consider in Sections 1.2, 2.1, 2.5.2, 3.1.2 and 4.1. The state-space of this model is one-dimensional and consists of the capital stock K_t only. In the second example, we extend the analysis to a two-dimensional state-space considering the stochastic growth model of Section 1.3. Finally, we model asset pricing. Towards this end, we introduce habit persistence and adjustment costs of capital into the stochastic growth model. The state-space of this model consists of the productivity shock, the stock of capital and past consumption.

6.3.1 The Deterministic Growth Model

The Model. In Section 1.2 we introduce the deterministic growth model. For your convenience, we restate the farmer's decision problem given in (1.8):

$$\max_{C_0, C_1, \ldots} U_0 = \sum_{t=0}^{\infty} \beta^t \frac{C_t^{1-\eta} - 1}{1 - \eta}, \quad \beta \in (0,1), \eta > 0,$$

s.t. (6.12)

$$\left.\begin{array}{rcl} K_{t+1} + C_t & \leq & K_t^\alpha + (1-\delta)K_t, \quad \alpha \in (0,1), \\ 0 & \leq & C_t, \\ 0 & \leq & K_{t+1}, \end{array}\right\} t = 0, 1, \ldots,$$

K_0 given,

where C_t is consumption in period t and K_t the farmer's stock of capital. Here, we assume that the current period utility function $u(C_t)$ has a constant elasticity of marginal utility with respect to consumption of $-\eta$. The production function $F(N, K_t) = K_t^\alpha$ is of the Cobb-Douglas type and capital depreciates at the rate $\delta \in (0,1]$.

The Euler equation of this problem is given by:

$$\left[\frac{C_{t+1}}{C_t}\right]^{-\eta} \beta \left(1 - \delta + \alpha K_{t+1}^{\alpha-1}\right) - 1 = 0. \tag{6.13}$$

From this equation we derive the steady state value of the capital stock:

$$K^* = \left[\frac{\alpha\beta}{1-\beta(1-\delta)}\right]^{1/(1-\alpha)}.$$

Implementation. The state-space X of the problem is one-dimensional and consists of the capital stock K_t. In order to perform the computation, we need to specify an upper and a lower bound for the state-space. We choose $X := [0.5K^*, 1.5K^*]$. Depending on the nature of our problem, we might want to specify a smaller or larger interval. For example, if we consider the transition dynamics from an initial capital stock K_0, we may choose an interval $[\underline{K}, \overline{K}]$ that contains K_0 and K^*, and choose the borders $\underline{K}$ and $\overline{K}$ to be close to these values.

In the first and second step of Algorithm 6.1.1, we choose a family of functions for the approximation. In particular, we approximate the consumption function $C(K)$ with the help of a Chebyshev polynomial of order p,

$$\hat{C}(\boldsymbol{\gamma}, K) := \sum_{j=0}^{p} \gamma_j T_j(\tilde{K}(K)),$$

where $\tilde{K}(K)$ maps the capital stock K into the interval $[-1, 1]$ according to equation (11.48).

In step 3, we define the residual function $R(\boldsymbol{\gamma}, K)$. We argued in the previous subsection that it is best to use a version of the Euler equation, where the fraction of current and future marginal utility appears. For this reason we use equation (6.13) as our starting point. We compute the residual $R(\boldsymbol{\gamma}, K)$ in the following steps:

1. Given a parameter vector $\boldsymbol{\gamma}$ and $K_0 \in [\underline{K}, \overline{K}]$ we use Algorithm 11.2.1 to compute $\hat{C}_0 := \hat{C}(\boldsymbol{\gamma}, K_0)$. At this step we will terminate the algorithm if the returned value of consumption is non-positive. This may occur if $\boldsymbol{\gamma}$ is far from the solution.
2. From $\hat{C}_0$ we compute the future stock of capital K_1 from the resource constraint:

$$K_1 = K^\alpha + (1-\delta)K - \hat{C}_0.$$

Here we must check whether K_1 is in $[\underline{K}, \overline{K}]$. If this condition is not satisfied, we must stop the algorithm: for values of K_1

outside the interval $[\underline{K}, \overline{K}]$ the transformed variable $\tilde{K}(K)$ is outside the interval $[-1, 1]$ where the Chebyshev polynomial is not defined. We know from Section 1.2 that the true solution converges to K^*. Therefore, the true policy function $C(K)$ always satisfies

$$\underline{K} < \underline{K}^\alpha + (1-\delta)\underline{K} - C(\underline{K}),$$
$$\overline{K} > \overline{K}^\alpha + (1-\delta)\overline{K} - C(\overline{K}).$$

Of course, a bad approximate solution does not need to satisfy this requirement. We invite you to discover what strange things can happen if you ignore this condition in the computation of a candidate solution. Just out-comment the respective line in the file `Ramsey2e.g`.

3. Given K_1 we use Algorithm 11.2.1 again to get $\hat{C}_1 := \hat{C}(\gamma, K_1)$.
4. In this final step we compute the residual from

$$R(\gamma, K_0) := \beta \left[\frac{\hat{C}_1}{\hat{C}_0}\right]^{-\eta} \left(1 - \delta + \alpha K_1^{\alpha-1}\right) - 1.$$

The fourth step of Algorithm 6.1.1 concerns the projection method. The least squares method requires the minimization of

$$\int_{\underline{K}}^{\overline{K}} R(\gamma, K)^2 dK$$

with respect to the parameter vector γ. We use Gauss-Chebyshev quadrature (see equation (11.76)) and approximate this integral by the sum

$$S(\gamma) := \frac{\pi(\overline{K} - \underline{K})}{2L} \sum_{l=1}^{L} R(\gamma, K(\tilde{K}_l))^2 \sqrt{1 - \tilde{K}_l^2},$$

where $\tilde{K}_l$ are the zeros of the L-th degree Chebyshev polynomial and $K(\tilde{K}_l)$ is the transformation of these zeros to the interval $[\underline{K}, \overline{K}]$ given by equation (11.49). The minimization of $S(\gamma)$ via a quasi Newton algorithm requires good starting values. With bad initial values it is not possible to evaluate S. It turns out that it is no trivial task to pick admissible points from which Algorithm 11.6.3 converges. In the case where an analytic solution exists we get starting values from a regression of the analytic solution on a Chebyshev polynomial. For this purpose we employ Algorithm 11.2.2. In all other cases we use a genetic search routine that provides an initial point for Algorithm 11.6.3.

For the Galerkin projection method we use again Gauss-Chebyshev quadrature. With this, we must solve the system of $p+1$ non-linear equations:

$$0 = \frac{\pi(\overline{K} - \underline{K})}{2L} \sum_{l=1}^{L} R(\boldsymbol{\gamma}, K(\tilde{K}_l)) T_i(\tilde{K}_l) \sqrt{1 - \tilde{K}_l^2}, \qquad (6.14)$$

$i = 0, 1, \ldots, p.$

The simplest method in terms of computer code required to specify the respective system of non-linear equations is the Chebyshev collocation method. Here, we determine the coefficients $\gamma_0, \ldots, \gamma_p$ from the conditions:

$$R(\boldsymbol{\gamma}, K(\tilde{K}_i)) = 0, \quad \forall i = 0, 2, \ldots, p, \qquad (6.15)$$

where, again, $\tilde{K}_i$ is the i-th zero of the Chebyshev polynomial of order $p+1$.

To solve both the non-linear system (6.14) and (6.15), we use the modified Newton-Raphson algorithm with line search explained in Section 11.5. Again, it is difficult to find good initial values. Our short cut to solve this problem was to regress the analytic solution on a Chebyshev polynomial using Algorithm 11.2.2 if an analytic solution is available. Otherwise we use the solution returned by the search algorithm employed to minimize $S(\boldsymbol{\gamma})$.

Results. The program Ramsey2e.g computes the different solutions. Table 6.1 displays the results for $p = 4$. The parameter values are $\alpha = 0.27$, $\beta = 0.994$, $\eta = 2$, and $\delta = 0.011$. The coefficients differ only slightly. They drop off nicely so that we are confident of having found a good solution. The last row of Table 6.1 shows the maximum absolute value of 100 Euler equation residuals computed on equally spaced points in the interval

Table 6.1

Coefficient	Least Squares	Galerkin	Collocation	Quadratic
γ_0	2.262612	2.262619	2.262620	0.021081
γ_1	0.477002	0.477001	0.476935	-0.000243
γ_2	-0.032233	-0.032274	-0.032398	
γ_3	0.004766	0.004764	0.004870	
γ_4	-0.000873	-0.000843	-0.000792	
EER	5.471E-6	5.377E-6	7.558E-6	3.864E-5

Notes: Euler equation residuals (EER) are computed as the maximum absolute value of 100 equally spaced points in the interval $[0.8K^*, 1.2K^*]$.

$[0.8K^*, 1.2K^*]$. The residuals are quite small for all three solutions and about one order of magnitude smaller than the Euler equation residual obtained from the quadratic policy function computed in Section 2.5.2. Comparing the different test and weighting functions, the collocation solution is slightly less precise than both the least squares and the Galerkin solution.

Figure 6.2 nicely shows the difference between a local and a global method to determine the policy function of a DGE model. It plots the 100 Euler equation residuals associated with the Galerkin solution and the quadratic policy function. Near the stationary solution of the model, there is no remarkable difference. Yet, to the right of $1.1K^*$ and to the left of $0.9K^*$ the precision of the quadratic solution rapidly worsens.

6.3.2 The Stochastic Growth Model with Non-Negative Investment

In Section 4.3.1 we employ discrete state-space methods to solve the stochastic growth model with a non-negativity constraint on investment. The solution of this model via the parameterized expectations approach is considered in Section 5.3.1. Here we compute a solution with the methods outlined in the first two sections of this chapter. We assume that you are by now familiar with this

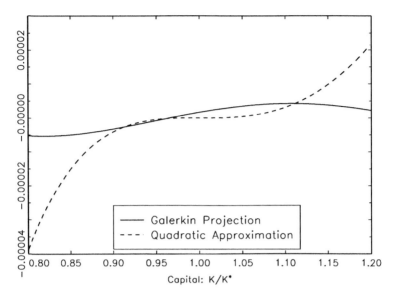

Figure 6.2: Euler Equation Residuals from the Deterministic Growth Model

model so that we can turn to the details of our implementation immediately. For your convenience, we repeat the first-order conditions from (5.12) that characterize the model's solution:

$$0 = C_t^{-\eta} - \mu_t - \beta E_t\left[C_{t+1}^{-\eta}(1 - \delta + \alpha Z_{t+1}K_{t+1}^{\alpha-1}) - \mu_{t+1}(1-\delta)\right], \tag{6.16a}$$

$$0 = Z_t K_t^\alpha + (1-\delta)K_t - C_t - K_{t+1}, \tag{6.16b}$$

$$0 = \mu_t[K_{t+1} - (1-\delta)K_t], \tag{6.16c}$$

$$0 \leq \mu_t, \tag{6.16d}$$

$$0 \leq K_{t+1} - (1-\delta)K_t. \tag{6.16e}$$

Implementation. We know from the previous discussion of this model that the consumption function has a kink (see Figure 4.2) at the points where the non-negativity constraint binds. Since kinked functions are difficult to approximate, we choose the conditional expectation on the rhs of (6.16a) as our target. As in Section 5.3.1, we use the exponential of a polynomial in $\ln K$ and $\ln Z$:

$$\psi(\gamma, Z, K) := \beta \exp\left(\sum_{i=0}^{p_1}\sum_{j=0}^{p_2} \gamma_{ij} T_i(\tilde{K}) T_j(\tilde{Z})\right),$$

where $\tilde{K}$ and $\tilde{Z}$ denote the transformations of $\ln K \in [\ln \underline{K}, \ln \overline{K}]$ and $\ln Z \in [\ln \underline{Z}, \ln \overline{Z}]$, respectively, to the interval $[-1, 1]$ as given by (11.48).

The state-space X of this model consists of all pairs $(K_t, Z_t) \in \mathbb{R}^2$, and we must choose a compact (that is, closed and bounded) subset X of this space to determine the parameters of ψ. There are two different considerations that guide our decision. First, we know from previous discussions of the model that the capital stock remains in a small neighborhood of the stationary capital stock of the deterministic growth model, if the level of total factor productivity Z_t stays close to its unconditional mean $Z = 1$. Since we want a good approximation of the model in this part of its state-space and not in those parts which the economy never visits, we will choose X as small as possible. Simulations of the process

$$\ln Z_t = \varrho \ln Z_{t-1} + \sigma \epsilon_t, \quad \epsilon_t \sim N(0, 1) \qquad (6.17)$$

helped to find lower and upper bounds for Z and simulations with the parameterized expectations solution provided the bounds of the capital stock. Without previous experience with the model trial and error must guide your choice of upper and lower bounds of the capital stock. For instance, the lower (upper) bound can be set to a small fraction (multiple) of the stationary capital stock. When a solution has been found, these bounds can be adjusted accordingly. There is, however, a second issue that we must consider. The domain of Chebyshev polynomials is the compact interval $[-1, 1]$ and we must map X into $[-1, 1] \times [-1, 1]$ via the transformation (11.48). It is, however, dangerous to use the same compact region chosen to determine the parameters of ψ for this purpose. In order to compute the residual function $R(\gamma, K, Z)$, we must evaluate conditional expectations. As before, we use Gauss-Hermite integration for this purpose. This algorithm also considers very extreme productivity levels Z that are beyond the bounds within which Z stays in simulations of the model. Furthermore, with extreme levels of Z savings may be either very high or very small and may put the capital stock outside the interval which we have specified. To prevent this, we use a different and much larger compact set $\tilde{X}$ as domain of the function ψ.

In our program SGNNI_c.for we compute the residual function from (6.8) in the following steps.

1. Given a pair (Z, K), we solve

$$C = \psi(\gamma, Z, K)^{-1/\eta}$$

and check the non-negativity constraint. If

$$K_1 := ZK^\alpha + (1-\delta)K - C \geq (1-\delta)K,$$

we accept this choice, else we put

$$C = ZK^\alpha,$$
$$K_1 = (1-\delta)K.$$

If $K_1 \in \tilde{X}$, we proceed to the next step; otherwise we stop and try a different vector γ or adjust the bounds of $\tilde{X}$.

2. Let $K_1(Z, K)$ denote the solution from the first step and let $Z_1 = e^{\varrho \ln Z + \sigma \epsilon}$, $\epsilon \sim N(0, 1)$ be the productivity level of the next period. We solve for

$$C_1 = \psi(\gamma, Z_1, K_1(Z, K))^{-1/\eta}.$$

Again, we must check whether this solution violates the non-negativity constraint on investment. Thus, if

$$K_2 = Z_1 K_1^\alpha + (1-\delta)K_1 - C_1 \geq (1-\delta)K_1$$

we accept and put $\mu_1 = 0$, else we set

$$C_1 = Z_1 K_1^\alpha,$$
$$\mu_1 = C_1^{-\eta} - \psi(\gamma, Z_1, K_1).$$

Given this, we can compute the expression

$$g(Z_1, Z, K) := C_1^{-\eta}(1 - \delta + \alpha Z_1 K_1^{\alpha-1}) - (1-\delta)\mu_1.$$

3. The conditional expectation on the rhs of (6.16a) is then

$$\phi(Z,K) := \beta \int_{-\infty}^{\infty} g(e^{\varrho z + \sigma \epsilon}, Z, K) \frac{e^{\frac{-\epsilon^2}{2}}}{\sqrt{2\pi}} d\epsilon.$$

In our program we compute this integral via Gauss-Hermite quadrature with four nodes.

As an alternative, one can approximate the AR(1)-process in equation (6.17) by a Markov chain with m states. Thus, if Z_i is the i-th element of the grid $\mathscr{Z} = \{Z_1, Z_2, \ldots, Z_m\}$ and if p_{ij}, $i, j = 1, 2, \ldots, m$ denotes the probability of moving from i to j, the conditional probability on the rhs of (6.16a) is approximated by

$$\phi(Z,K) := \beta \sum_{j=1}^{m} g(Z_j, Z_i, K) p_{ij}.$$

In any way, we are now done, and the residual function is defined by

$$R(\gamma, Z, K) = \phi(Z, K) - \psi(\gamma, Z, K).$$

Our program SGNNI_c.for has many options. You can choose the type of the polynomial (product base versus complete base), its degree, the projection type (least squares, Galerkin, or collocation), the bounds on K and Z that determine the set X, and the way to initialize the parameter vector. Specifically, you can use a former solution as starting value for a new one or use a genetic search routine. In addition, the program allows you to apply the linear policy function for λ_t found by the program Ramsey3a.g and estimate an initial parameter vector from the formulas given in (11.60). Note, however, that the program does not allow you to use the collocation solution together with a complete polynomial. A complete polynomial in two independent variables of degree p has $n = (p+1)(p+2)/2$ different parameters. Yet, there are $m = (p+1)^2 > n$ different zeros of the single Chebyshev polynomials. Which combination of n zeros out of m should we use to determine the parameters? Of course, there is a natural answer:

the solution that is best in terms of the Euler equation residual. Yet, even with a low degree of $p = 4$, this becomes a laborious task. To find the solution with the smallest Euler equation residual, we had to compare $l = m!/n!(m-n)! = 3,268,760$ different solutions.

Results. Table 6.2 presents the results from a few experiments that we conducted. The parameters of the model are as in our previous simulations, that is, $\alpha = 0.27$, $\beta = 0.994$, $\delta = 0.011$, $\eta = 2$, $\varrho = 0.9$. We considered two different values of $\sigma = 0.0072$ and $\sigma = 0.05$. For the smaller value, the non-negativity constraint never binds so that the model is identical to the stochastic growth model. It proved rather tricky to obtain the solutions. In some cases the linear solution provided a good starting value, in others our genetic search routine supplied acceptable initial values. The solutions shown in the first panel of the table were computed from the final solutions for $\sigma = 0.05$.

Table 6.2 supports several conclusions. First, consider the choice of the type of the polynomial. A complete polynomial with 15 parameters (the case $p = 4$) achieves about the same degree of accuracy as a product base polynomial with twenty parameters (the case $p_1 = 3$ and $p_2 = 4$). From our experiments (which are not all listed in the table) it is save to recommend complete polynomials instead of product base polynomials. For the least squares as well as for the Galerkin projection they provide the same degree of accuracy with fewer parameters than the latter family of polynomials.

Second, consider the kind of the projection. Least squares and Galerkin projection deliver about the same degree of accuracy. In the case of the smaller value of $\sigma = 0.0072$, we were not able to obtain the same degree of accuracy from the collocation solution. The last two rows of the first panel of Table 6.2 show that neither a product base polynomial with 12 nor with 16 parameters was able to reduce the Euler equation residual to about 2.E-8, which results from both the least squares and the Galerkin solution with 15 parameters. For the larger productivity shock, we obtain Euler equation residuals of the same size from all three methods with 15 ($p = 4$) and 12 ($p_1 = 2$ and $p_2 = 3$) parameters, respectively.

Table 6.2

Projection	Degree of Polynomial	Euler Equation Residual 90%	Euler Equation Residual 80%	DM-Statistic < 3.816	DM-Statistic > 21.920
			$\sigma = 0.0072$		
Least Squares	$p = 2$	5.542E-6	4.303E-6	1.7	3.3
	$p = 3$	1.104E-7	1.085E-7	1.8	3.2
	$p = 4$	2.220E-8	2.100E-8	1.8	3.2
Galerkin	$p = 2$	6.196E-6	4.863E-6	1.7	3.4
	$p = 3$	1.165E-7	1.151E-7	1.8	3.2
	$p = 4$	1.950E-8	1.650E-8	1.8	3.2
	$p_1 = 3, p_2 = 4$	1.817E-8	1.533E-8	1.8	3.2
Collocation	$p_1 = 2, p_2 = 3$	1.391E-6	1.294E-6	1.6	3.3
	$p_1 = 3, p_2 = 3$	3.347E-6	3.177E-6	1.8	3.0
			$\sigma = 0.05$		
Least Squares	$p = 2$	5.966E-4	4.676E-4	0.3	14.8
	$p = 3$	2.674E-4	1.540E-4	1.6	4.8
	$p = 4$	2.896E-4	1.906E-4	1.4	5.4
Galerkin	$p = 2$	6.177E-4	4.863E-4	0.3	15.1
	$p = 3$	2.905E-4	1.737E-4	1.5	5.2
	$p = 4$	2.661E-4	1.708E-4	1.5	5.3
	$p_1 = 3, p_2 = 4$	2.719E-4	1.501E-4	1.8	5.0
Collocation	$p_1 = 2, p_2 = 3$	2.550E-4	1.254E-4	1.6	5.6
	$p_1 = 3, p_2 = 3$	2.544E-4	1.340E-4	1.3	5.7

Notes: p is the degree of the complete polynomial, p_1 and p_2 refer to the dimensions of the product base polynomial. The Euler equation residuals are computed as maximum absolute value of 200^2 residuals computed on an equally spaced grid $\mathscr{K} \times \mathscr{Z}$. The size of the interval for K was chosen so that 90 (80) percent of the realizations of K out of 1,000 simulations with 3,000 points each are within the respective interval. The interval for Z was determined likewise.

But note, that the collocation solution with 16 parameters (the case $p_1 = 3$ and $p_2 = 3$) performs not really better than the one with 12 parameters.

Third, the Euler equation residuals computed over the 90 and 80 percent interval for the capital stock are about the same size. Being a global, non-linear method, the projection approach provides an equally precise solution over the relevant state-space of the model.

Fourth, compare the parameterized expectations (PE) solutions displayed in Table 5.1 with the results in Table 6.2. In the case of the small standard deviation $\sigma = 0.0072$, the least squares and the Galerkin solutions are almost an order of magnitude more accurate than the PE solution for $p = 2$. In addition, whereas it was not possible to obtain a more accurate solution from the PE approach, it was easy to reduce the Euler equation residuals from about 5.5E-6 to 2.0E-8 by increasing p from 2 to 4. On the other hand, for $\sigma = 0.05$, the PE solution is about as accurate as the solutions from the different projection methods. In this case, we have not been able to increase the precision markedly by using higher-order polynomials.

6.3.3 The Benchmark Model

Our solution of the benchmark model of Example 1.5.1 draws on the conclusions from the previous subsection. To facilitate the comparison with the parameterized expectations solution of Section 5.3.2 we approximate the rhs of the Euler equation (5.13d) by a complete Chebyshev polynomial of degree $p = 2$ and use Galerkin projection to determine the parameters of this function. The residual function $R(\boldsymbol{\gamma}, k, Z)$ is obtained as follows.

Given $\lambda = \psi(\boldsymbol{\gamma}, k, Z)$, we use equation (5.14) to determine working hours N and consumption c. Then, we compute the next-period capital stock k_1 from the budget constraint (5.13c). Let $Z_1 = e^{\varrho \ln Z + \sigma \epsilon}$ denote the next-period level of total factor productivity associated with Z and $\epsilon \sim N(0,1)$, so that $\lambda_1 = \psi(\boldsymbol{\gamma}, k_1, Z_1)$. We use (5.14) again to find N_1. In this way, we have determined

$$g(k, Z, \epsilon) = \lambda_1 (1 - \delta + \alpha e^{\varrho \ln Z + \sigma \epsilon} N_1^{1-\alpha} k_1^{\alpha-1}),$$

and the residual function is given by

$$R(\boldsymbol{\gamma}, k, Z) = \lambda - \beta a^{-\eta} \int_{-\infty}^{\infty} g(k, Z, \epsilon) \frac{e^{-\frac{\epsilon^2}{2}}}{\sqrt{2\pi}} d\epsilon.$$

Table 6.3

	Linear Approximation			Projection Methods					
				Galerkin $p=2$			Collocation $p_1=1, p_2=2$		
				Second Moments					
Variable	s_x	r_{xy}	r_x	s_x	r_{xy}	r_x	s_x	r_{xy}	r_x
Output	1.44	1.00	0.64	1.44	1.00	0.64	1.43	1.00	0.64
Investment	6.11	1.00	0.64	6.11	1.00	0.64	6.10	1.00	0.64
Consumption	0.56	0.99	0.66	0.56	0.99	0.66	0.56	0.99	0.66
Hours	0.77	1.00	0.64	0.77	1.00	0.64	0.77	1.00	0.64
Real Wage	0.67	0.99	0.65	0.67	0.99	0.65	0.67	0.99	0.65
	Euler Equation Residuals								
$[0.90; 1.10]k$	1.835E-4			1.543E-6			4.227E-5		
$[0.85; 1.15]k$	3.478E-4			1.993E-6			4.217E-5		
$[0.80; 1.20]k$	5.670E-4			3.770E-6			5.950E-5		
	DM-Statistic								
<3.816	2.0			2.7			1.5		
>21.920	3.4			3.0			5.3		

Notes: s_x:=standard deviation of variable x, r_{xy}:=cross correlation of variable x with output, r_x:=first order autocorrelation of variable x. All second moments refer to HP-filtered percentage deviations from a variable's stationary solution. Euler equation residuals are computed as maximum absolute value over a grid of 400 equally spaced points on the square $\mathcal{K} \times [\ln 0.95; \ln 1.05]$, where $\mathcal{K}$ is defined in the respective row of the left-most column. The 2.5 and the 97.5 percent critical values of the $\chi^2(11)$-distribution are displayed in the last two lines of the first column. The table entries refer to the percentage fraction out of 1,000 simulations where the DM-statistic is below (above) its respective critical value.

We compute the integral in this expression as before from the Gauss-Hermite formula (11.77) with four nodes.

Table 6.3 displays the results computed from our Fortran program `Benchmark.for`. This program has the same options as the program `SGNNI_c.for` so that you can experiment with different settings. The table shows two different solutions. Both use a polynomial with 6 parameters. The Euler equation residuals, the DM-statistic, and the second moments clearly show that the collocation solution with a product base polynomial is worse than the Galerkin solution with a complete polynomial. Compared with the parameterized expectations solution in Table 5.2 the Galerkin solution is an order of magnitude more precise than the PE solution. Note, however, that both solutions deliver the same second moments as the linear solution.

6.3.4 The Equity Premium Puzzle

The Puzzle. One of the most regarded puzzles in the theory of financial economics is the equity premium puzzle: Why has the average real return on stocks in the US been six percentage points higher than the return on US Treasury Bills over the last century?[6] In this chapter, we present a model of asset pricing in a production economy based on the work of JERMANN (1998).

The model is an extension of the stochastic growth model that you are, by now, most familiar with. In the latter model the expression

$$R_t := \alpha Z_t K_t^{\alpha-1} - \delta$$

(i.e., the marginal product of capital less the rate of depreciation) is the net return on one unit of output invested in the capital stock of a representative firm. We also know from this model that the household's lifetime utility does not change, if she trades one unit of consumption today against

$$\frac{u'(C_t)}{\beta E_t u'(C_{t+1})} = \frac{\Lambda_t}{\beta E_t \Lambda_{t+1}}$$

units of consumption tomorrow. Thus, the household is willing to pay

$$p_t := \beta E_t \frac{\Lambda_{t+1}}{\Lambda_t}$$

---

[6] An excellent overview of this issue is provided by KOCHERLAKOTA (1996). JAGANNATHAN, MCGRATTAN, and SCHERBINA (2001) argue that the equity premium has declined significantly in the last two decades and is likely to remain at a lower level on average as the transaction costs for trading stocks have been reduced substantially. For recent views on the puzzle and the efforts to solve it, see MEHRA (2003) and MEHRA and PRESCOTT (2003).

for a bond that promises one unit of consumption tomorrow for certain. For this reason we can use

$$r_t := \frac{1}{p_t} - 1 \equiv \frac{\Lambda_t}{\beta E_t \Lambda_{t+1}} - 1$$

as a measure of the risk free rate of return. Note that the time subscript t in this definition refers to the date on which the return becomes known. The return materializes in period $t+1$ when the bond pays one unit of consumption. The mean equity premium in the simple stochastic growth model is $E(R_{t+1} - r_t)$, where, as usual, $E(\cdot)$ denotes the unconditional mathematical expectation taken over the probability distribution of (Z, K, C).

In the simple stochastic growth model with less than full depreciation there is not much variation in the marginal product of capital, since investment is only a small portion of the stock of capital. One way to raise the variability of the stock of capital is to provide further incentives for investment. For instance, if the household's current period utility depends not only on current but also on past consumption, its desire to smooth consumption increases. This is usually referred to as habit persistence. A second way to obtain more variation in the return on equity is to allow for a variable price of shares. In the simple stochastic growth model the price of capital in terms of consumption goods is constant and equal to one, because it is possible to consume the stock of capital. The most common way to allow for a variable price of capital goods is to introduce adjustment costs.

In the following we extend the simple stochastic growth model along these two lines. We consider a decentralized economy inhabited by a continuum of identical households of mass one and a continuum of identical firms of the same size.

Households. The representative household provides one unit of labor to firms and earns the competitive real wage w_t. As a shareholder she is entitled to receive dividends d_t per unit of stocks S_t of the representative firm. The current price of stocks in terms of the consumption good is v_t. Thus, total income is $w_t + d_t S_t$. The household buys consumption goods C_t and additional shares $v_t(S_{t+1} - S_t)$. Her budget constraint, thus, is

$$v_t(S_{t+1} - S_t) \leq w_t + d_t S_t - C_t. \tag{6.18}$$

The household's current period utility function is specified in the following way:

$$u(C_t, C_{t-1}) := \frac{(C_t - bC_{t-1})^{1-\eta} - 1}{1 - \eta}, \quad b \in [0, 1), \eta > 0. \tag{6.19}$$

Habit persistence occurs if $b > 0$, otherwise we get the standard isoelastic current period utility function. The household maximizes expected lifetime utility

$$E_0 \sum_{t=0}^{\infty} \beta^t \frac{(C_t - bC_{t-1})^{1-\eta} - 1}{1 - \eta}, \quad \beta \in (0, 1),$$

subject to (6.18) and the initial number of shares S_0. Employing the techniques presented in Section 1.3, we derive the following first-order conditions:

$$\Lambda_t = (C_t - bC_{t-1})^{-\eta} - \beta b E_t (C_{t+1} - bC_t)^{-\eta}, \tag{6.20a}$$
$$\Lambda_t = \beta E_t \Lambda_{t+1} R_{t+1}, \tag{6.20b}$$
$$R_t := \frac{d_t + v_t}{v_{t-1}}. \tag{6.20c}$$

The term R_t gives the current period (ex post) gross rate of return on equities. As usual, Λ_t is the Lagrange multiplier of the budget constraint, and E_t denotes expectations conditional on information available at the beginning of the current period t.

Firms. The representative firm uses labor services N_t and capital services K_t to produce output according to

$$Y_t = Z_t N_t^{1-\alpha} K_t^{\alpha}. \tag{6.21}$$

The level of total factor productivity Z_t follows the AR(1)-process specified in equation (6.17). The firm finances its investment expenditures I_t by issuing new equities $v_t(S_{t+1} - S_t)$ and out of retained earnings RE_t:

$$I_t = v_t(S_{t+1} - S_t) + RE_t. \tag{6.22}$$

Investment expenditures increase the firm's current capital stock by

$$K_{t+1} - K_t = \phi(I_t/K_t)K_t - \delta K_t, \quad \delta \in (0,1]. \tag{6.23}$$

$\phi(I_t/K_t)$ is an increasing, concave function of its argument. The case $\phi(I_t/K_t) \equiv I_t/K_t$ specifies the capital accumulation equation in the standard model. As in Section 3.3.2 we parameterize this function by:

$$\phi(I_t/K_t) := \frac{a_1}{1-\zeta}\left(\frac{I_t}{K_t}\right)^{1-\zeta} + a_2, \quad \zeta > 0. \tag{6.24}$$

The firm's profits equal revenues Y_t less labor costs $w_t N_t$:

$$\Pi_t = Y_t - w_t N_t. \tag{6.25}$$

The amount RE_t of these profits are used to finance investment. The remaining profits are distributed as dividends to the firm's shareholders:

$$d_t S_t = \Pi_t - RE_t. \tag{6.26}$$

To motivate the firm's objective function, we consider the deterministic case first. The value of the firm at the beginning of time $t+1$ is given by

$$V_{t+1} = v_t S_{t+1}.$$

Using (6.22), (6.26), and (6.25) this may be expressed as

$$\begin{aligned}V_{t+1} = v_t S_{t+1} &= v_t S_t + I_t - RE_t, \\ &= v_t S_t + I_t + d_t S_t - \Pi_t, \\ &= \left(\frac{d_t + v_t}{v_{t-1}}\right) v_{t-1} S_t - (Y_t - w_t N_t - I_t),\end{aligned}$$

or, using the definition of R_t in (6.20c), as

$$V_{t+1} + (Y_t - w_t N_t - I_t) = R_t V_t.$$

Iterating this equation forward beginning with $t = 0$ and ending with $t = T$ yields:

$$V_0 = \frac{V_T}{R_0 R_1 \ldots R_{T-1}} + \sum_{t=0}^{T-1} \frac{Y_t - w_t N_t - I_t}{R_0 R_2 \ldots R_t}.$$

For the present value of the firm V_0 to be finite if T tends to infinity requires:

$$\lim_{T \to \infty} \frac{V_T}{R_0 R_1 \ldots R_{T-1}} = 0.$$

In effect, this condition rules out speculative bubbles. Thus, we end up with the following formula for the present value of the firm:

$$V_0 = \sum_{t=0}^{\infty} \varrho_t [Y_t - w_t N_t - I_t], \quad \varrho_t := \frac{1}{R_0 R_1 \cdots R_t}. \tag{6.27}$$

Note that the firm is not able to choose its discount factor. In equilibrium the household sector requires a return on equities given by

$$R_{t+1} = \frac{\Lambda_t}{\beta \Lambda_{t+1}}, \tag{6.28}$$

which follows from (6.20b) in the case of no aggregate uncertainty. As a consequence, the firm's value depends on the sequence of cash flows and the sequence of shadow prices Λ_t but not on the firm's dividend policy.[7]

The firm aims at maximizing its present value (6.27) subject to (6.23). The respective Lagrangean for this problem is

$$\mathscr{L} = \sum_{t=0}^{\infty} \varrho_t \Big\{ Z_t N_t^{1-\alpha} K_t^{\alpha} - w_t N_t - I_t \\ + q_t \big[\phi(I_t/K_t) K_t + (1-\delta) K_t - K_{t+1} \big] \Big\},$$

---

[7] This is not generally true. Here it follows because we neglect income and corporate taxes. See TURNOVSKY (2000), 292ff.

where q_t is the period t value of the Lagrange multiplier attached to the constraint (6.23).

The first-order conditions for the optimal choice of N_t, I_t, and K_{t+1} are:

$$w_t = (1-\alpha)Z_t N_t^{-\alpha} K_t^{\alpha}, \tag{6.29a}$$

$$q_t = \frac{1}{\phi'(I_t/K_t)}, \tag{6.29b}$$

$$q_t = \frac{1}{R_{t+1}}\Big\{\alpha Z_{t+1} N_{t+1}^{1-\alpha} K_{t+1}^{\alpha-1} - (I_{t+1}/K_{t+1}) \tag{6.29c}$$
$$+ q_{t+1}\big[\phi(I_{t+1}/K_{t+1}) + 1 - \delta\big]\Big\}.$$

In addition, the transversality condition

$$\lim_{t\to\infty} \varrho_t q_t K_{t+1} = 0 \tag{6.29d}$$

must hold.

The first condition determines labor input in the usual way and deserves no further comment, except that it implies

$$\Pi_t := Y_t - w_t N_t = \alpha Z_t N_t^{1-\alpha} K_t^{\alpha} = \alpha Y_t. \tag{6.30}$$

Given q_t, the shadow value of an additional unit of new capital in terms of the firm's output, the second equation can be solved for the optimal amount of investment expenditures I_t. We want adjustment costs of capital to play no role in the deterministic stationary state of the model. This has two consequences: q must equal one and I must equal δK. Using (6.24) and (6.29b) the first condition requires

$$a_1 = \delta^\zeta.$$

Via the second condition this in turn implies:

$$a_2 = \frac{-\zeta}{1-\zeta}\delta.$$

It is easy to see that for $\zeta > 0$ condition (6.29b) implies $q_t \to 0 \Rightarrow I_t \to 0$. Thus, there is always a solution featuring $q_t, I_t > 0$. Using equations (6.23) and (6.30) condition (6.29c) may be rewritten as

$$q_t = \frac{1}{R_{t+1}}\left\{Y_{t+1} - w_{t+1}N_{t+1} - I_{t+1} + q_{t+1}K_{t+2}\right\}\frac{1}{K_{t+1}}.$$

Iterating on this equation delivers

$$q_0 K_1 = \sum_{t=1}^{T} \varrho_t(Y_t - w_t N_t - I_t) + \varrho_T q_T K_{T+1}.$$

Taking the limit for $T \to \infty$, invoking the transversality condition (6.29d), and comparing the result to the definition of the present value of the firm in equation (6.27) establishes

$$q_0 K_1 = V_1.$$

Since the choice of the current period is arbitrary, we have just shown that $V_{t+1} = q_t K_{t+1}$. In words, q_t is the ratio of the firm's stock market value to the replacement costs of its capital stock.

This result carries over to the stochastic case to which we turn next. Since we have already seen that the management of the firm has to use the household's marginal valuation of wealth Λ_t, we define the expected present value of the firm in the following way:

$$V_0 = E_0 \sum_{t=0}^{\infty} \beta^t \frac{\Lambda_t}{\Lambda_{-1}} \left(Z_t N_t^{1-\alpha} K_t^\alpha - w_t N_t - I_t\right).$$

Proceeding in a way analogous to Section 1.3.2, we can derive first-order conditions. With regard to optimal labor input and the optimal amount of investment these conditions are equal to (6.29a) and (6.29b), respectively. The condition with respect to K_{t+1} is the obvious modification of (6.29c):

$$q_t = \beta E_t \frac{\Lambda_{t+1}}{\Lambda_t} \left(\alpha Z_{t+1}(K_{t+1}/N_{t+1})^{\alpha-1} - \frac{I_{t+1}}{K_{t+1}} \right.$$
$$\left. + q_{t+1}\left[\phi(I_{t+1}/K_{t+1}) + 1 - \delta\right]\right). \quad (6.29c')$$

Market Equilibrium. Since the size of the household sector is one and since leisure is not an argument of the household's utility function, total labor supply always equals unity: $N_t \equiv 1$. The household's budget constraint (6.18) together with definitions (6.22), (6.26), and (6.25) implies the economy's resource constraint:

$$Z_t K_t^\alpha = C_t + I_t. \tag{6.31}$$

Thus, the model's dynamics is governed by the stochastic Euler equations (6.20a) and (6.29c'), the capital accumulation equation (6.23), the resource constraint (6.31), and the investment function that derives from condition (6.29b).

Deterministic Stationary State. Remember that we have assumed that adjustment costs of capital play no role in the deterministic stationary state of the model, i.e., $q = 1$ and $\phi(I/K) = \delta$. Using this, as well as $\Lambda_{t+1} = \Lambda_t = \Lambda$ and $Z = 1$ in the Euler equation (6.29c') implies:

$$K = \left[\frac{\alpha \beta}{1 - \beta(1-\delta)} \right]^{1/1-\alpha}.$$

Hence, the deterministic stationary stock of capital coincides with the solution for the same variable in the simple deterministic growth model. From the resource constraint we get

$$C = K^\alpha - \delta K.$$

Finally, the Euler equation (6.20a) delivers the stationary value of Λ :

$$\Lambda = (1 - \beta b)[(1-b)C]^{-\eta}.$$

Implementation. We can solve for all period t variables, if we know q_t and Λ_t. These variables in turn depend on the predetermined variables K_t and C_{t-1} and the level of total factor productivity Z_t. Therefore, the state-space X of our model is a subspace of $\mathbb{R}^3$, given by

$$X := [\underline{K}, \overline{K}] \times [\underline{C}, \overline{C}] \times [\underline{Z}, \overline{Z}],$$

for suitable lower and upper bounds on K_t, C_{t-1}, and Z_t, respectively. As in the previous applications, we choose the intervals as small as possible, but pay attention that all variables remain in the respective interval in the simulations of the model. For the Chebyshev polynomials we choose larger intervals. In particular, the interval for the productivity shock must be large enough so that it encompasses the nodes of the Gauss-Hermite quadrature formula, which we employ to compute conditional expectations. Since both q_t and λ_t are non-negative variables, we employ exponentials of complete polynomials of degree p_i, $i = 1, 2$. The first polynomial $\psi^1(\gamma^1, K, C, Z)$ approximates the rhs of equation (6.29c') and, thus, determines the relative price of capital q. The second polynomial $\psi^2(\gamma^2, K, C, Z)$ approximates the conditional expectation on the rhs of equation (6.20a). The parameters of these functions are collected in the yet to be determined vectors γ^1 and γ^2. Before we consider this step, we explain our computations of the residual functions R^1 and R^2.

1. Given a triple (K, C, Z) we compute

   $$q_1 = \psi^1(\gamma^1, K, C, Z).$$

   Using equation (6.29b) and our parameterization of ϕ given in (6.24), we find

   $$I_1 = K(a_1 q_1)^{1/\varsigma}.$$

   The resource constraint (6.31) delivers

   $$C_1 = ZK^\alpha - I_1,$$

   and from the capital accumulation equation (6.23) we get

   $$K_2 = \phi(I_1/K)K + (1-\delta)K.$$

   Finally, we compute Λ_1 from

   $$\Lambda_1 = (C_1 - bC)^{-\eta} - \beta b \psi^2(\gamma^2, K, C, Z).$$

   Before we proceed, we check if C_1 and K_2 are in the domain of our polynomials.

2. Let $Z_1 = e^{\varrho \ln Z + \sigma \epsilon}$ with $\epsilon \sim N(0,1)$ denote the level of total factor productivity for an arbitrary realization of ϵ. We repeat the previous sequence of computations:

$$q_2 = \psi^1(\boldsymbol{\gamma}^1, K_2, C_1, Z_1),$$
$$I_2 = K_2(a_1 q_2)^{1/\varsigma},$$
$$C_2 = Z_1 K_2^\alpha - I_2,$$
$$\Lambda_2 = (C_2 - bC_1)^{-\eta} - \beta b \psi^2(\boldsymbol{\gamma}^2, K_2, C_1, Z_1)$$

to get

$$g^1(K, C, Z, \epsilon) := \beta(\Lambda_2/\Lambda_1)\big[\alpha Z_1 K_2^{\alpha-1} - (I_2/K_2)$$
$$+ q_2(\phi(I_2/K_2) + 1 - \delta)\big],$$
$$g^2(K, C, Z, \epsilon) := (C_2 - bC_1)^{-\eta}.$$

3. In the last step, we use these two functions to compute the residuals from the Euler equations (6.29c') and (6.20a):

$$R^1(\boldsymbol{\gamma}, K, C, Z) := q_1 - \int_{-\infty}^{\infty} g^1(K, C, Z, \epsilon) \frac{e^{\frac{-\epsilon^2}{2}}}{\sqrt{2\pi}} d\epsilon,$$

$$R^2(\boldsymbol{\gamma}, K, C, Z) := \psi^2(\boldsymbol{\gamma}^2, K, C, Z) - \int_{-\infty}^{\infty} g^2(K, C, Z, \epsilon) \frac{e^{\frac{-\epsilon^2}{2}}}{\sqrt{2\pi}} d\epsilon.$$

We employ the Gauss-Hermite formula with six points to compute the integrals in these equations.

Our program Equity.for determines the parameter vector from the Galerkin projection. Thus, it solves the set of equations

$$0 = \int_{\underline{K}}^{\overline{K}} \int_{\underline{C}}^{\overline{C}} \int_{\underline{Z}}^{\overline{Z}} R^i(\boldsymbol{\gamma}, K, C, Z) T_j(K) T_k(C) T_l(Z) dK dC dZ,$$
$$i = 1, 2, \quad j, k, l = 0, 1, \ldots p_i, \quad j + k + l \leq p_i. \tag{6.32}$$

The program approximates the three-fold integral with the Gauss-Chebyshev quadrature formula in three dimensions.

Notice that we do not need to solve for the share price v_t appearing in the definition of the return on equities $R_{t+1} := (d_{t+1} + v_{t+1})/v_t$. To see this, consider the proposition

$$R_{t+1} = \frac{\Pi_{t+1} - I_{t+1} + q_{t+1}K_{t+1}}{q_t K_{t+1}} = \frac{d_{t+1} + v_{t+1}}{v_t}. \tag{6.33}$$

The first term on the rhs equals the term in round brackets on the rhs of equation (6.29c') divided by q_t. We have shown above that the firm's total value at $t+1$ is given by $v_t S_{t+1} \equiv V_{t+1} = q_t K_{t+1}$. This allows us to replace $q_t K_{t+1}$ and $q_{t+1} K_{t+2}$ with $v_t S_{t+1}$ and $v_{t+1} S_{t+2}$, respectively. When we eliminate I_{t+1} by the rhs of equation (6.22), the first term on the rhs of (6.33) transforms into the second. Thus, we can compute the ex-post return on equities from the simulated times series for output Y_t, investment I_t, the stock of capital K_t, and the relative price of capital q_t. The conditional expectation $E_t \Lambda_{t+1}$ that appears in the definition of the risk free rate $r_t := \Lambda_t/(\beta E_t \Lambda_{t+1})$ is computed in a manner analogous to steps 2) and 3) above.

The program has several options to initialize the parameter vectors for the non-linear equations solver. The first option, genetic search, is rather time-consuming, if the degrees of the polynomials are high and if the quadrature formula uses many nodes. For instance, with 20 nodes in each dimension, the program must evaluate 8,000 times the residual functions R^i in order to compute the rhs of the system (6.32). One way to speed up this process, is to determine the initial parameters from the collocation solution. The second option uses the linear policy functions and the extension of Algorithm 11.2.2 to three dimensions to determine initial parameters. The problem with this approach is, that the linear policy functions may imply negative values for either q or Λ, because the six-point Gauss-Hermite formula uses rather extreme points for Z. The third option is to use a solution found in a previous step for a different set of parameters or different degrees p_i. The strategy that finally proved successful was genetic search for a collocation solution with $p_1 = p_2 = 2$ that could be used to determine the Galerkin solution. Note that even for $p_i = 2$ each polynomial has 10 parameters. We increased the degrees of both polynomials stepwise until the results with respect to the equity premium stabilized. In each step we used the previously found solution with zeros in the places of the yet unknown coefficients as starting values.

Calibration. Though there are prominent studies close to the model of the previous paragraph, namely JERMANN (1998) and BOLDRIN, CHRISTIANO, and FISHER (2001), from which we could have taken the parameters, we stick to our usual set of parameters and borrow only the additional parameter ζ from these studies. This allows us to compare the results to the stochastic growth model that we have considered in this and the previous chapters. Thus, we employ $\alpha = 0.27$, $\beta = 0.994$, $\eta = 2$, $\delta = 0.011$, $\varrho = 0.90$, $\sigma = 0.0072$. From the study of JERMANN (1998) we take the value of the elasticity of investment with respect to q of 0.23. In our notation, this implies $\zeta = 1/0.23$. We vary the habit persistence parameter to uncover its influence on the equity premium. We note, however, that for ζ as small as 0.23, our model does not imply a significant equity premium, even for b close to one.

Results. Table 6.4 shows that our model is able to generate a significant equity premium, if the household is sufficiently averse to changes in consumption. The statistics are averages from 500 simulations with 120 periods each. For the small value of $b = 0.1$, we found a good solution with $p_1 = 3$ and $p_2 = 2$ (30 parameters altogether). Yet, for $b = 0.8$ and $\eta = 3$, we had to use $p_1 = p_2 = 7$

Table 6.4

		$\eta = 2.0$		$\eta = 3.0$
	$b = 0.1$	$b = 0.5$	$b = 0.8$	$b = 0.8$
$R - 1$	0.62	0.71	1.26	1.41
$E(R - r)$	0.04	0.17	1.05	1.34

(240 parameters altogether) until a further increase in p_i did not change the equity premium noticeably. In this case we find an equity premium of about 5.5 percent p.a. (1.34 per quarter). The estimates for the U.S. economy between 1802 and 2000 presented in Table 1 of MEHRA (2003), range between 4.9 and 8.0 percent p.a., depending on the chosen time period. For our baseline parameters it is not possible to obtain a higher annual equity premium

by increasing η any further. For instance, JERMANN (1998) uses $\eta = 5$. In our model this implies a negative risk free rate since the denominator in $r_t = \Lambda_t/(\beta E_t \Lambda_{t+1})$ increases with a more curved utility function and since the risk free rate in the deterministic case is small: $r = (1/\beta) - 1$ yields an annual risk free rate of 2.4 percent. In a model with economic growth – as considered by JERMANN (1998) – this rate equals $r = (1/(\beta a^{-\eta})) - 1$. Using $a = 1.005$ and $\eta = 2$ as in our benchmark model, the annual risk free rate equals 6.6 percent. In this setting, it is possible to obtain a higher equity premium by raising η from 2 to 5 for a still positive and sizable risk free rate.

Considering the case of $b = 0.1$, where the equity premium is negligible, and remembering what we said about the adjustment cost parameter ζ, reveals that it is the combination of consumers that strife for a very smooth time profile of consumption and costly adjustment of capital that is able to explain the equity premium.

The ability of the model to predict a sizeable equity premium is sensitive to the assumption of a fixed supply of labor. If labor supply is endogenous, agents can smooth consumption over time quite effectively by adjusting their working hours. The burden placed on the stock of capital as a vehicle for consumption smoothing is greatly reduced. The variability of the relative price of capital declines and diminishes the equity premium. BOLDRIN, CHRISTIANO, and FISHER (2001) introduce frictions in the adjustment of labor by considering a two-sector model, where workers cannot move from one sector to the other within a given period. In this model, they are able to replicate the average equity premium.

Problems

6.1 Human Capital Accumulation

Consider the following discrete time version of LUCAS' (1988) model of growth through human capital accumulation. In this deterministic model the social planner solves the following problem:

$$\max \sum_{t=0}^{\infty} \beta^t \frac{C_t^{1-\eta} - 1}{1 - \eta}, \quad \beta \in (0,1), \ \eta > 0,$$

subject to

$$K_{t+1} = (u_t H_t)^\alpha K_t^{1-\alpha} + (1 - \delta) K_t - C_t,$$
$$H_{t+1} = A(1 - u_t) H_t + (1 - \delta) H_t, \quad A > 0,$$

K_0, H_0 given.

Here C_t is consumption in period t, K_t the stock of capital, H_t the stock of human capital. The size of the working population N is normalized to 1 so that u_t is the fraction of human capital adjusted labor $H_t N$ devoted to the production of output. The state variables of this model are physical capital K_t and human capital H_t. The control variables are consumption C_t and the fraction of hours spent in the production of output u_t. In the steady state of this model all variables grow at the rate $g_H = A(1 - u^*) + (1 - \delta)$, where u^* is the steady state value of u_t. Therefore, variables that are stationary (and, thus, remain within a compact space) are, for instance, $k_t := K_t/H_t$, $c_t := C_t/H_t$, and $h_{t+1} := H_{t+1}/H_t$. Use projection methods to approximate the functions $c(k_t, h_t)$ and $u(k_t, h_t)$. We propose the following values of the model's parameters: $\alpha = 0.27$, $\beta = 0.994$, $\eta = 2$, $\delta = 0.011$. Choose A so that the steady state growth rate is 0.005 per quarter. Compute the transitional dynamics of the model for both an economy with a relative shortage of physical and a relative shortage of human capital. Is there any difference?

6.2 The Equity Premium and Endogenous Labor Supply

In the model of Section 6.3.4 modify the instantaneous utility function of the household to include leisure:

$$u(C_t, C_{t-1}, 1 - N_t) := \frac{(C_t - bC_{t-1})^{(1-\eta)}(1 - N_t)^{\theta(1-\eta)} - 1}{1 - \eta}$$

and solve this model. Are you still able to produce a sizeable equity premium?

6.3 Oil Price Shocks

Consider the following model with a variable utilization rate of capital u_t and a second shock that represents exogenous variations in the price of imported oil p_t (this is adapted from FINN (1995)). The representative agent solves

$$\max E_0 \sum_{t=0}^{\infty} \beta^t \left[\ln C_t + \theta \ln(1 - N_t)\right], \quad \beta \in (0,1), \; \theta > 0,$$

subject to
$$K_{t+1} = (Z_t N_t)^\alpha (u_t K_t)^{1-\alpha} + (1 - \delta(u_t))K_t - C_t - p_t Q_t,$$
$$\delta(u_t) := \frac{u_t^\gamma}{\gamma},$$
$$\frac{Q_t}{K_t} = \frac{u_t^\zeta}{\zeta},$$
$$\ln Z_t = \ln Z + \ln Z_{t-1} + \epsilon_t^Z, \quad \epsilon_t^Z \sim N(0, \sigma^Z),$$
$$\ln p_t = \rho^p \ln p_{t-1} + \epsilon_t^p, \quad \epsilon_t^p \sim N(0, \sigma^p),$$
K_0 given.

As usual, C_t denotes consumption in period t, N_t are working hours, K_t is the stock of capital, and Q_t it the quantity of oil imported at the price of p_t. A more intense utilization of capital increases the amount of energy required per unit of capital. Thus, if the price of oil rises, capital utilization will decrease. Verify this claim as follows.

In this model, labor augmenting technical progress follows a random walk with drift rate $\ln Z$. Define the following stationary variables $c_t := C_t/Z_t$, $k_t := K_t/Z_{t-1}$, and $z_t := Z_t/Z_{t-1}$. The state variables of the model are k_t, z_t, and p_t. Solve the model for the consumption function $(C_t/Z_t) = c(k_t, z_t, p_t)$. Given this solution, compute the time path of the utilization rate of capital for a one-time oil price shock of the size of one standard deviation of ϵ^p. Use the following parameter values taken from FINN (1995): $\beta = 0.9542$, $\theta = 2.1874$, $\alpha = 0.7$, $\gamma = 1.4435$, $\zeta = 1.7260$, $\rho^p = 0.9039$, $\sigma^p = 0.0966$, $Z = 1.0162$, $\sigma^Z = 0.021$.

Part II
Heterogeneous Agent Models

Chapter 7

Computation of Stationary Distributions

Overview. This chapter introduces you to the modeling and computation of heterogeneous-agent economies. In this kind of problem, we have to compute the distribution of the individual state variable(s). While we focus on the computation of the stationary equilibrium in this chapter, you will learn how to compute the dynamics of such an economy in the next chapter.

The representative agent framework has become the standard tool for modern macroeconomics. It is based on the intertemporal calculus of the household that maximizes lifetime utility. Furthermore, the household behaves rationally. As a consequence, it is a natural framework for the welfare analysis of policy actions. However, it has also been subject to the criticism whether the results for the economy with a representative household carry over to one with heterogenous agents. In the real economy, agents are different with regard to many characteristics including their abilities, their education, their age, their marital status, their number of children, their wealth holdings, to name but a few. As a consequence it is difficult to define a representative agent. Simple aggregation may sometimes not be possible or lead to wrong implications. For example, if the savings of the households are a convex function of income and, therefore, the savings rate increases with higher income, the definition of the representative household as the one with the average income or median income may result in a consideration of a savings rate that is too low.[1] In addition, we are unable to study many important policy and welfare questions that

---

[1] To see this argument, notice that the rich (poor) households with a high (low) savings rate contribute much more (less) to aggregate savings than the household with average income.

analyze the redistribution of income among agents like, for example, through the reform of the social security and pensions system or by the choice of a flat versus a progressive schedule of the income tax.

In the remaining part of the book, agents are no longer homogeneous and cannot be represented by a single agent. For obvious reasons, we will not start to introduce the diversity of agents along its multiple dimensions at once, but we will first confine ourselves to the consideration of one source of heterogeneity. In the next section, therefore, we augment the standard Ramsey model by the real life feature that some agents are employed, while others are unemployed.[2] For simplicity, we assume that the agent cannot influence his employment probability, e.g. by searching harder for a new job or asking for a lower wage. In addition, agents cannot insure against the idiosyncratic risk of being unemployed. Accordingly, agents in our economy differ with regard to their employment status and their employment history. Those agents who were lucky and have been employed for many years are able to save more and build up higher wealth than their unlucky contemporaries who have been unemployed for longer periods of time. As a consequence, agents also differ with regard to their wealth. Besides, all agents are equal. In the second part of this chapter, we will compute the stationary distribution of the individual state variables. In the final section, we present two prominent applications from macroeconomic theory, the puzzle of the low risk-free interest rate and the distributional effects of a switch from an income tax to a consumption tax. In addition, we give you a short survey of the modern literature on the theory of income distribution.

---

[2] Different from the model of HANSEN (1985), we also assume that agents do not pool their income.

7.1 A Simple Heterogeneous-Agent Model with Aggregate Certainty

In Chapter 1, we present the deterministic infinite horizon Ramsey problem and show that the equilibrium of this economy is equivalent to the one of a decentralized economy and that the fundamental theorems of welfare economics hold. In this section, we consider heterogeneity at the household level, but keep the simplifying assumption that all firms are equal and, hence, can act as a representative firm. As a consequence, we most conveniently formulate our model in terms of a decentralized economy and study the behavior of the households and the firm separately.

As a second important characteristic of our model, we only consider idiosyncratic risk. In our economy, households can become unemployed and cannot insure themselves against this risk. However, there is no aggregate uncertainty. For example, the technology is deterministic. As you will find out, the economy will display a long-run behavior that is easily amenable to computational analysis. In the *stationary equilibrium* of the economy, the distribution of the state variable, the aggregate wage and the aggregate interest rate are all constant, while the employment status and the wealth level of the individual households vary.[3]

In our simple model, three sectors can be distinguished: households, production, and the government. Households maximize their intertemporal utility subject to their budget constraint. In order to insure against the risk of unemployment, they build up precautionary savings during good times. Firms maximize profits. The government pays unemployment compensation to the unemployed agents that is financed by an income tax. We will describe the behavior of the three sectors in turn.

Households. The economy consists of many infinitely lived individuals. In particular, we consider a continuum of agents of total

---

[3] Aggregate uncertainty will be introduced into the heterogeneous-agent extension of the Ramsey model in Chapter 8.

mass equal to one.[4] Each household consists of one agent and we will speak of households and agents interchangeably. Households differ only with regard to their employment status and their asset holdings. Households maximize their intertemporal utility

$$E_0 \sum_{t=0}^{\infty} \beta^t u(c_t), \qquad (7.1)$$

where $\beta < 1$ is the subjective discount factor and expectations are conditioned on the information set at time 0. At time zero, the agent knows his beginning-of-period wealth a_0 and his employment status $\epsilon_0 \in \{e, u\}$. If $\epsilon = e$ ($\epsilon = u$), the agent is employed (unemployed). The agent's instantaneous utility function is twice continuously differentiable, increasing and concave in his consumption c_t and has the following form:

$$u(c_t) = \frac{c_t^{1-\eta}}{1-\eta}, \quad \eta > 0, \qquad (7.2)$$

where η, again, denotes the coefficient of relative risk aversion. In the following, lowercase letters denote individual variables and uppercase letters denote aggregate variables. For example, c_t is individual consumption, while C_t is aggregate consumption in the economy. We, however, keep the notation that real prices are denoted by lower case letters, while nominal prices are denoted by upper case letters.

Agents are endowed with one indivisible unit of time in each period. If the agent is employed ($\epsilon = e$) in period t, he earns gross wage w_t. If the agent is unemployed ($\epsilon = u$) in period t, he receives unemployment compensation b_t. We will assume that $(1-\tau)w_t > b_t$, where τ denotes the income tax rate. The individual-specific employment state is assumed to follow a first-order Markov chain. The conditional transition matrix is given by:

$$\pi(\epsilon'|\epsilon) = Prob\{\epsilon_{t+1} = \epsilon'|\epsilon_t = \epsilon\} = \begin{pmatrix} p_{uu} & p_{ue} \\ p_{eu} & p_{ee} \end{pmatrix}, \qquad (7.3)$$

---

[4] This amounts to assume that the number of individual households is infinite and, if we index the household with $i \in [0,1]$, the probability that $i \in [i_0, i_1]$ is simply $i_1 - i_0$.

where, for example, $Prob\{\epsilon_{t+1} = e | \epsilon_t = u\} = p_{ue}$ is the probability that an agent will be employed in period $t+1$ given that the agent is unemployed in period t. Households know the law of motion of the employment status ϵ_t.

In our economy, unemployment is exogenous. We have not modeled any frictions which might be able to explain this feature. In this regard, we follow HANSEN and İMROHOROĞLU (1992) in order to simplify the exposition and the computation. Of course, it would be straightforward to introduce endogenous unemployment into this model. For example, various authors have used search frictions in the labor market in order to explain unemployment with the help of either endogenous search effort as in COSTAIN (1997) or HEER (2003) or endogenous separation from the firms as in DEN HAAN, RAMEY, and WATSON (2000). In addition, we assume that there are no private insurance markets against unemployment and unemployed agents only receive unemployment compensation from the government.[5]

The household faces the following budget constraint

$$a_{t+1} = \begin{cases} (1 + (1-\tau)r_t)a_t + (1-\tau)w_t - c_t & \text{if } \epsilon = e \\ (1 + (1-\tau)r_t)a_t + b_t - c_t & \text{if } \epsilon = u, \end{cases} \quad (7.4)$$

where r_t denotes the interest rate in period t. Interest income and wage income are taxed at rate τ. Each agent smoothes his consumption $\{c_t\}_{t=0}^{\infty}$ by holding the asset a. An agent accumulates wealth in good times ($\epsilon = e$) and runs it down in bad times ($\epsilon = u$). As a consequence, agents are also heterogeneous with regard to their assets a. We impose the asset constraint $a \geq a_{min}$, so that households cannot run down their assets below $a_{min} \leq 0$.

The first-order condition of the household that is not wealth-constrained can be solved by introducing the Lagrange multiplier λ and setting to zero the derivatives of the Lagrangean expression

---

[5] One possible reason why there are no private insurance markets against the risk of unemployment is moral hazard. Agents may be reluctant to accept a job if they may receive generous unemployment compensation instead. CHIU and KARNI (1998) show that the presence of private information about the individual's work effort helps to explain the failure of the private sector to provide unemployment insurance.

$$\mathscr{L} = E_0 \sum_{t=0}^{\infty} \{\beta^t [u(c_t) + \lambda_t (1_{\epsilon_t=u} b_t + (1 + (1-\tau)r_t)a_t$$
$$+ 1_{\epsilon_t=e}(1-\tau)w_t - a_{t+1} - c_t)]\}$$

with respect to c_t and a_{t+1}. $1_{\epsilon_t=e}$ ($1_{\epsilon_t=u}$) denotes an indicator function that takes the value one if the agent is employed (unemployed) in period t and zero otherwise. The first-order condition for the employed and unemployed agent in period t is

$$\frac{u'(c_t)}{\beta} = E_t \left[u'(c_{t+1})(1 + (1-\tau)r_{t+1}) \right]. \tag{7.5}$$

The solution is given by the policy function $c(\epsilon_t, a_t)$ that is a function of the employment status ϵ_t and the asset holdings a_t in period t. In particular, the policy function is independent of calendar time t. Together with (7.4), the policy function $c(\epsilon_t, a_t)$ also gives next-period asset holdings $a_{t+1} = a'(\epsilon_t, a_t)$.

Production. Firms are owned by the households and maximize profits with respect to their labor and capital demand. Production Y_t is characterized by constant returns to scale using capital K_t and labor N_t as inputs:

$$Y_t = N_t^{1-\alpha} K_t^{\alpha}, \quad \alpha \in (0,1). \tag{7.6}$$

In a market equilibrium, factors are compensated according to their marginal products and profits are zero:

$$r_t = \alpha \left(\frac{N_t}{K_t}\right)^{1-\alpha} - \delta, \tag{7.7a}$$

$$w_t = (1-\alpha) \left(\frac{K_t}{N_t}\right)^{\alpha}, \tag{7.7b}$$

where δ denotes the depreciation rate of capital.

Government. Government expenditures consist of unemployment compensation B_t which are financed by a tax on income. The government budget is assumed to balance in every period:

$$B_t = T_t, \tag{7.8}$$

where T_t denotes government revenues.

Stationary Equilibrium. First, we will analyze a stationary equilibrium. We may want to concentrate on the stationary equilibrium, for example, if we want to analyze the long-run effects of a permanent change in the government policy, e.g. a once-and-for-all change in the unemployment compensation b. In a stationary equilibrium, the aggregate variables and the factor prices are constant and we will drop the time indices if appropriate, e.g. for the aggregate capital stock K or the interest rate r and the wage w. Furthermore, the distribution of assets is constant for both the employed and unemployed agents, and the numbers of employed and unemployed agents are constant, too. The individual agents, of course, are not characterized by constant wealth and employment status over time. While we focus on a stationary distribution in this chapter, we will also analyze 1) the transition dynamics for a given initial distribution of the assets to the stationary distribution and 2) the movement of the wealth and income distribution over the business cycle in the next chapter.

For the description of the stationary equilibrium, we need to describe the heterogeneity in our economy. In this book, we use a very pragmatic and simple way to define the stationary equilibrium. In particular, we only use basic concepts from probability theory and statistics which all readers should be familiar with, namely the concept of a distribution function.[6] In the stationary equilibrium, the distribution of assets is constant and we will refer to it as either the stationary, invariant or constant distribution. In our particular model, we are aiming to compute the two distribution functions of the assets for the employed and unemployed agents, $F(e, a)$ and $F(u, a)$, respectively. The corresponding density functions are denoted by $f(e, a)$ and $f(u, a)$. The individual state space consists of the sets $(\epsilon, a) \in \mathcal{X} = \{e, u\} \times [a_{min}, \infty)$.

---

[6] A description of more general heterogeneous-agent economies might necessitate the use of more advanced concepts from measure theory. Since the algorithms and solution methods developed in this chapter do not require a thorough understanding of measure theory and should already be comprehensible with some prior knowledge of basic statistics, we dispense with an introduction into measure and probability theory. For a more detailed description of the use of measure theory in recursive dynamic models please see STOKEY and LUCAS with PRESCOTT (1989).

The concept of a stationary equilibrium uses a recursive representation of the consumer's problem. Let $V(\epsilon, a)$ be the value of the objective function of a household characterized by productivity ϵ and wealth a. $V(\epsilon, a)$ for the benchmark government policy is defined as the solution to the dynamic program:

$$V(\epsilon, a) = \max_{c, a'} \left[u(c) + \beta E \left\{ V(\epsilon', a') | \epsilon \right\} \right], \tag{7.9}$$

subject to the budget constraint (7.4), the government policy $\{b, \tau\}$, and the stochastic process of the employment status ϵ as given by (7.3).[7]

Definition. A stationary equilibrium for a given government policy parameter b is a value function $V(\epsilon, a)$, individual policy rules $c(\epsilon, a)$ and $a'(\epsilon, a)$ for consumption and next-period capital, a time-invariant density of the state variable $x = (\epsilon, a) \in \mathcal{X}$, $f(e, a)$ and $f(u, a)$, time-invariant relative prices of labor and capital $\{w, r\}$, and a vector of aggregates K, N, C, T, and B such that:

1. Factor inputs, consumption, tax revenues, and unemployment compensation are obtained aggregating over households:

$$K = \sum_{\epsilon \in \{e, u\}} \int_{a_{min}}^{\infty} a \, f(\epsilon, a) \, da, \tag{7.10a}$$

$$N = \int_{a_{min}}^{\infty} f(e, a) \, da, \tag{7.10b}$$

$$C = \sum_{\epsilon \in \{e, u\}} \int_{a_{min}}^{\infty} c(\epsilon, a) \, f(\epsilon, a) \, da, \tag{7.10c}$$

$$T = \tau(wN + rK), \tag{7.10d}$$

$$B = (1 - N)b. \tag{7.10e}$$

2. $c(\epsilon, a)$ and $a'(\epsilon, a)$ are optimal decision rules and solve the household decision problem described in (7.9).

---

[7] The solution obtained by maximizing (7.1) s.t. (7.4) and (7.3) corresponds to the solution obtained by solving (7.9) s.t. (7.4) and (7.3) under certain conditions on the boundedness of the value function $V(.)$ (see also Section 1.2.3). This correspondence has been called the *Principle of Optimality* by Richard Bellman.

3. Factor prices (7.7a) and (7.7b) are equal to the factors' marginal productivities, respectively.
4. The goods market clears:

$$N^{1-\alpha} K^\alpha + (1-\delta) K = C + K' = C + K. \tag{7.11}$$

5. The government budget (7.8) is balanced: $T = B$.
6. The distribution of the individual state variable (ϵ, a) is stationary:

$$F(\epsilon', a') = \sum_{\epsilon \in \{e,u\}} \pi(\epsilon'|\epsilon) \, F\left(\epsilon, a'^{-1}(\epsilon, a')\right) \tag{7.12}$$

for all $(\epsilon', a') \in \mathcal{X}$. Here, $a'^{-1}(\epsilon, a')$ denotes the inverse of the function $a'(\epsilon, a)$ with respect to its first argument a.[8] Accordingly, the distribution over states $(\epsilon, a) \in \mathcal{X}$ is unchanging.

Calibration. As we will often use the model as an example in subsequent sections, we will already assign numerical values to its parameters in this introductory part. Following İMROHOROĞLU (1989), periods are set equal to six weeks ($\approx 1/8$ of a year). Preferences and production parameters are calibrated as commonly in the dynamic general equilibrium models. In particular, we pick the values $\alpha = 0.36$ and $\eta = 2.0$. Our choice of $\beta = 0.995$ implies a real annual interest rate of approximately 4% before taxes. The employment probabilities are set such that the average duration of unemployment is 2 periods (=12 weeks) and average unemployment is 8%.[9] The employment transition matrix is given by:

$$\begin{pmatrix} p_{uu} & p_{ue} \\ p_{eu} & p_{ee} \end{pmatrix} = \begin{pmatrix} 0.5000 & 0.5000 \\ 0.0435 & 0.9565 \end{pmatrix}. \tag{7.13}$$

---

[8] In particular, we assume that $a'(\epsilon, a)$ is invertible. As it turns out, $a'(\epsilon, a)$ is invertible in our example economy in this chapter. In Section 7.2, we will also discuss the changes in the computation of the model that are necessary if $a'(\epsilon, a)$ is not invertible. This will be the case if the non-negativity constraint on assets is binding.

[9] Notice that unemployed agents stay unemployed with a probability of 0.5. As a consequence, the average duration of unemployment is simply $1/0.5=2$ periods. In Section 12.2, you will learn how to compute the stationary unemployment rate from the employment transition matrix.

The non-capital income of the unemployed household b amounts to 1.199 and is set equal to one fourth of the steady-state gross wage rate in the corresponding representative agent model,[10] where the gross interest rate is equal to the inverse of the discount factor β and, therefore, the capital stock amounts to $K = (\alpha/(1/\beta-1+\delta))^{1/(1-\alpha)} N$. In the literature, the ratio of unemployment compensation to net wage income is also called the replacement ratio which will be approximately equal to 25.6% in our model. In addition, the income tax rate is determined endogenously in the computation with the help of the balanced budget rule. Finally, the annual depreciation rate is set equal to 4% implying a six-week depreciation rate of approximately 0.5%.

7.2 The Stationary Equilibrium of a Heterogeneous-Agent Economy

With only very few exceptions, dynamic heterogeneous-agent general equilibrium models do not have any analytical solution or allow for the derivation of analytical results. Algorithms to solve heterogeneous-agent models with an endogenous distribution have only recently been introduced into the economic literature. Notable studies in this area are AIYAGARI (1994, 1995), DEN HAAN (1997), HUGGETT (1993), İMROHOROĞLU, İMROHOROĞLU, and JOINES (1995), KRUSELL and SMITH (1998) or RÍOS-RULL (1999). We will use Example 7.2.1 as an illustration for the computation of the stationary equilibrium of such an economy.

Example 7.2.1

Consider the following stationary distribution:

a) Households are allocated uniformly on the unit interval $[0, 1]$ and are of measure one. The individual household maximizes

---

[10] In such a model, the 'representative' household consists of $(1 - N)$ unemployed workers and N employed workers.

7.2 The Stationary Equilibrium of a Heterogeneous-Agent Economy

$$V(\epsilon, a) = \max_{c,a'} \left[\frac{c^{1-\eta}}{1-\eta} + \beta E\left\{V(\epsilon', a')|\epsilon\right\} \right],$$

s.t.

$$a' = \begin{cases} (1+(1-\tau)r)\, a + (1-\tau)w - c & \epsilon = e, \\ (1+(1-\tau)r)\, a + b - c & \epsilon = u, \end{cases}$$

$$a \geq a_{min},$$

$$\pi(\epsilon'|\epsilon) = Prob\{\epsilon_{t+1} = \epsilon'|\epsilon_t = \epsilon\} = \begin{pmatrix} p_{uu} & p_{ue} \\ p_{eu} & p_{ee} \end{pmatrix}.$$

b) The distribution of (ϵ, a) is stationary and aggregate capital K, aggregate consumption C, and aggregate employment N are constant.

c) Factors prices are equal to their respective marginal products:

$$r = \alpha \left(\frac{N}{K}\right)^{1-\alpha} - \delta,$$

$$w = (1-\alpha)\left(\frac{K}{N}\right)^{\alpha}.$$

d) The government budget balances: $B = T$.

e) The aggregate consistency conditions hold:

$$K = \sum_{\epsilon \in \{e,u\}} \int_{a_{min}}^{\infty} a\, f(\epsilon, a)\, da,$$

$$N = \int_{a_{min}}^{\infty} f(e, a)\, da,$$

$$C = \sum_{\epsilon \in \{e,u\}} \int_{a_{min}}^{\infty} c(\epsilon, a)\, f(\epsilon, a)\, da,$$

$$T = \tau(wN + rK),$$

$$B = (1-N)b.$$

The computation of the solution of Example 7.2.1 consists of two basic steps, the computation of the policy function and the computation of the invariant distribution. For this reason, we will apply several elements of numerical analysis that we introduced in the first part of this book. In order to solve the individual's optimization problem, we need to know the stationary factor prices and the tax rate. For a given triplet $\{K, N, \tau\}$, we can use the methods presented in Part I in order to compute the individual policy functions $c(\epsilon, a)$ and $a'(\epsilon, a)$. The next step is the basic new element that you have not encountered in the computation of representative agent economies. We need to compute the distribution of the individual state variables, aggregate the individual state variables, and impose the aggregate consistency conditions. The complete solution algorithm for Example 7.2.1 is described by the following steps:

Algorithm 7.2.1 (Computation of Example 7.2.1)

Purpose: *Computation of the stationary equilibrium.*

Steps:

Step 1: Compute the stationary employment N.
Step 2: Make initial guesses of the aggregate capital stock K and the tax rate τ.
Step 3: Compute the wage rate w and the interest rate r.
Step 4: Compute the household's decision functions.
Step 5: Compute the stationary distribution of assets for the employed and unemployed agents.
Step 6: Compute the capital stock K and taxes T that solve the aggregate consistency conditions.
Step 7: Compute the tax rate τ that solves the government budget.
Step 8: Update K and τ and return to step 2 if necessary.

In Step 1, we compute the stationary employment N. In our simple Example 7.2.1, employment N_t does not depend on the endogenous variables w_t, r_t, or the distribution of assets a_t in period t. N_t only depends on the number of employed in the previous period N_{t-1}. Given employment N_{t-1} in period $t-1$, we know that next-period employment is simply the sum of the lucky unemployed agents who find a job and the lucky employed agents that keep their job

$$N_t = p_{ue}(1 - N_{t-1}) + p_{ee} N_{t-1}. \tag{7.15}$$

Given any employment level N_0 in period 0, we can iterate over (7.15) for $t = 1, 2, \ldots$. In fact, if we use the probabilities $p_{ue} = 0.50$ and $p_{ee} = 0.9565$ from (7.13) and iterate some ten to twenty times for any given employment level $N_0 \in (0, 1)$, the percentage of employed people in the economy, or equally, the number of employed, N_t, converges to the so-called stationary employment $N = 0.92$. In essence, we are computing the invariant distribution of a simple 2-state Markov-chain. There are, however, more efficient methods in order to compute the stationary values of a Markov-chain process and we describe them in more detail in Section 12.2.

In Step 5, we compute the stationary distribution of assets for the employed and unemployed workers. The wealth distribution is continuous and, hence, is an infinite-dimensional object that can only be computed approximately. Therefore, in general, we apply other methods for its computation than in the case of a finite-state Markov-chain. Three different kinds of methods are presented in order to compute the invariant distribution $F(\epsilon, a)$ of the heterogeneous-agent model. First, we will compute the distribution function on a discrete number of grid points over the assets. Second, we will use Monte-Carlo simulations by constructing a sample of households and tracking them over time. And third, a specific functional form of the distribution function will be assumed and we will use iterative methods to compute the approximation.

Discretization of the Distribution Function. We first consider a method which relies upon the discretization of the state space. Our individual state space consists of two dimensions, the employment status ϵ and the wealth level a. However, the first state variable ϵ can only take two different values, $\epsilon \in \{e, u\}$, so that we only need to discretize the second state variable, the asset level a. Assume that we choose a grid over the state space with m points. If the policy function has been computed with the help of methods that rely upon the discretization of the state space, for example discrete value function approximation, we want to choose a finer grid for the computation of the state space following RÍOS-RULL (1999). Denote the distribution function by $F(\epsilon, a)$ and the density function by $f(\epsilon, a)$.

If we discretize the distribution function, the state variable (ϵ, a) can only take a discrete number of values $2m$. In this case, we are in essence trying to compute the Markov transition matrix between these states (ϵ, a). For the computation of the transition matrix between employment state ϵ, we presented several methods in the previous section and in Section 12.2. These methods are not all applicable for the computation of the transition matrix between the states (ϵ, a). In particular, with current computer technology, we will run into problems using the procedure `equivec1.g` to compute the ergodic distribution due to the curse of dimensionality because the Markov transition matrix has $(2m)^2$ entries. For reasonable values of grid points $2m$, we have a storage capacity problem and GAUSS, for example, will be unable to compute the ergodic matrix.[11]

In the following, we will present two iterative methods that rely upon the discretization of the state space in order to compute the discretized invariant distribution function. Both methods can be applied over a fine grid with a high number of points m. Algorithm 7.2.2 computes the invariant distribution function based on the equilibrium condition (7.12), while Algorithm 7.2.3 computes the invariant density function.

Algorithm 7.2.2 (Computation of the Invariant Distribution Function $F(\epsilon, a)$)

Purpose: *Computation of the stationary equilibrium.*

Steps:

Step 1: Place a grid on the asset space $\mathcal{A} = \{a_1 = a_{min}, a_2, \ldots, a_m = a_{max}\}$ such that the grid is finer than the one used to compute the optimal decision rules.

---

[11] The transition matrix between the $2m$ states mainly consists of zero entries, i.e. the matrix is sparse. As a consequence, we may still be able to apply the procedure `equivec1.g`; however, we have to change the computer code applying sparse matrix methods. In essence, we only store the non-zero entries. Gauss, for example, provides commands that handle sparse matrix algebra.

7.2 The Stationary Equilibrium of a Heterogeneous-Agent Economy 343

Step 2: Choose an initial piecewise distribution function $F_0(\epsilon = e, a)$ and $F_0(\epsilon = u, a)$ over the grid. The vectors have m rows each.

Step 3: Compute the inverse of the decision rule $a'(\epsilon, a)$.

Step 4: Iterate on

$$F_{i+1}(\epsilon', a') = \sum_{\epsilon = e, u} \pi(\epsilon', \epsilon) F_i \left(a'^{-1}(\epsilon, a'), \epsilon \right) \quad (7.16)$$

on grid points (ϵ', a').

Step 5: Iterate until F converges.

The Algorithm 7.2.1 that computes the stationary equilibrium of the heterogeneous-agent economy 7.2.1 and the Algorithm 7.2.2 that computes the invariant distribution function are implemented in the GAUSS program Rch7_disf.g. The individual policy functions are computed with the help of value function iteration with linear interpolation as described in Chapter 4. We compute the value function at $n = 200$ equidistant grid points a_j in the interval $[-2; 3,000]$. The interval is found by some trial and error. Of course, it should contain the steady state capital stock of the corresponding representative agent economy, $K = (\alpha/(1/\beta - 1 + \delta))^{1/(1-\alpha)} N = 247.6$. We would also love to choose an ergodic set so that once the individual's capital stock is inside the set, it stays inside the interval. As it turns out, this interval is rather large and we choose the smaller interval $[-2; 3,000]$ instead. In the stationary equilibrium, all employed agents have strictly positive net savings over the complete interval $[-2; 3,000]$. However, the number of agents that will have assets exceeding 1,500 is extremely small. In fact, fewer than 0.01% of the agents have assets in the range of $[1,500; 3,000]$ so that we can be very confident that our choice of the interval is not too restrictive. The reason for the low number of very rich people is the law of large numbers. We simulate the economy over 25,000 periods or more and sooner or later, the employed agents will loose their job and start decumulating their wealth again.

After we have computed the individual policy function $a'(\epsilon, a)$ for given capital stock K, unemployment compensation b, and income tax τ, we compute the invariant distribution function according to Algorithm 7.2.2. In step 1, we choose an equidistant grid with $m = 3n = 600$ points on $[-2; 3,000]$ for the computation of the distribution function.[12] In step 2, we initialize the distribution function with the equal distribution so that each agent has the steady-state capital stock of the corresponding representative agent economy.

In step 3, we compute the inverse of the policy function $a'(\epsilon, a)$, $a = a'^{-1}(\epsilon, a_j)$, over the chosen grid with $j = 1, \ldots, m$. Since the unemployed agent with low wealth may want to spend all his wealth and accumulate debt equal or exceeding $-a_{min}$, a' may not be invertible when $a' = a_{min}$. For this reason, we define $a'^{-1}(\epsilon, a_{min})$ as the maximum a such that $a'(\epsilon, a) = a_{min}$.[13] Furthermore, the computation of $a'(\epsilon, a)$ involves some type of interpolation, as $a'(\epsilon, a)$ is stored for only a finite number of values $n < m$. We use linear interpolation for the computation of $a'(\epsilon, a)$ for $a_j < a < a_{j+1}$.

In step 4, the invariant distribution is computed. F is computed for every wealth level $a' = a_j$, $j = 1, \ldots, m$, and $\epsilon = e, u$. In the computation, we impose two conditions: 1) If $a'^{-1}(\epsilon, a_j) < a_{min}$, $F(\epsilon, a_j) = 0$, and 2) if $a'^{-1}(\epsilon, a_j) \geq a_{max}$, $F(\epsilon, a_j) = g(\epsilon)$, where $g(\epsilon)$ denotes the ergodic distribution of the employment transition matrix. The first condition states that the number of employed (unemployed) agents with a current-period wealth below a_{min} is equal to zero. The second condition states that the number of the employed (unemployed) agents with a current-period wealth equal to or below a_{max} is equal to the number of all employed (unemployed) agents. In addition, as there may be some round-off errors in the computation of the next-period distribution $F_{i+1}(\epsilon', a')$, we normalize the number of all agents equal to one and multiply $F_{i+1}(e, a')$ and $F_{i+1}(u, a')$ by $0.92/F_{i+1}(e, a_{max})$ and $0.08/F_{i+1}(u, a_{max})$, respectively. Again, we need to use an interpolation rule, this time for the computation of $F_i(\epsilon, a)$. In (7.16), $a_0 = a'^{-1}(\epsilon, a_j)$, $j = 1, \ldots, m$, does not need to be a grid

---
[12] The grid over the asset space for the value function and the distribution function do not need to be equally spaced.
[13] HUGGETT (1993) establishes that a' is strictly non-decreasing in a.

7.2 The Stationary Equilibrium of a Heterogeneous-Agent Economy

point. As we have only stored the values of $F_i(\epsilon, a_0)$ for grid points $a = a_j$, $j = 1, \ldots, m$, we need to interpolate the value of F_i at the point a_0. We use linear interpolation for the computation of $F_i(\epsilon, a)$ for $a_j < a < a_{j+1}$.

Once we have computed the distribution function, we are also able to compute the aggregate capital stock in step 6 of the Algorithm 7.2.1. Therefore, we assume that the distribution of wealth a is uniform in any interval $[a_{j-1}, a_j]$. Thus, with the denotation $\Delta = F(\epsilon, a_j) - F(\epsilon, a_{j-1})$, we have

$$\int_{a_{j-1}}^{a_j} a f(\epsilon, a)\, da = \int_{a_{j-1}}^{a_j} a \frac{\Delta}{a_j - a_{j-1}}\, da =$$
$$\frac{1}{2} \frac{a^2 \Delta}{a_j - a_{j-1}}\bigg|_{a_{j-1}}^{a_j} = \frac{1}{2}\left(F(\epsilon, a_j) - F(\epsilon, a_{j-1})\right)(a_j + a_{j-1}).$$
(7.17)

With the help of this assumption, the aggregate capital can be computed as follows:

$$K = \sum_{\epsilon \in \{e, u\}} \int_{a_{min}}^{\infty} a\, f(\epsilon, a)\, da$$
$$\approx \sum_{\epsilon} \left(\sum_{j=2}^{m} (F(\epsilon, a_j) - F(\epsilon, a_{j-1})) \frac{a_j + a_{j-1}}{2} + F(\epsilon, a_1) a_1 \right).$$
(7.18)

In this computation, we assume that the distribution of the individual asset holdings is uniform in the interval $[a_{j-1}, a_j]$ for $j = 2, \ldots, m$. Of course, the accuracy of our computation will increase with a finer grid and increasing number of grid points m. If the capital stock K is close to the capital stock in the previous iteration, we are done. We stop the computation if two successive values of the capital stock diverge by less than 0.1%.

In the program Rch7_disf.g, we also increase the number of iterations over the invariant distribution as the algorithm slowly converges to the invariant aggregate capital stock K. We start with an initial number of 500 iterations i over $F_i(.)$ which we increase by 500 in each iteration to 25,000 iterations in the iteration $q = 50$ over the capital stock. In the first iterations over the capital stock, we do not need a high accuracy in the computation of the invariant distribution. It saves computational time to increase the accuracy as we get closer to the solution for the aggregate capital stock. Similarly, the value function is getting more accurate as the algorithm converges to the aggregate capital stock. The reason is that we use a better initialization of the value function in each iteration, namely the solution of the last iteration.

The divergence between the capital stocks in iteration 50 and 51 is less than 0.1% so that we stop the computation. The computational time is very long and amounts to 5 hours and 45 minutes using an Intel Pentium(R) M, 319 MHz machine. For our calibration, the invariant aggregate capital stock is $K = 243.7$. The implied values for the wage rate, the interest rate, and the tax rate are $w = 4.770$, $r = 0.513\%$, and $\tau = 1.724\%$. Notice that $\beta = 0.99500 \approx 0.99499 = 1/(1 + r(1-\tau))$, where the deviation is due to numerical round-off errors. As in the representative agent deterministic Ramsey model, the inverse of β is equal to the gross interest rate (after taxes). In the heterogeneous-agent economies of Example 7.2.1, this equation does not always need to hold. For our calibration, the wealth constraint $a \geq a_{min}$ is found to be non-binding. HUGGETT and OSPINA (2001) show that the stationary interest rate is always larger in any equilibrium with idiosyncratic shocks as long as the consumers are risk averse ($\eta > 0$) and if the liquidity constraint binds for some agents. We will also demonstrate this result to hold in the application of Section 7.3.1.

At this point, we need to draw your attention to an important issue. For our Example 7.2.1, it is rather the exception than the rule that Algorithm 7.2.2 converges. For instance, if you increase the number of simulations over the distribution from $\{500; 1,000; 1,500; \ldots ; 25,000\}$ to $\{2,500; 5,000; \ldots ; 12,5000\}$ while you iterate over the capital stock $q = 1, \ldots, 50$, the algorithm will not converge. Similarly, if we choose the uniform distribution over the interval $[-2; 3,000]$:

$$F(\epsilon, a) = \frac{a - a_{min}}{a_{max} - a_{min}}, \quad a \in [a_{min}, a_{max}]$$

for the initial distribution rather than the equal distribution:

$$F(\epsilon, a) = \begin{cases} 1 & \text{if } a \geq K \\ 0 & \text{else,} \end{cases}$$

where all agents hold the representative-agent economy steady-state capital stock, the algorithm does not converge either. Therefore, computing the stationary solution to Example 7.2.1 involves a lot of trial and error. Furthermore, as the computation time amounts to several hours, the solution might be very time-consuming.

Why is convergence so hard to achieve with the help of Algorithm 7.2.2? Consider what happens if we are not close to the stationary solution and, for example, our choice of the stationary capital stock is too low. As a consequence, the interest rate is too high and agents save a higher proportion of their income than in the stationary equilibrium. Consequently, if we choose rather too many time periods for the simulation of the distribution when we start the algorithm (and are far away from the true solution), the distribution of wealth among the employed agents becomes increasingly concentrated in the upper end of the wealth interval $[-2; 3,000]$. As a result, we have a new average capital stock that is much higher than the stationary capital stock. In the next iteration over the capital stock, we might, therefore, also choose a capital stock that is much higher than the stationary capital stock and an interest rate that is lower than the stationary rate. As a consequence, agents may now save a much lower proportion of their wealth than in the stationary equilibrium. For this reason, as we simulate the distribution over many periods, the distribution may now become increasingly centered in the lower part of the interval $[-2; 3,000]$. If we are unlucky, the distribution might alternate between one that is concentrated in the lower part of the interval for individual wealth and one that is concentrated close to the upper end of the interval.

The algorithm, furthermore, fails to converge at all if we do not fix the unemployment compensation b,[14] but, for example, calibrate it endogenously to amount to 25% of the net wage rate in each iteration over the capital stock. In this case, you will not be able to generate convergence even with the choice of the equal distribution for the initial distribution. Our choice of $b = 1.299$ serves as an anchor. If we do not fix it, b starts to alternate between high and low values and, as a consequence, precautionary savings of the employed agents also switch between low and high values, respectively. The convergence of the algorithm improves considerably if we could also fix the wage incomeof the agents. In fact, you will get to know two prominent applications from the literature in Sections 7.3.1 and 8.4.1, where we will exactly do this. By this device, we will be able to compute the stationary equilibrium in the models of HUGGETT (1993) and İMROHOROĞLU (1989) without any problems and convergence can be achieved for any initial distribution. In Section 7.3.2, you will encounter another example where convergence is not a problem. Different from Example 7.2.1, we will then introduce endogenous labor supply. In this case, richer agents supply less labor ceteris paribus and, as a consequence, the wage income decreases with higher wealth and so do savings. This mechanism, of course, improves convergence. In Chapter 8, where we compute the dynamics of the distribution endogenously, this problem does not occur either. In these models, as we will argue, an increase in the average capital stock during the simulation of a time series is then accompanied by a decrease in the endogenous interest rate and, hence, an endogenous reduction of the savings rate.

The convergence of the mean of the distribution during the final iteration over the capital stock is displayed in Figure 7.1. Notice that the rate of convergence is extremely slow. We also made this observation in all of our other applications: Convergence of the distributions' moments[15] only occurs after a substantial

---

[14] We encourage you to recompute Example 7.2.1 with the help of RCh7_disf.g for the cases discussed.

[15] The same result holds for the second and third moments of the distributions.

7.2 The Stationary Equilibrium of a Heterogeneous-Agent Economy 349

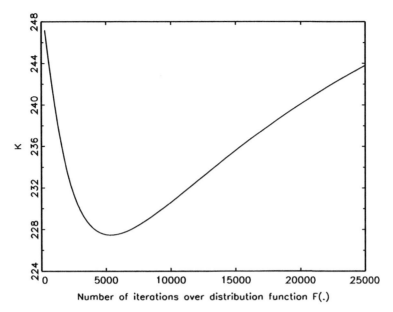

Figure 7.1: Convergence of the Distribution Mean

number of iterations well in excess of several thousands. It is for this reason that the computation of the stationary equilibrium of a heterogeneous-agent economy is extremely time-consuming.

Figure 7.1 also suggests that we should increase the number of iterations over the distribution function further to perhaps $n = 100,000$ or more.[16] In order to judge if our results are already accurate it is instructive to look at Figure 7.2 which displays the convergence of the aggregate capital stock K. At the first iteration over the capital stock, $q = 1$, we only use 500 iterations over the distribution functions and our value functions are highly inaccurate. For higher values of $q > 30$, our aggregate capital stock remains rather constant no matter if we iterate 15,000, 20,000 or 25,000 times over the distribution function (corresponding to q=30, 40, and 50, respectively). This result indicates that we have indeed found the stationary solution.

From the stationary distribution function that we computed with the help of Rch7_disf.g, we can also derive the invariant

---

[16] We encourage the reader to change the program RCh7_disf.g accordingly.

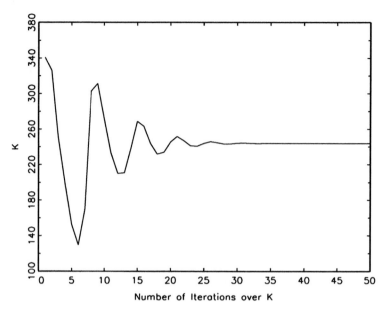

Figure 7.2: Convergence of K

density function. Assuming that the wealth distribution is uniform in the interval $[a_{j-1}, a_j]$, $a_j, a_{j-1} \in \mathcal{A}$, we compute the density such that $f(\epsilon, a) = (F(\epsilon, a_j) - F(\epsilon, a_{j-1}))/(a_j - a_{j-1})$ for $a \in [a_{j-1}, a_j]$. The invariant density function of the employed (unemployed) worker that is computed with the help of Algorithm 7.2.2 is displayed by the solid (broken) line in the Figure 7.3. Notice that the wealth constraint $a \geq a_{min}$ is non-binding and that the number of agents with wealth above $a = 1,000$ is almost zero. Therefore, our choice of the wealth interval $[a_{min}, a_{max}] = [-2, 3000]$ is sensible. Notice further, that, as observed empirically, the distribution is skewed to the left.

Discretization of the Density Function. Alternatively, we may approximate the continuous density function $f(\epsilon, a)$ by a discrete density function, which, for notational convenience, we also refer to as $f(\epsilon, a)$. Again, we discretize the asset space by the grid $\mathcal{A} = \{a_1 = a_{min}, a_2, \ldots, a_m = a_{max}\}$. We assume that the agent can only choose a next-period asset a' from the set $\mathcal{A}$. Of course, the optimal next-period capital stock $a'(\epsilon, a)$ will be

7.2 The Stationary Equilibrium of a Heterogeneous-Agent Economy 351

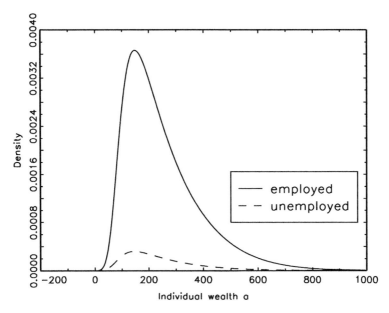

Figure 7.3: Invariant Density Function of Wealth

on the grid with a probability of zero. For this reason, we introduce a simple lottery: If the optimal next-period capital stock happens to lie between a_{j-1} and a_j, $a_{j-1} < a' < a_j$, we simply assume that the next-period capital stock will be a_j with probability $(a' - a_{j-1})/(a_j - a_{j-1})$ and a_{j-1} with the complementary probability $(a_j - a')/(a_j - a_{j-1})$. With these simplifying assumptions, we can compute the invariant discrete density function with the help of the following algorithm:

Algorithm 7.2.3 (Computation of the Invariant Density Function $f(\epsilon, a)$)

Purpose: *Computation of the stationary equilibrium.*

Steps:

Step 1: Place a grid on the asset space $\mathcal{A} = \{a_1 = a_{min}, a_2, \ldots, a_m = a_{max}\}$ such that the grid is finer than the one used to compute the optimal decision rules.

Step 2: Set $i = 0$. Choose initial discrete density functions $f_0(\epsilon = e, a)$ and $f_0(\epsilon = u, a)$ over that grid. The two vectors have m rows each.

Step 3: Set $f_{i+1}(\epsilon, a) = 0$ for all ϵ and a. i) For every $a \in \mathcal{A}$, $\epsilon \in \{e, u\}$, compute the optimal next-period wealth $a_{j-1} \leq a' = a'(\epsilon, a) < a_j$ and ii) for all $a' \in \mathcal{A}$ and $\epsilon' \in \{e, u\}$ the following sums:

$$f_{i+1}(\epsilon', a_{j-1}) = \sum_{\epsilon = e, u} \sum_{\substack{a \in \mathcal{A} \\ a_{j-1} \leq a'(\epsilon, a) < a_j}} \pi(\epsilon'|\epsilon) \frac{a_j - a'}{a_j - a_{j-1}} f_i(\epsilon, a),$$

$$f_{i+1}(\epsilon', a_j) = \sum_{\epsilon = e, u} \sum_{\substack{a \in \mathcal{A} \\ a_{j-1} < a'(\epsilon, a) < a_j}} \pi(\epsilon'|\epsilon) \frac{a' - a_{j-1}}{a_j - a_{j-1}} f_i(\epsilon, a).$$

Step 4: Iterate until f converges.

The Algorithm 7.2.3 is implemented in the GAUSS program Rch7_denf.g. The invariant discrete density function is computed with the same policy functions and parameterization that we were using for the approximation of the invariant distribution function. In particular, we use the equal distribution as initial distribution and increase the number of iterations over the density function from 500 to 25,000 by 500 in each iteration over the capital stock K. Again, we stop the computation as soon as two successive values of the capital stock diverge by less than 0.1% and the number of iterations over the density function is equal to 25,000.

The density function of the employed worker that is computed with the help of Algorithm 7.2.3 is displayed by the solid line with dots in Figure 7.4. The two density functions for the wealth of the employed worker computed with the help of the Algorithms 7.2.2 (solid line with squares) and 7.2.3 almost coincide and cannot be discerned. The two means $K = 243.7$ are identical. However, the computational time is much longer in the case of the discretized distribution function. The computation with the help of Algorithm 7.2.2 takes 40% longer than the one with Algorithm 7.2.3

7.2 The Stationary Equilibrium of a Heterogeneous-Agent Economy 353

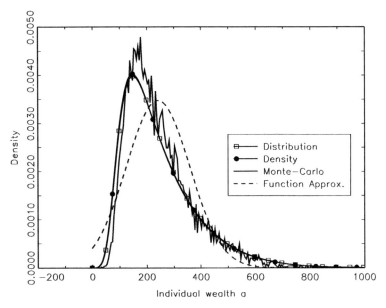

Figure 7.4: Invariant Density Function of Wealth for the Employed Worker

due to Step 3 where we compute the inverse of the policy function $a'(\epsilon, a)$. Table 7.1 summarizes the computational time and the first moment of the distribution for the various methods introduced in this section. In the last row, the number of iterations over the aggregate capital stock is presented.

Monte-Carlo Simulation. The second method to compute the invariant distribution is by means of Monte Carlo simulation. In this method, we choose a large sample of households, typically in excess of some thousands, and track their behavior over time. The household is subject to an employment shock which follows the Markov process (7.13). We simulate this individual employment shock with the help of a random number generator. As a consequence of these random draws, we may have too many or too few employed and unemployed agents so that their respective masses are not equal to those in the stationary distribution. Therefore, we will have to adjust these numbers at the end of each iteration over

Table 7.1

	Invariant Distribution	Invariant Density	Monte Carlo	Exponential Function $n=2$
Mean	243.7	243.7	243.4	246.6
Runtime	5:45	4:05	15:14	3:52
Iterations	51	51	54	63

Notes: Run time is given in hours:minutes on an Intel Pentium(R) M, 319 MHz computer. Iterations are over the aggregate capital stock K.

the distribution of the individual state variable. The algorithm is as follows:

Algorithm 7.2.4 (Computation of the Invariant Distribution Function $F(\epsilon, a)$ by Monte-Carlo Simulation)

Purpose: *Computation of the stationary equilibrium.*

Steps:

Step 1: Choose a sample size N.

Step 2: Initialize the sample. Each household $i = 1, \ldots, N$ is assigned an initial wealth level a_0^i and employment status ϵ_0^i.

Step 3: Compute the next-period wealth level $a'(\epsilon^i, a^i)$ for all $i = 1, \ldots, N$.

Step 4: Use a random number generator to obtain $\epsilon^{i'}$ for all $i = 1, \ldots, N$.

Step 5: Compute a set of statistics from this sample. We choose the mean and the standard deviation of a and ϵ.

Step 6: Iterate until the distributional statistics converge.

The algorithm is implemented in the program Rch7_mont.g. As an initial asset level, the agent is assigned the wealth level $a = 247.6$, which is equal to the steady-state capital stock in the corresponding representative-agent model. Similarly, the agent is employed with the ergodic employment probability $g(e)$ and unemployed with the complementary probability. The statistics of the sample distribution are the mean of the wealth and the standard deviations of the wealth and the employment status. We choose $N = 10,000$ individuals in order to keep the computational time to a reasonable amount and in order to demonstrate the necessity to choose a high number of individuals. Furthermore, we need to adjust the share of employed and unemployed agents in each iteration. As we use a random number generator in step 4, the number of employed agents does not need to be equal to the number of employed agents in the ergodic distribution, $Ng(e)$. If the number of employed agents in any iteration of the simulation is higher than the ergodic number, we select a random set of employed agents and change their employment status to 'unemployed' until the number of employed agents, again, is equal to the respective number in the ergodic distribution. If the number of unemployed agents is higher than the respective number in the ergodic distribution, we change the employment status of the unemployed agents in an analogous way.

We stop the computation after 50 iterations over the aggregate capital stock K. During the last iteration, we simulate the economy over 25,000 periods. The aggregate capital stock K amounts to 243.4 and diverges by less than 0.2% between two successive iterations. The distribution function that is computed with the help of Monte Carlo Simulation is displayed by the solid line in Figure 7.4. Notice that the distribution function has a lower variance than those computed with the help of Algorithms 7.2.2 and 7.2.3. It is also less smooth than these two distributions. In our application, the computational time becomes exorbitant and exceeds 15 hours. It is for this very reason that we do not recommend the use of Monte Carlo simulations in many applications.

Function Approximation. In this section, we introduce a third method to compute the invariant distribution function. In particular, we approximate the distribution function by a flexible functional form with a finite number of coefficients. In Chapter 6, we approximated the policy function with a linear combination of Chebyshev polynomials. Chebyshev polynomials, however, can take a value below zero. For this reason, it is advisable to use another class of functions. We follow DEN HAAN (1997) and use the class of exponential functions for the nth order approximation of the wealth holdings of the agents with employment status $\epsilon \in \{e, u\}$:

$$F(\epsilon, a) = 0 \qquad\qquad a < a_{min}, \qquad (7.20a)$$

$$F(\epsilon, a) = \rho_0^\epsilon \int_{-\infty}^{a} e^{\rho_1^\epsilon x^1 + \ldots + \rho_n^\epsilon x^n} \, dx \qquad a \geq a_{min}. \qquad (7.20b)$$

This approximation allows for a positive number of agents at the borrowing constraint $a = a_{min}$. Of course, this is a very desirable feature of the distribution function in the present case and might be very useful for models with binding constraints and heterogeneity.

For the exponential family, the first n moments capture the same information as the $n+1$ coefficients ρ_i. Suppose that we have found the first n moments of a distribution. In particular, we will use the first two moments, the mean μ^ϵ and the variance $(\sigma^\epsilon)^2$ for the wealth distribution of the employed and the unemployed, respectively. To find the values $\rho^\epsilon = (\rho_0^\epsilon, \rho_1^\epsilon, \rho_2^\epsilon)$, $\epsilon \in \{e, u\}$ that correspond to μ^ϵ and $(\sigma^\epsilon)^2$, we have to solve the following set of non-linear equations:

$$g(\epsilon) = \rho_0^\epsilon \int_{-\infty}^{a_{max}} e^{\rho_1^\epsilon a + \rho_2^\epsilon a^2} \, da, \qquad (7.21a)$$

$$\mu^\epsilon = \rho_0^\epsilon \int_{-\infty}^{a_{max}} \max(a, a_{min}) e^{\rho_1^\epsilon a + \rho_2^\epsilon a^2} \, da, \qquad (7.21b)$$

$$(\sigma^\epsilon)^2 = \rho_0^\epsilon \int_{-\infty}^{a_{max}} (\max(a, a_{min}) - \mu^\epsilon)^2 \, e^{\rho_1^\epsilon a + \rho_2^\epsilon a^2} \, da, \qquad (7.21c)$$

where $g(.)$, again, denotes the ergodic distribution of ϵ. The solution of this non-linear equations problem is not trivial, especially for a higher-order approximation n. As the problem is highly non-linear, a good first-order approximation is needed. In fact, some experimentation with a good starting value for ρ^ϵ might be necessary. Often, one might want to try to start with a low-order approximation of the exponential function, e.g. $n = 1$, and increase n subsequently. In our application, we will use the uniform distribution as an initial guess for $F(.)$.

7.2 The Stationary Equilibrium of a Heterogeneous-Agent Economy

Algorithm 7.2.5 (Approximation of $F(\epsilon, a)$ by an Exponential Function of Order 2)

Purpose: *Computation of the stationary equilibrium.*

Steps:

Step 1: Choose initial moments μ^ϵ and $(\sigma^\epsilon)^2$ for the wealth distribution for $\epsilon \in \{e, u\}$ and compute the corresponding parameters ρ^ϵ of the exponential distribution by solving the non-linear equation problem (7.21a)-(7.21c).

Step 2: Compute the moments of the next-period wealth distribution for the employed and unemployed agents, respectively, e.g. for the employed agent ($\epsilon = e$):

$$\mu^{e'} = \pi(e|e)\rho_0^e \int_{-\infty}^{a_{max}} \max(a'(a,e), a_{min}) e^{\rho_1^e a + \rho_2^e a^2} da$$

$$+ \pi(e|u)\rho_0^u \int_{-\infty}^{a_{max}} \max(a'(a,u), a_{min}) e^{\rho_1^u a + \rho_2^u a^2} da,$$

$$(\sigma^{e'})^2 = \pi(e|e)\rho_0^e \int_{-\infty}^{a_{max}} (\max(a'(a,e), a_{min}) - \mu^e)^2 e^{\rho_1^e a + \rho_2^e a^2} da$$

$$+ \pi(e|u)\rho_0^u \int_{-\infty}^{a_{max}} (\max(a'(a,u), a_{min}) - \mu^u)^2 e^{\rho_1^u a + \rho_2^u a^2} da,$$

and compute the parameters of the distribution function ρ^ϵ, $\epsilon \in \{e, u\}$, corresponding to the computed next-period moments μ' and σ'^2.

Step 3: Iterate until the moments μ^ϵ and σ^ϵ converge.

The GAUSS program RCh7_func.g implements the Algorithm 7.2.5. We parameterize the model and compute the value function in exactly the same way as in the other methods in this section. However, we do not use the equal distribution for the initialization of the distribution function as we would like to start with a continuous function. Therefore, in the first step of Algorithm 7.2.5, the function is approximated by the uniform distribution with $\rho_1^\epsilon = \rho_2^\epsilon = 0$ for $\epsilon \in \{e, u\}$ and $\rho_0^e = \rho_0^u = \frac{1}{a_{max} - a_{min}}$. We choose a smaller interval for individual wealth, $[a_{min}, a_{max}] = [-2; 1,000]$. The approximation, of course, is likely to be more accurate on a smaller interval and our computations in this section indicate that the number of agents with wealth exceeding 1,000 is practically zero. In the second step, we need to compute an integral. We will apply Gauss-Chebyshev quadrature as described in Section 11.3.2 using 20 nodes.

The Algorithm 7.2.5 needs more iterations over the capital stock in order to converge than the other algorithms and stops after 63 iterations. Of course, this is a consequence of our initialization of the distribution function. The computational time is close to the one for the computation of the density function and amounts to 3 hours 52 minutes. The average wealth of the distribution is higher than the one found with the help of the discretization methods presented in Algorithm 7.2.2 and 7.2.3 and amounts to $K = 246.6$. The density function approximated with the help of the Algorithm 7.2.5 is displayed by the broken line in Figure 7.4. Obviously, the density function is much more symmetric and described by smaller variance than in the case of the discretization methods and we are skeptical if the approximation of the density function with the exponential function is accurate.

In conclusion, we like to emphasize that our experience with the computation of the stationary distribution points to the following suggestions: Probably the first best try to compute the stationary distribution is by means of Algorithm 7.2.3 as implemented in the program Rch7_denf.g. If the functional form of the density function is similar to the one of a parameterized function, you may also want to try to approximate the density function using Algorithm 7.2.5. This involves some experience with functional approximation. Approximation methods, however, may better work locally. In our example, approximation over the complete state space is poor. Monte-Carlo simulations have the advantage that they are easy to implement. For our simple Example 7.2.1 with only one dimension for the (continuous) state space, discretization methods are much faster. For state spaces with higher dimension, however, Monte-Carlo simulation may become an important alternative. In Algorithms 7.2.2 and 7.2.3, and different from Algorithm 7.2.4, the computational time increases exponentially with the number of dimensions.

7.3 Applications

7.3.1 The Risk-Free Rate in Economies with Heterogeneous Agents and Incomplete Insurance

Two different phenomena have been observed in financial markets during the last hundred years: 1) the low risk-free rate and 2) the large equity premium. During the last 100 years, the average real return on US Treasury Bills has been about one percent. The average real return on US stocks has been six percent higher. The representative agent model has difficulties to resolve this problem as we discussed in Section 6.3.4. MEHRA and PRESCOTT (1985) show that the representative agent model can only explain the large equity premium and the low risk-free rate if the typical investor is implausibly risk averse. Consequently, the representative agent model in an Arrow-Debreu economy can be regarded as largely unsuccessful to explain the two observations from financial markets. KOCHERLAKOTA (1996) argues that one of the three assumptions of the representative-agent model needs to be abandoned in order to explain the two puzzles: 1) the standard utility function, 2) complete markets, and 3) costless trading. In this section, we try to explain the first phenomenon by abandoning the assumption of complete markets. We further consider a heterogeneous-agent economy in order to have both individuals who supply credit and individuals who demand credit. Following HUGGETT (1993), we compute the equilibrium interest rate which balances credit supply and credit demand and show that the consideration of incomplete asset markets implies a lower risk-free rate.

The Exchange Economy. HUGGETT (1993) considers a simple exchange economy without production. Agents receive an endowment of the only good in the economy. The endowment set $\mathcal{E}$ consists of only two values, $\mathcal{E} = \{e_h, e_l\}$ which we interpret again as in the previous section as the earnings during employment (e_h) and unemployment (e_l). The endowment (or employment) process follows a first-order Markov process with transition probability

$\pi(e'|e) = \text{Prob}(e_{t+1} = e'|e_t = e) > 0$ for $e', e \in \mathcal{E}$. The agent maximizes expected discounted utility:

$$E_0 \left[\sum_{t=0}^{\infty} \beta^t u(c_t) \right], \tag{7.22}$$

where $\beta < 1$ denotes the discount factor and instantaneous utility $u(.)$ is a CES function of consumption:

$$u(c) = \frac{c^{1-\eta}}{1-\eta}. \tag{7.23}$$

As in previous chapters, $1/\eta$ denotes the intertemporal elasticity of substitution.

Agents may hold a single asset. A credit balance of a units entitles the agent to a units of consumption goods this period. To obtain a credit balance of a' goods next period, the agent has to pay $a'q$ goods this period. q is the price of the next-period credit balances and we can interpret $r = 1/q - 1$ as the interest rate in the economy. In addition, there is a credit constraint so that agents cannot run a credit balance below $\bar{a} < 0$. The asset space is denoted by $\mathcal{A}$. Furthermore, assume that the central credit-authority who administers the credit balances has no transaction costs.

The budget constraint of the household is

$$c + a'q = a + e, \quad \text{where } a' \geq \bar{a}. \tag{7.24}$$

We can also formulate the individual's problem recursively with the help of the value function $v(.)$:

$$v(e, a; q) = \max_{c, a'} u(c) + \beta \sum_{e'} \pi(e'|e) v(e', a'; q') \tag{7.25}$$

subject to the budget constraint (7.24).

We consider a stationary equilibrium where the price q of the next-period credit balance a' is constant and the distribution of assets, $F(e, a)$, is invariant. Our definition of the stationary equilibrium allows for a positive mass of households at the borrowing constraint $\bar{a}$, $F(e, \bar{a}) \geq 0$. For $a \geq \bar{a}$, the distribution function $F(e, a)$ is associated with a density function $f(e, a)$. In a stationary equilibrium, furthermore, markets clear so that the average credit balance is equal to zero.

Definition. A stationary equilibrium for the exchange economy is a vector $(c(e, a), a'(e, a), q, F(e, a))$ satisfying:

1. $c(e, a)$ and $a'(e, a)$ are optimal decision rules given q.
2. Markets clear:

$$\sum_e \left(\int_{\bar{a}}^\infty c(e, a) f(e, a) \, da + c(e, \bar{a}) F(e, \bar{a}) \right) \qquad (7.26a)$$

$$= \sum_e \left(\int_{\bar{a}}^\infty e f(e, a) \, da + e F(e, \bar{a}) \right),$$

$$\sum_e \left(\int_{\bar{a}}^\infty a'(e, a) f(e, a) \, da + a'(e, \bar{a}) F(e, \bar{a}) \right) = 0. \qquad (7.26b)$$

3. $F(e, a)$ is a stationary distribution:

$$F(e', a') = \pi(e'|e_h) F(e_h, a_h) + \pi(e'|e_l) F(e_l, a_l), \qquad (7.27)$$

for all $a' \in \mathcal{A}$ and $e' \in \{e_l, e_h\}$ and with $a' = a'(e_h, a_h) = a'(e_l, a_l)$.

A detailed discussion of the equilibrium concept and the uniqueness and existence of the solution can be found in HUGGETT (1993). The model is also calibrated as in HUGGETT (1993). The endowments are set equal to $e_h = 1.0$ and $e_l = 0.1$. One model period corresponds to 8.5 weeks so that 6 periods are equal to one year. The transition probabilities are calibrated such that the average duration of the low endowment shock (unemployment) is two model periods and the standard deviation of annual earnings is 20%:

$$\pi(e'|e) = \begin{pmatrix} 0.925 & 0.075 \\ 0.500 & 0.500 \end{pmatrix}.$$

The equilibrium unemployment rate is 13%.

HUGGETT sets the discount factor equal to $\beta = 0.99322$ implying an annual discount rate of 0.96. In his benchmark case, the risk aversion coefficient η is set equal to 1.5. For the credit limit $\bar{a}$, he considers different values, $\bar{a} \in \{-2, -4, -6, -8\}$. A credit limit of -5.3 corresponds to one year's average endowment.

Programs. The model is computed with the help of the GAUSS routine RCh7_hug.g. The algorithm for this problem is analogous to the Algorithm 7.2.1. First, we make an initial guess of the interest rate r and compute the policy functions. Second, we compute the stationary equilibrium and the equilibrium average asset holdings. Finally, we update the interest rate and return to the first step, if necessary.

For the computation of the policy functions, we applied the techniques developed in Chapter 4. We compute the value function over a discrete grid $\mathcal{A}$. We choose an equispaced grid over $[\bar{a}, a_{max}]$. The upper limit of $\mathcal{A}$ can only be found by experimentation. We set $a_{max} = 4$ and find that agents do not hold assets in excess of a_{max} in the stationary equilibrium of our exchange economy. We further use 100 evenly spaced grid points on $\mathcal{A}$. The invariant distribution is computed over a finer grid. In particular, we use 300 grid points over the same interval.

The value function and optimal policy rules are computed with value function iteration following the Algorithm 4.2.1. In particular, we store the value of the value function at grid points and interpolate linearly between grid point. The value function is initialized assuming that each agent consumes his endowment infinitely and does not change his endowment type. The maximum value of the rhs of the Bellman equation is found by Golden Section search as described in Section 11.6.1. The optimal next-period assets of the employed and unemployed agents are displayed in Figures 7.5 and 7.6, respectively. Notice that only the employed agent has a higher next-period asset a' than the current period asset a and $a'(e, a) > a$ only for $a \leq 1$ (a' crosses the 45 degree line). In other words, the ergodic set for the asset is approximately $[-2, 1]$ and the chosen upper limit a_{max} is not binding. Even if the initial distribution has agents with $a > 1$, after the transition to the stationary equilibrium, no agent has a credit balance exceeding

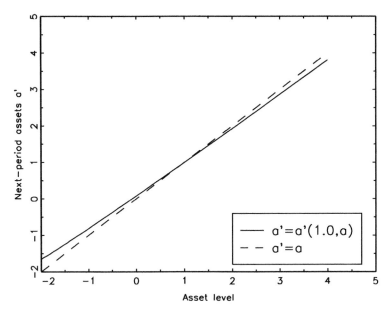

Figure 7.5: Next-Period Assets $a'(e_h, a)$ of the Employed Agent

a_{max}. The change in the asset level $a' - a$ is illustrated in Figure 7.7.

Once we have computed the decision functions $c(.)$ and $a'(.)$, we are able to compute the invariant distribution. We apply the methods of Section 7.2 and iterate over the density function applying Algorithm 7.2.3. We increase the number of iterations over the distribution from 5,000 to 25,000 while we iterate over the interest rate r.

The computation of the stationary equilibrium is almost identical to the one in the production economy 7.2.1 in the previous section with only one exception. In Section 7.2, we analyzed a production economy where the equilibrium interest rate can be computed from the marginal product of capital. In the present exchange economy, we can only guess the equilibrium price of next-period capital q which clears the credit market. We need to modify our computation as follows: First, make two initial guesses of the interest rate $r = 1/q - 1$. We choose the values $r_1 = 0\%$ and $r_2 = 1\%$, respectively. Next, compute the average asset hold-

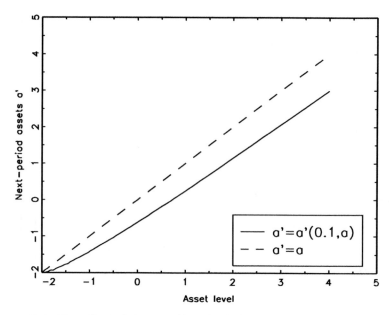

Figure 7.6: Next-Period Assets $a'(e_l, a)$ of the Unemployed Agent

ing of the economy for the two cases, a_1 and a_2. We compute the following guesses for the equilibrium interest rate with the help of the secant method which is described in more detail in Section 11.5.1. Given two points (a_s, r_s) and (a_{s+1}, r_{s+1}) we compute r_{s+2} from:

$$r_{s+2} = r_{s+1} - \frac{r_{s+1} - r_s}{a_{s+1} - a_s} a_{s+1}. \tag{7.28}$$

In order to improve convergence, we use extrapolation and use the interest rate $r = \phi r_{s+1} + (1 - \phi) r_s$ in the next iteration. We choose a value $\phi = 0.5$ in our computation.

We stopped the computation as soon as the absolute average asset level is below 10^{-5}. We need approximately 20 iterations over the interest rate with a computational time of 1 hour 5 minutes using an Intel Pentium(R) M, 319 MHz machine. The stationary distribution is displayed in Figure 7.8 for the employed agent (solid line) and unemployed agent (broken line), respectively. The mean of this distribution is equal to zero.

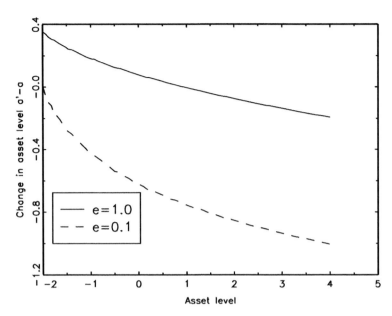

Figure 7.7: Change in Assets $a' - a$

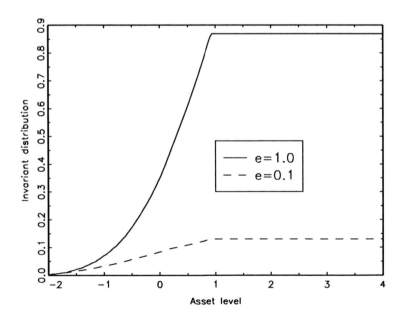

Figure 7.8: Stationary Distribution Function

Table 7.2

Credit limit $\bar{a}$	Interest rate r	price q
-2	-1.27%	1.0129
-4	0.196%	0.9983
-6	0.507%	0.9949
-8	0.627%	0.9938

Results. Table 7.2 presents the results from our computation.[17] Clearly, the interest rate is lower for a stricter credit limit. For a credit limit $\bar{a} = -2$ approximately equal to one half of the average income, the interest rate is even below zero. With a lower credit limit, the interest rate increases as agents can borrow more. For $\bar{a} = -8$, the interest rate is already equal to 0.63% implying an annual rate of 3.65%, which is much higher than the values we observe empirically. In the corresponding representative-agent economy, the risk-free rate is equal to the time preference rate $(1-\beta)/\beta = 0.682\%$. Notice that for a less binding credit constraint, the interest rate approaches the value of the representative agent economy. As noted above, the risk-free rate is strictly less than the time preference rate in a heterogeneous-agent economy with incomplete insurance markets and binding liquidity constraints.

In conclusion, we find that incomplete insurance (against the risk of a negative endowment shock) and credit constraints help to explain that the empirically observed risk-free rate of return is lower than the one found in standard representative-agent models. As a consequence, the representative agent model might not be appropriate for the analysis of some problems in finance, but rather the application of heterogeneous-agent models is warranted.

---

[17] Our results deviate less than 1% from Huggett's result. Notice that our interest rates are computed for one period equal to 1/6 of a year, while the corresponding numbers in Huggett's table 1 are computed for one year instead.

7.3.2 Heterogeneous Productivity and Income Distribution

Naturally, we are unable to study redistributive problems in the representative-agent model. The representative-agent model cannot answer the question how, for example, different fiscal policies affect the distribution of income and wealth. Furthermore, it does not provide an answer to the question how the dispersion of income and wealth arises in the first place.

The explanation of the income and the wealth distribution has been a central objective of the early literature on heterogeneous-agent models. In this section, we analyze how we can model the income heterogeneity of the economy. Like in most heterogeneous-agent models, the source of income heterogeneity like e.g. different levels of individual productivity or education is assumed to be exogenous.[18] Agents with different incomes build up different savings so that the wealth distribution can be computed endogenously and compared to the empirical distribution. We will find that our simple model is unable to replicate the empirical wealth distribution successfully and we will discuss possible solutions to this problem in the next chapters.

This section is organized as follows. First, empirical facts from the US and the German economy with regard to the distribution of wealth and income are reviewed.[19] Second, we discuss the standard way of introducing income heterogeneity into heterogeneous-agent models. Finally, we present a model with income heterogeneity and compute the endogenous invariant wealth distribution. We also analyze the steady-state effects of a fiscal policy reform that consists of a switch from a flat-rate income tax to a consumption tax.

Empirical Facts on the Income and Wealth Distribution.
US households hold different levels of wealth and income. To be precise, we define *earnings* to be wages and salaries plus a fraction

---

[18] As one of the few exceptions, HECKMAN, LOCHNER, and TABER (1998) model the decision to attend college or not endogenously.
[19] This is only a very brief presentation of facts and the interested reader is encouraged to consult any of the references cited in this section.

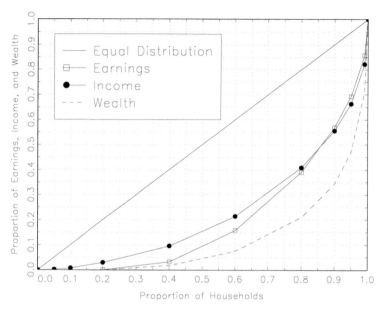

Figure 7.9: Lorenz Curve of US Wealth, Income, and Earnings in 1992

of business income, *income* as all kinds of revenue before taxes, and wealth as the net worth of households.[20] One striking feature of the US (and most industrialized and developed countries) is that wealth is much more unequally distributed than earnings and income. Using data from the 1992 Survey of Consumer Finances, DÍAZ-GIMÉNEZ, QUADRINI, and RÍOS-RULL (1997) compute Gini coefficients of income, earnings, and wealth equal to 0.57, 0.63, and 0.78, respectively. The Lorenz curves of US earnings, income, and wealth in 1992 are displayed in Figure 7.9.[21]

The distribution of income in many countries is a little less concentrated than the one in the US. For example, in Germany, the Gini coefficient of labor income amounts to 0.317, while the distribution of wages is even less concentrated with a Gini coef-

---

[20] For a more detailed definition, see DÍAZ-GIMÉNEZ, QUADRINI, and RÍOS-RULL (1997).

[21] The data on the US economy from the 1992 Survey of Consumer Finance is provided in DÍAZ-GIMÉNEZ, QUADRINI, and RÍOS-RULL (1997).

ficient equal to 0.275.²² Again, wealth is much more unequally distributed in Germany than earnings and the wealth distribution is characterized by a Gini coefficient in the range 0.59-0.89 depending on the assets included in the computation of wealth.²³

One crucial aspect for the analysis of redistributive effects of economic policy is the consideration of mobility. Households move up and down the different income, earnings, and wealth groups. Some people fulfil their and the American dream and become rich. Others have simply bad luck (such as an accident or a divorce) and become poor. A redistribution of income, therefore, may have multiple effects. For example, an increase in income taxes may help to finance a rise in unemployment benefits and redistributes income from the income-rich to the income-poor. This may increase welfare as utility is a concave function of consumption. On the other hand, higher income taxes reduce incentives both to supply labor and to accumulate savings. As a consequence, total income decreases and welfare is reduced because of the increased distortions in the economy. Redistribution comes at the expense of efficiency. If we also consider income mobility, the welfare effect of such a policy is reduced further. The reason is simple: income-poor agents may move up the income hierarchy and will also be harmed by higher taxes and a reduction in the efficiency of the economy in the future. Therefore, if we consider the redistribu-

---

[22] We computed the empirical Gini coefficient of gross wage income using the German Socio-Economic Panel (SOEP) data on annual individual labor income. The SOEP is a wide-ranging representative longitudinal study of private households. It provides information on all household members, consisting of Germans living in the Old and New German States, Foreigners, and recent Immigrants to Germany. The Panel was started in 1984. In 2002, there were more than 12,000 households, and nearly 24,000 persons sampled. For the computation, we deleted individuals with implausibly low or high implied hourly wage rates. We chose 7 DM as the lower limit and 200 DM as the upper limit. The number of deletions is small (about 0.17% at the top and about 6.5% at the bottom of the distribution).

[23] BOMSDORF (1989) analyzes Gini coefficients of the wealth distribution for different kinds of assets in the periods 1973, 1978, and 1983 for West Germany. Within each asset group, Gini coefficients are remarkably stable. The distribution of savings, securities, and real estate in 1983 are characterized by Gini coefficients equal to 0.59, 0.89, and 0.74, respectively.

tive effects of an economic policy in a heterogeneous-agent model, mobility is a crucial ingredient.

The US earnings mobility is presented in the following matrix which is taken from DÍAZ-GIMÉNEZ, QUADRINI, and RÍOS-RULL (1997):[24]

$$\begin{array}{c} \text{1989 Quintile} \\ \text{1984 Quintile} \begin{bmatrix} 0.858 & 0.116 & 0.014 & 0.006 & 0.005 \\ 0.186 & 0.409 & 0.300 & 0.071 & 0.034 \\ 0.071 & 0.120 & 0.470 & 0.262 & 0.076 \\ 0.075 & 0.068 & 0.175 & 0.465 & 0.217 \\ 0.058 & 0.041 & 0.055 & 0.183 & 0.663 \end{bmatrix} \end{array} \quad (7.29)$$

The matrix can be interpreted as follows: The entry in the first row, second column is equal to 0.116 and signifies that 11.6% of the households in the lowest earnings quintile in 1984 were in the second lowest earnings quintile in 1985. Notice that the entries in the diagonal are the maximums of each row so that there is a tendency to remain in the same earnings group. These values range between 40.9% and 85.8% and the low-income group is the least mobile group in the US. The income mobility is almost the same in Germany. For the 1980s, BURKHAUSER, HOLTZ-EAKIN, and RHODY (1997) find that, even though earnings are more unequally distributed in the US than in Germany, the patterns of the quintile to quintile mobility, surprisingly, are similar in the two countries.

Modeling Income Heterogeneity. In models of income heterogeneity, you have to introduce an exogenous source of such heterogeneity. Agents have either different abilities, inherit different levels of wealth or just happen to be unemployed after experiencing bad luck. In Example 7.2.1, agents face idiosyncratic risk of unemployment which they cannot insure against. In this section, we consider income heterogeneity. One can either assume that the individual's earnings y_t^i are stochastic or that labor productivity ϵ_t^i is stochastic. In the first case, labor income is an exogenous

---

[24] DÍAZ-GIMÉNEZ, QUADRINI, and RÍOS-RULL (1997) use data from the 1984, 1985, 1989 and 1990 Panel Study of Income Dynamics in order to compute the transition matrix.

variable, where in the latter case, agents may still be able to vary their labor supply so that labor income $y_t^i = \epsilon_t^i w_t n_t^i$, which is the product of individual productivity ϵ, wage w_t, and labor time n_t^i, is endogenous.

There have been many empirical studies on the time-series behavior of earnings and wages. For example, LILLARD and WILLIS (1978) estimate an AR(1) process for log earnings, while MACURDY (1982) considers an ARMA(1,2) equation for log earnings. They find substantial persistence in the shocks to earnings (the autoregressive coefficients equal 0.406 and 0.974 for annual data, respectively). More recently, some computable general equilibrium models with income heterogeneity and exogenous labor supply have used a regression to the mean process for log-labor earnings. Examples include AIYAGARI (1994), HUBBARD, SKINNER, and ZELDES (1995), HUGGETT (1996), or HUGGETT and VENTURA (2000). In these models, individual earnings y_t follow the process:

$$\ln y_t - \overline{\ln y} = \rho \left(\ln y_{t-1} - \overline{\ln y} \right) + \eta_t, \tag{7.30}$$

where $\eta_t \sim N(0, \sigma_\eta^2)$. ATKINSON, BOURGUIGNON, and MORISSON (1992) report that estimates of the regression towards the mean parameter ρ vary from 0.65 to 0.95 in annual data. In HUGGETT and VENTURA (2000) who study a life-cycle economy, the income is also age-dependent and follows the process:

$$\ln y_j - \overline{\ln y_j} = \rho \left(\ln y_{j-1} - \overline{\ln y_{j-1}} \right) + \eta_j, \tag{7.31}$$

where y_j is the income of the j-year-old household and $\eta_j \sim N(0, \sigma_\eta)$ and $\ln y_1 \sim N(\overline{\ln y_1}, \sigma_{y_1}^2)$. The parameters ρ, σ_{y_1}, and σ_η are calibrated in order to reproduce the Gini coefficient of US earnings of different cohorts and the overall economy on the one hand and the estimated variance of the persistence of the shocks to log earnings on the other hand.

Having specified the log earnings process as an AR(1)-process, we need to discretize the process for computational purpose. The earnings process can easily be approximated with a finite-state Markov chain using the method presented in Section 12.2.

In the following model, labor supply n is endogenous. Accordingly, earnings are endogenous and we cannot specify an exogenous earnings process. Rather, the exogenous variable is productivity ϵ or, similarly, the wage per unit labor, $w\epsilon$, as all agents face the same wage rate w per efficiency unity. Similar to related studies, e.g. VENTURA (1999) or CASTAÑEDA, DÍAZ-GIMÉNEZ, and RÍOS-RULL (1998b), we assume productivity ϵ to follow a first-order Markov chain with conditional transition probabilities given by:

$$\pi(\epsilon'|\epsilon) = Prob\{\epsilon_{t+1} = \epsilon'|\epsilon_t = \epsilon\}, \tag{7.32}$$

where $\epsilon, \epsilon' \in \mathcal{E} = \{\epsilon^1, \ldots, \epsilon^{n\epsilon}\}$. Empirical evidence provided by SHORROCKS (1976) suggests that the dynamics of productivity (and income) may be modeled slightly better by a second-order Markov chain, but the improvement in accuracy is rather small and does not justify the considerable increase in the model's complexity. The productivities $\epsilon \in \mathcal{E} = \{\epsilon^1, \ldots, \epsilon^{n\epsilon}\}$ are chosen to replicate the discretized distribution of hourly wage rates which, in our model, are proportional to productivity. The number of productivities is set equal to $n\epsilon = 5$. We also consider unemployment and let ϵ^1 characterize the state of unemployment by setting ϵ^1 equal to zero. The productivities $\{\epsilon^2, \epsilon^3, \epsilon^4, \epsilon^5\}$ are estimated from the empirical distribution of hourly wages in Germany in 1995. The productivity ϵ^i corresponds to the average hourly wage rate of earners in the $(i-1)$-th quartile. Normalizing the average of the four nonzero productivities to unity we arrive at

$$\{\epsilon^2, \epsilon^3, \epsilon^4, \epsilon^5\} = \{0.4476, 0.7851, 1.0544, 1.7129\}. \tag{7.33}$$

The transition probability into and out of unemployment, $\pi(\epsilon' = 0|\epsilon > 0)$ and $\pi(\epsilon' > 0|\epsilon = 0)$ where ϵ' represents next period's productivity, are chosen in order to imply an average unemployment rate of 10.95% and an average duration of unemployment equal to slightly more than one year (we assume that the average transition takes place in the middle of the year). Periods correspond to one year. Further, we assume that the probability to loose one's job does not depend on the individual productivity.

During unemployment, the worker's human capital depreciates or, equivalently, his productivity decreases. We assume that the worker can only reach productivity ϵ^2 after unemployment and set $\pi(\epsilon' = \epsilon^2 | \epsilon = 0) = 1 - \pi(\epsilon' = 0 | \epsilon = 0)$ and $\pi(\epsilon' > \epsilon^2 | \epsilon = 0) = 0$.[25] The remaining $(n\epsilon - 1)^2 = 16$ transition probabilities are calibrated such that (i) each row in the Markov transition matrix sums to one, (ii) the model economy matches the observed quartile transition probabilities of the hourly wage rate from 1995 to 1996 as given by the German Socio-economic panel data.[26] Our transition matrix is given by:

$$\pi(\epsilon'|\epsilon) = \begin{pmatrix} 0.3500 & 0.6500 & 0.0000 & 0.0000 & 0.0000 \\ 0.0800 & 0.6751 & 0.1702 & 0.0364 & 0.0383 \\ 0.0800 & 0.1651 & 0.5162 & 0.2003 & 0.0384 \\ 0.0800 & 0.0422 & 0.1995 & 0.5224 & 0.1559 \\ 0.0800 & 0.0371 & 0.0345 & 0.1606 & 0.6879 \end{pmatrix}. \quad (7.34)$$

You may want to compare the German wage mobility of the employed agents (the lower 4x4-matrix of (7.34) divided by $1 - 10.95\%$ in order to imply a mass equal to unity for the employed agents) with the US earnings mobility as described by (7.29). Notice, however, that (7.34) considers a 1-year transition period while (7.29) considers a time horizon of 5 years. If you assume that earnings follow an AR(1)-process, you may derive the 5-year transition matrix for Germany by multiplying (7.34) 4 times with itself.[27] If you compare these two matrices, you cannot help noticing that German workers are much more mobile than the US workers. While the diagonal elements in (7.29) are in the range 0.409-0.885, the corresponding elements in the 5-year transition

---

[25] Alternatively, we could have assumed that the worker's productivity does not decrease during unemployment. In this case, however, we had to introduce an additional state variable into the model which makes the computation and calibration even more cumbersome.

[26] A different approach is followed by CASTAÑEDA, DÍAZ-GIMÉNEZ, and RÍOS-RULL (1998b) who calibrate the transition matrix in order to replicate the U.S. earnings and wealth distribution as closely as possible. As a consequence, the diagonal elements of the transition matrix calibrated by CASTAÑEDA, DÍAZ-GIMÉNEZ, and RÍOS-RULL (1998b) are far larger than the empirical counterparts.

[27] See also Section 12.2.

matrix in Germany amount to values between 0.27-0.37. This result, however, is an artefact of our approximation. As pointed out above, the earnings process might be better modeled with the help of an AR(2) process as suggested by SHORROCKS (1976).

Modeling the Distributional Effects of Income Tax Reforms. In the following, we consider a heterogeneous-agent economy where agents differ with regard to their productivity and employment status. Agents are also mobile and, between periods, the productivity and employment status may change. As a consequence, individual labor income also changes. The model is able to account for both the observed heterogeneity in wage rates and the observed labor income mobility in Germany. In addition to the economy studied in Example 7.2.1, we model the household's labor supply decision. As a consequence, the labor income distribution is endogenous. As one major implication of our modeling framework, we are able to replicate the German labor income distribution quite closely. The model follows HEER and TREDE (2003).[28] Three sectors can be depicted: households, firms, and the government.

Households. Households are of measure one and infinitely-lived. Households are heterogeneous with regard to their employment status, their productivity ϵ^j, and their wealth k^j, $j \in [0,1]$.[29] Individual productivity $\epsilon^j \in \mathcal{E} = \{0, 0.4476, 0.7851, 1.0544, 1.7129\}$ follows the first-order finite-state Markov chain with conditional transition probabilities given by (7.32).

---

[28] HEER and TREDE (2003) also study the more complicated case of a progressive income tax. In this case, the policy function for labor supply does not have a continuous derivative and the computation is a little bit more complicated. The interested reader is referred to the original article. For the US economy, we know various other studies which consider the effects of a flat-rate tax versus a progressive income tax. VENTURA (1999) considers a life-cycle model, CASTAÑEDA, DÍAZ-GIMÉNEZ, and RÍOS-RULL (1998a) use a model similar to ours, but with a different calibration procedure for the Markov process (7.32), and CAUCUTT, İMROHOROĞLU, and KUMAR (2003) also model endogenous human capital formation.

[29] As we only consider one type of asset, we will refer to k as capital, wealth, and asset interchangeably.

Agents are not allowed to borrow, $k^j \geq 0$. In addition, the household faces a budget constraint. He receives income from labor n_t and capital k_t which he spends on consumption c_t and next-period wealth k_{t+1}:

$$k_{t+1}^j = (1+r)k_t^j + w_t n_t^j \epsilon_t^j - (1+\tau_c)c_t^j - \tau_y y_t^j + 1_{\epsilon=\epsilon^1} b_t, \quad (7.35)$$

where r_t, w_t, τ_c, and τ_y denote the interest rate, the wage rate, the consumption tax rate, and the tax rate on income y, respectively. $1_{\epsilon=\epsilon^1}$ is an indicator function which takes the value one if the household is unemployed ($\epsilon = \epsilon^1$) and zero otherwise. If the agent is unemployed, he receives unemployment compensation b_t. Taxable income is composed of interest income and labor income:

$$y_t^j = y_t^j(\epsilon_t^j, k_t^j) = rk_t^j + w_t n_t^j \epsilon_t^j. \quad (7.36)$$

Household j, which is characterized by productivity ϵ_t^j and wealth k_t^j in period t, maximizes his intertemporal utility with regard to consumption c_t^j and labor supply n_t^j:

$$E_0 \sum_{t=0}^{\infty} \beta^t u(c_t^j, 1 - n_t^j), \quad (7.37)$$

where $\beta < 1$ is a discount factor and expectations are conditioned on the information set of the household at time 0. Instantaneous utility $u(c_t, 1 - n_t)$ is assumed to be additively separable in the utility from consumption and the utility from leisure is given by:

$$u(c_t, 1 - n_t) = \frac{c_t^{1-\eta}}{1-\eta} + \gamma_0 \frac{(1-n_t)^{1-\gamma_1}}{1-\gamma_1}. \quad (7.38)$$

Our choice of the functional form for utility follows CASTAÑEDA, DÍAZ-GIMÉNEZ, and RÍOS-RULL (1998b). Most quantitative studies of general equilibrium model specify a Cobb-Douglas functional form of utility. In this case, however, the elasticity of individual labor supply with regard to wealth is larger than for the utility function (7.38) and, consequently, the distribution of working hours varies more (and is less in accordance with empirical observations) than for our choice of the utility function (7.38).[30]

---

[30] In Section 3.3.2, you learned about the preferences of GREENWOOD, HERCOWITZ, and HUFFMAN (1988) where the income effect on labor supply is zero.

Notice that this utility function is only applicable to an economy which is not growing over time. To see this point assume that we analyze a perfect-foresight economy with exogenous productivity growth at a rate $g > 0$ and no uncertainty. In steady state, capital, wages and consumption grow at rate $g > 0$, while labor supply is constant. The first-order condition of the household is given by

$$\gamma_0 \frac{(1-n_t)^{-\gamma_1}}{c_t^{-\eta}} = \frac{(1-\tau_y)\epsilon w_t}{1+\tau_c}. \qquad (7.39)$$

Consequently, for a steady state growth $c_{t+1}/c_t = w_{t+1}/w_t = 1+g$ with constant labor supply $n_t = n$, either $g \neq 0$ and $\eta = 1$ or $g = 0$.[31]

Production. Firms are owned by the households and maximize profits with respect to their labor and capital demand. Production Y_t is characterized by constant returns to scale using capital K_t and labor N_t as inputs:

$$Y_t = N_t^{1-\alpha} K_t^\alpha. \qquad (7.40)$$

In a market equilibrium, factors are compensated according to their marginal products and profits are zero:

$$r_t = \alpha \left(\frac{N_t}{K_t}\right)^{1-\alpha} - \delta, \qquad (7.41)$$

$$w_t = (1-\alpha) \left(\frac{K_t}{N_t}\right)^\alpha, \qquad (7.42)$$

where δ denotes the depreciation rate of capital.

Government. Government expenditures consist of government consumption G_t and unemployment compensation B_t. In our benchmark case, government expenditures are financed by an income tax and a consumption tax. We will compare the employment and distribution effects of two tax systems with equal tax revenues: (i) a flat-rate income tax structure and (ii) only a consumption tax ($\tau_y = 0$).

---

[31] See also the Appendix 2.

The government budget is balanced in every period so that government expenditures are financed by tax revenues T_t in every period t:

$$G_t + B_t = T_t. \tag{7.43}$$

Stationary Equilibrium. We will define a stationary equilibrium for a given government tax policy and a constant distribution $F(e, k)$ (and associated density $f(e, k)$) over the individual state space $(e, k) \in \mathcal{E} \times [0, \infty)$.

Definition. A *stationary equilibrium* for a given set of government policy parameters is a value function $V(\epsilon, k)$, individual policy rules $c(\epsilon, k)$, $n(\epsilon, k)$, and $k'(\epsilon, k)$ for consumption, labor supply, and next-period capital, respectively, a time-invariant distribution $F(\epsilon, k)$ of the state variable $(\epsilon, k) \in \mathcal{E} \times [0, \infty)$, time-invariant relative prices of labor and capital $\{w, r\}$, and a vector of aggregates K, N, B, T, and C such that:

1. Factor inputs, consumption, tax revenues, and unemployment compensation are obtained aggregating over households:

$$K = \sum_{\epsilon \in \mathcal{E}} \int_0^\infty k\, f(\epsilon, k)\ dk, \tag{7.44a}$$

$$N = \sum_{\epsilon \in \mathcal{E}} \int_0^\infty \epsilon\, n(\epsilon, k)\, f(\epsilon, k)\ dk, \tag{7.44b}$$

$$C = \sum_{\epsilon \in \mathcal{E}} \int_0^\infty c(\epsilon, k)\, f(\epsilon, k)\ dk, \tag{7.44c}$$

$$T = \tau_y \left(K^\alpha N^{1-\alpha} - \delta K\right) + \tau_c C, \tag{7.44d}$$

$$B = \int_0^\infty b\, f(\epsilon_1, k)\ dk. \tag{7.44e}$$

2. $c(\epsilon, k)$, $n(\epsilon, k)$, and $k'(\epsilon, k)$ are optimal decision rules and solve the household decision problem

$$V(\epsilon, k) = \max_{c, n, k'} \left[u(c, 1-n) + \beta E\left\{V(\epsilon', k') | \epsilon\right\}\right], \tag{7.45}$$

where ϵ' and k' denote next-period productivity and wealth, subject to the budget constraint (7.35), the tax policy, and

the stochastic mechanism determining the productivity level (7.32).
3. Factor prices (7.41) and (7.42) are equal to the factors' marginal productivities, respectively.
4. The goods market clears:

$$F(K, L) + (1 - \delta)K = C + K' + G = C + K + G. \qquad (7.46)$$

5. The government budget (7.43) is balanced: $G + B = T$.
6. The distribution of the individual state variables is constant:

$$F(\epsilon', k') = \sum_{\epsilon \in \mathcal{E}} \pi(\epsilon'|\epsilon) \, F(\epsilon, k), \qquad (7.47)$$

for all $k' \in [0, \infty)$ and $\epsilon' \in \mathcal{E}$ and with $k' = k'(\epsilon, k)$.[32]

Calibration. The model is calibrated as in HEER and TREDE (2003). The preference parameters are set equal to $\eta = 2$, $\gamma_0 = 0.13$, and $\gamma_1 = 10$. The latter two parameters are selected in order to imply an average working time of $\bar{n} = 32\%$ and a coefficient of variation for hours worked equal to $\sigma_n/\bar{n} = 0.367$. The empirical value for Germany for the coefficient of variation is equal to 0.385. The discount factor β amounts to 0.96. The productivities $\epsilon \in \{0, 0.4476, 0.7851, 1.0544, 1.7129\}$ imply a Gini coefficient of wages equal to 0.254, which compares favorably with the empirical counterpart (0.275). The Markov transition matrix is given by (7.34). The income tax rate is set equal to 17.4%, while the consumption tax rate is computed endogenously in order to imply a government consumption share in GDP equal to 19.6%. The replacement ratio of unemployment compensation b relative to the gross wage of the lowest wage quartile is equal to 52%, $b = 0.52\epsilon^2 w \bar{n}^2$, where $\bar{n}^2$ denotes the average working time of the lowest productivity workers. The production elasticity α is set equal to 0.36 and the annual depreciation rate is estimated at $\delta = 4\%$.

---

[32] Our definition of the stationary equilibrium, again, does not use advanced concepts of measure theory. In particular, our formulation of the characteristics of the stationary distribution assumes that the number of households with zero capital is zero. This will be the case for our calibration.

7.3 Applications

Computation. The solution algorithm for the benchmark case with a flat-rate income tax is described by the following steps:

1. Make initial guesses of the aggregate capital stock K, aggregate employment N, the consumption tax τ_c, and the value function $V(\epsilon, k)$.
2. Compute the wage rate w, the interest rate r, and unemployment compensation b.
3. Compute the household's decision functions $k'(\epsilon, k)$, $c(\epsilon, k)$, and $n(\epsilon, k)$.
4. Compute the steady-state distribution of assets.
5. Compute K, N, and taxes T that solve the aggregate consistency conditions.
6. Compute the consumption tax τ_c that solves the government budget.
7. Update K, N, and τ_c, and return to step 2 if necessary.

In step 3, the optimization problem of the household is solved with value function iteration. For this reason, the value function is discretized using an equispaced grid $\mathcal{K}$ of 1,000 points on the interval $[0, k^{max}]$. The upper bound on capital $k^{max} = 12$ is found to never be binding. The value function is initialized assuming that working agents supply 0.2 units of time as labor and that each agent consumes his current-period income infinitely. The matrix that stores the values of the value function has $1,000 \times 5$ entries. We also assume that the agent can only choose discrete values from the interval $[0, 1]$ for his labor supply. We choose an equispaced grid $\mathcal{N}$ of 100 points. The algorithm is implemented in the program RCh7_tax.g.

In order to find the maximum of the rhs of the Bellman equation (7.45), we need to iterate over the next-period capital stock $k' \in \mathcal{K}$ and the optimal labor supply $n' \in \mathcal{N}$ for every $k \in \mathcal{K}$ and $\epsilon^i, i = 1, \ldots, n\epsilon$. This amounts to $1,000 \cdot 100 \cdot 1,000 \cdot 4 + 1,000 \cdot 1,000$ iterations (the labor supply of the unemployed is equal to 0). In order to reduce the number of iterations, we can exploit the fact that the value function is a monotone increasing function of assets k, that consumption is strictly positive and monotone increasing in k, and that the labor supply is a monotone decreasing function of assets k. Therefore, given an optimal next-period capital stock $k'(\epsilon, k_i)$ and labor supply $n(\epsilon, k_i)$, we start the iteration over the next-period capital stock for the optimal next-period capital stock $k'(\epsilon, k_{i+1})$ at $k'(\epsilon, k_i)$ with $k_{i+1} > k_i$. Similarly, we start the iteration over the labor supply n at $n(\epsilon, k_i)$ and decrease the labor supply at each iteration in order to find $n(\epsilon, k_{i+1}) \leq n(\epsilon, k_i)$. We also stop the iteration as soon as $c \leq 0$. The number of iterations is reduced substantially by the exploitation of the monotonicity conditions.

During the first iterations over the aggregate capital stock, we do not need a high accuracy of the value function and the policy functions. Therefore, we iterate only 10 times over the value function and increase the number of iterations to 20 as the algorithm converges to the true solution. By this device, we save a lot of computational time. The computer program is already very time-consuming and runs approximately 5 hours. As a much faster alternative, we may compute the optimal labor supply functions with the help of the first-order condition (7.39) and you will be asked to perform this computation in the exercises. Using the time-consuming value function iteration over both the capital stock and the labor supply, however, might be a good starting point i) if you would like to compute a rough approximation of the final solution as an initial guess for more sophisticated methods or ii) if your policy function is not well-behaved. The latter case might arise in the presence of a progressive income tax where the optimal labor supply does not have a continuous first derivative.[33]

As soon as we have computed the optimal policy function, we might want to check the accuracy of our computation. For this reason, we compute the residual function for the two first-order conditions:

$$R^1(\epsilon, k) \equiv \frac{u_l\left(c(\epsilon, k), 1 - n(\epsilon, k)\right)(1 + \tau_c)}{u_c\left(c(\epsilon, k), 1 - n(\epsilon, k)\right)(1 - \tau_y)w\epsilon} - 1,$$

---

[33] Again, the interested reader is referred to either VENTURA (1999) or HEER and TREDE (2003) for further reference.

$$R^2(\epsilon, k) \equiv E\left[\beta \frac{u_c\left(c(\epsilon', k'), 1 - n(\epsilon', k')\right)}{u_c\left(c(\epsilon, k), 1 - n(\epsilon, k)\right)} \left(1 + r(1 - \tau_y)\right)\right] - 1.$$

The mean absolute deviations are about 1.07% and 3.71% for the two residual functions R^1 and R^2, respectively. The maximum deviations even amount to 11% and 47% for R^1 and R^2, respectively. For a closer fit, we either need to increase the number of grid points or to compute the optimal policy functions at points off the grid (see the exercises).

The remaining steps of the algorithm are straightforward to implement using the methods presented in the previous chapters. For the computation of the invariant distribution, in particular, we discretize the wealth density and compute it as described in the Algorithm 7.2.3.

Results. In Table 7.3, the effects of the two different tax policies on the aggregate capital stock K, the effective labor N, average working hours $\bar{n}$, the real interest rate r, the Gini coefficients of the labor income and the wealth distribution, and the variational coefficient of working time and effective labor are presented. In the stationary equilibrium, the unemployment rate is equal to 10.95%. Aggregate effective labor supply amounts to $N = 0.251$ with an average working time approximately equal to $\bar{n} = 0.324$. Working hours vary less than effective labor. The variational coefficient of working hours (effective labor) is equal to 0.367 (0.691) (see the last two columns of Table 7.3). The two variational coefficients are in very good accordance with the empirical estimates 0.385 (0.638) which we computed using data from the German Socio-Economic Panel during 1995-96. The higher variation of effective labor relative to working hours reflects the optimizing behavior of the working agents who work longer if they are more productive as the substitution effect of a rise in the wage predominates the income effect. The labor supply elasticity with regard to the wage rate, η_{nw}, is moderate, amounting to 0.213 for the average worker. Again, this compares favorably with the data. SIEG (2000), for example, estimates that elasticities for male labor supply are small and in the range between 0.02 and 0.2.

Table 7.3

Tax Policy	K	N	$\bar{n}$	r	Gini wen	Gini k	$\sigma_n/\bar{n}$	σ_{en}/N
τ_y	2.70	0.251	0.324	3.88%	0.317	0.406	0.367	0.691
τ_c	3.24	0.249	0.323	3.01%	0.316	0.410	0.366	0.685

Notes: τ_y refers to the case of a flat-rate income tax and τ_c to the case where the income tax rate is zero and the consumption tax rate τ_c is increased such that the government budget balances.

The aggregate capital stock amounts to $K = 2.70$ which is associated with a capital-output coefficient equal to $K/Y = 4.57$. During 1991-97, the empirical value of K/Y was equal to 5.0 (2.6) in Germany for the total economy (producing sector). The distribution of wealth, however, is not modeled in a satisfactory manner. In our model, the concentration of wealth is too low with a Gini coefficient equal to $\text{GINI}_{wealth} = 0.406$ and compares unfavorably with empirical estimates of the wealth Gini coefficient reported above (which are well in excess of 0.6). We will discuss the reasons why the simple heterogeneous-agent model of this section is unable to replicate the empirical wealth distribution in the next chapters.

In our second tax experiment, we set the income tax rate to zero and increase the consumption tax rate in order to generate the same tax revenues as in the benchmark case. The new steady-state consumption tax amounts to $\tau_c = 39.5\%$ (compared to 20.5% under tax policy (i)). As interest income is not taxed any more, households increase their savings. Accordingly, the aggregate capital stock K rises from 2.70 to 3.24. As labor is not taxed either any more, the incentives to supply labor increases on the one hand. On the other hand, average wealth of the agents is higher and, for this reason, labor supply decreases. The net effect is rather small so that employment approximately remains constant. Associated with these changes of the input factors is a strong decline of the interest rate r by 0.8 percentage points. The distribution effect of the tax reform is rather modest. The Gini coefficient of gross labor income almost remains constant and wealth is only a little more concentrated. Similarly, the coefficients of variation for labor supply and effective labor are hardly affected. In summary, the most marked effect of a switch to a consumption tax consists of a pronounced rise of savings.

Problems

7.1 Function Approximation
Compute the invariant distribution of Example 7.2.1 with the help of functional approximation as described in Algorithm 7.2.5. However, choose an exponential function of order $n = 3$ for the approximation of the density function.

7.2 The Risk-Free Rate of Return
a) Compute the model with production in Example 7.2.1 with $\beta = 0.96$ and for different levels of minimum asset levels, $a_{min} \in \{-2, -4, -8\}$, and show that the equilibrium interest rate decreases with a more binding credit constraint.

b) Compute the equilibrium prices in the exchange economy of HUGGETT (1993) for a higher coefficient of risk aversion $\eta = 3$ and compare your results with table 2 in HUGGETT (1993).

7.3 Unemployment Insurance and Moral Hazard
(adapted from HANSEN and İMROHOROĞLU (1992))

Consider the following extension of Example 7.2.1. The agents' utility function is now a function of both consumption and leisure,

$$u(c_t, l_t) = \frac{\left(c_t^{1-\sigma} l_t^\sigma\right)^{1-\eta}}{1-\eta}.$$

All agents are either offered an employment opportunity ($\epsilon = e$) or not ($\epsilon = u$). The Markov transition matrix is again described by (7.3). Agents that receive an employment offer may either accept the offer and work full-time, $n = 1 - l = 0.3$, or reject the offer and receive unemployment insurance b_t with probability $q(\epsilon_{t-1})$. In particular, the probability of unemployment benefits may be different for a *searcher*, $\epsilon_{t-1} = u$, and a *quitter*, $\epsilon_{t-1} = e$, $q(e) \neq q(u)$. Agents that turn down employment offers in order to extend unemployment spells may have different chances to receive unemployment benefits than quitters. Compute the stationary equilibrium of the model for the parameters of Example 7.2.1. In addition, set $\sigma = 0.67$. Compute the model for different replacement ratios $b_t/(1-\tau)w_t \in \{0.25, 0.5, 0.75\}$ and different probabilities to receive unemployment benefits $g(e) = g(u) = 0.9$, $g(e) = g(u) = 0.8$, $g(e) = 0.9, g(u) = 0.8$. How does the optimal unemployment insurance (as measured by the average value of the households) look like?

7.4 Income Tax Reform
Recompute the model of Section 7.3.2 implementing the following changes:
a) Compute the optimal labor supply with the help of the first-order condition (7.39) (do not forget to check if the constraint $0 \leq n \leq 1$ is binding). Therefore, you need to solve a non-linear equation.

b) Compute the optimal next-period capital k' where k' does not need to be a grid-point. Use linear interpolation to evaluate the value function between grid-points. Apply the Golden Section Search algorithm presented in the Section 11.6.1 in order to compute the maximum right-hand side of the Bellman equation.

7.5 **Superneutrality in the Sidrauski Model** (follows HEER, 2004)

As it is well-known, money is superneutral in the SIDRAUSKI (1967) model. A change of the money growth rate does not affect the real variables of the Ramsey model that is augmented by a monetary sector if 1) money demand is introduced with the help of money-in-the-utility and 2) labor supply is inelastic. Consider the following heterogeneous-agent extension of the standard Sidrauski model that consists of the three sectors households, firms, and the monetary authority:

Households. The household $j \in [0,1]$ lives infinitely and is characterized by her productivity ϵ_t^j and her wealth a_t^j in period t. Wealth a_t^j is composed of capital k_t^j and real money $m_t^j \equiv M_t^j / P_t$, where M_t^j and P_t denote the nominal money holdings of agent j and the aggregate price level, respectively. Individual productivity ϵ_t^j is assumed to follow a first-order Markov-chain with conditional probabilities given by:

$$\Gamma(\epsilon'|\epsilon) = Pr\{\epsilon_{t+1} = \epsilon' | \epsilon_t = \epsilon\},$$

where $\epsilon, \epsilon' \in \mathcal{E} = \{\epsilon_1, \ldots, \epsilon_n\}$.

The household faces a budget constraint. She receives income from labor l_t^j, capital k_t^j, and lump-sum transfers tr_t which she either consumes at the amount of c_t^j or accumulates in the form of capital or money:

$$k_{t+1}^j + (1 + \pi_{t+1})m_{t+1} = (1+r)k_t^j + m_t + w_t \epsilon_t^j l_t^j + tr_t - c_t^j,$$

where $\pi_t \equiv \frac{P_t - P_{t-1}}{P_{t-1}}$, r_t, and w_t denote the inflation rate, the real interest rate, and the wage rate in period t.

The household j maximizes life-time utility:

$$W = \sum_{t=0}^{\infty} \beta^t u(c_t^j, m_t^j, 1 - l_t^j)$$

subject to the budget constraint. The functional form of instantaneous utility $u(.)$ is chosen as follows:

$$u(c, m, 1-l) = \gamma \ln c + (1-\gamma) \ln m.$$

Labor supply is exogenous, $l = \bar{l} = 0.3$.

Production. Firms are also allocated uniformly along the unit interval and produce output with effective labor N and capital K. Let $F_t(k, m, \epsilon)$ (with associated density $f_t(k, m, \epsilon)$) denote the period-t distribution of the household with wealth $a = k + m$ and idiosyncratic productivity ϵ, respectively. Effective labor N_t is given by:

$$N_t = \sum_{\epsilon \in \mathcal{E}} \int_k \int_m \bar{l} \cdot \epsilon \cdot f_t(k, m, \epsilon) \, dm \, dk.$$

Effective labor N is paid the wage w. Capital K is hired at rate r and depreciates at rate δ. Production Y is characterized by constant returns to scale and assumed to be Cobb-Douglas:

$$Y_t = N_t^{1-\alpha} K_t^{\alpha}.$$

In a factor market equilibrium, factors are rewarded with their marginal product:

$$w_t = (1-\alpha) N_t^{-\alpha} K_t^{\alpha},$$
$$r_t = \alpha N_t^{1-\alpha} K_t^{\alpha-1} - \delta.$$

Monetary Authority. Nominal money grows at the exogenous rate θ_t:

$$\frac{M_t - M_{t-1}}{M_{t-1}} = \theta_t.$$

The seignorage is transferred lump-sum to the households:

$$tr_t = \frac{M_t - M_{t-1}}{P_t}.$$

a) Define a recursive stationary equilibrium which is characterized by a constant money growth rate θ and constant distribution $F(\epsilon, k, m)$.
b) Show that in the homogeneous-agent case, $\epsilon^j = \bar{\epsilon}$, money is super-neutral in the stationary equilibrium, i.e. the steady-state growth rate of money θ has no effect on the real variables of the model.
c) Compute the heterogeneous-agent model for the following calibration: Periods correspond to years. The number of productivities is set to $n = 5$ with

$$\mathcal{E} = \{0.2327, 0.4476, 0.7851, 1.0544, 1.7129\}.$$

Further, $\gamma = 0.990$, $\beta = 0.96$, $\alpha = 0.36$, and $\delta = 0.04$. The transition matrix is given by:

$$\pi(\epsilon'|\epsilon) = \begin{pmatrix} 0.3500 & 0.6500 & 0.0000 & 0.0000 & 0.0000 \\ 0.0800 & 0.6751 & 0.1702 & 0.0364 & 0.0383 \\ 0.0800 & 0.1651 & 0.5162 & 0.2003 & 0.0384 \\ 0.0800 & 0.0422 & 0.1995 & 0.5224 & 0.1559 \\ 0.0800 & 0.0371 & 0.0345 & 0.1606 & 0.6879 \end{pmatrix}.$$

Show that money is not superneutral (consider $\theta \in \{0, 5\%, 10\%\}$). Can you think of any reason for this result?

Chapter 8

Dynamics of the Distribution Function

Overview. This chapter presents methods in order to compute the dynamics of an economy that is populated by heterogenous agents. In the first section, we show that this amounts to compute the law of motion for the distribution function $F(\epsilon, a)$ of wealth among agents. In the second section, we concentrate on an economy without aggregate uncertainty. The initial distribution is not stationary. For example, this might be the case after a change in policy, e.g. after a change in the income tax schedule, or during a demographic transition, as many modern industrialized countries experience it right now. Given this initial distribution, we compute the transition to the new stationary equilibrium. With the methods developed in this section we are able to answer questions as to how the concentration of wealth evolves following a change in capital taxation or how the income distribution evolves following a change in the unemployment compensation system. In the third section, we consider a model with aggregate risk. There are many ways to introduce aggregate risk, but we will focus on a simple case. We distinguish good and bad times which we identify with the boom and recession during the business cycle. In good times, employment probabilities increase and productivity rises. The opposite holds during a recession. As one application, we study the income and wealth distribution dynamics over the business cycle in the final section of this chapter. We will need to find an approximation to the law of motion $F' = G(F)$ and introduce you to the method developed by KRUSELL and SMITH (1998).

8.1 Introduction

In the previous chapter, we have focused on the case of a stationary equilibrium where the distribution of wealth is invariant. If we want to compute the non-stationary state of an economy, we face severe problems. Consider Example 7.2.1 that we restate for your convenience. However, we will now also consider the case that the economy is not in the stationary equilibrium.

In our illustrative example, households maximize their intertemporal utility (7.1)

$$E_0 \sum_{t=0}^{\infty} \beta^t u(c_t),$$

subject to the budget constraint (7.4)

$$a_{t+1} = \begin{cases} (1 + (1-\tau_t)r_t) a_t + (1-\tau_t) w_t - c_t, & \text{if } \epsilon_t = e, \\ (1 + (1-\tau_t)r_t) a_t + b_t - c_t, & \text{if } \epsilon_t = u, \end{cases}$$

the employment transition probability (7.3)

$$\pi(\epsilon'|\epsilon) = Prob\{\epsilon_{t+1} = \epsilon' | \epsilon_t = \epsilon\} = \begin{pmatrix} p_{uu} & p_{ue} \\ p_{eu} & p_{ee} \end{pmatrix},$$

the aggregate consistency condition (7.10a)

$$K_t = \sum_{\epsilon_t \in \{e,u\}} \int_{a_{min}}^{\infty} a_t f_t(\epsilon_t, a_t) \, da_t, \tag{8.1}$$

where f_t denotes the density function corresponding to the distribution functions F_t. Notice also that, outside the stationary equilibrium, the income tax rate τ_t is no longer time-invariant.

The dynamics of the distribution are described by

$$F_{t+1}(\epsilon_{t+1}, a_{t+1}) = \sum_{\epsilon_t \in \{e,u\}} \pi(\epsilon_{t+1}|\epsilon_t) F_t\left(\epsilon_t, a_{t+1}^{-1}(\epsilon_t, a_{t+1})\right) \equiv G(F_t),$$

$$\tag{8.2}$$

where $a_{t+1}^{-1}(\epsilon_t, a_{t+1})$ is the inverse of the optimal policy $a_{t+1} = a_{t+1}(\epsilon_t, a_t)$ with regard to current period wealth a_t. Again, we assume that $a_{t+1}(.)$ is invertible which will be the case in our example economy. Given the distribution function F_t, we can compute (8.1) as in (7.18). Furthermore, (8.2) constitutes a functional equation as it describes a map G on a function space.

The factor prices depend on the aggregate capital stock K and the aggregate employment N:

$$w_t = w(K_t, N_t), \qquad (8.3)$$
$$r_t = r(K_t, N_t). \qquad (8.4)$$

The household's first-order condition with respect to its intertemporal consumption allocation depends on consumption in this and the next period, c_t and c_{t+1}:

$$u'(c_t) = \beta E_t \left[u'(c_{t+1}) \left(1 + (1 - \tau_{t+1}) r_{t+1}\right) \right]. \qquad (8.5)$$

Consumption in this and the next period for the employed worker, for example, is given by the budget constraint, $c_t = (1 + (1 - \tau_t) r_t) a_t + (1 - \tau_t) w_t - a_{t+1}$ and $c_{t+1} = (1 + (1 - \tau_{t+1}) r_{t+1}) a_{t+1} + (1 - \tau_{t+1}) w_{t+1} - a_{t+2}$, respectively. What do we need in order to compute the solution to (8.5)? The household observes the following current-period aggregate variables: the aggregate capital stock K_t, aggregate employment N_t, the wage rate w_t, the interest rate r_t, the tax rate τ_t, and the distribution of the assets $F_t(\epsilon_t, a_t)$. Her individual state space consists of her employment status ϵ_t and her individual assets a_t. The solution of (8.5), as we will argue in the following, consists of a time-invariant function $a'(\epsilon, a, F)$ which gives him the optimal next-period capital stock $a_{t+1} = a'(\epsilon_t, a_t, F_t)$ and also the optimal capital stock in two periods, $a_{t+2} = a'(\epsilon_{t+1}, a_{t+1}, F_{t+1})$. Different from the optimal policy function in the computation of the stationary state in Chapter 7, we also include the distribution F as an additional argument.[1]

---

[1] In our specific model, aggregate employment N is constant and we are able to drop it from the list of arguments. In other models with endogenous labor supply, N is also an additional argument of the policy functions, as we will argue below.

Why? In Chapter 7, the aggregate capital stock $K_t = K$ is constant. Therefore, the interest rate and the wage rate are constant, too. In the present model, K_t and, hence, r_t are not constant. As the solution of (8.5) clearly depends on r_t (via c_t and the budget constraint), K_t needs to be an argument of the policy function $a_{t+1} = a'(.)$ as well.[2] K_t, however, can be computed with the help of the distribution $F_t(\epsilon_t, a_t)$ using (8.1) and (7.18). Now we only need to explain why we also have to include the distribution of the individual states, $F_t(\epsilon_t, a_t)$, as an additional argument and do not only use the capital stock K_t instead. Consider again (8.5). The next-period interest rate r_{t+1} appears on the rhs of the equation. Therefore, the households need to predict r_{t+1}. In the stationary economy, this is not a problem: $r_{t+1} = r$. In the representative-agent economy, this is not a problem either: If the agent chooses the next-period capital stock a_{t+1}, he also knows that all other agents (with mass one) choose a_{t+1} such that the aggregate capital stock is given by $K_{t+1} = a_{t+1}$. In the heterogeneous-agent economy, however, the individual household is unable to infer the value of the next-period aggregate capital stock K_{t+1} from her own decision. She needs to know how all the other (infinitely-numbered) households in the economy decide and how much they save. As households with different wealth may also have different savings rates and incomes, she needs to know the distribution of the individual states and to sum the next-period assets over all households in order to compute K_{t+1} and, hence, r_{t+1}.[3] As a consequence, the distribution $F_t(\epsilon_t, a_t)$ is also an argument of the policy function. Put differently, if we consider different distributions $F_t(\epsilon_t, a_t)$ that are characterized by the same mean $\bar{a}_t = K_t$, we will have different next-period distributions $F_{t+1}(\epsilon_{t+1}, a_{t+1})$ which only by chance will all have the same mean $\bar{a}_{t+1} = K_{t+1}$. For this

---

[2] Alternatively, we could have used the variable r_t rather than K_t as an argument of $a'(.)$.

[3] In order to compute the savings of the other households, she also needs to know the policy functions $a'(\epsilon_t, a_t, F_t)$ of the other agents. As all agents, however, have the same optimization problem, the policy functions of all agents are identical. Consequently, as the individual household knows her own policy function, she also knows the policy functions of the other agents.

reason, $F_t(.)$ needs to be included as an additional argument of the policy function.

We are now ready to formulate the recursive problem. We will omit the time index t from the variables in the definition of the recursive equilibrium in order to keep the notation as simple as possible. The household maximizes her value function:

$$V(\epsilon, a, F) = \max_{c,a'} \left[u(c) + \beta E\left\{V(\epsilon', a', F')| \epsilon, F\right\}\right], \qquad (8.6)$$

subject to the budget constraint (7.4), the government policy $\{b, \tau\}$, the stochastic process of the employment status ϵ as given by (7.3), and the distribution dynamics (8.2). Again, the value function is a function of individual states ϵ and a, and the distribution $F(.)$. The distribution of assets, F, however, is an infinite-dimensional object and we cannot track it. Furthermore, finding the law of motion for the distribution, $G(F)$, is not trivial as G is a map from the set of functions (an infinite dimensional space) into itself.

8.2 Transition Dynamics

In this section, we consider the transition dynamics for given initial state in the economy with aggregate certainty as described by the following Example:[4]

Example 8.2.1
Households are allocated uniformly along the unit interval and are of measure one. The individual household maximizes

$$V(\epsilon, a, F) = \max_{c,a'} \left[\frac{c_t^{1-\eta}}{1-\eta} + \beta E\left\{V(\epsilon', a', F')| \epsilon, F\right\}\right],$$

s.t.

$$a' = \begin{cases} (1 + (1-\tau)r)\, a + (1-\tau)w - c, & \text{if } \epsilon = e, \\ (1 + (1-\tau)r)\, a + b - c, & \text{if } \epsilon = u, \end{cases}$$

---
[4] Please keep in mind that aggregate variables like r, w, or τ vary over time, even though we omitted the time index.

$$a \geq a_{min},$$

$$\pi(\epsilon'|\epsilon) = Prob\{\epsilon_{t+1} = \epsilon'|\epsilon_t = \epsilon\} = \begin{pmatrix} p_{uu} & p_{ue} \\ p_{eu} & p_{ee} \end{pmatrix}.$$

The distribution F of (ϵ, a) is described by the following dynamics:

$$F'(\epsilon', a') = \sum_{\epsilon \in \{e,u\}} \pi(\epsilon'|\epsilon)\, F(\epsilon, a'^{-1}(\epsilon, a', F)).$$

Factor prices are equal to their respective marginal products:

$$r = \alpha \left(\frac{N}{K}\right)^{1-\alpha} - \delta,$$

$$w = (1-\alpha)\left(\frac{K}{N}\right)^{\alpha}.$$

The aggregate consistency conditions hold:

$$K = \sum_{\epsilon \in \{e,u\}} \int_{a_{min}}^{\infty} a\, f(\epsilon, a)\, da,$$

$$C = \sum_{\epsilon \in \{e,u\}} \int_{a_{min}}^{\infty} c\, f(\epsilon, a)\, da,$$

$$T = \tau(wN + rK),$$

$$B = \int_{a_{min}}^{\infty} bf(u, a)\, da,$$

where f is the density function associated with F. The government policy is characterized by a constant replacement ratio $\zeta = b/(1-\tau)w$ and a balanced budget: $T = B$.

We will introduce two ways in order to approximate the dynamics of the distribution (8.2). The first way is to use partial information and has been applied by DEN HAAN (1997) and KRUSELL and SMITH (1998). The basic idea is that households do not use all the information at hand, i.e., the distribution F, but only use a little bit of information about F, for example the first moment. By this device, we reduce the infinite-dimensional problem of finding a law of motion for F to a finite-dimensional one. The second method is a shooting method which is only applicable to models with aggregate certainty. In this case, one assumes that one reaches the new stationary equilibrium after T periods and projects a transition path for the prices $\{w,r\}_{t=0}^{T}$ over the next T periods.[5] Given the dynamics of prices and the optimal policy functions, we can compute the dynamics of the distribution. From this, we can update the time path for the factor prices until the algorithm converges. We will present the two approaches in turn. Both approaches assume that the stationary equilibrium is stable and that the distribution function converges to the invariant distribution function.

8.2.1 Partial Information

In this subsection, we assume that agents only use partial information in order to predict the law of motion for the state variable(s) or, equivalently, are boundedly rational. Agents perceive the dynamics of the distribution $F' = G(F)$ in a simplified way. In particular, they characterize the distribution F by I statistics $m = (m_1, \ldots, m_I)$. In Chapter 7, we approximated the invariant distribution function with an exponential function. One might use the parameters ρ_i of the approximated exponential distribution function as statistics m_i, for example. In this section, we follow KRUSELL and SMITH (1998) and use the moments of the distribution function, instead. In particular, we only consider the simple case that agents only use the first moment m_1, i.e. the aggregate capital stock K. KRUSELL and SMITH (1998) find that the forecast error due to the omission of higher moments is extremely small.[6] The economic intuition for this result is straightforward. Higher moments of the wealth distribution only have an effect on

---

[5] If we considered aggregate uncertainty, we would have to project a distribution over the factor prices which would make the problem much more complicated, again.

[6] In Problem 8.1, you will be asked to verify this hypothesis. YOUNG (2005a) points out that higher moments do not influence nor are they influenced by the mean in this class of models. Therefore, they do not affect the forecasting of prices. In addition, he finds that the algorithm is robust to changes in the demographic structure, preferences, and curvature in the savings return.

aggregate next-period capital stock if agents of different wealth levels have different propensities to save out of wealth. However, most agents (except for the very poor ones, who, of course, do not contribute much to total savings) have approximately the same savings rate.[7] Therefore, the omission of higher moments is justified for the present case.

Accordingly, we assume that agents perceive the law of motion for m as follows:

$$m' = H_I(m). \tag{8.7}$$

Given the law of motion for m and the initial value of m, each agent optimizes his intertemporal consumption allocation by solving the following problem:

$$V(\epsilon, a, m) = \max_{c,a'} \left[u(c) + \beta E \left\{ V(\epsilon', a', m') | \epsilon, m \right\} \right], \tag{8.8}$$

subject to the budget constraint (7.4), the government policy $\{b, \tau\}$, the stochastic process of the employment status ϵ as given by (7.3), and the distribution dynamics (8.7). Again, the factor prices are computed as functions of the aggregate capital stock and employment, $w = w(K, N)$ and $r = r(K, N)$, where the aggregate capital stock is given by the first moment of the distribution $K = m_1$.[8] Similarly, we can compute the income tax rate τ and the unemployment compensation b from the balanced budget and for given replacement ratio ζ, aggregate capital K and employment N for every period t:

$$T = \tau N^{1-\alpha} K^\alpha = B = (1-N)b,$$

$$b = \zeta(1-\tau)w = \zeta(1-\tau)(1-\alpha)\left(\frac{K}{N}\right)^{-\alpha}.$$

---

[7] Empirically, high income households save a larger fraction than low income households in the US. HUGGETT and VENTURA (2000), however, show that age and relative permanent earnings differences across households together with the social security system are sufficient to replicate this fact. All these factors are absent from the model in Example 8.2.1.

[8] Again, we drop the time index from the variables in order to keep the notation simple.

The remaining problem is to approximate the law of motion for the moments m of the distribution, $m = m_1 = K$. We will choose a simple parameterized functional form for $H_I(m)$ following KRUSELL and SMITH (1998):

$$\ln K' = \gamma_0 + \gamma_1 \ln K. \tag{8.9}$$

Given the function H_I, we can solve the consumer's problem and compute optimal decision functions. For given initial distribution F_0 with mean K_0, we can simulate the behavior of the economy over time, and, in particular, are able to compute the law of motion for K and compare it to our projection (8.9). If the goodness of fit is not satisfactory, we might want to try a different functional form for H_I or try a higher order I. As it turns out, one moment, $I = 1$, and the functional form (8.9) are quite satisfactory.

The algorithm can be described by the following steps:

Algorithm 8.2.1 (Transition Dynamics with Bounded Rationality)

Purpose: *Computation of the transition dynamics of the distribution function for Example 8.2.1 with given initial distribution F_0 and the dynamics as given by (8.7).*

Steps:

Step 1: Choose the initial distribution of assets F_0 with mean K_0.
Step 2: Choose the order I of moments m.
Step 3: Guess a parameterized functional form for H_I and choose initial parameters of H_I.
Step 4: Solve the consumer's optimization problem and compute $v(\epsilon, a, m)$.
Step 5: Simulate the dynamics of the distribution.
Step 6: Use the time path for the distribution to estimate the law of motion for the moments m.
Step 7: Iterate until the parameters of H_I converge.
Step 8: Test the goodness of fit for H_I. If the fit is satisfactory, stop, otherwise increase I or choose a different functional form for H_I.

Calibration. The model of Example 8.2.1 is calibrated as the model of Example 7.2.1. In particular, the parameter values are given by $\alpha = 0.36$, $\beta = 0.995$, $\eta = 2$, $\delta = 0.005$, $\zeta = 0.25$,[9] and the employment transition matrix:

$$\begin{pmatrix} p_{uu} & p_{ue} \\ p_{eu} & p_{ee} \end{pmatrix} = \begin{pmatrix} 0.500 & 0.500 \\ 0.0435 & 0.9565 \end{pmatrix}.$$

The minimum wealth a_{min}, again, is set equal to -2.

Computation. The algorithm is implemented in the program RCh8_part.g. We choose an equispaced grid $\mathcal{A} = \{a_1, \ldots, a_n\} = \{-2, \ldots, 3000\}$ for wealth a with $n = 201$ nodes. We approximate the distribution over the same interval, but with $n_g = 603$ points. For the aggregate capital stock K, we also choose an equispaced grid $\mathcal{K} = \{K_1, \ldots, K_{n_K}\} = \{140, \ldots, 340\}$. The grid for the aggregate capital stock K consists of $n_K = 6$ nodes and its minimum and maximum values are approximately equal to the stationary equilibrium value of the capital stock, $K = 243.7, \pm 100$.

In the first step, we have to initialize the distribution function. We assume that at time period $t = 0$, the distribution is uniform over an interval approximately equal to $[-2, 300]$. The grid points that are closest to these values are -2 and 297.2 implying an aggregate capital stock K equal to the mean $\bar{K} = 147.6$. If we considered a policy change, e.g. an increase of unemployment benefits, we would have computed the invariant distribution of wealth prior to the policy change with the help of the methods developed in the previous chapter and would have used this distribution for our initialization of F. In the second step, we set the order I equal to one, i.e. consumers only use the first moment of the wealth distribution as information about the distribution F. In step 3, we choose the log-linear law of motion (8.9) for the capital stock and initialize the parameters $\gamma_0 = 0.09$ and $\gamma_1 = 0.95$.

---

[9] Different from Example 7.2.1, we, however, do not need to fix unemployment benefits b in order to ensure convergence of the algorithm, but can rather use the replacement ratio ζ instead. This facilitates the calibration because the replacement ratio ζ is readily observable from empirical data, contrary to the absolute amount of unemployment benefits b.

For the solution of the consumer's optimization problem in step 4, we resort to the methods presented in the first part of this book. In the computer program Rch8_part.g, we use value function iteration with linear interpolation. Our objective is to compute the value function $v(\epsilon, a, K)$ for $\epsilon = e, u$. As we only consider the first moment of the distribution F, the value function is only a function of the employment status ϵ, the individual wealth a, and the aggregate capital stock K. Given the coarse grid for K, we again use linear interpolation to approximate the value function at points off the grid points. The initial value function for the employed agent, $v^e = v(e, a, K)$, and the unemployed agent, $v^u = v(u, a, K)$, are computed at the grid points (a_i, K_j), $i = 1, \ldots, n$ and $j = 1, \ldots, n_K$, assuming that agents consume their current income permanently:

$$v_0^e(a_i, K_j) = \sum_{t=0}^{\infty} \beta^t u\left((1-\tau)r(K_j)a_i + (1-\tau)w(K_j)\right)$$

$$= \frac{1}{1-\beta} u\left((1-\tau)r(K_j)a_i + (1-\tau)w(K_j)\right),$$

$$v_0^u(a_i, K_j) = \frac{1}{1-\beta} u\left((1-\tau)r(K_j)a_i + b(K_j)\right).$$

The interest rate and the wage rate, of course, are functions of the aggregate capital stock K_j (and so are the unemployment benefits $b = \zeta(1-\tau)w(K_j)$).

For a given value function in iteration l, we can compute the value function of the employed agent, for example, in the next iteration $l+1$ from:

$$v_{l+1}^e(a_i, K_j) = \max_{a' \in \mathcal{A}} u(c) +$$
$$\beta \left\{ p_{ee} v_l^e \left(a', e^{\gamma_0 + \gamma_1 \ln K_j}\right) + p_{eu} v_l^u \left(a', e^{\gamma_0 + \gamma_1 \ln K_j}\right) \right\}$$

with

$$c = (1 + (1-\tau)r(K_j)) a_i + (1-\tau)w(K_j) - a'.$$

The value function is computed for every aggregate capital stock $K_j \in \mathcal{K}$ and $a_i \in \mathcal{A}$. The outer loop of the iteration is over the capital stock K_j. Given $K = K_j$, we can compute the factor prices w and r, unemployment compensation b, income taxes τ, and the next-period capital stock K'. For given w, r, b, τ, and K', we can compute the value function $v^e(a, K_j)$ and $v^u(a, K_j)$ at every grid point $a = a_i$. Notice that we do not have to compute the function $v^e(a', K')$ and $v^u(a', K')$ on the rhs of the Bellman equation for $a' \in \mathcal{A}$ at each iteration over the individual wealth $a_i \in \mathcal{A}$ but only once before we start the iteration over a because we know K' in advance. In the program Rch8_part, we store the value functions $v^e(a', K')$ and $v^u(a', K')$ for $K' = K'(K_j)$ and $a' = a_1, \ldots, a_n$ in the vectors ve1 and vu1, respectively, before we start the iteration over $a \in \mathcal{A}$. In order to find the optimum a', we only need to use the values from these one-dimensional vectors (or interpolate linearly between two values $a_m < a' < a_{m+1}$ of these vectors, respectively). The maximization of the rhs of Bellman's equation is performed using the Golden Section Search procedure explained in Section 11.6.1.

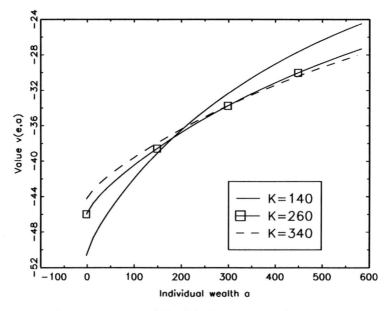

Figure 8.1: Value Function of the Employed Worker

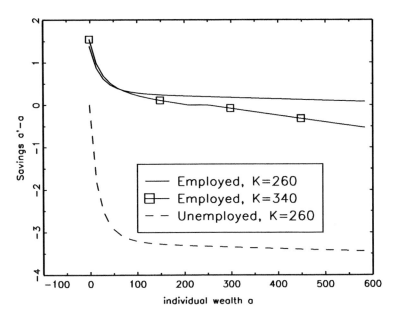

Figure 8.2: Savings of the Workers

The computed value function of the employed consumer is displayed in Figure 8.1. Since the value function of the unemployed worker displays the same behavior we do not show this function. The value function is a concave increasing function of individual wealth a. For the low aggregate capital stock $K = 140$ (solid line), the interest rate r is large and the wage rate w is low. For low wealth a, therefore, the value is lower than the value for a larger aggregate capital stock $K = 260$ or $K = 340$ (the solid line with squares and the broken line). At an intermediate wealth level a, approximately equal to 200, the value function of the agents is again higher for a low capital stock $K = 140$ compared to the other cases with a high capital stock K because the interest income ra becomes a more important component of total income.

The savings behavior of the households is displayed in Figure 8.2. Savings increase with higher interest rate r or, equally, lower capital stock K. The savings function $a'-a$ of the employed worker is presented by the solid line (solid line with squares) for aggregate capital stocks $K = 260$ ($K = 340$). Savings of the unemployed workers are smaller than those of the employed workers as they have lower wage income. The bottom curve in Figure 8.2 displays the savings function of the unemployed worker if the aggregate capital stock is equal to $K = 260$.

In step 5, we compute the dynamics of the distribution function. Given F_0, we can compute F_t from F_{t-1} with the help of the agent's savings function. The optimal policy functions off grid points (a, K) are computed with the help of linear interpolation. The dynamics of the distribution function are displayed in Figure 8.3 which presents the distribution function of the employed workers at period $t = 1$, $t = 10$, $t = 100$, and $t = 2,000$. After 2,000 iterations, the distribution function is stationary and the transition is complete. The mean of the distribution is already constant after 1,000 iterations and amounts to $\bar{K} = 246.9$. The convergence of the distribution's mean is displayed in Figure 8.4.

If you compare Figures 8.4 and 7.1, you cannot help noticing that convergence of the distribution's mean (and also of the higher moments) occurs much faster in Figure 8.4 than in Figure

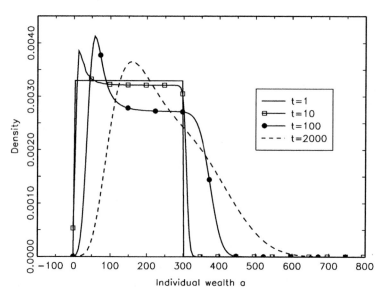

Figure 8.3: Dynamics of the Distribution Function over Time

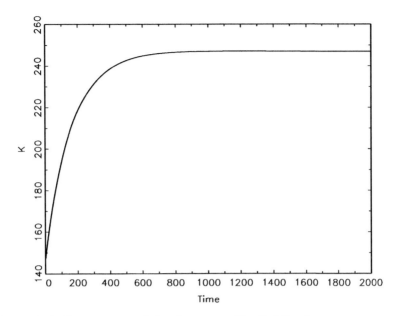

Figure 8.4: Convergence of the Aggregate Capital Stock

7.1, i.e. the distribution function approaches the stationary distribution much faster in the case where we model the transition of the aggregate capital stock. What is the reason for this observation? Assume that we start with a distribution that has an initial mean $\bar{a}_0$ below the stationary mean $\bar{K}$. In the computation of the stationary equilibrium in Chapter 7, we assumed that $K_t = \bar{K}$ in every period, while we use the aggregate capital stock $K_0 = \bar{a}_0$ in the Algorithm 8.2.1. Accordingly, the interest rate is lower in the economy with a constant interest rate than in the economy where we model the transition dynamics. Therefore, agents have lower savings in each period in the constant price economy and the mean of the distribution adjusts at a slower pace.

Consequently, step 5 in Algorithm 7.2.1 where we compute the stationary distribution is much more time-consuming than the corresponding step 5 in Algorithm 8.2.1. However, it would be wrong to conclude that Algorithm 8.2.1 is faster than Algorithm 7.2.1. Importantly, using Algorithm 8.2.1, we i) need to iterate over the law of motion for the aggregate capital stock and ii) have to compute the policy functions for a state space that is characterized by a higher dimension. As a consequence, the computational time may even be much higher in the latter case. In our example, computational time amounts to 3 hours 58 minutes using an Intel Pentium(R) M, 319 MHz computer which is approximately equal to the run time of the Algorithm 7.2.3 presented in Table 7.1. However, we have to consider that we only use a very coarse grid over the aggregate capital stock K in the computation of the value function. Therefore, if we only aim at computing stationary equilibria, we would rather apply the methods presented in Chapter 7.

We can use the time path of the capital stock displayed in Figure 8.4 to update the coefficients γ_0 and γ_1 (step 6 and 7). We use ordinary least squares regression (OLS) to compute the two coefficients (step 6). However, we only use the first 1,000 values for the capital stock $\{K_t\}_{t=0}^T$. Close to the stationary value of K, we only have observation points (K, K') where K and K' are almost equal and display little variation. In this regression, we get a very high R^2, almost equal to one, $R^2 = 1.000$. The computed dynamics (K, K') (simulated) and the regression line (as predicted by the households with the help of (8.9)) are almost identical. Obviously, the fit is extremely good.[10] In step 7, we update the parameters γ_0 and γ_1 until they converge. The final solution for the law of motion for the capital stock is given by

$$\ln K' = 0.0425835 + 0.9922636 \ln K. \tag{8.10}$$

This equation implies a stationary capital stock equal to $\bar{K} = e^{\frac{\gamma_0}{1-\gamma_1}} = 245.8$, which is a little lower than the one computed from the simulation ($\bar{K} = 246.9$). For γ_1 close to one, small errors in the estimation of γ_i, $i = 0, 1$, imply large errors in the computation of $\bar{K}$. For $\gamma_0 = 0.04262$ and $\gamma_1 = 0.9922636$, the stationary capital stock is already equal to $\bar{K} = 246.9$.

---

[10] DEN HAAN (2007) discusses the use of R^2 as a measure of accuracy. He points out that an R^2 equal to 0.99 may still hide large errors. We will not pursue his argument in more detail at this point, but refer the interested reader to his paper.

In the present model, K is a sufficient predictor for factor prices and taxes. We can compute the wage rate w, the interest rate r, the tax rate τ that balances the government budget, and the unemployment compensation if we only know K. In many economic applications, however, the distribution of wealth and its mean are not a sufficient statistic of factor prices. Consider the case of an elastic labor supply. Households maximize their utility by their choice of leisure. For example, if we assume instantaneous utility to be of the form

$$u(c, 1-n) = \frac{\left(c(1-n)^\theta\right)^{1-\eta}}{1-\eta}, \tag{8.11}$$

where n denotes labor supply and $1-n$ is leisure (the time endowment of the household is normalized to one). Labor income of the employed worker is simply the net wage rate times the working hours, $(1-\tau)wn$, and aggregate labor N in period t is given by

$$N = \int_{a_{min}}^{\infty} n(a; K, N)\, f(e, a)\, da, \tag{8.12}$$

where the labor supply of the unemployed is equal to zero. In this case, individual labor supply depends on individual wealth a and, consequently, aggregate labor supply N depends on the distribution of wealth.[11] In this case, we also need to estimate a prediction function for aggregate labor

$$N' = J(N, K), \tag{8.13}$$

that, for example, might take the log-linear form $\ln N' = \psi_0 + \psi_1 \ln N + \psi_2 \ln K$. The household maximizes intertemporal utility subject to the additional constraint (8.13) and the value function $v(\epsilon, a, K, N)$ has the aggregate labor N as an additional argument. Alternatively, you may try to specify aggregate employment N' as a function of next-period capital K:

$$N' = \tilde{J}(K'). \tag{8.14}$$

---

[11] Individual labor supply also depends on the wage rate and, hence, on K and N.

The latter specification has the advantage that the state space is smaller; aggregate employment N is not a state variable any more. Current-period capital K is used to forecast K' which, in turn, is used to forecast N'. You should choose the specification that provides a better fit as, for example, measured by the R^2.[12] Of course, the method developed in this chapter is still applicable to such more complicated problems and you will be asked to solve the growth model with endogenous labor supply in Problem 8.1 using (8.13). In Section 10.2.2, we will apply the Krusell-Smith algorithm to the solution of an OLG model using the forecasting function (8.14). In particular, we will choose the function form $\ln N' = \psi_0 + \psi_1 \ln K'$.

8.2.2 Guessing a Finite Time Path for the Factor Prices

In the previous section, we computed the value function as a function of the aggregate capital stock. If the model is getting more complex, e.g. if we consider endogenous labor supply, endogenous technology or multiple financial assets, the number of arguments in the value function rises and the computation becomes more cumbersome. In this section, we introduce another method for the computation of the transition path that only considers the individual variables as arguments of the value function (or policy functions). The only additional variable of both the value function and the policy functions is time t. The method presented in this section, however, is only applicable to deterministic economies.

Again, we consider the transition to a stationary equilibrium. For the computation, we assume that the stationary equilibrium is reached in finite time, after T periods. Typically, we choose T large enough, say $T = 1,000$ or higher. Furthermore, we can compute the stationary equilibrium at period $t \geq T$ with the help of the methods developed in the previous chapter. We also know the distribution of wealth in the initial period $t = 1$ and, therefore,

---

[12] DEN HAAN (2007) proposes alternative accuracy tests that we do not describe here.

the aggregate capital stock and the factor prices in period $t = 1$ and $t = T$. In order to compute the policy functions during the transition, we need to know the time path of the factor prices, or, equally, the time path of the aggregate capital stock. We start with an initial guess for the time path of the factor prices, compute the decision functions, and with the help of the initial distribution and the computed decision functions, we are able to compute the implied time path of the factor prices. If the initial guess of the factor prices is different from the values implied by our simulation, we update the guess accordingly. The algorithm can be described by the following steps:[13]

Algorithm 8.2.2 (Computation of Example 8.2.1)

Purpose: *Computation of the transition dynamics by guessing a finite-time path for the factor prices*

Steps:

Step 1: Choose the number of transition periods T.

Step 2: Compute the stationary distribution $\tilde{F}$ of the new stationary equilibrium. Initialize the first-period distribution function F^1.

Step 3: Guess a time path for the factor prices r and w, unemployment compensation b, and the income tax rate τ that balances the budget. The values of these variables in both periods $t = 1$ and $t = T$ are implied by the initial and stationary distribution, respectively.

Step 4: Compute the optimal decision functions using the guess for the interest rate r, the wage income w, the tax rate τ and the unemployment compensation b. Iterate backwards in time, $t = T - 1, \ldots, 1$.

Step 5: Simulate the dynamics of the distribution with the help of the optimal policy functions and the initial distribution for the transition from $t = 1$ to $t = T$.

---

[13] The algorithm follows RÍOS-RULL (1999) with some minor modifications.

Step 6: Compute the time path for the interest rate r, the wage w, unemployment compensation b, and the income tax rate τ, and return to step 3, if necessary.

Step 7: Compare the simulated distribution F^T with the stationary distribution function $\tilde{F}$. If the goodness of fit is poor, increase the number of transition periods T.

In step 4, we compute the optimal policy functions by backward iteration. In period T, we know the new stationary distribution, optimal policy functions, and the factor prices. For periods $t = T - 1, \ldots, 1$, we may compute the policy functions $c_t(\epsilon_t, a_t)$ and $a_{t+1}(\epsilon_t, a_t)$ for consumption and next-period assets with the methods developed in Part 1 of this book recursively.[14] For example, we may compute $c_t(\epsilon_t, a_t)$ and $a_{t+1}(\epsilon_t, a_t)$ for given policy functions $c_{t+1}(\epsilon_{t+1}, a_{t+1})$ and $a_{t+2}(\epsilon_{t+1}, a_{t+1})$ from the Euler equation (7.5) with the help of projection methods:[15]

$$\frac{u'(c_t(\epsilon_t, a_t))}{\beta} = E_t \left[u'(c_{t+1}(\epsilon_{t+1}, a_{t+1}))(1 + (1 - \tau_{t+1})r_{t+1}) \right],$$

$$\epsilon_t = e, u,$$

(8.15)

where $c_t(e, a_t) = (1 + r_t(1 - \tau_t))a_t + (1 - \tau_t)w_t - a_{t+1}(e, a_t)$ and $c_t(u, a_t) = (1 + r_t(1 - \tau_t))a_t + b_t - a_{t+1}(u, a_t)$ for the employed and unemployed worker, respectively. Alternatively, we may compute the optimal policy functions with value function iteration from the Bellman equation (7.9):

$$V_t(\epsilon_t, a_t) = \max_{c_t, a_{t+1}} \left[u(c_t) + \beta E_t \left\{ V_{t+1}(\epsilon_{t+1}, a_{t+1}) | \epsilon_t \right\} \right]. \qquad (8.16)$$

In period $t = T - 1$, again, we know the optimal next-period consumption policy c_T and the value function V_T which are equal

---

[14] Notice that with the present method, the policy functions are no longer time-invariant. Optimal consumption $c_t(.)$ depends on the period t via the factor prices w_t and r_t which are not arguments of the policy function. Therefore, we have to compute the optimal policy function in every period $t = 1, \ldots, T$.

[15] You will be asked to compute the transition dynamics using projection methods for the computation of the policy functions in the exercises.

to the stationary optimal consumption policy and value function, respectively. Notice that, in order to compute the policy functions from (8.16), we need to store V_t, $t = 1, \ldots, T$, but the value function is only a function of individual state variables ϵ and a. We iterate backwards in time and compute c_t given V_{t+1}.

As soon as we have computed the optimal consumption policy for $t = 1, \ldots, T$, with the help of the value function or the Euler equation, it is straightforward to simulate the behavior of the economy with the help of the first-period distribution function and compute the time path for the capital stock $\{K_t\}_{t=1}^T$.

Computation. The algorithm is implemented in the program RCh8_gues.g. The model of Example 8.2.1 is calibrated in exactly the same way as in the previous section and we also choose the same grid over the asset space $\mathcal{A}$ for the value function and the distribution function as in the programs RCh8_part.g and RCh7_denf.g. This is very convenient as it allows us to load the stationary policy function and distribution function as an input into the computation.[16] The transition time is set equal to $T = 2,000$ periods. In step 2, the initial distribution is chosen to be the uniform distribution over the interval of $[-2, 297.2]$ as in the previous section.

There are various ways to update the time path for $\{K_t\}_{t=0}^T$ in step 6. We may either resort to a parameterized recursive equation (8.9) as in the previous section and adjust the parameters γ_0 and γ_1 as in the program RCh8_part.g . Alternatively, we may use a tatonnement algorithm guessing an initial sequence $\{K_t\}_{t=0}^T$ and updating it after each iteration i, $K_t^i = K_t^{i-1} + \phi \left(K_t^{i-1} - K_t^i\right)$, $t = 2, \ldots, T-1$. This approach is used in the program RCh8_gues.g. A third approach is to use any standard non-linear equation solution method, e.g. Newton's method to find the sequence $\{K_t\}_{t=0}^T$ that implies the same sequence for the simulated model.[17] In the present case, the algorithm converges after 26 iterations over the

---

[16] The function and distribution are computed with the help of the program RCh7_denf.g as described in Chapter 7.
[17] In Section 10.2.2, we will study the transition for an Overlapping Generations model and use a quasi-Newton method in order to update the factor price time series.

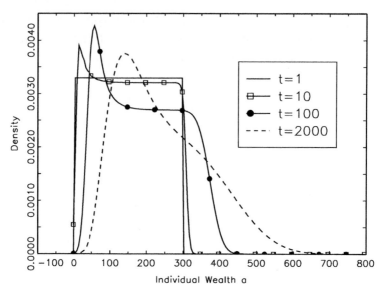

Figure 8.5: The Dynamics of the Distribution Function

sequence $\{K_t\}_{t=0}^{t=2,000}$. The computational time amounts to 7 hours 13 minutes and is longer than the one of Algorithm 8.2.1. Also keep in mind that, different from Algorithm 8.2.1, Algorithm 8.2.2 is using the new steady-state distribution as an input which requires an additional 4 hours of computation, while Algorithm 8.2.1 might need some time-consuming experimentation with an educative guess for the law of motion for the moments. The simulated time path and the projected time path of the capital stock are almost identical and the deviation only amounts to 0.1% on average during the transition.

The dynamics of the distribution over time is displayed in Figure 8.5. From the initial uniform distribution (solid line), the distribution slowly converges to the final distribution in period $T = 2,000$. The distribution at the end of the transition for both Algorithms 8.2.1 and 8.2.2 are compared to the new stationary distribution of wealth a in Figure 8.6. The three distributions have almost the same means, which deviate less than 1% from each other. However, the second moments vary as the right tail of

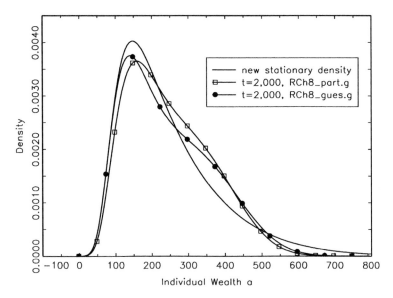

Figure 8.6: Goodness of Fit for the Stationary Distribution

the density functions after 2,000 periods is thinner than the one of the new stationary distribution. A longer transition period may even improve the fit.

8.3 Aggregate Uncertainty

So far, we have only considered individual risk in this chapter. Agents faced the idiosyncratic risk of getting unemployed, while the real interest rate and the factor prices were constant in the stationary state. Only during transition to the new steady state did factor prices vary. In this section, we also take a look at aggregate risk. As in Chapter 1, aggregate risk is introduced by a stochastic technology level Z_t in period t. In particular, the productivity shock follows a Markov process with transition matrix $\Gamma_Z(Z'|Z)$, where Z' denotes next-period technology level and $\pi_{ZZ'}$ denotes the transition probability from state Z to Z'. This assumption is not very restrictive. Given empirical evidence, we assumed in

Chapter 1 that productivity Z_t followed an AR(1)-process. As you also learn in Section 12.2, an AR(1)-process can easily be approximated by a finite Markov-chain.[18]

With stochastic technology level Z_t, aggregate production is given by:

$$Y_t = Z_t N_t^{1-\alpha} K_t^{\alpha}. \tag{8.17}$$

We assume competitive factor and product markets implying the factor prices:

$$w_t = Z_t(1-\alpha)N_t^{-\alpha}K_t^{\alpha}, \tag{8.18}$$
$$r_t = Z_t \alpha N_t^{1-\alpha} K_t^{\alpha-1} - \delta. \tag{8.19}$$

The individual employment probabilities, of course, depend on the aggregate productivity Z_t. In good times (high productivity Z_t), agents have higher employment probabilities than in bad times. The joint process of the two shocks, Z_t and ϵ_t, can be written as a Markov process with transition matrix $\Gamma(Z', \epsilon'|Z, \epsilon)$. We use $p_{Z\epsilon Z'\epsilon'}$ to denote the probability of transition from state (Z, ϵ) to state (Z', ϵ'). In the following, we restrict our attention to a very simple example. The economy only experiences good and bad times with technology levels Z_g and Z_b, respectively, where $Z_g > Z_b$. As before, agents are either employed ($\epsilon = e$) or unemployed ($\epsilon = u$). Consequently, the joint processes on (Z, ϵ) are Markov-chains with 4 states.

Households are assumed to know the law of motion of both $\{\epsilon_t\}$ and $\{Z_t\}$ and they observe the realization of both stochastic processes at the beginning of each period. Besides, the model is identical to the one in Example 8.2.1 and is summarized in the following:

Example 8.3.1

Households are of measure one. The individual household maximizes

---

[18] In the exercises, you will be asked to compute the solution for a heterogenous-agent economy with aggregate uncertainty where the productivity shocks follows an AR(1)-process using Tauchen's method.

$$V(\epsilon, a, Z, F) = \max_{c,a'} \left[\frac{c_t^{1-\eta}}{1-\eta} + \beta E\left\{ V(\epsilon', a', Z', F') \middle| \epsilon, Z, F \right\} \right],$$

s.t.

$$a' = \begin{cases} (1 + (1-\tau)r)\, a + (1-\tau)w - c & \text{if } \epsilon = e, \\ (1 + (1-\tau)r)\, a + b - c & \text{if } \epsilon = u, \end{cases}$$

$$a \geq a_{min},$$

$$\Gamma(Z', \epsilon' | Z, \epsilon) = \text{Prob}\left\{ Z_{t+1} = Z', \epsilon_{t+1} = \epsilon' | Z_t = Z, \epsilon_t = \epsilon \right\}$$

$$= \begin{pmatrix} p_{Z_g e Z_g e} & p_{Z_g e Z_g u} & p_{Z_g e Z_b e} & p_{Z_g e Z_b u} \\ p_{Z_g u Z_g e} & p_{Z_g u Z_g u} & p_{Z_g u Z_b e} & p_{Z_g u Z_b u} \\ p_{Z_b e Z_g e} & p_{Z_b e Z_g u} & p_{Z_b e Z_b e} & p_{Z_b e Z_b u} \\ p_{Z_b u Z_g e} & p_{Z_b u Z_g u} & p_{Z_b u Z_b e} & p_{Z_b u Z_b u} \end{pmatrix}.$$

The distribution of the individual states (ϵ, a) for given aggregate state variables (Z, K) in period t is denoted by $F(\epsilon, a; Z, K)$. The dynamics of the distribution of the individual states are described by the following equations:

$$F'(\epsilon', a'; Z', K') = \sum_{\epsilon} \Gamma(Z', \epsilon' | Z, \epsilon) F(\epsilon, a; Z, K),$$

where $a = a'^{-1}(\epsilon, a'; Z, K)$ is the inverse of the optimal policy function $a' = a'(\epsilon, a; Z, K)$ with respect to individual wealth a and

$$K' = \sum_{\epsilon} \int_a a'\, f(\epsilon, a; Z, K)\, da.$$

Again, f denotes the density function that is associated with F.

Factors prices are equal to their respective marginal products:

$$r = \alpha Z_t \left(\frac{N}{K}\right)^{1-\alpha} - \delta,$$

$$w = (1-\alpha) Z \left(\frac{K}{N}\right)^{\alpha}.$$

The aggregate consistency conditions hold:

$$K = \sum_{\epsilon} \int_a a\, f(\epsilon, a; Z, K)\, da,$$

$$N = \int_a f(e, a; Z, K)\, da,$$

$$C = \sum_{\epsilon} \int_a c(\epsilon, a; Z, K)\, f(\epsilon, a; Z, K)\, da,$$

$$T = \tau(wN + rK),$$
$$B = \int_a bf(u, a; Z, K)\, da.$$

The government policy is characterized by a constant replacement ratio $\zeta = b/(1-\tau)w$ and a balanced budget: $T = B$. _____

Due to the presence of aggregate uncertainty, there are three major changes in the computation of the model compared to the one in Section 8.2: 1) The employment levels fluctuate. 2) When we approximate the distribution function of wealth by its first I moments, for example, the value function is a function of the employment status ϵ, individual wealth a, the first I moments of wealth, and, in addition, aggregate technology Z. 3) The distribution of wealth is not stationary. We will discuss these three points in turn.

1. Individual employment probabilities depend on both the current employment status ϵ and the current and next-period productivity, Z and Z'. Given an employment distribution in period t, the next-period employment distribution depends on the technology level Z' because agents have a higher job finding probability in good times, $Z' = Z_g$, than in bad times, $Z' = Z_b$. As a consequence, we have an additional state variable in the model, namely aggregate employment. As the measure of households is normalized to one, aggregate employment is equal to $N_t = 1 - u_t$, where u_t is the unemployment rate of the economy in period t. As the factor prices are functions of both aggregate capital K_t and employment N_t, the households need to predict the law of motion for both state variables. Aggregate employment of the next period N', however, only depends on aggregate employment in the current period N and the technology level in this and the next-period, Z and Z', because we assume inelastic labor supply. As a consequence, the agents know that next-period aggregate employment is either N_g' if $Z' = Z_g$ or N_b' if $Z' = Z_b$ because they

know the transition matrix Γ, the current period employment N, and the technology level Z.[19]

We will simplify the analysis further following KRUSELL and SMITH (1998). In particular, we assume that the unemployment rate takes only two values u_g and u_b in good times and in bad times, respectively, with $u_g < u_b$. In order to simplify the dynamics of aggregate employment accordingly, the following restrictions have to be imposed on the transition matrix Γ:

$$u_Z \frac{p_{ZuZ'u}}{p_{ZZ'}} + (1 - u_Z) \frac{p_{ZeZ'u}}{p_{ZZ'}} = u_{Z'}, \qquad (8.20)$$

for $Z, Z' \in \{Z_g, Z_b\}$. Condition (8.20) implies that unemployment is u_g and u_b if $Z' = Z_g$ and $Z' = Z_b$, respectively. Consequently, we do not need to consider employment as an additional state variable in the special case (8.20) as the technology level Z' is a sufficient statistic for N'. Example 8.3.1 has already been formulated accordingly and the state variable is given by $\{\epsilon, a, Z, F\}$ rather than $\{\epsilon, a, Z, N, F\}$.[20]

2. In comparison with Example 8.2.1, the households' value function has an additional argument, the technology level Z. The Bellman equation can be formulated as follows:

$$V(\epsilon, a, Z, F) = \max_{c, a'} \left[u(c) + \beta E \left\{ V(\epsilon', a', Z', F') | \epsilon, Z, F \right\} \right].$$

The additional state variable Z has a finite number of values and the computation of the value function is analogous to the one in Section 8.2.1. In particular, the household is assumed to be boundedly rational and to use only the first I moments m in

---

[19] Furthermore, the law of large numbers holds.
[20] To be more precise, if the household knows the distribution $F(\epsilon, a)$, the argument N is redundant (even if Z' is not a sufficient statistic for N'), as he can compute aggregate employment N' with the help of $F'(\epsilon, a)$ and the aggregate consistency condition for N'. In the numerical computation, however, we assume that the household is boundedly rational and only uses the first I moments of the wealth distribution $F(.)$ as information. In this case, he is unable to compute N from the aggregate consistency conditions and we have to introduce N as an additional state variable into the value and policy functions.

order to predict the law of motion for the distribution $F(.)$ with $m_1 = K$:

$$V(\epsilon, a, Z, m) = \max_{c,a'} \left[u(c) + \beta E \left\{ V(\epsilon', a', Z', m') | \epsilon, Z, m \right\} \right].$$

3. In the economy with aggregate uncertainty, the distribution of capital is not stationary. The household's income and savings depend on the aggregate productivity level and, for this reason, the distribution of capital changes over time. Similarly, the law of motion of the aggregate capital stock depends on the productivity level Z and (8.7) needs to be modified:[21]

$$m' = H_I(m, Z). \tag{8.21}$$

In our economy with $Z \in \{Z_g, Z_b\}$, we will again analyze the simple case where the agents only use the first moment $\bar{a} = K$ to predict the law of motion for the aggregate capital stock in good and bad times, respectively, according to:

$$\ln K' = \begin{cases} \gamma_{0g} + \gamma_{1g} \ln K & \text{if } Z = Z_g, \\ \gamma_{0b} + \gamma_{1b} \ln K & \text{if } Z = Z_b. \end{cases} \tag{8.22}$$

As the aggregate productivity is a stochastic variable, we can only simulate the dynamics of the economy. We follow KRUSELL and SMITH (1998) and use 5,000 agents in order to approximate the population. We choose an initial distribution of assets a and employment status ϵ over the 5,000 households in period $t = 1$. In particular, we assume that every household is endowed with the initial asset holdings a_1 equal to the average capital stock of the economy and that the number of unemployed is equal to $u_1 \in \{u_g, u_b\}$. In the first iteration, the average capital stock is computed from the stationary Euler equation $1/\beta - \delta = \alpha(N/K)^{1-\alpha}$ with $N = 0.95$. We simulate the dynamics of the economy over 3,000 periods and discard the first 500 periods. As a consequence, the initialization of the distribution of

---

[21] In an economy, where (8.20) does not hold, employment N is an additional state variable and enters the function $H_I(m, Z, N)$ in (8.21) as an additional variable.

(a,ϵ) in period $t=1$ does not have any effect on our results for the statistics of the distribution in period 501-3,000.[22]

As in the previous section, we use the dynamics of the capital stock $\{K_t\}_{t=501}^{t=3,000}$ in order to estimate the law of motion for K_t in good and bad times, $Z_t = Z_g$ and $Z_t = Z_b$, respectively. For this reason, we separate the observation points (K_t, K_{t+1}) into two samples with either $Z_t = Z_g$ or $Z_t = Z_b$ and estimate the parameters $\{\gamma_0, \gamma_1\}$ for each subsample separately.

In order to simulate the dynamics of the households' wealth distribution, we use the optimal policy functions of the households. The optimal next-period asset level a' is a function of the employment status ϵ, the current period wealth a, the aggregate productivity level Z, and the aggregate capital stock K, $a' = a'(\epsilon, a, Z, K)$. We use value function iteration in order to compute the decision functions so that the individual asset level a and the aggregate capital stock K do not need to be a grid point a_i or K_j, respectively. Therefore, we have to use bilinear interpolation in order to compute the optimal next-period asset level a' off grid points in our simulation (compare Section 11.2.3).

Finally, we impose the law of large numbers on our simulation results. While we track the behavior of 5,000 agents, the fraction of unemployed agents does not need to be equal to u_g in good times and u_b in bad times. We use a random number generator in order to simulate the motion of the individuals' employment status according to their appropriate conditional probabilities. In each period t, we check if the fraction of unemployed is equal to either u_g or u_b. If not, we choose a corresponding sample of agents randomly and change their employment status accordingly. For example, if the number of unemployed agents is above $u_g \times 5,000$ in period t with $Z_t = Z_g$, we choose an unemployed agent at random

---

[22] This Monte-Carlo simulation is very time-consuming. In Chapter 10, we will consider a stochastic economy with 75 overlapping generations. If we simulate such an economy for 1,000 households in each generation, the computational time becomes a binding constraint given the current computer technology. Therefore, we will approximate the cross-sectional distribution by a piecewise linear function. ALGAN, ALLAIS, and DEN HAAN (2008) suggest the approximation of the distribution by a parameterized function and discuss various alternative approaches in the literature.

and switch his employment status to employed and continue this process until $u_t = u_g$.

The complete algorithm can be described by the following steps:[23]

Algorithm 8.3.1 (Computation of Example 8.3.1)

Purpose: *Computation of the dynamics in the heterogenous-agent economy with aggregate uncertainty assuming bounded rationality of the consumers*

Steps:

Step 1: Compute aggregate next-period employment N as a function of current productivity Z: $N = N(Z)$.
Step 2: Choose the order I of moments m.
Step 3: Guess a parameterized functional form for H_I in (8.21) and choose initial parameters of H_I.
Step 4: Solve the consumer's optimization problem and compute $V(\epsilon, a, Z, m)$.
Step 5: Simulate the dynamics of the distribution function.
Step 6: Use the time path for the distribution to estimate the law of motion for the moments m.
Step 7: Iterate until the parameters of H_I converge.
Step 8: Test the goodness of fit for H_I using, for example, R^2. If the fit is satisfactory, stop, otherwise increase I or choose a different functional form for H_I.

Computation. The algorithm is implemented in the program RCh8_unc.g. The computational time amounts to 7 hours 15 minutes on an Intel Pentium(R) M, 319 MHz computer. The parameterization is chosen for a model period equal to one year. We set the technology level equal to $Z_g = 1.03$ in good times and $Z_b = 0.97$ in bad times. The average duration of a boom or a recession is 5 years. Booms and recessions are of equal length so that the transition matrix Γ_Z is equal to:

---

[23] The algorithm follows KRUSELL and SMITH (1998) with some modifications.

$$\Gamma_Z = \begin{pmatrix} 0.8 & 0.2 \\ 0.2 & 0.8 \end{pmatrix}. \tag{8.23}$$

The following conditional employment probabilities are taken from CASTAÑEDA, DÍAZ-GIMÉNEZ, and RÍOS-RULL (1998b) who consider the annual employment mobility for the US economy:

$$\Gamma(\epsilon'|Z' = Z_g, Z = Z_g, \epsilon) = \begin{pmatrix} 0.9615 & 0.0385 \\ 0.9581 & 0.0492 \end{pmatrix},$$

$$\Gamma(\epsilon'|Z' = Z_b, Z = Z_b, \epsilon) = \begin{pmatrix} 0.9525 & 0.0475 \\ 0.3952 & 0.6048 \end{pmatrix}.$$

These employment probabilities imply ergodic distributions with unemployment rates $u_g = 3.86\%$ and $u_b = 10.73\%$, respectively. The conditional employment probabilities for the transition from good times to bad times, $Z = Z_g$ and $Z' = Z_b$ are calibrated such that all unemployed agents stay unemployed and that the unemployment rate is u_b in the next period using (8.20). Accordingly,

$$p_{Z_g e Z_b e} = \frac{1 - u_b}{1 - u_g} P_{Z_g Z_b}.$$

Similarly, the transition matrix from $Z = Z_b$ to $Z' = Z_g$ is calibrated so that all employed agents remain employed and the unemployment rate is equal to u_g in the next period, again making use of (8.20). The asset grids over individual wealth a, $\mathcal{A} = \{a_1 = 0, \ldots, a_{na} = 12\}$ and aggregate capital K, $\mathcal{K} = \{K_1 = 2.5, \ldots, K_{nk} = 5.5\}$, are chosen to be equispaced with $na = 101$ and $nk = 10$ nodes, respectively. The upper and lower bounds of these two intervals are found to be non-binding. The remaining parameters are also taken from CASTAÑEDA, DÍAZ-GIMÉNEZ, and RÍOS-RULL (1998b): $\alpha = 0.36$, $\beta = 0.96$, $\delta = 0.1$, and $\eta = 1.5$.

The optimal policy functions and the value functions behave as expected and, for this reason, we do not display them. Savings $a'(\epsilon, a)$ and consumption $c(\epsilon, a)$ increase with higher individual wealth a, while net savings $a' - a$ decline. In addition, households save a higher proportion of their income for higher interest rates r or, equally, lower aggregate capital K.

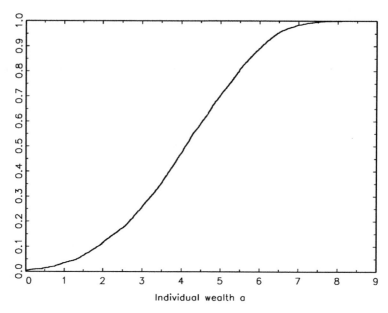

Figure 8.7: Distribution Function in Period $T = 3,000$

The mean capital stock in the economy with uncertainty is equal to $\bar{K} = 4.35$. The distribution of individual wealth in period $T = 3,000$ is graphed in Figure 8.7. In our simulation, the aggregate capital stock in the last period $t = 3,000$ has been equal to $K_{3,000} = 4.18$ and the economy has been in a recession, $Z_b = 0.97$. Notice, in particular, that the upper grid point of $\mathcal{A}$, $a_{na} = 12$, is not binding and the maximum wealth of the households is approximately equal to $a = 7.5$.

The law of motion for capital (8.22) is estimated at:

$$\ln K' = \begin{cases} 0.178 + 0.886 \ln K & \text{if } Z = Z_g, \\ 0.135 + 0.900 \ln K & \text{if } Z = Z_b. \end{cases} \quad (8.25)$$

Using (8.25), the mean prediction error of the capital stock amounts to 3.2%. The dynamics of the capital stock in our simulation are displayed in Figure 8.8. The standard deviation of capital[24] is equal to $\sigma_K = 0.195$. Our simple model falls short of

---

[24] The log of the time series of the aggregate capital stock K_t, output y_t, and aggregate consumption c_t have been HP-filtered with $\mu = 100$.

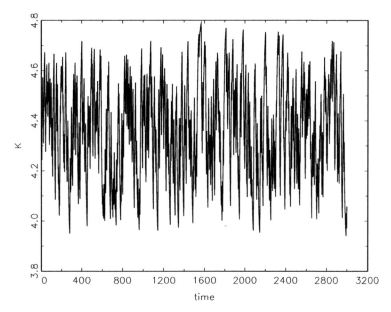

Figure 8.8: Time Path of the Aggregate Capital Stock K_t

replicating important business cycle characteristics. For example, the standard deviation of output ($\sigma_y = 0.458\%$) is much smaller than the one of consumption ($\sigma_c = 2.97\%$). In the next section, you will get to know two more elaborate models of the business cycle dynamics.

8.4 Applications

In this section, we will look at two prominent applications of computational methods for heterogenous-agent economies with uncertainty that consider business cycles dynamics. One of the first papers in the area of computable general equilibrium models of heterogenous-agent economies is the article by AYŞE İMROHOROĞLU (1989) published in the *Journal of Political Economy*. Her pioneering work, even though the model is only partial equilibrium, can be considered as the very first milestone in the literature on computable heterogeneous-agent economies that our second part of this book is concerned with.[25] We will recompute her benchmark equilibrium. She shows that the costs of business cycles depend on the assumption whether agents can borrow or not. Her equilibrium is partial in the sense that the factor prices are exogenous. As a consequence, agents do not need to project the cyclical behavior of the interest rate and the labor income. They only need to consider the probability of being employed in the next period. Therefore, the computation is straightforward applying the methods presented in Chapter 7.[26] In the second application, we consider the business cycle dynamics of the income distribution. Our model follows CASTAÑEDA, DÍAZ-GIMÉNEZ, and RÍOS-RULL (1998b) closely and we need to apply the methods developed in the previous section.

8.4.1 Costs of Business Cycles with Liquidity Constraints and Indivisibilities

The model. The model in İMROHOROĞLU (1989) is similar to the economy described in Example 8.2.1. There are many infinitely lived households of mass one who differ with regard to the assets a_t and their employment status ϵ_t. Households maximize their intertemporal utility

$$E_0 \sum_{t=0}^{\infty} \beta^t u(c_t), \qquad (8.26)$$

where $\beta < 1$ is the subjective discount factor and expectations are conditioned on the information set at time 0. At time zero,

---

[25] Moreover, Ayşe İmrohoroğlu was already publishing other important contributions in the field of computable heterogeneous-agent economies at this very early time, where the computer technology started to allow for such computations. Among others, she also made an important contribution to the study of the welfare costs of inflation that was published in the *Journal of Economic Dynamics and Control* in 1992.

[26] We, however, included this model in the present section because it also studies the effects of business cycle fluctuations.

the agent knows his beginning-of-period wealth a_0 and his employment status $\epsilon_0 \in \{e, u\}$. The agent's instantaneous utility function is a CES function of his consumption:

$$u(c_t) = \frac{c_t^{1-\eta}}{1-\eta}, \quad \eta > 0, \tag{8.27}$$

where η, again, denotes the coefficient of relative risk aversion.

If $\epsilon = e$ ($\epsilon = u$), the agent is employed (unemployed). If the agent is employed he produces $y(e) = 1$ units of income. If he is unemployed, he engages in home production and produces $y(u) = \theta$ units of consumption goods, where $0 < \theta < 1$. Furthermore, the agents cannot insure against unemployment.

İMROHOROĞLU (1989) considers two different economies: In the first economy, agents cannot borrow, $a \geq 0$. They can insure against fluctuations in their income by storing the asset. The budget constraint is given by:

$$a_{t+1} = a_t - c_t + y(\epsilon_t). \tag{8.28}$$

In the second economy, the agents can borrow at rate r_b. Agents can save assets by either lending at rate $r_l = 0$ or storing them. There is an intermediation sector between borrowing and lending households. The borrowing rate r_b exceeds the lending rate $r_b > r_l$. The intermediation costs, which are equal to the difference of the borrowing rate and the lending rate times the borrowed assets, are private costs and reduce total consumption.

In the case without business cycle fluctuations, the individual-specific employment state is assumed to follow a first-order Markov chain. The conditional transition matrix is given by:

$$\pi(\epsilon'|\epsilon) = Prob\{\epsilon_{t+1} = \epsilon'|\epsilon_t = \epsilon\} = \begin{pmatrix} p_{uu} & p_{ue} \\ p_{eu} & p_{ee} \end{pmatrix}, \tag{8.29}$$

where, for example, $Prob\{\epsilon_{t+1} = e|\epsilon_t = u\} = p_{ue}$ is the probability that an agent will be employed in period $t+1$ given that the agent is unemployed in period t.

In the case with business cycle fluctuations, the economy experiences good and bad times. In good times, employment is higher and both employed and unemployed agents have a higher probability to find a job. We can distinguish four states $s \in \{s_1, s_2, s_3, s_4\}$: $s = s_1$) the agent is employed in good times, $s = s_2$) the agent is unemployed in good times, $s = s_3$) the agent is employed in bad times, $s = s_4$) the agent is unemployed in bad times. The transition between the four states is described by a first-order Markov chain with conditional transition matrix $\pi(s'|s)$. The economies with and without business cycles have the same average unemployment rate.

Calibration. The model is calibrated for a model period of 6 weeks or approximately 1/8 of a year. The discount factor $\beta = 0.995$ implies an annual subjective time discount rate of approximately 4%. The relative coefficient of risk aversion η is set equal to 1.5. The annual borrowing rate is set equal to 8% corresponding to a rate of $r_b = 1\%$ in the model period.

The conditional transition matrices $\pi(\epsilon'|\epsilon)$ and $\pi(s'|s)$ are calibrated so that average unemployment is 8%, unemployment in good times and bad times is 4% and 12%, respectively. In the economy with business cycles, the average duration of unemployment is 1.66 and 2.33 periods (10 and 14 weeks) in good and bad times, respectively. Furthermore, the probability that good or bad times continue for another period is set equal to 0.9375 so that the average duration of good and bad times is equal to 24 months implying an average duration of the business cycle equal to 4 years. The transition matrices are then given by:

$$\pi(\epsilon'|\epsilon) = \begin{pmatrix} 0.5000 & 0.5000 \\ 0.9565 & 0.0435 \end{pmatrix}, \qquad (8.30)$$

and

$$\pi(s'|s) = \begin{pmatrix} 0.9141 & 0.0234 & 0.0587 & 0.0038 \\ 0.5625 & 0.3750 & 0.0269 & 0.0356 \\ 0.0608 & 0.0016 & 0.8813 & 0.0563 \\ 0.0375 & 0.0250 & 0.4031 & 0.5344 \end{pmatrix}. \qquad (8.31)$$

The Markov process described by matrix (8.31) implies average unemployment rates of 4.28% and 11.78% during good and bad times, respectively. Finally, the households' home production is equal to $\theta = 0.25$.

Computation. In the following, we describe the computation of the economy with business cycle fluctuations. The computation of the model is more simple than the one for the economy considered in Section 7.1. In Example 8.2.1 with the endogenous interest rate r, we had to pick an initial value of the interest rate, compute the decision functions and the invariant distribution and update the interest rate subsequently until it converged. In the present economy, the interest rate is given. We first compute the decision functions by value function iteration. The value function of the individual is a function of his assets a and the state s:

$$V(a,s) = \max_{c,a'} \left[u(c) + \beta E\left\{ V(a',s') | s \right\} \right] \tag{8.32}$$

$$= \max_{c,a'} \left[u(c) + \beta \sum_{s'} \pi(s'|s) V(a',s') \right].$$

From Chapter 4, we know how to solve this simple dynamic programming problem. In the program RCh83_imo.g, we use value function iteration with linear interpolation between grid points. The maximum of the rhs of the Bellman equation (8.32) is computed with Golden Section Search. We use $n_a = 301$ grid points for the asset space so that we have to store a matrix with $n_a \times 4 = 1204$ entries. The grid is chosen to be equispaced on the interval $[0,8]$ and $[-8,8]$ for the economy with only a storage technology and the economy with intermediation, respectively.

Consumption is an increasing function of income and is also higher in good times as agents have a higher expected next-period income (compare Figure 8.9). The optimal next-period asset $a'(a,s)$ is a monotone increasing function of assets a. Figure 8.10 displays the net savings $a' - a$ which are always negative for the unemployed agent and become negative for the employed agents at a wealth level approximately equal to 4 so that the ergodic set is contained in the interval $[0,8]$.

Next, we compute the invariant density function $f(a,s)$. The associated invariant distribution can be interpreted as the fraction of time that a particular individual spends in the different

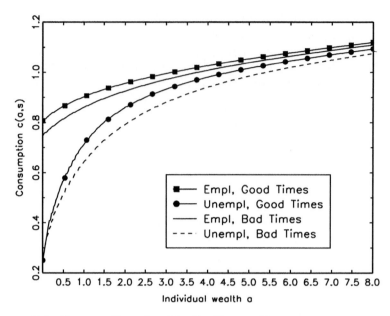

Figure 8.9: Consumption $c(a, s)$ in the Storage Economy

states (a, s). For an economy with business cycle fluctuations, the invariant distribution is the limit of the predictive probability distribution of an individual in n periods where n goes to infinity. We compute the invariant density function as described in Chapter 7 and approximate it by a discrete-valued function.[27] We use a finer grid over the asset space for the computation of the distribution than for the computation of the policy function. In particular, we compute the density function at $n_{ag} = 903$ equispaced points over the interval $[0, 8]$ and $[-8, 8]$, respectively. The invariant density function $f(a, s)$ can be computed from the following dynamics:

$$f'(a', s') = \sum_{a'=a'(a,s)} \sum_{s'} \pi(s'|s) f(a, s). \qquad (8.33)$$

As the optimal next-period asset level a' may not be a grid point, we simply assume that it will be on the lower or higher

---

[27] For notational convenience, we will also use the same function name $f(.)$ for the approximation.

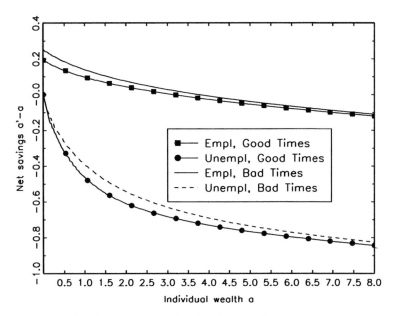

Figure 8.10: Net Savings $a' - a$ in the Storage Economy

neighboring point with a probability that corresponds to the distance from the higher or lower neighboring point, respectively (see Step 3 in Algorithm 7.2.3). The invariant density function $f(a, s)$ is displayed in Figure 8.11. The ergodic set is approximately $[0, 3.8]$ and the density is zero for $a > 3.8$.[28]

On average, assets are stored at the amount of $\bar{a} = 2.35$ in this economy. As the average employment rate is 8%, average income (which is equal to average consumption) is equal to $\bar{y} = 0.92 + 0.08 \times 0.25 = 0.94$.

The consumption and savings behavior in the economy with intermediation is different from the one in the economy with a

---

[28] Different from our density function, the density function computed by İMROHOROĞLU (1989) (Fig. 1 in her article) displays two spikes in the range 1.5-2.0 of individual wealth and maximum values of approximately 0.05 in good times. This, however, is an artefact of her computational methods. She only computes the policy functions at grid points and does not interpolate between grid points. As a consequence, our results differ to a slight degree and our policy functions and distribution functions are much smoother.

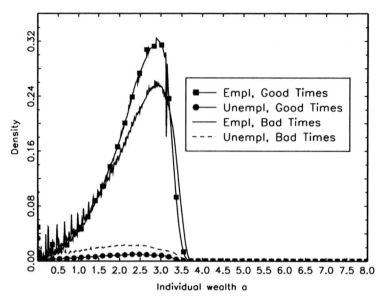

Figure 8.11: Invariant Density Function $g(a, s)$ in the Storage Economy

storage technology only. In particular, the consumption behavior changes around $a = 0$ as the interest rate on assets changes from the low lending rate $r^l = 0\%$ to the high borrowing rate $r^b = 8\%$ (see Figures 8.12 and 8.13). That is the reason why we have used value function iteration. If we had used a computational method like projection methods that does not rely on the discretization of the individual asset grid, we may have had problems in capturing this non-monotonicity of the first derivative of $a'(a, \epsilon)$ at $a = 0$.

The distribution of individual wealth in the economy with intermediation is graphed in Figure 8.14. The average of assets borrowed amounts to 0.510 and is not equal to the amount of assets saved (=0.287), because we only study a partial equilibrium. In a general equilibrium, the interest rate r^b and r^l would adjust in order to clear the capital market. The average income $\bar{y}$ is equal to the one in the economy with a storage technology only and amounts to 0.940. As, however, intermediation costs are private costs, average consumption is smaller than average income,

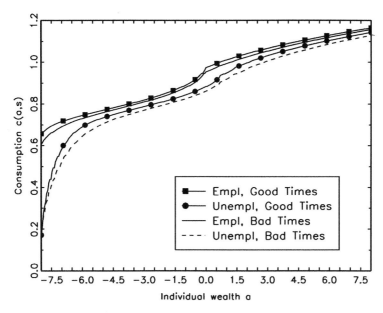

Figure 8.12: Consumption $c(a, s)$ in an Economy with Intermediation

$\bar{c} = 0.935 < 0.940 = \bar{y}$. The difference between average income and average consumption is simply the borrowing rate times the assets borrowed.

As one central problem of her work, İMROHOROĞLU (1989) computes the welfare gain from eliminating business cycle fluctuations. For this reason, she computes average utility in the economy with and without business cycle fluctuations, either using (8.30) or (8.31) for the state transition matrix of the economy. For the benchmark calibration, the elimination of business cycles is equivalent to a utility gain corresponding to 0.3% of consumption in the economy with a storage technology. If the relative risk aversion η is increased to 6.2, the welfare gain rises to 1.5% of consumption.[29] An intermediation technology significantly re-

---

[29] Notice that this is a huge welfare effect. LUCAS (1987) estimates the costs of business cycles to be very small and only equivalent to 0.1% of total US consumption. Different from the present model, agents can insure against the idiosyncratic risk in his model.

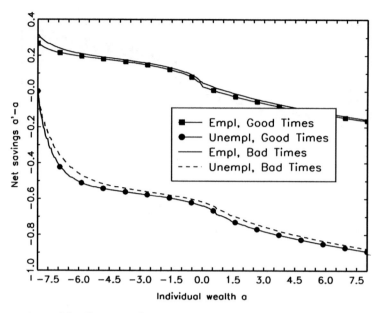

Figure 8.13: Net Savings $a' - a$ in an Economy with Intermediation

duces the business cycle costs. For $\eta = 1.5$, the fluctuations only cause a utility loss equivalent to 0.05% of consumption.

The computation of the welfare effects from business cycle fluctuations in İMROHOROĞLU (1989) is only sensible if the average asset holdings for the economies with and without business cycles do not change significantly. This is the case in İMROHOROĞLU (1989). HEER (2001a) considers an economy with endogenous prices where asset holdings are different in the economies with and without business cycles. Agents may hold much higher assets for precautionary reasons in a fluctuating economy. As a consequence, average asset holdings may change and, in a general equilibrium, average consumption may also change significantly. In his model, welfare changes that result from business cycle fluctuations are even more pronounced than in the present model. Similarly, STORESLETTEN, TELMER, and YARON (2001) and YOUNG (2005b) also derive much higher welfare costs of inflation. STORESLETTEN, TELMER, and YARON (2001) consider households with finite lifetime. In their model, the volatility of la-

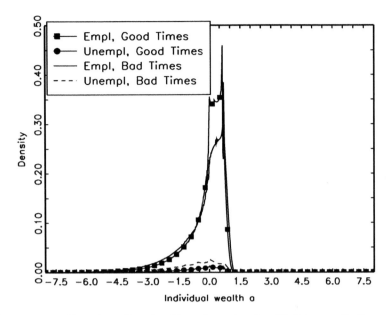

Figure 8.14: Invariant Density Function $g(a,s)$ with Intermediation Technology

bor income shocks depends on the business cycle. YOUNG (2005b) introduces an endogenous borrowing limit into the standard business cycle model so that repayment of the debt is ensured.

8.4.2 Business Cycle Dynamics of the Income Distribution

CASTAÑEDA, DÍAZ-GIMÉNEZ, and RÍOS-RULL (1998b) explore the business cycle dynamics of the income distribution both empirically and in a theoretical computable general equilibrium model. They find that, in the US, the income share earned by the lowest quintile is more procyclical and more volatile than the other income shares. In particular, the income shares earned by the 60%-95% group are even countercyclical, while the share earned by the top 5% is still acyclical.

To address these issues, they construct a heterogenous-agent economy with aggregate uncertainty based on the stochastic neoclassical growth model. The aggregate uncertainty is modeled as in Example 8.3.1 and follows a Markov process. Again, unemployment is higher during bad times and contributes to the explanation of the business cycle dynamics of the lowest income share. Contrary to the model by İMROHOROĞLU (1989) presented in the previous section, the aggregate capital stock and the interest rate are endogenous variables of the model. As one of their major results, cyclical unemployment helps to reconcile the model's behavior with the data on the dynamics of the income distribution.

In the following, we will present a slightly modified version of the model by CASTAÑEDA, DÍAZ-GIMÉNEZ, and RÍOS-RULL (1998b). In particular, we will introduce income mobility in their model and consider its effect on the cyclical behavior of the income shares of each income quintile. First, we describe the model. Second, we present the calibration and the computational method. We conclude with the presentations of our results.[30]

The Model. There are many infinitely lived households of mass one who differ with regard to the assets a_t, their employment status ϵ_t, and their efficiency type $i \in \{1, \ldots, 5\}$. The mass of type i household is equal to $\mu_i = 20\%$ for $i = 1, \ldots, 5$.

Households maximize their intertemporal utility[31]

$$E_0 \sum_{t=0}^{\infty} \beta^t u(c_t), \qquad (8.34)$$

where $\beta < 1$ is the subjective discount factor and expectations are conditioned on the information set at time 0. At time zero, the agent knows his beginning-of-period wealth a_0, his employment status $\epsilon_0 \in \{e, u\}$ and his efficiency type i. The agent's instantaneous utility function is a CES function of his consumption:

$$u(c_t) = \frac{c_t^{1-\eta}}{1-\eta}, \quad \eta > 0, \qquad (8.35)$$

---

[30] In Chapter 10, we will consider an Overlapping Generations model with elastic labor supply and further improve the modeling of the business cycle dynamics of the income distribution.

[31] For the sake of notational simplicity, we refrain from indexing individual variables like consumption, wealth, the employment status, and the efficiency index with a subscript $j \in [0, 1]$.

where η, again, denotes the coefficient of relative risk aversion.

The model is characterized by both idiosyncratic and aggregate risk. At the individual level, the household may either be employed ($\epsilon = e$) or unemployed ($\epsilon = u$). Aggregate risk is introduced by a stochastic technology level Z_t in period t. In particular, the productivity shock follows a Markov process with transition matrix $\Gamma_Z(Z'|Z)$, where Z' denotes next-period technology level and $\pi_{ZZ'}$ denotes the transition probability from state Z to Z'. The individual employment probabilities, of course, depend on the aggregate productivity Z_t. In good times (high productivity Z_t), agents have higher employment probabilities than in bad times. The joint process of the two shocks, Z_t and ϵ_t, can be written as a Markov process with transition matrix $\Gamma_i(Z', \epsilon'|Z, \epsilon)$ and depends on the efficiency type of the agent. We use $\pi_i(Z', \epsilon'|Z, \epsilon)$ to denote the probability of transition from state (Z, ϵ) to state (Z', ϵ') for an individual with efficiency type i. In the following, we restrict our attention to the simple case presented in Example 8.3.1. The economy only experiences good and bad times with technology levels Z_g and Z_b, respectively, $Z_g > Z_b$. Consequently, the joint processes on (Z, ϵ) are Markov-chains with 4 states for each efficiency type $i = 1, \ldots, 5$.

We study a simple extension of the model by CASTAÑEDA, DÍAZ-GIMÉNEZ, and RÍOS-RULL (1998b). In particular, different from their model, we assume that agents may change their efficiency type i. Given the empirical evidence on income mobility, however, we examine the effect of this assumption on the cyclical behavior of the income distribution.[32] We assume that the efficiency type i follows a Markov-chain $\pi(i'|i)$ that is independent of the aggregate productivity. Furthermore, the employment probability next period does only depend on the efficiency type of this period. In other words, $\pi_i(Z', \epsilon'|Z, \epsilon)$ is not a function of next-period type i'. The probability of an employed type i agent in the good state $Z = Z_g$ to be employed next period as a type

---

[32] In addition, the assumption of income mobility may change the wealth inequality in the model as we will argue below. Still, wealth heterogeneity is too small in both our model and the model by CASTAÑEDA, DÍAZ-GIMÉNEZ, and RÍOS-RULL (1998b).

i' agent in the bad state, for example, is given by the product $\pi(i'|i)\,\pi_i(e, Z_b|e, Z_g)$.

Households are assumed to know the law of motion of both $\pi_i(Z', \epsilon'|Z, \epsilon)$ and $\pi(i'|i)$ and they observe the realization of both stochastic processes at the beginning of each period. In good times, agents work $h(Z_g)$ hours, and, in bad times, agents work $h(Z_b)$ hours. Let ζ_i denote the efficiency factor of a type i agent. If employed, the agent receives the labor income $h(Z)\zeta_i w$; otherwise, he produces home production $\bar{w}$.

Let $N_i(Z)$ denote the number of employed households of type i for current productivity Z. We will calibrate these values below so that $N_i(Z)$ is constant for $Z \in \{Z_g, Z_b\}$ and does not depend on the history of the productivity level Z, $\{Z_\tau\}_{\tau=-\infty}^{\tau=t}$. The assumption that employment only depends on current productivity greatly simplifies the computation. Agents do not have to form expectations about the dynamics of the aggregate employment level but only need to consider aggregate productivity and the distribution of wealth. The aggregate labor input measured in efficiency units is given by $N(Z) = \sum_i \zeta_i h(Z) N_i(Z)$. For the technology level Z_t, aggregate production is given by:

$$Y_t = Z_t N_t^{1-\alpha} K_t^\alpha. \tag{8.36}$$

We assume competitive factor and product markets implying the factor prices:

$$w_t = Z_t(1-\alpha) N_t^{-\alpha} K_t^\alpha, \tag{8.37}$$
$$r_t = Z_t \alpha N_t^{1-\alpha} K_t^{\alpha-1} - \delta, \tag{8.38}$$

where δ denotes the rate of depreciation. Notice that the agents only need to forecast the aggregate capital stock K' (and, therefore, the dynamics of the distribution of capital) and the aggregate technology level Z' in order to form a prediction of the next-period factor prices w' and r', respectively, as we assume N' to be a function of Z' only.

In the following, we describe the household decision problem in a recursive form. Let F denote the distribution of the individual state variables $\{i, \epsilon, a\}$. For each household, the state variable consists of her efficiency type i, her employment status ϵ, her individual asset level a, the aggregate technology level Z, the aggregate capital stock K (which is implied by the distribution $F(.)$), and the distribution of efficiency types, employment, and individual wealth, $F(i, \epsilon, a)$.

The recursive problem can be formulated as follows:

$$V(i, \epsilon, a; Z, F) = \max_{c, a'} \left[u(c) + \beta E \left\{ V(i', \epsilon', a'; Z', F') | i, \epsilon, Z, F \right\} \right] \tag{8.39}$$

subject to the budget constraint:

$$a' = \begin{cases} (1+r)a + w\zeta_i h(Z) - c & \text{if } \epsilon = e, \\ (1+r)a + \bar{w} - c & \text{if } \epsilon = u, \end{cases} \tag{8.40}$$

and subject to (8.37) and (8.38), the stochastic process of the employment status ϵ and the aggregate technology Z, $\pi_i(Z', \epsilon'|Z, \epsilon)$, the agent's efficiency mobility as given by $\pi(i'|i)$, and the distribution dynamics $F' = G(F, Z, Z')$, where G describes the law of motion for the distribution F.

The definition of the equilibrium is analogous to the one in Example 8.3.1 and we will omit it for this reason. The interested reader is referred to Section 3.5.2 of CASTAÑEDA, DÍAZ-GIMÉNEZ, and RÍOS-RULL (1998b).

Calibration. The parameters, if not mentioned otherwise, are taken from the study of CASTAÑEDA, DÍAZ-GIMÉNEZ, and RÍOS-RULL (1998b).[33] Model periods correspond to 1/8 of a year ($\approx$ 6 weeks). The coefficient of relative risk aversion is set equal to $\eta = 1.5$ and the discount factor is set equal to $0.96^{1/8}$ implying an annual discount rate of 4%.

The authors assume that agents are immobile implying $\pi(i'|i) = 1$ if $i' = i$ and zero otherwise. BUDRÍA RODRÍGUEZ, DÍAZ-GIMÉNEZ, QUADRINI, and RÍOS-RULL (2002) provide an estimate of the US earnings transition matrix between the different earnings quintile from 1984 to 1989:[34]

---

[33] We would like to thank Victor Ríos-Rull for providing us with the calibration data on the transition matrices.

[34] See table 24 in their appendix.

$$P = \begin{pmatrix} 0.58 & 0.28 & 0.09 & 0.03 & 0.02 \\ 0.22 & 0.44 & 0.22 & 0.08 & 0.03 \\ 0.10 & 0.15 & 0.43 & 0.23 & 0.09 \\ 0.06 & 0.09 & 0.18 & 0.46 & 0.21 \\ 0.06 & 0.02 & 0.06 & 0.21 & 0.65 \end{pmatrix}. \tag{8.41}$$

We still have to transform this 5-year transition matrix into a 1/8-year transition matrix. Using the definition of the root of a matrix in equation (11.26), we can compute $P^{1/40}$ which we set equal to $\pi(i'|i)$:[35]

$$\pi(i'|i) = \begin{pmatrix} 0.983 & 0.015 & 0.001 & 0.000 & 0.000 \\ 0.011 & 0.974 & 0.013 & 0.001 & 0.000 \\ 0.003 & 0.007 & 0.974 & 0.013 & 0.002 \\ 0.001 & 0.004 & 0.010 & 0.976 & 0.010 \\ 0.002 & 0.000 & 0.001 & 0.010 & 0.987 \end{pmatrix}. \tag{8.42}$$

The 6 weekly earnings mobility is rather small as the entries on the diagonal of (8.42) are close to unity.[36] Therefore, we would expect little influence from the neglect of the income mobility on the results.

We use five types of households with efficiency $\zeta^i \in \{0.509, 0.787, 1.000, 1.290, 2.081\}$. The efficiency factors are chosen to be the relative earnings of the different income groups. The variation of hours worked of these 5 income groups between good and bad times are treated as if they were variations in employment rates. With the help of the coefficient of variation of average hours, the employment rates are calibrated as in Table 8.1.[37]

---

[35] The computation is performed by the procedure matroot in the program Rch83cas1.g. Furthermore, we set all negative entries of the matrix root equal to zero and normalize the sum of each row equal to one in the routine matroot. The error is rather small for our case (you may check this by computing $\pi(i'|i) \cdot \pi(i'|i) \cdots$ and compare it to the matrix P from (8.41)).

[36] In order to obtain (8.42) from (8.41), we have assumed that earnings follow an AR(1)-process. As we argued in Chapter 7, the behavior of earnings is much better described by an AR(2)-process. Due to the lack of high-frequency data on the earnings mobility, however, we do not have another choice.

[37] Please see the original article for a detailed description of the calibration procedure.

8.4 Applications

Table 8.1

i	$N(Z_g)$	$N(Z_b)$
1	0.8612	0.8232
2	0.9246	0.8854
3	0.9376	0.9024
4	0.9399	0.9081
5	0.9375	0.9125

Given the employment of type i households in good and bad times, $N_i(Z_g)$ and $N_i(Z_b)$, respectively, and the average duration of unemployment in good times (10 weeks) and in bad times (14 weeks), we are able to compute the matrices $\pi_i(\epsilon', Z'|\epsilon, Z)$ with $Z = Z'$. For this reason, we have to solve a system of 4 equations (including non-linear equations) which is carried out in the routine `transp` in the program `RCh83cas1.g`. Two equations are given by the conditions that agents are either employed or unemployed in the next period. Taking $\pi_i(\epsilon', Z_g|\epsilon, Z_g)$ as an example, we impose the following two conditions on the transition matrix:

$$\pi_i(e, Z_g|e, Z_g) + \pi_i(u, Z_g|e, Z_g) = \pi(Z_g|Z_g),$$
$$\pi_i(e, Z_g|u, Z_g) + \pi_i(u, Z_g|u, Z_g) = \pi(Z_g|Z_g).$$

Furthermore, the average duration of unemployment is 10 weeks or 10/6 periods in good times implying $\pi_i(u, Z_g|u, Z_g) = 4/10 \times \pi(Z_g|Z_g)$. The fourth condition is given by the equilibrium employment in good times, $N_i(Z_g)$. We impose as our fourth non-linear equation that the ergodic distribution of the employed agents is equal to $N_i(Z_g)$. The matrix $\pi_1(\epsilon', Z_g|\epsilon, Z_g)$, for example, is given by:

$$\pi_1(\epsilon', Z_g|\epsilon, Z_g) = \pi_1(\epsilon'|\epsilon) \cdot \pi(Z_g|Z_g)$$
$$= \begin{pmatrix} 0.9033 & 0.09067 \\ 0.6000 & 0.40000 \end{pmatrix} \cdot \pi(Z_g|Z_g).$$

As you can easily check, the ergodic distribution of $\pi_1(\epsilon'|\epsilon)$ is equal to $(0.8612, 0.1388)'$, the average duration of unemployment is 10 weeks, and the sum of each row is equal to one. Similarly, we are able to compute $\pi_i(\epsilon', Z_b|\epsilon, Z_b)$ for all $i = 1, \ldots, 5$.

It remains to compute the transition matrix $\pi(\epsilon', Z_b|\epsilon, Z_g)$ between good and bad times on the one hand and the transition matrix $\pi(\epsilon', Z_g|\epsilon, Z_b)$ between bad and good times on the other hand. First, we assume that all unemployed agents remain unemployed if the economy transits from good to bad times, $\pi_i(u, Z_b|u, Z_g) = \pi(Z_b|Z_g)$ and $\pi_i(e, Z_b|u, Z_g) = 0$ for all $i = 1, \ldots, 5$. Second, we assume that employments $N_i(Z_g)$ and $N_i(Z_b)$ are constant, respectively. For this reason, $N_i(Z_g)\pi_i(e, Z_b|e, Z_g) = N_i(Z_b)\pi(Z_b|Z_g)$ must hold. Together with the condition that $\pi_i(e, Z_b|e, Z_g) + \pi_i(u, Z_b|e, Z_g) = \pi(Z_b|Z_g)$, we have four conditions that help us to determine the matrix $\pi_i(\epsilon', Z_b|\epsilon, Z_g)$. For the computation of the matrix $\pi_i(\epsilon', Z_b|\epsilon, Z_g)$, we assume that all employed agents remain employed if the economy transits from the bad to the good state. Furthermore, we assume $N_i(Z_g)$ to be constant so that we also impose the restriction that $(1 - N_i(Z_g))\pi(Z_g|Z_b) = \pi_i(u, Z_g|u, Z_b)(1 - N_i(Z_b))$. Together with the two conditions that the sum of each row must be unity we can determine the matrix $\pi_i(\epsilon', Z_g|\epsilon, Z_b)$ for all $i = 1, \ldots, 5$.

The transition matrix between good and bad states is set equal to:

$$\pi(Z'|Z) = \begin{pmatrix} 0.9722 & 0.0278 \\ 0.0278 & 0.9722 \end{pmatrix},$$

implying equal length of booms and recession averaging 4.5 years. Furthermore, employment is constant both in good times and bad times, respectively, and the factor $Zh(Z)^{1-\alpha}$ is set equal to 1 and 0.9130 for $Z = Z_g$ and $Z = Z_b$, respectively. We assume that average working hours amount to $h(Z_g) = 32\%$ and $h(Z_b) = 30\%$ of the available time during good and bad times, respectively.[38] The production elasticity of capital is set equal to $\alpha = 0.375$ and the depreciation rate is equal to $1 - 0.9^{1/8}$.

---

[38] Together with the income mobility transition matrix, these are the only parameters that differ from the calibration of CASTAÑEDA, DÍAZ-GIMÉNEZ, and RÍOS-RULL (1998b).

Finally, the household production $\bar{w}$ is set equal to 25% of average earnings in the economy. In particular, the earnings during unemployment $\bar{w}$ are constant over the business cycle.

Computation. The solution is computed with the help of program RCh83cas1.g using the methods described in Section 7.2. In particular, we apply Algorithm 8.3.1 with the following steps 1-8:

Step 1: In the first step, we choose computational parameters and compute the aggregate employment levels in good and bad times,

$$N(Z_g) = \sum_i \mu_i \zeta_i h(Z_g) N_i(Z_g),$$
$$N(Z_b) = \sum_i \mu_i \zeta_i h(Z_b) N_i(Z_b).$$

The agents form very simple expectations about the next-period employment. Employment next period only depends on productivity in the next period: $N' = N'(Z')$. The policy functions are computed on the interval $\mathcal{A} \times \mathcal{K} = [a_{min}, a_{max}] \times [K_{min}, K_{max}] = [0, 800] \times [80, 400]$. The interval limits are found with some trial and error and do not bind. The policy and value functions are computed on an equispaced grid of the state space using $na = 50$ and $nk = 5$ grid points on the intervals $\mathcal{A}$ and $\mathcal{K}$, respectively.

As an initial guess for the interest rate, we use the steady state capital stock for the corresponding representative agent model as implied by $1/\beta = 1 + r - \delta$. For the computation of the distribution function $f(.)$, we, again, need to discretize the continuous variables of the individual state space. We use $na = 100$ equispaced points over the individual asset space $\mathcal{A}$. Furthermore, we have $ni = 5$ types of agents, $nz = 2$ states of the productivity, and $ne = 2$ states of employment.

Step 2: Agents need to predict next-period factor prices w' and r'. Factor prices are functions of both aggregate capital K' and aggregate employment N' as well as the exogenous technology level Z'. In order to predict the capital stock K', agents need to know the dynamics of the distribution. They only use partial information about the distribution, namely its first m moments. We choose $m = 1$. Agents only consider the aggregate capital stock as a statistic for the distribution. As argued above, this assumption is warranted if agents of different wealth have approximately equal savings rates. Therefore, the value function of the agents, $V(i, \epsilon, a, Z, K)$, and the consumption function, $c(i, \epsilon, a, Z, K)$, are functions of the individual efficiency type i, the employment status ϵ, the asset holdings a, the aggregate productivity Z, and the aggregate capital stock K.

The value function and the policy functions are both five-dimensional objects. This may impose some computational problems. For example, in older versions of Gauss, only two-dimensional objects can be stored. There are two ways to solve this problem. First, in our model, there is only a small number of efficiency types $i = 1, \ldots, 5$, two states of technology, $Z \in \{Z_g, Z_b\}$, and two employment status, $\epsilon \in \{e, u\}$. Consequently, we can store the two-dimensional value matrices $V(a, K; i, \epsilon, Z)$ for the $5 \times 2 \times 2 = 20$ different values of i, ϵ, and Z, separately. That's how we proceed. If the number of states is getting larger, of course, this procedure becomes cumbersome. In the latter case, you may want to store the value function in one matrix, reserving the first na rows for $i = 1$, $Z = Z_g$, $\epsilon = e$, the next na rows for $i = 2$, $Z = Z_g$, $\epsilon = e$, and so forth. In the second case, of course, it is very convenient for the computation to write a subroutine that returns you the value function $V(a, K; i, \epsilon, Z)$ for a state vector (i, ϵ, Z).

For the initialization of the consumption function for each (i, ϵ, Z), we assume that the agents consume their respective income. We further initialize the distribution of assets assuming that every agent holds equal wealth. The initial state of the economy is chosen by random choice. With probability 0.5, $Z = Z_g$. Otherwise, the bad state $Z = Z_b$ prevails. As we dispense of the first 100 simulated time periods, the initial choice of the distribution and the productivity does not matter.

Step 3: We impose again a very simple law of motion for the capital stock. As in (8.22), we assume that the aggregate capital stock follows a log-linear law of motion in good and bad times, respectively:

$$\ln K' = \begin{cases} \gamma_{0g} + \gamma_{1g} \ln K & \text{if } Z = Z_g, \\ \gamma_{0b} + \gamma_{1b} \ln K & \text{if } Z = Z_b. \end{cases} \quad (8.44)$$

We initialize the parameters as follows: $\gamma_{0g} = \gamma_{0b} = 0.09$ and $\gamma_{1g} = \gamma_{1b} = 0.95$.

Step 4: In this step, we compute the optimal next-period asset level $a'(i, \epsilon, a, Z, K)$ by value function iteration. Between grid points, we interpolate linearly. The maximization of the right-hand side of the Bellman equation is performed using the Golden Section Search Algorithm 11.6.1. We need to find the optimum for $50 \times 5 \times 5 \times 2 \times 2 = 5,000$ grid points. The computation is much faster i) if we compute and store the next-period value $V(i', \epsilon', a', Z', K')$ for all nk values $K'(K)$ where K' is computed from the dynamics (8.44), before we start iterating over i, ϵ, a and Z. ii) We make use of both the monotonicity of next-period asset level $a'(a, .)$ and the value function $V(a, .)$ with respect to a and the concavity of the value function $V(a, .)$ with respect to a'. In particular, we stop searching over the next-period asset grid a' if the rhs of the Bellman equation decreases and we do not search for the optimal next-period asset level for values of $a'(a_i)$ below $a'(a_{i-1})$ for $a_i > a_{i-1}$.

Step 5: In order to simulate the dynamics of the wealth distribution, we choose a sample of $nh = 5,000$ households. We divide the households in 10 subsamples (i, ϵ), $i = 1, \ldots, 5$, $\epsilon \in \{e, u\}$. We know that the relative numbers of these subsamples are equal to $N_i(Z)$ and $1 - N_i(Z)$, respectively, for $Z = Z_g$ and $Z = Z_b$. We initialize the distribution so that each agent has equal wealth in period 1. In particular, the average wealth in period 1 is equal to the aggregate capital stock in the economy.[39] The assets of the next period are computed with the help of the optimal decision rule $a'(a, K; i, \epsilon, Z)$ for each household. The aggregate capital stock of the economy is equal to average wealth in the economy. We further use a random number generator in order to find i) the productivity level of next period Z' using the transition matrix

---

[39] In the very first simulation, we use the aggregate capital stock as an initial guess that is computed from the steady-state of the corresponding representative-agent model.

$\pi(Z'|Z)$, ii) the employment status of the next period ϵ' using the transition matrix $\pi_i(\epsilon', Z'|\epsilon, Z)$ and iii) the efficiency type of the individual using the income mobility matrix $\pi(i'|i)$.

In the period t, we have a sample of 5,000 households with wealth holdings a_t and a distribution with mean K_t. The productivity level is equal to Z_t. The number of the employed households of type i, for example, may not be equal to $N_i(Z_t)$. For this reason, we choose a random number of agents and switch their employment status accordingly. We also may have to switch the productivity type i. For this reason, we start looking at the households with efficiency $i = 1$ and $\epsilon = e$. If their number is smaller than $N_1(Z_t)$ we switch the missing number of the households with $i = 2$ and $\epsilon = e$ to $i = 1$ and $\epsilon = e$ at random. Otherwise, we switch the surplus number of households with type $i = 1$ to type $i = 2$. We continue this process for $i = 1, \ldots, 5$, $\epsilon = e, u$. By this procedure, agents of type $i = 1$ may not be switched to agents of type $i = 4$, for example. We judge this to be a reasonable imposition of the law of large numbers.[40]

Step 6: We divide the simulated time series of the aggregate capital stock $\{K_t\}_{t=101}^{t=2,000}$ into two subsamples, with $Z_t = Z_g$ or $Z_t = Z_b$, respectively. For the two subsamples, we estimate the coefficients γ_0 and γ_1 of the equation (8.22) with the help of an OLS-regression.

Step 7: We continue this iteration until the estimated OLS regressors of the loglinear law of motion for the capital stock converge. As it turns out (step 8), the fit of the regression is very accurate with an R^2 close to one.

Results. The economy with efficiency mobility behaves very similarly to the one without efficiency mobility. For this reason, we concentrate on displaying the results for the former economy if not mentioned otherwise. The law of motion (8.44) is given by:

---

[40] These problems arising from the fact that the law of large numbers does not hold in our Monte-Carlo simulation do not show up in the methods that we present in Chapter 10. In this chapter, we will approximate the distribution function over the individual states by a piecewise linear function and simulate its dynamics.

$$\ln K' = \begin{cases} 0.0754 + 0.986 \ln K & \text{if } Z = Z_g, \\ 0.0620 + 0.988 \ln K & \text{if } Z = Z_b. \end{cases} \quad (8.45)$$

The stationary average aggregate capital stock amounts to $K = 219$.[41]

The distribution of earnings among the employed agents, $w\, h(Z)\, \zeta_i$, is more or less exogenous in our model and is proportional to the efficiency type ζ_i. Of course, the wage w is endogenous in our model. As home production is assumed to be constant over the business cycle, while the earnings of the employed agents increases during booms and decreases during recessions, the distribution of earnings is not constant over the business cycle. During booms, $Z = Z_g$, earnings are more concentrated and characterized by a Gini coefficient equal to 0.305. During a recession, the Gini coefficient of earnings drops to 0.291. The Gini coefficient of income (earnings plus interest income) is more volatile than the Gini coefficient of earnings because the concentration of wealth and the interest rate are procyclical. Consequently, the concentration of interest income and total income increases during booms. The Gini coefficients of income varies between 0.285 and 0.325 over the cycle. The Lorenz curve of income is displayed in Figure 8.15. The income shares are computed as averages over 2,000 periods. Notice that we are able to replicate the empirical distribution of income very closely.[42] The income distribution implied by the model is almost identical to the one in the US during 1946-84.

Table 8.2 reports the cyclical behavior of income shares for the US and for the model economy with varying efficiency types. The empirical correlations of US output and income shares are taken from Table 2 in CASTAÑEDA, DÍAZ-GIMÉNEZ, and RÍOS-RULL (1998b). The sample period, again, is 1948-86. The yearly output data is logged and detrended using a Hodrick-Prescott filter with

---

[41] For example, aggregate capital amounts to $K = 229$ in the economy without income mobility, and the law of motion for the capital stocks are given by $\ln K' = 0.0755 + 0.986 \ln K$ and $\ln K' = 0.0622 + 0.988 \ln K$ in good and bad times, respectively.

[42] The empirical values for the US income and wealth distribution during 1948-86 are provided in Table 1 and 6 of CASTAÑEDA, DÍAZ-GIMÉNEZ, and RÍOS-RULL (1998b), respectively.

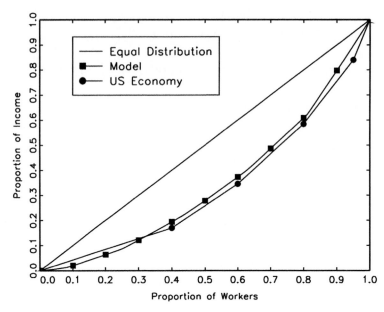

Figure 8.15: Lorenz Curve of Income

a smoothing parameter $\mu = 100$. The income share of the lower quintiles (0-60%) is procyclical, the income share of the fourth quintile and next 15% (60-95%) is anticyclical, while the top 5% of the income are acyclical.

In the third column of Table 8.2, we report the statistics computed from our simulation over 2,000 periods for the economy with time-varying efficiency types. The cyclical behavior of income shares in the economy without mobility is found to be almost identical to the one in the economy with mobility. Again, output is logged and detrended using the Hodrick-Prescott filter with $\mu = 100$ in order to compare it to the empirical numbers. Therefore, we need to compute annual averages of output and income and earnings shares for 2,000/8=250 years. The simulated correlation of income is only in good accordance with the empirical observations for the first and second income quintiles as well as for the 80-95% income percentile class. As one possible explanation for the rather poor modeling of the other percentiles, we do not allow for endogenous labor supply (which may result in

Table 8.2

Income Quintile	Correlation output and income	
	US	model
lowest quintile (0-20%)	0.53	0.79
second quintile (20-40%)	0.49	0.79
third quintile (40-60%)	0.31	-0.74
fourth quintile (60-80%)	-0.29	-0.80
next 15% (80-95%)	-0.64	-0.80
top 5% (95-100%)	0.00	-0.78

more procyclical behavior of the 3rd and 4th income quintiles) and we are not very successful in replicating the wealth distribution (which may result in more procyclical interest and profit income for the top 5% of the income distribution).

The most pronounced effect of income mobility on the distribution of the individual variables earnings, income, and wealth is on the concentration of wealth. There are two opposing effects of income mobility on wealth heterogeneity: In the economy with time-varying efficiency type, wealth-rich and income-rich agents of type $i = 2, 3, 4, 5$ accumulate higher savings for precautionary reasons in case that they move down the income ladder. This effect, of course, increases wealth concentration in our economy and we would expect the Gini coefficient of wealth to be higher in the economy with efficiency mobility for this reason. On the other hand, agents of type $i = 5$, for example, might have had efficiency type $i = 4$ or even lower in previous periods so that they have accumulated less wealth than agents who have had the efficiency type $i = 5$ forever. For this reason, wealth heterogeneity is less in an economy with time-varying efficiency types. As it turns out, the former effect dominates and wealth heterogeneity is lower in the case of no mobility. In both economies, the endogenous wealth concentration is much lower than observed empirically and the Gini coefficient of wealth a only amounts to 0.347 (0.298) in the

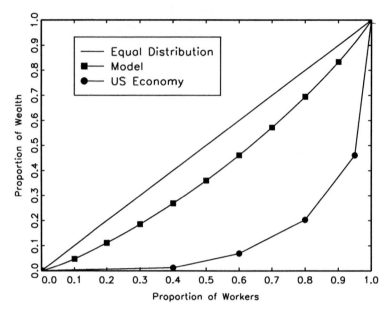

Figure 8.16: Lorenz Curve of Wealth

economy with varying efficiency types (no efficiency mobility). Figure 8.16 displays the Lorenz curve of our model economy with time-varying efficiency types and the US wealth distribution. In the next chapter, you will find out how we can improve the modeling of the wealth distribution.

8.5 Epilogue

In this chapter, we introduced you to the algorithm developed by and SMITH (1998). As you have learned, this algorithm is very time-consuming. In order to be implementable on a computer, you have to restrict the number of discrete points for the aggregate technology shock (or other shocks present in the model). In the applications of this chapter, we looked at only two distinct states of the technology shock, which we interpreted as boom and recession, respectively. In the following, we briefly discuss two alternative algorithms that are also applicable to models with continuously-valued variables for the aggregate technology.

REITER (2006) proposes a method that is related to one of the solution methods presented in Chapter 10, where we study the dynamics in Overlapping Generations Models. He computes the stationary distribution and the policy functions for the individuals at discrete points (between grid points he uses cubic spline interpolation). The policy functions are computed with the help of projection methods that you learned about in Chapter 6. For the computation of the dynamics for the aggregate variables he applies linear perturbation methods to the equilibrium conditions of the model. As the number of grid points for the individual capital stock may be quite large (1,000 points or more), the computation may become very time-consuming. As an alternative, he proposes to use a parametric approximation to the steady-state distribution in which case one may also apply higher-order perturbation methods.

In a similar vein, PRESTON and ROCA (2007) also apply perturbation methods to the solution of heterogenous-agent models with both idiosyncratic and aggregate shocks. The basic problem, of course, is the choice of the steady state at which you approximate the solution. REITER (2006) chooses the stationary non-stochastic steady state (by setting the aggregate technology shock to zero). With this choice, he faces the problem of approximating the behavior of an infinity of different households (distinguished by their individual wealth). PRESTON and ROCA, instead, overcome this problem by choosing a degenerate distribution of wealth where all individuals have equal wealth and productivity (equal to the non-stochastic steady state in the corresponding representative-agent model). In this case, the standard deviation of both individual wealth and productivity is zero. In their particular model, they use quadratic perturbation methods around this steady. The decision rules are functions of the variance of the technology shock, the variance of the distribution of the individual capital stock, and the covariance of the individual capital stock and individual productivity. In future work, it will be interesting to see how sensitive the algorithm of PRESTON and ROCA

(2007) is relative to the one of REITER (2006) and KRUSELL and SMITH (1998) with respect to the variance of the aggregate shock and the presence of non-linearities such as a liquidity or credit constraint. If, for example, the variance becomes large, the perturbation by PRESTON and ROCA (2007) is far from the assumed steady state of zero variance and the approximation may be even less accurate. The method of PRESTON and ROCA (2007), however, may have the advantage to be more readily applicable to models with more than one individual state variable.

Problems

8.1 Example 8.2.1

a) Assume that agents use the first two moments to forecast future factor prices in Example 8.2.1. Show that the consideration of an additional moment does not result in much higher accuracy in the prediction of the factor prices as compared to the case of one moment.

b) Assume that the initial distribution of the economy described in Example 8.2.1 is given by the stationary distribution and consider a policy that increases the replacement ratio of unemployment insurance to 40%. Compute the transition dynamics and assume that the income tax rate always adjusts in order to balance the budget. How does the wealth distribution change? Compute the Gini coefficients of the income and wealth distribution during the transition and in the new stationary state.

c) Compute the stationary state and the transition dynamics for the growth model 8.2.1 with leisure. Use the utility function (8.11) with $\sigma = 0.5$. Use the prediction function $\ln N' = \psi_0 + \psi_1 \ln N$ for aggregate employment N.

d) Implement the algorithm 8.2.2 using projection methods for the computation of the policy functions.

8.2 Aggregate Uncertainty

a) Assume that agents use the first two moments to forecast future factor prices in Example 8.3.1. Show that the consideration of an additional moment does not result in much higher accuracy in the prediction of the factor prices as compared to the case of one moment.

b) Assume that, in Example 8.3.1, technology z follows the first-order autoregressive process $z_t = \rho z_{t-1} + \eta_t$ with $\rho = 0.9$ and $\eta_t \sim N(0, 0.01)$. Compute a 5-state Markov-chain approximation of the AR(1)-process using Tauchen's method. Compute the model of Example 8.3.1. How do results change if you use 9 states instead of 5 states for the Markov-chain approximation?

c) Assume that the unemployment rate is not constant during booms or recessions. Assume that leisure is an argument of the utility function. How does the program Rch83cas1.g need to be adjusted?

8.3 Costs of Business Cycles

a) Compute the gain in average utility from eliminating the business cycle fluctuations in the model of İMROHOROĞLU (1989) presented in Section 8.3.1.

b) Assume that there is perfect insurance in the economy described in Section 8.3.1. Each agent receives the average income of the economy. By how much is the utility gain from the elimination of cyclical fluctuations reduced?

8.4 Dynamics of the Income Distribution

Compute the model of Section 8.4.2 with the same calibration except that $\pi(\epsilon', z_g | \epsilon, z_b) = \pi(\epsilon', z_b | \epsilon, z_b)$ and $\pi(\epsilon', z_b | \epsilon, z_g) = \pi(\epsilon', z_g | \epsilon, z_g)$. Notice that for this calibration, next-period aggregate employment N is not only a function of next-period aggregate productivity z', but also of current-period productivity and employment, $N' = N'(N, z, z')$. Recompute the mean Gini coefficients of income and earnings and the correlation of income and earnings with output.

Chapter 9

Deterministic Overlapping Generations Models

Overview. In this chapter, we introduce an additional source of heterogeneity. Agents do not only differ with regard to their individual productivity or their wealth, but also with regard to their age. First, you will learn how to compute a simple overlapping generations model (OLG model) where each generation can be represented by a homogeneous household. Subsequently, we study the dynamics displayed by the typical Auerbach-Kotlikoff model. We will pay particular attention to the updating of the transition path for the aggregate variables.

The previous two chapters concentrated on the computation of models based on the Ramsey model. In this chapter, we will analyze overlapping generations models. The central difference between the OLG model and the Ramsey model is that there is a continuous turnover of the population. The lifetime is finite and in every period, a new generation is born and the oldest generation dies. In such models, many cohorts coexist at any time. In the pioneering work on OLG models by SAMUELSON (1958) and DIAMOND (1965), the number of coexisting cohorts only amounts to two, the young and working generation on the one hand and the old and retired generation on the other hand. In these early studies of simple OLG models, SAMUELSON (1958) and DIAMOND (1965) focused on the analysis of theoretical problems, i.e. if there is a role for money and what are the effects of national debt, respectively.

The OLG model is a natural framework to analyze life-cycle problems such as the provision of public pensions, endogenous fertility, or the accumulation of human capital and wealth. In order to study the quantitative effects of economic policy, subsequent work has been directed towards the study of large scale numerical OLG models. Typically, cohorts are identified with the members of the population of the same age. One seminal work in this area is the study of dynamic fiscal policy by AUERBACH and KOTLIKOFF (1987).[1] In their work, the first cohort is identified with the 20-year-old cohort, who enters the labor market. Fifty-five different generations are distinguished so that at age 75, all agents die. In their 55-period overlapping generations model of a representative household, they show, among others, that a 60% benefit level of unfunded social security decreases welfare by approximately 5-6% of total wealth (depending on the financing of the social security expenditures).

In recent years, there has been a wide range of economic problems studied with the help of OLG models. In addition to the early work by Auerbach and Kotlikoff, subsequent authors have introduced various new elements in the study of overlapping generations, like, for example, stochastic survival probabilities, bequests, or individual income mobility, to name but a few. In this vein, HUGGETT and VENTURA (2000) look at the determinants of savings and use a calibrated life-cycle model to investigate why high income households save as a group a much higher fraction of income than do low income households as documented by US cross-section data. Relatedly, HUGGETT (1996) shows that the life-cycle model is able to reproduce the US wealth Gini coefficient and a significant fraction of the wealth inequality within age groups. HEER (2001b) studies the role of bequests in the explanation of observed wealth inequality.

The US tax system and the US social security system have also attracted substantial attention: İMROHOROĞLU (1998) analyzes the effects of capital income taxation, İMROHOROĞLU, İMROHOROĞLU, and JOINES (1998) evaluate the benefits of tax favored retirement accounts, and VENTURA (1999) considers the effects of a flat-rate versus a progressive income tax. The effects of social security and unemployment compensation are studied by

---

[1] Other early studies of life-cycle economies include SUMMERS (1981), AUERBACH, KOTLIKOFF, and SKINNER (1983), EVANS (1983), or HUBBARD and JUDD (1987).

İMROHOROĞLU, İMROHOROĞLU, and JOINES (1995), HUBBARD, SKINNER, and ZELDES (1995), and HEER (2003), among others. İMROHOROĞLU, İMROHOROĞLU, and JOINES (1995), for example, examine the effects of a change in the public pensions on economic welfare in a 60-period OLG model with liquidity constraints and income uncertainty. In their model, welfare may even increase following the introduction of unfunded social security. The OLG framework is also the natural framework in order to study questions related to the demographic transition. As the population is aging, the pension system gets under pressure. DE NARDI, IMROHOROĞLU, and SARGENT (1999) look at different policy plans in order to cope with the transition. HECKMAN, LOCHNER, and TABER (1998) explain the rising wage inequality since the 1960s with the enlarged cohorts of the Baby Boom. As one of the very few studies, HECKMAN, LOCHNER, and TABER (1998) endogenize the schooling choice of the young cohort.

The OLG model framework has also been successfully applied to the study of business cycle fluctuations or the pricing of assets and equities.[2] Business cycles will be the focus of attention in the next chapter. The list of recent applications is only selective and by no means exhaustive.

This chapter is organized as follows. In the first section, you will be introduced to the basic life-cycle model with age-dependent cohorts and we will compute the steady state. In the second section, the transition between two steady states is examined. In the following, we will focus on OLG models with perfect foresight both for the individual and the aggregate economy. OLG models with uncertainty will be considered in the next chapter.

9.1 The Steady State

In this section, we solve an overlapping generations model without uncertainty. All agents of one cohort are identical and their

---

[2] Please see RÍOS-RULL (1996), STORESLETTEN, TELMER, and YARON (2007), and BROOKS (2002), among others.

behavior is analyzed by means of the behavior of a representative agent.

9.1.1 An Illustrative Example

We will use a 60-period overlapping generations model as an illustration. The periods correspond to years. The model is a much simplified version of the economy studied by AUERBACH and KOTLIKOFF (1987).[3] Three sectors can be depicted: households, production, and the government.

Households. Every year, a generation of equal measure is born. The total measure of all generations is normalized to one. Their first period of life is period 1. A superscript s of a variable denotes the age of the generation, a subscript t denotes time. For example, c_t^s is the consumption of the s-year old generation at time t.

Households live $T + T^R = 40 + 20$ years. Consequently, the measure of each generation is $1/60$. During their first $T = 40$ years, agents supply labor n_t^s at age s in period t enjoying leisure $l_t^s = 1 - n_t^s$. After T years, retirement is mandatory ($n_t^s = 0$ for $s > T$). Agents maximize lifetime utility at age 1 in period t:

$$\sum_{s=1}^{T+T^R} \beta^{s-1} u(c_{t+s-1}^s, l_{t+s-1}^s), \qquad (9.1)$$

where β denotes the discount factor. Notice that, different from the discount factor β in the Ramsey model, β does not necessarily need to be below one in an OLG model to guarantee that lifetime utility is finite.[4]

Instantaneous utility is a function of both consumption and leisure:

$$u(c,l) = \frac{((c+\psi)l^\gamma)^{1-\eta} - 1}{1-\eta}. \qquad (9.2)$$

---

[3] For example, we do not consider different types of agents among one cohort and model the tax and pension system in a very stylized way.

[4] For restrictions on the size of β in economies with infinitely-lived agents, see DEATON (1991).

The small constant $\psi = 0.001$ is added in order to ensure that utility is finite even for zero consumption in the case of no income. This choice will turn out to be very convenient in the subsequent computations as we will be able to use a grid over the individual capital stock with a lower bound equal to zero.

Agents are born without wealth, $k_t^1 = 0$, and do not leave bequests, $k_t^{61} = 0$. Since capital k is the only asset held by individuals, the terms capital and wealth will henceforth be used interchangeably. Agents receive income from capital k_t^s and labor n_t^s. The real budget constraint of the working agent is given by

$$k_{t+1}^{s+1} = (1 + r_t)k_t^s + (1 - \tau_t)w_t n_t^s - c_t^s, \quad s = 1, \ldots, T, \qquad (9.3)$$

where r_t and w_t denote the interest rate and the wage rate in period t, respectively. Wage income in period t is taxed at rate τ_t. We can also interpret $\tau_t w_t n_t^s$ as the worker's social security contributions.

The first-order conditions of the working household are given by:

$$\frac{u_l(c_t^s, l_t^s)}{u_c(c_t^s, l_t^s)} = \gamma \frac{c_t^s + \psi}{l_t^s} = (1 - \tau_t)w_t, \qquad (9.4)$$

$$\frac{1}{\beta} = \frac{u_c(c_{t+1}^{s+1}, l_{t+1}^{s+1})}{u_c(c_t^s, l_t^s)}[1 + r_{t+1}] \qquad (9.5)$$

$$= \frac{\left(c_{t+1}^{s+1} + \psi\right)^{-\eta} \left(l_{t+1}^{s+1}\right)^{\gamma(1-\eta)}}{\left(c_t^s + \psi\right)^{-\eta} \left(l_t^s\right)^{\gamma(1-\eta)}}[1 + r_{t+1}].$$

During retirement, agents receive public pensions b irrespective of their employment history and the budget constraint of the retired worker is given by

$$k_{t+1}^{s+1} = (1 + r_t)k_t^s + b - c_t^s, \quad s = T + 1, \ldots, T + T^R. \qquad (9.6)$$

The first-order condition of the retired worker is given by (9.5) with $l_t^s = 1$.

Production. The production sector is identical to the one used in previous chapters. Firms are of measure one and produce output Y_t in period t with labor N_t and capital K_t. Labor N_t is paid the wage w_t. Capital K_t is hired at rate r_t and depreciates at rate δ. Production Y_t is characterized by constant returns to scale and assumed to be Cobb-Douglas:

$$Y_t = N_t^{1-\alpha} K_t^{\alpha}. \tag{9.7}$$

In a factor market equilibrium, factors are rewarded with their marginal product:

$$w_t = (1-\alpha) K_t^{\alpha} N_t^{-\alpha}, \tag{9.8}$$
$$r_t = \alpha K_t^{\alpha-1} N_t^{1-\alpha} - \delta. \tag{9.9}$$

Government. The government uses the revenues from taxing labor in order to finance its expenditures on social security:

$$\tau_t w_t N_t = \frac{T^R}{T+T^R} b. \tag{9.10}$$

Following a change in the provision of public pensions b or in gross labor income $w_t N_t$, the labor income tax rate τ_t adjusts in order to keep the government budget balanced.

Equilibrium. The concept of equilibrium applied in this section uses a recursive representation of the consumer's problem following STOKEY and LUCAS with PRESCOTT (1989). This specification turns out to be very amenable to one of the two solution methods described in this section. For this reason, let $V^s(k_t^s, K_t, N_t)$ be the value of the objective function of the s-year old agent with wealth k_t^s. K_t and N_t denote the aggregate capital stock and employment. $V^s(k_t, K_t, N_t)$ is defined as the solution to the dynamic program:

$$V^s(k_t^s, K_t, N_t) = \begin{cases} \max_{k_{t+1}^{s+1}, c_t^s, l_t^s} \left[u\left(c_t^s, l_t^s\right) + \beta V^{s+1}(k_{t+1}^{s+1}, K_{t+1}, N_{t+1}) \right], \\ \qquad s = 1, \ldots, T \\ \max_{k_{t+1}^{s+1}, c_t^s} \left[u\left(c_t^s, 1\right) + \beta V^{s+1}(k_{t+1}^{s+1}, K_{t+1}, N_{t+1}) \right], \\ \qquad s = T+1, \ldots, T+T^{R-1}, \end{cases}$$

$$\tag{9.11}$$

subject to (9.3) and (9.6), respectively, and

$$V^{T+T^R}(k_t^{T+T^R}, K_t^{T+T^R}, N_t^{T+T^R}) = u(c_t^{T+T^R}, 1). \quad (9.12)$$

The value function $V^s(.)$, in particular, depends on the aggregate state variables K_t and N_t that determine the wage rate w_t and the interest rate r_t in period t via (9.8) and (9.9), and, in addition, τ_t with the help of the balanced budget (9.10). We did not include τ_t as an argument of the value function as it is implied by the values of K_t and N_t. Furthermore, $V^s(.)$ depends on the age s of the household, but not on calendar time t.

An equilibrium for a given government policy b and initial distribution of capital $\{k_0^s\}_{s=1}^{T+T^R}$ is a collection of value functions $V^s(k_t^s, K_t, N_t)$, individual policy rules $c^s(k_t^s, K_t, N_t)$, $n^s(k_t^s, K_t, N_t)$, and $k^{s+1}(k_t^s, K_t, N_t)$, relative prices of labor and capital $\{w_t, r_t\}$, such that:

1. Individual and aggregate behavior are consistent:

$$N_t = \sum_{s=1}^{T} \frac{n_t^s}{T+T^R}, \quad (9.13)$$

$$K_t = \sum_{s=1}^{T+T^R} \frac{k_t^s}{T+T^R}. \quad (9.14)$$

   The aggregate labor supply N_t is equal to the sum of the labor supplies of each cohort, weighted by its mass $1/(T+T^R) = 1/60$. Similarly, the aggregate capital supply is equal to the sum of the capital supplies of all cohorts.

2. Relative prices $\{w_t, r_t\}$ solve the firm's optimization problem by satisfying (9.8) and (9.9).

3. Given relative prices $\{w_t, r_t\}$ and the government policy b, the individual policy rules $c^s(.)$, $n_t^s(.)$, and $k_{t+1}^s(.)$ solve the consumer's dynamic program (9.11)-(9.12).

4. The goods market clears:

$$N_t^{1-\alpha} K_t^{\alpha} = \sum_{s=1}^{T+T^R} \frac{c_t^s}{T+T^R} + K_{t+1} - (1-\delta)K_t. \quad (9.15)$$

5. The government budget (9.10) is balanced.

Calibration. Our model just serves as an illustration. Therefore, we calibrate our model with the functional forms and parameters as commonly applied in DGE life-cycle models. Our benchmark case is characterized by the following calibration: $\eta = 2$, $\beta = 0.99$, $\alpha = 0.3$, $\delta = 0.1$, replacement ratio $\zeta = \frac{b}{(1-\tau)w\bar{n}} = 0.3$ (where $\bar{n}$ denotes the average labor supply in the economy), $T = 40$, $T^R = 20$. γ is chosen in order to imply a steady state labor supply of the working agents approximately equal to $\bar{n} = 35\%$ of available time and amounts to $\gamma = 2.0$. The small constant ψ is set equal to 0.001.

9.1.2 Computation of the Steady State

In this section, we compute the steady state that is characterized by a constant distribution of the capital stock over the generations, $\{k_t^s\}_{s=1}^{60} = \{k_{t+1}^s\}_{s=1}^{60} = \{\bar{k}^s\}_{s=1}^{60}$. In the steady-state economy, the aggregate capital stock and aggregate employment are constant, $K_t = K$ and $N_t = N$, respectively. As a consequence, prices w and r are constant, too, and so are taxes τ. Therefore, in the steady state, the computation of the equilibrium is simplified, as for given aggregate capital stock K and employment N, the value function and the individual policy function are only functions of the age s and individual wealth k^s. For notational convenience, we drop the time index t in this section and will only reintroduce it in the next section.

The general solution algorithm is described by the following steps:

Algorithm 9.1.1 (Computation of the Stationary Equilibrium of the OLG Model in Section 9.1)

Purpose: *Computation of the stationary equilibrium.*

Steps:

Step 1: Make initial guesses of the steady state values of the aggregate capital stock K and employment N.

Step 2: Compute the values w, r, and τ, which solve the firm's Euler equations and the government budget.
Step 3: Compute the optimal path for consumption, savings, and employment for the new-born generation by backward induction given the initial capital stock $k^1 = 0$.
Step 4: Compute the aggregate capital stock K and employment N.
Step 5: Update K and N and return to step 2 until convergence.

In step 3, the household's optimization problem needs to be solved. Our aim is to compute the steady-state distribution of capital $\{\bar{k}^s\}_{s=1}^{60}$. There are basically two different numerical techniques in order to solve this problem in an economy with perfect foresight. Assume that we would like to compute the optimal next-period capital stock $k^{s+1}(k^s, K, N)$, current consumption $c^s(k^s, K, N)$, and current labor supply $n^s(k^s, K, N)$. Then, we may either compute the policy functions only for $k^s = \bar{k}^s$ or we may compute the policy function over an interval $[k_{min}, k_{max}]$. In the first case, we have simultaneously computed the distribution of individual capital. This method, however, is only applicable to OLG models without idiosyncratic risk, as we will argue below.

In the second case, we compute the time path of savings, employment, and consumption using the optimal decision functions and the initial condition $k^1 = 0 = \bar{k}^1$. With the help of $k^2(k^1, K, N)$, we can compute $\bar{k}^2 = k^2(\bar{k}^1, K, N)$ and similarly k^s, $s = 3, \ldots, 60$. If we consider OLG models with heterogeneity and idiosyncratic risk, this will be the only workable procedure. Therefore, it is important to sort out if idiosyncratic risk and income mobility are important for the economic problem that you study. In Section 8.4.2, we found that idiosyncratic income risk does not help to improve the modeling of the income distribution business cycle dynamics in the infinite-life model with heterogenous agents. HUGGETT, VENTURA, and YARON (2007) analyze an overlapping generations model with heterogeneity in initial abilities, wealth, and human capital and also consider idiosyncratic shocks to human capital which they estimate from US data. They find that initial endowments of human capital and wealth are more important for the explanation of inequality than idiosyncratic shocks over the lifetime. Next, we describe the two methods for the computation of the steady state in turn.

Direct Computation of the Steady State Distribution. In order to illustrate the direct computation of the steady-state distribution, consider the first-order conditions of the working household with regard to labor supply and next-period capital stock, (9.4) and (9.5), respectively. Inserting the working households budget (9.3) in these two equations, we derive the following two steady-state equations for $s = 1, \ldots, T-1$:

$$(1-\tau)w = \gamma \frac{(1+r)k^s + (1-\tau)wn^s - k^{s+1} + \psi}{1-n^s}, \qquad (9.16)$$

$$\frac{1}{\beta} = \frac{\left((1+r)k^{s+1} + (1-\tau)wn^{s+1} - k^{s+2} + \psi\right)^{-\eta}}{\left((1+r)k^s + (1-\tau)wn^s - k^{s+1} + \psi\right)^{-\eta}} \\ \times \frac{(1-n^{s+1})^{\gamma(1-\eta)}}{(1-n^s)^{\gamma(1-\eta)}} [1+r]. \qquad (9.17)$$

Similarly, (9.16) also holds for $s = T$, while (9.17) needs to be adjusted:

$$\frac{1}{\beta} = \frac{\left((1+r)k^{T+1} + b - k^{T+2} + \psi\right)^{-\eta}}{\left((1+r)k^T + (1-\tau)wn^T - k^{T+1} + \psi\right)^{-\eta}} \\ \times \frac{1}{(1-n^T)^{\gamma(1-\eta)}} [1+r]. \qquad (9.18)$$

For the retired agent, the labor supply is zero, $n^s = 0$, and the Euler equation is given by:

$$\frac{1}{\beta} = \frac{\left((1+r)k^{s+1} + b - k^{s+2} + \psi\right)^{-\eta}}{\left((1+r)k^s + b - k^{s+1} + \psi\right)^{-\eta}} [1+r] \qquad (9.19)$$

for $s = T+1, \ldots, T+T^R - 1 = 41, \ldots, 59$. Remember that the optimal capital stock after death is also set equal to zero, $k^{61} \equiv 0$. The equations (9.16)-(9.19) for $s = 1, \ldots, 59$ constitute a system of 59+40=99 equations in the 59+40=99 unknowns $\{k^s\}_{s=2}^{60}$ and

$\{n^s\}_{s=1}^{40}$. Therefore, we have the same type of problem that we already encountered in Section 3.1.1 where we solve the finite-horizon Ramsey. We, again, need to compute a non-linear equations system in n unknowns, in our case with $n = 99$. However, as you may have learned by now, the computation of such large-scale non-linear problems may become cumbersome. Therefore, we better make further use of the recursive structure of the problem.

In the program RCh91d.g, we compute the solution of this problem. We know that agents are born without wealth at age 1, $k^1 = 0$ and do not leave bequests. Therefore, $k^{61} = 0$. Let us start by providing an initial guess of the wealth in the last period of life, k^{60}. With the help of this initial guess and the retired worker's first-order condition (9.19) at age $s = 59$, we are able to compute k^{59}. In this case, we only have to solve a non-linear equation problem with one unknown. Having computed k^{s+1} and k^{s+2} for the retired agent, we simply iterate backwards and compute k^s for $s = 59, 58, \ldots, 41$. From (9.16) for $s = 40$ and (9.18), we are able to compute n^{40} and k^{40}. We continue to compute k^s and n^s with the help of the values n^{s+1}, k^{s+1}, and k^{s+2} found in the previous two iterations and with the help of equations (9.16) and (9.17) until we have computed k^1 and n^1. If $k^1 = 0$, we are finished. Otherwise, we need to update our guess for k^{60} and recompute the distribution of individual capital and labor supply, $\{k^s\}_{s=1}^{60}$ and $\{n^s\}_{s=1}^{40}$. Notice, in particular, that we need to iterate backwards. We cannot start with a guess of k^2 given $k^1 = 0$ and iterate forwards in the presence of endogenous labor supply. With exogenous labor supply, we would also be able to find the optimal capital distribution with forward iteration (why?).

Finally, we need to mention how we update successive values for k^{60}. In RCh91d.g, we apply the *Secant Method* that we present in Section 11.5.[5] Successive values of k^{60} are found by:

$$k_{i+2}^{60} = k_{i+1}^{60} - \frac{k_{i+1}^{60} - k_i^{60}}{k_{i+1}^1 - k_i^1} k_{i+1}^1,$$

---

[5] Alternatively, you can also apply Newton's method. You will be asked to perform this in Problem 9.1.

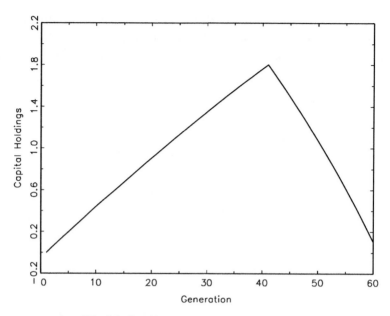

Figure 9.1: Age-Wealth Profile

where the subscript i denotes the number of the iteration. As the first two guesses for k^{60}, we choose the values $k_1^{60} = 0.15$ and $k_2^{60} = 0.2$. After 5 iterations, we find the absolute value of k_5^1 to be below 10^{-8}.

The solution for $\{\bar{k}^s\}_{s=1}^{60}$ is displayed in Figure 9.1. Typically for the life-cycle model, savings k^s increase until retirement at age $s = T$ and decline monotonically thereafter. The aggregate capital stock amounts to $K = 0.937$. Optimal labor supply is graphed in Figure 9.2. The labor supply declines with increasing age s because older agents hold higher stocks of capital. As a consequence, marginal utility of income declines for older age. Average working time amounts to 0.354 so that aggregate employment is equal to $N = 0.236$. The steady state values of pensions, the interest rate, and taxes are given by $b = 0.0977$, $r = 1.42\%$, and $\tau = 13.0\%$, respectively.

This direct method of computing the policy functions at single values of the state space only is very fast and accurate. It is also applicable to more complex models with many types of agents

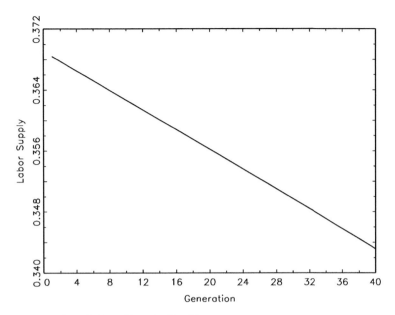

Figure 9.2: Age-Labor Supply Profile

and/or assets. In Problem 9.3 we ask you to solve an OLG model with 5 different types of agents in each generation and with a portfolio choice on capital and money. The basic challenge is to come up with a good initial guess. Therefore you are asked to compute the solution for the model without money and just one representative agent in each generation and find the solution step by step using homotopy methods.

The direct computation should be applied whenever possible. However, this will not always be feasible as in models with idiosyncratic uncertainty. In order to understand this point, assume that we introduce an autocorrelated shock to productivity so that next-period income is stochastic and depends on the current period income. For the sake of the argument, let us assume that we have $n = 5$ different levels of individual income in each period and that the transition between these states is described by a Markov chain. In this case, of course, agents build up different levels of wealth during their working life depending on their income history. How many different types would we have to distinguish at age 41? At age 1, all have equal (zero) wealth. At age 2, we have 5 types of agents who differ with regard to their period 1 income and hence with regard to their savings (and wealth in period 2). At age 3, we have $5 \times 5 = 25$ different types of agents. If we continue like this, we have to distinguish 5^{40} different agents at age 41 who all hold different levels of wealth. During retirement, the number of different agents does not increase because all agents receive equal retirement benefits. Therefore, if we compute the optimal savings path recursively with the direct method, we would have to apply Algorithm 9.1.1 9.09×10^{27} times![6] In such an economy, of course, the only feasible alternative solution method consists of computing the policy functions over an interval of the state space. This method is described next.

Computation of the Policy Functions. In order to compute the age-wealth profile of the steady state, $\{\bar{k}^s\}_{s=1}^{60}$, we may also compute the optimal policy function $k^{s+1}(k^s, K, N)$ for each cohort s over an interval $k^s \in [k^s_{min}, k^s_{max}]$. As we do not know the age-wealth profile in advance, we will start to compute the policy functions for each age over the same interval $[k^s_{min}, k^s_{max}] = [k_{min}, k_{max}]$. In later iterations, we may adapt the state space for each cohort s.[7] Having computed the policy functions, it is easy to find the solution $\{\bar{k}^s\}_{s=1}^{60}$. We simply start with $k^1 = \bar{k}^1$ and compute $k^2(k^1) = k^2(0) = \bar{k}^2$. Similarly, we compute $\bar{k}^{s+1}$ with the help of $k^{s+1}(\bar{k}^s, \bar{K}, \bar{N})$ for $s = 2, \ldots, T + T^R - 1$.

There are various methods in order to compute the policy functions. We will discuss value function iteration and projection methods that you have already encountered in the Chapter 4 and Chapter 6 for the solution of the Ramsey problem. We discuss these methods in turn and start with value function iteration in an economy with finite lifetime.

Value Function Iteration. A straightforward method of approximating the value function $V^s(k^s)$, $s = 1, \ldots, T+T^R$, involves

---

[6] $5^{40} = 9.0949470 \times 10^{27}$.

[7] The adaption of the age-specific asset grid may not be a feasible strategy in the case of heterogeneous agents among the same cohort, a problem that you will encounter in Section 9.2.

tabulating it for a finite number n_k of points on the state space starting in the last period of life, $T + T^R$, and iterating backwards in time to the period $s = 1$. The maximization occurs over the interval $[k_{min}, k_{max}]$, which, in particular, must contain the steady state, a point, which is only determined as the outcome of our computation. In the last period $T + T^R$, the value function $V^{T+T^R}(k^{T+T^R})$ is given by (9.12) with $c^{T+T^R} = (1+r)k^{T+T^R} + b$. For a given table of values for $V^{s+1}(k^{s+1})$ on the grid $[k_{min}, k_{max}]$, the approximate retired agent's maximum at age s on the right-hand side of (9.11)-(9.12) can be found by choosing the largest value for $V^{s+1}(k^{s+1})$ given k^s, which we store as $k^{s+1}(k^s)$. Together with the two neighboring points on the asset grid, we bracket the maximum and apply a Golden Section Search to find the maximum of the Bellman equation (9.11). To get values of the value function $V^{s+1}(.)$ off gridpoints, we interpolate linearly or cubically.

At this point, we need to emphasize a crucial difference between finite-horizon and infinite-horizon problems. Differently from value function iteration in infinite-horizon models, we know the value of the agent in the last period of his life, $V^{60} = u(c^{60}, l^{60})$ with $c^{60} = (1+r)k^{60} + b$ and $l^{60} = 1.0$. As a consequence, we do not have the problem to provide an initial guess for the value function. This feature also holds for the other solution methods of finite-horizon problems, e.g. the projection method presented below. Given the value $V^{60}(k^s, K, N)$ for $k^s \in [k_{min}, k_{max}]$, we can find the value function of the different cohorts, $V^s(.)$, $s = 59, \ldots, 1$ with only one iteration. As a consequence, the computation of the policy functions is much faster in most applications with finite horizons than in infinite-horizon problems. Notice, however, that the need for storage capacity increases as the number of policy functions is multiplied by the number of different age cohorts.

The dynamic programming problem of the working agent (9.11) involves the maximization over an additional control, the labor supply n^s. A standard procedure to solve this kind of problem consists of choosing the largest value over a grid on the labor supply $[n_{min}, n_{max}]$. As a consequence, the optimal next period capital stock together with the optimal labor supply decision is found by iterating over a two-dimensional grid. For reasonable required accuracy, we often find this procedure to already imply prohibitive storage capacity and computing speed in order to be a useful method on personal computers. Instead, we only iterate over a one-dimensional grid of the capital stock and solve the household's Euler equation (9.4) and budget constraint (9.3) for given current and next period capital stock (k^s, k^{s+1}). For our choice of the functional form for utility $u(.)$, we can solve these two equations even directly for c^s and n^s for given k^s and k^{s+1}. Notice that this procedure does not restrict the controls c^s and n^s to lie on any grid.

The solution is computed with the help of value function iteration in the program RCh91v.g. Concerning our computation details, wealth is bounded below by $k_{min} = 0$, while maximum wealth is set equal to $k_{max} = 5.0$, which is found to never be binding.[8] Furthermore, we choose an equispaced grid over the capital stock $[k_{min}, k_{max}]$ of $n_k = 50$ points. The required storage capacity associated with this algorithm is equal to $(2 \times T + T^R)n_k = 500$ numbers. The user can choose between linear and cubic spline interpolation. The age-wealth profile computed with value function iteration is almost identical to the one displayed in Figure 9.1. Our results are summarized in Table 9.1.

The aggregate capital stock and aggregate employment amount to $K = 0.948$ (0.942) and $N = 0.237$ (0.236) for the linear (cubic spline) interpolation. Notice that in the case of cubic spline interpolation between grid points, the aggregate capital stock diverges less from the aggregate capital stock found with the direct method described above. This difference is a good measure of accuracy as the latter solution can be expected to coincide with the true solution (in the case of direct computation of the steady-state distribution, the accuracy of the non-linear equation solution and the divergence of $\bar{k}^1$ from zero are both less than 10^{-8}). In addition, cubic spline interpolation is faster than linear interpolation, even though only to a small extent. While value function iteration with linear interpolation takes 12 minutes and 22 seconds,

---

[8] In our model, we abstract from any inequality constraints such as $c \geq 0$ or $k \geq 0$ because these constraints do not bind (except in period 1 with $\bar{k}^1 \equiv 0.0$).

Table 9.1

Method	K	N	Run Time
Direct computation	0.937	0.236	00:04
Value function iteration			
— linear interpolation	0.948	0.237	12:22
— cubic spline	0.942	0.236	11:37
Projection method	0.941	0.237	00:10

Notes: Run time is given in minutes:seconds on an Intel Pentium(R) M, 319 MHz computer.

cubic spline interpolation only takes 11 minutes and 37 seconds. In good accordance with our findings for the solution of the stochastic Ramsey model with value function iteration in Chapter 4, we also find that the cubic spline interpolation, even though it requires more function evaluations, is faster in the computation of the OLG model than linear interpolation because the Golden Section Search converges much faster.

Projection Methods. Alternatively, we compute the steady state solution $\{\bar{k}^s\}_{s=1}^{60}$ with the help of projection methods that we introduced in Chapter 6. For this reason, we approximate the consumption function $c^s(k^s, K, N)$, $s = 1, \ldots, 60$, and the labor supply $n^s(k^s, K, N)$, $s = 1, \ldots, 40$, with Chebyshev polynomials of order n_c and n_n over the interval $[k_{min}, k_{max}]$, respectively:

$$c^s(k^s, K, N) = \frac{1}{2} ac_0^s + \sum_{j=1}^{n_c} ac_j^s T_j(z(k^s)),$$

$$n^s(k^s, K, N) = \frac{1}{2} an_0^s + \sum_{j=1}^{n_n} an_j^s T_j(z(k^s)),$$

where $z(k^s) = (2k^s - k_{min} - k_{max})/(k_{max} - k_{min})$ is the linear transformation that maps $k^s \in [k_{min}, k_{max}]$ into the interval $[-1, 1]$.[9]

---

[9] See also Section 11.2.6 on Chebyshev Polynomials where we describe the transformation in more detail.

We choose orthogonal collocation to compute the coefficients ac_j^s and an_j^s from equations (9.4) and (9.5). In the case of the retired worker, for example, we solve the system of n_c+1 nonlinear equations at the values z that are the $n_c + 1$ (transformed) zeros of the Chebyshev polynomial T_{n_c}. In order to solve the nonlinear-equations problem, we use a quasi-Newton method. The initial guess for the coefficients ac^s and an^s are the coefficients ac^{s+1} and an^{s+1} for $s < T + T^R$. For $s = T + T^R$, we are able to compute the exact values of c^{T+T^R} at $2n_c$ Chebyshev interpolation nodes because we know that the household consumes all his income and his wealth in the last period. Therefore, we can approximate the function in period $t + T^R$ by least squares with the help of Algorithm 11.2.2. For $s = T$, we need to provide an initial guess of the coefficients for labor supply, an^{40}. We use an inelastic labor supply function, $n^{40}(k^s) = 0.3$ in order to initialize the coefficients again making use of Algorithm 11.2.2.

The program RCh91p.g computes the steady-state solution with the help of projection methods. Concerning our computational details, we chose a degree of approximation n_c equal to 3. By this choice, nc_3 and nc_3/nc_2 are less than 10^{-6} and 10^{-3}, respectively, and we can be confident that our approximation is acceptable. Similarly, we choose $n_n = 3$. We also choose the same interval over the state space, $[k_{min}, k_{max}] = [0,5]$, as in the case of the value function iteration. The computed Chebyshev coefficients drop off nicely because the decision functions of the household can be described by polynomial functions of small degree quite accurately. Besides, all parameter values are exactly the same as in the case of value function iteration.

The results from the solution of the steady state distribution with the help of the projection method almost coincide with those from the value function iteration with cubic spline interpolation (see Table 9.1). In the former, the aggregate capital stock amounts to $K = 0.941$ and employment is equal to $N = 0.237$. The optimal policy functions for consumption differs by less than 0.1% over the range $[k_{min}, k_{max}] = [0,5]$ between these two methods. Importantly, however, the algorithm based on projection methods is 60 times faster than the one based on value function iteration and only takes 10 seconds.

At this point, let us reconsider the results in Table 9.1 and mention one word of caution. In accordance with the results presented in Table 9.1, we recommend to use direct computation whenever possible. In Chapter 10, we introduce both individual and aggregate uncertainty. In these cases, direct computation is not feasible and one might conjecture that the projection method is preferable to value function iteration with cubic splines due to the much shorter computational time. However, in many cases, the introduction of uncertainty requires the consideration of much larger intervals for the state space intervals over which we have to approximate the policy function. In these cases, we often find that the quality of the projection method deteriorates[10] or it might be extremely difficult to come up with a good initial guess. In fact, the search for a good initial guess might be more time-consuming than the use of value function iteration methods or the initial guess might be found with the help of value function iteration. For this reason, we cannot give a general recommendation which method is preferable and the researcher may have to try different methods and find the most accurate and fastest one with trial and error.

9.2 The Transition Path

In their seminal work, AUERBACH and KOTLIKOFF (1987) have laid the groundwork for the modern analysis of dynamic fiscal policy. Typically, they analyze the question how a particular policy affects the welfare of different generations. For example, how does a change in the pension replacement ratio, i.e. the ratio of pensions to net wage income, affect the lifetime utility of present and future cohorts of the population. In their analysis, they assume that the economy is in a steady state in period 0 that, for example, is characterized by a replacement ratio of 30%. At the

---

[10] For example, using projection methods we may be unable to preserve the shape (e.g. the concavity) of the policy function.

beginning of period 1, the government announces an unexpected change of pension policy, for example a decrease of the replacement ratio to 20% that becomes effective in period t. Agents have perfect foresight and already adjust their behavior in time period 1 and all subsequent periods. After a certain number of transition periods, the economy converges to the new steady state. The number of transition periods are taken as approximately 2-3 times the number of generations. AUERBACH and KOTLIKOFF (1987), for example, assume in their 55-overlapping generations model that the economy has reached the new steady state after 150 periods.

In the following, we will study the computation of the transition path in a model with perfect foresight. First, we present a simple stylized 6-period model, which we have chosen for illustrative purpose. Subsequently, we describe our basic algorithm for its solution. The main insights also carry over to larger-scale models. If we consider a 6-period model, the transition is complete after some 20 periods and we have to predict the time path of the aggregate variables in our model. In the 6-period model, these aggregate variables will be the aggregate capital stock and employment. Therefore, we will have to predict 40 values. For a most simple initial guess and a simple updating scheme of the transition path, the iteration over the time path of the aggregate variables will converge. However, this does not need to be the case in more complex models where we have to predict time paths consisting of some hundred or even thousand variables. In the next section, you will get to know such a much more complex 75-period OLG model of the demographic transition. In this case, we need to apply much more sophisticated updating schemes of the transition path.[11] In the second part of this section, we, therefore, will introduce you to three different ways to update the transition path: linear, Newton's and Broyden's methods.

---

[11] In our own work, we have found examples where simple Newton-Raphson methods or linear updating schemes do not converge, for example in the model of HEER and IRMEN (2008).

9.2.1 A Stylized 6-Period Model

In the spirit of AUERBACH and KOTLIKOFF (1987), we will compute the transition dynamics associated with a long-run once-and-for-all change of fiscal policy in the following. In particular, we look at an unexpected change of the replacement ratio from 30% to 20% which is announced and becomes effective in period 1. While AUERBACH and KOTLIKOFF (1987) consider a 55-period model in their original work, we distinguish only 6 generations in our model. The periods in our model can be interpreted as decades. Of course, the main idea of the solution method is unaffected by this innocent assumption.

During the first 4 decades, the agents are working, while during the last two decades of their life, they are retired. Besides, the model is exactly the same as the one described in Section 9.1. For your convenience, we have summarized the description of the economy in Example 9.2.1. As we consider decades rather than years, we also need to adjust the calibration of the discount factor β and the depreciation rate δ. The new values are also summarized in Example 9.2.1.

Example 9.2.1
6-Period Overlapping Generations Model. Households live 6 periods. Each generation is of measure 1/6. The first 4 periods, they are working, the last two periods, they are retired and receive pensions. Households maximize lifetime utility at age 1 in period t:

$$\sum_{s=1}^{6} \beta^{s-1} u(c_{t+s-1}^s, l_{t+s-1}^s).$$

Instantaneous utility is a function of both consumption and leisure:

$$u(c,l) = \frac{((c+\psi)l^\gamma)^{1-\eta} - 1}{1-\eta}$$

The working agent of age s faces the following budget constraint in period t:

$$k_{t+1}^{s+1} = (1+r_t)k_t^s + (1-\tau_t)w_t n_t^s - c_t^s, \quad s=1,\ldots,4.$$

The budget constraint of the retired worker is given by

$$k_{t+1}^{s+1} = (1+r_t)k_t^s + b_t - c_t^s, \quad s = 5, 6$$

with $k_t^1 = k_t^7 \equiv 0$ and $l_t^5 = l_t^6 = 1$. Total time endowment is normalized to one and allocated to work and leisure, $1 = n_t + l_t$.

Production Y_t is characterized by constant returns to scale and assumed to be Cobb-Douglas:

$$Y_t = N_t^{1-\alpha} K_t^\alpha.$$

In a factor market equilibrium, factors are rewarded with their marginal product:

$$w_t = (1-\alpha) N_t^{-\alpha} K_t^\alpha,$$
$$r_t = \alpha N_t^{1-\alpha} K_t^{\alpha-1} - \delta.$$

Furthermore, the government budget is balanced in every period t:

$$\tau_t w_t N_t = \frac{2}{6} b_t.$$

In equilibrium, individual and aggregate behavior are consistent:

$$N_t = \sum_{s=1}^{4} \frac{n_t^s}{6},$$

$$K_t = \sum_{s=1}^{6} \frac{k_t^s}{6},$$

and the goods market clears:

$$K_t^\alpha N_t^{1-\alpha} = \sum_{s=1}^{6} \frac{c_t^s}{6} + K_{t+1} + (1-\delta) K_t.$$

In period 0, the economy is in the steady state associated with the parameter values $\beta = 0.90$, $\eta = 2.0$, $\gamma = 2.0$, $\alpha = 0.3$, $\delta = 0.40$, and a replacement ratio of pensions relative to net wage earnings equal to $\zeta = \frac{b_t}{(1-\tau)w_t \bar{n}_t} = 30\%$, where $\bar{n}_t$ is the average labor supply in the economy. The small constant ψ is set equal to 0.001. In period $t=1$, the government announces a change of the replacement ratio to $\zeta = 20\%$, that becomes instantaneously effective in period 1.

9.2.2 Computation of the Transition Path

The Auerbach-Kotlikoff problem in Example 9.2.1 is solved in six basic steps that are described in the following Algorithm 9.2.1:

Algorithm 9.2.1 (Computation of the Transition Dynamics for the Perfect Foresight 6-Period OLG Model of Example 9.2.1)

Purpose: *Computation of the transition dynamics.*

Steps:

Step 1: Choose the number of transition periods t_c.
Step 2: Compute the initial and final steady state solution for the periods $t = 0$ and $t = t_c + 1$, respectively.
Step 3: Provide an initial guess for the time path of the aggregate variables $\{K_t^0, N_t^0\}_{t=1}^{t_c}$.
Step 4: Compute the transition path.
Step 5: If the new value $\{K_t^1, N_t^1\}_{t=1}^{t_c}$ is close to the starting value, stop. Otherwise update the initial guess and return to Step 4.
Step 6: If the aggregate variables in period t_c are not close to those in the new steady state, increase t_c and return to step 3 using the transition path from the last iteration in the formulation of an initial guess.

In step 1, we need to assume that the transition only lasts a finite number of periods in order to compute the transition. Typically, if $T + T^R$ denotes the number of generations, researchers pick a number of transition periods approximately equal to $3 \times (T + T^R)$, which is usually found to be sufficient in order to guarantee convergence to the new steady state. We will choose $t_c = 20$ model periods corresponding to 200 years. As it will turn out, this number of periods is sufficiently high and the transition will be complete. The computation is implemented in the program RCh92AK6.g.

In step 2, we compute the old and the new steady state using the methods described in Section 9.2.1 above. In particular,

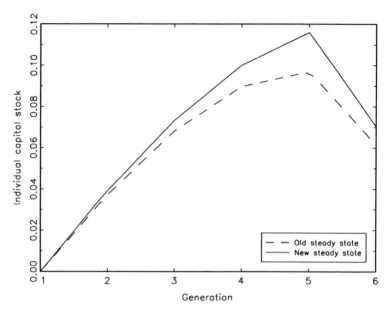

Figure 9.3: Age-Capital Profile in the New and in the Old Steady State

for this simple problem we are able to use direct computation. The age-wealth profile and the age-labor supply profile for the two steady states are displayed in the Figures 9.3 and 9.4, respectively. Notice that savings increase in the new steady state as the government reduces pensions and the agents accumulate private savings for old age. Since the government reduces pensions, it is also able to cut wage taxes in order to keep the government budget balanced. Taxes τ are reduced from 13.04% to 9.09%. Consequently, the labor supply is higher in the new steady state than in the old steady state. The aggregate capital stock and employment amount to 0.0665 (0.0589) and 0.233 (0.228) in the new (old) steady state with replacement ratio of 20% (30%), respectively.

In step 3, we provide a guess for the dynamics of the capital stock and employment, $\{K_t, N_t\}_{t=1}^{t_c}$. We know that $K_0 = 0.0589$ ($N_0 = 0.228$) and $K_{t_c+1} = 0.0665$ ($N_{t_c+1} = 0.233$). As an initial guess, we simply interpolate linearly between these values. Given the time path of the aggregate state variables, we can compute

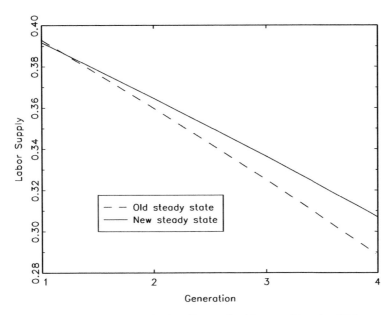

Figure 9.4: Age-Labor Supply Profile in the New and in the Old Steady State

wages, the interest rates, pensions, and the tax rate from the first-order conditions of the firm and the balanced budget constraint.

Computation of the Transition Path for Given Factor Prices, Taxes, and Pensions. In step 4, we need to compute the transition between the old and the new steady state. For this reason, the two steady states need to be saddlepoint stable, an issue that we turn to in Section 10.2 and which you are asked to show in Problem 10.3 in Chapter 10. Given the sequence of factor prices, taxes, and pensions, we can compute the capital stock and labor supply of the s-year old household in period t, $s = 1, \ldots, 6$, starting in the last period of the transition t_c and going backward in time. As in the case for the computation of the steady state, we use the first-order conditions of the households to compute the capital stock and the labor supply of the household born in period $t = 20, 19, \ldots, 0, -1, -2, -3, -4$:

$$\gamma \frac{c_{t+s-1}^s + \psi}{1 - n_{t+s-1}^s} = (1 - \tau_{t+s-1})w_{t+s-1}, \quad s = 1, \ldots, 4 \quad (9.20\text{a})$$

$$\frac{1}{\beta} = \frac{(c_{t+s}^{s+1} + \psi)^{-\eta}(1 - n_{t+s}^{s+1})^{\gamma(1-\eta)}}{(c_{t+s-1}^{s} + \psi)^{-\eta}(1 - n_{t+s-1}^{s})^{\gamma(1-\eta)}}, \quad s = 1, \ldots, 5 \tag{9.20b}$$

with $n_t^5 = n_t^6 = 0$. Furthermore, we substitute consumption from the budget constraint, $c_t^s = (1 - \tau_{t+s-1})w_{t+s-1}n_{t+s-1}^s + (1 + r_{t+s-1})k_{t+s-1}^s - k_{t+s}^{s+1}$ and use $k_t^1 = k_t^7 = 0$ so that (9.20) is a system of 9 non-linear equations in the 9 unknowns $\{k_t^2, k_{t+1}^3, k_{t+2}^4, k_{t+3}^5, k_{t+4}^6, n_t^1, n_{t+1}^2, n_{t+2}^3, n_{t+3}^4\}$. In the program RCh92AK6.g, this non-linear equations problem is solved in the procedure rftr. The sequences of the factor prices, pensions, and income tax rates have to be specified as global variables. We can use this routine in all periods of the transition and also in the steady state. For example, during our first iteration over the aggregate capital stock and labor supply, we use the time sequences

$$\{K_{20}^0, K_{21}^0, \ldots, K_{25}^0\} = \{0.661, 0.665, \ldots, 0.665\},$$
$$\{N_{20}^0, N_{21}^0, \ldots, N_{25}^0\} = \{0.2330, 0.2332, \ldots, 0.2332\},$$

where the values for the periods $t = 21, \ldots, 25$ are equal to the new steady state values. From these sequences we compute the factor prices $\{w_t^0, r_t^0\}_{t=20}^{25}$, the tax rate $\{\tau_t^0\}_{t=20}^{25}$, and the pensions $\{b_t^0\}_{t=20}^{25}$. We store them as global variables and compute the policy of the household born in period $t = 20$, $\{k_{20}^1, k_{21}^2, \ldots, k_{25}^6, n_{20}^1, \ldots, n_{23}^4\}$. We continue in the same way for the agents born in $t = 19, \ldots, 1$.

For the agents that are born prior to period 1, $t = 0, \ldots, -4$, we need to modify our computation. As an example, let us consider the computation of the policy functions for the household born in period $t = 0$. We assumed that the change in policy is unexpected. Therefore, the agent does not know in period $t = 0$ that the policy change will be affected in period $t = 1$ and, hence, that the factor prices, tax rates, and pensions will be different from the old steady-state value starting in period $t = 1$. Therefore, we cannot simply use the vectors $\{K_0^0, K_1^0, \ldots, K_5^0\}$ and $\{N_0^0, N_1^0, \ldots, N_5^0\}$ and the corresponding factor prices, tax rates, and pensions together with the non-linear equations system (9.20) in order to

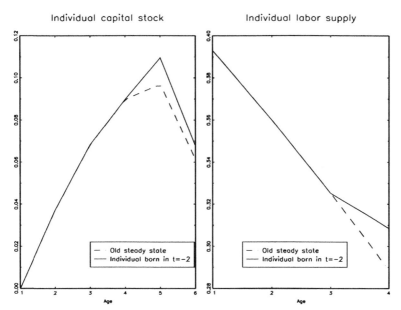

Figure 9.5: Capital-Age and Labor-Age Profile in the Old Steady State and for the Household Born in Period $t = -2$

compute the optimal allocation. In period 0, the household behaves exactly as the household in the old steady state. Accordingly, his savings and his labor supply in the first period of his life are also equal to those of the 1-year old household in the old steady state, $k^2 = 0.0372$ and $n^1 = 0.393$. Therefore, we modify the procedure `rftr` in the program `RCh92AK6.g` and substitute the two first-order conditions (9.20a) and (9.20b) for $s = 1$ by the condition that k^2 and n^1 are equal to the old steady-state values. We proceed in the same way for $t = -1, \ldots, -4$.

In Figure 9.5, we illustrate the capital-age and labor age-profile for the household born in period $t = -2$ by the solid line. At age $s = 4$ in period $t = 1$, he learns about the change in policy. He adjust his labor supply and savings in this period. Consequently, n^4 and k^5 are different from the old steady values that are depicted by the broken line. k^4 is still determined by the household's behavior in period 0.

We stop our computation for the household that is born in period $t = -4$ because the households born in periods $t = -5, -6, \ldots$ do not have any effect on the aggregate capital stock and employment during the transition as they are not alive in period 1.

It is straightforward to compute the aggregate capital stock and employment in each period $t = 1, \ldots, 20$ from the savings and labor supply of the households that are alive in period t:

$$K_t = \sum_{s=1}^{6} k_t^s, \quad N_t = \sum_{s=1}^{4} n_t^s.$$

Of course, we update the aggregate capital stock and employment for $t, t+1, \ldots, t+5$ directly after the computation of the optimal savings and labor supply of the household born in period t so that we do not have to store the optimal policies for all generations.

The computation with the direct method is fast and accurate. The computation for the savings and labor supply of each generation takes only fractions of a second and the accuracy is equal to the one of the non-linear equations solver (10^{-10}). As we already mentioned in Section 9.1, the direct computation of the first-order conditions with non-linear equations methods may not be feasible in more complex models. In the application of the next section, for example, we will not be able to use it, but have to resort to the more time-consuming value function iteration method instead.

Updating Schemes. In step 5, we need to update the time path for the aggregate variables $\{K_t, N_t\}_{t=1}^{t_c=20}$. We will consider three methods: 1. simple linear updating, 2. the Newton Raphson method and 3. Broyden's method. 1. With linear updating, we simply compute the new capital stock K_t and employment N_t as a weighted average of the old and the new value in iteration i over the transition path, $K_t^{i+1} = \phi K_t^i + (1-\phi) K_t^{i*}$, where K_t^i denotes the value of the capital stock used in the last iteration and K_t^{i*} is the value that is found in iteration i by averaging the individual capital stocks of the households alive in period t. In the program RCh92AK6.g, we choose $\phi = 0.8$. Convergence of the

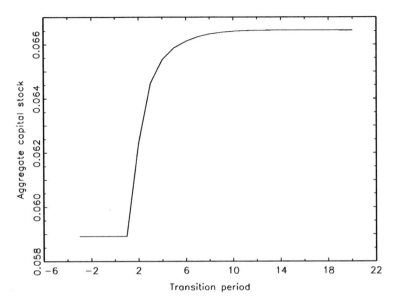

Figure 9.6: Transition from the Old to the New Steady State

time paths for the capital stock and employment $\{K_t, N_t\}_{t=0}^{20}$ occurs after 14 iterations. The computation takes 0.34 seconds on an Intel Pentium(R) M, 319 MHz computer.

The computed dynamics of the capital stock are displayed in Figure 9.6. Obviously, the economy has converged from the old to the new steady state aggregate capital stock, from $\bar{K} = 0.0589$ to $\bar{K} = 0.0665$. In period 0, the economy is in old steady state. All agents have chosen their next-period capital stock k_1^s, $s = 1, \ldots, 6$, assuming that there is no change in the fiscal policy. Consequently, the capital stock of an s-year old generation in period 1, k_1^s, is also equal to the capital stock of the s-year old generation in period 0, k_0^s. Accordingly, the aggregate capital stock is equal in these two periods, $\bar{K} = K_0 = K_1$. Only in period 2 does the capital stock K_t start to change. In period 20, the last period of the transition, the capital stock K_{20} is equal to 0.0665 and only diverges from the new steady state $\bar{K} = 0.0665$ by 0.010%.

2. In step 5, we are looking for the solution of the non-linear equation

$$\mathbf{g}(K_1^i, K_2^i, \ldots, K_{20}^i, N_1^i, N_2^i, \ldots, N_{20}^i) = \begin{bmatrix} K_1^{i*} - K_1^i \\ K_2^{i*} - K_2^i \\ \vdots \\ K_{20}^{i*} - K_{20}^i \\ N_1^{i*} - N_1^i \\ N_2^{i*} - N_2^i \\ \vdots \\ N_{20}^{i*} - N_{20}^i \end{bmatrix} = 0.$$

In order to apply the Newton Raphson algorithm, we have to compute the Jacobian matrix which is a 20 × 20 matrix for our Example 9.2.1. Let $\mathbf{x^i}$ denote our stacked column vector $(K_1^i, K_2^i, \ldots, K_{20}^i, N_1^i, N_2^i, \ldots, N_{20}^i)'$ and $J(\mathbf{x^i})$ the Jacobian matrix that results from the differentiation of the above equation $\mathbf{g}(\mathbf{x^i})$. In the next step, we update the time path for the aggregate variables according to (11.90), $\mathbf{x}^{i+1} = \mathbf{x}^i - J(\mathbf{x}^i)^{-1}\mathbf{g}(\mathbf{x}^i)$. In the program RCh92AK6, the solution for the aggregate variables is found after two iterations. The run time amounts to 3.45 seconds as the computation of the Jacobian matrix is relatively time-consuming. Our results are summarized in Table 9.2.

Table 9.2

Method	Run Time	Iterations
Linear Update	0:34	14
Newton	3:45	2
Broyden		
— Jacobian matrix	1:91	2
— Steady state derivatives	0:13	3

Notes: Run time is given in seconds:hundreth of seconds on an Intel Pentium(R) M, 319 MHz computer. In the Broyden updating step, a first initialization of the Jacobian matrix is either provided by the Jacobian of the non-linear system describing the transition path or by using the derivatives of the non-linear equations that are describing the final steady state for an approximation of the Jacobian.

3. In many applications that are based upon the OLG framework, the number of generations and transition periods is much higher than in Example 9.2.1 and we may have to solve a system $\mathbf{g}(\mathbf{x})$ in several hundred variables. You will get to know such an application in the next section where the dimension of the Jacobian matrix amounts to 900×900. In these cases, the computation time for the Jacobian matrix becomes prohibitive, especially if we need to iterate many times in step 5, and not only twice as in the present Example 9.2.1. In these cases, we advocate the Broyden algorithm that is described in more detail in Section 11.5.2. This algorithm is identical to the Newton Raphson algorithm except that you do not compute the Jacobian matrix in each step but rather use an approximation for the update. In the program RCh92AK6 , you may choose between two different ways to initialize the Jacobian matrix in the first iteration. In the first case, you compute the actual Jacobian matrix. In the second case, we use an initialization that has been suggested by LUDWIG (2007). In particular, we assume that i) the choice of K_t^i (N_t^i) only has an effect on the capital stock K_t^{i*} (employment N_t^{i*}) in the same period and ii) the effect is identical to the one in the final steady state. Therefore, we set all elements off the diagonal in the Jacobian matrix equal to zero and initialize the elements on the diagonal with the partial derivative of the variable in the respective nonlinear equation that is describing the final steady state. The two conditions for the final steady state in period 21 are given by:

$$\mathbf{h}(K_{21}, N_{21}) = \begin{bmatrix} h^1(K_{21}, N_{21}) \\ h^2(K_{21}, N_{21}) \end{bmatrix} = \begin{bmatrix} K_{21}^* - K_{21} \\ N_{21}^* - N_{21} \end{bmatrix} = \mathbf{0}.$$

According to this equation, the capital stock K_{21} and employment N_{21} and associated factor prices w_{21} and r_{21} imply individual savings and labor supply that add up to K_{21}^* and N_{21}^*. Therefore, we have to compute the partial derivatives $\partial h^1(K_{21}, N_{21})/\partial K_{21}$ and $\partial h^2(K_{21}, N_{21})/\partial N_{21}$.[12]

---

[12] In addition, you may also initialize the elements of the Jacobian matrix that describe the contemporaneous effects of K_t^i (N_t^i) on N_t^{i*} (K_t^{i*}) using the cross derivatives $\partial h^1(K_{21}, N_{21})/\partial N_{21}$ and $\partial h^2(K_{21}, N_{21})/\partial K_{21}$.

In Table 9.2, you notice that the Broyden algorithm is much faster than the Newton algorithm, especially if we use the steady state derivatives in order to form an initial guess of the Jacobian matrix. In this case, the gain in speed is considerable as we only have to find the derivatives of a two-dimensional non-linear equations system that is describing the steady state rather than the 40-dimensional non-linear equations system that is describing the transition. Convergence with the Broyden algorithm is slower than with the Newton algorithm, but the slower convergence is usually outweighed by the gain in speed in the computation of the Jacobian matrix.

As another alternative, many studies consider a variant of the Gauss-Seidel algorithm. In Section 11.5.2, we introduce you to the details of the Gauss-Seidel algorithm, and you are asked to apply this algorithm to the solution of the model in this section in Problem 9.6. In our experience, the Broyden algorithm seems to dominate the other updating schemes in more complex models in terms of convergence and robustness. This is also confirmed by findings of LUDGWIG (2007) who advocates a hybrid algorithm for the solution of complex OLG models with more complicate non-linear transitional dynamics that combines the Gauss-Seidel and Broyden's method.

9.3 Application: The Demographic Transition

In the following, we will consider the transition dynamics in a more sophisticated model. As an example, we analyze the demographic transition in an economy with 75 overlapping generations. In this model, we need to find the time path for a three-dimensional vector consisting of the capital stock K, employment L, and government transfers tr over a time horizon of 300 periods. In essence, we have to solve a non-linear equations system of 900 variables. As one possible approach to this problem, we will propose Broyden's method that you got to know in the previous section and that is also described in more detail in Section 11.5.2.

9.3.1 The Model

We analyze the effects of a (very simplified) demographic transition on savings and factor prices in a model with overlapping generations and heterogeneous agents. There are three sectors in the economy: households, firms, and the government. Workers build up savings for old age. Firms maximize profits. The government collects taxes and social security contributions and runs a balanced budget.

Demographics and Timing. A period, t, corresponds to one year. At each t, a new generation of households is born. Newborns have a real life age of 21 denoted by $s = 1$. All generations retire at age 66 ($s = R = 46$) and live up to a maximum age of 95 ($s = J = 75$). At t, all agents of age s survive until age $s+1$ with probability ϕ_s where $\phi_0 = 1$ and $\phi_J = 0$.[13]

Let $N_t(s)$ denote the number of agents of age s at t. We assume that population grows at the exogenous rate $g_N = 1.1\%$ until the year 2000 corresponding to $t = 0$. Afterwards, the population growth rate unexpectedly drops to 0% and remains equal to zero permanently. At $t = 0$, we assume that the economy is in a steady state.

Households. Each household comprises one representative worker. Households maximize intertemporal utility at the beginning of age 1 in period t:

$$\max \sum_{s=1}^{J} \beta^{s-1} \left(\Pi_{j=1}^{s} \phi_{t+j-1, j-1} \right) u(c_{t+s-1}(s), l_{t+s-1}(s)), \quad (9.21)$$

---

[13] For simplicity, we assume that survival probabilites for the s-aged agent are constant over time. Obviously, survival probabilities will continue to increase for some time in most countries.

where instantaneous utility $u(c,l)$ is a function of consumption c and labor supply l:[14]

$$u(c,l) = \frac{\left(c^\gamma (1-l)^{1-\gamma}\right)^{1-\eta}}{1-\eta}, \quad \eta > 0, \quad \gamma \in (0,1); \tag{9.22}$$

here, $\beta > 0$ denotes the discount factor.

Households are heterogeneous with regard to their age, s, their individual labor efficiency, $e(s,j)$, and their wealth, ω. We stipulate that an agent's efficiency $e(s,j) = \bar{y}_s \epsilon_j$ depends on its age, $s \in \mathcal{S} \equiv \{1, 2, ..., 75\}$, and its efficiency type, $\epsilon_j \in \mathcal{E} \equiv \{\varepsilon_1, \varepsilon_2\}$. We choose the age-efficiency profile, $\{\bar{y}_s\}$, in accordance with the US wage profile. The permanent efficiency types ϵ_1 and ϵ_2 are meant to capture differences in education and ability. We use Γ to denote the unique invariant distribution of $e_j \in \mathcal{E}$.

The net wage income in period t of an s-year old household with efficiency type j is given by $(1 - \tau_w - \tau_b) w_t e(s,j) l_t(s)$, where w_t denotes the wage rate per efficiency unit in period t. The wage income is taxed at rate τ_w. Furthermore, the worker has to pay contributions to the pension system at rate τ_b. A retired worker receives pensions $b(s,j)$ that depend on his efficiency type j. Clearly, $b(s,j) = 0$ for $s < R$.

Households are born without assets at the beginning of age $s = 1$, hence $\omega_t(1) = 0$. Parents do not leave bequests to their children and all accidental bequests are confiscated by the government. This element of the model that is absent from the models of the previous chapters in this book is necessary in the presence of stochastic survival probabilities. We could have introduced bequests and a parent-child link into the model, which, however, greatly complicates the computation (see HEER, 2001b). As an alternative, we could have assumed the presence of perfect annuity markets as in KRUEGER and LUDWIG (2006), for example. In this case, the end-of-period assets of the dying households are shared equally by the surviving members of the same cohort.

---

[14] Different from previous sections, we use l rather than n for the denotation of the labor supply as we use the denotation N and L for the population size and the aggregate labor supply, respectively.

The household earns interest r_t on his wealth $\omega_t \in \mathbb{R}$. Capital income is taxed at rate τ_r. In addition, households receive lump-sum transfers tr_t from the government. As a result, the budget constraint at t of an s-year old household with productivity type j and wealth ω_t is:

$$b_t(s,j) + (1 - \tau_w - \tau_b)w_t e(s,j)l_t(s) + [1 + (1-\tau_r)r_t]\omega_t(s)$$
$$+ tr_t = c_t(s) + \omega_{t+1}(s+1).$$

Firms. At each t, firms produce output, Y_t, according to the following constant-returns-to-scale production function:

$$Y_t = A_t L_t^{1-\alpha} K_t^{\alpha}. \tag{9.23}$$

Productivity A_t grows at the exogenous rate g_A.[15] Profit maximization gives rise to the first-order conditions:

$$\frac{\partial Y_t}{\partial K_t} = r_t + \delta = \alpha k_t^{\alpha-1}, \tag{9.24}$$

$$\frac{\partial Y_t}{\partial L_t} = w_t = (1-\alpha)k_t^{\alpha}, \tag{9.25}$$

where $k_t \equiv K_t/A_t L_t$ denotes the capital per effective labor in period t. Again, w, r, and δ denote the wage rate, the interest rate, and the depreciation rate, respectively.

Government. The government collects income taxes T_t in order to finance its expenditures on government consumption G_t and transfers Tr_t. In addition, it confiscates all accidental bequests Beq_t. The government budget is balanced in every period t:

$$G_t + Tr_t = T_t + Beq_t. \tag{9.26}$$

In view of the tax rates τ_w and τ_r, the government's tax revenues are:

$$T_t = \tau_w w_t L_t + \tau_r r_t \Omega_t, \tag{9.27}$$

where Ω_t is aggregate wealth at t.

Government spending is a constant fraction of output:

$$G_t = \bar{g} Y_t.$$

---

[15] HEER and IRMEN (2008) consider a model of the demographic transition with endogenous growth.

Social Security. The social security system is a pay-as-you-go system. The social security authority collects contributions from the workers in order to finance its pension payments to the retired agents. Pensions are a constant fraction of net labor income of the productivity type j:

$$b_t(s,j) = \begin{cases} 0 & s < R \\ \zeta(1 - \tau_w - \tau_b)w_t \epsilon_j & s \geq R. \end{cases} \quad (9.28)$$

In equilibrium, the social security budget is balanced and will be defined below. The replacement ratio of net pensions, $\zeta = \frac{b_t}{(1-\tau_w-\tau_b)w_t}$, is assumed to be constant. In this case, the contribution rate τ_b has to adjust in order to balance the social security budget.[16] In order to simplify notation, we do not index τ_b by time t.

Stationary Equilibrium. In the stationary equilibrium, individual behavior is consistent with the aggregate behavior of the economy, firms maximize profits, households maximize intertemporal utility, and factor and goods' markets are in equilibrium. To express the equilibrium in terms of stationary variables only, we have to divide aggregate quantities by $A_t L_t$ and individual variables and prices by A_t. Therefore, we define the following stationary aggregate variables:

$$k_t \equiv \frac{K_t}{A_t L_t}, \quad \tilde{B}eq_t \equiv \frac{Beq_t}{A_t L_t}, \quad \tilde{T}_t = \frac{T_t}{A_t L_t},$$

$$\tilde{G}_t = \frac{G_t}{A_t L_t}, \quad \tilde{C}_t = \frac{C_t}{A_t L_t}, \quad \tilde{Y}_t = \frac{Y_t}{A_t L_t},$$

and stationary individual variables:

$$\tilde{c}_t \equiv \frac{c_t}{A_t}, \quad \tilde{w}_t \equiv \frac{w_t}{A_t}, \quad \tilde{b}_t \equiv \frac{b_t}{A_t}, \quad \tilde{\omega}_t \equiv \frac{\omega_t}{A_t}, \quad \tilde{tr}_t \equiv \frac{tr_t}{A_t}.$$

Let $F_t(\tilde{\omega}, s, j)$ denote the distribution of individual wealth $\tilde{\omega}$, age s, and the efficiency type j in the period t.

---

[16] In Problem 9.5 you are also asked to compute the case that i) the social security contribution rate τ_b is constant, while ζ adjusts, and ii) that the government increases the retirement age by 5 years for those agents born after 2020.

9.3 Application: The Demographic Transition

A stationary equilibrium for a government policy $\{\tau_r, \tau_w, \tau_b, \bar{g}, \zeta, tr\}$ and initial distribution $F_0(\tilde{\omega}, s, j)$ in period 0 corresponds to a price system, an allocation, and a sequence of aggregate productivity indicators $\{A_t\}$ that satisfy the following conditions:

1. Population grows at the rate $g_{N,t} = \frac{N_{t+1}}{N_t} - 1$.
2. Capital market equilibrium: aggregate wealth is equal to aggregate capital:

$$\Omega_t = K_t.$$

3. Households maximize the intertemporal utility (9.21) subject to the budget constraint:

$$\tilde{b}_t(s,j) + (1 - \tau_w - \tau_b)\tilde{w}_t e(s,j) l_t(\tilde{\omega}, s, j) + $$
$$+ [1 + (1 - \tau_r)r_t]\tilde{\omega}_t(s,j) + \tilde{tr}_t$$
$$= \tilde{c}_t(s,j) + \tilde{\omega}_{t+1}(s+1,j)(1 + g_A).$$

This gives rise to the two first-order conditions:

$$\frac{1-\gamma}{\gamma} \frac{\tilde{c}_t(s,j)}{1 - l_t(s,j)} = (1 - \tau_w - \tau_b)\tilde{w}_t e(s,j) \tag{9.29}$$

and

$$\tilde{c}_t(s,j)^{\gamma(1-\eta)-1}(1 - l_t(s,j))^{(1-\gamma)(1-\eta)} = \beta(1+g_A)^{\gamma(1-\eta)-1}\phi_{t,s}$$
$$\times [1 + (1-\tau_r)r_{t+1}]\,\tilde{c}_{t+1}(s+1,j)^{\gamma(1-\eta)-1}$$
$$\times (1 - l_{t+1}(s+1,j))^{(1-\gamma)(1-\eta)}.$$
$$\tag{9.30}$$

Individual labor supply $l_t(\tilde{\omega}, s, j)$, consumption $c_t(\tilde{\omega}, s, j)$, and optimal next period assets $\tilde{\omega}'_t(\tilde{\omega}, s, j)$ of period t are functions of the individual state variables $\tilde{\omega}$, j, and s, and also depend on the period t.

4. Firms maximize profits satisfying (9.24) and (9.25).
5. The aggregate variables labor supply L_t, bequests Beq_t, consumption C_t, and taxes T_t are equal to the sum of the individual variables.

6. The government budget is balanced.

$$\bar{g}k_t^\alpha + \tilde{tr}_t \frac{N_t}{L_t} = \tilde{T}_t + \tilde{B}eq_t.$$

7. The budget of the social security system is balanced.
8. The goods market clears.
9. The distribution F_t evolves according to

$$F_{t+1}(\tilde{\omega}', s+1, j) = \sum_{\tilde{\omega}'=\tilde{\omega}'_t(\tilde{\omega},s,j)} \phi_t F_t(\tilde{\omega}, s, j), \quad s = 1, \ldots, 74,$$

and for the newborns

$$F_{t+1}(0, 1, j) = N_{t+1}(1) \times \Gamma(\epsilon_j).$$

The model is calibrated following HEER and IRMEN (2008). Parameters are chosen such that $\eta = 2.0$, $\beta = 0.99$, $\{\epsilon_1, \epsilon_2\} = \{0.57, 1.43\}$, $G/Y = 19.5\%$, $\tau_w = 24.8\%$, $\tau_r = 42.9\%$, and $\zeta = 15\%$. γ is set equal to 0.32 to imply an average labor supply approximately equal to 0.3. In addition, we use the survival probabilities for the year 2000 as estimated by the UNITED NATIONS (2002). The survival probabilities decrease with age and are presented in Figure 9.7.[17]

The mean efficiency index $\bar{y}_s$ of the s-year-old worker is taken from HANSEN (1993), and interpolated to in-between years. As a consequence, the model is able to replicate the cross-section age distribution of earnings of the US economy. Following İMROHOROĞLU, İMROHOROĞLU, and JOINES (1995), we normalize the average efficiency index to one. The mean efficiency of the s-year old agents $\bar{y}_s$ is displayed as the solid line in Figure 9.8. Notice that the age-productivity profile is hump-shaped and earnings peak at age 50.

For comparison purpose, we also graph the age-productivity profile for the German economy (broken line). The productivity of age s is computed with the help of the average hourly wages of

---

[17] We would like to thank Alexander Ludwig and Dirk Krueger for the provision of the data.

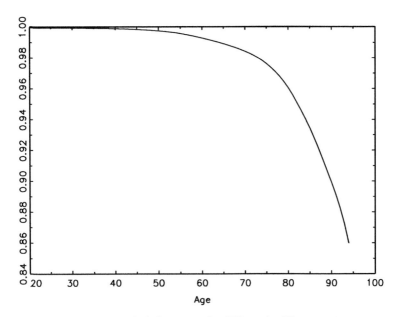

Figure 9.7: Survival Probabilities in the US in the Year 2000

the s-year old during the years 1990-97 following the method of HANSEN (1993). Average productivity is normalized to one. We further interpolated the productivity-age profile with a polynomial function of order 3. We use data from the Cross National Data Files for West Germany during 1990-97 which are extracted from the GSOEP.[18] As it is obvious from inspection of Figure 9.8, the productivity-age profiles of the US and Germany almost coincide.

9.3.2 Computation

In the following paragraphs, we will describe the computation of the transition dynamics. We choose a time horizon of 300 years

---

[18] We only consider agents who were working 1,500 hours per year or more and who earned a wage in excess of one Euro. The number of observations for each generation ranges between 154 (for the 20-year old) and 765 (for the 29-year old). We would like to thank Mark Trede for providing us with the data.

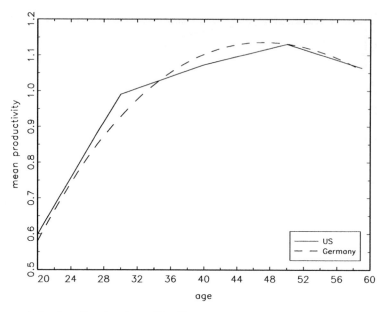

Figure 9.8: Age-Productivity Profile

which we may interpret as the years 2000-2300 corresponding to the periods $t = 0, \ldots, 300$. We start with an initial guess of the time path for the aggregate variables $\{K, L, tr\}_{t=1}^{300}$ and iterate as long as it converges. The allocation in the period $t = 0$ is given and corresponds to the initial steady state.

The computation of the transition is very time-consuming. In each iteration, we have to compute the optimal allocation for all individual generations that are born in the years $1926, 1927, \ldots, 2299, 2300$ separately since each generation faces a different factor price sequence and hence chooses a different allocation. We also have to consider the generations born prior to 2000 because they are still alive in the year 2000 and their savings and labor supply contribute to the aggregate capital stock and employment, respectively. Therefore, we have to go back in time until the year 1926 when the oldest generation that is still alive in 2000 was born. The solution of the perfect foresight model with Broyden's method is described by the following steps:

Algorithm 9.3.1 (Computation of the Transition Dynamics for the Perfect Foresight OLG Model in Section 9.3 with a Broyden Algorithm)

Purpose: *Computation of the transition dynamics.*

Steps:

Step 1: *Compute the initial and final steady state solution for the periods $t = 0$ and $t = 301$, respectively.*
Step 2: *Compute the demographics.*
Step 3: *Provide an initial guess for the time path of the aggregate variables $\{\tilde{K}_t^0, L_t^0, \tilde{tr}_t^0\}_{t=1}^{300}$.*
Step 4: *Compute the transition.*
Step 5: *If the new value $\{\tilde{K}_t^1, L_t^1, \tilde{tr}_t^1\}_{t=1}^{300}$ is close to the starting value, stop. Otherwise update the initial guess with the help of Broyden's method and return to Step 4.*

The algorithm is implemented in program RCh93.g. In Step 1, we compute the initial and the final steady state (with $g_N = 1.1\%$ and $g_N = 0\%$, respectively) with the help of direct computation. Therefore, we start with a simple model. We first consider an OLG model with inelastic labor supply, $l_t^s \equiv 0.3$. In this case, also aggregate employment L_t is exogenous and we can compute the social contribution rate τ_b from the social security budget. The steady state is computed in the routine getk in the program. Importantly, the non-linear equations system consists of two equations. The two unknowns are the aggregate capital stock $\tilde{K}$ and government transfers $\tilde{tr}$ in the steady state. The two equations reflect the conditions that the sum of the individual assets equals the aggregate capital stock and that the government budget is balanced.

The computation of the individual allocations $\{k^s(\epsilon)\}_{s=1}^{75}$ for given $\tilde{K}$, N, τ_b, and transfers $\tilde{tr}$ is very fast as it amounts to the solution of a linear equations system. In order to see this consider the intertemporal first-order condition for the one-year old agent and notice that the terms involving the labor supply $l(1) = l(2) = 0.3$ drop out of the equation:

$$\tilde{c}(1)^{\gamma(1-\eta)-1} = \beta(1+g_A)^{\gamma(1-\eta)-1}\phi_1\left[1+(1-\tau_r)r_{t+1}\right]\tilde{c}(2)^{\gamma(1-\eta)-1},$$

which can be reduced into a linear equation in $c(1)$ and $c(2)$:

$$c(1) = \kappa c(2),$$

with $\kappa = (1+g_A)\left(\beta\phi_1\left[1+(1-\tau_r)r_{t+1}\right]\right)^{1/(\gamma(1-\eta)-1)}$. Once we replace $c(1)$ and $c(2)$ with the help of the budget constraint, we have found a linear (!) equation in $k(2)$ and $k(3)$ ($k(1) = 0$ is known). Similarly, we can find another 73 linear equations involving $k(3),\ldots,k(75)$ by starting from the first-order conditions for the agents aged $s = 2,\ldots,74$. The solution of a linear equations system can be computed very fast via the LU-decomposition described in Section 11.1.8. It takes only fractions of a second to solve our problem. We store the capital-age profile as an initial guess for the direct computation of the steady state. Next, we compute the steady state with elastic labor supply. The non-linear equations system in the aggregate variables $\tilde{K}$, L, and $\tilde{tr}$ is solved in the routine getvaluess. As an additional equation, we include the condition that the sum of the individual labor supplies in efficiency units is equal to aggregate labor supply L. Given the vector $\{\tilde{K}, L, \tilde{tr}\}$, we can compute w, r, and τ_b and solve the individual optimization problem calling the routine Sys1. This amounts to the computation of a problem in 240 non-linear equations that consists of the first-order conditions of the households. For the working and retired agents, we have to solve the Euler equations (9.30) for $s = 1,\ldots,75$ and $j = 1,2$. The optimal labor supply is computed from (9.29) for $s = 1,\ldots,45$, $j = 1,2$. As our initial guess for the labor supply for all agents, we use $l_t(s) \equiv 0.3$. The initial guess for the optimal capital stock is taken from the solution of the model with inelastic labor supply.

Notice that we define the aggregate variables, factor prices, transfers, and social security contributions over the 75-period lifetime of the household as a global variable in our program. In the case of the steady state, these sequences are constant, of course. When we call the routine Sys1, it computes the allocation of the household for any sequence of these variables. In particular, we are also able to use it for the computation of the household problem during the transition where the aggregate variables are not vectors of constants.

At this point, let us mention one generalization. So far, we have assumed that we are in a steady state at the beginning of the transition. Of course, this does not need to be the case. For example, consider the case of the German economy that was experiencing a structural break in the year 1989 in the form of the reunification with a former socialist part of the country. As a consequence, it may be a little far-fetched to assume that Germany has reached a steady state meanwhile. Similarly, if we want to study the question of demographic transition in the US, the assumption of a steady state today would probably be too simplifying as fertility and mortality rates have not been stationary in the US over the recent decades.

How can we compute the initial steady state in this case? As you will find out shortly, in order to compute the transition, we need to know the allocation of all agents who are alive at the beginning of the transition. Accordingly, we need to know the sequence of the factor prices, tax rates, and social security contribution rates that are important for their allocation decision. Since our oldest agents are aged 75, we need to know the time series for the last 75 periods. If we are in a steady state, this does not pose a problem since all aggregate variables are constant. If we are out of the steady state, the issue is more problematic. One typical approach to the solution of this problem is used by KRUEGER and LUDWIG (2007), among others. They study the demographic transition in the US (among other countries) starting in the year 2000. They assume that the economy was in a steady state in 1950 and start the computation of the transition in this year imposing the demographic development of the US population during 1950-2000 exogenously. Even if the US were not in a steady state in 1950, the allocation in the year 2000 is hardly affected by this initialization because most of the households whose decisions depend on the behavior of the economy prior to 1950 do not live any more.

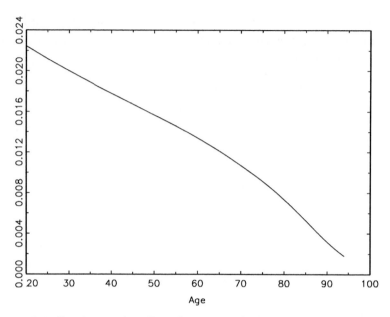

Figure 9.9: Stationary Age Distribution in the Initial Steady State

In Step 2, we first initialize the number of the transition periods. In our case, we assume that the transition takes 300 periods. As mentioned above, you should choose a number that is at least three times higher than the maximum age of the households. As we will find out, 300 periods is already quite short in our case. Next we compute the mass of the population and individual generations during the transition with the help of the population growth rates and the survival probabilites. In Figure 9.9, we display the stationary distribution of the generations that is associated with these survival probabilities. The total mass of the population is normalized to one in the initial steady state.

In the year 2001 corresponding to period $t = 1$, the population growth rate is assumed to fall from 1.1% to 0% permanently. As a consequence, the demographics change. We assume that the 1-year old household (corresponding to the 20-year old) consists of one person and also has one child. Consequently, the demographic structure of the economy is still changing for some time until the one-year old generation has approached its new population share

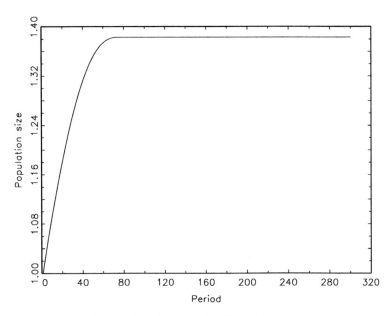

Figure 9.10: Population Size During the Transition

in the final steady-state. The transition of the population size is displayed in Figure 9.10. The new mass of the population in the final steady state is equal to 1.38.

At first sight, it seems puzzling that the mass of the population is still growing even though the population growth rate drops to zero. In order to understand the basic mechanism that is at work here consider a model with two generations. Let B_t denote the mass of the total population, which consists of the mass of the agents born in period $t-1$ (the old ones), N_{t-1}, and those born in period t (the young ones), N_t. Consequently, $B_t = N_t + N_{t-1}$. Until period $t = 0$, the population grows at rate g_N, $N_t = (1+g_N)N_{t-1}$ implying

$$B_0 = N_0 + N_{-1} = N_0 + \frac{N_0}{1+g_n} = \frac{2+g_N}{1+g_N}N_0.$$

If we normalize B_0 to one, $N_0 = (1+g_N)/(2+g_N)$. In period $t = 1$, the population growth rate drops to zero and

$$B_1 = N_0 + N_1 = N_0 + N_0 = 2\frac{1+g_N}{2+g_N} > 1.$$

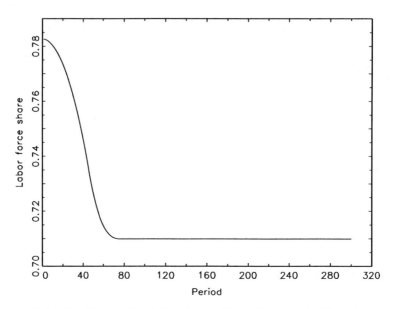

Figure 9.11: Decline of the Labor Force Share During the Transition

Since we have 75 overlapping generations in our model, the transition is more time-consuming, of course. In the computation of the solution, we have do keep in mind that the mass of the total population is growing during the transition. Often we have to divide the aggregate sums of the individual variables by this number.

The main effect of the demographic transition results from the decline in the labor force share. As fewer young workers are born, the share of the retired agents rises and the burden of the pensions increases. The development of the labor force share is graphed in Figure 9.11. In our economy, we observe a considerable drop of the labor share from 78% to 71%. In addition, we also have to notice that the composition of the labor force changes. In particular, the share of older agents in the labor force increases and, therefore, average productivity of the worker rises as well.

In Step 3, we provide an initial guess for the time path of the aggregate variables $\{\tilde{K}_t^0, L_t^0, \tilde{tr}_t^0\}_{t=1}^{300}$. We assume a linear law of motion for K, L, and tr, starting from the initial steady state value in period $t = 1$ and reaching the new steady state in period $t = 301$.[19]

Given this sequence for the endogenous variables, we call the procedure `getvaluetrans` in the program `RCh93.g` in Step 4. With the help of the aggregate variables, we can compute all factor prices, transfers, and the social security contribution rate that are necessary for the computation of the individual optimization problem. We start the computation of the individual policy functions in the last period of the transition, $t = 300$, and iterate backwards. In each period, we compute the optimal policy functions for the households born in period t. Therefore, we assign the factor prices to global variables and call the routine `sys1`. In each period $t = 1, \ldots, 300$, we have to aggregate the capital stock and labor supply of the generations currently alive. Therefore, when we consider a generation born in period t, we use its allocation, $\{k_{t+s-1}(s), l_{t+s-1}(s)\}_{s=1}^{s=75}$ and add the individual capital stock and labor supply to the aggregate capital stock $\tilde{K}_{t+s-1}$ and employment L_{t+s-1} for $s = 1, \ldots, 75$. Of course, we have to multiply the individual variables by the measure of the generation with productivity j that we computed in Step 2. As we iterate over the periods t, we do not have to store the allocation of the generation born in period t. We only use the allocation of the generation born in t as an initial guess for the one born in $t - 1$ that we compute in the next iteration.

Given the aggregate consistency conditions and the government budget constraint, we can compute the new time sequence $\{\tilde{K}_t^{i*}, L_t^{i*}, \tilde{tr}_t^{i*}\}_{t=1}^{t=300}$. In Step 5, we update our prior guess $\{\tilde{K}_t^i, L_t^i, \tilde{tr}_t^i\}_{t=1}^{t=300}$. This amounts to the solution of the 900 equations $\tilde{K}_t^{i*} - \tilde{K}_t^i = 0$, $L_t^{i*} - L_t^i = 0$, and $\tilde{tr}_t^{i*} - \tilde{tr}_t^i = 0$, $t = 1, \ldots, 300$. Standard Newton-Raphson methods will break down as we are trying to compute the Jacobian matrix with a dimension of 900×900 in each step. A workable solution to this problem is Broyden's algorithm as described in Section 11.5.2. In order to economize

---

[19] If we had assumed the existence of perfect annuity markets rather than postulating that accidental bequests are confiscated by the government, we would have needed only the two endogenous variables $\{K, L\}$ since these variables would have already implied the government transfers.

on computational time we use (11.94) for the update of the inverse matrix of the Jacobian matrix. The only remaining problem is to find an initial value of the Jacobian matrix. As described in the previous section, we use the Jacobian matrix in the final steady state as an approximation for the Jacobian matrix in all periods.[20] It is straightforward to compute the derivative of our function getvaluess with respect to the final steady state values $\tilde{K}_{301}$, L_{301}, and $\tilde{tr}_{301}$. Given the Jacobian matrix in the final steady state, we compute the Kronecker product of this matrix and an identity matrix of dimension 300×300. In essence, we are assuming that the aggregate variables in period t, $\{\tilde{K}_t, L_t, \tilde{tr}_t\}$, do not have an impact on the behavior in the other periods and that the economy behaves alike in every period. In our problem, we find out that this approximation of the Jacobian matrix J performs in a very satisfactory way and its computation is very fast, amounting to a matter of seconds.

In order to improve convergence in our program RCh93.g, we also imply a line search over the values $\mathbf{x}^i = \{\tilde{K}_t^i, L_t^i, \tilde{tr}_t^i\}_{t=1}^{t=300}$. Assume we have computed the next step size

$$d\mathbf{x} = -J(\mathbf{x}^i)^{-1} \mathbf{f}(\mathbf{x}^i),$$

with the help of the value returned by the routine getvaluetrans. We then apply Algorithm 11.5.3 from Chapter 11 in order to find an increase $\lambda\, d\mathbf{x}$ that improves our fit, $0 < \lambda \leq 1$. In case we do not find a decrease of the function value, we reinitialize our Jacobian matrix with our first initialization and return to step 4. In our computation, however, this step is not necessary.

We stop the computation as soon as we have found a solution, where the sum of the squared deviations of two successive values $\mathbf{x}^i$ is less than 0.001. In this case, the maximum percentage difference between two individual values of $\tilde{K}_t^i$ and L_t^i with the new values $\tilde{K}_t^{i*}$ and L_t^{i*} is approximately equal to 0.8% and 0.01%, respectively. With Broyden's method, we need 4 iterations. The computation is very time-consuming and amounts to 8 hours 21

---

[20] In particular, we are also using the final steady-state values of the cross derivatives $\partial(\tilde{K}_t^{i*} - \tilde{K}_t^i)/\partial L_t^i$, $\partial(\tilde{K}_t^{i*} - \tilde{K}_t^i)/\partial \tilde{tr}_t^i$, ... for the initialization.

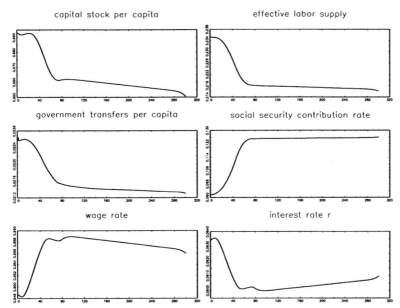

Figure 9.12: Transition Dynamics of Aggregate Variables and Factor Prices

minutes on an Intel Pentium(R) M, 319 MHz machine. The resulting time paths of the aggregate variables and factor prices is graphed in Figure 9.12. As you can see by simple inspection, we may even have considered a longer transition period of 400 periods or even more as we do not observe a smooth approximation of the final steady state, but rather some curvature.

9.3.3 Results

The declining labor force share decreases total employment in our economy. As a consequence, the capital intensity increases and wages go up, while the interest rate declines. The transition of the factor prices is illustrated in Figure 9.12.

How does the decline of the population growth rate affect the savings behavior of the households? In the left column of Figure 9.13, we depict the savings behavior of the low-productivity and the high productivity agents in the initial and final steady state,

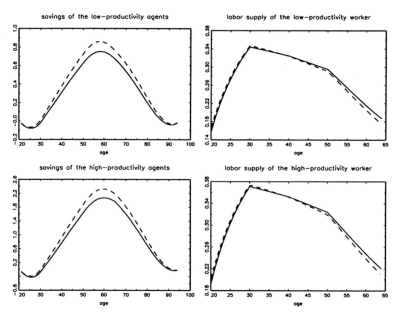

Figure 9.13: Steady State Behavior in the Economy with Constant (solid line) and Growing (broken line) Population

respectively. Obviously, savings of the high-productivity workers are higher than those of the low-productivity workers because their labor income is higher as well. Both agents dissave during their first years.[21]

If you compare the savings behavior in the economy with the growing population ($g_N = 1.1\%$, broken line) with the one in the constant-population economy ($g_N = 0$, solid line), you find out that households have higher average savings per capita in the case of a growing population. As the main explanation, social contributions are lower in the growing population so that workers receive a higher net income and can save more.

In the right column of Figure 9.13, we present the labor supply of the low and the high-productivity workers in the economy with a constant and a growing population, respectively. High-productivity workers have a higher labor supply than low-

---

[21] In Section 10.2.2, we also consider the case where we impose a credit constraint $\omega \geq 0$ in a model with heterogeneous agents.

productivity workers because they have higher wage rates per working hour. In our model, the substitution effect is stronger than the income effect. When we compare the constant-population with the growing-population economy, we find that in the former, older agents work longer, while in the latter, the younger agents are supplying more labor. This observation is explained by the higher wealth of the older workers in the growing economy. In addition, workers substitute labor intertemporally so that households supply more labor in young years in the growing economy which is characterized by higher interest rates (compare Figure 9.12). However, the quantitative effects are small.

Problems

9.1 Recompute the illustrative example in Section 9.1.1 using direct computation with the help of the program RCh91d. However, instead of the Secant method use Newton's method instead. Therefore, write a routine that computes the capital stock k^1 for given k^{60}. Solve the non-linear equation $k^1(k^{60}) = 0$.

9.2 Earnings-Related Pensions

Consider the steady state of the model in Section 9.1 with a constant wage and interest rate. Pension payments b are assumed to be lump-sum irrespective of the individual's earnings history and contributions to social security. As a more realistic description of pension payments in modern industrial countries, let pension payments depend on average life-time earnings. In addition, the government provides minimum social security b_{min} in old age. More formally, for an individual with earnings history $\{n^s w\}_{s=1}^T$, annual pension payments are calculated by the formula

$$b = \epsilon \sum_{s=1}^{T} \frac{n^s w}{T} + b_{min}, \quad 0 \leq \epsilon < 1.$$

As a consequence, the individual state variables of the value function of the retired agent are given by individual wealth k and annual pension payments b, while the individual state variables of the young agent are given by his wealth k and his accumulated earnings.

Furthermore, the working agent maximizes his labor supply taking the intertemporal effect on his entitlement to pension payments into account. Accordingly, his first-order condition with respect to labor supply in the steady state is given by

$$\frac{u_l(c^s, l^s)}{u_c(c^s, l^s)} = (1-\tau)w + \beta^{T+1-s} \frac{\partial V^{T+1}(k^T, b, K, N)}{\partial b} \epsilon \frac{w}{T},$$

where the second additive term on the right-hand side of the equation reflects the increase of old-age utility from an increase in labor supply through its effect on pensions.

Compute the stationary equilibrium and show that an initial increase of ϵ from 0 to 0.1 increases employment and the welfare as measured by the value of the newborn generation $V^1(0, 0, K, N)$.

9.3 Money-Age Distribution.

In this problem, you will compute the money-age distribution and compare the model's cross-section correlation of money with income and wealth to its empirical counterparts. The model follows HEER, MAUSSNER, and MCNELIS (2007).

Consider an economy with overlapping generations. The total measure of all households is equal to one. Households live a maximum of $T = 60$ years and face a stochastic survival probability ϕ_s from age s to $s+1$. The first 40 years, they are working supplying one unit of labor inelastically, and the remaining years, they retire. Households differ with regard to age s and their productivity type $j = 1, \ldots, 5$. Each productivity class j is of equal measure. Households hold two assets, real money $m_t = M_t/P_t$ and capital k_t. The household h maximizes life-time utility:

$$\left[\sum_{s=1}^{T} \beta^{s-1} \left(\Pi_{j=1}^{s} \phi_s \right) u(c_{hs}, m_{hs}), \right] \quad (9.31)$$

where β and c denote the discount factor and real consumption, respectively. A role for money is introduced by assuming money in the utility:

$$u(c, m) = \frac{\left(c^\gamma m^{1-\gamma} \right)^{1-\sigma}}{1 - \sigma}. \quad (9.32)$$

Individual productivity $e(s, j) = \bar{y}_s \epsilon_j$ depends on its age, $s \in \{1, 2, ..., 75\}$ and its efficiency type, $\epsilon_j \in \{0.5, 0.75, 1, 1.25, 1.5\}$. The s-year old agent receives income from capital k_{hs} and labor $e(s, j)w$ in each period s of his life. After retirement agents do not work, $e(s, j) = 0$ for $s \geq 41$. The budget constraint of the s-year old household h is given by:[22]

$$(1 - \tau_r) r k_{hs} + (1 - \tau_w - \eta) w e(s, z_h) + b(\bar{e}_{hs}) + tr + k_{hs} + m_{hs}$$
$$= c_{hs} + k_{hs+1} + m_{hs+1}(1 + \pi) - Seign,$$

where $Seign$ and $\pi = P_t/P_{t-1}$ denote seignorage and the inflation factor between two successive periods $t - 1$ and t, respectively. Note that in the stationary equilibrium π is a constant and equals the money growth factor. Real interest income is taxed at the rate τ_r. In addition, the households receive transfers tr from the government.

Social security benefits $b(s, j)$ depend on the agent's age s as well as on his productivity type j as follows:

$$b(s, j) = \begin{cases} 0 & \text{for } s < 41 \\ \zeta(1 - \tau_w) w \epsilon_j & \text{for } s \geq 41. \end{cases}$$

The net replacement ratio ζ amounts to 30%.

Output is produced with effective labor N and capital K. Effective labor N is paid the wage w. Production Y is characterized by constant returns to scale and assumed to be Cobb-Douglas:

---

[22] At the end of the final period, $k_{hT+1} = M^h_{hT+1,t} \equiv 0$.

$$Y = N^{1-\alpha}K^\alpha,$$

with $\alpha = 0.35$. In a factor market equilibrium, factors are rewarded with their marginal product:

$$w = (1-\alpha)N^{-\alpha}K^\alpha,$$
$$r = \alpha N^{1-\alpha}K^{\alpha-1} - \delta.$$

Capital depreciates at the rate $\delta = 0.08$.

The government consists of the fiscal and monetary authority. Nominal money grows at the exogenous rate μ:

$$\frac{M_{t+1} - M_t}{M_t} = \mu. \tag{9.33}$$

Seignorage $Seign = M_{t+1} - M_t$ is transferred lump-sum.

The government uses the revenues from taxing income and aggregate accidental bequests Beq in order to finance its expenditures on government consumption G, government transfers tr, and transfers to the one-year old households $\tilde{m}$. We assume that the first-period money balances $\tilde{m}$ are financed by the government:

$$G + tr + \tilde{m} = \tau_r r k + \tau_w N + Beq.$$

Transfers tr are distributed lump-sum to all households. Furthermore, the government provides social security benefits $Pens$ that are financed by taxes on labor income:

$$Pens = \theta w N.$$

In a stationary equilibrium, aggregate variables are equal to the sum of the individual variables, households maximize intertemporal utility, firms maximize profits, the factor and goods markets clear, and the government and social security budget are balanced.

In order to compute the model use the efficiency-age profile $\{y_s\}_{s=1}^{60}$ and the survival probabilities $\{\phi_s\}_{s=1}^{60}$ that you find in the programs RCh93.g (ef1.fmt and sp2.fmt). The remaining parameters are calibrated as follows: The money endowment of the newborn generation is equal to 20% of the average money holdings in the economy. Furthermore, we set $\beta = 1.01$, $\sigma = 2.0$, $\mu = 0.04$, $\{\tau_r, \tau_w\}=\{0.429, 0.248\}$, $G/Y = 0.19$. Calibrate γ so that the velocity of money PY/M is equal to 6.0.

a) Compute the steady state. Use direct computation. First compute the model without money and productivity heterogeneity. Then introduce different productivity types before you also consider money. Graph the wealth-age and money-age profile.

b) Compute the Gini coefficients of the wage, income, and capital distribution. Do they match the empirical numbers that you encountered in Chapter 7?
c) Compute the cross-section correlation of money with total income and capital. Compare to the empirical values that amount to 0.22 and 0.25 during 1994-2001 (see HEER, MAUSSNER, and MCNELIS, 2007). Can you think of any reasons why the correlations are higher in our model? How should we improve upon the modeling of the money demand in OLG models?

9.4 Recompute Example 9.2.1.
   a) Use value function iteration with cubic spline interpolation in order to compute the policy functions of the households.
   b) Assume instead that households know the change in policy in period t 6 periods in advance. Compare the transition dynamics with the case where the change in policy is unexpected.

9.5 Recompute the model in Section 9.3 for the following two cases:
   a) Assume that the government keeps the social security contribution rate τ_b constant and that the replacement ratio (pensions) adjusts in order to keep the government budget balanced.
   b) The change in the population growth rate in period $t = 0$ is expected.
   c) The government announces in period $t = 20$ that it increases the retirement age from $R = 65$ to $R = 70$ for all those agents that are born after $t = 20$. Again distinguish between the two cases that i) the replacement rate and ii) the contribution rate remain constant during the transition.

   How do you need to adjust the program RCh93.g? What are the effects on the transition paths of the factor prices?

9.6 **Gauss-Seidel Algorithm.** In their original work, AUERBACH and KOTLIKOFF (1987) compute the transition with the help of the Gauss-Seidel Algorithm. In this problem, we ask you to compute the model in Section 9.3 with the help of the Gauss-Seidel algorithm. Assume that the economy has reached the final steady state in period $t = 200$.
   a) Compute the initial and the final steady states.
   b) As an initial guess for the transition, specify a linear law of motion for $\{K_t^0, L_t^0, tr_t^0\}_{t=0}^{t=199}$.
   c) Compute $\{K_{199}^1, L_{199}^1, tr_{199}^1\}$ given that all other aggregate variables are equal to the initial values $\{K_t^0, L_t^0, tr_t^0\}_{t=0}^{t=198}$. Therefore, you have to write a routine that computes the savings and labor supply of all households that are alive in period $t = 199$ given the factor prices and transfers over their lifetime, respectively. As an input, you need to provide your initial value of $\{K_{199}^1, L_{199}^1, tr_{199}^1\}$.

d) Compute $\{K^1_{198}, L^1_{198}, tr^1_{198}\}$ given $\{K^0_t, L^0_t, tr^0_t\}^{t=197}_{t=0}$ and $\{K^1_{199}, L^1_{199}, tr^1_{199}\}$ in the same way as above.
e) Continue to compute $\{K^1_t, L^1_t, tr^1_t\}$, $t = 197, \ldots, 1$ and return to step c) until convergence.

Compare the computational time with our Broyden algorithm.

Chapter 10

Stochastic Overlapping Generations Models

Overview. In this chapter, we introduce both idiosyncratic and aggregate uncertainty into the OLG model. The methods that we will apply for the computation of these models are already familiar to you from previous chapters and will only be modified in order to allow for the more complex age structure of OLG models. In particular, we will apply the log-linearization from Chapter 2, the algorithm for the computation of the stationary distribution from Chapter 7, and the Algorithm by KRUSELL and SMITH (1998) from Chapter 8 for the solution of the non-stochastic steady state and the business cycle dynamics of the OLG model.

In the following, we will first introduce individual stochastic productivity in the standard OLG model, and, then, aggregate stochastic productivity. In the first section, agents have different productivity types. Different from the traditional Auerbach-Kotlikoff models, agents are subject to idiosyncratic shocks and may change their productivity types randomly. As a consequence, the direct computation of policies and transition paths is no longer feasible. As an interesting application, we are trying to explain the empirically observed wealth heterogeneity. In the second section, we introduce aggregate uncertainty and study the business cycle dynamics of the OLG model.

10.1 Individual Uncertainty

One of the main aims of the heterogeneous-agent literature in the 1990s has been the explanation of the high concentration of wealth. In the US economy, the distribution of wealth is characterized by a Gini coefficient equal to 0.78 according to estimates by DÍAZ-GIMÉNEZ, QUADRINI, and RÍOS-RULL (1997) and BURDÍA RODRÍGUEZ, DÍAZ-GIMÉNEZ, QUADRINI, and RÍOS-RULL (2002). One main explanatory factor, of course, is the unequal distribution of earnings. However, when we added heterogeneous productivity into the Ramsey model in Section 7.3.2, the model failed to replicate the observed wealth concentration. In the present chapter, we add another important determinant of the wealth distribution in addition to heterogeneous individual productivity: life-cycle savings. Agents accumulate wealth in order to finance consumption in old age. For this reason, we will consider an overlapping generation model in the following.[1]

Our OLG model for the study of the wealth distribution is characterized by the following features:

1. life-cycle savings,
2. uncertain lifetime,
3. uncertain earnings,
4. lump-sum pensions,

and follows HUGGETT (1996) closely.

Uncertain earnings also generate additional wealth heterogeneity as income-rich agents increase their precautionary savings in order to ensure against the bad luck of a fall in individual earnings. As a consequence, the discount factor β^{-1} is higher than the real interest rate $1 + r$. Therefore, if the lifetime is certain, consumption increases over lifetime, even into the final years of life. Empirically, however, the consumption-age profile is hump-shaped in the US. For this reason, we also introduce stochastic survival in order to improve the model's quality.[2] If agents have lower surviving probabilities in old age, consumption is hump-shaped again because future periods of life are discounted at a higher rate.

---

[1] As an alternative way to model life-cycle savings, CASTAÑEDA, DÍAZ-GIMÉNEZ, and RÍOS-RULL (2003) consider the standard Ramsey model with heterogeneous productivity. In addition, they assume that agents retire and die with a certain probability, respectively. In the former case, agents receive pensions which are lower than labor income.

[2] Uncertain lifetime has already been introduced in the model of the demographic transition in Section 9.3.1.

In our model, three sectors can be depicted: households, production, and the government. Households maximize discounted lifetime utility. They inherit no wealth and leave no bequests. Firms maximize profits. Output is produced with the help of labor and capital. The government provides unfunded public pensions which are financed by a tax on wage income.

Households. Every year, a generation of equal measure is born. The total measure of all generations is normalized to one. As we only study steady state behavior, we concentrate on the study of the behavior of an individual born at the beginning of period 1. Her first period of life is period 1. A subscript t of a variable denotes the age of the generation, the measure of generation t is denoted by μ_t.

Households live a maximum of $T + T^R$ years. Lifetime is stochastic and agents face a probability s_t of surviving up to age t conditional on surviving up to age $t-1$. During their first T years, agents supply labor $\bar{h}$ inelastically. After T years, retirement is mandatory. Agents maximize lifetime utility:

$$E_1 \left[\sum_{t=1}^{T+T^R} \beta^{t-1} \left(\Pi_{j=1}^{t} s_j \right) u(c_t) \right], \tag{10.1}$$

where β and c_t denote the discount factor and consumption at age t, respectively. The instantaneous utility function $u(c)$ is the CRRA (constant relative-risk aversion) function:[3]

$$u(c) = \frac{c^{1-\eta} - 1}{1 - \eta}, \tag{10.2}$$

where η denotes the coefficient of relative risk aversion.

Heterogeneous labor earnings are introduced in a similar way as in Section 9.3.1. The worker's labor productivity $e(z,t)$ is also stochastic such that the idiosyncratic labor productivity z is subject to a shock. The shock z follows a Markov process and takes only a finite number n_z of possible values in the set

---

[3] Different from equation (9.2), we do not include a small constant ψ in the utility function because we do not consider the case of a zero income.

$Z = \{z^1 = \underline{z}, \ldots, z^{n_z} = \bar{z}\}$ with $z^i < z^{i+1}$ for $i = 1, \ldots, n_z - 1$. Again, the shocks z are independent across agents and the law of large numbers holds (there is an infinite number of agents) so that there is no aggregate uncertainty. The labor productivity process is calibrated in detail below.

Agents are born without wealth, $k_1 = 0$, and do not leave altruistic bequests to their children. All accidental bequests are confiscated by the state and used for public consumption. Agents receive income from capital k_t and labor n_t and face a borrowing limit $k \geq \underline{k}$. The budget constraint of the working agent is given by

$$k_{t+1} = (1 + r)k_t + (1 - \tau)w\bar{h}e(z, t) - c_t, \quad t = 1, \ldots, T, \quad (10.3)$$

where r and w denote the interest rate and the wage rate per efficiency unit of labor, respectively. Wage income is taxed at rate τ.

During retirement, agents receive public pensions b irrespective of their employment history. The budget constraint of the retired agent is given by

$$k_{t+1} = (1 + r)k_t + b - c_t, \quad t = T + 1, \ldots, T + T^R. \quad (10.4)$$

Production. Firms are of measure one and produce output with effective labor N and capital K. Effective labor N is paid the wage w. Capital K is hired at rate r and depreciates at rate δ. Production Y is characterized by constant returns to scale and assumed to be Cobb-Douglas:

$$Y = N^{1-\alpha} K^\alpha. \quad (10.5)$$

In a factor market equilibrium, factors are rewarded with their marginal product:

$$w = (1 - \alpha)N^{-\alpha}K^\alpha, \quad (10.6)$$
$$r = \alpha N^{1-\alpha}K^{\alpha-1} - \delta. \quad (10.7)$$

Government. The government uses the revenues from taxing labor in order to finance its expenditures on social security:

$$\tau w N = \sum_{t=T+1}^{T+T^R} \mu_t b. \tag{10.8}$$

Following a change in the provision of public pensions b, the labor income tax rate τ adjusts in order to keep the government budget balanced. Government consumption G is exogenous and is financed by accidental bequests.

Stationary Equilibrium. The applied concept of equilibrium uses a recursive representation of the consumer's problem following STOKEY and LUCAS with PRESCOTT (1989). Let $V_t(k_t, z_t)$ be the value of the objective function of the t-year old agent with wealth k_t and idiosyncratic productivity level z_t. $V_t(k_t, z_t)$ is defined as the solution to the dynamic program:

$$V_t(k_t, z_t) = \max_{k_{t+1}, c_t} \left\{ u(c_t) + \beta s_{t+1} E\left[V_{t+1}(k_{t+1}, z_{t+1}) | z_t\right] \right\}, \tag{10.9}$$

subject to (10.3) or (10.4) and $k \geq \underline{k}$. Optimal decision rules for consumption $c_t(k, z)$ and next-period capital stock $k_{t+1}(k, z)$ at age t are functions of wealth k and the idiosyncratic productivity shock z.

We further need to describe the distribution of wealth and productivity in our economy. Remember that μ_t is the mass of the t-year old agents and that the total mass of all generations is equal to one. Furthermore, let $F_t(k, z)$ denote the probability distribution of the individual states $(k, z) \in \mathcal{X}$ across age t agents. In our model, the individual capital stock k is also bounded from above as the agents cannot save more than they earn over their finite lifetimes. Let $\bar{k}$ denote the upper bound. Accordingly, the state space $\mathcal{X} = (\underline{k}, \bar{k}) \times Z$ is bounded, too. The t-year old agents with a capital stock and productivity equal or below k and z, respectively, will make up a proportion of $\mu_t F_t(k, z)$ of all agents in the economy. The distribution $F_t(k, z)$ has the property that $F_t(\bar{k}, \bar{z}) \equiv 1.0$ for all t. Furthermore, the initial distribution $F_1(k, z)$ is given by the exogenous initial distribution of labor endowment $e(z, 1)$, as all agents are born with zero assets. The distribution of individual states across agents is given by the following recursive equation for all $(k_{t+1}, z_{t+1}) \in \mathcal{X}$ and $t = 1, \ldots, T + T^R - 1$:

$$F_{t+1}(k_{t+1}, z_{t+1}) = \sum_{z_t \in Z} \pi(z_{t+1}|z_t) \cdot F_t\left((k_{t+1})^{-1}(k_{t+1}, z_t), z_t\right),$$

(10.10)

where $\pi(z_{t+1}|z_t)$ denotes the exogenously given transition probability from productivity state z_t to z_{t+1} and $(k_{t+1})^{-1}(k_{t+1}, z_t)$ denotes the inverse of the function for the optimal next-period capital stock $k_{t+1}(k_t, z_t)$ with respect to its first argument k_t.[4] Obviously, our concept of a stationary distribution corresponds closely to the one introduced in Chapter 7 for the infinite-horizon Ramsey model.

We will consider a stationary equilibrium where factor prices and aggregate capital and labor are constant and the distribution of wealth is stationary. The following properties characterize the stationary equilibrium:

1. Individual and aggregate behavior are consistent. The aggregate variables effective labor N, capital K, and consumption C are equal to the sum of the individual variables.
2. Relative prices $\{w, r\}$ solve the firm's optimization problem by satisfying (10.6) and (10.7).
3. Given relative prices $\{w, r\}$ and the government policy b, the individual policy rules $c_t(.)$ and $k_{t+1}(.)$ solve the consumer's dynamic program (10.9).
4. The government budget (10.8) is balanced.
5. Government consumption G equals accidental bequests.
6. The goods market clears:

$$K^\alpha N^{1-\alpha} = C + G + \delta K.$$

(10.11)

7. The distributions F_t, $t = 1, \ldots, T + T^R - 1$, are consistent with individual behavior and follow (10.10).

Calibration Periods correspond to years. Agents are born at real lifetime age 20 which corresponds to $t = 1$. They work $T = 40$ years corresponding to a real lifetime age of 59. They live a maximum life of 60 years ($T^R = 20$) so that agents do not become older

---

[4] Please see also footnote 8 in Chapter 7.

Table 10.1

Preferences	Production
$\beta = 1.011$	$\alpha = 0.36$
$\eta = 1.5$	$\delta = 0.06$
	$\bar{h} = 0.30$

than real lifetime age 79. We use the same survival probabilities that are presented in Figure 9.7. ψ_{60} is set equal to zero.

The model parameters are presented in Table 10.1. If not mentioned otherwise, the model parameters are taken from HUGGETT (1996). The discount rate β is set equal to 1.011. We use the estimate by Hurd (1989) that accounts for mortality risk. Notice again that, different from infinite-lifetime models like the ones in previous chapters, the discount factor β does not need to be smaller than one in finite-lifetime models. The credit limit is set at $\underline{k} = 0$. Huggett uses a coefficient of relative risk aversion equal to $\eta = 1.5$. The capital share of output α and the depreciation rate of capital δ are set equal to 0.36 and 0.06, respectively.

The labor endowment process is given by $e(z,t) = e^{z_t + \bar{y}_t}$, where $\bar{y}_t$ is the mean log-normal income of the t-year old. The mean efficiency index $\bar{y}_t$ of the t-year-old worker is taken from HANSEN (1993), and is presented in Figure 9.8. The idiosyncratic productivity shock z_t follows a Markov process. The Markov process is given by:

$$z_t = \rho z_{t-1} + \epsilon_t, \tag{10.12}$$

where $\epsilon_t \sim N(0, \sigma_\epsilon)$. Huggett uses $\rho = 0.96$ and $\sigma_\epsilon = 0.045$. Furthermore, we follow HUGGETT (1996) and choose a log-normal distribution of earnings for the 20-year old with $\sigma_{y_1} = 0.38$ and mean $\bar{y_1}$. As the log endowment of the initial generation of agents is normally distributed, the log efficiency of subsequent agents will continue to be normally distributed. This is a useful property of the earnings process, which has often been described as log-normal in the literature. We discretize the state space Z using $n_z = 9$ values. The states z are equally spaced and range from

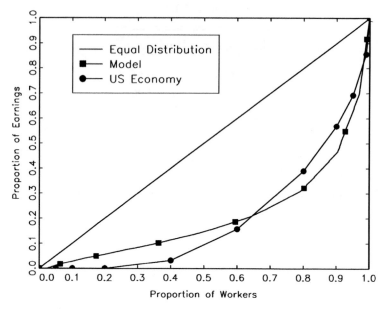

Figure 10.1: Lorenz Curve of US and Model Earnings

$-2\sigma_{y_1}$ to $2\sigma_{y_1}$. The probability of having productivity shock z_1 in the first period of life is computed by integrating the area under the normal distribution. The transition probabilities are computed using the Algorithm 12.2.1. As a consequence, the efficiency index $e(z,t)$ follows a finite Markov-chain. Furthermore, we set the shift length equal to $\bar{h} = 0.3$.

The earnings process is exogenous in our model. The Lorenz curve for the earnings in our model and for the US are displayed in Figure 10.1. The inequality of earnings for the model economy and for the US are similar. In our model, the lowest quintile of earners has a higher labor income share than observed empirically, while the top quintile earns a higher income share than those in the US.[5] Hence, we have two countervailing effects on the Gini coefficient. In our model, the Gini coefficient of labor income is equal to 0.413 and matches empirical values as reported in Chapter 7 quite closely.

---

[5] The source of the US data is described in Chapter 8.

Finally, the government provides pensions b. The replacement ratio of pensions relative to average net wages is set equal to 30%.

Computation. The solution algorithm follows Algorithm 9.1.1 closely and consists of the following steps:

Step 1: Parameterize the model and compute aggregate employment N.

Step 2: Make initial guesses of the steady state values of the aggregate capital stock K and the social security contribution rate τ.

Step 3: Compute the values w, r, and b, which solve the firm's Euler equation and the government budget.

Step 4: Compute the household's decision functions by backward induction.

Step 5: Compute the optimal path for consumption and savings for the new-born generation by forward induction given the initial capital stock $k_1 = 0$.

Step 6: Compute the aggregate capital stock K.

Step 7: Update K and return to step 3 until convergence.

The algorithm is implemented in the program Rch101.g. In step 4, a finite-time dynamic programming problem is to be solved. Again, we solve this problem with value function iteration with linear interpolation between grid points. We choose an equispaced grid with $\underline{k} = 0$, $\bar{k} = 40$, and $n_k = 601$. Associated with every optimal next period capital stock $k_{t+1}(k_t, z_t)$ is an optimal consumption policy $c_t(k_t, z_t) = (1+r)k_t + b - k_{t+1}(k_t, z_t)$ for the retired agent and $c_t(k_t, z_t) = (1+r)k_t + (1-\tau)w\bar{h}e(z,t) - k_{t+1}(k_t, z_t)$ for the working agent, respectively.

In step 5, we compute the endogenous wealth distribution in every generation over an equispaced grid of the asset space $[\underline{k}, \bar{k}] \times Z$ with $2n_k \cdot n_z$ points. We start with the newborn generation at $t = 1$ with zero wealth. Furthermore, we know the distribution of the idiosyncratic productivity at age 1. Given the distribution of the capital stock and the productivity at age t, we can compute the distribution at age $t + 1$ from (10.10) by using the optimal decision functions of the agents, $k_{t+1}(k_t, z_t)$, and the transition probabilities for the idiosyncratic productivities. We continue to compute the distribution for $t = 2, \ldots, 60$. Notice that, for given factor prices and policy functions, we can compute the endogenous stationary distribution in the OLG model with one iteration only. In the Ramsey model, on the other hand, we do not know the distribution of the wealth among agents in the stationary equilibrium or in any period prior to it.

Finally, in step 7, we use extrapolation to stabilize the sequence, i.e. let K^i and K^* denote the starting value in the i-th iteration and the computed endogenous value of the capital stock, respectively, then $K^{i+1} = \phi K^i + (1-\phi) K^*$. We set ϕ equal to 0.8.

Results. Figure 10.2 displays the average wealth over the lifetime. As you know by now, the hump-shape of the profile is typical for the life-cycle model. Agents build up savings during working life, and assets start to fall after retirement. Therefore, wealth heterogeneity is higher in the OLG model than in the standard Ramsey model as agents have different savings at different ages. Furthermore, we have many agents who are liquidity constrained and only have zero wealth, especially the young agents with low productivity. In the Ramsey model of Chapter 8, all agents hold strictly positive wealth and, for this reason, wealth heterogeneity is much lower.

Average wealth in the economy amounts to $K = 3.94$. For our choice of the earnings process, aggregate effective employment is equal to $N = 0.386$ so that the interest rate equals $r = 2.15\%$. The equilibrium social security contribution rate amounts to $\tau = 9.75\%$. The wealth distribution of the model economy and the US economy are displayed in Figure 10.3. The model economy is characterized by a much more equal wealth distribution than the US economy. The Gini coefficient of the wealth distribution in our model is equal to 0.587 and is below the one for the US economy (that is approximately equal to 0.78). However, wealth is much more concentrated than earnings on the one hand, and, on the other hand, the model generates more wealth heterogeneity than the Ramsey model with heterogeneous productivity presented in Section 7.3.2.

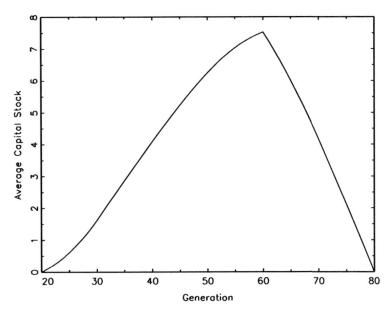

Figure 10.2: Age-Wealth Profile

There are numerous reasons why the endogenous wealth heterogeneity of our model is smaller than observed empirically:

1. Pensions are not related to the earnings history of the recipient. If the earnings-rich agents get higher pensions, one might suppose that wealth heterogeneity would also be higher. However, as earnings-poor agents also know that they will only receive small pensions, they will also save more for precautionary reasons.[6]

2. We neglect any asset-based means tests of social security. HUBBARD, SKINNER, and ZELDES (1995) show that, in the presence of social insurance programs with means tests, low-income households are likely to hold virtually no wealth across lifetime. Unemployment and asset-based social insurance would imply a much higher proportion of agents with zero or near-zero wealth.

---

[6] In our own research, we only encountered applications where the introduction of earnings-related benefits decreased wealth heterogeneity (as measured by the Gini coefficient).

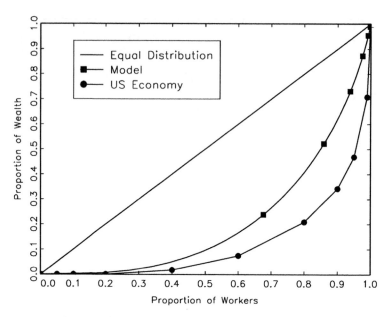

Figure 10.3: Lorenz Curve of US and Model Wealth

3. Furthermore, agents are not unemployed. HEER (2003) studies a life-cycle economy with endogenous search unemployment. Working agents may loose their job at an exogenous rate; higher search effort increases the job finding probability, but searching for a job also causes a disutility for the agent. HEER (2003) shows that the replacement rate of unemployment insurance has only a very small effect on wealth heterogeneity. Even though income is distributed from the income-rich agents to the income-poor workers with the help of unemployment insurance, higher unemployment insurance also increases endogenous unemployment so that the number of unemployment recipients increases. As a consequence, the wealth Gini coefficient changes by less than one percentage point if the replacement ratio of unemployment insurance increases from 0% to 50% or even to 100%; for a replacement ratio exceeding 70%, wealth heterogeneity even starts to increase again.

4. We neglect bequests. For example, KESSLER and MASSON (1989), considering France, find that only 36% of the households receive any inheritances and those who do are about 2.4

times richer than the representative household. HEER (2001b) considers an OLG model where parents leave altruistic and accidental bequests to their children. He, however, finds, that bequests are able to explain only a small fraction of observed wealth heterogeneity. The main reasons are that i) also poor agents may receive bequests and ii) agents who expect a high inheritance in the future also spend more on consumption. Importantly, however, HEER (2001b) only considers intergenerational transfers of physical wealth, but not transfers of human wealth. Rich parents may have rich children because they may invest in their college education, for example. LOURY (1981) analyzes parental human capital investment in their offspring. The allocation of training and hence the earnings of the children depend on the distribution of earnings among the parents. BECKER and TOMES (1979) present a model framework comprising both human and non-human capital transfers from parents to children. The introduction of human capital transfers in an OLG model in order to explain the observed wealth heterogeneity is a promising question for future research.

5. In our model, agents are not allowed to borrow against anticipated bequests implying a credit limit $k \geq 0$. For lower binding constraints, $k < 0$, wealth heterogeneity increases as demonstrated by HUGGETT (1996). In particular, the proportion of agents holding zero and negative assets increases.

Accounting for these features in our model is likely to result in an increase of wealth inequality for agents characterized by low to high asset holdings, however, we are sceptical as to whether it proves successful in reproducing the observed wealth concentration among the very rich. As one of the very few exceptions to these modeling choices (known to us),[7] QUADRINI (2000) presents a promising approach in order to explain the high concentration

---

[7] QUADRINI and RÍOS-RULL (1997) present a review of studies of wealth heterogeneity in computable general equilibrium models with uninsurable idiosyncratic exogenous shocks to earnings, including business ownership, higher rates of return on high asset levels, and changes in health and marital status, among others. A more recent survey of facts and models is provided by CAGETTI and DE NARDI (2006).

of wealth among the very rich agents. He introduces entrepreneurship into a dynamic general equilibrium model.

10.2 Aggregate Uncertainty

In this section, we introduce aggregate uncertainty in the standard OLG model. As one prominent application consider the effects of aging and the public pension system on the equity premium.[8] A higher share of older agents is likely to increase the returns from stocks relative to that from bonds. Old agents prefer to hold a large part of their wealth in the form of safe assets like bonds because their (rather safe) non-financial wealth in the form of discounted pensions is rather small. Younger agents may prefer to invest predominantly in risky assets like stocks as their total wealth mainly consists of discounted lifetime labor income that is characterized by relatively little risk.[9] Aging may now increase the demand of bonds relative to stocks and, thus, raise the equity premium. If, however, public pension systems are changed from pay-as-you-go to fully funded, total savings may increase and, if the pension funds invest the additional savings primarily in the stock market, the equity premium may fall. BROOKS (2002) explores the impact of the Baby Boom on stock and bond returns quantitatively in a model with 4 overlapping generations and predicts a sharp rise in the equity premium when the Baby Boomers retire. As an important step to answering this question in a more realistic setting, STORESLETTEN, TELMER, and YARON (2007) consider an OLG model with annual periods and analyze the effects of idiosyncratic risk and life-cycle aspects for asset pricing.

Obviously, in models with aggregate uncertainty, we cannot study the transition dynamics any more as the time path is stochastic. In order to see this point assume that the US is in a steady state today (period $t = 0$) and that there is a sudden unexpected and permanent decline in the fertility rate. If aggregate

---

[8] Please see also Section 6.3.4 of this book on the equity premium puzzle.
[9] There are numerous other variables than age that influence the portfolio decision of the households as, for example, housing.

technology were a deterministic variable we could compute the transition path just like in Section 9.2. In this case, agents would have to predict the time path for the factor prices. We would know that after some 200-300 periods the economy is close to the new steady state and that we may stop the computation. If technology is stochastic, however, agents can only form expectations about the time path of factor prices and the number of possible time paths becomes infinite. Assume that technology can only take two different values. Even in this case, we had to compute some 2^n different transition paths with n denoting the number of periods. Given our experience it is save to assume that in a model with annual periods, n should be in the range 200-300. The computational costs become unbearable.[10] Therefore, we will confine the analysis of OLG models with aggregate uncertainty to the study of the dynamics around the steady state.

In the following, we will describe two methods for the computation of the dynamics close to the steady-state that you have already encountered in previous chapters of the book. First, we will consider models without idiosyncratic uncertainty. In these models, we can compute the steady state by solving directly for the individual state variables with the help of non-linear equation solvers. The method has been described in Section 9.1. Even though the state space may be quite large including some hundred variables it is often possible to compute the log-linearization. In the next subsection, we will use this method to study the business cycle dynamics of an OLG model with 60 generations. Second, we consider an OLG model with both idiosyncratic and aggregate uncertainty in Subsection 10.2.2. As the most practical approach to the solution of such a problem, we advocate the algorithm of KRUSELL and SMITH (1998). We will use the latter method in order to compute the business cycle dynamics of the income distribution. We will compare our results with those from the model with infinitely-lived households of Section 8.4.2.

---

[10] As one possible solution to this problem, one can use Monte-Carlo simulation techniques to compute multiple possible transition paths and the associated distribution for the factor prices during the transition. We will not pursue this method here.

10.2.1 Log-Linearization

There are only few studies that apply linear approximation methods to large-scale economies OLG models. As one exception, Ríos-Rull (1996) also considers the dynamics in a stochastic lifecycle model.[11] In our own work (Heer and Maussner, 2007), we consider the redistributive effects of inflation following an unanticipated monetary expansion. In the following, we will illustrate the numerical and analytical methods with the help of a 60-period OLG model that is described in Example 10.2.1. The model is a simple extension of Example 9.2.1. In particular, we rather consider 60 than 6 different generations and add a technology shock ϵ_t to production. The (logarithmic) aggregate technology level follows the AR(1)-process:

$$\ln Z_t = \rho \ln Z_{t-1} + \epsilon_t, \qquad (10.13)$$

where ϵ_t is i.i.d., $\epsilon_t \sim N(0, \sigma^2)$. Production, therefore, is given by

$$Y_t = Z_t N_t^{1-\alpha} K_t^{\alpha}.$$

The household forms rational expectations about future income and future prices and maximizes expected lifetime utility. Besides, the model is identical to the one described in Example 9.2.1.

Example 10.2.1
60-period Overlapping Generations Model with Aggregate Uncertainty.
Households live 60 periods. Each generation is of measure 1/60. The first 40 periods, they are working, the last 20 periods, they are retired and receive pensions. Households maximize expected lifetime utility at age 1 in period t:

$$E_t \sum_{s=1}^{60} \beta^{s-1} u(c_{t+s-1}^s, l_{t+s-1}^s), \quad l = 1 - n.$$

---
[11] Different from our algorithm in this section, he concentrates on the analysis of a pareto-optimal economy and studies the problem of a central planner. In particular, he uses the LQ-Approximation presented in Section 2.3 in order to compute the solution of this model. Our approach also allows for the computation of the dynamics in a stochastic decentralized economy.

Instantaneous utility is a function of both consumption and leisure:

$$u(c,l) = \frac{(cl^\gamma)^{1-\eta} - 1}{1-\eta}.$$

The working agent of age s faces the following budget constraint in period t:

$$k_{t+1}^{s+1} = (1+r_t)k_t^s + (1-\tau_t)w_t n_t^s - c_t^s, \quad s = 1, \ldots, 40.$$

The budget constraint of the retired worker is given by

$$k_{t+1}^{s+1} = (1+r_t)k_t^s + b - c_t^s, \quad s = 41, \ldots, 60,$$

with $k_t^{61} \equiv 0$ and $l_t^{51} = l_t^{52} = \ldots = l_t^{60} \equiv 1.0$. Pensions b are constant.

Production Y_t is characterized by constant returns to scale and assumed to be Cobb-Douglas:

$$Y_t = Z_t N_t^{1-\alpha} K_t^\alpha,$$

where $\ln Z_t$ follows the AR(1)-process:

$$\ln Z_t = \rho \ln Z_{t-1} + \epsilon_t,$$

and ϵ_t is i.i.d., $\epsilon_t \sim N(0, \sigma^2)$.

In a factor market equilibrium, factors are rewarded with their marginal product:

$$\begin{aligned} w_t &= (1-\alpha)Z_t N_t^{-\alpha} K_t^\alpha, \\ r_t &= \alpha Z_t N_t^{1-\alpha} K_t^{\alpha-1} - \delta. \end{aligned}$$

Furthermore, the government budget is balanced in every period t:

$$\tau_t w_t N_t = \frac{20}{60} b.$$

In equilibrium, individual and aggregate behavior are consistent:

$$N_t = \sum_{s=1}^{40} \frac{n_t^s}{60},$$

$$K_t = \sum_{s=1}^{60} \frac{k_t^s}{60},$$

and the goods market clears:

$$Z_t N_t^{1-\alpha} K_t^\alpha = \sum_{s=1}^{60} \frac{c_t^s}{60} + K_{t+1} - (1-\delta)K_t.$$

The parameter values are chosen as follows: $\beta = 0.99$, $\eta = 2.0$, $\gamma = 2.0$, $\alpha = 0.3$, $\delta = 0.04$, and a non-stochastic replacement ratio of pensions relative to net wage earnings equal to $\zeta = \frac{b}{(1-\tau)w\bar{n}} = 30\%$, where $\bar{n}$ is the average labor supply in the non-stochastic steady state of the economy. The parameters of the AR(1) for the technology are set equal to $\rho = 0.814$ and $\sigma = 0.0142$. These parameters correspond to annual frequencies by a quarterly AR(1)-process for the Solow residual with parameter 0.95 and 0.00763, which are the parameters in PRESCOTT (1986).[12]

For the economy described in Example 10.2.1, we can compute the non-stochastic steady state with the help of the methods described in Section 9.1. The non-stochastic steady state is characterized by a constant technology level, $Z_t = Z = 1$. Furthermore, all individual and aggregate variables are constant, too, and are denoted by a variable without time index. For example, k^s and K denote the non-stochastic steady state capital stock of the individual at age s and the non-stochastic steady state aggregate capital stock, respectively. For our calibration, we compute the following economy-wide values: $K = 1.856$, $N = 0.2293$, $b = 0.1175$, $\tau = 13.04$, $w = 1.311$, $r = 2.938\%$.

Log-Linearization. In Section 9.2, we analyzed the transition dynamics in OLG models. We refrained from showing that the economy displays saddlepoint stability, even though our analysis requires determinancy and stability. In the following, we will show that, indeed, the model in Example 10.2.1 is stable. Therefore, we first need to log-linearize the equations characterizing the economy around the non-stochastic steady state applying the methods of Chapter 2. These equations, in particular, consist of the first-order conditions of the households and the firm, the budget constraint of the households, and the government budget constraint.

---

[12] The correspondence between the quarterly and annual parameters of the AR(1) process is shown in the Appendix 5 of this chapter.

10.2 Aggregate Uncertainty

The first-order conditions of the households for $s = 1, \ldots, 60$ in period t are analogous to the equations (9.4) and (9.5) for labor supply and next-period capital stock, respectively:

$$u_l(c_t^s, l_t^s) = \gamma (c_t^s)^{1-\eta} (1 - n_t^s)^{\gamma(1-\eta)-1} = \lambda_t^s (1 - \tau_t) w_t, \quad (10.14)$$

$$\lambda_t^s = (c_t^s)^{-\eta} (l_t^s)^{\gamma(1-\eta)}, \quad (10.15)$$

$$\frac{1}{\beta} = E_t \left\{ \frac{\lambda_{t+1}^{s+1}}{\lambda_t^s} [1 + r_{t+1}] \right\}. \quad (10.16)$$

Log-linearization of (10.14)-(10.16) around the non-stochastic steady state results in:

$$(1 - \eta)\hat{c}_t^s + (1 - \gamma(1 - \eta)) \frac{n^s}{1 - n^s} \hat{n}_t^s = \hat{\lambda}_t^s - \frac{\tau}{1 - \tau}\hat{\tau}_t + \hat{w}_t,$$
$$s = 1, \ldots, 40, \quad (10.17)$$

$$\hat{\lambda}_t^s = -\eta \hat{c}_t^s - \gamma(1 - \eta) \frac{n^s}{1 - n^s} \hat{n}_t^s, \quad s = 1, \ldots, 40, \quad (10.18)$$

$$\hat{\lambda}_t^s = -\eta \hat{c}_t^s, \quad s = 41, \ldots, 60, \quad (10.19)$$

$$\hat{\lambda}_t^s = E_t \hat{\lambda}_{t+1}^{s+1} + \frac{r}{1+r} E_t \hat{r}_{t+1}, \quad s = 1, \ldots, 59. \quad (10.20)$$

Furthermore, we need to log-linearize the working household's budget constraint (9.3) around the steady state for the one-year old with $k^1 \equiv 0$:

$$k^2 \hat{k}_{t+1}^2 = -\tau w n^1 \hat{\tau}_t + (1-\tau) w n^1 \hat{w}_t + (1-\tau) w n^1 \hat{n}_t^1 - c^1 \hat{c}_t^1, \quad (10.21)$$

and for $s = 2, \ldots, 40$:

$$k^{s+1} \hat{k}_{t+1}^{s+1} = (1 + r) k^s \hat{k}_t^s + r k^s \hat{r}_t - \tau w n^s \hat{\tau}_t + (1 - \tau) w n^s \hat{w}_t$$
$$+ (1 - \tau) w n^s \hat{n}_t^s - c^s \hat{c}_t^s. \quad (10.22)$$

Log-linearization of the retired agent's budget constraint (9.6) around the non-stochastic steady state results in:

$$k^{s+1} \hat{k}_{t+1}^{s+1} = (1 + r) k^s \hat{k}_t^s + r k^s \hat{r}_t - c^s \hat{c}_t^s, \quad s = 41, \ldots, 59.$$

Finally, consumption at age $s = 60$ is given by:

$$c^{60} \hat{c}_t^{60} = (1 + r) k^{60} \hat{k}_t^{60} + r k^{60} \hat{r}_t. \quad (10.23)$$

Therefore, we have 60 controls c_t^s, $s = 1, \ldots, 60$, 40 controls n_t^s, $s = 1, \ldots, 40$, 60 costates λ_t^s, $s = 1, \ldots, 60$, and 59 predetermined variables k_t^s, $s = 2, \ldots, 60$. We also have $60 + 40 + 60 + 59 = 219$ equations. We have three further endogenous variables w_t, r_t, and τ_t. The wage rate is given by the marginal product of labor:

$$w_t = (1-\alpha) Z_t K_t^\alpha N_t^{-\alpha} = (1-\alpha) Z_t \left(\sum_{s=2}^{60} \frac{k_t^s}{60} \right)^\alpha \left(\sum_{s=1}^{40} \frac{n_t^s}{60} \right)^{-\alpha}.$$

Log-linearization results in:

$$\hat{w}_t = \hat{Z}_t + \alpha \sum_{s=2}^{60} \frac{k^s}{K} \frac{1}{60} \hat{k}_t^s - \alpha \sum_{s=1}^{40} \frac{n^s}{N} \frac{1}{60} \hat{n}_t^s. \qquad (10.24)$$

Similarly, we derive the percentage deviation of the interest rate, $\hat{r}_t$, from its non-stochastic steady state $r = \alpha N^{1-\alpha} K^{\alpha-1}$:

$$\hat{r}_t = \hat{Z}_t - (1-\alpha) \sum_{s=2}^{60} \frac{k^s}{K} \frac{1}{60} \hat{k}_t^s + (1-\alpha) \sum_{s=1}^{40} \frac{n^s}{N} \frac{1}{60} \hat{n}_t^s. \qquad (10.25)$$

The government budget $\tau w N = (1/3) \times b$ is the remaining equation that we need to approximate locally around the non-stochastic steady state:

$$\hat{\tau}_t = -\hat{w}_t - \sum_{s=1}^{40} \frac{n^s}{N} \frac{1}{60} \hat{n}_t^s. \qquad (10.26)$$

Equations (10.24)-(10.26) constitute three further equations in the three endogenous variables w_t, r_t, and τ_t. Finally, we have the law of motion for the exogenous state variable Z_t:

$$\hat{Z}_{t-1} = \rho \hat{Z}_{t+1} + \epsilon_t. \qquad (10.27)$$

Local Stability of the Non-Stochastic Steady State. Our log-linearization of the 60-period Auerbach-Kotlikoff model in Example 10.2.1 is described by equations (10.17)-(10.27). In order to conduct a local stability analysis, it is convenient to express our system of stochastic difference equations in the form (2.47) of Chapter 2:

$$C_u \mathbf{u}_t = C_{x\lambda} \begin{bmatrix} \mathbf{x}_t \\ \boldsymbol{\lambda}_t \end{bmatrix} + C_z \mathbf{z}_t, \tag{10.28a}$$

$$D_{x\lambda} E_t \begin{bmatrix} \mathbf{x}_{t+1}, \\ \boldsymbol{\lambda}_{t+1} \end{bmatrix} + F_{x\lambda} \begin{bmatrix} \mathbf{x}_t \\ \boldsymbol{\lambda}_t \end{bmatrix} = D_u E_t \mathbf{u}_{t+1} + F_u \mathbf{u}_t \tag{10.28b}$$
$$+ D_z E_t \mathbf{z}_{t+1} + F_z \mathbf{z}_t.$$

Therefore, we define:

$$\mathbf{u}_t = \left[\hat{c}_t^1, \hat{c}_t^2, \ldots, \hat{c}_t^{60}, \hat{n}_t^1, \hat{n}_t^2, \ldots, \hat{n}_t^{40}, \hat{r}_t, \hat{w}_t, \hat{\tau}_t \right]',$$

$$\mathbf{x}_t = \left[\hat{k}_t^2, \hat{k}_t^3, \ldots, \hat{k}_t^{60} \right]',$$

$$\boldsymbol{\lambda}_t = \left[\hat{\lambda}_t^1, \hat{\lambda}_t^2, \ldots, \hat{\lambda}_t^{59} \right]',$$

$$\mathbf{z}_t = \hat{Z}_t.$$

Notice that λ_t^{60} is not a costate variable because it is implied by (10.23) and (10.15), and, for this reason, rather constitutes a control variable than a costate. If we included λ^{60} in $\mathbf{u}_t$, the matrix $D_{x\lambda} - D_u C_u^{-1} C_{x\lambda}$ would not be invertible! Thus, we substitute $\hat{\lambda}_{t+1}^{60}$ in (10.20) by $-\eta \hat{c}_{t+1}^{60}$.

In the contemporary equations system (10.28a), the first 40 equations represent the first-order condition of the households with respect to labor, (10.17), the next 59 equations represent the equality of the costate variable λ_t^s, $s = 1, \ldots, 59$, and the marginal utility of consumption at age s, (10.18), the next equation is given by the consumption in period 60, (10.23), and the last three equations are the equations (10.24), (10.25) and (10.26) for the wage rate, the interest rate, and the government budget, respectively. For the matrix C_u, we get the following convenient partition:

$$C_u = \begin{bmatrix} A_{11} & A_{12} & A_{13} \\ A_{21} & A_{22} & A_{23} \\ A_{31} & A_{32} & A_{33} \end{bmatrix},$$

with the 40×60 submatrix A_{11} and the 40×40 submatrix A_{12}:

$$A_{11} = \begin{bmatrix} (1-\eta) & 0 & \cdots & 0 \\ 0 & (1-\eta) & \cdots & 0 \\ \vdots & \vdots & \ddots & \vdots \\ 0 & 0 & \cdots & (1-\eta) \end{bmatrix},$$

$$A_{12} = \begin{bmatrix} \Delta_1 & 0 & 0 & \cdots & 0 \\ 0 & \Delta_2 & 0 & \cdots & 0 \\ \vdots & \vdots & \vdots & \ddots & \vdots \\ 0 & 0 & 0 & \cdots & \Delta_{40} \end{bmatrix}, \Delta_s := \left(1 - \gamma(1-\eta)\right)\frac{n^s}{1-n^s},$$

and the 40×3 submatrix A_{13}:

$$A_{13} = \begin{bmatrix} 0 & -1 & \frac{\tau}{1-\tau} \\ \vdots & \vdots & \vdots \\ 0 & -1 & \frac{\tau}{1-\tau} \end{bmatrix}.$$

The 60×60 matrix A_{21} and the 60×40 matrix A_{22} together with the 60×3 matrix A_{23} represent (10.18) and (10.23):

$$A_{21} = \begin{bmatrix} -\eta & 0 & \cdots & 0 \\ 0 & -\eta & \cdots & 0 \\ \vdots & \vdots & \ddots & \vdots \\ 0 & 0 & \cdots & -\eta \\ 0 & 0 & \cdots & c^{60} \end{bmatrix},$$

$$A_{22} = \begin{bmatrix} \Delta_1 & 0 & 0 & \cdots & 0 \\ 0 & \Delta_2 & 0 & \cdots & 0 \\ \vdots & \vdots & \vdots & \ddots & \vdots \\ 0 & 0 & 0 & \cdots & \Delta_{40} \\ 0 & 0 & 0 & \cdots & 0 \\ \vdots & \vdots & \vdots & \ddots & \vdots \\ 0 & 0 & 0 & \cdots & 0 \end{bmatrix}, \Delta_s = -\gamma(1-\eta)\frac{n^s}{1-n^s},$$

$$A_{23} = \begin{bmatrix} 0 & 0 & 0 \\ 0 & 0 & 0 \\ \vdots & \vdots & \vdots \\ -rk^{60} & 0 & 0 \end{bmatrix}.$$

The last three rows are given by the 3×60 matrix $A_{31} = \mathbf{0}$, the 3×40 matrix A_{32} and the 3×3 matrix A_{33}:

$$A_{32} = \begin{bmatrix} \alpha \frac{n^1}{N} \frac{1}{60} & \alpha \frac{n^2}{N} \frac{1}{60} & \cdots & \alpha \frac{n^{40}}{N} \frac{1}{60} \\ -(1-\alpha) \frac{n^1}{N} \frac{1}{60} & -(1-\alpha) \frac{n^2}{N} \frac{1}{60} & \cdots & -(1-\alpha) \frac{n^{40}}{N} \frac{1}{60} \\ \frac{n^1}{N} \frac{1}{60} & \frac{n^2}{N} \frac{1}{60} & \cdots & \frac{n^{40}}{N} \frac{1}{60} \end{bmatrix},$$

$$A_{33} = \begin{bmatrix} 0 & 1 & 0 \\ 1 & 0 & 0 \\ 0 & 1 & 1 \end{bmatrix}.$$

The matrix $C_{x\lambda}$ is represented by:

$$\begin{bmatrix} 0 & 0 & \cdots & 0 & 1 & 0 & \cdots & 0 \\ 0 & 0 & \cdots & 0 & 0 & 1 & \cdots & 0 \\ & & \vdots & & & & & \\ 0 & 0 & \cdots & 0 & 1 & 0 & \cdots & 0 \\ 0 & 0 & \cdots & 0 & 0 & 1 & \cdots & 0 \\ & & \vdots & & & & & \\ 0 & 0 & \cdots & (1+r)k^{60} & 0 & 0 & \cdots & 0 \\ \alpha \frac{k^2}{K} \frac{1}{60} & \alpha \frac{k^3}{K} \frac{1}{60} & \cdots & \alpha \frac{k^{60}}{K} \frac{1}{60} & 0 & 0 & \cdots & 0 \\ -(1-\alpha) \frac{k^2}{K} \frac{1}{60} & -(1-\alpha) \frac{k^3}{K} \frac{1}{60} & \cdots & -(1-\alpha) \frac{k^{60}}{K} \frac{1}{60} & 0 & 0 & \cdots & 0 \\ 0 & 0 & \cdots & 0 & 0 & 0 & \cdots & 0 \end{bmatrix},$$

and, finally, the remaining matrix C_z from (10.28a) is equal to:

$$C_z = [0, 0, \ldots, 0, 0, \ldots, 0, 1, 1, 0]^T.$$

The dynamic equation system (10.28b) is characterized by the matrices $D_{x\lambda}$, $\bar{D}_{x\lambda}$, D_u, F_u, D_z, and F_z. The first 59 rows of these matrices represent the first-order conditions of the household with respect to k_{t+1}^{s+1}, $s = 1, \ldots, 59$, as described by (10.20). In the 59th equation, we have replaced $\hat{\lambda}_{t+1}^{60}$ by the percentage deviation of the marginal utility of consumption of the 60-year old, $-\eta \hat{c}_{t+1}^{60}$ as explained above. The remaining 59 equations are the budget constraints of the household at age $s = 1, \ldots, 59$:

$$D_{x\lambda} = \begin{bmatrix} 0 & 0 & \cdots & 0 & 0 & \cdots & 0 & 0 & -1 & \cdots & 0 \\ & & \vdots & & & & & & & & \\ 0 & 0 & \cdots & 0 & 0 & \cdots & 0 & 0 & 0 & \cdots & 0 \\ k^2 & 0 & \cdots & 0 & 0 & \cdots & 0 & 0 & 0 & \cdots & 0 \\ 0 & k^3 & \cdots & 0 & 0 & \cdots & 0 & 0 & 0 & \cdots & 0 \\ & & \vdots & & & & & & & & \\ 0 & 0 & \cdots & 0 & k^{42} & \cdots & 0 & 0 & 0 & \cdots & 0 \\ & & \vdots & & & & & & & & \end{bmatrix},$$

$$F_{x\lambda} = \begin{bmatrix} 0 & 0 & \cdots & 0 & 0 & \cdots & 0 & 1 & 0 & \cdots & 0 \\ & & & & & \vdots & & & & & \\ 0 & 0 & \cdots & 0 & 0 & \cdots & 0 & 0 & 0 & \cdots & 1 \\ 0 & 0 & \cdots & 0 & 0 & \cdots & 0 & 0 & 0 & \cdots & 0 \\ -(1+r)k^2 & 0 & \cdots & 0 & 0 & \cdots & 0 & 0 & 0 & \cdots & 0 \\ & & & & & \vdots & & & & & \\ 0 & 0 & \cdots & -(1+r)k^{41} & 0 & \cdots & 0 & 0 & 0 & \cdots & 0 \\ & & & & & \vdots & & & & & \end{bmatrix},$$

$$D_u = \begin{bmatrix} 0 & 0 & \cdots & 0 & 0 & 0 & \cdots & 0 & \frac{r}{1+r} & 0 & 0 \\ & & \vdots & & & & & & & & \\ 0 & 0 & \cdots & -\eta & 0 & 0 & \cdots & 0 & \frac{r}{1+r} & 0 & 0 \\ 0 & 0 & \cdots & 0 & 0 & 0 & \cdots & 0 & 0 & 0 & 0 \\ 0 & 0 & \cdots & 0 & 0 & 0 & \cdots & 0 & 0 & 0 & 0 \\ & & \vdots & & & & & & & & \\ 0 & 0 & \cdots & 0 & 0 & 0 & \cdots & 0 & 0 & 0 & 0 \\ & & \vdots & & & & & & & & \end{bmatrix},$$

and $D_z = F_z = \mathbf{0}$. For expositional reasons, we decompose the matrix F_u into convenient submatrices:

$$F_u = \begin{bmatrix} B_{11} & B_{12} & B_{13} \\ B_{21} & B_{22} & B_{23} \end{bmatrix},$$

with the 59×60 submatrix $B_{11} = \mathbf{0}$, 59×40 submatrix $B_{12} = \mathbf{0}$, and 59×3 submatrix $B_{13} = \mathbf{0}$. The submatrix B_{21} of dimension 59×60 is given by:

$$B_{21} = \begin{bmatrix} -c^1 & 0 & \cdots & 0 & 0 \\ 0 & -c^2 & \cdots & 0 & 0 \\ \vdots & \vdots & \vdots & \vdots & \vdots \\ 0 & 0 & \cdots & -c^{59} & 0 \end{bmatrix}.$$

The submatrix B_{22} of dimension 59×40 describes the coefficients of the terms $\hat{n}_t$:

$$B_{22} = \begin{bmatrix} (1-\tau)wn^1 & 0 & \cdots & 0 \\ 0 & (1-\tau)wn^2 & \cdots & 0 \\ & & \vdots & \\ 0 & 0 & \cdots & (1-\tau)wn^{40} \\ 0 & 0 & \cdots & 0 \\ & & \vdots & \\ 0 & 0 & \cdots & 0 \end{bmatrix}.$$

Finally, the 59×3 submatrix B_{23} is as follows:

$$B_{23} = \begin{bmatrix} 0 & (1-\tau)wn^1 & -\tau wn^1 \\ rk^2 & (1-\tau)wn^2 & -\tau wn^2 \\ rk^3 & (1-\tau)wn^3 & -\tau wn^3 \\ & \vdots & \\ rk^{40} & (1-\tau)wn^{40} & -\tau wn^{40} \\ rk^{41} & 0 & 0 \\ & \vdots & \\ rk^{59} & 0 & 0 \end{bmatrix}.$$

This system of equations can be solved with the methods introduced in Chapter 2. In particular, we can reduce the system to the equation systems (2.51):

$$E_t \begin{bmatrix} \mathbf{x}_{t+1} \\ \boldsymbol{\lambda}_{t+1} \end{bmatrix} = W \begin{bmatrix} \mathbf{x}_t \\ \boldsymbol{\lambda}_t \end{bmatrix} + R\mathbf{z}_t,$$

$$W = \left(D_{x\lambda} - D_u C_u^{-1} C_{x\lambda}\right)^{-1} \left(F_{x\lambda} - F_u C_u^{-1} C_{x\lambda}\right),$$

$$R = \left(D_{x\lambda} - D_u C_u^{-1} C_{x\lambda}\right)^{-1}$$
$$\times \left[\left(D_z + D_u C_u^{-1} C_z\right) \Pi + \left(F_z - F_u C_u^{-1} C_z\right)\right].$$

In our problem, the matrix $D_{x\lambda} - D_u C_u^{-1} C_{x\lambda}$ is invertible and we can compute the matrix W. The economy displays local saddlepoint stability around the non-stochastic steady state if and only if the number of eigenvalues of W inside the unit circle is equal to the number of predetermined variables. As it turns out, the matrix W of the dynamic system (10.28a)-(10.28b) has 59 eigenvalues with absolute value less than one which is exactly the number of predetermined variables k_t^s, $s = 2, \ldots, 59$.[13] Therefore, our economy is locally stable.[14]

Business Cycle Dynamics. How do the business cycle dynamics of the OLG model compare with those of the standard Ramsey model? For this reason, we look at the impulse response functions of our OLG model and also compute artificial time series for output Y_t, investment $I_t = K_{t+1} - (1-\delta)K_t$, consumption C_t, working hours N_t, and the real wage w_t. The impulse responses and statistics are computed with the help of program RCh1021.g, which only takes seconds for the computation. The impulse responses of the technology level Z and the endogenous variables Y, I, K, C, and N are presented in Figure 10.4. Notice that we used years rather than quarters as time periods which is usually not the case in business cycle studies that are based on the stochastic Ramsey model. The impulse responses are similar to those in the RBC model. Interestingly, however, employment even undershoots its long-run steady state value along the adjustment path after 4 years.

Analogous to our procedure in Section 2.4, we use the linear policy function for $\mathbf{x}$, $\mathbf{x}_{t+1} = L_x^x \mathbf{x}_t + L_z^x \mathbf{z}_t$, and the GAUSS random number generator rndn to simulate time series data. The logs of the results are passed to the HP-Filter (with $\lambda = 100$ for annual data) in order to get percentage deviations from the stationary solution. Table 10.2 presents the second moments from the filtered series for the OLG model. Be careful with comparing the results obtained from the annual periods of the OLG model with those

---

[13] In the exercises, you are asked to show that Example 9.2.1 also displays local stability.

[14] See LAITNER (1990) for a detailed analysis of local stability and determinancy in Auerbach-Kotlikoff models.

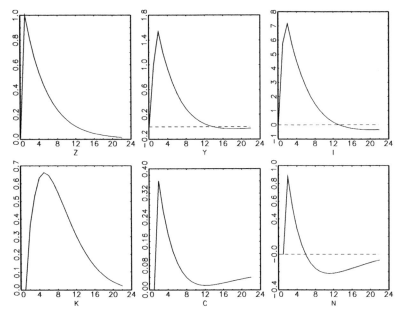

Figure 10.4: Impulse Responses in the OLG Model

presented in Table 1.2 from quarterly periods for the stochastic Ramsey model.

The cyclical behavior of the US economy during 1956-87 is presented in parentheses in Table 10.2.[15] The table shows that all variables in our model are not volatile enough. Furthermore, consumption in our model varies as much as output, while this is obviously not the case for the US economy. The correlations of investment, hours, and consumption with output in our model, however, are in good accordance with the US data.

10.2.2 The Algorithm of Krusell and Smith in Overlapping Generations Models

The Algorithm proposed by KRUSELL and SMITH (1998) that you learned about in Section 8.3 can also be applied to economies

---

[15] The data is taken from Table 4 in RÍOS-RULL (1996).

Table 10.2

Variable	s_x	r_{xy}	r_x
Output	0.454	1.00	0.78
	(2.23)	(1.00)	
Investment	1.60	0.55	0.36
	(8.66)	(0.82)	
Consumption	0.455	0.80	0.78
	(1.69)	(0.86)	
Hours	0.456	0.47	0.78
	(1.88)	(0.94)	
Real Wage	1.04	−0.07	0.40

Notes: s_x:=standard deviation of HP-filtered simulated series of variable x, r_{xy}:=cross correlation of variable x with output, r_x:=first order autocorrelation of variable x. Numbers in parenthesis give the empirical magnitudes computed from US yearly data between 1956 and 1987.

with finite lifetime with some minor modifications. The individual state space is simply characterized by an additional dimension which is age. Therefore, the simulation step becomes more time-consuming. Besides, we have not encountered any other limitations in the application of the Krusell-Smith algorithm to finite-lifetime economies in our experience. In particular, the goodness of fit for the law of motion for a particular functional form is almost identical to the one in infinite-lifetime models. Given the current computer technology, however, the algorithm is still very time-consuming. Below we will present a simple example that takes us some 20 hours to compute with an Intel Pentium(R) M, 319 MHz machine, even though technology as the only stochastic aggregate variable is assumed to take only two different values. Therefore, adding more stochastic aggregate variables may serious impede computational time.

In the following, we will apply the Krusell-Smith algorithm to an overlapping generations business cycle model.[16] The analysis in

---

[16] The exposition follows HEER (2007).

this section is very closely related to that of the infinite-lifetime model in Section 8.4.2. Hereinafter, we study the business cycle dynamics of the income distribution in an OLG model with aggregate uncertainty. For this reason, let us briefly review our results from Chapter 8. In Table 8.2, we presented the empirical correlation between output and income shares as estimated by CASTAÑEDA,DÍAZ-GIMÉNEZ, and RÍOS-RULL (1998b). The US income distribution is highly, but not perfectly procyclical for the low income quintiles, countercyclical for the top 60-95%, and acyclical for the top 5%. In their model, cyclical fluctuations result from the stochastic technology level. During a boom, the number of unemployed workers decreases. As a consequence, the relative income share of the lower income quintiles rises at the expense of the higher income quintiles. However, the income shares are almost perfectly correlated with output, either positively or negatively. Therefore, we also fail to replicate the income dynamics of the very income-rich which is acyclical.

In the following, we present a simple business cycle model with overlapping generations and elastic labor supply in order to improve the modeling of the cyclical income distribution dynamics. We consider households with different productivity types. In addition, individual productivity is also age-dependent and subject to an idiosyncratic shock so that we are able to match both the observed income and wealth heterogeneity. The latter feature, of course, is also important for the study of the factor income distribution dynamics because we also aim for the replication of the cyclical movements of the capital income. Aggregate uncertainty is introduced in the form of a shock on aggregate production technology.

In our model, the almost perfect correlation of the lower income quintiles with output is reduced as the high-productivity agents have a more elastic labor supply than their low-productivity contemporanies.[17] In addition, the share of the top 5% of the income earners is almost acyclical as i) many of the income-rich agents are

---

[17] HEER and MAUSSNER (2007) show that this does not need to be the case in the presence of progressive income taxation.

wealth-rich retired agents and ii) the wealth-rich workers also have a less elastic labor supply than the wealth-poor workers. During an economic expansion, both wages and pensions increase. Pensions are tied to the current wage rate. However, workers increase their labor supply, which is not possible for retired workers. Therefore, the income share of workers increases and is procyclical.

An OLG Model of the Income Distribution Business Cycle Dynamics. In the model, three different sectors are depicted: households, firms, and the government. Households differ with regard to their individual productivity and are also subject to idiosyncratic productivity risk. They maximize discounted lifetime utility with regard to their intertemporal consumption, capital, and labor supply. Firms are competitive and maximize profits. The government provides pensions which it finances with a tax on wage income.

Households. Households live 70 periods. Periods are equal to one year. Households are born at age 1 (corresponding to real lifetime age 20). Each generation is of measure 1/70. The first 45 periods, they work, the last 25 periods, they are retired and receive pensions. Households maximize expected lifetime utility at age 1 in period t:

$$E_t \sum_{s=1}^{70} \beta^{s-1} u(c_{t+s-1}^s, l_{t+s-1}^s), \qquad (10.29)$$

where s denotes age. Instantaneous utility is a function of both consumption c and leisure l:

$$u(c, l) = \frac{(c^\gamma l^{1-\gamma})^{1-\eta} - 1}{1 - \eta}.$$

The total time endowment is equal to one and allocated between leisure l and work n, $n + l = 1$.

The worker's labor productivity $e(s, \epsilon, z) = \epsilon z e^{\bar{y}_s}$ depends on the agent's permanent efficiency type $\epsilon \in \mathcal{E} = \{\epsilon_1, \epsilon_2\}$, his idiosyncratic stochastic productivity $z \in \mathcal{Z} = \{z_1, z_2\}$, and his age $s \in \mathcal{S}$. This modeling of labor productivity has often been applied in DGE analysis for the following reasons: i) Differences in the permanent efficiency type ϵ help to generate the wage heterogeneity that is observed empirically. In our case, two different efficiency types are enough to achieve this aim. ii) Workers will build up precautionary savings if they face idiosyncratic productivity risk z. Therefore, the wealth distribution becomes more heterogenous in better accordance with reality. iii) The age-dependent component $\bar{y}_s$ helps to explain differences in the age-income distribution that is important to explain the movement of the cross-section factor shares.

In each period t, an equal measure of 1-year old workers of productivity types $e(1, \epsilon_i, z_j)$, $i = 1, 2$, $j = 1, 2$, is born. During working age, $s = 1, \ldots, 44$, the process for idiosyncratic productivity z_s is a Markov chain:

$$\pi(z'|z) = Prob\{z_{s+1} = z'|z_s = z\} = \begin{pmatrix} \pi^z_{11} & \pi^z_{12} \\ \pi^z_{21} & \pi^z_{22} \end{pmatrix}. \qquad (10.30)$$

Depending on his efficiency type ϵ, the agent receives pensions $b_t(\epsilon) = \epsilon \bar{b}_t$ in old age that are financed by a social security tax $\tau_{w,t}$ on the young workers' wage income.

Let k, w, and r denote the individual capital stock, the wage rate, and the interest rate, respectively. The working agent of age s faces the following budget constraint in period t:

$$k^{s+1}_{t+1} = (1 + r_t)k^s_t + (1 - \tau_{w,t})w_t e(s, \epsilon, z)n^s_t - c^s_t, \quad s = 1, \ldots, 45. \qquad (10.31)$$

The budget constraint of the retired worker is given by

$$k^{s+1}_{t+1} = (1 + r_t)k^s_t + b_t(\epsilon) - c^s_t, \quad s = 46, \ldots, 70. \qquad (10.32)$$

Agents are born without capital at age 1, $k^1_t \equiv 0$, and do not work in old age, $l^s_t = 1$ for $s \geq 46$. In addition, we impose a borrowing constraint with $k^s_t \geq 0$.

Firms. Firms are competitive and produce output using capital K and labor N. Production Y is characterized by constant returns to scale and assumed to be Cobb-Douglas:

$$Y_t = A_t N_t^{1-\alpha} K_t^\alpha.$$

The aggregate technology level $A_t \in \{A_1, A_2\}$ follows a 2-state Markov process:

$$\pi(A'|A) = Prob\{A_{t+1} = A'|A_t = A\} = \begin{pmatrix} \pi_{11}^A & \pi_{12}^A \\ \pi_{21}^A & \pi_{22}^A \end{pmatrix}. \quad (10.33)$$

In a factor market equilibrium, factors are rewarded with their marginal product:

$$w_t = (1-\alpha) A_t N_t^{-\alpha} K_t^\alpha, \quad (10.34)$$
$$r_t = \alpha A_t N_t^{1-\alpha} K_t^{\alpha-1} - \delta. \quad (10.35)$$

Capital K depreciates at rate δ.

Government. The government provides pensions to the retired agents. Pensions are proportional to the current-period wage rate with the replacement ratio being denoted by ζ. In addition, we distinguish between the two cases: pensions are either lump-sum or depend on the permanent efficiency type ϵ:

$$b_t = \begin{cases} \zeta w_t \bar{n} & \text{lump-sum,} \\ \zeta \epsilon w_t \bar{n} & \text{efficiency-dependent.} \end{cases}$$

$\bar{n}$ denotes the average labor supply in the economy in the non-stochastic steady state (with $A \equiv 1$). Therefore, pensions of the retired agents do not increase if the contemporary workers increase their labor supply.

Stationary Equilibrium. In the stationary equilibrium, individual behavior is consistent with the aggregate behavior of the economy, households maximize intertemporal utility, firms maximize profits, and factor and goods' markets are in equilibrium. Let $F_t(k, s, \epsilon, z)$ denote the distribution of individual wealth k, age s, the efficiency type ϵ, and idiosyncratic productivity z in the period t.

A stationary equilibrium for a government policy $\{\zeta\}$ and initial distribution $F_0(k, s, \epsilon, z)$ in period 0 corresponds to a price system, an allocation, and a sequence of aggregate productivity indicators $\{A_t\}$ that satisfy the following conditions:

1. Households maximize the intertemporal utility (10.29) subject to the budget constraint (10.31) or (10.32), and the dynamics of the idiosyncratic productivity level z, (10.30). This gives rise to the following first-order conditions:

$$\frac{1-\gamma}{\gamma}\frac{c_t^s}{1-n_t^s} = (1-\tau_{w,t})w_t e(s,\epsilon,z),$$

$$\frac{(1-n_t^s)^{(1-\gamma)(1-\eta)}}{(c_t^s)^{1-\gamma(1-\eta)}} = \beta E_t \frac{\left(1-n_{t+1}^{s+1}\right)^{(1-\gamma)(1-\eta)}}{\left(c_{t+1}^{s+1}\right)^{1-\gamma(1-\eta)}}[1+r_{t+1}].$$

Individual labor supply $n_t(k,s,\epsilon,z)$, consumption $c_t(k,s,\epsilon,z)$, and optimal next period capital stock $k'_t(k,s,\epsilon,z)$ in period t are functions of the individual state variables $\{k,s,\epsilon,z\}$ and also depend on the period t.

2. Firms maximize profits satisfying (10.34) and (10.35).
3. The aggregate variables employment N_t, capital K_t, consumption C_t, and pensions B_t are equal to the sum of the individual variables.
4. The government budget is balanced:

$$B_t = \tau_{w,t} w_t N_t.$$

In particular, the contribution rate $\tau_{w,t}$ adjusts in each period.
5. The goods' market clears:

$$C_t + K_{t+1} - (1-\delta)K_t = Y_t.$$

6. The cross-sectional distribution F_t evolves as

$$F_{t+1}(k', s+1, \epsilon, z') = \sum_z \pi(z'|z) \sum_{k=(k'_t)^{-1}(k',\epsilon,s,z)} F_t(k,s,\epsilon,z),$$

where $(k'_t)^{-1}(.)$ denotes the inverse of the policy function $k'_t(.)$.[18] For the newborns with efficiency type $\epsilon \in \{\epsilon_1, \epsilon_2\}$ and idiosyncratic productivity z in $\{z_1, z_2\}$ in period $t+1$, the distribution is given by:

$$F_{t+1}(0, 1, \epsilon, z) = \frac{1}{4 \times 70}.$$

---
[18] In the model, $k'(.)$ is a strictly monotone increasing function of k.

Calibration. We choose the parameter values $\beta = 0.99$, $\eta = 2.0$, $\gamma = 0.28$, $\alpha = 0.35$, $\delta = 0.08$ that are standard in the business cycle literature and have been applied repeatedly in this book. The Markov process (10.33) of aggregate technology level is calibrated so that the average duration of one cycle is equal to 6 years:

$$\pi(A'|A) = \begin{pmatrix} 2/3 & 1/3 \\ 1/3 & 2/3 \end{pmatrix}. \tag{10.36}$$

Aggregate technology is chosen so that the mean $\bar{A}$ is equal to one and the annual standard deviation of output is approximately equal to 2% implying $\{A_1, A_2\} = \{0.98, 1.02\}$.

The calibration of the individual productivity $e(s, \epsilon, z)$ is chosen in accordance with KRUEGER and LUDWIG (2007). In particular, we pick $\{\epsilon_1, \epsilon_2\} = \{0.57, 1.43\}$ so that the average productivity is one and the implied variance of labor income for the new entrants at age $s = 1$ is equal to the value reported by STORESLETTEN, TELMER, and YARON (2007). The annual persistence of the idiosyncratic component z is chosen to be 0.98. In addition, idiosyncratic productivity has a conditional variance of 8%, implying $\{z_1, z_2\} = \{0.727, 1.273\}$, and

$$\pi(z'|z) = \begin{pmatrix} 0.98 & 0.02 \\ 0.02 & 0.98 \end{pmatrix}. \tag{10.37}$$

The age-efficiency $\bar{y}_s$ profile is taken from HANSEN (1993).[19] The calibration implies an average labor supply approximately equal to $\bar{n} = 0.3$ and a Gini coefficient of income (wealth) equal to 0.42 (0.58) in good accordance with empirical observations, even though the values are lower than those of most recent studies on the empirical wealth and income distribution. As pointed out before, BUDRÍA RODRÍGUEZ, DÍAZ-GIMÉNEZ, QUADRINI, and RÍOS-RULL (2002) find a value of 0.55 (0.80) for the income Gini (wealth Gini) for the US economy.

The replacement ratio of average pensions relative to net wage earnings is equal to $\zeta = \frac{\bar{b}_t}{(1-\tau_{w,t})w_t\bar{n}} = 30\%$, with $\bar{n} = 0.3$.

---

[19] See Section 9.3.2.

Computation. In order to compute the OLG model with aggregate uncertainty, we use the algorithm of KRUSELL and SMITH (1998). The GAUSS program Rch1022.g implements the algorithm that is described by the following steps:

Algorithm 10.2.1 (Krusell-Smith Algorithm for OLG Models)

Purpose: *Computation of the OLG model with individual and aggregate uncertainty*

Steps:

Step 1: Compute the non-stochastic steady state with $A \equiv 1$. Store the policy functions and the steady-state distribution of $\{k, s, \epsilon, z\}$.

Step 2: Choose an initial parameterized functional form for the law of motion for the aggregate next-period capital stock $K' = g(K, A)$ and employment $N' = h(K', A')$.

Step 3: Solve the consumer's optimization problem as a function of the individual and aggregate state variables, $\{k, s, \epsilon, z; K, A\}$.

Step 4: Simulate the dynamics of the distribution function.

Step 5: Use the time path for the distribution to estimate the law of motion for K' and N'.

Step 6: Iterate until the parameters converge.

Step 7: Test the goodness of fit for the functional form using, for example, R^2. If the fit is satisfactory, stop, otherwise choose a different functional form for $g(.)$ and/or $h(.)$.

In the first step, the non-stochastic steady state allocation is computed with standard methods. In particular, we discretize the individual state space using a grid over the individual asset space k of 50 points and interpolate linearly between points to evaluate the policy functions off grid points. The policy functions $k'(k, s, \epsilon, z)$ and $n(k, s, \epsilon, z)$ are computed from the first-order conditions of the household starting in the last period of life, $s = 70$. In the last period of his life, the retired agent consumes all his income.

Therefore, $k'(k, 70, \epsilon, z) = 0$ for all grid points $\{k, 70, \epsilon, z\}$. In the next iteration, we consider the household of age $s = 69$. Special care has to be taken with regard to possible corner solutions $k' = 0$. For the grid point $\{k, s, \epsilon, z\}$, we evaluate the residual function for $k' = 0$:

$$rf(k, s, \epsilon, z) = (c_t^s)^{\gamma(1-\eta)-1} - \beta E_t \left(c_{t+1}^{s+1}\right)^{\gamma(1-\eta)-1} [1 + r_{t+1}],$$

with $c^{s+1} = c(k', s+1, \epsilon, z)$. Remember that we have stored the policy function c^{s+1} during the previous iteration. If the residual function is larger or equal zero, then the optimal next-period capital stock is equal to zero, $k'(k, s, \epsilon, z) = 0$. Otherwise, an interior solution with $k' > 0$ exists that solves the above equation and we can apply our non-linear equations solver `FixvMN1`. The computation is carried out in the routine `rfold` of the program `Rch1022.g`.

For the working agent, we also have to take care of the corner solution $n = 0$. In order to facilitate the computation, we eliminate the labor supply n from the budget constraint with the help of the first-order condition for the labor supply implying:

$$c_t^s = \gamma \left[(1 - \tau_{w,t})e(s, \epsilon, z)w_t + (1 + r_t)k - k'\right], \quad (10.38)$$

$$n_t^s = 1 - \frac{1-\gamma}{\gamma} \frac{c_t^s}{(1 - \tau_{w,t})e(s, \epsilon, z)w_t}. \quad (10.39)$$

Just like in the case of the retired agent, we compute the residual function from the Euler equation of the working agent:

$$rf(k, s, \epsilon, z) = \frac{(1 - n_t^s)^{(1-\gamma)(1-\eta)}}{(c_t^s)^{1-\gamma(1-\eta)}}$$

$$- \beta E_t \frac{\left(1 - n_{t+1}^{s+1}\right)^{(1-\gamma)(1-\eta)}}{\left(c_{t+1}^{s+1}\right)^{1-\gamma(1-\eta)}} [1 + r_{t+1}].$$

The optimal next-period policy functions c^{s+1} and n^{s+1} have been stored in previous iterations. For the 45-year old worker, the next period labor supply is zero as he will retire. In order to find the optimal policy functions, we first evaluate the residual function for $k' = 0$ to find out whether we have a corner solution or not. If n_t^s

as computed from (10.39) is below zero, we recompute the residual function setting $n_t^s = 0$. While the first computation is done in the procedure rfyoung, the second one is carried out in the procedure rfyoung1 in the program Rch1022.g. If the residual is below zero, $k' = 0$ is the optimal solution, otherwise, we solve the non-linear equation for k'. Again, we have to check if the optimal solution from rfyoung implies $n \geq 0$. Otherwise, we have to compute k' with the help of the routine rfyoung1.

In order to solve the non-linear equations problem, it is helpful to find a good starting value. In fact, we try different initial values and take the one that implies the lowest absolute value for the residual function. Possible candidate solutions include the optimal next-period capital stock k' for the agent i) that is one year older, but otherwise equal with regard to $\{k, \epsilon, z\}$ or ii) that has a capital stock which is the adjacent grid point. We also try iii) $k' = 0$ or iv) $k' = k$. As a consequence, we do not encounter the problem that our computation breaks down because we have to evaluate the utility function for $c < 0$.

In step 1, we iterate over the aggregate capital stock and employment to find the non-stochastic steady-state. The optimal policy functions for the steady state are stored in order to use them as an initial guess for the policy functions in step 3. Similarly, we save the non-stochastic steady state distribution and use it as initial distribution for the simulation of the stochastic economy in step 4.

In the second step, we postulate the following laws of motion for the next-period capital stock and employment:

$$K' = \exp[\theta_0 + \theta_1 \ln(K) + \theta_2 \mathbf{1}_{A'=A_1} + \theta_3 \mathbf{1}_{A'=A_1} \ln(K)],$$
$$N' = \exp[\kappa_0 + \kappa_1 \ln(K') + \kappa_2 \mathbf{1}_{A'=A_1} + \kappa_3 \mathbf{1}_{A'=A_1} \ln(K')].$$

Notice in particular that next-period employment is a function of next-period capital stock K' and next-period aggregate productivity A' only. Therefore, employment N is not an aggregate state variable. As an initialization, we set $\theta_2 = \theta_3 = \kappa_1 = \kappa_2 = \kappa_3 = 0$. We choose $\theta_1 = 0.9$ and compute θ_0 and κ_0 so that $K' = K$ and $N' = N$ correspond to their non-stochastic steady state values, respectively.

As our solution, we find the following laws of motion:
$$K' = e^{0.0610+0.0126\ln(K)+0.9076\,\mathbf{1}_{A'=A_1}-0.0043\,\mathbf{1}_{A'=A_1}\ln(K)},$$
$$N' = e^{-1.265+0.0179\ln(K')-0.1751\,\mathbf{1}_{A'=A_1}+0.0064\,\mathbf{1}_{A'=A_1}\ln(K')}.$$

In step 3, we compute the individual policy functions as functions of the individual and aggregate state variables for given law of motion for K' and N'. For this reason, we choose a rather loose grid for the aggregate capital stock K as the curvature of the policy function with respect to this argument is rather low. We find that 7 points are sufficient. Furthermore, we choose 80% and 120% of the non-stochastic steady state aggregate capital stock as the lower and upper boundary for this interval. In our simulations, the aggregate capital stock always remains within these boundaries.

Starting with the non-stochastic steady state distribution as our initial distribution $F_0(k,s,\epsilon,z)$, we compute the dynamics of the economy using the Algorithm 7.2.3. We use a pseudo-random number generator in order to simulate the technology level $\{A_t\}$ over 200 periods repeatedly. Given the distribution in period t, $F_t(k,s,\epsilon,z)$, we can compute the next-period distribution, $F_{t+1}(k,s,\epsilon,z)$, with the help of the policy functions $k'(k,s,\epsilon,z;K,A)$ and $n(k,s,\epsilon,z;K,A)$. In addition, we can compute aggregate production and the income shares of the different quintiles.

Let us emphasize one point at this place. Many studies on OLG models with aggregate uncertainty consider a sample of 1,000 households for each generation or so and simulate their behavior. We find that this method has several disadvantages. First, it is very time consuming. We instead advocate to store the actual distribution at the grid points $\{k,s,\epsilon,z\}$ as in Algorithm 7.2.3. This procedure requires less storage capacity. Importantly, the computation of the next-period distribution is much faster than the simulation of some 1,000 households in each generation. Second, if we simulate the behavior of the household sample for each generation, we will have to use a random number generator in order to switch the agents type from z to z'. As we are only using some 1,000 agents, the law of large numbers does not need to hold and the percentage of the agents with $z' = z_1$ and $z' = z_2$ is not equal to 50%, respectively. Therefore, during our simulation, we always have to adjust the number of agents with productivity $z' = z_1$ ($z' = z_2$) to one half in each generation which involves some arbitrariness as we have to select some households whose productivity is changed ad hoc.[20]

Finally, in step 6, we update the parameters by estimating the law of motions for the simulated time series with the help of OLS. We stop the algorithm as soon as the maximum change of the θ_i and κ_j is below 0.001. In our last iteration, the R^2 in the two regressions of the law of motion exceeds 0.999, respectively. Therefore, we can be confident that our postulated laws of motion $g(.)$ and $h(.)$ are satisfactory. The computation of Rch1022.g takes some 20 hours on an Intel Pentium(R) M, 319 MHz machine.

Business Cycle Dynamics of the Income Distribution. Figure 10.5 describes the behavior of our economy in the non-stochastic steady state. In the top row, we graph the average wealth and labor supply of each generation, while the average total income of each generation and the efficiency-age profiles $e(s, \epsilon, z)$ for the four productivity types $\{\epsilon_i, z_j\}$ for $i = 1, 2$, $j = 1, 2$, are displayed in the bottom row. Agents accumulate savings until retirement age $s = 45$ (corresponding to real lifetime age 64 in the Figure 10.5) and dissave thereafter. Total income (wage and interest income before taxes plus pensions) peaks at real lifetime age 50. Our average-age profiles accord very well with empirical observations in BUDRÍA RODRÍGUEZ, DÍAZ-GIMÉNEZ, QUADRINI, and RÍOS-RULL (2002). Based on the 1998 data from the Survey of Consumer Finances they find that US household income, earnings, and wealth peak around ages 51-55, 51-55, and 61-65, respectively.

In order to compute the correlation of the income distribution with output, we simulate the dynamics of our economy repeatedly over 200 periods. One of these simulations is illustrated in Figure 10.6. In the lower picture, we graph the dynamics of out-

---

[20] Please compare Section 8.3.

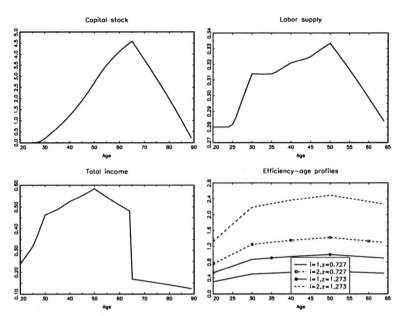

Figure 10.5: Non-Stochastic Steady State Age-Profiles

put.[21] If the technology level jumps from A_1 to A_2 or vice versa, this is also instantaneously reflected in the movement of the production level. In the upper picture, we graph the behavior of the Gini coefficient of total income. Obviously, total income is highly procyclical. The correlation coefficient of the total income Gini coefficient with output amounts to 0.87. As a simple explanation, the high-productivity workers increase their labor supply by a higher percentage than the low-productivity workers when the wage rates increases during an economic expansion.

Table 10.3 shows in detail the behavior of the income quintiles. In the first entry row, we display the empirical correlations of output with the 1st, 2nd, 3rd, and 4th income quintiles, and the 80-95% and 95-100% income groups for the US economy, respectively.[22] In the second row, you find the values as resulting

---

[21] Logarithmic output has been detrended using the Hodrick-Prescott filter with smoothing parameter $\lambda = 100$.

[22] The estimates are reproduced from Table 4 in CASTAÑEDA, DÍAZ-GIMÉNEZ, and RÍOS-RULL (1998b).

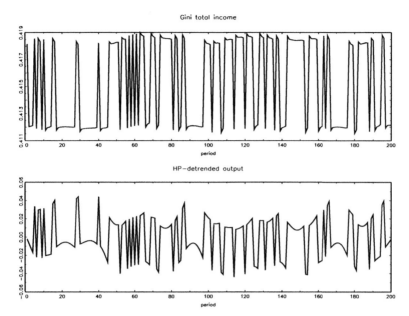

Figure 10.6: Time Series Simulation

from the simulation of the most preferred model of CASTAÑEDA, DÍAZ-GIMÉNEZ, and RÍOS-RULL (1998b). The last two lines display the values obtained from simulating our economy for the two cases that pensions are either proportional to the individual efficiency ϵ or lump-sum. Obviously, the model with lump-sum pensions is our preferred model (last row). In this case, the income share of the first and fourth income quintile and the top 5% group match the empirical correlations almost perfectly, while the correlations of the 2nd and 3rd income quintiles with output are negative and of opposite sign compared to the empirical ones.

In our model, the dynamics of the income distribution are mainly driven by the intertemporal substitution of labor. During an economic expansion, wages increase and labor (replacement) income is redistributed 1) from low-productivity to high productivity workers, 2) old wealth-rich to young wealth-poor workers, as the latter groups increase their labor supply to a larger extent than the former, respectively. In addition, 3) income of the working agents increases relative to the one of retired agents. In

Table 10.3

	0-20%	20-40%	40-60%	60-80%	80-95%	95-100%
US	0.53	0.49	0.31	-0.29	-0.64	0.00
Castañeda et al. (1998)	0.95	0.92	0.73	-0.56	-0.90	-0.84
our model i) $b_t(\epsilon) = \epsilon \bar{b}_t$	-0.15	-0.07	-0.08	-0.01	0.31	0.03
ii) $b_t(\epsilon) = \bar{b}_t$	0.40	-0.47	-0.11	-0.24	0.60	0.04

Notes: Entries in rows 1 and 2 are reproduced from Table 4 in Castañeda et al. (1998b). Annual logarithmic output has been detrended using the Hodrick-Prescott filter with smoothing parameter $\lambda = 100$.

our economy with overlapping generations, the highest income quintile consists of the workers aged 50-60 with high productivity as these agents have the highest wage income and relatively high interest income. Since these agents also hold relatively high wealth, they do not increase their labor supply as much as the younger high-productivity workers. As a consequence, the total income share of the top 5% income earners is almost acyclical.

The lowest income quintile in our economy consists of the very old retired workers (aged 80 and above in real lifetime) and the young workers with low productivity ϵ_1 and z_1 (aged 20-30 in real lifetime). Since the pension income falls relative to the wage income during an economic expansion, the correlation of output with the income share of the first quintile is not close to unity as in CASTAÑEDA, DÍAZ-GIMÉNEZ, and RÍOS-RULL (1998b). Therefore, the introduction of overlapping generations, pensions, and elastic labor may help to improve the modeling of the income distribution business cycles dynamics.

Appendix 5: Parameters of the AR(1)-Process with Annual Periods

In this Appendix, we derive the parameters (ρ, σ) that we were using for the AR(1)-process with annual periods in Section 10.2.1. In particular, we choose (ρ, σ) so that they correspond to the parameters of the AR(1) with quarterly periods, $(\rho^q, \sigma^q) = (0.95, 0.00763)$.

Let z_t^q denote the logarithm of the technology level in the model with quarterly periods that follows the AR(1)-process:

$$z_{t+1}^q = \rho^q z_t^q + \epsilon_{t+1}^q,$$

where $\epsilon_t^q \sim N\left(0, (\sigma^q)^2\right)$. Similarly,

$$z_{t+2}^q = \rho^q z_{t+1}^q + \epsilon_{t+2}^q,$$
$$z_{t+3}^q = \rho^q z_{t+2}^q + \epsilon_{t+3}^q,$$
$$z_{t+4}^q = \rho^q z_{t+3}^q + \epsilon_{t+4}^q.$$

Let z_T^a denote the logarithm of the technology level in the corresponding model with annual periods that follows the AR(1)-process:

$$z_{T+1}^q = \rho z_T^q + \epsilon_{T+1},$$

where $\epsilon_T \sim N\left(0, \sigma^2\right)$.

If we identify the technology level z^q at the beginning of the quarters t, $t+4$, $t+8$ with the annual technology level z^a at the beginning of the periods T, $T+1$, $T+2$, we find:

$$\begin{aligned}
z_{T+1}^a = z_{t+4}^q &= \rho^q z_{t+3}^q + \epsilon_{t+4}^q, \\
&= \rho^q \left(\rho^q z_{t+2}^q + \epsilon_{t+3}^q\right) + \epsilon_{t+4}^q, \\
&= (\rho^q)^2 z_{t+2}^q + \rho^q \epsilon_{t+3}^q + \epsilon_{t+4}^q, \\
&= (\rho^q)^3 z_{t+1}^q + (\rho^q)^2 \epsilon_{t+2}^q + \rho^q \epsilon_{t+3}^q + \epsilon_{t+4}^q, \\
&= (\rho^q)^4 z_t^q + (\rho^q)^3 \epsilon_{t+1}^q + (\rho^q)^2 \epsilon_{t+2}^q + \rho^q \epsilon_{t+3}^q + \epsilon_{t+4}^q, \\
&= (\rho^q)^4 z_T^a + (\rho^q)^3 \epsilon_{t+1}^q + (\rho^q)^2 \epsilon_{t+2}^q + \rho^q \epsilon_{t+3}^q + \epsilon_{t+4}^q.
\end{aligned}$$

Accordingly, we can make the following identifications:

$$\rho = (\rho^q)^4$$
$$\epsilon_T = (\rho^q)^3 \epsilon_{t+1}^q + (\rho^q)^2 \epsilon_{t+2}^q + \rho^q \epsilon_{t+3}^q + \epsilon_{t+4}^q.$$

Therefore,

$$\begin{aligned}
\operatorname{var}(\epsilon) &= \sigma^2 \\
&= \operatorname{var}\left(\epsilon^q(1 + \rho^q + (\rho^q)^2 + (\rho^q)^3)\right) \\
&= \left(1 + (\rho^q)^2 + (\rho^q)^4 + (\rho^q)^6\right)(\sigma^q)^2.
\end{aligned}$$

For $(\rho^q, \sigma^q) = (0.95, 0.00763)$, we get $\rho = 0.814$ and $\sigma = 0.0142$.

Problems

10.1 Concentration of Wealth
Consider the model described in Section 10.1.
a) Recompute the model for a less stricter borrowing constraint where the agent can borrow up to the average wage in the economy, $(1-\tau)w\bar{h}N/\sum_{t=1}^{T}\mu_t$. How does this affect the Gini coefficient of wealth?
b) Compute the effect of higher public pensions on the wealth heterogeneity. For this reason, increase the replacement ratio to 50%.
c) Compute the model assuming that all accidental bequests are transferred lump-sum to the households in equal amounts. How does this affect the concentration of wealth as measured by the Gini coefficient?
d) Compute the model assuming that labor supply is endogenous. Use the utility function and calibration presented in Example 10.2.1.

10.2 Business Cycle Dynamics of Aggregate Variables
Consider the model described in Section 10.2.1. Recompute the model for quarterly frequencies. Be careful to recalibrate β and δ. What are the effects on business cycle statistics for the aggregate variables?

10.3 Stability
Show that the economy described in Example 9.2.1 is saddlepoint stable.

10.4 Business Cycle Dynamics of the Income Distribution
Consider the model described in Section 10.2.2. Recompute the model for quarterly frequencies. Be careful to recalibrate β and δ. What are the effects on business cycle statistics for the income shares?

10.5 Redistributive Effects of Cyclical Government Spending
Introduce exogenous government spending G_t into the model in Section 10.2.2. Assume that government spending follows the AR(1)-process

$$\ln G_t = \rho \ln G_{t-1} + (1-\rho)\ln G + \varepsilon_t,$$

with $\varepsilon \sim N(0, \sigma^2)$, $\rho = 0.7$, and $\sigma = 0.007$. Assume further that government expenditures are financed with a proportional tax on factor income and that the government budget balances in each period.
a) Reformulate the model.
b) Compute the non-stochastic steady state assuming that government expenditures amount to 19% of total production. What are the values for the non-stochastic steady state tax rates?
c) Discretize the AR(1)-process for government consumption choosing three values. Let the middle point correspond to the one in the non-stochastic steady state. Use the Markov-chain Approximation algorithm from Section 12.2.

d) Compute the business cycle dynamics for the model. The state space consists of $\{k, s, \epsilon, z; A, K, G\}$. Households predict the next-period income tax rate using a law of motion equivalent to the one for N'.
e) How do cyclical government spending affect the income distribution? Simulate a time series where the government expenditure are increased above the steady state level for one period and fall back to the steady state level thereafter. Plot the impulse response functions of the total income Gini index.

Part III
Tools

Chapter 11

Numerical Methods

11.1 A Quick Refresher in Linear Algebra

In this section we provide some elementary and some more advanced, but very useful concepts and techniques from linear algebra. Most of the elementary material gathered here is found in any undergraduate textbook on linear algebra as, e.g., LANG (1987). For the more advanced subjects BRONSON (1989) as well as GOLUB and VAN LOAN (1996) are good references. In addition, many texts on econometrics review matrix algebra, as, e.g., GREENE (2003), Appendix A, or JUDGE et al. (1982), Appendix A.

11.1.1 Complex Numbers

A complex number c is an object of the form $c = \alpha + i\beta$, where the symbol i designates the imaginary unit, whose square is defined to equal minus unity, i.e., $i^2 = -1$ or $i = \sqrt{-1}$. The set of all those numbers is denoted by the symbol $\mathbb{C}$.

In the definition of c the real number α is called the real part, and the real number β is called the imaginary part of the complex number c. If we measure α on the abscissa and β on the ordinate c is a point in the plane, sometimes called the Gaussian plane. Instead of representing c by the pair (α, β), we may also use polar coordinates. If θ is the angle (measured in radians) between the horizontal axis and the vector from the origin to the point (α, β), then $c = r(\cos\theta + i\ \sin\beta)$ as shown in Figure 11.1. According to Pythagoras' theorem, the length of the vector is equal to $r =$

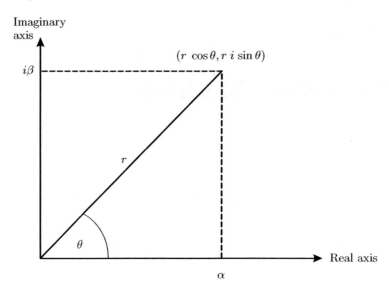

Figure 11.1: Gaussian Plane

$\sqrt{\alpha^2 + \beta^2}$. r is called the modulus (or simply absolute value $|c|$) of the complex number c.

The complex conjugate of c, is denoted by $\bar{c}$ and given by $\bar{c} = \alpha - i\beta$.

Addition and multiplication of complex numbers $c_1 = \alpha_1 + i\beta_1$ and $c_2 = \alpha_2 + i\beta_2$ are defined by the following formulas:

$$c_1 + c_2 = \alpha_1 + \alpha_2 + i(\beta_1 + \beta_2),$$
$$c_1 c_2 = (\alpha_1 + i\beta_1)(\alpha_2 + i\beta_2)$$
$$= (\alpha_1 \alpha_2) - (\beta_1 \beta_2) + i(\alpha_1 \beta_2 + \alpha_2 \beta_1).$$

In polar coordinates, the product $c_1 c_2$ is given by[1]

$$c_1 c_2 = r_1 r_2 [\cos(\theta_1 + \theta_2) + i \sin(\theta_1 + \theta_2)].$$

---

[1] This follows from the trigonometric formulas

$$\cos(\theta_1 + \theta_2) = \cos(\theta_1)\cos(\theta_2) - \sin(\theta_1)\sin(\theta_2),$$
$$\sin(\theta_1 + \theta_2) = \sin(\theta_1)\cos(\theta_2) + \cos(\theta_1)\sin(\theta_2).$$

See, e.g., SYDSÆTER, STRØM, and BERCK (1999), p. 15.

Thus the vector representing c_1 is stretched by r_2 and rotated counterclockwise by θ_2 radians. If $c_1 = c_2$ this implies $c^2 = r^2[(\cos(2\theta) + i\sin(2\theta)]$ or, more generally:

$$c^t = r^t[\cos(t\theta) + i\sin(t\theta)]. \tag{11.1}$$

Since $\sin(x)$ and $\cos(x)$ are in $[-1, 1]$ for all $x \in \mathbb{R}$, this implies

$$\lim_{t \to \infty} c^t = (0, i0) \equiv 0 \text{ for } r \in (0, 1). \tag{11.2}$$

Thus, if the modulus of a complex number is smaller than one, its tth power converges to the origin of the Gaussian plane, if $t \to \infty$. Sometimes we say that a complex number is inside (on or outside) the unit circle. The unit circle is the circle around the origin of the Gaussian plane with radius equal to one. Thus, complex numbers inside (on or outside) this circle have modulus less (equal to or greater) than unity.

11.1.2 Vectors

A real (complex) vector of dimension n is a n-tuple of numbers $x_i \in \mathbb{R}$ ($x_i \in \mathbb{C}$) $i = 1, 2, \ldots n$, denoted by

$$\mathbf{x} = \begin{bmatrix} x_1 \\ x_2 \\ \vdots \\ x_n \end{bmatrix}.$$

The space of all n-tuples is $\mathbb{R}^n$ ($\mathbb{C}^n$). Vector addition and scalar multiplication are defined by

$$\mathbf{y} = a + b\mathbf{x} = \begin{bmatrix} a + bx_1 \\ a + bx_2 \\ \vdots \\ a + bx_n \end{bmatrix}.$$

11.1.3 Norms

Norms are measures of distance. Since the distance of **x** from the zero vector is the length of **x**, norms are also measures of vector length. More formally, a norm on $\mathbb{R}^n$ (and similarly on $\mathbb{C}^n$) is a real valued function $\|\mathbf{x}\|$ that obeys:

$$\|\mathbf{x}\| \geq 0 \text{ for all } \mathbf{x} \in \mathbb{R}^n, \text{ and } \|\mathbf{x}\| = 0 \text{ if and only if } \mathbf{x} = \mathbf{0} \in \mathbb{R}^n,$$
$$\|a\mathbf{x}\| = |a| \cdot \|\mathbf{x}\| \text{ for all } \mathbf{x} \in \mathbb{R}^n \text{ and } a \in \mathbb{R},$$
$$\|\mathbf{x} + \mathbf{y}\| \leq \|\mathbf{x}\| + \|\mathbf{y}\| \text{ for all } \mathbf{x}, \mathbf{y} \in \mathbb{R}^n. \tag{11.3}$$

The most common examples of norms on $\mathbb{R}^n$ are

1. the ℓ_∞ or sup norm: $\|\mathbf{x}\|_\infty := \max\limits_{1 \leq i \leq n} |x_i|$, where $|x_i|$ denotes the absolute value of x_i.
2. the ℓ_2 or Euclidean norm: $\|\mathbf{x}\|_2 := \left(\sum_{i=1}^n x_i^2\right)^{1/2}$.

11.1.4 Linear Independence

A set of n vectors $\mathbf{x}_i$, $i = 1, 2, \ldots n$ is linearly independent if and only if the solution to

$$\mathbf{0} = a_1 \mathbf{x}_1 + a_2 \mathbf{x}_2 + \cdots + a_n \mathbf{x}_n$$

is $a_1 = a_2 = \cdots = a_n = 0$. A set $\mathcal{B} := \{\mathbf{v}_1, \mathbf{v}_2, \ldots, \mathbf{v}_n\}$ of n linearly independent vectors is a basis $\mathcal{B}$ for $\mathbb{R}^n$, since any element $\mathbf{x} \in \mathbb{R}^n$ can be represented by a linear combination of the elements of $\mathcal{B}$, i.e.,

$$\mathbf{x} = \sum_{i=1}^n a_i \mathbf{v}_i \quad \forall \mathbf{x} \in \mathbb{R}^n.$$

11.1.5 Matrices

A real (complex) matrix A with typical element $a_{ij} \in \mathbb{R}$ ($a_{ij} \in \mathbb{C}$) is the following n-by-m array of real numbers:

11.1 A Quick Refresher in Linear Algebra

$$A = (a_{ij}) := \begin{bmatrix} a_{11} & a_{12} & \cdots & a_{1m} \\ a_{21} & a_{22} & \cdots & a_{2m} \\ \vdots & \vdots & \ddots & \vdots \\ a_{n1} & a_{n2} & \cdots & a_{nm} \end{bmatrix}.$$

If $n = m$, A is called a square matrix. Other special matrices encountered in the main text are:

$$\underbrace{\begin{bmatrix} a_{11} & 0 & \cdots & 0 \\ 0 & a_{22} & \cdots & 0 \\ \vdots & \vdots & \ddots & \vdots \\ 0 & 0 & \cdots & a_{nn} \end{bmatrix}}_{\text{diagonal matrix}}, \underbrace{\begin{bmatrix} a_{11} & a_{12} & \cdots & a_{1n} \\ 0 & a_{22} & \cdots & a_{2n} \\ \vdots & \vdots & \ddots & \vdots \\ 0 & 0 & \cdots & a_{nn} \end{bmatrix}}_{\text{upper triangular matrix}}, \underbrace{\begin{bmatrix} 1 & 0 & \cdots & 0 \\ 0 & 1 & \cdots & 0 \\ \vdots & \vdots & \ddots & \vdots \\ 0 & 0 & \cdots & 1 \end{bmatrix}}_{\text{identity matrix}}.$$

If we consider the matrix $A = (a_{ij})$ as the row vector

$$[\underbrace{a_{11}, a_{21}, \ldots a_{n1}}_{\text{column 1}}, \underbrace{a_{12}, \ldots, a_{n2}}_{\text{column 2}}, \ldots, \underbrace{a_{1n} \ldots, a_{nn}}_{\text{column } n}],$$

we may apply the definition of any vector norm to this "long" vector to find the corresponding matrix norm. For instance, the ℓ_2 norm of A is

$$\|A\| = \left(\sum_{j=1}^{n} \sum_{i=1}^{n} a_{ij}^2 \right)^{1/2}.$$

Matrix addition and scalar multiplication are defined componentwise:

$$C = A + dB = \begin{bmatrix} a_{11} + db_{11} & a_{12} + db_{12} & \cdots & a_{1m} + db_{1m} \\ a_{21} + db_{21} & a_{22} + db_{22} & \cdots & a_{2m} + db_{2m} \\ \vdots & \vdots & \ddots & \vdots \\ a_{n1} + db_{n1} & a_{n2} + db_{n2} & \cdots & a_{nm} + db_{nm} \end{bmatrix}$$
(11.4)

for $A, B, C \in \mathbb{R}^{n \times m}$ and $d \in \mathbb{R}$. Thus, matrix addition obeys the following rules:

$$A + B = B + A, \qquad (11.5a)$$
$$A + (B + C) = (A + B) + C. \qquad (11.5b)$$

The product of two matrices $A \in \mathbb{R}^{n \times m}$ and $B \in \mathbb{R}^{m \times n}$, is the $n \times n$ matrix $C = (c_{ij})$, defined by

$$c_{ij} = \sum_{k=1}^{m} a_{ik} b_{kj}. \tag{11.6}$$

The Kronecker product $\otimes$ of two matrixes A and B is the following expression:

$$A \otimes B = \begin{bmatrix} a_{11}B & a_{12}B & \cdots & a_{1m}B \\ a_{21}B & a_{22}B & \cdots & a_{2m}B \\ \vdots & \vdots & \ddots & \vdots \\ a_{n1}B & s_{n2}B & \cdots & a_{nm}B \end{bmatrix}. \tag{11.7}$$

For suitable matrices A, B, C, and D matrix multiplication satisfies the following rules

$$AB \neq BA, \tag{11.8a}$$
$$A(B+C) = AB + AC, \tag{11.8b}$$
$$A(BC) = (AB)C, \tag{11.8c}$$
$$A(B+C)D = ABD + ACD. \tag{11.8d}$$

The vec operator transforms a n by m matrix A into an nm by 1 vector by stacking the columns:

$$\text{vec}(A) = \begin{bmatrix} a_{11} \\ a_{21} \\ \vdots \\ a_{n1} \\ a_{12} \\ a_{22} \\ \vdots \\ a_{n2} \\ \vdots \\ a_{1m} \\ a_{2m} \\ \vdots \\ a_{nm} \end{bmatrix} \tag{11.9}$$

The following rules apply for the vec operator:

$$\text{vec}(A + B) = \text{vec}(A) + \text{vec}(B), \tag{11.10a}$$

$$\begin{aligned}\text{vec}(AB) &= (I \otimes A)\,\text{vec}(B) \\ &= (B' \otimes I)\,\text{vec}(A),\end{aligned} \tag{11.10b}$$

$$\begin{aligned}\text{vec}(ABC) &= (C' \otimes A)\,\text{vec}(B) \\ &= (I \otimes AB)\,\text{vec}(C) \\ &= (C'B \otimes I)\,\text{vec}(A).\end{aligned} \tag{11.10c}$$

The trace of a square matrix A is the sum of the elements of its main diagonal, i.e.,

$$\text{tr}\,A = \sum_{i=1}^{n} a_{ii}. \tag{11.11}$$

The determinant of a 2×2 matrix A, denoted by either $|A|$ or $\det(A)$, is defined by

$$|A| = a_{11}a_{22} - a_{12}a_{21}. \tag{11.12}$$

There is a recursive formula to compute the determinant of an arbitrary square matrix of dimension n. Using an arbitrary row (say i) or column (say j), the formula is:

$$|A| = \sum_{j=1}^{n} a_{ij}(-1)^{i+j}|A_{ij}| = \sum_{i=1}^{n} a_{ij}(-1)^{i+j}|A_{ij}|, \tag{11.13}$$

where A_{ij} is the matrix obtained from A by deleting the i-th row and j-th column. This expansion gives the determinant of A in terms of a sum of determinants of $n - 1$ matrices. These can be reduced further to determinants of $n - 2$ matrices and so forth until the summands are 2×2 matrices, computed from equation (11.12).

The rank of an arbitrary $n \times m$ matrix A is the maximal number of linearly independent rows of A. This also equals the maximal number of linearly independent columns of A.

The transpose of A, denoted by A' or A^T, is the $m \times n$ matrix obtained by interchanging the rows and columns of A:

$$A' = (a'_{ij}) = (a_{ji}) = \begin{bmatrix} a_{11} & a_{21} & \cdots & a_{n1} \\ a_{12} & a_{22} & \cdots & a_{n2} \\ \vdots & \vdots & \ddots & \vdots \\ a_{1m} & a_{2m} & \cdots & a_{nm} \end{bmatrix}.$$

In the case of a complex matrix, we use the prime ' or the superscript T to denote conjugate complex transposition. Thus, A' is the matrix whose element in the ij-th position is the complex conjugate of a_{ji}.

The inverse of a square matrix A, denoted $A^{-1} = (a^{ij})$ (note that we use superscripts to indicate the typical element of an inverse matrix) solves the problem $AA^{-1} = I$. If it exists, the inverse is unique and given by

$$a^{ij} = \frac{a_{ij}(-1)^{i+j}|A_{ji}|}{|A|}. \tag{11.14}$$

If $|A| = 0$, the inverse does not exist. It is an implication of the expansion formula (11.13) that matrices with a row (or column) of zeros or with linearly dependent rows (or columns) have no inverse. In general, an invertible (non-invertible) matrix is named non-singular (singular).

The inverse of a partitioned matrix A is related to the blocks of A via:

$$A := \begin{bmatrix} A_{11} & A_{12} \\ A_{21} & A_{22} \end{bmatrix}, \quad A^{-1} = \begin{bmatrix} A^{11} & A^{12} \\ A^{21} & A^{22} \end{bmatrix},$$

$$A^{11} = \left(A_{11} - A_{12}A_{22}^{-1}A_{12}\right)^{-1}, \tag{11.15a}$$
$$A^{12} = -A^{11}A_{12}A_{22}^{-1}, \tag{11.15b}$$
$$A^{21} = -A_{22}^{-1}A_{21}A^{11}, \tag{11.15c}$$
$$A^{22} = A_{22}^{-1} + A_{22}^{-1}A_{12}A^{11}A_{12}A_{22}^{-1}. \tag{11.15d}$$

A square matrix A is symmetric, if it equals its transpose: $A = A'$. The transpose operator obeys the following rules:

$$(A')' = A, \tag{11.16a}$$
$$(A+B)' = A' + B', \tag{11.16b}$$
$$(AB)' = B'A', \tag{11.16c}$$
$$(A^{-1})' = (A')^{-1}. \tag{11.16d}$$

11.1.6 Linear and Quadratic Forms

Let $\mathbf{a} = (a_1, a_2, \ldots, a_n)'$ and $\mathbf{x} = (x_1, x_2, \ldots, x_n)'$ denote two n-dimensional column vectors. The dot product

$$z = \mathbf{a}'\mathbf{x} = \sum_{i=1}^{n} a_i x_i \qquad (11.17)$$

with given $\mathbf{a}$ is called a linear form. The column vector of partial derivatives of z with respect to x_i, $i = 1, 2, \ldots, n$, denoted by ∇z, is obviously given by:

$$\nabla z := \frac{\partial \mathbf{a}'\mathbf{x}}{\partial \mathbf{x}} = \mathbf{a} = (\mathbf{a}')'. \qquad (11.18)$$

Since $z = z' = \mathbf{x}'\mathbf{a}$ we also have

$$\frac{\partial \mathbf{x}'\mathbf{a}}{\partial \mathbf{x}} = \mathbf{a}. \qquad (11.19)$$

A direct application of these findings are the following two rules:

$$\frac{\partial \mathbf{u}'B\mathbf{x}}{\partial \mathbf{x}} = (\mathbf{u}'B)' = B'\mathbf{u}, \qquad (11.20\text{a})$$

$$\frac{\partial \mathbf{u}'B\mathbf{x}}{\partial \mathbf{u}} = B\mathbf{x}, \qquad (11.20\text{b})$$

where $\mathbf{u} \in \mathbb{R}^m$, $B \in \mathbb{R}^{m \times n}$, and $\mathbf{x} \in \mathbb{R}^n$.

Let $A = (a_{ij})$ denote a $n \times n$ square matrix and $\mathbf{x} = (x_1, x_2, \ldots, x_n)'$ a n-dimensional column vector. The expression

$$q = \mathbf{x}'A\mathbf{x}, \quad q \in \mathbb{R}, \qquad (11.21)$$

is a quadratic form. If $q \geq 0$ ($q \leq 0$) for each non-zero vector $\mathbf{x}$, the matrix A is said to be positive (negative) semi-definite. If $q > 0$ ($q < 0$), A is positive (negative) definit. Let $B \in \mathbb{R}^{n \times m}$, $\mathbf{x} \in \mathbb{R}^n$, and $\mathbf{v} = B\mathbf{x}$. Since

$$\mathbf{v}'\mathbf{v} = \sum_{i=1}^{m} v_i^2 = \mathbf{x}'B'B\mathbf{x} \geq 0 \; \forall \mathbf{x},$$

the square matrix $A := B'B$ is obviously positive definite. Using the rule for matrix multiplication given in (11.6), equation (11.21) can be written in several ways:

$$q = \sum_{i=1}^{n} \sum_{j=1}^{n} a_{ij} x_i x_j,$$

$$= \sum_{i=1}^{n} a_{ii} x_i^2 + \sum_{i=1}^{n} \sum_{\substack{j=1 \\ j \neq i}}^{n} a_{ij} x_i x_j,$$

$$= \sum_{i=1}^{n} a_{ii} x_i^2 + \sum_{i=1}^{n} \sum_{j=1+i}^{n} (a_{ij} + a_{ji}) x_i x_j.$$

Setting $\tilde{a}_{ij} = \tilde{a}_{ji} \equiv (a_{ij} + a_{ji})/2$, it is obvious that we can assume without loss of generality that the matrix A is symmetric. Using this assumption, it is easy to show that the column vector of first partial derivatives of q with respect to x_i, $i = 1, 2, \ldots, n$, is given by

$$\nabla q := \frac{\partial \mathbf{x}' A \mathbf{x}}{\partial \mathbf{x}} = (A + A') \mathbf{x} = 2 A \mathbf{x}. \tag{11.22}$$

11.1.7 Eigenvalues and Eigenvectors

Let $A \in \mathbb{R}^{n \times n}$. A right eigenvector of A is a vector $\mathbf{v}$ that solves

$$A \mathbf{v} = \lambda \mathbf{v} \quad \Leftrightarrow \quad (A - \lambda I) \mathbf{v} = \mathbf{0}. \tag{11.23}$$

Similarly, the solution of $\mathbf{v}' A = \lambda \mathbf{v}'$ is named a left eigenvector of A. The system of n linear equations (11.23) has non-trivial solutions $\mathbf{v} \neq \mathbf{0}$, if the determinant $|A - \lambda I|$ vanishes. The condition $|A - \lambda I| = 0$ results in a polynomial of degree n in λ. It is well known from the Fundamental Theorem of Algebra (see, e.g., HIRSCH and SMALE (1974), pp. 328ff.) that this polynomial has n roots, which may be real, complex, or multiples of each other. These roots are the eigenvalues of the matrix A. Solving equation (11.23) for a given λ_i gives the associated eigenvector $\mathbf{v}_i$. Thus, eigenvectors are vectors that either stretch or shrink when multiplied by A. If $\mathbf{v}_i$ solves (11.23) and c is an arbitrary scalar, then $c\mathbf{v}_i$ also solves (11.23). Therefore, eigenvectors are unique up to a scalar multiple and, thus, may be normalized to have unit length.

There are two important relations between the elements of A and its eigenvalues:

$$\sum_{i=1}^{n} \lambda_i = \sum_{i=1}^{n} a_{ii}, \tag{11.24a}$$

$$\prod_{i=1}^{n} \lambda_i = |A|. \tag{11.24b}$$

In words: the sum of the eigenvalues of A equals the trace of A, and the determinant of A equals the product of the n eigenvalues.

Note that equation (11.23) is a special case of

$$(A - \lambda I)^m \mathbf{v}_m = \mathbf{0}$$

for $m = 1$. If there are non-trivial solutions $\mathbf{v}_m$ for $m \geq 2$ but not for $m - 1$, the vector $\mathbf{v}_m$ is called a generalized right eigenvector of rank m for the square matrix A. The space spanned by the (generalized) eigenvectors of A is called the eigenspace of A. The eigenspace can be partitioned in three subspaces formed by generalized eigenvectors that belong to the eigenvalues with

1. modulus less than one (stable eigenspace, E^s),
2. modulus equal to one (center eigenspace, E^c),
3. modulus greater than one (unstable eigenspace, E^u).

11.1.8 Matrix Factorization

Matrix factorizations play an important role in the solution of systems of linear difference equations. They are also used to solve systems of linear equations. Here, we touch on the Jordan, the Schur, the LU, and the Cholesky factorization.

Jordan Factorization. Consider the case of n distinct real eigenvalues and associated eigenvectors $\mathbf{v}_1, \mathbf{v}_2, \ldots, \mathbf{v}_n$ of a square matrix A. The matrix

$$P = [\mathbf{v}_1, \mathbf{v}_2, \ldots, \mathbf{v}_n]$$

transforms A into a diagonal matrix Λ with the eigenvalues $\lambda_1, \lambda_2, \ldots, \lambda_n$ on its main diagonal:

$$\Lambda = P^{-1} A P.$$

In the general case of real and complex eigenvalues, possibly with multiplicity $m > 1$, it may not be possible to diagonalize A. Yet there exists a matrix M (in general a complex matrix) of a set of linearly independent generalized eigenvectors (which is not unique) that puts A in Jordan canonical form:

$$A = MJM^{-1}, \quad J = \begin{bmatrix} J_1 & 0 & \cdots & 0 \\ 0 & J_2 & \cdots & 0 \\ \vdots & \vdots & \ddots & \vdots \\ 0 & 0 & \cdots & J_K \end{bmatrix}, \quad (11.25)$$

where the Jordan blocks $J_k \in \mathbb{C}^{m \times m}$, $k = 1, 2, \ldots, K$ are given by

$$J_k = \begin{bmatrix} \lambda_k & 1 & 0 & 0 & \cdots & 0 \\ 0 & \lambda_k & 1 & 0 & \cdots & 0 \\ 0 & 0 & \lambda_k & 1 & \cdots & 0 \\ \vdots & \vdots & \vdots & \vdots & \ddots & \vdots \\ 0 & 0 & 0 & 0 & \cdots & 1 \\ 0 & 0 & 0 & 0 & \cdots & \lambda_k \end{bmatrix},$$

and λ_k refers to an eigenvalue of A with multiplicity $m \geq 1$. Note, that if λ_k is a unique eigenvalue (i.e., has multiplicity $r = 1$) than $J_k = \lambda_k$. The Jordan blocks are determined uniquely. They can be ordered in J according to the absolute value of the eigenvalues of A.

There is also a real Jordan factorization of A, where each complex root $\lambda_j = \alpha_j + i\beta_j$ in J_k is represented by a matrix

$$\begin{bmatrix} \alpha_j & -\beta_j \\ \beta_j & \alpha_j \end{bmatrix},$$

and the ones on the upper right diagonal are replaced by two-dimensional identity matrix I_2.

Consider a matrix $A \in \mathbb{R}^{n \times n}$ whose n eigenvalues λ_i are all real and non-negative (that is, A is positive semidefinite). Let $\Lambda^{1/2} = (\sqrt{\lambda_i})$ be the diagonal matrix with the square roots of the eigenvalues along the main diagonal. Then

$$A^{1/2} = P\Lambda^{1/2}P^{-1},$$

because

$$A^{1/2}A^{1/2} = P\Lambda^{1/2}P^{-1}P\Lambda^{1/2}P^{-1} = P\Lambda P^{-1} = A.$$

It is easy to show by induction that for any $r = 1, 2, \ldots$

$$A^{1/r} = P\Lambda^{1/r}P^{-1}, \quad \Lambda^{1/r} = (\lambda_i^{1/r}). \tag{11.26}$$

We use this definition of the root of a matrix in Section 8.4.2 to compute a 1/8 year transition matrix out of a 5 year transition matrix.

Schur Factorization. The Schur factorization of a square matrix A is given by

$$A = TST^{-1}. \tag{11.27}$$

The complex matrix S is upper triangular with the eigenvalues of A on the main diagonal. It is possible to choose T such that the eigenvalues appear in any desired order along the diagonal of S. The transformation matrix T has the following properties:

1. its complex conjugate transpose T' equals the inverse of T,
2. therefore: $TT' = TT^{-1} = I$, i.e., T is an unitary matrix,
3. all eigenvalues of T have absolute value equal to 1.

LU and Cholesky Factorization. Consider a system of linear equations

$$\left.\begin{aligned} a_{11}x_1 + a_{12}x_2 + \cdots + a_{1n}x_n &= b_1, \\ a_{21}x_1 + a_{22}x_2 + \cdots + a_{2n}x_n &= b_2, \\ &\vdots = \vdots, \\ a_{n1}x_1 + a_{n2}x_2 + \cdots + a_{nn}x_n &= b_n \end{aligned}\right\} \Leftrightarrow A\mathbf{x} = \mathbf{b}. \qquad (11.28)$$

We assume that the square matrix A has full rank, i.e., there are no linearly dependent rows or columns in A. In this case it is possible to factorize A as follows

$$A = LU, \qquad (11.29)$$

$$L = \begin{bmatrix} 1 & 0 & 0 & \cdots & 0 \\ l_{21} & 1 & 0 & \cdots & 0 \\ l_{31} & l_{32} & 1 & \cdots & 0 \\ \vdots & \vdots & \vdots & \ddots & \vdots \\ l_{n1} & l_{n2} & l_{n3} & \cdots & 1 \end{bmatrix}, \ U = \begin{bmatrix} u_{11} & u_{12} & u_{13} & \cdots & u_{1n} \\ 0 & u_{22} & u_{23} & \cdots & u_{2n} \\ 0 & 0 & u_{33} & \cdots & u_{3n} \\ \vdots & \vdots & \vdots & \ddots & \vdots \\ 0 & 0 & 0 & \cdots & u_{nn} \end{bmatrix}.$$

If A is symmetric and positive definite, its Cholesky factor is the lower triangular matrix L that solves

$$LL' = A. \qquad (11.30)$$

Both the LU and the Cholesky factorization can be used to solve the linear system (11.28). Let $\tilde{\mathbf{x}} := U\mathbf{x}$. Then it is easy to solve the system

$$L\tilde{\mathbf{x}} = \mathbf{x}$$

by forward substitution:

$$\begin{aligned} \tilde{x}_1 &= b_1, \\ \tilde{x}_2 &= b_2 - l_{21}\tilde{x}_1, \\ \tilde{x}_3 &= b_3 - l_{31}\tilde{x}_1 - l_{32}\tilde{x}_2, \\ \vdots &= \vdots \end{aligned}$$

Given the solution for $\tilde{\mathbf{x}}$, one gets the desired solution for $\mathbf{x}$ via backward substitution from $U\mathbf{x} = \tilde{\mathbf{x}}$:

$$x_n = \frac{\tilde{x}_n}{u_{nn}},$$

$$x_{n-1} = \frac{1}{u_{n-1\,n-1}} \left(\tilde{x}_{n-1} - u_{n-1\,n}x_n\right),$$

$$x_{n-2} = \frac{1}{u_{n-2\,n-2}} \left(\tilde{x}_{n-2} - u_{n-2\,n-1}x_{n-1} - u_{n-2\,n}x_n\right),$$

$$\vdots = \vdots$$

The solution of a system of linear equations via its LU or Cholesky factorization is the strategy that underlies linear equations solvers. For instance, the LAPACK routine dgesv.for uses this procedure as well as the IMSL subprogram DLSARG. In Gauss the command $x = b/A$ solves (11.28) via the LU factorization. Yet another factorization used to solve linear systems is the QR factorization

$$A = QR, \quad QQ^T = I, \quad R = \begin{bmatrix} r_{11} & r_{12} & r_{13} & \cdots & r_{1n} \\ 0 & r_{22} & r_{23} & \cdots & r_{2n} \\ 0 & 0 & r_{33} & \cdots & r_{3n} \\ \vdots & \vdots & \ddots & \vdots & \vdots \\ 0 & 0 & 0 & \cdots & r_{nn} \end{bmatrix} \quad (11.31)$$

which provides $R\mathbf{x} = Q^T\mathbf{b} =: \tilde{\mathbf{x}}$. The solution can then be found via backward substitution. It is beyond the scope of this text to deal with algorithms that compute any of the above mentioned factorizations.[2] In Gauss the command {S,T}=Schtoc(Schur(A)) can be used to get the matrices S and T from the matrix A. In Fortran the subroutine ZGEES from LAPACK can be used for the same purpose.[3] Whereas ZGEES has an option to order the eigenvalues on the main diagonal of S, the Schtoc command returns S with unordered eigenvalues. However, Givens rotations may be used to order the eigenvalues in S.

---

[2] A good reference on this subject is GOLUB and VAN LOAN (1996).
[3] The LAPACK Fortran 77 routines can be downloaded from www.netlib.com/lapack for free. They are also included in the CXML library being shipped with Compaq's Digital Fortran compiler.

11.1.9 Givens Rotation

Consider the symmetric matrix $G \in \mathbb{C}^{n \times n}$ defined by

$$G := \begin{bmatrix} 1 & 0 & \cdots & 0 & 0 & \cdots & 0 \\ 0 & 1 & \cdots & 0 & 0 & \cdots & 0 \\ \vdots & \vdots & \ddots & \vdots & \vdots & \ddots & \\ 0 & 0 & \cdots & b & c & \cdots & 0 \\ 0 & 0 & \cdots & -\bar{c} & \bar{b} & \cdots & 0 \\ \vdots & \vdots & \vdots & \vdots & \vdots & \ddots & \\ 0 & 0 & 0 & 0 & 0 & \cdots & 1 \end{bmatrix} \begin{matrix} \\ \\ \\ \leftarrow \text{row } i \\ \leftarrow \text{row } i+1 \\ \\ \end{matrix}$$

$$\underset{\text{column } i, i+1}{\uparrow \quad \uparrow}$$

and the upper triangular matrix $S \in \mathbb{C}^{n \times n}$. Choose the complex numbers b and c as follows:

$$b = \frac{s_{ii+1}}{r}, \quad c = \frac{s_{i+1i+1} - s_{ii}}{r}, \quad r := \sqrt{s_{ii+1}^2 + (s_{i+1i+1} - s_{ii})^2}.$$

In this case G is also an unitary matrix, $GG' = I$, so that

$$A = T(GG')S(GG')T = (TG)(G'SG)(G'T').$$

As an exercise you may want to verify that pre-multiplying S with G' and post-multiplying S with G interchanges s_{ii} and s_{i+1i+1}. The new transformation matrix putting A into the newly ordered matrix $G'SG$ is given by TG. Via a number of such pairwise Givens rotations the eigenvalues on the main diagonal of S can be brought into any desired order.

11.2 Function Approximation

There are numerous instances where we need to approximate functions of one or several variables. In some cases we need a local approximation around a given point x_0. For instance, in Chapter 2, the linear-quadratic approximation method requires a quadratic approximation of the return function at the stationary equilibrium. In other cases we must approximate functions over a given interval. Think of the value function in Chapter 1, or the policy function in Chapter 4.

Usually, local approximations rest on Taylor's theorem, which we review in Section 11.2.1. The simplest case of function approximation over a given interval is linear interpolation, which we discuss in Section 11.2.3. In Section 11.2.4, cubic spline interpolation is presented which also preserves the smoothness of a function. Linear and cubic spline interpolation are special cases of polynomial approximation dealt with in Section 11.2.5. Among the various families of polynomials, orthogonal polynomials have very desirable properties. From this class, we consider Chebyshev polynomials in Section 11.2.6. Finally, we briefly touch on neural networks.

11.2.1 Taylor's Theorem

Consider a function f of a single variable $x \in U$, where U is an open subset of $\mathbb{R}$. Taylor's theorem states the following:[4]

Theorem 11.2.1 *Let $f : [a,b] \to \mathbb{R}$ be a $n+1$ times continuously differentiable function on (a,b), let $\bar{x}$ be a point in (a,b). Then*

$$f(\bar{x}+h) = f(\bar{x}) + f^{(1)}(\bar{x})h + f^{(2)}(\bar{x})\frac{h^2}{2} + \cdots + f^{(n)}(\bar{x})\frac{h^n}{n!}$$
$$+ f^{(n+1)}(\xi)\frac{h^{n+1}}{(n+1)!}, \quad \xi \in (\bar{x}, \bar{x}+h).$$

In this statement $f^{(i)}$ is the i–th derivative of f evaluated at the point $\bar{x}$. The derivative that appears in the rightmost term of this formula is evaluated at some unknown point between $\bar{x}$ and

---
[4] Statements of this theorem appear in any calculus textbook and in most mathematics for economists texts. JUDD (1998), p. 23, states the theorem for the singe variable case; p. 239 of the same book presents the formula for the n-variable case.

$\bar{x} + h$. When we neglect this term, the formula approximates the function f at $\bar{x}$ and the approximation error is of order $n + 1$. By this we mean that the error is proportional to h^{n+1} where the constant of proportionality is given by $C = f^{n+1}(\xi)/(n+1)!$.

There is also a version of this theorem for the n-variable case. To present it, we need a fair amount of additional notation. Let $\mathbf{a} := [a_1, a_2, \ldots, a_n]$, define

$$|\mathbf{a}| := \sum_{i=1}^{n} a_i, \ \forall a_i = 0, 1, \ldots,$$
$$\mathbf{a}! := a_1! a_2! \ldots a_n!,$$
$$\mathbf{x}^{\mathbf{a}} := x_1^{a_1} x_2^{a_2} \ldots x_n^{a_n},$$
$$D_i f(\mathbf{x}) := \frac{\partial f(\mathbf{x})}{\partial x_i},$$
$$D_i^{a_i} := \underbrace{D_i D_i \ldots D_i}_{a_i \text{ times}},$$
$$D^{\mathbf{a}} f(\mathbf{x}) := D_1^{a_1} D_2^{a_2} \ldots D_n^{a_n}.$$

Then, the following holds:

Theorem 11.2.2 *Let $U \subset \mathbb{R}^n$ be an open subset, $\mathbf{x} \in U$, $\mathbf{h} \in \mathbb{R}^n$ so that $\mathbf{x} + t\mathbf{h} \in U$ for all $t \in [0.1]$. Assume that $f : U \to \mathbb{R}$ is $(k+1)$-times continuously differentiable. Then, there is a $\lambda \in [0, 1]$, so that*

$$f(\mathbf{x} + \mathbf{h}) = \sum_{|\mathbf{a}| \leq k} \frac{D^{\mathbf{a}} f(\mathbf{x})}{\mathbf{a}!} \mathbf{h}^{\mathbf{a}} + \sum_{|\mathbf{a}| = k+1} \frac{D^{\mathbf{a}} f(\mathbf{x} + \lambda \mathbf{h})}{\mathbf{a}!} \mathbf{h}^{\mathbf{a}}.$$

Note that $D_i^0 \equiv 1$ and that summation is over all n-tuples $[a_1, a_2, \ldots, a_n]$, which sum to $0, 1, 2, \ldots, k$ (or $k+1$).

An immediate corollary of this theorem is the quadratic approximation of f at $\mathbf{x}$: assume that $k = 2$. Let

$$\nabla f(\mathbf{x}) := [D_1 f(\mathbf{x}), D_2 f(\mathbf{x}), \ldots, D_n f(\mathbf{x})]'$$

denote the column vector of first partial derivatives and let

$$H(\mathbf{x}) := \begin{bmatrix} D_1 D_1 f(\mathbf{x}) & D_1 D_2 f(\mathbf{x}) & \cdots & D_1 D_n f(\mathbf{x}) \\ D_2 D_1 f(\mathbf{x}) & D_2 D_2 f(\mathbf{x}) & \cdots & D_2 D_n f(\mathbf{x}) \\ \vdots & \vdots & \ddots & \vdots \\ D_n D_1 f(\mathbf{x}) & D_n D_2 f(\mathbf{x}) & \cdots & D_n D_n f(\mathbf{x}) \end{bmatrix}$$

be the Hesse matrix of second partial derivatives (which is symmetric if f is two times continuously differentiable). Then

$$f(\mathbf{x}+\mathbf{h}) \approx f(\mathbf{x}) + [\nabla f(\mathbf{x})]'\mathbf{h} + \frac{1}{2}\mathbf{h}'H(\mathbf{x})\mathbf{h}, \tag{11.32}$$

where the approximation error $\phi(\mathbf{h})$, with $\phi(\mathbf{0}) = 0$, has the property

$$\lim_{\substack{\mathbf{h} \to 0 \\ \mathbf{h} \neq 0}} \frac{\phi(\mathbf{h})}{\|\mathbf{h}\|^2} = 0.$$

Similarly, the linear approximation is given by:

$$f(\mathbf{x}+\mathbf{h}) \approx f(\mathbf{x}) + [\nabla f(\mathbf{x})]'\mathbf{h}, \tag{11.33}$$

where the error $\phi(\mathbf{h})$ now obeys

$$\lim_{\substack{\mathbf{h} \to 0 \\ \mathbf{h} \neq 0}} \frac{\phi(\mathbf{h})}{\|\mathbf{h}\|} = 0.$$

Consider a map $\mathbf{f} : X \to Y$ that maps points $\mathbf{x}$ of the open subset $X \subset \mathbb{R}^n$ into points $\mathbf{y}$ of the open subset $Y \subset \mathbb{R}^m$:

$$\mathbf{y} = \mathbf{f}(\mathbf{x}) \Leftrightarrow \begin{cases} y_1 = f^1(x_1, x_2, \ldots, x_n), \\ y_2 = f^2(x_1, x_2, \ldots, x_n), \\ \vdots = \vdots \\ y_m = f^m(x_1, x_2, \ldots, x_n). \end{cases} \tag{11.34}$$

If we apply Taylor's theorem to each component of $\mathbf{f}$, we get the linear approximation of the non-linear map $\mathbf{f}$ at a point $\bar{\mathbf{x}} \in X$:

$$\mathbf{y} \simeq \mathbf{f}(\bar{\mathbf{x}}) + J(\bar{\mathbf{x}})(\mathbf{x} - \bar{\mathbf{x}}). \tag{11.35}$$

The matrix

$$J(\bar{\mathbf{x}}) := \begin{bmatrix} f_1^1(\bar{\mathbf{x}}) & f_2^1(\bar{\mathbf{x}}) & \cdots & f_n^1(\bar{\mathbf{x}}) \\ f_1^2(\bar{\mathbf{x}}) & f_2^2(\bar{\mathbf{x}}) & \cdots & f_n^2(\bar{\mathbf{x}}) \\ \vdots & \cdots & \ddots & \vdots \\ f_1^m(\bar{\mathbf{x}}) & f_2^m(\bar{\mathbf{x}}) & \cdots & f_n^m(\bar{\mathbf{x}}) \end{bmatrix} \tag{11.36}$$

$$f_j^i(\bar{\mathbf{x}}) := \frac{\partial f^i(\bar{x}_1, \bar{x}_2, \ldots, \bar{x}_n)}{\partial x_j}$$

is called the Jacobian matrix of $\mathbf{f}$ at the point $\bar{\mathbf{x}}$.

11.2.2 Implicit Function Theorem

In this book many if not all systems of non-linear equations that we have encountered are not given in explicit form $\mathbf{y} = \mathbf{f}(\mathbf{x})$, as considered in the previous paragraph. Rather the relation between $\mathbf{y} \in \mathbb{R}^m$ and $\mathbf{x} \in \mathbb{R}^n$ is implicitly defined via

$$\mathbf{g}(\mathbf{x}, \mathbf{y}) = \mathbf{0}_{m \times 1}, \tag{11.37}$$

where $\mathbf{g} : U \to V$, U is a subset of $\mathbb{R}^n \times \mathbb{R}^m$ and V a subset of $\mathbb{R}^m$. The implicit function theorem[5] allows us to compute the derivative of $\mathbf{y} = \mathbf{f}(\mathbf{x})$ at a solution $(\bar{\mathbf{x}}, \bar{\mathbf{y}})$ of (11.37).

Theorem 11.2.3 (Implicit Function Theorem) *Let U be an open subset in a product $U_1 \times U_2$, $U_1 \subset \mathbb{R}^n$, $U_2 \subset \mathbb{R}^m$ and let $\mathbf{g} : U \to V \subset \mathbb{R}^m$ be a p-times continuously differentiable map. Let $(\bar{\mathbf{x}}, \bar{\mathbf{y}}) \in U$ with $\bar{\mathbf{x}} \in U_1$ and $\bar{\mathbf{y}} \in U_2$. Let $\mathbf{g}(\bar{\mathbf{x}}, \bar{\mathbf{y}}) = \mathbf{0}_{m \times 1}$. Assume that $D_y(\mathbf{g}(\bar{\mathbf{x}}, \bar{\mathbf{y}})) : U_2 \to V$ is invertible. Then there exists an open ball B, centered at $\bar{\mathbf{x}} \in U_1$ and a continuous map $\mathbf{f} : B \to U_1 \to U_2$ such that $\bar{\mathbf{y}} = \mathbf{g}(\bar{\mathbf{x}})$ and $\mathbf{g}(\mathbf{x}, \mathbf{f}(\mathbf{y})) = \mathbf{0}_{m \times 1}$ for all $\mathbf{x} \in B$. If B is a sufficiently small ball, then $\mathbf{f}$ is uniquely determined, and p-times continuously differentiable.*

The expression D_y denotes the $m \times m$ matrix of partial derivatives of $\mathbf{g}$ with respect to the variables $y_1, y_2, \ldots, y_m$ evaluated at $(\bar{\mathbf{x}}, \bar{\mathbf{y}})$:

---

[5] See, e.g., LANG (1983), p. 529, Theorem 5.4.

$$D_y(\mathbf{g}(\bar{\mathbf{x}},\bar{\mathbf{y}})) = \begin{bmatrix} \frac{\partial g^1(\bar{\mathbf{x}},\bar{\mathbf{y}})}{\partial y_1} & \frac{\partial g^1(\bar{\mathbf{x}},\bar{\mathbf{y}})}{\partial y_2} & \cdots & \frac{\partial g^1(\bar{\mathbf{x}},\bar{\mathbf{y}})}{\partial y_m} \\ \frac{\partial g^2(\bar{\mathbf{x}},\bar{\mathbf{y}})}{\partial y_1} & \frac{\partial g^2(\bar{\mathbf{x}},\bar{\mathbf{y}})}{\partial y_2} & \cdots & \frac{\partial g^2(\bar{\mathbf{x}},\bar{\mathbf{y}})}{\partial y_m} \\ \vdots & \vdots & \ddots & \vdots \\ \frac{\partial g^m(\bar{\mathbf{x}},\bar{\mathbf{y}})}{\partial y_1} & \frac{\partial g^m(\bar{\mathbf{x}},\bar{\mathbf{y}})}{\partial y_2} & \cdots & \frac{\partial g^m(\bar{\mathbf{x}},\bar{\mathbf{y}})}{\partial y_m} \end{bmatrix}.$$

If this matrix is invertible (as required by Theorem 11.2.3), we obtain the Jacobian of $\mathbf{f}$ at $\bar{\mathbf{x}}$ by differentiating $\mathbf{g}(\mathbf{x}, \mathbf{f}(\mathbf{x}))$ with respect to $\mathbf{x}$:

$$J(\bar{\mathbf{x}}) := \mathbf{f}_x(\bar{\mathbf{x}}) = -D_y^{-1}(\bar{\mathbf{x}}, \bar{\mathbf{x}}) D_x(\bar{\mathbf{x}}, \bar{\mathbf{x}}), \qquad (11.38)$$

where $D_x(\cdot)$ is analogously defined as $D_y(\cdot)$.

11.2.3 Linear Interpolation

Linear interpolation is simple and shape preserving. This property is important, if we use interpolation to approximate the value function, which is known to be concave and increasing.[6]

Consider Figure 11.2 that depicts the graph of a given function f. Suppose we want to approximate $f(x)$ at a given point x with the property $x_1 < x < x_2$. Linear interpolation uses the point

$$\hat{f}(x) := f(x_1) + \frac{f(x_2) - f(x_1)}{x_2 - x_1}(x - x_1). \qquad (11.39)$$

Thus, f is approximated by the line through $(x_1, f(x_1))$ and $(x_2, f(x_2))$.

In many applications (such as value function iteration with interpolation between grid-points) the function f is known only at a given number of points $x_1, x_2, \ldots$. In this case it is helpful to have a procedure that finds the neighboring points $x_i < x < x_{i+1}$ and returns $\hat{f}(x)$. Our Gauss procedure LIP in the file Function.src (and the Fortran subroutine LIP in the file Function.for) does

---
[6] There are so-called *shape-preserving* methods which, however, have been produced for mainly one-dimensional problems. COSTANTINI and FONTANELLA (1990) consider shape-preserving bivariate interpolation.

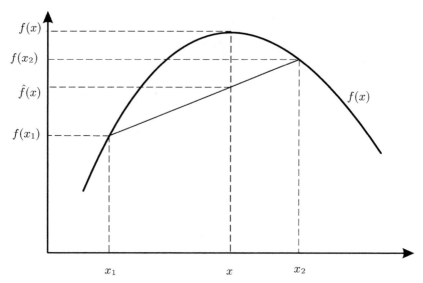

Figure 11.2: Linear Interpolation

this. It takes the vector of grid-points $\mathbf{x} = [x_1, x_2, \ldots, x_n]$ and the corresponding vector $\mathbf{y} = [f(x_1), f(x_2), \ldots, f(x_n)]$ as well as the point x as input, locates x in the grid, and returns $\hat{f}(x)$ given by (11.39).

The extension to the two-dimensional case is straightforward. Assume that we want to approximate a function $f(x_1, x_2) \in \mathbb{R}$ at a point (x_1, x_2) where $x_1 \in [x_{10}, x_{1n}]$ and $x_2 \in [x_{20}, x_{2m}]$. Furthermore, the function values are stored for all grid-points (x_{1i}, x_{2j}), $y_{ij} = f(x_{1i}, x_{2j})$, with $i = 0, 1, \ldots, n$, $j = 0, \ldots, m$. First, we need to find the four neighboring points (x_{1i}, x_{2j}), (x_{1i+1}, x_{2j}), (x_{1i}, x_{2j+1}), and (x_{1i+1}, x_{2j+1}) such that $x_{1i} \leq x_1 < x_{1i+1}$ and $x_{2i} \leq x_2 < x_{2i+1}$. Define

$$t = \frac{x_1 - x_{1i}}{x_{1i+1} - x_{1i}}, \quad u = \frac{x_2 - x_{2i}}{x_{2i+1} - x_{2i}}.$$

The approximation with the help of bilinear interpolation is given by:

$$\hat{f}(x_1, x_2) = (1-t)(1-u)y_{ij} + t(1-u)y_{i+1,j} + tuy_{i+1,j+1} + (1-t)uy_{i,j+1}.$$

Obviously, the function value and the approximation value coincide at the grid-points $\hat{f}(x_{1i}, x_{2j}) = y_{ij}$, $\hat{f}(x_{1,i+1}, x_{2j}) = y_{i+1,j}$,

$\hat{f}(x_{1i}, x_{2,j+1}) = y_{i,j+1}$, and $\hat{f}(x_{1,i+1}, x_{2,j+1}) = y_{i+1,j+1}$. Our Gauss procedure Bilinear performs the bilinear interpolation requiring the grid $[x_{10}, x_{1n}]$ and $[x_{20}, x_{1m}]$ together with the matrix of the function values (y_{ij}) as inputs. Our routine for bilinear interpolation is BLIP in Function.src and Function.for, respectively.

11.2.4 Cubic Splines

In the previous section, you learned about piecewise linear approximation of a function. Often we are interested in preserving the smoothness of a function. For example, we know that the value function is a smooth function in the Ramsey problem considered in Chapter 4. With piecewise linear or even polynomial approximation, the function may not be differentiable at the grid-points, even though this may be required for the solution of the economic problem. In the following, we will consider one of the simplest types of approximation with the help of a differentiable piecewise polynomial function that is called cubic spline interpolation.

Assume that we approximate the function $f(x)$ by a function $s(x)$ over the grid $\mathbf{x} = [x_0, x_1, \ldots, x_n]$, $x_i \in \mathbb{R}$ with corresponding functions values $\mathbf{y} = [y_0, y_1, \ldots, y_n]$ with $y_i = f(x_i) \in \mathbb{R}$. On each subinterval $[x_{i-1}, x_i]$, $i = 1, \ldots, n$, we will approximate $f(x)$ with a cubic function $s(x) = a_i + b_i x + c_i x^2 + d_i x^3$. On the computer, you will have to store a list of $n+1$ grid-points x_i and the $4n$ coefficients a_i, b_i, c_i, d_i. We impose the following conditions:

1) The approximation is exact at the grid-points, $y_i = s(x_i)$:

$$y_i = a_i + b_i x_i + c_i x_i^2 + d_i x_i^3, \quad i = 1, \ldots, n,$$

$$y_i = a_{i+1} + b_{i+1} x_i + c_{i+1} x_i^2 + d_{i+1} x_i^3, \quad i = 0, \ldots, n-1.$$

2) The first and the second derivatives agree on the nodes:

$$b_i + 2c_i x_i + 3d_i x_i^2 = b_{i+1} + 2c_{i+1} x_i + 3d_i x_i^2, \quad i = 1, \ldots, n-1,$$

$$2c_i + 6d_i x_i = 2c_{i+1} + 6d_{i+1} x_i, \quad i = 1, \ldots, n-1.$$

These conditions amount to $4n - 2$ linear equations in the $4n$ unknowns a_i, b_i, c_i, d_i leaving us two conditions short of fixing the coefficients. In most applications, we do not know the derivatives at the endpoints of the interval, x_0 and x_n. Two possible solutions to fix this problem is to either set them to zero, $s'(x_0) = s'(x_n) = 0$, which is called the natural spline or to use the slope of the secant lines over $[x_0, x_1]$ and $[x_{n-1}, x_n]$, respectively:

$$s'(x_0) = \frac{y_1 - y_0}{x_1 - x_0} = b_1 + 2c_1 x_0 + 3d_1 x_0^2,$$

$$s'(x_n) = \frac{y_n - y_{n-1}}{x_n - x_{n-1}} = b_n + 2c_n x_n + 3d_n x_n^2.$$

The latter is also called the Secant Hermite spline. Cubic splines are very easy to program and very fast to compute since the resulting set of equations is not only linear in the coefficients $a_i, b_i, c_i,$ and d_i, but also tridiagonal. We implemented the cubic spline interpolation following PRESS, TEUKOLKSY, VETTERLING, and FLANNERY(1992), Section 3.3. First, you have to call the routine cspline once providing the data points (x_i, y_i) and getting the coefficients (a_i, b_i, c_i, d_i) as output. Calling this routine, you also have the option between the natural and secant Hermite spline. After this call, you can use splint any time you would like to approximate the function at a point $x \in [x_0, x_n]$. Both routines are in Function.src and Function.for, respectively.

11.2.5 Families of Polynomials

Bases for Function Spaces. The formula given in (11.39) is a special case of the more general formula

$$f(x) = \sum_{i=0}^{n} \alpha_i \varphi_i(x),$$

with $n = 1$, $\varphi_i(x) := x^i$, $\alpha_0 = [x_2 f(x_1) - x_1 f(x_2)]/(x_2 - x_1)$, and $\alpha_1 = [f(x_2) - f(x_1)]/(x_2 - x_1)$. To understand the idea behind this formula, remember that a vector $\mathbf{x} \in \mathbb{R}^n$ can be represented as a linear combination of n linearly independent vectors $\mathcal{B} := \{\mathbf{v}_1, \mathbf{v}_2, \ldots \mathbf{v}_n\}$ of $\mathbb{R}^n$. The collection of vectors $\mathcal{B}$ is said to build a base of the vector space $\mathbb{R}^n$. If the members of $\mathcal{B}$ are mutually orthogonal (i.e., $\mathbf{v}'_i \mathbf{v}_j = 0$ for $i \neq j$) and normal (i.e., $\mathbf{v}'_i \mathbf{v}_i = 1$) the base is called an orthonormal base.

Now, consider the set of all continuous functions that map the interval $[a, b]$ to the real line. Like $\mathbb{R}^n$, this set, denoted by $C[a, b]$, is a vector space. The monomials $x^i, i = 0, 1, \ldots$ build a base $\mathcal{B}$, for this space, i.e., every member of $C[a, b]$ can be represented by

$$\sum_{i=0}^{\infty} \alpha_i x^i.$$

For this reason it is common to use a linear combination of the first p members of this base to approximate a continuous function $f(x) \in C[a, b]$:

$$f(x) \simeq \alpha_0 + \alpha_1 x + \alpha_2 x^2 + \cdots + \alpha_p x^p.$$

Yet, this may not always be a good choice. For instance, if we use a regression of $y = f(x)$ on $(1, x, x^2, ..., x^p)$ to determine $\boldsymbol{\alpha} := (\alpha_0, \alpha_1, \ldots, \alpha_p)'$, as we actually do in the parameterized expectations approach considered in Chapter 3, we may face the problem of multicollinearity (i.e., nearly linear dependence among the x^i), since for large i, x^i and x^{i+1} may be difficult to distinguish. Bases that consists of polynomials that are – in an appropriate sense – orthogonal circumvent this problem.

Orthogonal Polynomials. To motivate the notion of orthogonality in a function space, consider the following problem. Assume we want to approximate $f(x) \in C[a, b]$ by

$$\hat{f}(x) := \sum_{i=1}^{n} \alpha_i \varphi_i(x),$$

where $\mathcal{P} := (\varphi_0(x), \varphi_1(x), \ldots)$ is some family of polynomials. Suppose further that there is a weight function $w(x)$ on $[a, b]$. A weight function is a function that has a finite integral

$$\int_a^b w(x)dx < \infty$$

and that is positive almost everywhere on $[a, b]$.[7] Our goal is to choose the parameters $\alpha_i, i = 0, 1, \ldots n$ such that the weighted sum of squared errors $R(\boldsymbol{\alpha}, x) := f(x) - \hat{f}(\boldsymbol{\alpha}, x)$ over all $x \in [a, b]$ attains a minimum:[8]

$$\min_{\boldsymbol{\alpha}} \int_a^b w(x) \left[f(x) - \sum_{i=0}^n \alpha_i \varphi_i(x) \right]^2 dx. \qquad (11.40)$$

The first order conditions for this problem are

$$0 = 2 \int_a^b w(x) \left[f(x) - \sum_{j=0}^n \alpha_j \varphi_j(x) \right] \varphi_i(x) dx, \; i = 0, 1, \ldots, n,$$

which may be rewritten as

$$\int_a^b w(x) f(x) \varphi_i(x) dx = \sum_{j=0}^n \alpha_j \int_a^b w(x) \varphi_j(x) \varphi_i(x) dx, \qquad (11.41)$$
$$i = 0, 1, \ldots, n.$$

If the integral on the rhs of (11.41) vanishes for $i \neq j$ and equals a constant ζ_j for $i = j$, it will be easy to compute α_i from

$$\alpha_i = \frac{1}{\zeta_i} \int_a^b w(x) f(x) \varphi_i(x) dx.$$

This motivates the following definition of orthogonal polynomials: A set of functions $\mathcal{P}$ is called orthogonal with respect to the weight function $w(x)$ if and only if:

$$\int_a^b w(x) \varphi_i(x) \varphi_j(x) dx = \begin{cases} 0 & \text{if } i \neq j, \\ \zeta_i & \text{if } i = j. \end{cases} \qquad (11.42)$$

If in addition $\zeta_i = 1 \; \forall i$, the set of functions is said to be orthonormal. Among the families of orthonormal polynomials are the Chebyshev polynomials used extensively in Chapter 4.

---

[7] Intuitively, the qualifier 'almost everywhere' allows $w(x)$ to be non-positive on a very small set of points. This set must be so small that its size – technically, its measure – equals zero.

[8] This is called a continuous least squares approximation of $f(x)$.

11.2.6 Chebyshev Polynomials

Definition. The domain of Chebyshev polynomials is the interval $[-1, 1]$, and the i-th member of this family is defined by

$$T_i(x) = \cos(i \arccos x). \tag{11.43}$$

The weight function for which $\int_{-1}^{1} w(x) T_i(x) T_j(x) dx = 0$ for $i \neq j$ is given by

$$w(x) := \frac{1}{\sqrt{1-x^2}}. \tag{11.44}$$

In particular, the following holds:

$$\int_{-1}^{1} \frac{T_i(x) T_j(x)}{\sqrt{1-x^2}} dx = \begin{cases} 0 & \text{if } i \neq j, \\ \frac{\pi}{2} & \text{if } i = j \geq 1, \\ \pi & \text{if } i = j = 0. \end{cases} \tag{11.45}$$

Thus, if we use

$$\hat{g}(\boldsymbol{\alpha}, x) := \frac{1}{2}\alpha_0 + \sum_{i=1}^{n} \alpha_i T_i(x) \tag{11.46}$$

to approximate $g(x) \in C[-1, 1]$ the coefficients of the continuous least squares approximation are given by

$$\alpha_i = \frac{2}{\pi} \int_{-1}^{1} \frac{g(x) T_i(x)}{\sqrt{1-x^2}} dx. \tag{11.47}$$

Notice that in (11.46), α_0 is multiplied by the factor $1/2$ so that (11.47) also holds for $i = 0$ where the integral (11.45) for $i = j = 0$ is equal to $\zeta_0 = \pi$.

Most often, of course, we are interested in approximating a function f on the interval $[a, b]$ where a and b do not necessarily coincide with the values -1 and 1, respectively. Suppose that we have a function $f(z)$, $f : [a, b] \to R$ and want to compute a polynomial approximation over $[a, b]$ that corresponds to the Chebyshev approximation over $x \in [-1, 1]$ with weighting function (11.44). This can simply be done by defining the transformation

$$X(z) = \frac{2z}{b-a} - \frac{a+b}{b-a}, \quad z \in [a,b] \tag{11.48}$$

and the reverse transformation

$$Z(x) = \frac{(x+1)(b-a)}{2} + a, \quad x \in [-1,1]. \tag{11.49}$$

With these transformations, we can define the function $g(x) = f(Z(x))$ on the interval $[-1, 1]$ with approximation

$$\hat{f}(z;\alpha) = \sum_{i=0}^{n} \alpha_i T_i\left(X(z)\right). \tag{11.50}$$

The coefficients of the continuous least squares approximation are then given by

$$\alpha_j = \frac{2}{\pi} \int_a^b \frac{f(z) T_j(X(z))}{\sqrt{1-(X(z))^2}}\, dz. \tag{11.51}$$

Properties. Chebyshev polynomials (11.43) have many other properties which make them a prime candidate in numerical applications. Importantly, we can compute a Chebyshev polynomial of order $i+1$, if we know the values of the Chebyshev polynomials of order i and $i-1$.[9] This property of the Chebyshev polynomial family helps economizing on computational time. In particular, the Chebyshev polynomials satisfy the following recursive scheme:

$$T_{i+1}(x) = 2x T_i(x) - T_{i-1}(x). \tag{11.52}$$

The recurrence relation (11.52) can be shown by introducing the substitution $\theta = \arccos x$. With this substitution, (11.43) can be rewritten as

$$T_i(\theta(x)) = T_i(\theta) = \cos(i\theta). \tag{11.53}$$

Furthermore, applying the trigonometric identities

---

[9] There exist different families which satisfy such a recursive scheme, e.g. the Legendre or Hermite polynomials.

$$T_{i+1}(\theta) = \cos((i+1)\theta) = \cos(i\theta)\cos\theta - \sin(i\theta)\sin\theta,$$
$$T_{i-1}(\theta) = \cos((i-1)\theta) = \cos(i\theta)\cos\theta + \sin(i\theta)\sin\theta,$$

we get

$$T_{i+1}(\theta) = 2\cos(i\theta)\cos\theta - T_{i-1}(\theta),$$

or

$$T_{i+1} = 2xT_i(x) - T_{i-1}(x). \tag{11.54}$$

The first four Chebyshev polynomials are

$$\begin{aligned} T_0(x) &= \cos(0 \cdot \arccos x) = 1, \\ T_1(x) &= \cos(1 \cdot \arccos x) = x, \\ T_2(x) &= 2xT_1(x) - T_0(x) = 2x^2 - 1, \\ T_3(x) &= 2xT_2(x) - T_1(x) = 4x^3 - 3x. \end{aligned}$$

Notice that the Chebyshev polynomial $T_i(x)$ is a polynomial of degree i with leading coefficient 2^{i-1}. The Chebyshev polynomials T_1, T_2, and T_3 are displayed in Figure 11.3.

The recursive formula (11.52) yields an efficient way to evaluate the polynomial at given point x, which we present in the following algorithm:

Algorithm 11.2.1 (Chebyshev Evaluation)

Purpose: *Evaluate a n-th degree Chebyshev polynomial at x*

Steps:

Step 1: Initialize: use the $n+1$-vector **y** *to store the values of $T_i(x)$ for $i = 0, 1, \ldots, n$. Put $y[1] = 1$ and $y[2] = x$.*
Step 2: For $i = 2, 3, \ldots, n-1$ compute:

$$y_{i+1} = 2xy_i - y_{i-1}.$$

Step 3: Return $\sum_{i=0}^{n} a_i y_i$.

In our files Function.src and Function.for, respectively, you will find the procedure ChebEval1 that implements this algorithm.

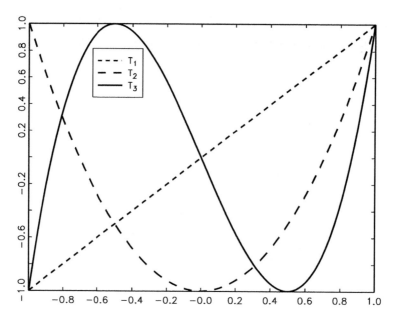

Figure 11.3: Chebyshev Polynomials T_1, T_2 and T_3

Zeros. Consider the sequence of points

$$\bar{x}_k := \cos\left(\frac{2k-1}{2n}\pi\right), \quad k = 1, 2, \ldots, n. \tag{11.55}$$

Using the substitution $\theta_k = \arccos(x_k)$ we get $n\theta_k = \pi(2k-1)/2$. Since the cosine function cuts the abscissa at $\pi/2$, $(3/2)\pi$, $(5/2)\pi, \ldots$, the points $\bar{x}_k$ are the zeros of the n-th degree Chebyshev polynomial. Now, for $i, j < n$, Chebyshev polynomials satisfy a discrete version of the orthogonality relation:

$$\sum_{k=1}^{m} T_i(\bar{x}_k)T_j(\bar{x}_k) = \begin{cases} 0 & i \neq j, \\ m/2 & i = j \neq 0, \\ m & i = j = 0. \end{cases} \tag{11.56}$$

Computation of the Chebyshev Coefficients. There are three possible ways. First, we may compute the integral on the rhs of equation (11.51) using the techniques presented in 11.3.2. Second, we may choose the n-dimensional vector $\boldsymbol{\alpha}$ such that f and $\hat{f}$ coincide at n points. Third, we can determine the coefficients from a regression of $f(x_i)$ on x_i, $i = 1, 2, \ldots, m$, using $m > n$ points. Since the second approach is a special case of the third for $m = n$, we consider the latter.

It can be shown that the maximal interpolation error attains a minimum, if the n interpolation nodes coincide with the n zeros of the n-th degree Chebyshev polynomial $T_n(x)$.[10] Using the $m > n$ zeros of $T_m(x)$ in a regression produces an even smoother approximation. The coefficients in this regression can be determined analytically as follows: Assume we want to approximate $f(x) \in C[a, b]$ by a n-th degree Chebyshev polynomial. Let $\bar{x} = [\bar{x}_1, \bar{x}_2, \ldots, \bar{x}_m]$ denote the m zeros of $T_m(x)$. The corresponding points in the interval $[a, b]$ are $\bar{z}_k := Z(\bar{x}_k)$ (see (11.49)), so that $\bar{y}_k = f(\bar{z}_k)$. We choose $\boldsymbol{\alpha} = [\alpha_0, \alpha_1, \ldots, \alpha_{n-1}]$ to minimize the sum of squared prediction errors at the nodes $\bar{z}_k$:

$$\min_{\boldsymbol{\alpha}} \sum_{k=1}^{m} \left[\bar{y}_k - \sum_{j=0}^{n-1} \alpha_j T_j(X(\bar{z}_k)) \right]^2.$$

The respective first order conditions are:

$$\sum_{k=1}^{m} T_0 \bar{y}_k = \sum_{j=0}^{n-1} \alpha_j \sum_{k=1}^{m} T_0 T_j(\bar{x}_k) = m\alpha_0,$$

$$\sum_{k=1}^{m} \bar{y}_k T_1(\bar{x}_k) = \sum_{j=0}^{n-1} \alpha_j \sum_{k=1}^{m} T_1(\bar{x}_k) T_j(\bar{x}_k) = (m/2)\alpha_1,$$

$$\vdots = \vdots, \qquad (11.57)$$

$$\sum_{k=1}^{m} \bar{y}_k T_{n-1}(\bar{x}_k) = \sum_{j=0}^{n-1} \alpha_j \sum_{k=1}^{m} T_{n-1}(\bar{x}_k) T_j(\bar{x}_k) = (m/2)\alpha_{n-1},$$

where the respective rhs follow from (11.56). This provides Algorithm 11.2.2, which we implement in the program ChebCoef (see the files Function.src and Function.for, respectively).

---

[10] For a formal proof of this minimax property of Chebyshev zeros see any introductory textbook on numerical analysis such as BURDEN and FAIRES (2001).

Algorithm 11.2.2 (Chebyshev Regression)

Purpose: *Approximate $f(z) \in C[a,b]$ with $\sum_{j=0}^{n-1} \alpha_j T_j(x)$.*

Steps:

Step 1: Choose the degree $n-1$ of the approximating Chebyshev polynomial. Compute $m \geq n$ Chebyshev interpolation nodes $\bar{x}_k$ from (11.55) and adjust the nodes to the interval $[a,b]$ using (11.49).

Step 2: For $k = 1, 2, \ldots, m$, compute $\bar{y}_k = f(\bar{z}_k)$.

Step 3: Compute the Chebyshev coefficients: $\alpha_0 = (1/m) \sum_{k=1}^{m} \bar{y}_k$. For $i = 1, 2, \ldots, n-1$ the coefficients are given by:

$$\alpha_i = \frac{2}{m} \sum_{k=1}^{m} \bar{y}_k T_i(\bar{x}_k).$$

Examples. In order to demonstrate the performance of the computation of Chebyshev coefficients we compute the Chebyshev approximation of $f(x) = e^x$ and of

$$g(x) = \begin{cases} 0 & \text{if } x < 1, \\ (x-1) & \text{if } x \geq 1. \end{cases}$$

The latter type of function might often be encountered in economic problems with constraints. In Chapter 3, gross investment is assumed to be nonnegative. As another example, assume that agents supply labor elastically, instead. If the wage is below unemployment compensation, they do not work and labor supply is equal to zero. For a wage exceeding unemployment compensation, they supply labor and, if the income effect is less than the substitution effect, labor supply increases with the wage rate. The optimal labor supply may look similar to the function $g(x)$.

Figure 11.4 depicts e^x and its second degree Chebyshev polynomial approximation. If we use the 3 zeros of T_3 as interpolation nodes, the maximum absolute error between e^x and its approximation in the interval $[0,1]$ is 0.0099. With 10 data points it drops to 0.0093. However, if we use the fifth degree approximation with

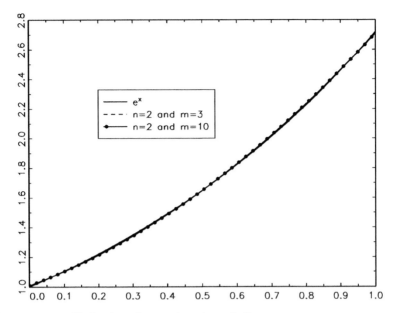

Figure 11.4: Chebyshev Approximation of e^x

10 data points the error drops below $(1.17) \times 10^{-6}$. In this case, the graph of e^x and the graph of its approximation virtually coincide in Figure 11.4.

Table 11.1 shows that the value of the Chebyshev coefficients drop off rapidly. This result is not surprising. In fact, one can show the following theorem:[11]

Theorem 11.2.4 *If $f \in C^k[-1,1]$ has a Chebyshev representation $f(x) = \sum_{i=1}^{\infty} \alpha_i T_i(x)$, then there is a constant c such that*

$$|\alpha_i| \leq \frac{c}{i^k}, \quad i \geq 1. \tag{11.58}$$

This theorem also gives a hint for the choice of the degree n of the approximating polynomial. If the α_i are falling rapidly and if α_n is small, then we can be more confident to ignore higher-order polynomial terms. Notice further that the values of the first 4 coefficients do not change if we increase the degree of the Chebyshev

---

[11] See JUDD (1998), Theorem 6.4.2.

Table 11.1

Coefficient	$n=2$, $m=10$	$n=5$, $m=10$
α_0	1.753	1.753
α_1	0.850	0.850
α_2	0.105	0.105
α_3		0.0087
α_4		0.0005
α_5		0.000027

polynomial from $n=2$ to $n=5$. Of course, this is obvious from (11.57) if we keep m constant.

As we have just learned, smooth functions can be approximated quite accurately by Chebyshev polynomials. However, Chebyshev approximation is less apt for the approximation of functions displaying a kink, like the function $g(x) = \max(0, x-1)$, or step functions. The function $g(x)$ is not differentiable at $x=1$. The approximation by Chebyshev interpolation (i.e., $m = n+1$) and Chebyshev regression are displayed in Figure 11.5. Notice that with regression, we are better able to approximate the kink at $x=1$ than with interpolation. As the degree of the Chebyshev polynomial increases, the approximation is getting closer.

11.2.7 Multidimensional Approximation

Choice of Bases. Even in the simple stochastic growth model the domain of the policy function is already a subset of $\mathbb{R}^2$. So how can we generalize the polynomial approximation to the n-dimensional case? One approach is to use the n-fold tensor product base. Let x_i denote the i-th element of $\mathbf{x} = (x_1, x_2, \ldots, x_n)$ and use $\varphi_k(x_i)$ for the k-th member of a family of polynomials. For instance $\varphi_k(x_i) \equiv x_i^k$. The set

$$\mathscr{T} := \left\{ \prod_{i=1}^{n} \varphi_{k_i}(x_i) \,\middle|\, k_i = 0, 1, \ldots p \right\}$$

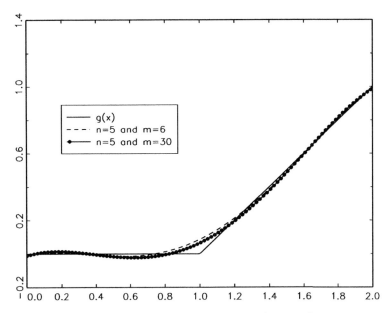

Figure 11.5: Chebyshev Approximation of $\max\{0, x-1\}$

is the n-fold tensor product base. The linear combination of the $(1+p)^n$ elements of $\mathscr{T}$ can be used to approximate $f(\mathbf{x})$. For instance, in the stochastic growth model $\mathbf{x} = (K, Z)$, and for $p = 2$ and $\varphi_k(x_i) = x_i^k$ the set $\mathscr{T}$ is given by

$$\{K^0 Z^0, K^0 Z^1, K^0 Z^2, K^1 Z^0, K^1 Z^1, K^1 Z^2, K^2 Z^0, K^2 Z^1, K^2 Z^2\}$$
$$\equiv \{1, Z, Z^2, K, KZ, KZ^2, K^2, K^2 Z, K^2 Z^2\}.$$

This set grows exponentially with the dimension n of $\mathbf{x}$. A smaller set that delivers as good an approximation (in terms of asymptotic convergence) as the tensor product base is the complete set of polynomials of degree p in n variables, denoted $\mathscr{P}_p^n$. This set is derived by considering the p-th order approximation of $f(\mathbf{x})$. As we know from Theorem 11.2.2, this approximation involves the following products:

$$\mathscr{P}_p^n = \left\{ (x_1^{k_1} x_2^{k_2} \cdots x_n^{k_n}) \middle| \sum_{i=1}^n k_i = j, k_i \geq 0, j = 0, 1, 2, \ldots, p \right\}$$

Thus, for $\mathbf{x} = (K, Z)$ and $p = 2$, the set is

$$\mathscr{P}_2^2 = \{\underbrace{K^0 Z^0}_{j=0}, \underbrace{K^1 Z^0, K^0 Z^1}_{j=1}, \underbrace{K^2 Z^0, K^1 Z^1, K^0 Z^2}_{j=2}\},$$
$$= \{1, K, Z, K^2, KZ, Z^2\}.$$

More generally, we can build a complete set of polynomials of total degree p in n variables from any family of polynomials by replacing $x_i^{k_i}$ with $\varphi_{k_i}(x_i)$ in the definition of $\mathscr{P}_p^n$.

Chebyshev Approximation in Two Dimensions. The parameters of a Chebyshev approximation in a multidimensional framework also derive from the minimization of an appropriate sum of squares. We illustrate this approach for the two-dimensional case. Higher dimensions are handled analogously. Let $f(z_1, z_2)$ be a function on $[a, b] \times [c, d]$ that we would like to approximate by a two-dimensional Chebyshev polynomial[12]

$$\sum_{j_1=0}^{n_1} \sum_{j_2=0}^{n_2} \alpha_{j_1 j_2} T_{j_1}(X(z_1)) T_{j_2}(X(z_2)). \tag{11.59}$$

We need $m_1 \geq n_1 + 1$ and $m_2 \geq n_2 + 1$ points and choose them as the zeros of the m_1-dimensional and m_2-dimensional Chebyshev polynomial, adjusted to the interval $[a, b]$ and $[c, d]$, respectively. Let

$$\bar{y}_{k_1 k_2} := f(Z(\bar{x}_{1 k_1}), Z(\bar{x}_{2 k_2})),$$

and consider the least squares criterion

$$\min \sum_{k_1=1}^{m_1} \sum_{k_2=1}^{m_2} \left[\bar{y}_{k_1 k_2} - \sum_{j_1=0}^{n_1} \sum_{j_2=0}^{n_2} \alpha_{j_1 j_2} T_{j_1}(\bar{x}_{1 k_1}) T_{j_2}(\bar{x}_{2 k_2}) \right]^2.$$

The first order condition with respect to $\alpha_{j_1 j_2}$ yields:

---

[12] Remember, $X(z)$ is the linear transformation of points in $[a, b]$ or $[c, d]$ to $[-1, 1]$ defined in (11.48).

$$\sum_{k_1=1}^{m_1}\sum_{k_2=1}^{m_2} \bar{y}_{k_1 k_2} T_{j_1}(\bar{x}_{1k_1}) T_{j_2}(\bar{x}_{2k_2})$$

$$= \sum_{k_1=1}^{m_1}\sum_{k_2=1}^{m_2}\sum_{i_1=0}^{n_1}\sum_{i_2=0}^{n_2} \alpha_{i_1 i_2} T_{i_1}(\bar{x}_{1k_1}) T_{i_2}(\bar{x}_{2k_2}) T_{j_1}(\bar{x}_{1k_1}) T_{j_2}(\bar{x}_{2k_2})$$

$$= \sum_{i_1=0}^{n_1}\sum_{i_2=0}^{n_2} \alpha_{i_1 i_2} \underbrace{\sum_{k_1=1}^{m_1} T_{i_1}(\bar{x}_{1k_1}) T_{j_1}(\bar{x}_{1k_1})}_{\substack{=0 \quad \text{if} \quad j_1 \neq i_1 \\ =m_1/2 \text{ if } j_1 = i_1 \neq 0 \\ =m_1 \quad \text{if } j_1 = i_1 = 0}} \underbrace{\sum_{k_2=1}^{m_2} T_{i_2}(\bar{x}_{2k_2}) T_{j_2}(\bar{x}_{2k_2})}_{\substack{=0 \quad \text{if} \quad j_2 \neq i_2 \\ =m_2/2 \text{ if } j_2 = i_2 \neq 0 \\ =m_2 \quad \text{if } j_2 = i_2 = 0}}.$$

Therefore, we get the following estimator:

$$\begin{aligned}
\alpha_{00} &= \frac{1}{m_1 m_2} \sum_{k_1=1}^{m_1}\sum_{k_2=1}^{m_2} \bar{y}_{k_1 k_2}, \\
\alpha_{0j_2} &= \frac{1}{m_1}\frac{2}{m_2} \sum_{k_1=1}^{m_1}\sum_{k_2=1}^{m_2} \bar{y}_{k_1 k_2} T_{j_2}(\bar{x}_{2k_2}), \\
\alpha_{j_1 0} &= \frac{2}{m_1}\frac{1}{m_2} \sum_{k_1=1}^{m_1}\sum_{k_2=1}^{m_2} \bar{y}_{k_1 k_2} T_{j_1}(\bar{x}_{1k_1}), \\
\alpha_{j_1 j_2} &= \frac{2}{m_1}\frac{2}{m_2} \sum_{k_1=1}^{m_1}\sum_{k_2=1}^{m_2} \bar{y}_{k_1 k_2} T_{j_1}(\bar{x}_{1k_1}) T_{j_2}(\bar{x}_{2k_2}).
\end{aligned} \quad (11.60)$$

11.2.8 Neural Networks

Instead of linear combinations of polynomials neural networks use non-linear approximation schemes. A single-layer neural network is a function of the form

$$\Phi(\mathbf{a}, \mathbf{x}) := h\left(\sum_{i=1}^{n} a_i g(x_i)\right),$$

where h and g are scalar functions. In the left panel of Figure 11.6 the first row of nodes represents the function g processing the inputs x_i. The result is aggregated via summation, as indicated by the arrows to the single node which represents the function h that delivers the final output y. In the single hidden-layer feedforward network displayed in the right panel of Figure 11.6 the function g delivers its output to a second row of nodes. There, this input is processed by another function G, say, before it is aggregated and passed on to the function h.

Formally, the single hidden-layer feedforward network is given by:

$$\Phi(\mathbf{a}, \mathbf{b}, \mathbf{x}) := h\left(\sum_{j=1}^{m} b_j G\left[\sum_{i=1}^{n} a_{ij} g(x_i)\right]\right).$$

The function G is called the hidden-layer activation function. A common choice for G is the sigmoid function

$$G(x) = \frac{1}{1 + e^{-x}}.$$

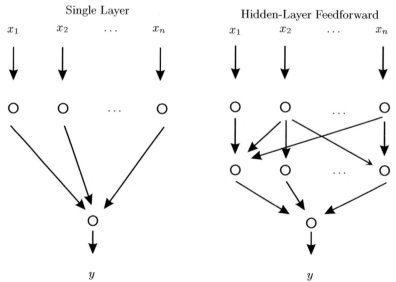

Figure 11.6: Neural Networks

Neural networks are efficient functional forms for approximating multidimensional functions. Often they require less parameters for a given accuracy than polynomial approximations.[13]

In the case of the stochastic growth model, which we consider inter alia in Section 5.1, DUFFY and MCNELIS (2001) approximate the conditional expectation that appears in the Euler equation (5.1b) by the following single hidden-layer feedforward neural network with six parameters:

$$\Phi(\gamma, K, Z) = \gamma_1 + \frac{\gamma_2}{1 + e^{-\gamma_3 K - \gamma_4 Z}} + \frac{1}{1 + e^{-\gamma_5 K - \gamma_6 Z}}.$$

11.3 Numerical Differentiation and Integration

11.3.1 Differentiation

Many of our algorithms require derivatives. Think of the Newton-Raphson algorithm or the linear quadratic approximation method. In the simplest case of a real valued function of one variable, $y = f(x)$, the obvious choice is the analytical derivative $f'(x)$. Yet, if $f'(x)$ is given by a complicated formula, mistakes easily sneak into the computer code. It may even be impossible to derive an explicit expression for the derivative at all. Think of the sum of squares in the case of the parameterized expectations approach. If the Jacobian matrix of a vector valued function or the Hesse matrix of a function of many independent variables are required, analytical derivatives – if available at all – require many lines of computer code; something which is failure-prone. Therefore, we use numerical derivatives in almost all of our computer programs.

This section provides some background on numerical differentiation and presents two algorithms that approximate the Jacobian matrix of a vector valued function and the Hesse matrix of a real valued function, respectively. The related program code can be used in place of built-in routines, as, e.g., Gradp and Hessp in

---
[13] See SARGENT (1993), p. 58f and the literature cited there.

Gauss or DFDJAC and DFDHES from the IMSL library of Fortan subroutines.

First Difference Formulas. The basis of numerical derivative formulas is Taylor's Theorem. Consider Theorem 11.2.1 for the case $n = 1$. We get

$$f(\bar{x} + h) = f(\bar{x}) + f^{(1)}(\bar{x})h + f^{(2)}(\xi)\frac{h^2}{2}. \tag{11.61}$$

Thus, we may approximate the first derivative by the formula[14]

$$D_{FD}f(\bar{x}, h) := \frac{f(\bar{x} + h) - f(\bar{x})}{h}. \tag{11.62}$$

This is known as the forward difference formula. The approximation error is proportional to h, since from (11.61):

$$\left|D_{FD}f(\bar{x}, h) - f^{(1)}(\bar{x})\right| = \left|f^{(2)}(\xi)/2\right| h.$$

Thus, the error is of first order. The backward difference formula derives from Taylor's theorem for $-h$ in place of h. Its error is also of first order. Now consider Taylor's theorem for $n = 2$, h, and $-h$:

$$f(\bar{x} + h) = f(\bar{x}) + f^{(1)}(\bar{x})h + f^{(2)}(\bar{x})\frac{h^2}{2} + f^{(3)}(\xi_1)\frac{h^3}{6}, \tag{11.63a}$$

$$f(\bar{x} - h) = f(\bar{x}) - f^{(1)}(\bar{x})h + f^{(2)}(\bar{x})\frac{h^2}{2} - f^{(3)}(\xi_2)\frac{h^3}{6}, \tag{11.63b}$$

and subtract the second line from the first. The quadratic term disappears and from

$$f(\bar{x} + h) - f(\bar{x} - h) = 2f^{(1)}(\bar{x})h + \left(f^{(3)}(\xi_1) + f^{(3)}(\xi_2)\right)\frac{h^3}{6}$$

we find the approximation

$$D_{CD}f(\bar{x}, h) := \frac{f(\bar{x} + h) - f(\bar{x} - h)}{2h} \tag{11.64}$$

---

[14] As in Section 11.2.1, we use the symbol D^i to denote the i-th derivative of f. Subscripts denote the kind of approximation.

known as central difference formula. Letting C denote the maximum of $(f^{(3)}(\xi_1)+f^{(3)}(\xi_2))/6$ in $[\bar{x},\bar{x}+h]$, we see that the approximation error is proportional to Ch^2 and, thus, of second order. When we add equation (11.63a) to equation (11.63b) the first derivative terms cancel and we get the central difference formula for the second derivative:

$$D^2_{CD}f(\bar{x},h) := \frac{f(\bar{x}+h)+f(\bar{x}-h)-2f(\bar{x})}{h^2}, \qquad (11.65)$$

whose approximation error is bound by Ch and, thus, of first order.

Choice of h. From the previous discussion it might seem to be a good idea to choose h as small as possible. But remember the finite precision of computer arithmetic. Suppose your PC is able to represent, say, the first 10 digits to the right of the decimal point of any floating point number correctly. If h is too small, the first and second term in the numerator of equation (11.62) may differ only in the eleventh digit and the computed derivative is highly unreliable.

Suppose the error in computing $f(\bar{x})$ and $f(\bar{x}+h)$ is $\bar{e}$ and e_h, respectively. At least, $\bar{e}$ and e_h equal the machine epsilon ϵ, i.e., the smallest positive number for which the statement $1+\epsilon > 1$ is true on your machine. However, if $f(x)$ is the result of complicated and involved computations, the actual error may be much larger. We want to find an upper bound on the total error $E(\delta,h)$ that results when we use $\tilde{f}(\bar{x}) := f(\bar{x})+\bar{e}$ and $\tilde{f}(\bar{x},h) := f(\bar{x}+h)+e_h$ to compute $D_{FD}f(\bar{x},h)$, where $\bar{e}, e_h \leq \delta$ for some $\delta \geq \epsilon$.

$$E(\delta,h) := \left| f'(\bar{x}) - \frac{\tilde{f}(\bar{x}) - \tilde{f}(\bar{x}+h)}{h} \right|$$

$$\leq \underbrace{|f'(\bar{x}) - D_{FD}f(\bar{x},h)|}_{\leq Ch} + \underbrace{\frac{|\bar{e}-e_h|}{h}}_{\leq 2\delta/h},$$

$$\leq Ch + \frac{2\delta}{h}, \quad C := \max_{\xi \in [\bar{x},\bar{x}+h]} \frac{f^2(\xi)}{2}.$$

Setting the derivative of this upper bound with respect to h to zero and solving for h gives the step size that provides the smallest upper bound:

$$h^* = \sqrt{\frac{2\delta}{C}}. \tag{11.66}$$

If we perform the same exercise with respect to the central difference formulas (11.64) and (11.65) we find that the optimal choice of h is

$$h^{**} = \sqrt[3]{\frac{2\delta}{C}}, \quad C := \max_{\xi_1,\xi_2 \in [\bar{x},\bar{x}+h]} \frac{f^{(3)}(\xi_1) + f^{(3)}(\xi_2)}{6}. \tag{11.67}$$

Computation of the Jacobian. It is easy to apply the above results to a vector valued function $\mathbf{f} : \mathbb{R}^n \to \mathbb{R}^m$. Let $f^i(\mathbf{x})$, $\mathbf{x} = [x_1, x_2, \ldots, x_n]$ denote the i-th component function of $\mathbf{f}$. Using the central difference formula (11.64) we may approximate the element f^i_j of the Jacobian matrix at the point $\bar{\mathbf{x}}$ by

$$f^i_j := \frac{\partial f^i(\bar{\mathbf{x}})}{\partial x_j} \simeq \frac{f(\bar{x} + \mathbf{e}_j h) - f(\bar{x} - \mathbf{e}_j h)}{2h}, \tag{11.68}$$

where $\mathbf{e}_j$ is the unit (row) vector with one in the j–th position and zeros elsewhere.

If the x_i differ considerably in size, we set h proportional to x_j using

$$h_j = h^{**} \max\{|x_j|, 1\}. \tag{11.69}$$

Our program CDJac (see the file Differentiation.scr for the Gauss version and the file Differentiation.for for the Fortran version) uses equation (11.68) together with this choice of h_j (and $h^{**} = \sqrt[3]{\epsilon}$ as default) to compute the Jacobian of a user supplied routine that evaluates $f^i(\bar{x})$, $i = 1, 2, \ldots, m$ at $\bar{x}$.

Computation of the Hesse Matrix.
Suppose we want to compute the elements of the Hesse matrix of $f : \mathbb{R}^n \to \mathbb{R}$ given by

$$H(\bar{x}) := \begin{bmatrix} h_{11} & h_{12} & \cdots & h_{1n} \\ h_{21} & h_{22} & \cdots & h_{2n} \\ \vdots & \vdots & \ddots & \vdots \\ h_{n1} & h_{n2} & \cdots & h_{nn} \end{bmatrix}, \quad h_{ij} := \frac{\partial^2 f(\bar{x})}{\partial x_i \partial x_j}.$$

There are two possibilities. Note, that the Hesse matrix equals the Jacobian matrix of the gradient of f. Thus, if an analytic expression for the gradient of f is easy to program, one can use this as an input to a procedure that approximates the Jacobian. This gives a better approximation than the use of difference formulas for second partial derivatives.[15] If this is not an option, one can apply the central difference formula for the second derivative of a function in one variable to compute the diagonal elements of H.[16] This gives:

$$h_{ii} \simeq \frac{f(\bar{x} + \mathbf{e}_i h_i) + f(\bar{x} - \mathbf{e}_i h_i) - 2f(\bar{x})}{h_i^2}. \tag{11.70}$$

There are several choices for the off-diagonal elements of H. From a third order expansion of f at $\bar{x}$, we can get the following equations:[17]

$$f(\bar{x} + h_i + h_j) = f(\bar{x}) + f_i(\bar{x})h_i + f_j(\bar{x})h_j + (1/2)h_{ii}h_i^2$$
$$+ (1/2)h_{jj}h_j^2 + h_{ij}h_i h_j + C_1,$$

$$f(\bar{x} + h_i - h_j) = f(\bar{x}) + f_i(\bar{x})h_i - f_j(\bar{x})h_j + (1/2)h_{ii}h_i^2$$
$$+ (1/2)h_{jj}h_j^2 - h_{ij}h_i h_j + C_2,$$

$$f(\bar{x} - h_i + h_j) = f(\bar{x}) - f_i(\bar{x})h_i + f_j(\bar{x})h_j + (1/2)h_{ii}h_i^2$$
$$+ (1/2)h_{jj}h_j^2 - h_{ij}h_i h_j + C_3,$$

$$f(\bar{x} - h_i - h_j) = f(\bar{x}) - f_i(\bar{x})h_i - f_j(\bar{x})h_j + (1/2)h_{ii}h_i^2$$
$$+ (1/2)h_{jj}h_j^2 + h_{ij}h_i h_j + C_4,$$

---

[15] The error of the central difference formula for the first derivative is of second order, whereas the error from the central difference formula for the second derivative is of first order.
[16] In the following we use h_i proportional to $\max\{|x_i|, 1\}$ as in (11.69).
[17] See, e.g., JUDD (1998), p. 239, for Taylor's formula in the case of many independent variables.

where $C_k, k = 1, 2, 3, 4$ are sums of the mixed third partial derivatives of f and of third order.[18] If we add the first and the last equation and subtract the second and third equation from this sum, we find the following four-point formula:

$$h_{ij} \simeq \frac{1}{4h_ih_j}\Big[f(\bar{x} + \mathbf{e}_ih_i + \mathbf{e}_jh_j) - f(\bar{x} - \mathbf{e}_ih_i + \mathbf{e}_jh_j) \\ - f(\bar{x} + \mathbf{e}_ih_i - \mathbf{e}_jh_j) + f(\bar{x} - \mathbf{e}_ih_i - \mathbf{e}_jh_j)\Big], \tag{11.71}$$

whose approximation error is bound by $Ch := h\sum_k |C_k|$. Our procedure CDHesse (see the file Differentiation.src for the Gauss version and Differentiation.for for the Fortran version) uses (11.70) and (11.71). This agrees with the suggestion of HANSEN and PRESCOTT (1995) for the quadratic approximation of the current period return function.

11.3.2 Numerical Integration

Newton-Cotes Formulas. Basically, there are two different approaches to compute an integral $\int_a^b f(x)dx$ numerically.[19] The first idea is to approximate the function $f(x)$ by piecewise polynomials and integrate the polynomials over subdomains of $[a, b]$. For example, the Trapezoid rule evaluates the function $f(x)$ at the end points $x = a$ and $x = b$ and uses the linear Lagrange polynomial

$$P_1(x) = \frac{x-b}{a-b}f(a) + \frac{x-a}{b-a}f(b) \tag{11.72}$$

---

[18] For instance,

$$C_1 := (1/6)(f_{iii}h_i^3 + f_{jjj}h_j^3 + f_{iij}h_i^2h_j + f_{jji}h_ih_j^2),$$

where the third partial derivatives are evaluated at some point between $\bar{x}$ and $\bar{x} + \mathbf{e}_ih_i + \mathbf{e}_jh_j$ (see Theorem 11.2.2). Since one can always choose $h_i = ah, h_j = bh$ for some h, all terms on the rhs of the previous equation are of third order.

[19] In fact, there is a third approach that we do not pursue here. It considers the related problem to solve an ordinary differential equation.

to approximate $f(x)$. Integration of P_1 over $[a,b]$ results in the formula

$$\int_a^b f(x)dx \approx \frac{b-a}{2}[f(a)+f(b)]. \quad (11.73)$$

If we use higher-order polynomials or a higher number of subdomains, more generally, we derive a Newton-Cotes formula for the approximation of the integral which evaluates the integral at a number of points:

$$\int_a^b f(x)dx \approx \sum_{i=1}^n a_i f(x_i). \quad (11.74)$$

Gaussian Formulas. In Newton-Cotes formulas, the coefficients a_i are chosen so that the local approximation is correct and the nodes x_i are chosen arbitrarily; usually, the x_i are equidistant. The second approach, which we will pursue in all quadrature applications of this book, is to choose both the weights a_i and the nodes x_i optimally in order to provide a good approximation of $\int_a^b f(x)dx$. It is obvious that we increase the degrees of freedom at our disposal if we choose both the nodes x_i and the weights a_i simultaneously rather than just the weights a_i in order to get a good approximation. Essentially, the resulting Gaussian quadrature formulas have twice the order than the Newton-Cotes formulas for the same number of function evaluations.[20]

The following theorem highlights the importance of orthogonal families of polynomials for numerical integration:[21]

Theorem 11.3.1 *Suppose that $\{\varphi_i(x)\}_{i=0}^\infty$ is an orthonormal family of polynomials with respect to the weight function $w(x)$ on $[a,b]$ with $\varphi_i(x) = q_i x^i + q_{i-1} x^{i-1} + \ldots + q_0$. Let $\bar{x}_i$, $i=1,\ldots,n$, be the n zeros of φ_n. Then $a < \bar{x}_1 < \cdots < \bar{x}_n < b$, and if $f \in C^{(2n)}[a,b]$, then*

---

[20] Notice, however, that higher order does not always translate into higher accuracy.
[21] See also Judd (1998), Theorem 7.2.1.

$$\int_a^b w(x)f(x)dx = \sum_{i=1}^n \omega_i f(\bar{x}_i) + \frac{f^{2n}(\zeta)}{q_n^2(2n)!}, \qquad (11.75)$$

for some $\zeta \in [a,b]$, where

$$\omega_i = -\frac{q_{n+1}/q_n}{\varphi_n'(\bar{x}_i)\varphi_{n+1}(\bar{x}_i)} > 0.$$

Accordingly, we can evaluate the integral of a polynomial of degree $2n-1$ exactly by applying formula (11.75). Usually, one does not have to compute the nodes and weights, since they are kept in tables. It is a nice property of the Chebyshev polynomials that their weights ω_i are constant. The Gauss-Chebyshev quadrature formula for a function $f(x)$ on the interval $[-1,1]$ is defined by:

$$\int_{-1}^1 \frac{f(x)}{\sqrt{1-x^2}}dx = \frac{\pi}{n}\sum_{i=1}^n f(\bar{x}_i) + \frac{\pi}{2^{2n-1}}\frac{f^{(2n)}(\zeta)}{(2n)!}$$

for some $\zeta \in [-1,1]$, where the quadrature nodes $\bar{x}_i$ are the zeros of the Chebyshev polynomial $T_n(x)$ as presented in (11.55).

For integrals of the form $\int_a^b f(z)dz$, we use (11.49) to adjust $[-1,1]$ to $[a,b]$. Since the linear transformation (11.49) implies

$$dz = \frac{b-a}{2}dx,$$

we can derive the following approximation:

$$\int_a^b f(z)dz = \int_{-1}^1 f(Z(x))\frac{b-a}{2}\frac{\sqrt{1-x^2}}{\sqrt{1-x^2}}dx \qquad (11.76)$$

$$\approx \frac{\pi(b-a)}{2n}\sum_{i=1}^n f\left(\frac{(\bar{x}_i+1)(b-a)}{2}+a\right)\sqrt{1-\bar{x}_i^2},$$

where the $\bar{x}_i$, again, are the Chebyshev zeros from (11.55).

Very often we have to compute (conditional) expectations. In these instances it is natural to refer to the Hermite polynomials, since their weight function is given by $w(x) := e^{-x^2}$. Suppose z is distributed normally with mean μ and variance σ^2. Then,

$$E(f(z)) := (2\pi\sigma^2)^{-1/2} \int_{-\infty}^{\infty} f(z) e^{[-(z-\mu)^2/2\sigma^2]} dz.$$

Since

$$x = \frac{z-\mu}{\sqrt{2}\sigma}$$

has a standard normal distribution (i.e., $E(x) = 0$ and $\text{var}(x) = 1$), we get

$$E(f(z)) = \pi^{-1/2} \int_{-\infty}^{\infty} f\left(\sqrt{2}\sigma x + \mu\right) e^{-x^2} dx,$$

where we used

$$dz = \sqrt{2}\sigma dx.$$

This integral can be approximated by the Gauss-Hermite quadrature formula

$$E(f(z)) \simeq \pi^{-1/2} \sum_{i=1}^{n} w_i f\left(\sqrt{2}\sigma x_i + \mu\right). \quad (11.77)$$

For $n = 2, \ldots, 5$ the integration nodes x_i and weights w_i are given in Table 11.2.

Multidimensional Integration. Even the stochastic growth model has a state space of dimension two. When we use least squares or Galerkin projection to solve this model or models whose state space has an even higher dimension, we must compute multiple integrals. The most natural way to do this, is to use product rules. For instance, if we want to compute the integral of $f(z_1, \ldots, z_n)$ over the n-dimensional rectangle $[a_1, b_1] \times [a_2, b_2] \times \ldots [a_n, b_n]$ the Gauss-Chebyshev quadrature (11.76) implies

$$\int_{a_1}^{b_1} \cdots \int_{a_n}^{b_n} f(z_1, \ldots, z_n) dz_1 \ldots dz_n$$

$$\simeq \frac{\pi^n (b_1 - a_1) \ldots (b_n - a_n)}{(2m)^n} \sum_{i_1=1}^{m} \cdots \sum_{i_n=1}^{m} f(Z(\bar{x}_1), \ldots, Z(\bar{x}_n))$$

$$\times \sqrt{1 - \bar{x}_{i_1}^2} \ldots \sqrt{1 - \bar{x}_{i_n}^2}. \quad (11.78)$$

Table 11.2

n	x_i	ω_i
2	-0.7071067811	0.8862269254
	0.7071067811	0.8862269254
3	-1.224744871	0.2954089751
	0.0000000000	1.18163590
	1.224744871	0.2954089751
4	-1.650680123	0.08131283544
	-0.5246476232	0.8049140900
	1.650680123	0.8049140900
	0.5246476232	0.08131283544
5	-2.02018287	0.01995324205
	-0.9585724646	0.3936193231
	0.0000000000	0.9453087204
	0.9585724646	0.3936193231
	2.02018287	0.01995324205

Source: JUDD (1998), Table 7.4

In this formula $Z(x_i)$ denotes the linear transformation given in equation (11.49), and $\bar{x}_i$ is the i-th zero of the Chebyshev polynomial of degree m. The problem with product rules is the curse of dimensionality. It requires m^n function evaluations to compute the approximate integral. If f itself is time consuming to evaluate, computational time becomes a binding constraint, even for n as small as 4. Monomial formulas are derived from the problem to exactly integrate a weighted product of monomials over a subset D of $\mathbb{R}^n$. A large number of specific formulas derive from this approach. A good source for those formulas is STROUT (1971). A formula that is particularly helpful to compute the expectation $E(f(\mathbf{x}))$ if $\mathbf{x} \in \mathbb{R}^n$ has a multivariate standard normal distribution, is the following:

$$(2\pi)^{-n/2} \int_{\mathbb{R}^n} f(\mathbf{x}) e^{-\sum_{i=1}^n x_i^2} d\mathbf{x} \simeq \frac{1}{2n} \sum_{i=1}^n f(\pm\sqrt{n/2}\mathbf{e}_i), \quad (11.79)$$

where $\mathbf{e}_i = (0, \ldots, 0, 1, 0, \ldots 0)$ denotes the i-th unit vector. To apply this rule to the general case of a random normal vector z with mean $\boldsymbol{\mu}$ and covariance matrix Σ, we use the change of variable technique.[22] The linear transformation

$$\mathbf{x} = \frac{\Sigma^{-1/2}}{\sqrt{2}}(\mathbf{z}-\boldsymbol{\mu})$$

implies that $E(f(\mathbf{z}))$ can be expressed as an integral function of $\mathbf{x}$:

$$E(f(\mathbf{z})) = (2\pi)^{-n/2}|\Sigma|^{-1/2}\int_{\mathbb{R}^n} f(\mathbf{z}) e^{\frac{-1}{2}(\mathbf{z}-\boldsymbol{\mu})'\Sigma^{-1}(\mathbf{z}-\boldsymbol{\mu})} d\mathbf{z}$$

$$= \pi^{-n/2}\int_{\mathbb{R}^n} f\left(\sqrt{2}\Sigma^{1/2}\mathbf{x}+\boldsymbol{\mu}\right) e^{-\sum_{i=1}^{n} x_i^2} d\mathbf{x}.$$

This integral can be approximated by formula (11.79). In the files Integration.src and Integration.for we provide several procedures for numerical integration.

11.4 Stopping Criteria for Iterative Algorithms

Most, if not all of our algorithms are iterative. Think of the value function iterations presented in Chapter 1 or the fixed point iterations used in Chapter 3. For those algorithms we must know when to stop them.

Stopping criteria can be based on two questions:[23]

1. Have we solved the problem?
2. Have we ground to a halt?

Consider the problem to find the root of the system of non-linear equations $\mathbf{f}(\mathbf{x}) = \mathbf{0}$. To answer the first question we must decide when $\mathbf{f}(\mathbf{x})$ is close to zero. To answer the second question we must decide when two successive points $\mathbf{x}^{s+1}$ and $\mathbf{x}^s$ are close together so that we can reasonably assume the sequence is near its limit point.

---

[22] See, e.g., Theorem 7.5.3 in JUDD (1998).
[23] See DENNIS and SCHNABEL (1983), p. 159.

To tackle both problems we need measures of distance, or, more generally, vector norms as defined in equation (11.1). Given a vector norm, we will be speaking of a vector sequence $(\mathbf{x}^s)_{s=1}^\infty$ converging to a point $\mathbf{x}^*$, if $\lim_{s\to\infty} \|\mathbf{x}^s - \mathbf{x}^*\| = 0$. A key property of a convergent series is the rate at which it converges to its limit. We say that $\mathbf{x}^s$ converges at rate q to $\mathbf{x}^*$, if there exists a constant $c \in [0,1)$ and an integer $\bar{s}$ such that

$$\|\mathbf{x}^{s+1} - \mathbf{x}^*\| \leq c\|\mathbf{x}^s - \mathbf{x}^*\|^q \text{ for all } s \geq \bar{s}. \tag{11.80}$$

If q in (11.80) equals 1 (2), we say that the vector series converges linearly (quadratically). If there is a sequence $(c_s)_{s=1}^\infty$ that converges to zero,

$$\|\mathbf{x}^{s+1} - \mathbf{x}^*\| \leq c_s\|\mathbf{x}^s - \mathbf{x}^*\|,$$

then we say the sequence $(\mathbf{x}_s)_{s=1}^\infty$ converges superlinearly.

With these definitions at hand we may accept $\mathbf{x}^c$ as a solution of $\mathbf{f}(\mathbf{x}) = 0$ if

$$\|\mathbf{f}(\mathbf{x}^c)\|_\infty < \epsilon, \ \epsilon \in \mathbb{R}. \tag{11.81}$$

Care must be taken with respect to the scaling of $\mathbf{f}$. For example, if $f^j \in [10^{-5}, 10^{-4}] \ \forall j$ and $\epsilon = 10^{-3}$, any $\mathbf{x}$ will cause us to stop. If the f^j differ greatly in magnitude, applying (11.81) may be overly restrictive. Therefore, before applying (11.81) the x_i should be scaled so that the f^j have about the same magnitude at points not near the root.

An answer to the second question can be based on the rule

$$\frac{|x_i^s - x_i^{s+1}|}{1 + |x_i^s|} \leq \epsilon \ \forall \ i = 1, 2, \ldots, n, \ \epsilon \in \mathbb{R}_{++}. \tag{11.82}$$

It tests whether the change in the i-th coordinate of $\mathbf{x}$ is small relative to the magnitude of x_i^s. To circumvent the possibility of $x_i \simeq 0$, $1 + |x_i^s|$ instead of $|x_i^s|$ is used in the denominator. However, if $\forall i$ x_i is much smaller than unity this criterium indicates convergence too early. Therefore, if the typical value of x_i, $typ\ x_i$, say, is known, DENNIS and SCHNABEL (1983), p. 160 recommend

$$\frac{|x_i^s - x_i^{s+1}|}{\max\{|x_i^s|, |typ\ x_i|\}} \le \epsilon\ \forall i = 1, 2, \ldots, n, \epsilon \in \mathbb{R}_{++}. \tag{11.83}$$

In some cases, like, e.g., in iterations over the value function, it is known that

$$\|\mathbf{x}^{s+1} - \mathbf{x}^*\| \le c\|\mathbf{x}^s - \mathbf{x}^*\|, 0 \le c < 1 \text{ for all } s \ge 1.$$

Thus the properties of norms given in (11.3) imply

$$\|\mathbf{x}^s - \mathbf{x}^*\| \le \frac{\|\mathbf{x}^s - \mathbf{x}^{s+1}\|}{1-c}.$$

Using

$$\|\mathbf{x}^s - \mathbf{x}^{s+1}\| \le \epsilon(1-c), \ \epsilon \in \mathbb{R}_{++} \tag{11.84}$$

as stopping rule secures that the error $\|\mathbf{x}^s - \mathbf{x}^*\|$ in accepting $\mathbf{x}^{s+1}$ as solution is always bounded from above by ϵ.

In Section 11.5.2 we present a globally convergent extension of the Newton-Raphson algorithm 11.5.2. It is based on finding the minimizer $\mathbf{x}^* \in \mathbb{R}^n$ of a real valued function $f(\mathbf{x})$. Therefore, in addition to the stopping criteria discussed so far, we need criteria that tell us, when we are close to the minimum of $f(\mathbf{x})$. A necessary condition for any minimum is

$$f_i(\mathbf{x}^*) = 0, \quad i = 1, 2, \ldots, n,$$

where $f_i(\mathbf{x}^*)$ denotes the partial derivative of f with respect to its i-th argument evaluated at $\mathbf{x}^*$. Let

$$\nabla f := [f_1, f_2, \ldots, f_n]'$$

denote the column vector of partial derivatives (the gradient of f). Then, a natural choice seems to stop, if at the k-th step

$$\|\nabla f(\mathbf{x}^k)\| \le \epsilon$$

for a small positive number ϵ. However, this criterium is sensitive with respect to the scale of f. To see this, suppose $f(\mathbf{x})$ are the costs of producing the quantities x_i, $i = 1, 2, \ldots, n$ in US \$. Now, if instead we measure costs in thousands of dollars, so that $\tilde{f} = S_f f$ with $S_f = 10^{-3}$ the algorithm would already stop if $S_f \|\nabla f(\mathbf{x}^s)\| \leq \epsilon$. To circumvent this problem, we could use

$$\frac{\|\nabla f(\mathbf{x}^k)\|}{\max\{|typ\ f|, |f|\}} \leq \epsilon, \tag{11.85}$$

which is independent of the scale of f. Here, again, we use $\max\{|typ\ f|, |f|\}$ instead of $1+|f|$ in the denominator to allow for the typical value of f, $typ\ f$, to be much smaller than 1. However, (11.85) is not independent of the scale of x_i, $i = 1, 2, \ldots, n$. For instance, let $f(x) := (S_x x)^2$, where S_x is a scaling factor for x and assume $|typ f| \equiv 1 < (S_x x^k)^2$. In this case the lhs of (11.85) yields

$$\frac{2}{|S_x x^k|}.$$

Here, again, the algorithm stops the sooner the larger is the scale – tons instead of kilos – for x. An obvious measure that is free of both the scale of f and of x_i is the partial elasticity of f with respect to x_i:

$$\frac{f_i(\mathbf{x}^k) x_i}{f(\mathbf{x}^k)}.$$

To account for either $x_i^k \simeq 0$ or $f(\mathbf{x}^k) \simeq 0$, DENNIS and SCHNABEL (1983), p. 160 recommend the following stopping criterium:

$$\left| \frac{f_i(\mathbf{x}^k) \max\{|x_i|, typ\ x_i\}}{\max\{|f(\mathbf{x}^k)|, typ\ f\}} \right| < \epsilon, \quad \forall i = 1, 2, \ldots, n. \tag{11.86}$$

11.5 Non-Linear Equations

There are many problems where we must solve non-linear equations. For instance, in Section 4.3.2 we must solve the household's first order condition for working hours (4.15) in oder to compute the utility associated with a given savings decision k'. Or, think of the deterministic extended path algorithm presented in Chapter 3 that boils down to solve a large system of non-linear equations. In the next subsection we describe two well-known methods that locate the zero of a function of a single variable. Subsection 11.5.2 considers systems of non-linear equations.

11.5.1 Single Equations

Bisection. Suppose we want to solve the equation $f(x) = 0$ for $x \in [a, b]$. If f is continuous and if $f(a)$ and $f(b)$ are of opposite sign, the intermediate value theorem tells us that there is a $x^* \in [a, b]$ for which $f(x^*) = 0$. The bisection method constructs a series of shrinking intervals I_j, $j = 1, 2, \ldots$ that bracket the solution to any desired degree. Figure 11.7 illustrates this approach. The first interval is given by $I_1 = [a, p_1]$ with $p_1 = a + (b - a)/2$. Since f changes its sign in I_1, that is $f(a)f(p_1) < 0$, we know that $x^* \in I_1$. In the next step we consider the smaller interval $I_2 = [a, p_2]$ with $p_2 = a + (p_1 - a)/2$. At the boundaries of I_2, f

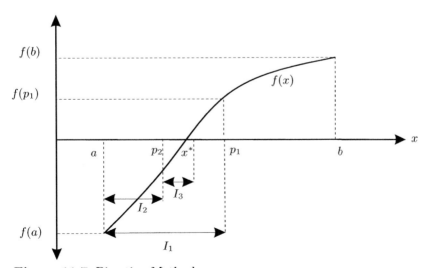

Figure 11.7: Bisection Method

has the same sign, $f(a)f(p_2) > 0$. Thus, the zero must be to the right of p_2. For this reason we now adjust the lower bound and choose $I_3 = [p_2, p_2 + (p_1 - p_2)/2]$. Continuing in this way gets us closer and closer to x^*.

The bisection method, which we summarize in Algorithm 11.5.1, is a derivative free method, and thus, can be applied to problems where f is not differentiable. Our Gauss program `Fixp2` implements this algorithm.

Algorithm 11.5.1 (Bisection)

Purpose: *Approximate the solution x^* of $f(x) = 0$ in $I = [a, b]$.*

Steps:

Step 1: Initialize: Choose a tolerance ϵ_1 and a parameter convergence criterium ϵ_2 and a maximum number of iterations n and set $i = 1$.

Step 2: Compute $fa = f(a)$.

Step 3: Compute $p = a + (b-a)/2$.

Step 4: Compute $fp = f(p)$.

Step 5: Check for convergence: If $|fp| < \epsilon_1$ or $(b-a)/2 < \epsilon_2$ or $i = n$ stop.

Step 6: Adjust the boundaries: If $fa \times fp > 0$, replace a with p and fa with fp, else replace b with p. Increase i by one and return to Step 3.

Newton-Raphson Method. Newton's method or, as it is also known, the Newton-Raphson method, uses the linear approximation of f to locate the zero x^*. Since it converges quadratically, it is much faster than the bisection method.

In Figure 11.8 the domain of the function $f(x)$ is the set of nonnegative real numbers $\mathbb{R}_+$. Consider the point x_0. We approximate f linearly around x_0. This gives $g^0(x) := f(x_0) + f'(x_0)(x - x_0)$, where $f'(x_0)$ is the slope of f at x_0. The root of $g^0(x)$ is given by

$$0 = f(x_0) + f'(x_0)(x'_1 - x_0) \quad \Rightarrow \quad x'_1 = x_0 - \frac{f(x_0)}{f'(x_0)}.$$

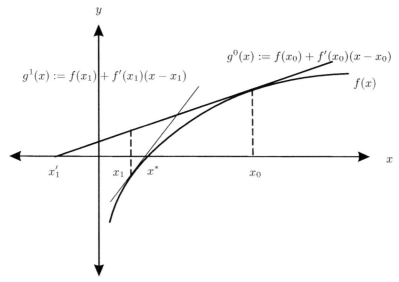

Figure 11.8: Modified Newton-Raphson Method

Yet, $x_1' < 0$ where $f(x)$ is not defined. Hence, we choose a point x_1 between x_1' and x_0. Approximating f at x_1 and solving for the root of $g^1(x) = f(x_1) + f'(x_1)(x - x_1)$ takes us close to x^*.

The method where one iterates over

$$x_{s+1} = x_s - \frac{f(x_s)}{f'(x_s)} \qquad (11.87)$$

until $f(x_{s+1}) \approx 0$ is called the Newton-Raphson method. The modified Newton-Raphson method takes care of regions where f is not defined and backtracks from x_{s+1} along the direction $f'(x_s)$ to a point x_{s+1}' at which f can be evaluated.

There are problems where it is impossible or very costly (in terms of computational time) to compute the derivative of f. For instance, in Section 7.3.1 we compute the stationary distribution of an exchange economy with credit constraints. In this problem, there is no analytical expression for the function that relates the economy's interest rate to average asset holdings. In these situations we use the slope of the secant that connects two points $(x_s, f(x_s))$ and $(x_{s+1}, f(x_{s+1}))$ in place of $f'(x_s)$ in (11.87) (see Figure 11.9). This provides the secant method:

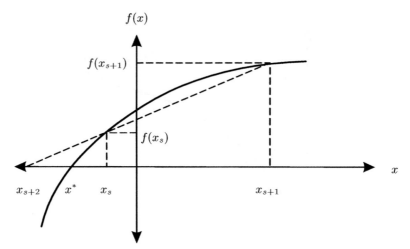

Figure 11.9: Secant Method

$$x_{s+2} = x_{s+1} - \frac{x_{s+1} - x_s}{f(x_{s+1}) - f(x_s)} f(x_s). \tag{11.88}$$

It can be shown that both the iterative scheme (11.87) and (11.88) converge to the solution x^* under suitable conditions.[24] Furthermore, they are easily generalized to the multi-variable framework.

11.5.2 Multiple Equations

Assume we want to solve the system of n equations in the unknowns $\mathbf{x} = [x_1, x_2, \ldots, x_n]$:

$$\left.\begin{aligned} 0 &= f^1(x_1, x_2, \ldots, x_n), \\ 0 &= f^2(x_1, x_2, \ldots, x_n), \\ &\vdots = \vdots \\ 0 &= f^n(x_1, x_2, \ldots, x_n), \end{aligned}\right\} \iff \mathbf{0} = \mathbf{f}(\mathbf{x}). \tag{11.89}$$

---

[24] See, e.g., DENNIS and SCHNABEL (1983), Theorem 2.4.3 and Theorem 2.6.3.

As in the single equation case there are simple, derivative free methods, as well as extensions of the Newton-Raphson and secant method.

Gauss-Seidel Method. This method starts with a point $\mathbf{x}^s = [x_1^s, x_2^s, \ldots, x_n^s]$, and obtains a new point $\mathbf{x}^{s+1}$ by solving

$$0 = f^1(x_1^{s+1}, x_2^s, \ldots, x_n^s),$$
$$0 = f^2(x_1^{s+1}, x_2^{s+1}, \ldots, x_n^s),$$
$$\vdots = \vdots,$$
$$0 = f^n(x_1^{s+1}, x_2^{s+1}, \ldots, x_n^{s+1}).$$

This process is continued until two successive solutions $\mathbf{x}^{s+1}$ and $\mathbf{x}^s$ are close together, as defined by either condition (11.82) or (11.83). Thus, the problem of solving n equations simultaneously is reduced to solving n single equations in one variable x_i^{s+1}. Depending on the nature of the functions f^i these solutions may be either obtained analytically – if it is possible to write $x_i^{s+1} = h^i(\mathbf{x}_{-i}^s)$, where $\mathbf{x}_{-i}^s$ is the vector $\mathbf{x}^s$ without its ith element – or by any of the methods considered in the previous subsection.

Figure 11.10 illustrates that the sequence of points constructed in this way may well diverge from the true solution (x_1^*, x_2^*). A set of sufficient conditions for the convergence of the Gauss-Seidel iterations is derived by CARNAHAN, LUTHER, and WILKES (1969), p.308. Assume there is a neighborhood $\mathcal{N}(\mathbf{x}^*)$ of $\mathbf{x}^*$ defined by $|x_i - x_i^*| < \epsilon$, $\epsilon > 0$, for all $i = 1, 2, \ldots, n$ and a positive number $K < 1$ so that the partial derivatives of f^i satisfy

$$\sum_{j \neq i} \left| \frac{\partial f^i}{\partial x_j}(\mathbf{x}) \right| + \left| 1 - \frac{\partial f^i}{\partial x_i}(\mathbf{x}) \right| < K, \quad \forall i = 1, 2, \ldots, n$$

for all $\mathbf{x} \in \mathcal{N}(\mathbf{x}^*)$. Then, the Gauss-Seidel iterations converge to $\mathbf{x}^*$ for each $\mathbf{x}^s \in \mathcal{N}(\mathbf{x}^*)$.[25]

---

[25] This condition derives from condition (5.37) in CARNAHAN, LUTHER, and WILKES (1969), p.308, if we define the functions $F^i(\mathbf{x})$ as $F^i(\mathbf{x}) = x_i - f^i(\mathbf{x})$.

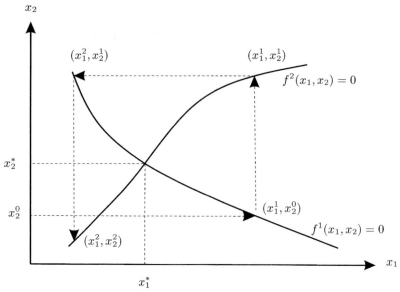

Figure 11.10: Gauss-Seidel Iterations

The Newton-Raphson Method. The Newton-Raphson method considered in Subsection 11.5.1 is based on a linear approximation of $f(x)$. In the multi-variable case the linear approximation of $\mathbf{f}(\mathbf{x})$ at a point $\mathbf{x}^s$ is

$$\mathbf{g}(\mathbf{x}) := \mathbf{f}(\mathbf{x}^s) + J(\mathbf{x}^s)\mathbf{w}, \quad \mathbf{w} := (\mathbf{x} - \mathbf{x}^s),$$

with the Jacobian matrix J defined in (11.36). The zero of $\mathbf{g}(\mathbf{x}^{s+1})$ is

$$\mathbf{x}^{s+1} = \mathbf{x}^s - J(\mathbf{x}^s)^{-1}\mathbf{f}(\mathbf{x}^s). \tag{11.90}$$

To establish the convergence of the sequence of iterates (11.90) we need a few more definitions. Let $\|\cdot\|$ denote a given vector or matrix norm, depending on the respective context.[26] We define an open ball with center $\mathbf{x}^s$ and radius r, $\mathcal{N}(\mathbf{x}^s, r)$, as the collection of all $\mathbf{x} \in \mathbb{R}^n$ whose distance to $\mathbf{x}^s$ is less than r:

$$\mathcal{N}(\mathbf{x}^s, r) := \{\mathbf{x} \in \mathbb{R}^n : \|\mathbf{x} - \mathbf{x}^s\| < r\}.$$

---

[26] See Section 11.1 on the definition of vector and matrix norms.

The Jacobian matrix $J(\mathbf{x})$ is a map of points in $\mathbb{R}^n$ to points in $\mathbb{R}^{n \times n}$. It is said to be Lipschitz on $\mathcal{N}(\mathbf{x}^s)$ with constant γ if for $\mathbf{x}^1, \mathbf{x}^2 \in \mathcal{N}(\mathbf{x}^s)$ the following condition holds

$$\|J(\mathbf{x}^1) - J(\mathbf{x}^2)\| \leq \gamma \|\mathbf{x}^1 - \mathbf{x}^2\|.$$

This is a stronger condition than the continuity of J. It can be shown that a sufficient condition for J to be Lipschitz is that J is continuously differentiable, i.e., that it belongs to the class of C^1 functions.[27] In the one-dimensional case $f(x) = 0$ this requires the function f to be twice continuously differentiable. The following theorem, taken from DENNIS and SCHNABEL (1983), p. 90, states that the sequence of points $\mathbf{x}^0, \mathbf{x}^1, \ldots$ converges quadratically to $\mathbf{x}^*$, if $\mathbf{x}^0$ is sufficiently close to $\mathbf{x}^*$.

Theorem 11.5.1 *Let $\mathbf{f} : \mathbb{R}^n \to \mathbb{R}^n$ be continuously differentiable in an open convex set $\mathcal{D} \subset \mathbb{R}^n$. Assume that there exists $\mathbf{x}^* \in \mathbb{R}^n$ and $r, \beta > 0$, such that $\mathcal{N}(\mathbf{x}^*, r) \subset \mathcal{D}$, $\mathbf{f}(\mathbf{x}^*) = \mathbf{0}$, $J(\mathbf{x}^*)^{-1}$ exists with $\|J(\mathbf{x}^*)^{-1}\| \leq \beta$, and J is Lipschitz with constant γ on $\mathcal{N}(\mathbf{x}^*, r)$. Then there exists $\epsilon > 0$ such that for all $\mathbf{x}^0 \in \mathcal{N}(\mathbf{x}^*, \epsilon)$ the sequence $\mathbf{x}^1, \mathbf{x}^2, \ldots$ generated by*

$$\mathbf{x}^{s+1} = \mathbf{x}^s - J(\mathbf{x}^s)^{-1} f(\mathbf{x}^s), \quad s = 0, 1, \ldots,$$

is well defined, converges to $\mathbf{x}^*$, and obeys

$$\|\mathbf{x}^{s+1} - \mathbf{x}^*\| \leq \beta\gamma \|\mathbf{x}^s - \mathbf{x}^*\|^2, \quad s = 0, 1, \ldots.$$

If the initial guess $\mathbf{x}^0$ is not as close to the final solution as required by this theorem, the algorithm may hit points for which $\mathbf{f}$ is not defined (as the point x_1' in Figure 11.7). To circumvent this case, we specify upper and lower bounds $[\underline{\mathbf{x}}, \bar{\mathbf{x}}]$ such that $\mathbf{f}$ is well defined for all $\mathbf{x} \in [\underline{\mathbf{x}}, \bar{\mathbf{x}}]$.

Putting all pieces together, provides Algorithm 11.5.2. We implemented the single equation version of this algorithm in the Gauss procedure `Fixp1` in the file `NLEQ.src`. For the multi-equation version we provide two implementations. The procedure

---

[27] A prove of this statement can be found in HIRSCH and SMALE (1974), p. 163f.

`FixvMN1` can be used, if you have no a priori knowledge about the domain of $\mathbf{f}$ (as is the case, for instance, in the parameterized expectations approach presented in Chapter 5). In this case, the procedure returning $\mathbf{f}(\mathbf{x})$ must return a Gauss missing value code if it is not possible to evaluate $\mathbf{f}$ at $\mathbf{x} + \mathbf{w}$. The procedure than backtracks from $\mathbf{x} + \mathbf{w}$ towards $\mathbf{x}$. If you know the boundaries (as in the application of the deterministic extended path approach of Chapter 3) you can use `FixvMN2`. Both implementations allow you to either use the Gauss command `gradp` to compute the Jacobian matrix or our routine `CDJac` (see Section 11.3.1). Both versions of the program compute $\mathbf{x}^{s+1}$ in equation (11.90) from the solution of the linear system

$$J(\mathbf{x}^s)\mathbf{w}^{s+1} = -\mathbf{f}(\mathbf{x}^s), \quad \mathbf{w}^{s+1} = \mathbf{x}^{s+1} - \mathbf{x}^s,$$

via the LU factorization of the Jacobian matrix. Fortran versions of both procedures are available in the source file `MNR.for`.

Algorithm 11.5.2 (Modified Newton-Raphson)

Purpose: *Approximate the solution* $\mathbf{x}^*$ *of* (11.89).

Steps:

Step 1: Initialize: choose $\mathbf{x}^0 \in [\underline{\mathbf{x}}, \bar{\mathbf{x}}]$.
Step 2: Compute $J(\mathbf{x}^0)$ *the Jacobian matrix of* $\mathbf{f}$ *at* $\mathbf{x}^0$ *and solve* $J(\mathbf{x}^0)\mathbf{w} = -\mathbf{f}(\mathbf{x}^0)$. *If* $\mathbf{x}^1 = \mathbf{x}^0 + \mathbf{w} \notin [\underline{\mathbf{x}}, \bar{\mathbf{x}}]$ *choose* $\lambda \in (0,1)$ *such that* $\mathbf{x}^2 = \mathbf{x}^0 + \lambda \mathbf{w} \in [\underline{\mathbf{x}}, \bar{\mathbf{x}}]$ *and set* $\mathbf{x}^1 = \mathbf{x}^2$.
Step 3: Check for convergence: if $\|\mathbf{f}(\mathbf{x}^1)\|_\infty < \epsilon$ *and/or* $|x_i^1 - x_i^0|/(1 + |x_i^0|) \leq \epsilon \forall i$ *for a given tolerance* $\epsilon \in \mathbb{R}_{++}$ *stop, else set* $\mathbf{x}^0 = \mathbf{x}^1$ *and return to step 2.*

Broyden's Secant Update. In systems with many variables the computation of the Jacobian matrix slows down the algorithm considerably and may even prohibit the use of the modified Newton-Raphson method. For instance, the problem presented in Section 9.3.2 involves 900 variables and each function evaluation requires several minutes. As a consequence, the computation of the Jacobian in Step 2 of Algorithm 11.5.2 with the help of numerical differentiation is a matter of days rather than hours or minutes. In general, for a system of n equations in n unknowns, Newton's method requires at least $2n^2 + n$ scalar functional evaluations in each step.[28]

Broyden's method overcomes this problem. Instead of computing the Jacobian matrix at each step of the iterations, it updates the most recent estimate of this matrix using only n function evaluations. The method is an extension of the secant-method given in (11.88) to the multivariate case.

Let $A^s := J(\mathbf{x}^s)$ denote the estimate of the Jacobian matrix at step s of the iterations, $\mathbf{w}^{s+1} = \mathbf{x}^{s+1} - \mathbf{x}^s$ the step from the point $\mathbf{x}^s$ to $\mathbf{x}^{s+1}$, and $\mathbf{y}^{s+1} := \mathbf{f}(\mathbf{x}^{s+1}) - \mathbf{f}(\mathbf{x}^s)$. The extension of the secant formula $f'(x^s) \simeq (f(x^{s+1}) - f(x^s))/(x^{s+1} - x^s)$ to the n-variable case implies

$$A^{s+1}\mathbf{w}^{s+1} = \mathbf{y}^{s+1}. \tag{11.91}$$

Yet, this equation determines just n of the n^2 unknown elements of A^{s+1}. As shown by DENNIS and SCHNABEL (1983), p. 170f, the additional condition

$$A^{s+1}\mathbf{z} = A^s\mathbf{z} \text{ with } \left(\mathbf{x}^{s+1} - \mathbf{x}^s\right)^T \mathbf{z} = 0 \tag{11.92}$$

minimizes the difference between two successive linear approximations of $\mathbf{f}(\mathbf{x})$ at $\mathbf{x}^s$ and $\mathbf{x}^{s+1}$ subject to condition (11.91). The two conditions (11.91) and (11.92) uniquely determine A^{s+1} via the update formula

$$A^{s+1} = A^s \frac{\left[\mathbf{y}^{s+1} - A^s\mathbf{w}^{s+1}\right](\mathbf{w}^{s+1})^T}{(\mathbf{w}^{s+1})^T(\mathbf{w}^{s+1})}. \tag{11.93}$$

In some applications, even the initial computation of the Jacobian $J(\mathbf{x}_0)$ may be too time-consuming. In these cases, the identity matrix is often used as an initial guess for A_0.[29]

---

[28] $2n^2$ evaluations to obtain the approximate Jacobian matrix with the help of the central difference formula (11.68) and n evaluations to compute $f^i(\mathbf{x})$, $i = 1, 2, \ldots, n$.

[29] One has to be careful, though, with the initialization of the Jacobian A_0 as the sequence A^s does not need to converge to the true matrix $J(\mathbf{x}^*)$.

There are two ways to accelerate the iterations further. 1) Suppose we use the QR factorization (11.31) of A^s to solve the linear system $A^s \mathbf{w}^{s+1} = -\mathbf{f}(\mathbf{x}^s)$. In this case it is possible to update QR instead of A^s. Since the QR factorization of an $n \times n$ matrix requires $(4/3)n^3$ floating point operations (flops), whereas its QR update requires at a maximum $26n^2$ flops,[30] this can save considerable time in systems with many unknowns n. 2) There is also an update formula for the inverse of A^s, denoted by $(A^s)^{-1}$, that derives from the Sherman-Morrison formula:[31]

$$(A^{s+1})^{-1} = (A^s)^{-1} + \frac{\left[\mathbf{w}^{s+1} - (A^s)^{-1}\mathbf{y}^{s+1}\right](\mathbf{w}^{s+1})^T (A^s)^{-1}}{(\mathbf{w}^{s+1})^T (A^s)^{-1} \mathbf{y}^{s+1}}. \qquad (11.94)$$

DENNIS and SCHNABEL (1983), Theorem 8.2.2 show that Broyden's algorithm converges superlinearly (see Section 11.4 on the different rates of convergence). However, the lower rate of convergence vis-à-vis the Newton-Raphson algorithm is usually outweighed by the faster computation of the secant update of the approximate Jacobian matrix. The secant method with an update of the QR factorization is implemented in the Fortran program hybrd1, which is part of a freely available collection of routines named MINPACK that can be used to solve unconstrained optimization problems and to find the roots of a system of non-linear equations. A slightly adjusted version of hybrd1 is included in our Fortran programs where the solution of non-linear equations is part of the algorithm.

If the initial guess $\mathbf{x}^0$ is bad, it may happen that the Newton-Raphson iterations with or without Broyden's secant approximation of the Jacobian matrix fail to converge to the solution $\mathbf{x}^*$. We next discuss two approaches that facilitate convergence: the line search and the trust region approach.

In the computation of the demographic transition problem in Section 9.3, we allow for the re-specification of the Jacobian, if the algorithm fails to converge and use an alternative initialization.

[30] See GOLUB and VAN LOAN (1996), p. 225 and 608.

[31] See, for example, DENNIS and SCHNABEL (1983), p. 188.

Line Search. This strategy forces the algorithm to converge to the solution from any starting point in the domain of the vector valued function **f**. It is based on two observations:

1. The solution to $\mathbf{f}(\mathbf{x}) = \mathbf{0}$ is also a minimizer of

$$g(\mathbf{x}) := (1/2)\mathbf{f}(\mathbf{x})^T\mathbf{f}(\mathbf{x}) = (1/2)\sum_{i=1}^{n}(f^i(x_1,\ldots,x_n))^2.$$

2. The Newton-Raphson step at $\mathbf{x}^s$,

$$\mathbf{w} = -J(\mathbf{x}^s)^{-1}\mathbf{f}(\mathbf{x}^s),$$

is a descent direction for g.

To see the latter, note that the linear approximation (see equation (11.33)) of g at $\mathbf{x}^s$ is given by

$$\hat{g}(\mathbf{x}^{s+1}) \simeq g(\mathbf{x}^s) + [\nabla g(\mathbf{x}^s)]^T \underbrace{(\mathbf{x}^{s+1} - \mathbf{x}^s)}_{\mathbf{w}},$$

where ∇g denotes the gradient of g, i.e., the column vector of first partial derivatives of g, which equals:

$$\nabla g(\mathbf{x}^s) = J(\mathbf{x}^s)^T\mathbf{f}(\mathbf{x}^s). \tag{11.95}$$

Therefore

$$g(\mathbf{x}^{s+1}) - g(\mathbf{x}^s) \simeq [\nabla g(\mathbf{x}^s)]^T\mathbf{w} = \mathbf{f}(\mathbf{x}^s)^T J(\mathbf{x}^s)(-J(\mathbf{x}^s)^{-1}\mathbf{f}(\mathbf{x}^s))$$
$$= -\mathbf{f}(\mathbf{x}^s)^T\mathbf{f}(\mathbf{x}^s) \leq 0.$$

The idea is, thus, to move in the Newton-Raphson direction, and check, whether going all the way actually reduces g. If not, we move back towards $\mathbf{x}^s$ until we get a sufficient reduction in g. The details of this procedure are from DENNIS and SCHNABEL (1983), who show that this algorithm converges to a minimum of g except in rare cases (see their Theorem 6.3.3 on p. 121). Let

$$h(\lambda) := g(\mathbf{x}^s + \lambda\mathbf{w})$$

denote the restriction of g to the line through $\mathbf{x}^s$ in the direction $\mathbf{w}$. We look for a step of size $\lambda \in (0,1]$ that reduces $g(\mathbf{x}^s)$ at least by $\lambda \alpha \nabla g(\mathbf{x}^s)\mathbf{w}$ for a small $\alpha \in (0, 1/2)$, i.e.,

$$g(\mathbf{x}^s + \lambda \mathbf{w}) \leq g(\mathbf{x}^s) + \lambda \alpha [\nabla g(\mathbf{x}^s)]^T \mathbf{w}. \tag{11.96}$$

DENNIS and SCHNABEL (1983) recommend $\alpha = 10^{-4}$. At first we try the full Newton-Raphson step, and hence, put $\lambda_1 = 1$. If λ_1 fails to satisfy (11.96), we approximate h by a parabola,

$$y := a\lambda^2 + b\lambda + c$$

and choose λ_2 as the minimizer of this function. This delivers:

$$\lambda_2 = -\frac{b}{2a}.$$

We get a and b from:

$$\left. \begin{array}{l} h(0) = g(\mathbf{x}^s) =: c, \\ h(1) = g(\mathbf{x}^s + \mathbf{w}) =: a + b + c, \\ h'(0) = \nabla g(\mathbf{x}^s)\mathbf{w} =: b. \end{array} \right\} \Rightarrow \left\{ \begin{array}{l} a = h(1) - h(0) - h'(0), \\ b = h'(0), \\ c = h(0). \end{array} \right.$$

Therefore:

$$\lambda_2 = -\frac{b}{2a} = \frac{-h'(0)}{2(h(1) - h(0) - h'(0))}. \tag{11.97}$$

Note that $\lambda_2 < (1/2)$ if $g(\mathbf{x}^s + \mathbf{w}) > g(\mathbf{x}^s)$ and $\lambda_2 = 1/[2(1-\alpha)]$. Since too small or too large steps can prevent the algorithm from converging to the minimum of g, we require $\lambda_2 \in [0.1, 0.5]$.[32]

If the quadratic approximation was not good, λ_2 may still violate (11.96). In this case we approximate h by a cubic function:

$$y := a\lambda^3 + b\lambda^2 + c\lambda + d.$$

The parameters of this approximation must solve the following system of equations

---

[32] See DENNIS and SCHNABEL (1983) for examples.

$$a\lambda_1^3 + b\lambda_1^2 + c\lambda_1 + d = h(\lambda_1) = g(\mathbf{x}^s + \lambda_1 \mathbf{w}),$$
$$a\lambda_2^3 + b\lambda_2^2 + c\lambda_2 + d = h(\lambda_2) = g(\mathbf{x}^s + \lambda_2 \mathbf{w}),$$
$$c = h'(0) = \nabla g(\mathbf{x}^s)\mathbf{w}, \tag{11.98}$$
$$d = h(0) = g(\mathbf{x}^s),$$

and the minimizer of y is the solution to

$$\lambda_3 = \frac{-b + \sqrt{b^2 - 3ac}}{3a}. \tag{11.99}$$

If $\alpha < (1/4)$ this solution is always real.[33] Here, again we avoid too large or too small steps by restricting λ_3 to

$$\lambda_3 \in [0.1\lambda_2, 0.5\lambda_2].$$

If λ_3 still violates (11.96) we approximate h at the points $\mathbf{x}^s$, $\mathbf{x}^s + \lambda_2 \mathbf{w}$, and $\mathbf{x}^s + \lambda_3 \mathbf{w}$, solve (11.98) and (11.99) for λ_4 and continue this procedure until λ_k satisfies (11.96). To prevent the line search to get trapped in an endless loop, we check at each step whether λ_k is larger than some minimal value λ_{min}. We choose λ_{min} so that $\lambda < \lambda_{min}$ implies convergence according to the parameter convergence criterium ϵ. For example, consider the convergence criterium (11.83), define

$$\Delta_i := \frac{|x_i^s - x_i^{s+1}|}{\max\{|x_i^s|, |typ\ x_i|\}},$$

and $\Delta = \arg\max\{\Delta_1, \Delta_2, \ldots, \Delta_n\}$. Then $\lambda_{min} = \epsilon/\Delta$. If the line search is used in a pure minimization routine, where (11.86) is used to stop the algorithm, $\lambda < \lambda_{min}$ should never occur. If it nevertheless does, this usually indicates that the ϵ used in (11.83) is to large relative to the ϵ used in (11.86). If $\lambda < \lambda_{min}$ occurs in a non-linear equation solver, the calling program should verify whether the minimum of g as defined above, is also a zero of f.

Algorithm 11.5.3 summarizes the line search. Both, our non-linear equations solver and our minimization routine use versions of this algorithm. See `MNRStep` in the file `MNR.for` or in `NLEQ.src`

---

[33] See DENNIS and SCHNABEL (1983), p. 129.

(for the Gauss version) and `QNStep` in `Optimization.for` or `Optimization.src`, respectively.

Algorithm 11.5.3 (Line Search)

Purpose: *Find a step size that achieves a sufficient decrease in the value of a function to be minimized.*

Steps:

Step 1: Initialize: Choose $\alpha = 10^{-4}$, compute λ_{min}, put $\lambda_k = 1$, and $k = 1$.

Step 2: If λ_k satisfies (11.96) stop and return λ_k, else increase k by 1 and proceed to the next step.

Step 3: If $k = 2$ solve (11.97) for λ_2, yet restrict the solution to the interval $\lambda_2 \in [0.1, 0.5]$.

If $k > 2$ solve (11.98) and (11.99) using the two most recent values of λ, say λ_{k-1} and λ_{k-2}, and restrict the solution to the interval $\lambda_k \in [0.1\lambda_{k-1}, 0.5\lambda_{k-1}]$.

In any case put $\lambda = \lambda_k$. If $\lambda > \lambda_{min}$ return to step 2, else stop and let the calling program know that no further decrease of g can be achieved within the given parameter tolerance ϵ.

Trust Region. This approach specifies an open ball $\mathscr{N}(\mathbf{x}^s, \delta)$ of radius δ at $\mathbf{x}^s$ (the trust region) in which it assumes that the linear approximation of $\mathbf{f}$ is sufficiently good. Then it computes a direction $\mathbf{w}$ that minimizes

$$\hat{g}(\mathbf{x}) := 0.5\big[\mathbf{f}(\mathbf{x}^s) + J(\mathbf{x}^s)\mathbf{w}\big]^T \big[\mathbf{f}(\mathbf{x}^s) + J(\mathbf{x}^s)\mathbf{w}\big]$$

subject to $\|\mathbf{w}\|_2 \leq \delta$.

Figure 11.11 illustrates the approximate solution to this problem.[34] If the Newton-Raphson step $\mathbf{w}^{NR}$ from $\mathbf{x}^s$ to $\mathbf{x}^{NR_1}$ remains in $\mathscr{N}$ it is taken. If the Newton-Raphson step forces the algorithm to leave $\mathscr{N}$ (the point $\mathbf{x}^{NR_2}$ in Figure 11.11), the steepest decent direction is considered. This direction is given by the gradient of

---

[34] See DENNIS and SCHNABEL (1983), p. 130ff.

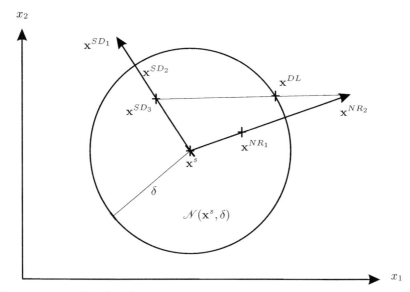

Figure 11.11: Dogleg Step

g (see (11.95)). The algorithm first tries to minimize $\hat{g}$ along this direction. If the point

$$\mathbf{x}^{SD_1} = \mathbf{x}^s - \mu \nabla g(\mathbf{x}^s), \quad \mu = \frac{\|\nabla g(\mathbf{x}^s)\|_2^2}{[\nabla g(\mathbf{x}^s)]^T [J(\mathbf{x}^s)]^T J(\mathbf{x}^s) \nabla g(\mathbf{x}^s)}$$

is outside $\mathcal{N}$, the algorithm moves to the point

$$\mathbf{x}^{SD_2} = \mathbf{x}^s - \frac{\delta}{\|\nabla g(\mathbf{x}^s)\|_2} g(\mathbf{x}^s)$$

on the boundary of $\mathcal{N}$. Otherwise the point

$$\mathbf{x}^{DL} = \mathbf{x}^s + \mathbf{w}^{DL},$$
$$\mathbf{w}^{DL} = \mathbf{w}^{SD} + \lambda[\mathbf{w}^{NR} - \mathbf{w}^{SD}],$$
$$\mathbf{w}^{NR} = -J(\mathbf{x}^s)\mathbf{f}(\mathbf{x}^s),$$
$$\mathbf{w}^{SD} = -\mu \nabla g(\mathbf{x}^s),$$

is selected. This point is on the intersection of the convex combination between the steepest decent point $\mathbf{x}^{SD_3}$ and the Newton-Raphson point $\mathbf{x}^{NR_2}$ with the boundary of $\mathcal{N}$. The step from $\mathbf{x}^s$

to this point is called the dogleg step, and the parameter λ is the positive root of the quadratic equation

$$0 = \lambda^s + \lambda \frac{2}{\alpha} \left[\mathbf{w}^{NR} - \mathbf{w}^{SD} \right]^T \mathbf{w}^{SD} + \frac{[\mathbf{w}^{SD}]^T \mathbf{w}^{SD} - \delta^2}{\alpha},$$

$$\alpha := \left[\mathbf{w}^{NR} - \mathbf{w}^{SD} \right]^T \left[\mathbf{w}^{NR} - \mathbf{w}^{SD} \right].$$

The initial radius of the trust region is usually set to a multiple, 1, 10, or 100, say, of $\|\mathbf{x}^0\|_2$. This radius is shortened, if it is not possible to reduce g sufficiently. DENNIS and SCHNABEL (1983), p. 143ff. recommend the line search algorithm to compute $\lambda \in (0.1, 0.5)$ so that $\delta^{s+1} = \lambda \delta^s$. The implementation of the trust region approach in the Fortran program hybrd1 just puts $\delta^{s+1} = 0.5\delta^s$, if the actual reduction of the function value $\Delta^a := g(\mathbf{x}^s) - g(\mathbf{x}^{s+1})$ is less than 10% of the predicted reduction $\Delta^p := g(\mathbf{x}^s) - \hat{g}(\mathbf{x}^{s+1})$. If $\Delta^a \in (0.1, 0.5)\Delta^p$, the trust radius is not changed. It is set to $\delta^{s+1} = \max\{\delta^s, 2\|\mathbf{x}^{s+1} - \mathbf{x}^s\|\}$ if $\Delta^a \in (0.5, 0.9)\Delta^p$. If the actual reduction amounts to $\Delta^a \in (0.9, 1.1)\Delta^p$ the program doubles the radius.

11.6 Numerical Optimization

There are some algorithms where we must find the minimizer of a given function.[35] Think of the non-linear least squares problem encountered in the parameterized expectations approach of Chapter 4 or think of the maximization step as part of Algorithm 4.2.1. In other algorithms we are free to choose whether to solve the system of first order conditions that characterizes the optimal solution or to employ numerical optimization tools. Sometimes one line of attack may work while the other performs poorly. Here we describe three well known tools from numerical optimization. The golden section search is a simple means of locating the maximizer of a single valued function in a given interval $[a, b]$. The Gauss-Newton approach is tailored to non-linear least squares problems,

---

[35] Since the maximizer of $-f(\mathbf{x})$ is identical to the minimizer of $f(\mathbf{x})$, we can restrict ourselves to minimization problems.

while the BFGS quasi-Newton method is suitable to a wide class of unconstrained maximization problems. Finally, we consider stochastic algorithms.

11.6.1 Golden Section Search

This method locates the maximum of a single peaked function $f(x)$ in the interval $I = [A, D]$. The idea is to shrink the interval around the true maximizer x^* in successive steps until the midpoint of the remaining interval is a good approximation to x^* (see Figure 11.12).

Assume we have two more function evaluations at points B and C, respectively. It is obvious from Figure 11.12 that for $f(B) > f(C)$ the maximum lies in the shorter interval $[A, C]$. In the opposite case $f(B) < f(C)$ the maximizer is located in $[B, D]$. The question is, how should we choose B and C?

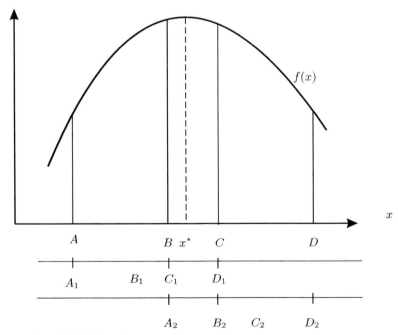

Figure 11.12: Golden Section Search

There are two reasonable principles that will guide our choice. First, note that we do not know in advance whether we end up with $[A, C]$ or $[B, D]$. Our aim is to reduce the interval as much as possible. The unfavorable case is to end up with the larger of the two intervals. We exclude this possibility by choosing B and C so that both intervals are of the same size:

$$\overline{AC} = \overline{BD} \Rightarrow \overline{AB} = \overline{CD}. \tag{11.100}$$

Consider what happens, if $[A_1, D_1] = [A, C]$ is the new interval. Since we know $f(B)$, we need only one more function evaluation to find the next smaller interval. The second principle that we employ is that $[A_1, D_1]$ is a scaled down replication of $[A, D]$, i.e., the points B_1 and C_1 divide $[A_1, D_1]$ the same way as did B and C with $[A, D]$:

$$p := \frac{\overline{AC}}{\overline{AD}} = \frac{\overline{A_1 C_1}}{\overline{A_1 D_1}} \Rightarrow \frac{\overline{AC}}{\overline{AD}} = \frac{\overline{AB}}{\overline{AC}}, \tag{11.101a}$$

$$\frac{\overline{AB}}{\overline{AC}} = \frac{\overline{A_1 B_1}}{\overline{A_1 C_1}}. \tag{11.101b}$$

Symmetrically, if it turns out that the new interval is $[A_2, D_2] = [B, D]$, we demand:

$$p = \frac{\overline{AB}}{\overline{AC}} = \frac{\overline{B_2 D_2}}{\overline{A_2 D_2}}, \tag{11.102a}$$

$$\frac{\overline{CD}}{\overline{BD}} = \frac{\overline{C_2 D_2}}{\overline{B_2 D_2}}. \tag{11.102b}$$

Equation (11.100) and (11.101a) (as well as (11.100) and (11.102a)) imply the condition

$$\frac{1-p}{p} = p.$$

Solving this quadratic equation in p delivers:

$$p = \frac{\sqrt{5}-1}{2} \approx 0.618. \qquad (11.103)$$

This is the fraction by which we are able to shrink the interval in successive iterations. It divides each interval into the so called golden sections. Thus, in the first step we choose points B and C according to

$$B = A + (1-p)\overline{AD},$$
$$C = A + p\overline{AD}.$$

In the next step we choose $[A_1, D_1] = [A, C]$ if $f(B) > f(C)$ and $[A_2, D_2] = [B, D]$ otherwise. In the first case, we put $A_1 = A$, $C_1 = B$, and $D_1 = C$. Condition (11.101b) gives

$$B_1 = pC_1 + (1-p)A_1.$$

In the second case we put $A_2 = B$, $B_2 = C$, and $D_2 = D$. The new point C_2 is given by (11.102b):

$$C_2 = pB_2 + (1-p)D_2.$$

Summarizing, we can construct the following iterative scheme to bracket x^*:

Algorithm 11.6.1 (Golden Section Search)

Purpose: *Find the maximizer of a single peaked function $f(x)$ in the interval $[\underline{x}, \overline{x}]$.*

Steps:

Step 1: Initialize: Set $A = \underline{x}$, $D = \overline{x}$ and compute

$$B = pA + (1-p)D,$$
$$C = (1-p)A + pD,$$
$$p = +(\sqrt{5}-1)/2,$$

and store $f(B)$ in fB and $f(C)$ in fC.

Step 2: *If $fB > fC$ replace D by C, C by B, and fC by fB. Find the new B from $B = pC + (1-p)A$ and store $f(B)$ in fB.*
Otherwise: replace A by B, B by C, and fB by fC. Find the new C from $C = pB + (1-p)D$ and store $f(C)$ in fC.

Step 3: *Check for convergence: if $|D - A| < \epsilon \max\{1, |B| + |C|\}$ stop and return B, else repeat the previous step.*

Our procedure GSS implements this algorithm. Its inputs are the pointer to the procedure that returns $f(x)$ and the boundaries of the interval in which the maximum lies.

11.6.2 Gauss-Newton Method

Algorithms that solve non-linear least squares problems are adapted from procedures that solve the more general problem of finding the minimizer of a real valued function. The solution that we propose is known as the damped Gauss-Newton method.[36] To introduce this algorithm we return to the more common notion of seeking to minimize

$$S(\boldsymbol{\gamma}) := \frac{1}{T}\sum_{i=1}^{T}(y_i - f(\boldsymbol{\gamma}, \mathbf{x}_i))^2, \quad \mathbf{x}_i = (x_{i1}, x_{i2}, \ldots, x_{in}). \quad (11.104)$$

with respect to the parameter vector $\boldsymbol{\gamma} = (\gamma_1, \gamma_2, \ldots, \gamma_p)'$.

The minimizer $\boldsymbol{\gamma}^*$ must solve the set of first order conditions

$$\frac{\partial S}{\partial \gamma_j} = \frac{-2}{T}\sum_{i=1}^{T}(y_i - f(\boldsymbol{\gamma}^*, \mathbf{x}_i))\frac{\partial f}{\partial \gamma_j}(\boldsymbol{\gamma}^*, \mathbf{x}_i) = 0, \quad (11.105)$$
$$j = 1, 2, \ldots, p.$$

Instead of solving this system of p non-linear equations in $\boldsymbol{\gamma}$ the simple Gauss-Newton method operates on a linearized minimization problem. Suppose we have an initial guess $\boldsymbol{\gamma}_s$ and consider

---
[36] See DENNIS and SCHNABEL (1983), Chapter 10.

the linear approximation of f at this vector:[37]

$$f(\gamma, \mathbf{x}_i) \simeq f(\gamma_s, \mathbf{x}_i) + [\nabla f(\gamma_s, \mathbf{x}_i)]'(\gamma - \gamma_s),$$

where $\nabla f(\cdot)$ is the column vector of the first partial derivatives of f with respect to $\gamma_j, j = 1, 2, \ldots, p$ evaluated at the given γ_s. Put

$$\bar{y}_i := y_i - f(\gamma_s, x_i),$$
$$\bar{\mathbf{x}}_i := \nabla f(\gamma_s, \mathbf{x}_i),$$
$$\bar{\gamma} = \gamma - \gamma_s.$$

The solution to the linear least squares problem

$$\min_{\bar{\gamma}} \sum_{i=1}^{T} [\bar{y}_i - \bar{\mathbf{x}}_i \bar{\gamma}]^2$$

is provided by the well known formula

$$\bar{\gamma} = (\bar{X}'\bar{X})^{-1}\bar{X}'\bar{\mathbf{y}},$$
$$\bar{X} := [\bar{\mathbf{x}}_1, \bar{\mathbf{x}}_2, \ldots, \bar{\mathbf{x}}_T], \bar{\mathbf{y}} = [\bar{y}_1, \bar{y}_2, \ldots, \bar{y}_T]'.$$

The simple Gauss-Newton method chooses

$$\gamma_{s+1} = \gamma_s + \underbrace{(\bar{X}'\bar{X})^{-1}\bar{X}'\bar{\mathbf{y}}}_{=:d\gamma}$$

as the next value of γ. Along $d\gamma$ the sum of squares S is decreasing. To see this, note that

$$\nabla S(\gamma) := \frac{-2}{T}\bar{X}'\bar{\mathbf{y}}$$

is the (column) vector of partial derivatives of S evaluated at γ. Therefore,

$$[\nabla S(\gamma_s)]'d\gamma = \frac{-2}{T}\underbrace{\bar{\mathbf{y}}'\bar{X}}_{=:\mathbf{z}'}\underbrace{(\bar{X}'\bar{X})^{-1}}_{=:A}\underbrace{\bar{X}'\bar{\mathbf{y}}}_{=:\mathbf{z}} < 0.$$

---
[37] See equation (11.33).

This follows from the fact that the matrix $\bar{X}'\bar{X}$ and thus its inverse A is positive definite.[38]

If γ_{s+1} is not the minimizer of S, f is linearized at the new value of γ_{s+1} and the related linear least squares problem is solved again to deliver γ_{s+2}. These steps are repeated until convergence.

If the initial value of γ is not near the (local) minimizer, this method may fail to converge, much like the Newton-Raphson method considered in Algorithm 11.5.2. The damped Gauss-Newton method uses the line search from Algorithm 11.5.3 to force the iterations downhill towards a local minimum. Indeed, since the sum of squares (11.104) is bounded from below and since the gradient of a polynomial is continuously differentiable and thus Lipschitz, these iterations satisfy the conditions of Theorem 6.3.3 from DENNIS and SCHNABEL (1983). As a consequence, using the damped Gauss-Newton method will take us to a local minimum of $S(\gamma)$. We use the stopping rule (11.86) (see 11.4) to terminate the algorithm.[39]

Taking all pieces together, the damped Gauss-Newton algorithm proceeds as follows:

Algorithm 11.6.2 (Damped Gauss-Newton)

Purpose: *Find the mimizier of the non-linear least squares problem (11.104)*

Steps:

Step 1: Initialize: Choose a vector γ_0 and stopping criteria $\epsilon_1 \in \mathbb{R}_{++}$ and $\epsilon_2 \in \mathbb{R}_{++}$, $\epsilon_1 >> \epsilon_2$. Put $s = 0$.

Step 2: Linearize $f(\gamma, \mathbf{x}_i)$ at γ_s and put

---

[38] See Section 11.1.6 on definite quadratic forms.

[39] Indeed, since Theorem 6.3.3. from DENNIS and SCHNABEL (1983) establishes convergence of

$$\frac{\nabla S(\gamma_s)'(\gamma_{s+1} - \gamma_s)}{\|\gamma_{s+1} - \gamma_s\|_2}$$

but not of γ_s, it makes sense, to try criterion (11.86) at first. Our line search procedure will warn us, if it is not possible to decrease S further, even if (11.86) is not met.

$$\bar{y}_i = y_i - f(\gamma_s, \mathbf{x}_i), \quad \bar{\mathbf{y}} = [\bar{y}_1, \bar{y}_2, \ldots, \bar{y}_T]',$$
$$\bar{\mathbf{x}}_i = [\nabla f(\gamma_s, \mathbf{x}_i)]', \quad \bar{X} = [\bar{\mathbf{x}}_1, \bar{\mathbf{x}}_2, \ldots, \bar{\mathbf{x}}_T].$$

Step 3: Compute γ_{s+1}: Solve the linear system

$$\bar{X}'\bar{X}\bar{\gamma} = \bar{X}'\bar{y}$$

for $\bar{\gamma}$. Use Algorithm 11.5.3 with ϵ_2 to find the step length d and put

$$\gamma_{s+1} = \gamma_s + d\bar{\gamma}.$$

Step 4: Check for convergence: Use criterion (11.86) with ϵ_1 to see whether the algorithm is close to the minimizer. If so, stop. If not, and if the line search was successful, increase s by one and return to Step 2. Otherwise stop and report convergence to a nonoptimal point.

We provide an implementation of this algorithm in Fortran. Look for the file GaussNewton.for. The procedure allows the user to either supply his own routine for the computation of the gradient of f or to use built-in forward difference methods (or our routines described in Section 11.3.1) to approximate the gradient. Note that the matrix $\bar{X}$ is the Jacobian matrix of the vector valued function

$$\begin{bmatrix} z_1 \\ z_2 \\ \vdots \\ z_T \end{bmatrix} = \begin{bmatrix} f(\gamma, \mathbf{x}_1) \\ f(\gamma, \mathbf{x}_2) \\ \vdots \\ f(\gamma, \mathbf{x}_T) \end{bmatrix}.$$

Thus, if you write a subroutine that returns the vector $\mathbf{z} = [z_1, z_2, \ldots, z_T]'$ and pass this routine to another routine that approximates the Jacobian matrix of a vector valued function, as, e.g., the gradp routine in Gauss, the output of this routine is $\bar{X}$.

11.6.3 Quasi-Newton

In this section we introduce the so called BFGS method to locate the minimizer of a function of several variables. This method derives from Newton's method, which we describe next.

Newton's Method. Suppose you want to minimize $y = f(\mathbf{x})$ on an open subset U of $\mathbb{R}^n$. Newton's method solves this problem by considering the quadratic approximation (see equation (11.32))

$$\hat{f}(\mathbf{x}_0 + \mathbf{h}) = f(\mathbf{x}_0) + [\nabla f(\mathbf{x}_0)]'\mathbf{h} + \frac{1}{2}\mathbf{h}'H(\mathbf{x}_0)\mathbf{h}.$$

In this formula $\nabla f(\mathbf{x}_0)$ is the column vector of first partial derivatives of f with respect to x_i, $i = 1, 2, \ldots, n$, and H is the Hesse matrix of second partial derivatives. Minimizing $\hat{f}$ with respect to the vector $\mathbf{h}$ requires the following first order conditions to hold:[40]

$$\nabla f(\mathbf{x}_0) + H(\mathbf{x}_0)\mathbf{h} = 0.$$

Solving for $\mathbf{x}_1 = \mathbf{x}_0 + \mathbf{h}$ provides the following iterative formula:

$$\mathbf{x}_1 = \mathbf{x}_0 - H(\mathbf{x}_0)^{-1}\nabla f(\mathbf{x}_0). \tag{11.106}$$

It is well known that iterations based on this formula converge quadratically to the minimizer $\mathbf{x}^*$ of $f(\mathbf{x})$, if the initial point $\mathbf{x}_0$ is sufficiently close to the solution $\mathbf{x}^*$.[41] Note, that the second order conditions for a local minimum require the Hesse matrix to be positive semidefinite in a neighborhood of $\mathbf{x}^*$.[42] Furthermore, using $\nabla f(\mathbf{x}_0) = -H(\mathbf{x}_0)\mathbf{h}$ in the quadratic approximation formula gives

$$\hat{f}(\mathbf{x}_1) - f(\mathbf{x}_0) = -(1/2)\mathbf{h}'H(\mathbf{x}_0)\mathbf{h}.$$

Thus, if the Hessian is positive definite (see Section 11.1 on definite matrices), the Newton direction is always a decent direction.

---

[40] See Section 11.1.6 on the differentiation of linear and quadratic forms.
[41] This follows from Theorem 11.5.1, since the iterative scheme (11.106) derives from the Newton-Raphson method applied to the system of first order conditions $\nabla f(\mathbf{x}) = \mathbf{0}$.
[42] See, e.g., SUNDARAM (1996), Theorem 4.3.

The computation of the Hesse matrix is time consuming. Furthermore, there is nothing that ensures this matrix to be positive definite far away from the solution. So called quasi-Newton methods tackle these problems by providing secant approximations to the Hesse matrix. In addition, they implement line search methods that direct the algorithm downhill and, thus, help to ensure almost global convergence. The secant method that has proven to be most successful was discovered independently by Broyden, Fletcher, Goldfarb, and Shanno in 1970. It is known as the BFGS update formula.

BFGS Secant Update. The BFGS quasi-Newton method replaces the Hessian in (11.106) by a positive definite matrix H_k that is updated at each iteration step k. The identity matrix I_n can be used to initialize the sequence of matrices. Consider the following definitions:

$$\mathbf{x}_{k+1} - \mathbf{x}_k = -H_k^{-1}\nabla f(\mathbf{x}_k), \quad (11.107a)$$

$$\mathbf{w}_k := \mathbf{x}_{k+1} - \mathbf{x}_k, \quad (11.107b)$$

$$\mathbf{z}_k := \nabla f(\mathbf{x}_{k+1}) - \nabla f(\mathbf{x}_k), \quad (11.107c)$$

$$H_{k+1} := H_k + \frac{\mathbf{z}_k \mathbf{z}_k'}{\mathbf{z}_k' \mathbf{w}_k} - \frac{H_k \mathbf{w}_k \mathbf{w}_k' H_k'}{\mathbf{w}_k' H_k \mathbf{w}_k}, \quad (11.107d)$$

where the last line defines the BFGS update formula for the secant approximation of the Hesse matrix.

The following theorem provides the foundation of the BFGS method:[43]

Theorem 11.6.1 *Let $f : \mathbb{R}^n \to \mathbb{R}$ be twice continuously differentiable in an open convex set $D \subset \mathbb{R}^n$, and let $H(\mathbf{x})$ be Lipschitz. Assume there exists $\mathbf{x}^* \in D$ such that $\nabla f(\mathbf{x}^*) = \mathbf{0}$ and $H(\mathbf{x}^*)$ is nonsingular and positive definite. Then there exist positive constants ϵ, δ such that if $\|\mathbf{x}_0 - \mathbf{x}^*\|_2 \leq \epsilon$ and $\|H_0 - H(\mathbf{x}^*)\| \leq \delta$, then the positive definite secant update (11.107) is well defined, $\{\mathbf{x}_k\}_{k=1}^{\infty}$ remains in D and converges superlinearly to $\mathbf{x}^*$.*

---

[43] See Theorems 9.1.2 and 9.3.1 of DENNIS and SCHNABEL (1983).

Instead of updating the approximate Hessian H_k one can also start with a positive definite approximation of the inverse of H_k, say $A_k := H_k^{-1}$. The next iterate of $\mathbf{x}_k$ is then given by

$$\mathbf{x}_{k+1} = \mathbf{x}_k - A_k \nabla f(\mathbf{x}_k).$$

This involves only vector addition and matrix multiplication, whereas (11.106) requires the solution of a system of linear equations. The BFGS update formula for A_k is given by (see PRESS ET AL. (2001), p. 420):

$$A_{k+1} = A_k + \frac{\mathbf{w}_k \mathbf{w}_k'}{\mathbf{w}_k' \mathbf{z}_k} - \frac{(A_k \mathbf{z}_k)(A \mathbf{z}_k)'}{\mathbf{z}_k' A_k \mathbf{z}_k} + (\mathbf{z}_k A_k \mathbf{z}_k) \mathbf{u}_k \mathbf{u}_k',$$

$$\mathbf{u}_k := \frac{\mathbf{w}_k}{\mathbf{w}_k' \mathbf{z}_k} - \frac{A_k \mathbf{z}_k}{\mathbf{z}_k' A_k \mathbf{z}_k}.$$

(11.108)

Yet another approach is to use the fact that a positive definite matrix H_k has a Cholesky factorization $L_k L_k' = H_k$, where L_k is a lower triangular matrix. Using this factorization, it is easy to solve the linear system $(L_k L_k')(\mathbf{x}_1 - \mathbf{x}_0) = -\nabla f(\mathbf{x}_0)$ by forward and backward substitution (see Section 11.1.8). Thus, instead of updating H_k, one may want to update L_k. GOLDFARB (1976) provides the details of this approach, which underlies the Gauss routine QNewton.

The BFGS iterations may be combined with the line search algorithm 11.5.3 to enhance global convergence. Indeed, if the Hesse matrix of $f(\mathbf{x})$ (not its approximation!) is positive definite for all $\mathbf{x} \in \mathbb{R}^n$ a Theorem due to Powell (see DENNIS and SCHNABEL (1983), Theorem 9.51 on p. 211) establishes global convergence.[44]

Taking all pieces together provides Algorithm 11.6.3, which is available in the Gauss command QNewton and in the ISML subroutine DUMINF. Our versions of the BFGS method are the

---

[44] Note, this does not imply that a computer coded algorithm does indeed converge. Finite precision arithmetic accounts for differences between the theoretical gradient, the theoretical value of f and the approximate Hessian.

Fortran subroutines QuasiNewton (secant update of H_k) in the file QN.FOR) and the Gauss program QuasiNewton (secant update of A_k) in the file Optimization.src.

Algorithm 11.6.3 (BFGS Quasi-Newton)

Purpose: *Minimize $f(\mathbf{x})$ in $U \subset \mathbb{R}^n$.*

Steps:

Step 1: Initialize: Choose $\mathbf{x}_0$, stopping criteria $\epsilon_1 \in \mathbb{R}_{++}$ and $\epsilon_2 \in \mathbb{R}_{++}$, $\epsilon_1 \gg \epsilon_2$, and either $A_0 = I_n$ or $H_0 = I_n$. Put $k = 0$.

Step 2: Compute the gradient $\nabla f(\mathbf{x}_k)$ and solve for $\mathbf{w}_k$ either from

$$H_s \mathbf{w}_k = -\nabla f(\mathbf{x}_s)$$

or from

$$\mathbf{w}_k = -A_k \nabla f(\mathbf{x}_k).$$

Step 3: Use Algorithm 11.5.3 with ϵ_2 to find the step length s, and put

$$\mathbf{x}_{k+1} = \mathbf{x}_k + s\mathbf{w}_k.$$

Step 4: Check for convergence: Use criterion (11.86) with ϵ_1 to see whether the algorithm is close to the minimizer. If so, stop. If not, and if the line search was successful, proceed to Step 5. Otherwise stop and report convergence to a nonoptimal point.

Step 5: Use either (11.107d) or (11.108) to get A_{k+1} or H_{k+1}, respectively. Increase k by one and return to Step 2.

11.6.4 Genetic Algorithms

The Gauss-Newton as well as the BFGS quasi-Newton method start from a given initial guess and move uphill along the surface of the objective function until they approach a maximizer.

Thus, they may not be able to find the global maximizer. Genetic algorithms, instead, search the set of possible solutions globally.

Terminology. Genetic algorithms (GAs) use operators inspired by natural genetic variation and natural selection to evolve a set of candidate solutions to a given problem. The terminology used to describe GAs is from biology. The set of candidate solutions is called a population, its members are referred to as chromosomes, and each iteration step results in a new generation of candidate solutions. In binary-coded GAs chromosomes are represented by bit strings of a given length l. Each bit is either on (1) or off (0). In real-coded GAs a chromosome is a point in an m-dimensional subspace of $\mathbb{R}^m$. A chromosomes fitness is its ability to solve the problem at hand. In most problems the fitness is determined by a real valued objective function that assigns higher numbers to better solutions.

Basic Structure. The evolution of a population of chromosomes consists of four stages:

1. selection of parents,
2. creation of offspring (crossover),
3. mutation of offspring,
4. and the final selection of those members of the family that survive to the next generation.

The encoding of the problem (binary or floating point) and the operators used to perform selection, crossover, and mutation constitute a specific GA. The many different choices that one can make along these dimensions give rise to a variety of specific algorithms that are simple to describe and program. Yet, at the same time, this variety is a major obstacle to any general theory that is able to explain why and how these algorithms work.[45] Intuitively, and very generally, one can think of GAs as contractive mappings operating on metric spaces whose elements are populations.[46] A mapping f is contractive if the distance between $f(x)$ and $f(y)$

---

[45] MITCHELL (1996) as well as MICHALEWICZ (1999) review the theoretical foundations of genetic algorithms.
[46] See, MICHALEWICZ (1999), p.68ff.

is less than the distance between x and y. Under a contractive mapping an arbitrary initial population will converge to a population where each chromosome achieves the same (maximum) fitness value that is the global solution to the problem at hand. The problem with this statement is that it gives no hint as to how fast this convergence will take place, and whether specific operators accelerate or slow down convergence. Therefore, many insights in the usefulness of specific GAs come from simulation studies.

In the following we restrict ourselves to real-coded GAs. This is motivated by the kind of problems to which we apply GAs. The methods presented in Chapter 5 and Chapter 6 rest on the approximation of unknown functions by linear combinations of members of a family of polynomials. The problem is to find the parameters γ_i that constitute this approximation. Usually, we have no idea about the domain of γ_i. Therefore, it is difficult to decide about the length l of the binary strings, which determines the precision of the solution. Furthermore, using floating point numbers avoids the time consuming translation to and from the binary alphabet. Yet another advantage of real-coded GAs is their capacity for the local fine tuning of the solutions.[47]

Choice of Initial Population. The initial population of a real-coded GA is chosen at random. If there are no a priori restrictions on the candidate solutions one can use a random number generator to perform this task. In our applications we use draws from the standard normal distribution. When we pass a randomly chosen chromosome to the routine that evaluates the candidate's fitness it may happen that the chromosome violates the model's restrictions. For instance, in the parameterized expectations approach, a time path may become infeasible. In this case, the program returns a negative number and our initialization routine discards the respective chromosome. Alternatively, one may want to assign a very small fitness number to those chromosomes. After all,

---

[47] Advantages and disadvantages of real-coded GAs vis-à-vis binary-coded GAs are discussed by HERRERA, LOZANO, and VERDEGAY (1998). In their experiments most real-coded GAs are better than binary-coded GAs in minimizing a given function.

bad genes can mutate or generate reasonable good solutions in the crossover process.

Selection of Parents. There are many different ways to choose parents from the old generation to produce offspring for the new generation. The most obvious and simplest approach is sampling with replacement, where two integers from the set $1, 2, \ldots, n$ that index the n chromosomes of the population are drawn at random. More in the spirit of natural selection, where fitter individuals usually have a better chance to reproduce, is the concept of fitness-proportionate selection. Here, each chromosome $i = 1, 2, \ldots, n$ has a chance to reproduce according to its relative fitness $p(i) = f(i)/\sum_i f(i)$, where $f(i)$ denotes the fitness of chromosome i. The following code implements this selection principle:

Algorithm 11.6.4 (Fitness-Proportionate Selection)

Purpose: *Choose a chromosome from the old generation for reproduction*

Steps:

Step 1: For $i = 1, 2, \ldots, n$ compute $p(i) = f(i)/\sum_i f(i)$.
Step 2: Use a random number generator that delivers random numbers uniformly distributed in $[0, 1]$ and draw $y \in [0, 1]$.
Step 3: For $i = 1, 2, \ldots, n$ compute $q(i) = \sum_{j=1}^{i} p(j)$. If $q(i) \geq y$ select i and stop.

In small populations the actual number of times an individual is selected as parent can be far from its expected value $p(i)$. The concept of stochastic universal sampling avoids this possibility and gives each chromosome a chance to be selected as parent that is between the floor and the ceiling of $p(i)n$.[48] Rather than choosing one parent after the other stochastic universal sampling selects n parents at a time. Each member of the old generation is assigned a slice on a roulette wheel, the size of the slice being proportionate to the chromosomes fitness $f(i)$. There are n equally spaced

---

[48] The floor of x is the largest integer i_1 with the property $i_1 \leq x$ and the ceiling is the smallest integer i_2 with the property $x \leq i_2$.

pointers and the wheel is spun ones. For instance, in Figure 11.13 the chromosome $i = 1$ with relative fitness $p(1)$ is not selected, whereas chromosome 4 is selected twice. Stochastic universal sampling can be implemented as follows[49]

Algorithm 11.6.5 (Stochastic Universal Sampling)

Purpose: *Choose n parents from the old generation for reproduction.*

Steps:

Step 1: For $i = 1, 2, \ldots, n$ compute the relative fitness $r(i) = f(i)/(\sum_i f(i)/n)$ so that $\sum_i r(i) = n$.
Step 2: Use a random number generator that delivers random numbers uniformly distributed in $[0, 1]$ and draw $y \in [0, 1]$.
Step 3: Put $i = 1$.
Step 4: Compute $q(i) = \sum_{j=1}^{i} r(j)$.
Step 5: If $q(i) > y$ select i and increase y by 1.
Step 6: Repeat Step 5 until $q(i) \leq y$.
Step 7: Terminate if $i = n$, otherwise increase i by 1 and return to Step 4.

The major problem with both fitness proportionate and stochastic universal sampling is "premature convergence". Early in the search process the fitness variance in the population is high, and under both selection schemes the small number of very fit chromosomes reproduces quickly. After a few generations they and their descendants build a fairly homogenous population that limits further exploration of the search space. A selection scheme that deals with this problem is sigma scaling. Let σ denote the standard deviation of fitness and $\bar{f} = \sum_{i=1}^{n} f(i)/n$ the average fitness. Under sigma scaling chromosome i is assigned a probability of reproduction according to

$$p(i) := \begin{cases} 1 + \frac{f(i)-\bar{f}}{2\sigma} & \text{if } \sigma(t) \neq 0, \\ 1 & \text{if } \sigma(t) = 0. \end{cases}$$

---
[49] See MITCHELL (1996), p. 167.

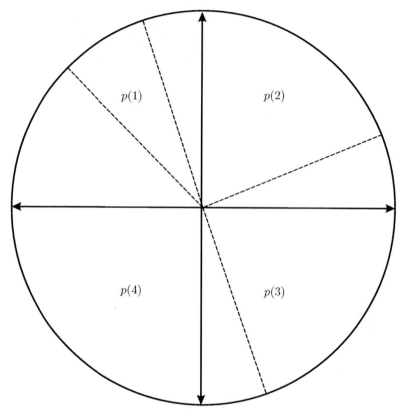

Figure 11.13: Stochastic Universal Sampling

An addition to many selection methods is "elitism": the best chromosome in the old generation replaces the worst chromosome in the new generation irrespective of whether it was selected for reproduction.[50]

Crossover. In nature the chromosomes of most species are arrayed in pairs. During sexual reproduction these pairs split and the child's chromosomes are the combination of the chromosomes of its two parents. Crossover operators mimic this process. Following HERRERA, LOZANO, and VERDEGAY (1998), p. 288ff, we describe some of these operator for real-coded GAs, where $P_1 = (p_1^1, p_1^2, \ldots, p_1^m)$ and $P_2 = (p_2^1, p_2^2, \ldots, p_2^m)$ denote the chromosomes

---

[50] See MITCHELL (1996) for further selection schemes.

of two parents, and $C_1 = (c_1^1, c_1^2, \ldots, c_1^m)$ and $C_2 = (c_2^1, c_2^2, \ldots, c_2^m)$ are their children.

1. **Simple crossover:** A position $i = 1, 2, \ldots, n-1$ is randomly chosen. The two children are:
$$C_1 = (p_1^1, p_1^2, \ldots, p_1^i, p_2^{i+1}, \ldots, p_2^m),$$
$$C_2 = (p_2^1, p_2^2, \ldots, p_2^i, p_1^{i+1}, \ldots, p_1^m).$$

2. **Shuffle crossover:** For each position $i = 1, 2, \ldots, n$ draw a random number $\lambda \in [0, 1]$. If $\lambda < 0.5$ put
$$c_1^i = p_1^i,$$
$$c_2^i = p_2^i,$$
else put
$$c_1^i = p_2^i,$$
$$c_2^i = p_1^i.$$

3. **Linear crossover:** Three offspring are built according to
$$c_1^i = \frac{1}{2}p_1^i + \frac{1}{2}p_2^i,$$
$$c_2^i = \frac{2}{3}p_1^i - \frac{1}{2}p_2^i,$$
$$c_3^i = -\frac{1}{2}p_1^i + \frac{3}{2}p_2^i,$$
and two most promising are retained for the next generation.

4. **Arithmetical crossover:** A scalar $\lambda \in [0, 1]$ is randomly chosen (or given as constant) and the chromosomes of child 1 and child 2 are build from
$$c_1^i = \lambda p_1^i + (1 - \lambda) p_2^i,$$
$$c_2^i = (1 - \lambda) p_1^i + \lambda p_2^i.$$

5. **BLX-α crossover:** One child is generated, where for each $i = 1, 2, \ldots, m$ the number c^i is randomly (uniformly) chosen from the interval
$$[p_{min} - \alpha \Delta, p_{max} + \alpha \Delta],$$
$p_{max} := \max\{p_1^i, p_2^i\}$, $p_{min} := \min\{p_1^i, p_2^i\}$, $\Delta := p_{max} - p_{min}$. HERRERA, LOZANO, and VERDEGAY (1998) report good results for $\alpha = 0.5$.

Mutation. In nature, mutations, i.e., sudden changes of the genetic code, result either from copying mistakes during sexual reproduction or are triggered in the living organism by external forces as, e.g., by radiation. In binary-coded GAs the mutation operator randomly selects a position in a bit string and changes the respective bit from 0 to 1 or vice versa. Mutation operators designed for real-codes GAs also randomly select an element of a chromosome and either add or subtract another randomly selected number. Non-uniform operators decrease this number from generation to generation towards zero and, thus, allow for the local fine-tuning of the candidate solutions. The experiments of HERRERA, LOZANO, and VERDEGAY (1998) show that non-uniform mutation is very appropriate for real-coded GAs. In our algorithm we use the following operator suggested by MICHALEWICZ (1999), p. 128. Let c_i denote the i-th element in a child chromosome selected for mutation and c'_i the mutated element. The operator selects

$$c'_i = \begin{cases} c_i + \Delta(t) & \text{if a random binary digit is 0} \\ c_i - \Delta(t) & \text{if a random binary digit is 1} \end{cases} \quad (11.109)$$
$$\Delta(t) := y(1 - r^{(1-(t/T)^b)}),$$

where y is the range of c_i and $r \in [0, 1]$ is a random number. t is the current generation and T the maximal number of iterations. Since we do not know the range of the parameters of the expectations function in advance, we draw y from a standard normal distribution. The parameter b defines the degree of non-uniformity. MICHALEWICZ (1999) suggests $b = 2$ and HERRERA, LOZANO, and VERDEGAY (1998) use $b = 5$.

Final Selection. Whether a final selection among children and parents is undertaken depends upon the choice of selection method of parents. If parents are chosen at random with replacement from generation $\mathcal{P}(t)$ one needs a final fitness tournament between parents and children to exert selection pressure. In this case the initial heterogeneity in the population decreases quickly and reasonable good solutions emerge within a few generations. However, this tight selection pressure may hinder the algorithm to sample the solution space more broadly so that only local optima are found. Therefore, there is a trade-off between tight selection and short run-time on the one hand and more precise solutions and a longer run-time on the other hand.

Implementation. This sketch of the building blocks of GAs, which is by no means exhaustive, demonstrates that the researcher has many degrees of freedom in developing his own implementation. Therefore, it is a good idea to build on GAs that have performed good in previous work.

DUFFY and MCNELIS (2002) used a genetic algorithm to find the parameters of the approximate expectations function.[51] They choose four parents at random (with replacement) from the old generation. With a probability of 0.95 the best two of the four will have two children. With equal probability of selection crossover is either arithmetical, single point, or shuffle. The probability of mutations in generation T, $\pi(t)$, is given by

$$\pi(t) = \mu_1 + \mu_2/t, \tag{11.110}$$

where $\mu_1 = 0.15$ and $\mu_2 = 0.33$. Mutations are non-uniform as given in (11.109) with $b = 2$, and there is a final fitness tournament between parents and children. The two members of the family with the best fitness pass to the new generation. In addition, the best member of the old generation replaces the worst member of the new generation (elitism).

The Fortran 95 subroutine `Search1.for` implements this GA. The user can supply the following parameters in the file `GSP1.txt`:

---

[51] In the notation used in Section 3.1.2, their solution is the minimizer of

$$\frac{1}{T} \sum_{t=1}^{T} [\phi(\gamma, \mathbf{u}_{t+1}) - \psi(\gamma, \mathbf{x}_t)]^2,$$

which does not correspond to the definition of the PEA solution found in the theoretical work of MARCET and MARSHALL (1992), (1994), which we use in Section 3.1.2.

Another application of a GA to the stochastic growth model is the paper of GOMME (1997), who solves for the policy function. His procedure replaces the worst half of solutions with the best half, plus some noise.

- npop: the size of the population,
- ngen: the number of iterations (generations),
- probc: the probability of crossover,
- mu1: the first parameter in (11.110),
- mu2: the second parameter in (11.110),
- mu3: the parameter b in (11.109).

In the Fortran 95 subroutine Search2.for we provide a more flexible implementation of a GA to solve for the parameters of the expectations function. The user can choose between two selection methods: stochastic universal sampling and the method used in Search1.for. We do not provide an option for sigma scaling, since, from our experiments, we learned that a sufficiently high probability of mutation prohibits population heterogeneity from shrinking too fast. In addition to arithmetical, single point, and shuffle crossover we allow for BLS-α and linear crossover. This is motivated by the good results obtained for these two operators in the experiments of HERRERA, LOZANO, and VERDEGAY (1998). The user can decide either to use a single operator throughout or to apply all of the operators with equal chance of selection. The program uses the same mutation operator as Search1.for. If stochastic universal sampling is used, there is no final fitness tournament. The two children always survive, except they provide invalid solutions (i.e., if it is not possible to compute the sequence $\{u_{t+1}(\gamma)\}_{t=0}^{T}$. If this happens, they are replaced by their parents.

The basic structure of both implementation is summarized in the following algorithm.

Algorithm 11.6.6 (Genetic Algorithm)

Purpose: *Find the minimum of a user defined objective function.*

Steps:

Step 1: Initialize: Set $t = 1$. Choose at random an initial population of candidate solutions $\mathcal{P}(t)$ of size n.

Step 2: Find a new set of solutions $\mathcal{P}(t+1)$: Until the size of $\mathcal{P}(t+1)$ is n, repeat these steps:

Step 2.1: Select two parents from the old population $\mathcal{P}(t-1)$.

Step 2.2: Produce two offspring (crossover).

Step 2.3: Perform random mutation of the new offspring.

Step 2.4: Depending upon the selection method in Step 2.1, either evaluate the fitness of parents and offspring and retain the two fittest or pass the two children to the next generation.

Step 3: If t=ngen terminate, otherwise return to Step 2.

Chapter 12

Various Other Tools

12.1 Difference Equations

Dynamic models are either formulated in terms of difference or differential equations. Here we review a few basic definitions and facts about difference equations.

12.1.1 Linear Difference Equations

Consider a function x that maps $t \in \mathbb{R}$ into $x(t) \in \mathbb{R}$. In practice, we do not observe economic variables x at every instant of time t. Most economic data are compiled at a yearly, quarterly, or monthly frequency. To account for that fact, we consider the function x only at equally spaced points in time: $x(t), x(t+h), x(t+2h), \ldots$, and usually normalize $h \equiv 1$. It is then common to write x_t instead of $x(t)$.

The first difference of x_t, Δx_t, is defined as

$$\Delta x_t := x_t - x_{t-1},$$

and further differences are computed according to

$$\Delta^2 x_t := \Delta x_t - \Delta x_{t-1} = x_t - 2x_{t-1} + x_{t-2},$$
$$\Delta^3 x_t := \Delta^2 x_t - \Delta^2 x_{t-1} = x_t - 3x_{t-1} + 3x_{t-2} - x_{t-3},$$
$$\vdots$$
$$\Delta^n x_t := \Delta^{n-1} x_t - \Delta^{n-1} x_{t-1}.$$

A difference equation of order n relates the function x to its n differences. The simplest of these equations is

$$\Delta x_t = x_t - x_{t-1} = ax_{t-1}, \quad a \in \mathbb{R}. \tag{12.1}$$

In this equation x_{t-1} and its first difference Δx_t are linearly related (only addition and scalar multiplication are involved). Furthermore, the coefficient at x_{t-1} does not depend on t. Therefore, equation (12.1) is a called a first order linear difference equation with constant coefficient. The unknown in this equation is the function x. For this reason equation (12.1) is a functional equation.

Assume we know the time $t = 0$ value x_0. We can then determine all future (or past) values of x_t by iterating forwards (or backwards) on (12.1):

$$\begin{aligned} x_1 &= \lambda x_0, \quad \lambda := 1 + a, \\ x_2 &= \lambda x_1 = \lambda^2 x_0, \\ x_3 &= \lambda x_2 = \lambda^3 x_0, \\ &\vdots, \\ x_t &= \lambda x_{t-1} = \lambda^t x_0. \end{aligned}$$

In most applications we are interested in the limiting behavior of x as $t \to \infty$. The previous derivations show that x approaches zero for every initial $x_0 \in \mathbb{R}$ if and only if $|\lambda| < 1$. This behavior is called asymptotic stability. Note, that this result also applies to complex numbers $a, x_0 \in \mathbb{C}$ (see equation (11.2)).

Now, consider the generalization of (12.1) to n variables $\mathbf{x} := [x_1, x_2, \ldots, x_n]' \in \mathbb{R}^n$:

$$\mathbf{x}_t = A\mathbf{x}_{t-1}. \tag{12.2}$$

What are the properties of the n by n matrix A that ensure that $\mathbf{x}_t$ is asymptotically stable? To answer this question we use the Jordan factorization of $A = MJM^{-1}$ (see equation (11.25)) to transform (12.2) into a simpler system. First, we define new variables $\mathbf{y}_t = M^{-1}\mathbf{x}_t$. Second, we multiply (12.2) from the left by M^{-1} to get

$$\underbrace{M^{-1}\mathbf{x}_t}_{=\mathbf{y}_t} = M^{-1}A\,\underbrace{\mathbf{x}_{t-1}}_{M\mathbf{y}_{t-1}},$$

$$\mathbf{y}_t = \underbrace{M^{-1}AM}_{=J}\mathbf{y}_{t-1},$$

$$\mathbf{y}_t = J\mathbf{y}_{t-1}. \tag{12.3}$$

Since J is a block-diagonal matrix, the new system is decoupled into K independent blocks:

$$\mathbf{y}_{kt} = J_k \mathbf{y}_{kt-1},$$

where the size of the vector $\mathbf{y}_{kt}$ equals the multiplicity m of the kth eigenvalue of A. For instance, if A has n distinct real or complex eigenvalues λ_i, equation (12.3) simplifies to

$$\mathbf{y}_t = \begin{bmatrix} \lambda_1 & 0 & 0 & \cdots & 0 \\ 0 & \lambda_2 & 0 & \cdots & 0 \\ \vdots & \vdots & \vdots & \ddots & \vdots \\ 0 & 0 & 0 & 0 & \lambda_n \end{bmatrix} \mathbf{y}_{t-1} \Leftrightarrow y_{it} = \lambda_i y_{it-1}, i = 1, 2, \ldots, n.$$

It is, thus, obvious that the transformed system is asymptotically stable if the absolute value of all eigenvalues is less than unity. But if $\mathbf{y}_t$ converges towards the zero vector so does the vector $\mathbf{x}_t = M\mathbf{y}_t$. Though less obvious, it can be shown that this also holds in the general case where A may have multiple eigenvalues.[1] Thus, we have the following theorem:

Theorem 12.1.1 *The linear system of difference equations* (12.2) *is asymptotically stable,*

$$\lim_{t \to \infty} \mathbf{x}_t = 0_{n \times 1},$$

if and only if every eigenvalue of A is less than unity in modulus.

Now suppose that only $n_1 < n$ eigenvalues have modulus less than unity while the remaining $n_2 = n - n_1$ eigenvalues exceed unity.

---

[1] See MURATA (1977), p. 85.

Since we may choose M so that the stable eigenvalues appear in the first blocks of J, we can partition J into

$$J = \begin{bmatrix} P_{n_1 \times n_1} & 0_{n_1 \times n_2} \\ 0_{n_2 \times n_1} & Q_{n_2 \times n_2} \end{bmatrix}$$

and $\mathbf{y}_t$ into $\mathbf{y}_t = [\mathbf{y}_{1t}, \mathbf{y}_{2t}]'$, $\mathbf{y}_{1t} = [y_{1t}, y_{2t}, \ldots, y_{n_1 t}]'$ and $\mathbf{y}_{2t} = [y_{n_2 t}, y_{n_2+1 t}, \ldots, y_{nt}]'$, so that (12.3) is given by

$$\mathbf{y}_{1t} = P \mathbf{y}_{1 t-1},$$
$$\mathbf{y}_{2t} = Q \mathbf{y}_{2 t-1}.$$

Since all the eigenvalues of P are inside the unit circle the vector $\mathbf{y}_{1t}$ approaches the zero vector as $t \to \infty$. The vector $\mathbf{y}_{2t}$, however, is farther and farther displaced from the origin as $t \to \infty$, since all the eigenvalues of Q are outside the unit circle. If we are free to choose the initial $\mathbf{y}_0$, we put $\mathbf{y}_{20} = \mathbf{0}_{n_1 \times 1}$, and, thus, can ensure that $\mathbf{y}_0$ and hence $\mathbf{x}_0 = M \mathbf{y}_0$ converges to the zero vector as $t \to \infty$. By choosing $\mathbf{y}_0 = [y_{10}, \ldots, y_{n_1 0}, 0, \ldots 0]$ we restrict the system to the stable eigenspace of the matrix A.[2]

12.1.2 Non-Linear Difference Equations

Let $f^i : \mathbb{R}^n \to \mathbb{R}, i = 1, 2, \ldots, n$ denote arbitrary differentiable functions. A system of n non–linear first–order difference equations is defined by the following set of equations:

$$\begin{bmatrix} x_{1t} \\ x_{2t} \\ \vdots \\ x_{nt} \end{bmatrix} = \begin{bmatrix} f^1(x_{1 t-1}, x_{2 t-1}, \ldots, x_{n t-1}) \\ f^2(x_{1 t-1}, x_{2 t-1}, \ldots, x_{n t-1}) \\ \vdots \\ f^n(x_{1 t-1}, x_{2 t-1}, \ldots, x_{n t-1}) \end{bmatrix}. \quad (12.4)$$

In a more compact notation this can be written as

$$\mathbf{x}_t = \mathbf{f}(\mathbf{x}_{t-1}).$$

---

[2] Remember, from Section 11.1.7, this is the set spanned by the generalized eigenvectors of A with modulus less than one.

Assume there is a point $\mathbf{x}^*$ that satisfies

$$\mathbf{x}^* = \mathbf{f}(\mathbf{x}^*).$$

Such a point is called a fixed point, a rest point or, in more economic terms, a stationary equilibrium. What can be said about the asymptotic behavior of $\mathbf{x}_t$ under the map $\mathbf{f}$? Is there a relation between the linear system (12.2) and the non-linear system? To deal with these questions consider the linear approximation of $\mathbf{f}$ at $\mathbf{x}^*$ (see equations (11.35) and (11.36) for details):

$$\mathbf{f}(\mathbf{x}+\mathbf{h}) \simeq \mathbf{f}(\mathbf{x}^*) + J(\mathbf{x}^*)\mathbf{h}, \ \mathbf{h} = \mathbf{x} - \mathbf{x}^*,$$

where $J(\mathbf{x}^*)$ is the Jacobian matrix of $\mathbf{f}$. Since $\mathbf{x}^* = \mathbf{f}(\mathbf{x}^*)$, the linear approximation of the system of non-linear difference equations (12.4) at $\mathbf{x}^*$ is given by

$$\bar{\mathbf{x}}_t = J(\mathbf{x}^*)\bar{\mathbf{x}}_{t-1}, \quad \bar{\mathbf{x}}_t := \mathbf{x}_t - \mathbf{x}^*. \qquad (12.5)$$

The relation between the non-linear system and the linearized system is the subject of the following theorem:[3]

Theorem 12.1.2 (Hartman-Grobman) *Let* $\mathbf{f} : \mathbb{R}^n \to \mathbb{R}^n$ *be a* C^1 *diffeomorphism with a hyperbolic fixed point* $\mathbf{x}^*$. *Then there exists a homeomorphism* $\mathbf{h}$ *defined on some neighborhood* U *of* $\mathbf{x}^*$ *such that* $\mathbf{h}(\mathbf{f}(\mathbf{x})) = J(\mathbf{x}^*)\mathbf{h}(\mathbf{x})$ *for all* $\mathbf{x} \in U$.

A map $\mathbf{f}$ is a homeomorphism if

1. it is a continuous one-to-one map of some subset $U \subset \mathbb{R}^n$ onto the set $Y \subset \mathbb{R}^n$, i.e., $\mathbf{f}(\mathbf{x}_1) = \mathbf{f}(\mathbf{x}_2) \Rightarrow \mathbf{x}_1 = \mathbf{x}_2$ and $\mathbf{f}(U) = Y$,
2. whose inverse $\mathbf{f}^{-1}$ is also continuous.

If both $\mathbf{f}$ and $\mathbf{f}^{-1}$ have continuous first derivatives, the homeomorphism $\mathbf{f}$ is a C^1 diffeomorphism. Finally, $\bar{\mathbf{x}}$ is a hyperbolic fixed point of $\mathbf{f}$, if the Jacobian matrix $J(\bar{\mathbf{x}})$ has no eigenvalues on the unit circle.

---
[3] See, e.g., GUCKENHEIMER and HOLMES (1983), p. 18, Theorem 1. 4 1 for a statement and PALIS and DE MELO (1982), p. 60ff for a proof.

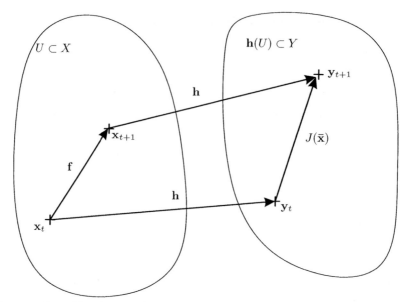

Figure 12.1: Topological Conjugacy Between **f** and $J(\bar{\mathbf{x}})$

Figure 12.1 illustrates Theorem 12.1.2. The image of the point $\mathbf{x}_t$ under the non-linear map **f** is given by $\mathbf{x}_{t+1}$. If we map $\mathbf{x}_{t+1}$ into the set $\mathbf{h}(U) \subset Y$ we get $\mathbf{y}_{t+1}$. Yet, we arrive at the same result, if we first map $\mathbf{x}_t$ into Y via the non-linear change of coordinates **h** and then apply the linear operator $J(\bar{\mathbf{x}})$ to $\mathbf{y}_t$. Two maps that share this property are called topological conjugates. This allows us to infer the dynamics of $\mathbf{x}_t$ near $\bar{\mathbf{x}}$ from the dynamics of the linear system (12.5) near the origin. Since we already know that the linear system is asymptotically stable if all the eigenvalues of $J(\bar{\mathbf{x}})$ are inside the unit circle, we can conclude from Theorem 12.1.2 that under this condition all $\mathbf{x}_0$ sufficiently close to $\bar{\mathbf{x}}$ will tend to $\bar{\mathbf{x}}$ as $t \to \infty$. A fixed point with this property is called locally asymptotically stable.

We can also extend our results with respect to the case where the matrix A in (12.2) has n_1 eigenvalues inside and $n_2 = n - n_1$ eigenvalues outside the unit circle to the non-linear system of difference equations (12.4). For that purpose we define two sets. The local stable manifold of $\bar{\mathbf{x}}$ is the set of all $\mathbf{x} \in U$ that tend to $\bar{\mathbf{x}}$ as $t \to \infty$:

$$W^s_{loc}(\bar{\mathbf{x}}) := \left\{\mathbf{x} \in U : \lim_{t \to \infty} \mathbf{f}^t(\mathbf{x}) \to \bar{\mathbf{x}} \text{ and } \mathbf{f}^t(\mathbf{x}) \in U \,\forall t \geq 0\right\}.$$

Here $\mathbf{f}^t(\cdot)$ is recursively defined via $\mathbf{f}^t = \mathbf{f}(\mathbf{f}^{t-1}(\cdot))$. The local unstable manifold is the set of all $\mathbf{x} \in U$ that tend to $\bar{\mathbf{x}}$ as we move backwards in time:

$$W^u_{loc}(\bar{\mathbf{x}}) := \left\{\mathbf{x} \in U : \lim_{t \to -\infty} \mathbf{f}^t(\mathbf{x}) \to \bar{\mathbf{x}} \text{ and } \mathbf{f}^t(\mathbf{x}) \in U \,\forall t \leq 0\right\}.$$

Together with Theorem 12.1.2 the next theorem shows that if we restrict the initial point $\mathbf{x}_0$ to lie in the stable eigenspace of $J(\bar{\mathbf{x}})$ then for $\bar{\mathbf{x}}_0$ sufficiently close to $\bar{\mathbf{x}}$ the dynamics of the linear system mimics the dynamics of the non-linear system on the local stable manifold $W^s_{loc}(\bar{\mathbf{x}})$:[4]

Theorem 12.1.3 (Stable Manifold Theorem) *Let* $\mathbf{f} : \mathbb{R}^n \to \mathbb{R}^n$ *be a* C^1 *diffeomorphism with a hyperbolic fixed point* $\mathbf{x}^*$. *Then there are local stable and unstable manifolds* W^s_{loc}, W^u_{loc}, *tangent to the eigenspaces* $E^s_{\bar{\mathbf{x}}}$, $E^u_{\bar{\mathbf{x}}}$ *of* $J(\bar{\mathbf{x}})$ *and of corresponding dimensions.*

Figure 12.2 illustrates this theorem. Note, that any time path that is neither in the local stable nor in the local unstable manifold also diverges from $\bar{\mathbf{x}}$ as $t \to \infty$, as the path represented by the broken line.

12.2 Markov Processes

Markov processes are an indispensable ingredient of stochastic DGE models. They preserve the recursive structure that these models inherit from their deterministic relatives. In this section we review a few results about these processes that we have used repeatedly in the development of solution methods and in applications.

---

[4] See, e.g., GUCKENHEIMER and HOLMES (1983), p. 18, Theorem 1.4.2 for a statement of this theorem and PALIS and DE MELO (1982), p. 75ff for a proof. GRANDMONT (1988) provides more detailed theorems that relate the solution of the non-linear system (12.4) to the solution of the linear system (12.2).

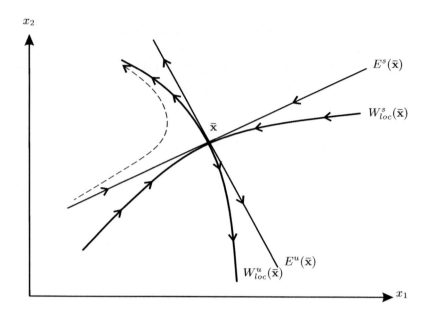

Figure 12.2: Local Stable and Unstable Manifold

Stochastic Processes. A stochastic process is a time sequence of random variables $\{Z_t\}_{t=0}^{\infty}$. If the members Z_t of this sequence have a countable number of realizations $Z_t \in \{z_1, z_2, \ldots, z_n\}$ the process is discrete valued as opposed to a continuous valued process whose realizations are taken from an interval of the real line $Z_t \in [a, b] \subseteq \mathbb{R}$. This interval is known as the support of the process. We say that the elements of a stochastic process are identically and independently distributed (iid for short), if the probability distribution is the same for each member of the process Z_t and independent of the realizations of other members of the process $Z_{t+s}, s \neq 0$. In this case the probability of the event $[Z_1 = z_1, Z_2 = z_2, \ldots Z_T = z_T]$ is given by

$$Prob[Z_1 = z_1, Z_2 = z_2, \ldots Z_T = z_T]$$
$$= Prob(Z_1 = z_1) \times Prob(Z_2 = z_2) \times \cdots \times Prob(Z_T = z_T).$$

A stochastic process has the Markov property, if the probability distribution of Z_{t+1} only depends upon the realization of Z_t.

The AR(1) Process. An example of a Markov process is the first-order autoregressive processs (AR(1) for short)

$$Z_t = (1-\varrho)\bar{Z} + \varrho Z_{t-1} + \epsilon_t, \quad \varrho \in [0,1), \ \epsilon_t \sim N(0,\sigma^2). \quad (12.6)$$

The random variable ϵ_t, the so called innovations of the AR(1)-process, are iid draws from a normal distribution with mean 0 and variance σ^2. Given Z_t, next period's shock Z_{t+1} is normally distributed with mean $E(Z_{t+1}|Z_t) = (1-\varrho)\bar{Z} + \varrho Z_t$ and variance $\text{var}(Z_{t+1}|Z_t) = \sigma^2$. Since higher order autoregressive processes can be reduced to first-order vector autoregressive processes the first-order process plays a prominent role in the development of stochastic Ramsey models. As an example, consider the second-order autoregressive process

$$Z_t = \varrho_1 Z_{t-1} + \varrho_2 Z_{t-2} + \epsilon_t. \quad (12.7)$$

Defining $X_t = Z_{t-1}$ equation (12.7) can be written as

$$Z_{t+1} = \varrho_1 Z_t + \varrho_2 X_t + \epsilon_t,$$
$$X_{t+1} = Z_t,$$

which is a first-order vector autoregressive process in $(Z_t, X_t)'$ with innovations $(\epsilon_t, 0)'$.

Markov Chains. Markov chains are discrete valued Markov processes. They are characterized by three objects:

1. The column vector $\mathbf{z} = [z_1, z_2, \ldots, z_n]'$ summarizes the n different realizations of Z_t.
2. The probability distribution of the initial date $t=0$ is represented by the vector $\boldsymbol{\pi}_0 = [\pi_{01}, \pi_{02}, \ldots, \pi_{0n}]'$, where π_{0i} denotes the probability of the event $Z_0 = z_i$.
3. The dynamics of the process is represented by a transition matrix $P = (p_{ij})$, where p_{ij} denotes the probability of the event $Z_{t+1} = z_j | Z_t = z_i$, i.e., the probability that next period's state is z_j given that this period's state is z_i. Therefore, $p_{ij} \geq 0$ and $\sum_{j=1}^{m} p_{ij} = 1$.

Thus, given $Z_t = z_i$ the conditional expectation of Z_{t+1} is $E(Z_{t+1}|Z_t = z_i) = P_i \mathbf{z}$, where P_i denotes the i-th row of P and the conditional variance is $\text{var}(Z_{t+1}|Z_t = z_i) = \sum_j P_{ij}(z_j - P_i\mathbf{z})^2$. The probability distribution of Z_t evolves according to

$$\boldsymbol{\pi}'_{t+1} = \boldsymbol{\pi}'_t P. \tag{12.8}$$

Computation of the Ergodic Distribution. The limit of (12.8) for $t \to \infty$ is the time invariant, stationary, or ergodic distribution of the Markov chain $(\mathbf{z}, P, \boldsymbol{\pi}_0)$. It is defined by

$$\boldsymbol{\pi}' = \boldsymbol{\pi}'P \iff (I - P')\boldsymbol{\pi} = \mathbf{0}. \tag{12.9}$$

Does this limit exist? And if it exists, is it independent of the initial distribution $\boldsymbol{\pi}_0$? The answer to both questions is yes, if either all $p_{ij} > 0$ or, if for some integer $k \geq 1$ all elements of the matrix

$$P^k := \underbrace{P \times P \cdots \times P}_{k-\text{elements}}$$

are positive, i.e., $p_{ij}^k > 0$ for all (i, j). This latter condition states that it is possible to reach each state j in at least k steps from state i.[5] Obviously, this is a weaker condition than $p_{ij} > 0$ for all (i, j). As an example, consider the transition matrix

$$P = \begin{pmatrix} 0.0 & 1.0 \\ 0.9 & 0.1 \end{pmatrix},$$

for which

$$P^2 = P \times P = \begin{pmatrix} 0.9 & 0.1 \\ 0.09 & 0.91 \end{pmatrix}.$$

We need to compute the invariant distribution in many applications. For instance, in Section 7.2 we must solve for the stationary distribution of employment in oder to find the stationary distribution of assets. The states of the respective Markov chain are

---

[5] See, e.g., LJUNGQVIST and SARGENT (2004), Theorem 1 and Theorem 2.

$z_1 = e$ and $z_2 = u$, where e (u) denotes (un)employment, and π_{01} ($\pi_{02} = 1 - \pi_{01}$) is the probability that a randomly selected agent from the unit interval is employed in period $t = 0$. The transition matrix P is given by

$$P = \begin{pmatrix} p_{uu} & p_{ue} \\ p_{eu} & p_{ee} \end{pmatrix} = \begin{pmatrix} 0.5000 & 0.5000 \\ 0.0435 & 0.9565 \end{pmatrix},$$

where p_{uu} (p_{ue}) denotes the probability that an unemployed agent stays unemployed (becomes employed).

One obvious way to find the stationary distribution is to iterate over equation (12.8) until convergence. When we start with an arbitrary fraction of unemployed and employed agents of $(0.5, 0.5)$, say, and iterate over (12.8) we get the sequence in Table 12.1, which converges quickly to $(0.08, 0.92)$, the stationary probabilities of being (un)employed.

Table 12.1

Iteration No.	π_u	π_e
0	0.500000	0.500000
1	0.271750	0.728250
2	0.167554	0.832446
3	0.119988	0.880012
4	0.098275	0.901725
5	0.088362	0.911638
10	0.080202	0.919798
20	0.080037	0.919963

Another procedure to compute the stationary distribution of a Markov chain is by means of Monte Carlo simulations. For the two-state chain of the previous example this is easily done: assume an initial state of employment z_{0i}, for example $z_{02} = e$. Use a uniform random number generator with the support $[0, 1]$. If the random number is less than 0.9565, $z_{12} = e$, otherwise the agent is unemployed in period 1, $z_{11} = u$. In the next period, the agent is either employed or unemployed. If employed, the agent remains employed if the random number of this period is less than 0.9565 and becomes unemployed otherwise. If unemployed, the agent remains unemployed if the random number of this period is less than 0.5 and becomes employed otherwise. Continue this process for T periods and count the number of times the agent is either employed or unemployed. The relative frequencies will converge slowly to the ergodic distribution according to the Law of Large Numbers. In our computation, we get the simulation results displayed in Table 12.2. Notice that this procedure converges very

Table 12.2

Iteration No.	π_u	π_e
10	0.10	0.90
100	0.12	0.88
1000	0.063	0.937
10000	0.0815	0.9185
100000	0.0809	0.9191
500000	0.0799	0.9201

slowly. Furthermore, if the Markov chain has more than $n = 2$ states this becomes a very cumbersome procedure. For this reason, we will usually employ a third, more direct way to compute the ergodic distribution. Observe that the definition of the invariant distribution (12.9) implies that π is an eigenvector to the eigenvalue of one of the matrix $-P'$, where π has been normalized so that $\sum_{i=1}^{n} \pi_i = 1$. Solving the eigenvalue problem for the matrix given above gives $\pi_1 = 0.0800$ and $\pi_2 = 0.920$. An equivalent procedure uses the fact that the matrix $I - P'$ has rank $n-1$ (given that P' has rank n) and that the π_i must sum to one. Therefore, the vector π must solve the following system of linear equations:

$$\pi' \begin{bmatrix} p_{11}-1 & p_{12} & \cdots & p_{1,n-1} & 1 \\ p_{21} & p_{22}-1 & \cdots & p_{2,n-1} & 1 \\ \vdots & \vdots & \vdots & \vdots & \vdots \\ p_{n-1,1} & p_{n-1,2} & \cdots & p_{n-1,n-1}-1 & 1 \\ p_{n1} & p_{n2} & \cdots & p_{n,n-1} & 1 \end{bmatrix} = (0,\ldots,0,1).$$

We provide the procedure `equivec1.g` to perform this task.

Markov Chain Approximations of AR(1) Processes. In Section 1.3.3 we extend the value function iteration method from Section 1.2.3 to solve the stochastic Ramsey model when the productivity shock is a finite state Markov chain. Empirically, however, the shift parameter of the production function resembles an AR(1)-process. Fortunately, TAUCHEN (1986) develops a method for choosing values for the realizations and the transition matrix so that the resulting Markov chain closely mimics the underlying continuous valued autoregressive process.

Consider the process

$$Z_{t+1} = \varrho Z_t + \epsilon_t, \quad \epsilon_t \sim N(0, \sigma_\epsilon^2).$$

The unconditional mean and variance of this process are 0 and $\sigma_Z^2 = \sigma_\epsilon^2/(1-\varrho^2)$.[6] TAUCHEN (1986) proposes to choose a grid $\mathscr{Z} = [z_1, z_2, \ldots, z_m]$ of equidistant points $z_1 < z_2 < \ldots, < z_m$, whose upper end point is a multiple, say λ, of the standard deviation of the autoregressive process, $z_m = \lambda \sigma_Z$ and whose lower end point is $z_1 = -z_m$. For a given realization $z_i \in \mathscr{Z}$ the variable $z := \varrho z_i + \epsilon$ is normally distributed with mean ϱz_i and variance σ_ϵ^2. Let dz denote half of the distance between two consecutive grid points. The probability that z is in the interval $[z_j - dz, z_j + dz]$ is given by

$$prob(z_j - dz \leq z \leq z_j + dz) = \pi(z_j + dz) - \pi(z_j - dz)$$

where $\pi(\cdot)$ denotes the cumulative distribution function of the normal distribution with mean ϱz_i and variance σ^2. Equivalently, the variable $v := (z - \varrho z_i)/\sigma_\epsilon$ has a standard normal distribution. Thus, the probability to switch from state z_i to state z_j for $j = 2, 3, \ldots, m-1$, say p_{ij}, is given by the area under the probability density function of the standard normal distribution in the interval

$$\left[\frac{z_j - \varrho z_i - dz}{\sigma_\epsilon}, \frac{z_j - \varrho z_i + dz}{\sigma_\epsilon}\right].$$

The probability to arrive at state z_1 is the area under the probability density in the interval $[-\infty, z_1 + dz]$. Since $\sum_j p_{ij} = 1$, the

---

[6] See, e.g., HAMILTON (1994), p. 53.

probability to go from any state i to the upper bound z_m is simply $p_{im} = 1 - \sum_{j=1}^{m-1} p_{ij}$.

We summarize this method in the following steps:

Algorithm 12.2.1 (Markov Chain Approximation)

Purpose: *Finite state Markov chain approximation of first order autoregressive process*

Steps:

Step 1: Compute the discrete approximation of the realizations: Let ϱ and σ_ϵ denote the autoregressive parameter and the standard deviation of innovations, respectively. Select the size of the grid by choosing $\lambda \in \mathbb{R}_{++}$ so that $z_1 = -\lambda \sigma_\epsilon / \sqrt{1 - \varrho^2}$. Choose the number of grid points m. Put $step = -2z_1/(m-1)$ and for $i = 1, 2, ..., m$ compute $z_i = z_1 + (i-1)step$.

Step 2: Compute the transition matrix $P = (p_{ij})$: Let $\pi(\cdot)$ denote the cumulative distribution function of the standard normal distribution. For $i = 1, 2, \ldots, m$ put

$$p_{i1} = \pi\left(\frac{z_1 - \varrho z_i}{\sigma_\epsilon} + \frac{step}{2\sigma_\epsilon}\right),$$
$$p_{ij} = \pi\left(\frac{z_j - \varrho z_i}{\sigma_\epsilon} + \frac{step}{2\sigma_\epsilon}\right) - \pi\left(\frac{z_j - \varrho z_i}{\sigma_\epsilon} - \frac{step}{2\sigma_\epsilon}\right),$$
$$j = 2, 3, \ldots, m-1,$$
$$p_{im} = 1 - \sum_{j=1}^{m-1} p_{ij}.$$

TAUCHEN (1986) reports the results of Monte Carlo experiments that show that choosing $m = 9$ and $\lambda = 3$ gives an adequate representation of the underlying AR(1)-process. Our Gauss procedure MarkovAR in the file ToolBox.src implements the above algorithm. It takes ϱ, σ_ϵ, λ, and m as input and returns the vector $\mathbf{z} = [z_1, z_2, ..., z_m]'$ and the transition matrix P.

12.3 DM-Statistic

In this section we consider the DM-statistic proposed by DEN HAAN and MARCET (1994). It is measure of the accuracy of an approximate solution of a stochastic DGE model, based on the residuals of the model's Euler equations.

Single Equation. For the sake of concreteness let us return to the stochastic growth model in Example 1.3.2. The ex-post forecast error obtained from the Euler equation (3.1b),

$$C_t^{-\eta} = \beta E_t \left[C_{t+1}^{-\eta}(1 - \delta + \alpha Z_{t+1} K_{t+1}^{\alpha-1}) \right],$$

is defined by

$$y_t := \beta \left[C_{t+1}^{-\eta}(1 - \delta + \alpha Z_{t+1} K_{t+1}^{\alpha-1}) \right] - C_t^{-\eta}.$$

Any deviation of y_t from zero is due to forecast errors. Since the household's expectations are rational, the forecast errors are uncorrelated with any variable whose realization is known to the household prior to period $t+1$. Put differently, it should not be possible to predict y_t from past information on, say, consumption C and the productivity shock Z.

Let us state this proposition in more formal terms. Consider the linear regression model

$$y_t = \sum_{i=1}^{n} a_i x_{ti} + \epsilon_t, \quad t = 1, 2, \ldots, T. \tag{12.10}$$

The x_{it} are the n variables that we use to test our proposition. For instance, this list may include consumption and the productivity shock at various lags. The error term ϵ_t captures all deviations of y_t from zero that the household cannot predict from the information conveyed by the row vector $\mathbf{x}_t := [x_{t1}, x_{t2}, \ldots, x_{tn}]'$. When we say y_t is unpredictable, we posit $\mathbf{a} = [a_1, a_2, \ldots, a_n]' = \mathbf{0}$. A bad solution, however, should violate this condition. Using the usual econometric notation, $\mathbf{y} := [y_1, y_2, \ldots, y_T]'$ and $X = [\mathbf{x}_1, \mathbf{x}_2, \ldots, \mathbf{x}_T]$, the normal equations of the least squares estimator of $\mathbf{a}$, denoted by $\hat{\mathbf{a}}$, may be written as

$$X'X\hat{\mathbf{a}} = X'\mathbf{y}.$$

Thus, $E(\hat{\mathbf{a}}) = \mathbf{a} = \mathbf{0}$, is equivalent to

$E(X'\mathbf{y}) = \mathbf{0}.$

The sample analog of $E(X'\mathbf{y})$ is

$$\mathbf{q} := \begin{bmatrix} \frac{1}{T}\sum_{t=1}^{T} y_t x_{t1} \\ \frac{1}{T}\sum_{t=1}^{T} y_t x_{t2} \\ \vdots \\ \frac{1}{T}\sum_{t=1}^{T} y_t x_{tn} \end{bmatrix}. \tag{12.11}$$

Of course, given any time series of y_t and $\mathbf{x}_t$ computed from a solution of the model, the vector $\mathbf{q}$ is never precisely equal to the zero vector, as is the estimate $\hat{\mathbf{a}}$. DEN HAAN and MARCET (1994) propose a Wald-type statistic to test, whether any deviations of (12.11) from zero are only due to sampling variability. Specifically, they propose the statistic

$$\mathrm{DM}(n) := T\mathbf{q}'\left[\mathrm{v\hat{a}r}(\mathbf{q})\right]^{-1}\mathbf{q},$$

where $\mathrm{v\hat{a}r}(\mathbf{q})$ is a consistent estimate of the variance of $\mathbf{q}$. This variance is given by:

$$\begin{aligned} \mathrm{var}(\mathbf{q}) &:= E[(\mathbf{q} - E(\mathbf{q}))(\mathbf{q} - E(\mathbf{q}))'] = E[\mathbf{q}\mathbf{q}'], \\ &= E[X'\mathbf{y}\mathbf{y}'X] = E[X'(X\mathbf{a} + \boldsymbol{\epsilon})(\boldsymbol{\epsilon}' + \mathbf{a}'X')X], \\ &= E[(X'X\mathbf{a} + X'\boldsymbol{\epsilon})(\boldsymbol{\epsilon}'X + \mathbf{a}'X'X)] = E[X'\boldsymbol{\epsilon}\boldsymbol{\epsilon}'X]. \end{aligned}$$

It is well known from WHITE (1980) that a consistent estimator of $E(X'\boldsymbol{\epsilon}\boldsymbol{\epsilon}'X)$ is given by

$$\mathrm{v\hat{a}r}(\mathbf{q}) = \frac{1}{T}X'\hat{\Sigma}X, \quad \hat{\Sigma} = \begin{bmatrix} \hat{\epsilon}_1^2 & 0 & 0 & \cdots & 0 \\ 0 & \hat{\epsilon}_2^2 & 0 & \cdots & 0 \\ \vdots & \vdots & \vdots & \ddots & \vdots \\ 0 & 0 & 0 & \cdots & \hat{\epsilon}_T^2 \end{bmatrix}, \tag{12.12}$$

where $\hat{\epsilon}_t = y_t - X\hat{\mathbf{a}}$ is the estimated error for observation t. This estimate is based on the assumption that the errors in the regression (12.10) are not autocorrelated. This assumption can be violated, if the conditional expectation on the rhs of the Euler equation includes variables dated $t+2$ and later. Consistent covariance estimators for this case can be found in the literature on the generalized method of moments estimator.[7] Note, however, that non of our applications belongs to this class of problems. The asymptotic distribution of the DM statistic is χ^2 with n degrees of freedom.[8] Replacing vâr($\mathbf{q}$) by the estimator (12.12) the DM-statistic can be rewritten as

$$\mathrm{DM}(n) = \mathbf{y}'X \left[\sum_t \mathbf{x}_t \mathbf{x}'_t \hat{\epsilon}_t^2 \right]^{-1} X'\mathbf{y}. \tag{12.13}$$

Any approximate solution never exactly satisfies the condition $E(X'\mathbf{y}) = \mathbf{0}$. Hence, if the researcher uses a very large sample size T the statistic will discover this and reject the null. Therefore, the DM-test is the more stringent, the larger T is.

To reduce the type I error (rejection of the null when it is true) DEN HAAN and MARCET (1994) propose the following procedure: For a given sequence of shocks compute the approximate solution for a large T; use this solution, draw a new sequence of shocks for a sample size T_2 much smaller than T, compute the respective time path of the model's variables and calculate the DM-statistic for these observations. Repeat this very often[9] and compute the percentage of the DM-statistic that is below the lower or above the upper 2.5 percent critical values of the $\chi^2(m)$ distribution, respectively. If these fractions differ markedly from the theoretical 5 percent, this indicates an inaccurate solution.

Multiple Equations. The DM-statistic is also applicable to models with more than one Euler equation. The simplest thing to do, of course, is to compute this statistic for every single equation. However, this neglects the fact that the respective equations are interrelated and it does not provide an answer to the question

---
[7] See, e.g., NEWEY and WEST (1987). .
[8] See DEN HAAN and MARCET (1994).
[9] In their examples, DEN HAAN and MARCET (1994) compute 500 realizations of DM with a sample size of T_2=3,000 and $T = 29,000$.

whether the approximate solution in general is sufficiently accurate. Fortunately it is not difficult to generalize the presentation from the previous paragraph to the case of m Euler equations.

Let $\mathbf{y}_j := [y_{j1}, y_{j2}, \ldots, y_{jT}]$ denote the residual computed from the model's j-th Euler equation, $j = 1, 2, \ldots, m$. Then we wish to test, whether the nm column vector

$$\mathbf{q} := \begin{bmatrix} X'\mathbf{y}_1/T \\ X'\mathbf{y}_2/T \\ \vdots \\ X'\mathbf{y}_m/T \end{bmatrix} \tag{12.14}$$

is close to the zero vector. Note that we use the same set of explanatory variables X in each of the m regressions. The variance of $\mathbf{q}$ is given by

$$\mathrm{var}(\mathbf{q}) = E \begin{bmatrix} X'\mathbf{y}_1\mathbf{y}_1'X & \cdots & X'\mathbf{y}_1\mathbf{y}_m'X \\ \vdots & \ddots & \vdots \\ X'\mathbf{y}_m\mathbf{y}_1'X & \cdots & X'\mathbf{y}_m\mathbf{y}_m'X \end{bmatrix},$$

$$= E \begin{bmatrix} X'\boldsymbol{\epsilon}_1\boldsymbol{\epsilon}_1'X & \cdots & X'\boldsymbol{\epsilon}_1\boldsymbol{\epsilon}_m'X \\ \vdots & \ddots & \vdots \\ X'\boldsymbol{\epsilon}_m\boldsymbol{\epsilon}_1'X & \cdots & X'\boldsymbol{\epsilon}_m\boldsymbol{\epsilon}_m'X \end{bmatrix},$$

where $\boldsymbol{\epsilon}_j = [\epsilon_{1j}, \epsilon_{2j}, \ldots, \epsilon_{Tj}]'$ is the vector of errors in the j-th regression of $\mathbf{y}_j$ on the vector $\mathbf{a}_j$ and X. A consistent estimate of this matrix in the case of heteroscedastic but serially uncorrelated errors is given by

$$\hat{\mathrm{var}}(\mathbf{q}) := \frac{1}{T} \sum_{t=1}^{T} \begin{bmatrix} \hat{\epsilon}_{1t}^2 & \hat{\epsilon}_{1t}\hat{\epsilon}_{2t} & \cdots & \hat{\epsilon}_{1t}\hat{\epsilon}_{mt} \\ \hat{\epsilon}_{2t}\hat{\epsilon}_{1t} & \hat{\epsilon}_{2t}^2 & \cdots & \hat{\epsilon}_{2t}\hat{\epsilon}_{mt} \\ \vdots & \vdots & \ddots & \vdots \\ \hat{\epsilon}_{mt}\hat{\epsilon}_{1t} & \hat{\epsilon}_{mt}\hat{\epsilon}_{2t} & \cdots & \hat{\epsilon}_{mt}^2 \end{bmatrix} \otimes \mathbf{x}_t'\mathbf{x}_t, \tag{12.16}$$

where $\otimes$ denotes the Kronecker product. The statistic

$$\mathrm{DM}(nm) = T\mathbf{q}'\left[\hat{\mathrm{var}}(\mathbf{q})\right]^{-1}\mathbf{q}$$

with $\mathbf{q}$ and $\hat{\mathrm{var}}(\mathbf{q})$ as defined in (12.14) and (12.16), respectively, is asymptotically distributed as a $\chi^2(nm)$ random variable.

12.4 The HP-Filter

In this section we consider the Hodrick-Prescott or for short the HP-filter that has been used in numerous studies to derive the cyclical component of a time series. This filter is proposed in a discussion paper by ROBERT HODRICK and EDWARD PRESCOTT that circulated in the nineteen eighties and which was recently published.[10]

Let $(y_t)_{t=1}^T$ denote the log of a time series that may be considered as realization of a non-stationary stochastic process. The growth component $(g_t)_{t=1}^T$ of this series as defined by the HP-Filter is the solution to the following minimization problem:

$$\min_{(g_t)_{t=1}^T} \sum_{t=1}^{T}(y_t - g_t) + \lambda \sum_{t=2}^{T-1}[(g_{t+1} - g_t) - (g_t - g_{t-1})]^2. \quad (12.17)$$

The parameter λ must be chosen by the researcher. Its role can be easily seen by considering the two terms to the right of the minimization operator. If λ were equal to zero, the obvious solution to (12.17) is $y_t = g_t$, i.e., the growth component were set equal to the original series. As λ gets large and larger it becomes important to keep the second term as small as possible. Since this term equals the growth rate of the original series between two successive periods, the ultimate solution for $\lim_\lambda \to \infty$ is a constant growth rate g. Thus, by choosing the size of the weight λ the filter returns anything between the original time series and a linear time trend.

The first order conditions of the minimization problem imply the following system of linear equations:

$$A\mathbf{g} = \mathbf{y}, \quad (12.18)$$

where $\mathbf{g} = [g_1, g_2, \ldots, g_T]'$, $\mathbf{y} = [y_1, y_2, \ldots, y_T]'$, and A is the tridiagonal matrix

---

[10] See HODRICK and PRESCOTT (1980) and (1997), respectively.

$$A = \begin{bmatrix} 1+\lambda & -2\lambda & \lambda & 0 & 0 & \cdots & 0 & 0 & 0 \\ -2\lambda & 1+5\lambda & -4\lambda & \lambda & 0 & \cdots & 0 & 0 & 0 \\ \lambda & -4\lambda & 1+6\lambda & -4\lambda & \lambda & \cdots & 0 & 0 & 0 \\ 0 & \lambda & -4\lambda & 1+6\lambda & -4\lambda & \cdots & 0 & 0 & 0 \\ 0 & 0 & \lambda & -4\lambda & 1+6\lambda & \cdots & 0 & 0 & 0 \\ \vdots & \vdots & \vdots & \vdots & \vdots & \ddots & \vdots & \vdots & \vdots \\ 0 & 0 & 0 & 0 & 0 & \cdots & 1+6\lambda & -4\lambda & \lambda \\ 0 & 0 & 0 & 0 & 0 & \cdots & -4\lambda & 1+5\lambda & -2\lambda \\ 0 & 0 & 0 & 0 & 0 & \cdots & \lambda & -2\lambda & 1+\lambda \end{bmatrix}.$$

Note, that A can be factored in[11]

$$A = I + \lambda K'K,$$

$$K = \begin{bmatrix} 1 & -2 & 1 & 0 & 0 & \cdots & 0 & 0 & 0 \\ 0 & 1 & -2 & 0 & 0 & \cdots & 0 & 0 & 0 \\ 0 & 0 & 1 & -2 & 1 & \cdots & 0 & 0 & 0 \\ \vdots & \vdots & \vdots & \vdots & \vdots & \ddots & \vdots & \vdots & \vdots \\ 0 & 0 & 0 & 0 & 0 & \cdots & 1 & -2 & 1 \end{bmatrix},$$

which shows that A is positive definite.[12] Linear algebra routines that use sparse matrix methods[13] can be used to solve the system (12.18). These methods require considerably less workspace than methods that operate on the matrix A. For instance, the Fortran subroutine `DLSLQS` available in the `IMSL` library requires only the main and the two upper codiagonals of A, i.e., a $3 \times T$-matrix, whereas general linear system solvers require the full $T \times T$ matrix A. Our implementation of the HP-Filter in the Gauss procedure `HPFilter` in the file `Toolbox.src` uses the command `bandsolpd` to solve (12.18).

---

[11] See BRANDNER and NEUSSER (1990), p. 5.
[12] A matrix A is called positive definite, if for each vector $\mathbf{x} \neq \mathbf{0}$

$$\mathbf{x}'A\mathbf{x} > 0.$$

The matrix $I + \lambda K'K$ clearly satisfies this requirement, since

$$\mathbf{x}'[I + \lambda K'K]\mathbf{x} = \sum_{i=1}^{T} x_i^2 + \lambda \sum_{i=1}^{T} z_i^2, \quad \mathbf{z} := K\mathbf{x}.$$

[13] A sparse matrix is a matrix that has most of its entries set to zero. This can be used to reduce the size of the memory in which the matrix is stored on a computer and to develop fast algorithms that operate with these matrices.

The cyclical component of **y**,

$$\mathbf{c} = \mathbf{y} - \mathbf{g} = [I - A^{-1}]\mathbf{y},$$

remains unchanged if a linear time trend

$$\mathbf{a} := \begin{bmatrix} a_1 + a_2 \\ a_1 + 2a_2 \\ \vdots \\ a_1 + Ta_2 \end{bmatrix}$$

is added to the time series $(y_t)_{t=1}^T$. To see this, note that[14]

$$\mathbf{c} = [I - A^{-1}][\mathbf{y} + \mathbf{a}] = [I - A^{-1}]\mathbf{y} + \underbrace{[I - A^{-1}]\mathbf{a}}_{=\mathbf{0}}.$$

The usual choice of the filter weight is $\lambda = 1600$ for quarterly data. It rests on the observation that with this choice the filter "removes all cycles longer than 32 quarters leaving shorter cycles unchanged" (BRANDNER and NEUSSER (1990), p. 7). For yearly data RAVN and UHLIG (2001) propose $\lambda = 6.5$ whereas BAXTER and KING (1999) advocate for $\lambda = 10$.

---

[14] This statement can be proven by noting that

$$[I - A^{-1}]\mathbf{a} = \mathbf{0} \Leftrightarrow A^{-1}[A - I]\mathbf{a} = \mathbf{0} \Leftrightarrow [A - I]\mathbf{a} = \mathbf{0},$$

and considering the product on the rightmost side of this statement.

References

Aiyagari, Rao S. 1994. Uninsured Idiosyncratic Risk and Aggregate Saving. *Quarterly Journal of Economics.* Vol. 109. pp. 659-84.

Aiyagari, Rao S. 1995. Optimal Capital Income Taxation with Incomplete Markets, Borrowing Constraints and Constant Discounting. *Journal of Political Economy.* Vol. 103. pp. 1158-75.

Algan, Yann, Oliver Allais, and Wouter J. den Haan. 2008. Solving Heterogeneous-Agent Models with Parameterized Cross-Sectional Distributions. *Journal of Economic Dynamics and Control.* Vol. 32 .pp. 875-908.

Ambler, Steve and Alain Paquet. 1996. Fiscal spending shocks, endogenous government spending, and real business cycles. *Journal of Economic Dynamics and Control.* Vol. 20. pp. 237-56.

Amisano, Gianni and Carlo Giannini. 1997. Topics in Structural VAR Econometrics, 2nd Ed. Berlin: Springer.

Antony, Jürgen and Alfred Maußner. 2008. A Further Note on a new Class of Solutions to Dynamic Programming Problems Arising in Economic Growth. Universität Augsburg - Volkswirtschaftliche Diskussionsreihe Nr. 297.

Auerbach, Alan J. and Laurence J. Kotlikoff. 1987. Dynamic Fical Policy, Cambridge: Cambridge University Press.

Auerbach, Alan J., Laurence J. Kotlikoff, and J. Skinner. 1983. The Efficiency Gains from Dynamic Tax Reform. *International Economic Review.* Vol. 24. pp. 81-100.

Aruoba, S. Boragan, Jesús Fernández-Villaverde, and Juan F. Rubio-Ramírez. 2006. Comparing Solution Methods for Dynamic Equilibrium Economies. *Journal of Economic Dynamics and Control.* Vol. 30. pp. 2477-2508.

Baxter, Marianne and Robert G. King. 1993. Fiscal policy in general equilibrium. *American Economic Review.* Vol. 83. pp. 315-334.

Baxter, Marianne and Robert G. King. 1999. Measuring Business Cycles: Approximate Band-Pass Filters for Economic Time Series. *Review of Economics and Statistics.* pp. 575-593.

Becker, Gary S. and Nigel Tomes. 1979. An Equilibrium Theory of the Distribution of Income and Intergenerational Mobility. *Journal of Political Economy.* Vol. 87. pp. 1153-89.

Benhabib, Jess, Richard Roberson, and Randall Wright. 1991. Homework in Macroeconomics: Household Production and Aggregate Fluctuations, *Journal of Political Economy*, Vol. 99, pp. 1166-87

Benhabib, Jess and Aldo Rustichini. 1994 .A Note on a New Class of Solutions to Dynamic Programming Problems arising in Economic Growth. *Journal of Economic Dynamics and Control.* Vol. 18. pp. 807-813.

Benigno , Pierpaolo and Michal Woodford. 2007. Linear-Quadratic Approximation of Optimal Policy Problems. Mimeo.

Bergin, Paul R. and Robert C. Feenstra. 2000. Staggered Price Setting, Translog Preferences, and Endogenous Persistence. *Journal of Monetary Economics.* Vol. 45. pp. 657-680.

Blanchard, Oliver J. and Charles M. Kahn. 1980. The Solution of Linear Difference Models Under Rational Expectations. *Econometrica.* Vol. 48. pp. 1305-1311.

Boldrin, Michele, Lawrence C. Christiano and Jonas D.M. Fisher. 2001. Habit Persistence, Asset Returns and the Business Cycle. *American Economic Review.* Vol. 91. pp. 149-166.

Bomsdorf, Eckart. 1989. Die personelle Vermögensverteilung in der Bundesrepublik Deutschland 1973, 1978 und 1983. *Vierteljahreshefte zur Wirtschaftsforschung.* Heft 4.

Brandner, Peter and Klaus Neusser. 1990. Business Cycles in Open Economies: Stylized Facts for Austria and Germany. Austrian Institute for Economic Research. Working Papers No. 40.

Brock, William A. and Leonard Mirman. 1972. Optimal Economic Growth and Uncertainty: The Discounted Case. *Journal of Economic Theory*. Vol. 4. pp. 479-513.

Bronson, Richard. 1989. Theory and Problems of Matrix Operations. New York: McGraw-Hill.

Brooks, Robin. 2002. Asset-Market Effects of the Baby Boom and Social-Security Reform. *American Economic Review*, Vol. 92. pp. 402-06.

Browning, Martin, Lars Peter Hansen and James J. Heckman. 1999. Micro Data and General Equilibrium Models. In John B. Taylor and Michael Woodfors (Eds.). Handbook of Macroeconomics. Vol. 1A. Amsterdam: North-Holland. pp. 543-633.

Budría Rodríguez, Santiago, Javier Díaz-Giménez, Vincenzo Quadrini, and José-Victor Ríos-Rull. 2002. Updated Facts on the U.S. Distributions of Earnings, Income, and Wealth. *Federal Reserve Bank of Minneapolis Quarterly Review*. Vol. 26. pp. 2-35.

Burden, Richard L. and J. Douglas Faires. 2001. Numerical Analysis, Seventh Edition. Pacific Grove: Brooks/Cole

Burkhauser, Richard V., Douglas Holtz-Eakin and Stephen E. Rhody. 1997. Labor Earnings Mobility and Inequality in the United States and Germany during the Growth Years of the 1980s. *International Economic Review*. Vol. 38. pp. 775-94.

Burnside, Craig. 1999. Real Business Cycle Models: Linear Approximation and GMM Estimation. Mimeo. Revision 7, May 1.

Calvo, Guillermo A. 1983. Staggered Prices in a Utility-Maximizing Framework. *Journal of Monetary Economics*. Vol. 12. pp. 383-398.

Canova, Fabio. 2007. Methods for Applied Macroeconomic Research. Princeton, NJ: Princeton University Press.

Carnahan, Brice, H. A. Luther, and James O. Wilkes. 1969. Applied Numerical Methods. New York: John Wiley & Sons.

Cass, David. 1965. Optimum Growth in an Aggregative Model of Capital Accumulation. *Review of Economic Studies*. Vol. 32. pp. 233-240.

Castañeda, Ana, Javier Díaz-Giménez and José-Victor Ríos-Rull. 1998a. Earnings and Wealth Inequality and Income Taxation: Quantifying the Trade-Offs of Switching to a Proportional Tax in the US. Mimeo.

Castañeda, Ana, Javier Díaz-Giménez and José-Victor Ríos-Rull. 1998b. Exploring the income distribution business cycle dynamics. *Journal of Monetary Economics*. Vol. 42. pp. 93-130.

Castañeda, Ana, Javier Díaz-Giménez and José-Victor Ríos-Rull. 2003. Accounting for the US inequality. *Journal of Political Economy*. Vol. 111. pp. 818-57.

Caucutt, Elisabeth M., Selahattin İmrohoroğlu and Krishna B. Kumar. 2003. Growth and welfare analysis of tax progressivity in a heterogeneous-agent model. *Review of Economic Dynamics*. Vol. 6. pp. 546-77.

Chari, Varadaraian V., Patrick J. Kehoe and Ellen R. McGrattan. 2000. Sticky Price Models of the Business Cycle: Can the Contract Multiplier Solve the Persistence Problem? *Econometrica*. Vol. 68. pp. 1151-1179.

Cho, Jang-Ok and Thomas F. Cooley. 1995. The Business Cycle with Nominal Contracts. *Economic Theory*. Vol. 6. pp. 13-33.

Chow, Gregory C. 1997. Dynamic Economics. Optimization by the Lagrange Method. New York, Oxford: Oxford University Press.

Christiano, Lawrence J., Martin Eichenbaum, and Charles L. Evans. 1997. Sticky Price and Limited Participation Models of Money: A Comparison. *European Economic Review*. Vol. 41. pp. 1201-1249.

Christiano, Lawrence J., Martin Eichenbaum, and Charles L. Evans. 1999. Monetary Policy Shocks: What Have We Learned and to What End? In John B. Taylor and Michael Woodford (Eds.). Handbook of Macroeconomics. Vol. 1A. Amsterdam: Elsevier. pp. 65-148.

Christiano, Lawrence J. and Richard M. Todd. 1996. Time to Plan and Aggregate Fluctuations. *Federal Reserve Bank of Minneapolis Quarterly Review*. Vol. 20. pp. 14-27.

Christiano, Lawrence J. and Jonas D.M. Fisher. 2000. Algorithms for Solving Dynamic Models with Occasionally Binding Constraints. *Journal of Economic Dynamics and Control.* Vol. 24. pp. 1179-1232.

Cochrane, John H. 1998. What do the VARs Mean? Measuring the Output Effects of Monetary Policy. *Journal of Monetary Economics.* Vol. 41. pp. 277-300.

Cogley, Timothy and James M. Nason. 1995. Output Dynamics in Real-Business-Cycle Models. *American Economic Review.* Vol. 85. pp. 492-511.

Constantini, Paolo and Fabio Fontanella. 1990. Shape-preserving Bivariate Interpolation. *SIAM Journal of Numerical Analysis.* Vol. 27. pp. 488-506.

Cooley, Thomas F., Gary D. Hansen. 1989. The Inflation Tax in a Real Business Cycle Model. *American Economic Review.* 79. pp. 733-748.

Cooley, Thomas F. and Gary D. Hansen. 1995. Money and the Business Cycle. In Thomas F. Cooley (Ed.). Frontiers of Business Cycle Research. Princeton, NJ: Princeton University Press. pp. 175-216.

Cooley, Thomas F. and Gary D. Hansen. 1998. The Role of Monetary Shocks in Equilibrium Business Cycle Theory: Three Examples. *European Economic Review.* Vol. 42. pp. 605-617.

Cooley, Thomas F. and Edward C. Prescott. 1995. Economic Growth and Business Cycles. In Thomas F. Cooley (Ed.). Frontiers of Business Cycle Research. Princeton, NJ: Princeton University Press. pp. 1-38.

Correia, Isabel, Joao Neves, and Sergio Rebelo. 1995. Business Cycles in a Small Open Economy. *European Economic Review.* Vol. 39. pp. 1089-1113.

Deaton, Angus. 1991. Saving and liquidity constraints. *Econometrica.* Vol. 59. pp. 1221-48.

Debreu, Gerard. 1954. Valuation Equilibrium and Pareto Optimum. *Proceedings of the National Academy of Science.* Vol. 40. pp. 588-592.

DeJong, David N. with Chetan Dave. 2007. Structural Macroeconomics. Princeton, NJ: Princeton University Press

De Nardi, Mariachristina, Selahattin İmrohoroğlu and Thomas J. Sargent. 1999. Projected US Demographics and Social Security. *Review of Economic Dynamics*. Vol. 2. pp. 575-615.

Den Haan, Wouter J. 1997. Solving Dynamic Models with Aggregate Shocks and Heterogenous Agents. *Macroeconomic Dynamics*. Vol. 1. pp. 335-386.

Den Haan, Wouter J. 2007. Assessing the Accuracy of the Law of Motion in Models with Heterogeneous Agents, mimeo.

Den Haan, Wouter J. and Albert Marcet. 1990. Solving the Stochastic Growth Model by Parameterizing Expectations. *Journal of Business & Economic Statistics*. Vol. 8. pp. 31-34.

Den Haan, Wouter J. and Albert Marcet. 1994. Accuracy in Simulations. *Review of Economic Studies*. Vol. 61. pp. 3-17.

Den Haan, Wouter J., Garey Ramey and Joel C. Watson. 2000. Job Destruction and the Propagation of Shocks. *American Economic Review*. Vol. 90. pp. 482-98.

Dennis, John E. and Robert B. Schnabel. 1983. Numerical Methods for Unconstrained Optimization and Nonlinear Equations: Lehrbuch. Englewood Cliffs, NJ: Prentice-Hall.

Diamond, Peter. 1965. National Debt in a Neoclassical Growth Model. *American Economic Review*. Vol. 55. pp. 1126-50.

Díaz-Giménez, Javier, Vincenzo Quadrini and José-Victor Ríos-Rull. 1997. Dimensions of Inequality: Facts on the US Distributions of Earnings, Income, and Wealth. *Federal Reserve Bank of Minneapolis Quarterly Review*. Vol. 21. pp. 3-21.

Diebold, Francis X. and Robert S. Mariano. 1995 . Comparing Predictive Accuracy. *Journal of Business and Economic Statistics*. Vol. 13. pp. 253-263.

Dotsey, Michael, and Peter Ireland. 1996. The welfare costs of inflation in general equilibrium. *Journal of Monetary Economics*. Vol. 37. pp. 29-47.

Duffy, John and Paul D. McNelis. 2001. Approximating and simulating the stochastic growth model: Parameterized expectations, neural networks, and the genetic algorithm. *Journal of Economic Dynamics and Control*. Vol. 25. pp. 1273-1303.

Eichenbaum, Martin and Jonas D. M. Fisher. 2004. Evaluating the Calvo Model of Sticky Prices. NBER Working Paper No. W10617.

Erosa, Andrés, and Gustavo Ventura. 2002. On inflation as a regressive consumption tax. *Journal of Monetary Economics*. Vol. 49. pp. 761-95.

Evans, George W. and Seppo Honkapohja. 2001. Learning and Expectations in Macroeconomics. Princeton, Oxford: Pinceton University Press.

Evans, Owen J. 1983. Tax Policy, the Interest Elasticity of Saving, and Capital Accumulation: Numerical Analysis of Theoretical Models. *American Economic Review.* Vol. 83. pp. 398-410.

Fair, Ray C. and John B. Taylor. 1983. Solution and Maximum Likelihood Estimation of Dynamic Nonlinear Rational Expectations Models. *Econometrica.* Vol. 51. pp. 1169-1185.

Farmer, Roger E. A. 1993. The Macroeconomics of Self-Fulfilling Prophecies. Cambridge, MA, London: MIT Press.

Favero, Carlo A. 2001. Applied Macroeconometrics. Oxford: Oxford University Press.

Finn, Mary G. 1995. Variance Properties of Solow's Productivity Residual and their Cyclical Implications. *Journal of Economic Dynamics and Control.* Vol. 19. pp. 1249-1281.

Gagnon, Joseph E. 1990. Solving the Stochastic Growth Model by Deterministic Extended Path. *Journal of Business & Economic Statistics.* Vol. 8. pp. 35-36.

Galí, Jordi. 2008. Monetary Policy, Inflation, and the Business Cycle. Princeton and Oxford: Princeton University Press

Goldfarb, Donald. 1976. Factorized Variable Metric Methods for Unconstrained Optimization *Mathematics of Computation.* Vol. 30. pp. 796-811.

Golub, Gene H. and Charles F. Van Loan. 1996. Matrix Computations. 3rd. Ed. Baltimore and London: The Johns Hopkins University Press.

Gomme, Paul. 1997. Evolutionary Programming as a Solution Technique for the Bellman Equation. Federal Reserve Bank of Cleveland Working Paper No. 9816.

Gomme, Paul and Paul Rupert. 2007. Theory, Measurment, and Calibration of Macroeconomic Models. *Journal of Monetary Economics.* Vol. 54. pp. 460-497.

Grandmont, Jean-Michel. 1988. Nonlinear Difference Equations, Bifurcations and Chaos: An Introduction. CEPREMAP Working Paper No 8811.

Greene, William H. 2003. Econometric Analysis. 5th Ed. Upper Saddle River, NJ: Prentice Hall.

Greenwood, Jeremy, Zvi Hercowitz and Gregory W. Huffman. 1988. Investment, Capacity Utilization, and the Real Business Cycle. *American Economic Review.* Vol. 78. pp. 402-417.

Griffoli, Tommaso M. 2007. DYNARE User Guide. Mimeo.

Grüner, Hans Peter and Burkhard Heer. 2000. Optimal Flat-rate Taxes on Capital, A reexamination of Lucas' Supply Side Model', *Oxford Economic Papers*, Vol. 52, pp. 289-305

Hairault, Jean-Oliver and Franck Portier. 1993. Money, New-Keynesian Macroeconomics and the Business Cycle. *European Economic Review.* Vol. 37. pp. 1533-1568.

Hamilton, James D. 1994. Time Series Analysis. Princeton, NJ: Princeton University Press.

Hansen, Gary D. 1985. Indivisible Labor and the Business Cycle *Journal of Monetary Economics.* Vol. 16. pp. 309-327.

Hansen, Gary D. 1993. The cyclical and secular behavior of the labor input: comparing efficiency units and hours worked. *Journal of Applied Econometrics.* Vol. 8. pp. 71-80.

Hansen, Gary D. and Edward C. Prescott. 1995. Recursive Methods for Computing Equilibria of Business Cycle Models. In Thomas F. Cooley (Eds.). Frontiers of Business Cycle Research. Princeton, NJ: Princeton University Press. pp. 39-64.

Hansen, Gary D. and Ayse İmrohoroğlu. 1992. The role of Unemployment Insurance in an Economy with Liquidity Constraints and Moral Hazard. *Journal of Political Economy.* Vol. 100. no. 1. pp. 118-42.

Harris, Milton. 1987. Dynamic Economic Analysis. Oxford u.a.: Oxford University Press.

Heckman, James J., Lance Lochner, and Christopher Taber. 1998. Explaining Rising Wage Inequality: Explorations with a Dynamic General Equilibrium Model of Labor Earnings with Heterogeneous Agents. *Review of Economic Dynamics.* Vol. 1. pp. 1-58.

Heer, Burkhard. 2001a. On the welfare gain from stabilizing cyclical fluctuations. *Applied Economic Letters.* Vol. 8. pp. 331-34.

Heer, Burkhard. 2001b. Wealth Distribution and Optimal Inheritance Taxation in Life-Cycle Economies. *Scandinavian Journal of Economics.* Vol. 103. pp. 445-65.

Heer, Burkhard. 2003. Employment and Welfare Effects of a Two-Tier Unemployment Compensation System. *International Tax and Public Finance.* Vol. 10. pp. 147-68.

Heer, Burkhard. 2004. Nonsuperneutrality of money in the Sidrauski model with heterogenous agents. *Economics Bulletin.* Vol. 5. pp. 1-6.

Heer, Burkhard. 2007. On the modeling of the income distribution business cycle dynamics. *CESifo working paper.* No. 1945.

Heer, Burkhard, and Andreas Irmen. 2008. Population Growth, Pensions, and Economic Growth. *CESifo working paper.* forthcoming.

Heer, Burkhard, and Alfred Maußner. 2004. Projection methods and the curse of dimensionality, mimeo.

Heer, Burkhard, and Alfred Maußner. 2007. The Burden of Unanticpated Inflation: Analysis of an Overlapping Generations Model with Progressive Income Taxation and Staggered Prices. Mimeo.

Heer, Burkhard and Alfred Maußner. 2008. Computation of Business Cycle Models: A Comparision of Numerical Methods. *Macroeconomic Dynamics.* Vol. 12. pp. 641-663.

Heer, Burkhard, Alfred Maußner, and Paul McNelis. 2007. The Money-Age Distribution: Empirical Facts and Limited Monetary Models. *CESifo working paper.* No. 1917.

Heer, Burkhard and Mark Trede. 2003. Efficiency and Distribution Effects of a Revenue-neutral Income Tax Reform. *Journal of Macroeconomics.* Vol. 25. pp. 87-107.

Hercowitz, Zvi and Michael Sampson. 1991. Output Growth, the Real Wage, and Employment Fluctuations. *American Economic Review.* Vol. 81. pp. 1215-1237.

Herrera, Fransisco, Manuel Lozano and José L. Verdegay. 1998. Tackling Real-Coded Genetic Algorithms: Operators and Tools for Behavioural Analysis. *Artificial Intelligence Review.* Vol. 12. pp. 265-319.

Hirsch, Morris W. and Stephen Smale. 1974. Differntial Equations, Dynamical Systems, and Linear Algebra. New York: Academic Press.

Hodrick, Robert J. and Edward C. Prescott. 1980. Post-War U.S. Business Cycles: An Empirical Investigation. University of Warwick, Discussion Paper No. 451.

Hodrick, Robert J. and Edward C. Prescott. 1997. Postwar U.S. Business Cycles: An Empirical Investigation. *Journal of Money, Credit, and Banking.* Vol. 29. pp. 1-16.

Hoffman, Dennis L., Robert H. Rasche and Margie A. Tieslau. 1995. The Stability of Long-Run Money Demand in Five Industrial Countries. *Journal of Monetary Economics.* Vol. 35. pp. 317-339.

Holland, Allison, and Andrew Scott. 1998. The Determinants of UK Business Cycles, *Economic Journal*, Vol. 108, pp. 1067-1092

Hubbard, Robert G. and Kenneth L. Judd. 1987. Social security and individual welfare: precautionary saving, borrowing constraints, and the payroll tax. *American Economic Review.* Vol. 77. pp. 630-46.

Hubbard, Robert G., Jonathan Skinner and Stephen P. Zeldes. 1995. Precautionary Saving and Social Insurance. *Journal of Political Economy.* Vol. 103. pp. 360-99.

Huggett, Mark. 1993. The risk-free rate in heterogenous-agent incomplete-insurance economies. *Journal of Economic Dynamics and Control.* Vol. 17. pp. 953-69.

Huggett, Mark. 1996. Wealth Distribution in Life-Cycle Economies. *Journal of Monetary Economics.* Vol. 38. pp. 469-94.

Huggett, M. and Sandra Ospina. 2001. On aggregate precautionary savings: When is the third derivative irrelevant? *Journal of Monetary Economics.* Vol. 48. pp. 373-96.

Huggett, Mark and Gustavo Ventura. 2000. Understanding why high income households save more than low income households. *Journal of Monetary Economics*. Vol. 45. pp. 361-397.

Huggett, Mark, Gustavo Ventura, and Amir Yaron. 2007. Sources of Lifetime Inequality.NBER Working Paper No. 13224.

Hurd, Michal D. 1989. Mortality Risk and Bequests. *Econometrica*. Vol. 57. pp. 799-813.

İmrohoroğlu, Ayse. 1989. Cost of Business Cycle with Indivisibilities and Liquidity Constraints. *Journal of Political Economy*. Vol. 97. pp. 1364-83.

İmrohoroğlu, Ayse. 1992. Welfare Costs of Inflation under Imperfect Insurance. *Journal of Economic Dynamics and Control*. Vol. 16. pp. 79-91.

İmrohoroğlu, Ayse, Selahattin İmrohoroğlu, and Douglas Joines. 1995. A life cycle analysis of social security. *Economic Theory*. Vol. 6. pp. 83-114.

İmrohoroğlu, Ayse, Selahattin İmrohoroğlu, and Douglas Joines. 1998. The Effect of Tax-Favored Retirement Acccounts on Capital Accumulation. *American Economic Review*. Vol. 88. pp. 749-68.

İmrohoroğlu, Selahattin. 1998. A Quantitative Analysis of Capital Income Taxation. *International Economic Review*. Vol. 39. pp. 307-28.

Jagannathan, Ravi, Ellen R. McGrattan and Anna Scherbina. 2001. The Declining U.S. Equity Premium. NBER Working Paper No. 8172.

Jermann, Urban J. 1998. Asset Pricing in Production Economies. *Journal of Monetary Economics*. Vol. 41. pp. 257-275.

Judd, Kenneth L. 1998. Numerical Methods in Economics. Cambridge, MA, London: MIT Press.

Judge, George G., R. Carter Hill, William E. Griffiths and Helmut Lütkepohl. 1988. Introduction to the Theory and Practice of Econometrics. 2nd. Ed. New York: John Wiley & Sons.

Kamihigashi, Takashi. 2002. A Simple Proof of the Necessity of the Transversality Condition. *Journal of Economic Theory*. Vol. 20. pp. 427-433.

Kessler, Denis and André. Masson. 1989. Bequest and Wealth Accumulation: Are Some Pieces of the Puzzle Missing? *Journal of Economic Perspectives*. Vol. 3. pp. 141-52.

Keynes, John M. 1930. F.P. Ramsey. *Economic Journal*. Vol. 40. pp. 153-154.

Kim, Jinill, Sunghyun Kim, Ernst Schaumburg, and Christopher A. Sims. 2005. Calculating and Using Second Order Accurate Solutions of Discrete Time Dynamic Models. Mimeo

King, Robert G., Charles I. Plosser and Sergio Rebelo. 1988. Production, Growth and Business Cycles I, The Basic Neoclassical Model. *Journal of Monetary Economics*. Vol. 21. pp. 195-232.

King, Robert G., Charles I. Plosser and Sergio Rebelo. 1988. Production, Growth and Business Cycles II, New Directions. *Journal of Monetary Economics*. Vol. 21. pp. 309-341.

King, Robert G. and Sergio T. Rebelo. 1993. Low Frequency Filtering and Real Business Cycles. *Journal of Economic Dynamics and Control*. Vol. 17. pp. 207-231.

King, Robert G. and Mark W. Watson. 1998. The Solution of Singular Linear Difference Systems Under Rational Expectations. *International Economic Review*. Vol. 39. pp. 1015-1026.

King, Robert G. and Mark W. Watson. 2002. System Reduction and Solution Algorithms for Singular Linear Difference Systems under Rational Expectations. *Computational Economics*. Vol. 20. pp. 57-86.

Kocherlakota, Narayana R. 1996. The Equity Premium: It's Still a Puzzle. *Journal of Economic Literature*. Vol. 34. pp. 42-71.

Koopmans, Tjalling C. 1965. On the Concept of Optimal Economic Growth. In The Econometric Approach to Development Planning. Amsterdam: North-Holland. pp. 225-287.

Kremer, Jana. 2001. Arbeitslosigkeit, Lohndifferenzierung und wirtschaftliche Entwicklung. Lohmar, Köln: Josef Eul Verlag.

Krueger, Dirk, and Alexander Ludwig. 2007. On the Consequences of Demographic Change for Rates of Returns to Capital, and the Distribution of Wealth and Welfare. *Journal of Monetary Economics*. Vol. 54. pp 49-87.

Krussell, Per and Anthony A. Smith. 1998. Income and Wealth Heterogeneity in the Macroeconomy. *Journal of Political Economy.* Vol. 106. pp. 867-96.

Kydland, Finn E. and Edward C. Prescott. 1982. Time to Built and Aggregate Fluctuations. *Econometrica.* Vol. 50. pp. 1345-1370.

Laitner, John. 1990. Tax changes and phase diagrams for an Overlapping Generations model. *Journal of Political Economy.* Vol. 98. pp. 193-220.

Lang, Serge. 1986. Introduction to Linear Algebra. New York: Springer Verlag.

Lang, Serge, 1997. Undergraduate Analysis. Second Edition. New York: Springer Verlag.

Leeper, Eric M. and Christopher A. Sims. 1994. Toward a Modern Macroeconomic Model Usable for Policy Analysis. NBER Macroeconomics Annual.

Lillard, Lee A. and Robert J. Willis. 1978. Dynamic aspects of earnings mobility. *Econometrica.* Vol. 46. pp. 985-1012.

Linnemann, Ludger. 1999. Sectoral and Aggregate Estimates of the Cyclical Behavior of Markups: Evidence from Germany. *Weltwirtschaftliches Archiv.* Vol. 135. pp. 480-500.

Linnemann, Ludger and Andreas Schabert. 2003. Fiscal Policy in the New Keynesian Synthesis. *Journal of Money, Credit, and Banking.* Vol. 35. pp. 911-929

Ljungqvist, Lars and Thomas J. Sargent. 2004. Recursive Macroeconomic Theory. 2nd Ed. Cambridge, MA, London: MIT Press.

Lombardo, Giovanni and Alan Sutherland. 2007. Computing Second-Order Accurate Solutions for Rational Expectation Models Using Linear Solution Methods. *Journal of Economic Dynamics and Control.* Vol. 31. pp. 515-530.

Long, John B. and Charles I. Plosser. 1983. Real Business Cycles. *Journal of Political Economy.* Vol. 91. pp. 39-69.

Loury, Glenn C. 1981. Intergenerational transfers and the distribution of earnings. *Econometrica.* Vol. 49. pp. 843-67.

Lucas, Robert E. 1987. *Models of Business Cycles.* New York: Blackwell.

Lucas, Robert E. 1988. On the Mechanics of Economic Development. *Journal of Monetary Economics.* Vol. 22. pp. 3-42.

Lucas, Rober. E. 1990. Supply-Side Economics: An Analytical Review, *Oxford Economic Papers*, Vol. 42, pp. 3-42

Lucke, Bernd. 1998. Theorie und Empirie realer Konjunkturzyklen. Heidelberg: Physica-Verlag.

Ludwig, Alexander. 2007. The Gauss-Seidel-Quasi-Newton Method: A Hybrid Algorithm for Solving Dynamic Economic Models. *Journal of Economic Dynamics and Control.* Vol. 31. pp 1610-32.

MaCurdy, Thomas E. 1982. The use of time series processes to model the error structure of earnings in longitudinal data analysis. *Journal of Econometrics.* Vol. 18. pp. 83-114.

Mankiw, Gregory N. 2000. Macroeconomics. 4th Ed. New York: Worth Publishers.

Marcet, Albert and David A. Marshall. 1992. Convergence of Approximate Model Solutions to Rational Expectations Equilibria Using the Method of Parameterized Expectations. Kellogg Graduate School of Management. Working Paper No. 73.

Marcet, Albert and David A. Marshall. 1994. Solving Nonlinear Rational Expectations Models by Parameterized Expectations: Convergence to Stationary Solutions. Manuscript.

Marcet, Albert and Guido Lorenzoni. 1999. The Parameterized Expectations Approach: Some Practical Issues. In Ramon Marimon and Andrew Scott (Eds.). Computational Methods for the Study of Dynamic Economies. Oxford: Oxford University Press. pp. 143-171.

Mas-Colell, Andreu, Michael D. Whinston and Jerry R. Green. 1995. Microeconomic Theory. New York, Oxford: Oxford University Press.

Maußner, Alfred. 1999. Unvollkommene Gütermärkte, Konjunktur und Wachstum. Wolfgang Franz et al. (Eds.). Trend und Zyklus. Tübingen: Mohr Siebeck. pp. 121-151.

McCandless, George. 2008. The ABCs of RBCs. Cambrdige, MA and London: Harvard University Press

McGrattan, Ellen R. 1999. Application of Weighted Residual Methods to Dynamic Economic Models. In Ramon Marimon and Andrew Scott. Computational Methods for the Study of Dynamic Economies. Oxford and New York: Oxford University Press. pp. 114-142.

Mehra, Rajnish. 2003. The Equity Premium: Why Is It a Puzzle? *Financial Analysts Journal.* Vol. 59. pp. 2003, 54-69.

Mehra, Rajnish and Edward C. Prescott. 1985. The Equity Premium: A Puzzle. *Journal of Monetary Economics.* Vol.15(2). pp. 145-62.

Mehra, Rajnish and Edward C. Prescott. 2003. The Equity Premium in Retrospect. NBER Working Paper No. 8172.

Michalewicz, Zbigniew 1999. Genetic Algorithms+Data Structures=Evolution Programs. 3rd. Ed. Berlin, Heidelberg und New York: Springer.

Mitchell, Melanie. 1996. An Introduction to Genetic Algorithms. Cambridge, MA, London: MIT Press.

Murata, Yasuo. 1977. Mathematics for Stability and Optimization of Economic Systems. New York: Academic Press.

Muth, John F. 1961. Rational Expectations and the Theory of Price Movements. *Econometrica.* Vol .29. pp. 315-335.

Nelson, Charles R. and Charles I. Plosser. 1982. Trends and Random Walks in Macroeconomic Time Series, Some Evidence and Implications. *Journal of Monetary Economics.* Vol. 10. pp. 139-162.

Newey, Whitney K. and Kenneth D. West. 1987. A Simple, Positive Semi-Definite, Heteroskedasticity and Autocorrelation Consistent Covariance Matrix. *Econometrica.* Vol. 55. pp. 703-708.

Palis, Jacob and Welington de Melo. 1982. Geometric Theory of Dynamical Systems. New York: Springer.

Plosser, Charles I. 1989. Understanding Real Business Cycles. *Journal of Economic Perspectives.* Vol. 3. pp. 51-77.

Prescott, Edward C. 1986. Theory ahead of business cycle measurement. *Carnegie Rochester Series on Public Policy.* Vol. 25. pp. 11-44.

Press, William H., Saul A. Teukolsky, William T. Veterling and Brian P. Flannery. 1992. *Numerical recipes in FORTRAN:*

the art of scientific computing. 2nd edition. Cambridge: Cambridge University Press.

Preston, Bruce, and Mauro Roca. 2007. Incomplete Markets, Heterogeneity, and Macroeconomic Dynamics. NBER Working Paper No. 13260.

Puterman, Martin L. and Moon Chirl Shin. 1978. Modified Policy Iteration Algorithms for Discounted Markov Decision Problems. *Management Science.* Vol. 24. pp. 1127-1237.

Puterman, Martin L. and Shelby Brumelle. 1979. On the Convergence of Policy Iteration in Stationary Dynamic Programming. *Mathematics of Operations Research.* Vol. 4. pp. 1979, 60-69.

Quadrini, Vincenzo. 2000. Entrepreneurship, Saving and Social Mobility. *Review of Economic Dynamics.* Vol. 3. pp. 1-40.

Quadrini, Vincenzo and José-Victor Ríos-Rull. 1997. Understanding the U.S. Distribution of Wealth. *Federal Reserve Bank of Minneapolis Quarterly Review.* Vol. 21. pp. 22-36.

Radner, Roy. 1966. Optimal Growth in a Linear-Logarihmic Econom. *International Economic Review.* Vol. 7. pp. 1-33.

Ramsey, Frank. 1928. A Mathematical Theory of Saving. *Economic Journal.* Vol. 38. pp. 543-559.

Ravn, Morten and Harald Uhlig. 2001. On Adjusting the HP-Filter for the Frequency of Observations. CEPR Discussion Paper No. 2858.

Reiter, Michael. 2006. Solving Heterogenous Agent Models by Projection and Perturbation. Universitat Pompeu Fabra. mimeo.

Ríos-Rull, José-Victor. 1996. Life-Cycle Economies and Aggregate Fluctuations. *Review of Economic Studies.* Vol. 63. pp. 465-89.

Ríos-Rull, José-Victor. 1999. Computation of Equilibria in Heterogenous-Agent Models. In Marimon, R., and A. Scott (eds.). *Computational Methods for the Study of Dynamic Economies.* Oxford: Oxford University Press.

Romer, Paul. 1991. Increasing Returns and New Developments in the Theory of Growth. In Wiliam A. Barnett et al. (Eds.). Equilibrium Theory and Applications. Cambridge, MA.: Cambridge University Press. pp. 83-110.

Rotemberg, Julio J. 1987. The New Keynesian Microfoundations. NBER Macroeconomics Annual. Vol. 2. pp. 69-104.

Rotemberg, Julio J. and Michael Woodford. 1995. Dynamic General Equilibrium Models with Imperfectly Competitive Product Markets. In Thomas F. Cooley (Ed.). Frontiers of Business Cycle Research. Princeton, NJ: Princeton University Press. pp. 243-293.

Samuelson, Paul A. 1958. An exact consumption-loan model of interest, with or without the social contrivance of money. *Journal of Political Economy.* Vol. 66. pp. 467-82.

Sargent, Thomas J. 1987. Macroeconomic Theory, 2nd edition. San Diego: Academic Press.

Sargent, Thomas J. 1993. Bounded Rationality in Macroeconomics. Oxford: Clarendon Press.

Schmitt-Grohé, Stephanie and Martin Uribe. 2004. Solving Dynamic General Equilibrium Models Using a Second-Order Approximation to the Policy Function. *Journal of Economic Dynamics and Control.* Vol. 28. pp. 755-775.

Shorrocks, Anthony F. 1976. Income Mobility and the Markov Assumption. *Economic Journal.* Vol. 86. pp. 566-578.

Sidrauski, Miguel. 1967. Rational Choice and Patterns of Growth in a Monetary Economy. *American Economic Review.* Vol. 57. pp. 534-44.

Sieg, Holger. 2000. Estimating a dynamic model of household choices in the presence of income taxation. *International Economic Review.* Vol. 43. no. 3. pp. 637-68.

Simon, Herbert A. 1957. Models of Man: Social and Rational; Mathematical Essays on Rational Human Behavior in Society Setting. New York: John Wiley.

Solow, Robert M. 1988. Growth Theory, An Exposition. New York, Oxford: Oxford University Press.

Starr, Ross M. 1997. General Equilibrium Theory, An Introduction. Cambridge: Cambridge University Press.

Stokey, Nancy, Robert E. Lucas and Edward C. Prescott. 1989. *Recursive methods in economic dynamics.* Cambridge, MA.: Harvard University Press.

Storesletten, Kjetil, Chris I. Telmer, and Amir Yaron. 2001. The Welfare Costs of Business Cycles Revisited: Finite Lives and Cyclical Variation in Idiosyncratic Risk. *European Economic Review.* Vol. 45. pp. 1311-39.

Storesletten, Kjetil, Chris Telmer, and Amir Yaron. 2007. Asset pricing with idiosyncratic risk and overlapping generations. *Review of Economic Dynamics,* Vol. 10. pp. 519-48.

Summers, Lawrence H. 1981. Capital Taxation and Accumulation in a Life Cycle Growth Model. *American Economic Review.* Vol. 71. pp. 533-44.

Sundaram, Rangarajan K. 1996. A First Course in Optimization Theory. Cambridge: Cambridge University Press.

Sydsæter, Knut, Arne Strøm and Peter Berck. 1999. Economists' Mathematical Manual. Third Edition. Berlin: Springer.

Takayama, Akira. 1985. Mathematical Economics. 2nd Ed. Cambridge: Cambridge University Press.

Tauchen, George. 1986. Finite State Markov-Chain Approximations to Univariate and Vector Autoregressions. *Economics Letters.* Vol. 20. pp. 177-181.

Taylor, John B. and Harald Uhlig. 1990. Solving Nonlinear Stochastic Growth Models: A Comparision of Alternative Solution Methods. *Journal of Business & Economic Statistics.* Vol. 8. pp. 1-17.

Turnovsky, Stephen J. 2000.Methods of Macroeconomic Dynamics, Second Edition. Cambridge, MA., London: MIT Press.

Uhlig, Harald. 1999. A Toolkit for Analysing Nonlinear Dynamic Stochastic Models Easily. In Ramon Marimon and Andrew Scott (Eds.). Computational Methods for the Study of Dynamic Economies. Oxford: Oxford University Press.

United Nations . 2002. World Population Prospects: The 2002 Revision. United Populations Division. New York: United Nations

Ventura, Gustavo. 1999. Flat-Rate Tax Reform: A Quantitative Exploration. *Journal of Economic Dynamics and Control.* Vol. 23. pp. 1425-58.

Walsh, Carl E. 2003. Monetary Theory and Policy. 2nd Ed. Cambridge, MA., London: MIT Press.

Walsh, Carl E. 2005. Labor Market Search, Sticky Prices, and Interest Rate Rules. *Review of Economic Dynamics*. Vol. 8. pp. 829-849.

White, Halbert. 1980. A Heteroskedasticity-Consistent Covariance Matrix Estimator and a Direct Test for Heteroskedasticity, *Econometrica*, Vol. 48, pp. 817-838

Young, Eric R. 2005a. Approximate Aggregation. University of Virginia, mimeo.

Young, Eric R. 2005b. Risk Sharing and the Welfare Costs of Inflation. University of Virginia, mimeo.

Name Index

Aiyagari, S.R., 338, 371
Algan, Y., 417
Allais, O., 417
Ambler, S., 170
Amisano, G., 54
Antony, J., 23
Aruoba, S. B., 62
Atkinson, P., 371
Auerbach, A.J., 451, 452, 454, 469–471, 505

Baxter, M., 170, 665
Becker, G.S., 519
Bellman, R.E., 14, 336
Benhabib, J., 23, 204
Benigno, P., 89, 90
Berck, P., 42, 556
Bergin, P.R., 143
Blanchard, O.J., 106
Boldrin, M., 322, 323
Bomsdorf, E., 369
Bourguignon, F., 371
Brandner, P., 664, 665
Brock, W., 4
Bronson, R., 555
Brooks, R., 453, 520
Browning, M., 50
Brumelle, S., 214
Budría Rodríguez, S., 435, 508, 540, 545
Burden, R.L, 585
Burkhauser, R.V., 370
Burnside, C., 106

Cagetti, M., 519
Calvo, G.A., 144, 155, 169
Canova, F., XI, 47, 49, 52, 54
Carnahan, B., 611
Cass, D., 4
Castañeda, A., 372–375, 419, 422, 431–433, 435, 438, 443, 508, 546–548
Caucutt, E.M., 374
Chari, V.V., 143
Chiu, W.H., 333
Cho, J.O., 143
Chow, G.C., 11
Christiano, L.J., 63, 142, 143, 155, 253, 268, 270, 291, 322, 323
Cochrane, J.H., 155
Cogley, T., 55
Cooley, T.F., 47, 57, 143, 281–283
Correia, I., 175, 189, 192, 193
Costain, J.S., 333
Costantini, P., 575

Dave, C., XI, 47, 49, 52
de Melo, W., 649, 651
De Nardi, M., 453, 519
Deaton, A., 454
Debreu, G., 41
DeJong, D.N., XI, 47, 49, 52
Den Haan, W.J., 63, 64, 246, 253, 254, 282, 283, 333, 338, 356, 394, 404, 417, 658, 660, 661

Dennis, J.E., 603, 604, 606, 613, 615–620, 622, 626, 628, 631, 632
Diamond, P., 451
Díaz-Giménez, J., 368, 370, 372–375, 419, 422, 431–433, 435, 438, 443, 508, 540, 545–548
Diebold, F. X., 64
Dotsey, M, 239
Duffy, J., 253, 593, 641

Eichenbaum, M., 143, 155, 268, 270
Erosa, A., 239, 241
Euler, L., 12
Evans, C.L., 143, 155, 268, 270
Evans, G.W., 250
Evans, O.J., 452

Fackler, P.L., X
Fair, R.C, 175
Faires, J.D., 585
Farmer, R.E., 106
Favero, C.A., 54
Feenstra, R.C., 143
Fernández-Villaverde, J., 62
Finn, M.G., 325
Fisher, J.D.M., 63, 155, 253, 291, 322, 323
Flannery, , 578
Fontanella, F., 575

Gagnon, J.E., 175
Galí, J., XI
Giannini, C., 54
Goldfarb, D., 632
Golub, G.H., 555, 569, 616
Gomme, P., 47, 57, 641
Grandmont, J.M., 651
Green, J. R., 41
Greene, W.H., 250, 555
Greenwood, J., 192, 375
Griffiths, W.E., 250
Griffoli, T.M., 131
Grüner, H.P., 202

Guckenheimer, J., 649, 651

Hairault, J.O., 143, 151, 169
Hamilton, J.D., 54, 223, 657
Hansen, G.D., 44, 51, 89, 91, 143, 281–283, 330, 333, 384, 488, 489, 513, 540, 598
Hansen, L.P., 50
Harris, M., 14
Heckman, J.J., 50, 367, 453
Heer, B., 61, 63, 155, 194, 202, 223, 224, 276, 296, 333, 374, 378, 380, 385, 430, 452, 453, 470, 484, 485, 488, 503, 518, 519, 522, 534, 535
Hercowitz, Z., 21, 192, 375
Herrera, F., 635, 638–640, 642
Hill, R.C., 250
Hirsch, M.W., 564, 613
Hodrick, R.J., 663
Hoffman, D.L., 152
Holland, A., 202
Holmes, J., 649, 651
Holtz-Eakin, D., 370
Honkapohja, S., 250
Hubbard, R.G., 371, 452, 453, 517
Huffman, G.W., 192, 375
Huggett, M., 338, 344, 346, 348, 359, 361, 362, 371, 384, 396, 452, 459, 508, 513, 519

İmrohoroğlu, A., 333, 337, 338, 348, 374, 384, 421–423, 429, 430, 432, 449, 452, 453, 488
İmrohoroğlu, S., 338, 452, 453, 488
Ireland, P., 239
Irmen, A., 470, 485, 488

Jagannathan, Ravi, 311
Jermann, U.J., 311, 322, 323
Joines, D.H., 338, 452, 453, 488

Judd, K.L., X, 89, 210, 258, 286, 296, 452, 571, 587, 597, 603
Judge, G.G., 250, 555
Juillard, M., 131

Kahn, C.M., 106
Kamihigashi, T., 13, 30
Karni, E., 333
Kehoe, P.J., 143
Kessler, D., 518
Keynes, J.M., 4
Kim, J., 131
Kim, S., 131
King, R.G., 44, 50, 51, 106, 170, 665
Klein, P., 106
Kocherlakota, N.R., 311, 359
Koopmans, T., 4
Kotlikoff, L.J., 451, 452, 454, 469–471, 505
Kremer, J., 212
Krueger, D., 484, 488, 493, 540
Krusell, P., 338, 389, 394, 395, 397, 415, 416, 418, 448, 521, 533, 541
Kumar, K.B., 374
Kydland, F.E., 44, 131, 138, 142

Laitner, J., 532
Lang, S., 90, 555, 574
Leeper, E.M., 143
Lillard, L.A., 371
Linnemann, L., 152, 172
Ljungqvist, L., XI, 654
Lochner, L., 367, 453
Lombardo, G., 119
Long, J.B., 21
Lorenzoni, G., 253, 255
Loury, G.C., 519
Lozano, M., 635, 638–640, 642
Lucas, R.E., XI, 11, 14, 26, 31, 202, 324, 335, 429, 456, 511
Lucke, B., 51, 52

Ludwig, A., 481, 482, 484, 488, 493, 540
Luther, H.A., 611
Lütkepohl, H., 250

MaCurdy, T.E., 371
Mankiw, G.N., 144
Marcet, A., 63, 64, 246, 249, 252–255, 282, 283, 641, 658, 660, 661
Mariano, R. S., 64
Marimon, R., X
Marshall, D.A., 249, 252, 254, 641
Mas-Colell, A., 41
Masson, A., 518
Maußner, A., 23, 61, 63, 155, 156, 194, 223, 224, 276, 296, 503, 522, 535
McCandless, G., XI
McGrattan, E.R., 143, 286, 311
McNelis, P.D., 253, 503, 593, 641
Mehra, R., 311, 322, 359
Michalewicz, Z., 634, 640
Miranda, M.J., X
Mirman, L., 4
Mitchell, M., 634, 637, 638
Morisson, C., 371
Murata, Y., 647
Muth, J.F., 27

Nason, J.M., 55
Nelson, C.R., 36
Neusser, K., 664, 665
Neves, J., 175, 189, 192, 193
Newey, W.K., 661

Ospina, S., 346

Palis, J., 649, 651
Paquet, A., 170
Plosser, C.I., 21, 36, 44, 50, 51
Portier, F., 143, 151, 169
Prescott, E.C., XI, 11, 14, 26, 31, 44, 47, 48, 57, 89, 91, 131, 138, 142, 311, 335, 359, 456, 511, 524, 598, 663

Press, W.H., 578
Preston, B., 447, 448
Puterman, M.L., 214, 215

Quadrini, V., 368, 370, 435, 508, 519, 540, 545

Radner, R., 21
Ramey, G., 333
Ramsey, F., 4
Rasche, R.H., 152
Ravn, M., 665
Rebelo, S., 44, 50, 51, 175, 189, 192, 193
Reddy, J.N., 286
Reiter, M., 447, 448
Rhody, S.E., 370
Ríos-Rull, J.V., 338, 341, 368, 370, 372–375, 407, 419, 422, 431–433, 435, 438, 443, 453, 508, 519, 522, 533, 540, 545–548
Roca, M., 447, 448
Rogerson, R., 204
Romer, P.M., 11
Rotemberg, J.J., 151, 152
Rustichini, A., 23
Rubio-Ramírez, J. F., 62
Rupert, P., 47, 57

Sampson, M., 21
Samuelson, P.A., 451
Sargent, T.J., XI, 250, 453, 593, 654
Schabert, A., 172
Schaumburg, E., 131
Scherbina, A., 311
Schmitt-Grohé, S., 101, 119, 125, 131
Schnabel, R.B., 603, 604, 606, 613, 615–620, 622, 626, 628, 631, 632
Scott, A., X, 202
Shin, M.C., 215
Shorrocks, A.F., 372, 374

Sidrauski, M., 385
Sieg, H., 381
Simon, H., 250
Sims, C.A., 131, 143
Skinner, J., 371, 452, 453, 517
Smale, S., 564, 613
Smith, A.A., 338, 389, 394, 395, 397, 415, 416, 418, 446, 448, 521, 533, 541
Solow, R.M., 35
Starr, R.M., 41
Stokey, N.L., XI, 11, 14, 26, 31, 335, 456, 511
Storesletten, K., 430, 453, 520, 540
Strøm, A., 42, 556
Strout, A.H., 602
Summers, L.H., 452
Sundaram, R.K., 6, 630
Sutherland, A., 119
Sydsæter, K., 42, 556

Taber, C., 367, 453
Takayama, A., 39
Tauchen, G., 223, 657, 658
Taylor, J.B., 175
Telmer, C.I., 430, 453, 520, 540
Teukolsky, S.A., 578
Tieslau, M.A., 152
Todd, R.M., 142
Tomes, N., 519
Trede, M., 374, 378, 380, 489
Turnovsky, S.J., 315

Uhlig, H., 106, 665
Uribe, M., 101, 119, 125, 131

Van Loan, C.F., 555, 569, 616
Ventura, G., 239, 241, 371, 372, 374, 380, 396, 452, 459
Verdegay, J., 635, 638–640, 642
Vetterling, W.T., 578

Walsh, C.E., 143, 155
Watson, M.W., 106, 333
West, K.D., 661

Whinston, M. D., 41
White, H., 660
Wilkes, J.O., 611
Willis, R.J., 371
Woodford, M., 89, 90, 151
Wright, R., 204

Yaron, A., 430, 453, 459, 520, 540
Young, E.R., 395, 430

Zeldes, S.P., 371, 453, 517

Subject Index

Accuracy checks, 135, 188, 219, 262, 266, 301, 307, 310, 586, 588
Accuracy measures, 61–64, 297, 658
Adaptive learning, 249–252
Age-labor supply profile, 463, 474
Age-productivity profile, 488
Age-wealth profile, 462, 466, 474, 517
Approximation methods
    continuous least squares, 580, 581
    interpolation, *see* Interpolation
    linear, 77–83, 98–113
    linear quadratic, 89–98
    local, 526, 570
    log-linear, 106, 113, 524–526
    multidimensional, **588**, 590, 593
    neural networks, *see* Neural network
    polynomial, 355, 467–469, **578**, 584, 588
    quadratic, 76, 114–131, 572, 618, 630
    shape preserving, 575
Asset
    asset market, incomplete, 359–366
    asset-based means test, 517
    constraint, *see* Constraint
    distribution, 335–358, 391
    holdings, 333, 416, 430, 519
    pricing model, 286, 298, 311

Auerbach-Kotlikoff model, 451, 469–473, 507, 526
Autoregressive process
    ARMA(1,2), 371
    first-order (AR(1)), 48, 50, 151, 171, 173, 189, 222, 229, 234, 292, 306, 313, 371, 373, 412, 436, 522, 524, **653**, 657, 658
    second-order (AR(2)), 374, 436, **653**
    vector autoregressive, 87, 107, 268

Backward iteration, 461, 646
Banking deposits, 268, 272
Banking sector, 268–269
Bellman equation, **14**, 207, 209, 215, 221, 223, 227, 233, 235, 238, 289, 336, 362, 379, 400, 465
BFGS, *see* Quasi-Newton method
Bilinear interpolation, *see* Interpolation, bilinear
Bisection method, 607–608
Borrowing rate, 423
Broyden algorithm, *see* Broyden's method
Broyden's method, 478, 481, 482, 490, 497, 498, 506, 614–616
Bubbles, 103, 315
Budget constraint, *see* Constraint
Business cycle

benchmark model, **44**
fluctuations, 425

Calibration, 44–51, 204, 276, 279, 322, 337–338, 346, 372–373, 378, 398, 424–425, 429, 435–439, 458, 512–515, 540
Calvo price setting, 144
Capital
    adjustment costs, 155, 298, 312, 318
    aggregate capital stock, 335, 456, 458, 468, 524
    capital accumulation, 314, 318, 319
    capital goods, 57
    capital income, 49
    capital stock, 295
    depreciation, 5, 27, 43, **50**, 57, 258, 311, 334, 338, 434, 471
    gestation period, 138
    income, 452, 455, 510
    marginal product of, 17, 245, 294, 311, 456, 523
    net return, 311
    planning phase, 138
    price of capital, 312
    rental rate of, 41
    time path of, 31, 104, 474
    time to build, 138
    user costs of capital, 57
Cash-in-advance, 268, 270, 278
Certainty Equivalence Principle, 86–87
Certainty, aggregate, 331, 393, 394
Change of variables, 299, 304, **581**
Chebyshev, 580–588
    coefficients, 468, **584**, 586
    collocation, *see* Collocation method
    evaluation, **583**
    interpolation theorem, 296
    nodes, 296, 468
    polynomials, 293, 294, 296, 299–301, 467, **581**, 590
    regression, 293, **585**
    zeros, 296, 585, 600
Choleski factorization, *see* Matrix factorization
Cobb-Douglas, *see* Production Function
Collocation method, **289, 290, 296**, 301, 468
Complex numbers, 555–557
Conditional expectations function, 245–247, 266
Consistency conditions, aggregate, 339, 390, 394, 415
Constant elasticity of substitution (CES) utility, *see* Utility function
Constraint
    asset constraint, 333, 360
    binding constraint, 8, 243
    budget constraint, 43, 144, 265, 270, 272, 318, 331, 336
    credit constraint, 333, 360
    liquidity constraint, 422–430, 453, 516
    non-negativity constraint, **7**, 12, 256
    resource constraint, **5**, 44, 91, 318, 319
Consumption
    consumption function, 295, 299
    feed-back rule, 131
    marginal utility of, 294, 295
    policy, 409, 467, 511
    time path of, 43, 104, 459
Continuation methods, *see* Homotopy
Contraction mapping theorem, 210–211
Control variable, *see* Variable
Convergence
    distribution function, 348
    linear, 214, 215, 604

quadratic, 214, 604
rate of, 604
superlinear, 604
Credit constraint, *see* Constraint
Cubic spline interpolation, *see* Interpolation, cubic splines

Demographic transition, 483–501
Den Haan-Marcet statistic, *see* DM-statistic
Density function, 30, 335, 336, 341, 350–353, 657
    invariant, 351, 425
Depreciation, *see* Capital
Derivative
    numerical, 593–598
Deterministic growth model, 4–25, 77, 116, 176, 208, 298
Difference equations, 527, **645**, 645–651
    asymptotic stability, 646, 647, 650
    fixed point, 649
    linear, 645–648
    non-linear, 82, 648–651
    stochastic, 89, 102, 106
Dimensionality
    curse of, 207, 243, 342, 602
Dirac delta function, *see* Weight function
Discount factor, **9**, 40, 51, 95, 147, 149, 315
Discretization
    density function, 350–353
    distribution function, 341–350
Distribution
    approximation of, 341–350, 354–358
    ergodic, 344, 355, 356, 419
    invariant, 341, 342, 344, 354
    money-age, 502
    stationary, 335, 389, 459–464
Dividend, 144, 156, 270, 312

DM-statistic, 63–64, 135, 137–138, 189, 237, 263, 267, 297, 310, 658–662
Dynamic programming, *see* Programming

Earnings
    distribution of, 367–374, 443, 488, 508, 519
    inequality, 367–374, 514
    mobility, 367–374, 436
    retained earnings, 313
Economic growth, *see* Growth
Economy, decentralized, 40–44, 331
Eigenspace, **565**, 648, 651
    center, **565**
    stable, 80, **565**
    unstable, **565**
Eigenvalue, 113, 184, 252, **564**, 566, 567
Eigenvector, **564**, 566, 656
    generalized, **565**
Employment
    distribution, 414
    history, 330, 455, 510
    mobility, 419
    probability, 330, 337, 433
    stationary, 340
    status, 330, 333, 391, 393, 417
    transition matrix, 337, 344, 398
    transition probability, 390
Equilibrium
    competitive, **41**, 331
    decentralized, 40, 331, 454, 472, 523
    general, **41**
    partial, 428
    rational expectations equilibrium, 249
    stationary, **18**, 49, 331, 335–341, 377, 458–460, 502, 511–512
    utility maximizing, 44, 131
Equity
    premium, 311–323, 359

premium puzzle, 286, 311–323
return on equity, 51, 315
risk free rate of return, 321
Ergodic set, 343, 425
Error bounds, 237, 594, 595, 598, 605
Euclidean norm, **558**
Euler equation, 3, 11–13, 289, 294, 318, 320, 459–461, 659
    logarithmic preferences, 91
    residual, 62–63, 117, 123, 124, 135–137, 237
    stochastic, **26**, 28–30, 87, 318
Euler's theorem, **42**
Exchange economy, 359–362
Expectations
    conditional, 27, 30, 85, 245, 246, 285, 292–294, 303, 313, 321, 422
Exponential function, class of, 355–358

Financial intermediary, see Banking sector
Finite difference method, 594–596
Firm, 41–42, 313–317
    monopolistically competitive, 144, 154
    stock market value, 314, 315, 317
    total value, 321
Forward iteration, 646
Frictions, nominal, 144, 152, 156
Function
    density, see Density function
    homogenous of degree one, **35**, 38, 41
    homogenous of degree zero, 38
    indicator function, 334
    objective function, 84
    policy function, 85–86, 91, 98, 111, 334, 343
    production function, see Production function
    residual function, 287, 289, 290, 305, 306, 319
    return function, 87, 91
    sigmoid function, 592
    space, 286, 391, 579
    utility function, see Utility function
    value, see Value function
    weight, see Weight function
Functional equation, 12, 14, 30, 62, 286, 291, 646

Galerkin method, **288**, 289, **290**, 301
Gauss-Chebyshev quadrature, 296, 300, 301, 358, 600, 601
Gauss-Hermite quadrature, 306, 601
Gauss-Newton algorithm, 275, 276, 626–629
    damped, 628
Gauss-Seidel method, 482, 505, 611
Gaussian formulas, see Numerical integration
Gaussian plane, 555, 557
Genetic algorithm, 258, 633–643
    binary-coded, 634
    choice of initial population, 635
    chromosome, 634
    chromosomes fitness, 634
    creation of offspring, 634
    crossover, 638
    final selection, 640
    fitness variance, 637
    fitness-proportionate selection, 636
    mutation, 640
    population, 634
    premature convergence, 637
    real-coded, 634
    sampling with replacement, 636
    sigma scaling, 637
    stochastic universal sampling, 636
Genetic search, see Genetic algorithm

German Socio-Economic Panel GSOEP, 369, 373, 381
Gini coefficient, 507
    of earnings, 368, 443
    of income, 368, 381, 443, 540, 546
    of labor income, 514
    of wages, 368
    of wealth, 368, 381, 382, 445, 452, 516, 518, 540
    West Germany, 369
Givens rotation, 113, 569–570
Golden section search, 362, 425, 623–626
Government
    budget, 334, 377, 405, 456, 472, 474, 511, 523, 526
    policy, 335, 377, 393, 457, 470
    revenues, 334, 376, 510
    spending and business cycles, 170, 171
Growth
    balanced growth path, **35**, 37
    deterministic, 39
    difference stationary, 35–37
    economic growth, **34**
    trend stationary, 35–37

Habit persistence, 155, 298, **312**, 313
Hansen-Prescott algorithm, 89–95
Hesse matrix, 96, 115, 119, 122, 130, **573**, 593, 597, 630–632
    numerical approximation, 597
    secant approximation of, 631
Hodrick-Prescott filter (HP-filter), 55, 135, 532, 663–665
Homotopy, 180, 257–258
Household, 42–44, 144–145, 270–272, 312–313
    production(home production), 423, 434, 439

Howard's improvement algorithm, *see* Policy function iteration

Implicit function theorem, 77, 81, 90, 99, 100, **574**
Impulse response function, **52**, 53, 55, 153–155, 196, 277, 532
Income
    tax, 330
    capital income, 338, 452, 455, 510
    concentration of interest, 443
    current, 399
    cyclical behavior of income shares, 432, 444
    dispersion of, 367
    distribution of, 330, 369, 389, 422, 431–446, 518
    effect, 278, 381
    heterogeneity of, 367, 370
    mobility, 369, 432, 433, 445, 452
    tax, 332, 374, 389, 396, 452
Indicator function, 375
Inflation
    anticipated, 268, 276
    current inflation rate, 144
    expected, 144
    inflationary expectations effect, 268, 277
Initial guess, 177, 211, 225, 262, 300, 301, 307, 321, 615, 633
Insurance, incomplete, 359–362
Integration, *see* Gauss-Chebyshev quadrature, *see* Gauss-Hermite quadrature
Intermediate value theorem, 607
Interpolation, 227
    bilinear, 229, 234, 417, 576–577
    Chebyshev, 296, 583
    cubic splines, 216, 231, 237, 447, 466, 505, 577–578

linear, 216, 343, 399, 466, 515, 575–576
multidimensional, 588
Investment, **5**, 50, 139, 313
expenditures, 313, 314

Jacobian matrix, 78, 80, 82, 102, 130, 266, 480–482, 497, 498, **574**, 593, 597, 612–616, 629, 649
forward difference, 96
numerical approximation, 596
Jordan factorization, *see* Matrix factorization

Kronecker product, **560**, 662
Krusell-Smith algorithm, 395–397, 533
Kuhn-Tucker
first-order conditions, **7**, 12, 260, 261, 272, 274
Theorem, **6**

Labor
effective, 34, 57, 381, 510
efficiency level of, 36
labor input, 316, 317
marginal product of, 33, 38, 526
market, 42
productivity of, 33, 370, 509
Labor demand, **57**, 274, 376
Labor supply, 33–34, 42, 318, 323, 454, 457, 467, 502, 509, 511, 524
elasticity, 381
endogenous, 37, 372, 406
exogenous, 33
feed-back rule, 131
schedule, **58**
time path of, 43
Lagrangean function, **12**, **28**, 37, 43, 45, 139, 271, 315
Lagrangean multiplier, **7**, 88, 89, 107, 313, 316

Law of large numbers, 343
Law of motion
productivity shocks, 132
stochastic linear, 84
Learning dynamics, 249–252
Least squares
method, 290, 291, 300, 468
nonlinear, 251, **255**
recursive, 250
Leibniz rule, 241
Leisure, 33–34, 38, 318, 375, 405, 454
Lending rate, 423
Life-cycle model, *see* Overlapping generations model, 452
Life-cycle savings, 508
Line search, 617–622
Linear algebra, 555–570
Linear interpolation, *see* Interpolation, linear
Linear-quadratic (LQ) model, 84–89
Linearization methods, *see* Approximation methods, linear
Liquidity effect, 268, 277, 279
Lorenz curve, 514, 517
of earnings, 368, 514
of income, 368, 443
of wealth, 368, 446, 516
LU factorization, *see* Matrix factorization

Machine epsilon, 595
Manifold
stable, 650
unstable, 651
Markov chain, 222, 234, 306, 463, 653–658
2-state, 341
finite state, 341, 514, 657
first order, 332, 372
Markov chain approximation of AR(1) process, **657**
second order, 372
Markov process, 509, 652–658

Markov property, 247, **652**
Matrix
  addition, 557, 559
  complex, 558
  conjugate complex transposition, 562
  determinant, **561**, 564
  diagonal, 559
  Givens rotation, 569
  identity, 89, 559
  inverse, 562
  invertible, 562
  main diagonal, 108, 561
  negative definite, 86
  negative semidefinite, 84, 563
  non-invertible, 562
  non-singular, 562
  partitioned, 108
  positive definite, 564, 630, 664
  positive semidefinite, 564
  rank, 561
  scalar multiplication, 557, 559
  semidefinite, 84, 563, 630
  singular, 562
  square, 85, 559
  symmetric, 84, 562, 568
  trace, 561
  transition matrix, 30, **653**
  transpose, 561
  unitary, 567
  upper triangular, 559
Matrix factorization
  Cholesky factorization, 568, 569
  Jordan factorization, 565, 566, 646
  LU factorization, 568, 569, 614
  QR factorization, 569, 616
  Schur factorization, 79, 102, 108, 567, 569
Mean
  conditional, 657
  long-run, 37
  unconditional, 657

Method of undetermined coefficients, 24, **66**, 73
Modified policy iteration, 215, 218, 219, 226, 229, 231
Monetary aggregate, 151
Monetary growth rule, 145, 270
Monetary policy, 145, 153, 173, 268, 275
Money
  cash balances, 270, 272
  cash-in-advance, 143, 268, 270, 278
  elasticity of demand for real money balances, 152
  in the utility function, 143, 385
  liquidity effect, 268, 277, 279
  neutrality of, 143, 145, 153
  outside money, 143
  real money balances, 143, 144
  Sidrauski model, 385
  superneutral, 273
  superneutrality, 385
  supply, 145, 151
  transaction costs, 143, 144, 151, 154
  velocity of, 150, 153
Money balances, see Money
Monomial formulas, 253, 254, 287, 293, 579, 602
Monopolistic competition, 144, 154
Monte-Carlo simulation, 285, 292, 353–355
Multicollinearity, 275, 579

National accounts, 49, 56
Natural spline, 578
Neoclassical growth model, see Ramsey model
Neural network, 591–593
  hidden-layer activation function, 592
  hidden-layer feedforward, 592
  single hidden-layer feedforward, 592

single-layer, 591
Neutrality of money, *see* Money
Newton's method, 630–631
Newton-Raphson method, 608–614
    globally convergent extension, 617–622
    modified, 301, 609, 613–616
Non-linear equations solver, 256, 257, 262, 275
Norm, 214, 558
    Euclidean, 558
    sup, 558
Normal good, 34, 58
Numerical differentiation, 593–598
    central differences, 595, 597
    first difference formulas, 594–595
    forward differences, 594, 629
    numerical derivative, 593–598
Numerical integration, 598–603
    Gaussian formulas, 599–601
    linear Lagrange polynomial, 598
    multidimensional, 601–603
    Newton-Cotes formulas, 598–599
    Trapezoid rule, 598
Numerical optimization, 622–643

OLG, *see* Overlapping generations model
Open economy model, 189–199
Optimal policy functions, *see* Policy functions
Optimization, *see* Numerical optimization
Orthogonal polynomials, *see* Polynomials
Overlapping generations model
    aggregate uncertainty, 520–548
    business cycle dynamics, 536–548
    demographic transition, 482–501
    deterministic, 451–501
    individual uncertainty, 507–520

steady state, 453–469
stochastic, 507–548
transition dynamics, 469–482

Partial information, 395–406, 439
Pensions, 455
    earnings-related, 502
    lump-sum pensions, 508
    replacement ratio, 469, 515, 524
Perfect foresight models, *see* Overlapping generations model
Perturbation methods
    linear, 77–83, 98–114, 131
    quadratic, 114–131
Phase diagram, 16–21
Phillips curve
    New Keynesian, 131, 143–157
    traditional, 144
Policy function, **14**, 20, 31, 209, 285, 294, 295, 297, 334, 343
    time invariant, **14**
Policy function iteration, 213–215
Polynomials, 578–591
    n-fold tensor product base, 588
    Chebyshev polynomials, 355, 467, 581–588, 590
    complete set of, 589
    Hermite polynomials, 600
    Legendre polynomials, 582
    linear Lagrange polynomials, 598
    orthogonal, 579–580
    orthonormal, 579
    tensor product base, 589
Predetermined variable, *see* Variable
Prediction error, 247, 420
Price
    Calvo-pricing, 144
    price index, aggregate, 146
    price setting, 145, 155, 156
Principle of optimality, **14**, 336
Probability, 26

Subject Index   701

conditional, 306
density function, 657
distribution, 27, 32, 312, 426, 511
ergodic distribution, 292
Production economy, 311, 363
Production function, 41, 298
    aggregate, **41**, 412
    Cobb-Douglas, 91, 456, 510, 523
    constant returns to scale, 334, 456, 510, 523
    marginal product, 334, 394
    neoclassical, 36
    properties, **5**
Productivity level, aggregate, 416
Profits, 41, 146, 147, 149, 269, 314
Programming
    dynamic, 3, **13**, 425
    non-linear, **4**
    stochastic dynamic, **30**
Projection function, 291, 295, 297, 467
Projection methods, 285–297, 300
    algorithm, 291
    approximating function, 293
    finite-element methods, 286
    in OLG models, 467
    residual function, 294, 295
    weighted residual methods, 285

QR factorization, *see* Matrix factorization
Quadratic form, **84**, **563**
Quadratic objective function, 84
Quasi-Newton method, 300, 630–633
    BFGS, 468, 631–633
    Newton direction, 630
    Newton's method, *see* Newton's method

Ramsey model
    finite-horizon deterministic, 4–6, 176–179
    infinite-horizon deterministic, 10–11, 77–82, 91–95, 115–117, 179–181, 208–209, 286, 289, 294, 297–302
    infinite-horizon stochastic, 26–28, 44–46, 99–106, 117–124, 131–138, 181–184, 228–232, 235–237, 244–247, 286, 289, 292, 298, 311, 312
    with non-negative investment, 232–235, **259**, 302–309
Random number generator, 353, 417, 441
Rate of interest
    nominal, 152, 268, 269
    risk-free, 330, 359–366
    risk-free rate puzzle, 330
Rational expectations, **28**, 64, 175, 183, 184, 189, 232, 243
Rationality, bounded, 250, 397, 418
Recursive methods, XI, 209, 221, 227, 235
Representative agent, 42, 49, 131, 247, 296
Residual function, *see* Function
Restrictions, *see* Constraints
Returns to scale, constant, **35**, 36, 456, 510, 523
Riccati equation, 86
Rigidities, nominal, 143, 152, 154, 155
Risk aversion, 509
    relative risk aversion, coefficient of, 423, 509, 513
Risk, idiosyncratic, 330, 370, 411, 429

Saddle path, 16–21, 77, 179
Savings, 34
    behavior, 401
    function, 402
    precautionary, 331
    rate, 348, 396
    share of, 35

Schur factorization, *see* Matrix factorization
Secant Hermite Spline, 578
Secant method, 364, 461, **609**
Seignorage, 386, 503
Shock, 33–34
    anticipated, 153
    monetary shock, 143, 155, 268, 276, 278
    productivity shock, 298, 522, 657
    technology shock, 292
    unanticipated, 152
Shooting method, 394
Simulation method, *see* Monte-Carlo simulation
Social planner, **84**
Social security, 510, 517
    contributions, 455, 502, 515
    system, 396
Solow residual, 524
Sparse matrix methods, 342, 664
Spline, *see* Interpolation, cubic spline
State space, 295
    discretization of, 341, 358, 465, 513
    individual, 335, 377, 391, 439
State variable, *see* Variable
Stationary solution, *see* Steady state
Steady state, 18–21, 376, 411, 458, 460, 470, 524, 526
Stochastic growth model, *see* Ramsey model
Stochastic process
    autoregressive, *see* autoregressive process, *see* autoregressive process
    continuous valued, 652
    covariance stationary, 36
    difference stationary, 36
    discrete valued, 652
    non-stationary, 663
    trend stationary, 36
    white noise, 37

Stopping criteria, 603–606
Substitution
    effect, 34
    inter-temporal, 34
    intra-temporal, 33
    marginal rate of, **8**, 9, 245
Superneutrality of money, *see* Money

Tax
    consumption tax, 330, 367, 378
    income tax, 330, 382, 452
    income tax rate, 332, 382, 396, 407
    income tax reform, 374–381
    labor income tax rate, 455, 475
    revenues, 334, 376, 456, 510
    system, 452
Taylor series, 571, 589
    expansion, 96, 597
    second order approximation, 92
Taylor's theorem, 75, 571–574
Technical progress, 34–35
    disembodied, 34
    embodied, 34
    labor augmenting, 35
Time series
    artificial, 135
    cyclical component of, 55, 665
    second moments, 55, 91, 135
Time to Build Model, 138–143
Topological conjugates, 650
Total factor productivity, 318
Transformation matrix, **94**, 567
Transition matrix, 332, 373, 398, 411, 463, 512, **653**
    conditional, 423
Transversality condition, 13, 17, 18, 20, 30, 103, 316, 317
Trend
    linear, 36, 663
    path, 35

Uncertainty, 26, 507

aggregate, 331, 520–533
individual, 507–520
Undetermined coefficients, *see* Method of undetermined coefficients
Unemployment
compensation, 331, 335, 375, 396, 517
cyclical, 144, 432
duration of, 337, 372
replacement ratio, 338, 378, 518
risk, 331
Unit circle, 83, 87, 107, 108, 111, 113, 184, 196, 532, 557, 648, 649
Unit root, 194, 195
Utility function, 298
constant elasticity of substitution (CES), 423
current period utility function, 313
elasticity of marginal utility, 50, 258, 298
expected lifetime utility, 26, 313
instantaneous, 405, 423
isoelastic current period utility function, 313
lifetime utility, 8, 26, 311
marginal utility, 8
one-period, 10, 26
recursive, **9**
time additive separable (TAS), 9

Value function, **14**, 30, 85, 285, 336, 343, 401, 457, 464
Value function iteration, 209, 213, 217, 379, 380, 464, 466, 515
and concavity, 211–213, 441
and monotonicity, 211–213, 441
Variable
control, 86, 89, 93, 95, 97, 98, 124, 164–166, 184, 186, 195, 243, 324, 527
costate, 89, 91, **107**, 124, 184, 527
predetermined, 84, 318, 526, 532
state variable, 85, 87, 95, 107, 243, 245, 271, 274, 275, 292
state variable, distribution of, 434
state variable, non-stochastic, 84
state variable, with given initial condition, 107
state variable, without given initial condition, 107
stochastic, 27
Variance, conditional, 654
Variational coefficient
effective labor, 381, 383
labor supply, 383
working hours, 381
vec operator, 560–561
Vector, 557–558
addition, 557
basis, 558
control vector, **84**, 85
gradient, 96, 251, 605, 628
norm, 558
scalar multiplication, 557
space, 286, 564
state vector, **84**

Wage income, 333, 348, 402, 407, 455, 469, 524
Wald statistic, 660
Wealth
average, 441
concentration of, 369, 382, 445, 507
distribution, 341, 347, 356, 381, 395, 417, 441, 452, 507, 511, 515, 516

heterogeneity, 445, 507, 518
level, 331, 341, 370, 396, 425, 463
Weight function, **579**, 581, 600
Dirac delta function, 290, 296
Weighted residual methods, *see* Projection methods
Weighting function, 290, 291, 295, 302
Welfare
analysis, 329
effects, 430